# CROWELL'S HANDBOOK
# OF WORLD OPERA

# CROWELL'S HANDBOOK OF WORLD OPERA

COMPILED BY

FRANK LEDLIE MOORE

INTRODUCTION BY DARIUS MILHAUD

A CROWELL REFERENCE BOOK

THOMAS Y. CROWELL COMPANY, NEW YORK

ESTABLISHED 1834

# INTRODUCTION

This book on opera is absolutely the source of information that we need. The general public as well as the musicologist will be able to use it, because everything concerning opera is mentioned. It is like a series of dictionaries, one for the operas—their background, their story, their cast; another for the composers, with a list of their theatrical works; another for the characters in operas. Even first lines and titles of famous numbers, a glossary of technical expressions, and a list of complete operas recorded are to be found; also an index of famous musical themes, the chronology of operas with references to general history, to opera history, and to first performances year by year from the thirteenth century to the present day.

Here everybody can find everything about opera through its long and glorious history. This book not only will be treasured by musicians, but will enrich every school, college, or university library.

I wish the fruits of Frank Moore's indefatigable research the great success it deserves.

DARIUS MILHAUD

# PREFACE

*Crowell's Handbook of World Opera* has been designed to give you as much information as possible about all the operas that have importance of one kind or another for our time. Within these pages it will be possible for you to track down nearly any reference that may cross your mind in the course of reading about or listening to opera. Whether you begin with the first line or the nickname of an aria, or the name of some character recalled from a performance, the reference you find here will lead you on to more knowledge about the opera concerned and the people who may have been involved in it. If you are a singer, there are special indexes of vocal numbers arranged according to voice to help you build your repertoire. If you want to know about composers, conductors, and others, the biographical section will help you. For history see the chronology, and for technical facts or some practical definitions of different styles, the glossary.

In the sixty pages of musical themes two objectives governed the choice of material. I wanted first to give as full an illustration of the musical texture of certain great works as was practical, and second to introduce to those who have not heard them certain melodies of matchless beauty from the lesser-known works. Hence you will find *Boris Godunov* and *Carmen* well represented, plus samples such as the Lamento d'Arianna, which is all that remains to us of one of Monteverdi's greatest works.

As I gathered facts for this volume I received help from many. I listened as opera fans of earlier days recalled anecdotes that brought light for me into shadowy places. I hope the book itself will repay them for their contributions. Publicly I want to thank Nicolas Slonimsky, who went over the manuscript in detail and made many corrections, and Gorton Carruth who quietly whittled my concepts of the book into proper shape to present to you.

F. L. M.

# CONTENTS

INTRODUCTION BY DARIUS MILHAUD                                           v

PREFACE                                                                 vii

THE OPERAS                                                                I

THE PEOPLE IN OPERA                                                      184

THE CHARACTERS IN THE OPERAS                                            308

FIRST LINES AND TITLES OF FAMOUS MUSICAL NUMBERS                        493

CHRONOLOGY OF OPERA                                                     537

GLOSSARY                                                                560

THEMES OF THE MOST FAMOUS MUSICAL NUMBERS                               593

RECORDINGS OF COMPLETE OPERAS                                          654

SPECIAL INDEXES                                                         663

    Sopranos, Mezzo-sopranos, Contraltos, Male contraltos, Tenors, Baritones, Basses    663

    Composers, Librettists, Conductors                                  666

    Roles for: Soprano, Mezzo-soprano, Contralto, Tenor, Baritone, Bass, Chorus;
        Speaking roles, Silent roles, Children's roles                   669

    Arias for: Soprano, Mezzo-soprano, Contralto, Tenor, Baritone, Bass        678

    Duets, Trios, Quartets, Quintets, Sextets, Choruses                  682

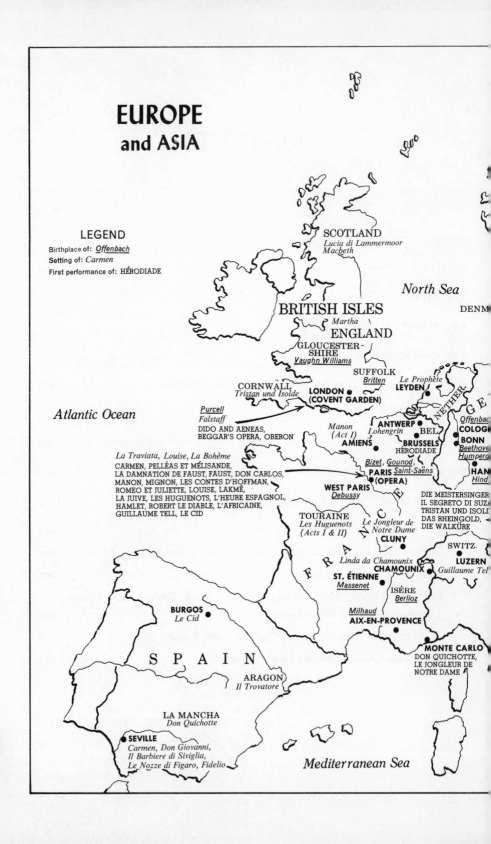

# EUROPE
## and ASIA

### LEGEND
Birthplace of: _Offenbach_
Setting of: _Carmen_
First performance of: HÉRODIADE

*North Sea*

SCOTLAND
_Lucia di Lammermoor_
_Macbeth_

DENM

## BRITISH ISLES
_Martha_
### ENGLAND
GLOUCESTER-
SHIRE
_Vaughn Williams_

SUFFOLK
_Britten_

_Le Prophète_
LEYDEN

CORNWALL
_Tristan und Isolde_

LONDON ●
(COVENT GARDEN)

*Atlantic Ocean*

_Purcell_
_Falstaff_
DIDO AND AENEAS,
BEGGAR'S OPERA, OBERON

_Manon_
(Act 1)

ANTWERP ●
_Lohengrin_
AMIENS ●

BRUSSELS ●
HÉRODIADE

BEL

NETHER

_Offenbac_
COLOG ●

BONN ●
_Beethove_
_Humpero_

GE

_La Traviata, Louise, La Bohème_
CARMEN, PELLÉAS ET MÉLISANDE,
LA DAMNATION DE FAUST, FAUST, DON CARLOS,
MANON, MIGNON, LES CONTES D'HOFFMAN,
ROMEO ET JULIETTE, LOUISE, LAKMÉ,
LA JUIVE, LES HUGUENOTS, L'HEURE ESPAGNOL,
HAMLET, ROBERT LE DIABLE, L'AFRICAINE,
GUILLAUME TELL, LE CID

_Bizet, Gounod,_
_Saint-Saëns_
PARIS ●
(OPERA)

WEST PARIS
_Debussy_

HAN ●
_Hind_

DIE MEISTERSINGER
IL SEGRETO DI SUZA
TRISTAN UND ISOLI
DAS RHEINGOLD,
DIE WALKÜRE

F R A N C E

TOURAINE
_Les Huguenots_
(Acts I & II)

_Le Jongleur de_
_Notre Dame_
CLUNY ●

_Linda da Chamounix_
CHAMOUNIX ●

SWITZ.

LUZERN ●
_Guillaume Tel_

ST. ÉTIENNE ●
_Massenet_

ISÈRE ●
_Berlioz_

_Milhaud_
AIX-EN-PROVENCE ●

BURGOS ●
_Le Cid_

S P A I N

ARAGON ●
_Il Trovatore_

LA MANCHA
_Don Quichotte_

SEVILLE ●
_Carmen, Don Giovanni,_
_Il Barbiere di Siviglia,_
_Le Nozze di Figaro, Fidelio_

MONTE CARLO ●
DON QUICHOTTE,
LE JONGLEUR DE
NOTRE DAME

*Mediterranean Sea*

Fliegende Holländer

ST. PETERSBURG
(LENINGRAD)
*Borodin, Stravinsky*
BORIS GODUNOV, LA FORZA DEL DESTINO,
KHOVANTSCHINA, PIQUE-DAME, PRINCE IGOR,
RUSSLAN AND LUDMILLA

VIATKA
*Tschaikovsky*

NOVGOROD
*Rimsky-Korsakov*
*Sadko*

PSKOV
*Mussorgsky*

MOSCOW
*Boris Godunov, Khovantschina*
EUGENE ONEGIN, LE COQ D'OR,
SADKO

*mlet*
ELSINORE

SCANDINAVIA

SMOLENSK
*Glinka*

R U S S I A

*Meyerbeer*
DER FREISCHÜTZ,
I GIOIELLI DELLA MADONNA
BERLIN

LOHENGRIN, HÄNSEL UND GRETEL,
SAMSON ET DALILA

*ch*
*user*

ELEKTRA, TANNHÄUSER,
DER ROSENKAVALIER,
DER FLIEGENDE HOLLÄNDER,
SALOME

DRESDEN

LEIPZIG *Wagner*
EUTH

PARSIFAL, SIEGFRIED,
GÖTTERDÄMMERUNG

*Gluck*
WEIDENWANG
PRAGUE

DON GIOVANNI,
PRODANÁ NEVĚSTA

EKATERINOSLAV
*Prokofiev*

BOHEMIA
LEITOMISCHL
*Smetana*

CZECHO.

*BERG*
*H*
*rauss*

*Die Meistersinger*

*Prodaná Nevěsta,*
*Der Freischütz*

SALZBURG
*Mozart*

VIENNA
*Berg*
*Der Rosenkavalier*
ORFEO ED EURIDICE,
LE NOZZE DI FIGARO,
ALCESTE, FIDELIO, DIE ZAUBERFLÖTE,
EURYANTHE, COSÌ FAN TUTTE,
DIE ENTFÜHRUNG AUS DEM SERAIL, MARTHA

AUST.

HUNGARY

TRANSYLVANIA
*Bartok*

Black Sea

CHINA
*Turandot*

JAPAN
*Madama Butterfly*

INDIA
*Lakmé*

Pacific
Ocean

*Indian Ocean*

CEYLON
*Les Pêcheurs*
*de Perles*

Don Pitcher

I PAGLIACCI, OTELLO, MADAMA BUTTERFLY,
FALSTAFF, ANDREA CHÉNIER,
L'AMORE DEI TRE RE, LA GIOCONDA,
L'ELISIR D'AMORE, FEDORA

Don Pitcher

## Mediterranean Sea

CYPRUS
*Otello*

Samson et Dalila GAZA

JERUSALEM
*Salome, Hérodiade*

CAIRO
MEMPHIS ● AIDA

*Aida,
Die Zauberflöte,*

E G Y P T

TROY
(DARDANELLES)
*Les Troyens*

MYCENAE ●
*Elektra*

*Alceste, La Favola d'Orfeo,
Orfeo ed Euridice,*

## Mediterranean Sea

TURIN ●
LA BOHÈME,
MANON LESCAUT

MILAN
(LA SCALA) ●

*Donizetti*
BERGAMO

VERONA ●
*Romeo et
Juliette*

CREMONA ●
*Monteverdi*

PADUA ●
*Boito*

VENICE ●
*La Gioconda*

RIGOLETTO, LA TRAVIATA,
ERNANI, SIMON BOCCANEGRA

MANTUA
*Rigoletto*
LA FAVOLA D'ORFEO

PARMA ●
*Verdi*

LUCCA ●
*Puccini*

LEGHORN ●
*Mascagni*

GENOA ●
*Simon Boccanegra*

PESARO ●
*Rossini*

FLORENCE ●
(*Florence is the birthplace of Opera, 1597*)
MACBETH

I T A L Y

ROME ●
*Tosca*

TOSCA, IL TROVATORE,
UN BALLO IN MASCHERA,
IL BARBIERE DE SIVIGLIA,
CAVALLERIA RUSTICANA

FOGGIA ●
*Giordano*

NAPLES ●
*Leoncavallo*
I Gioielli della Madonna
LUCIA DI LAMMERMOOR

CALABRIA
*I Pagliacci*

CATANIA ●
*Bellini*

SICILY
*Cavalleria Rusticana*

# ITALY, GREECE
and the
EASTERN MEDITERRANEAN

## LEGEND

Birthplace of: *Bellini*
Setting of: *I Pagliacci*
First performance of: MACBETH

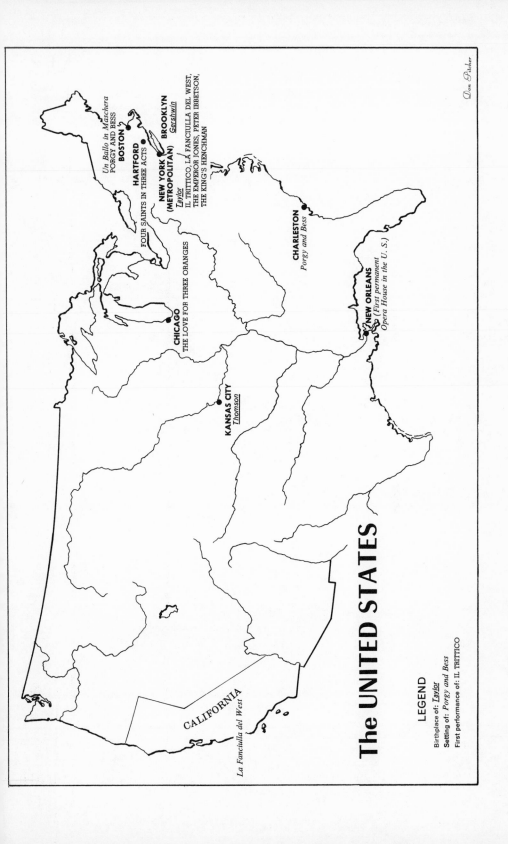

Don Pitcher

# The UNITED STATES

*Un Ballo in Maschera*
**BOSTON** PORGY AND BESS

**HARTFORD**
FOUR SAINTS IN THREE ACTS

**BROOKLYN** *Gershwin*

**NEW YORK
(METROPOLITAN)** *Taylor*
IL TRITTICO, LA FANCIULLA DEL WEST,
THE EMPEROR JONES, PETER IBBETSON,
THE KING'S HENCHMAN

**CHARLESTON**
*Porgy and Bess*

**CHICAGO**
THE LOVE FOR THREE ORANGES

**NEW ORLEANS**
(First permanent
*Opera House in the U. S.*)

**KANSAS CITY**
*Thomson*

CALIFORNIA

*La Fanciulla del West*

## LEGEND

Birthplace of: <u>*Taylor*</u>
Setting of: *Porgy and Bess*
First performance of: IL TRITTICO

# CROWELL'S HANDBOOK
# OF WORLD OPERA

# THE OPERAS

The operas in this section are listed in alphabetical order according to title. Information about each one is arranged as follows:

**Name of the Opera**
   Its composer
   Its librettist(s)
   The source of the story

*Number of acts and scenes*
   Place and date of first performance
   Other significant first performances

For the more important operas there follow, then, the cast of characters, a synopsis, and, where pertinent, notes. In the listing of first performances, six theaters appear as names only. These are:

   Comique—L'Opéra Comique, Paris, France
   Covent Garden—London, England
   Drury Lane—London, England
   La Scala—Milan, Italy
   Metropolitan—New York City
   Opéra—L'Académie Royale de Musique, Paris, France

The abbreviation (*rev.*) indicates a revised version. Other abbreviations are as follows:

| | |
|---|---|
| S—Soprano | T—Tenor |
| MS—Mezzo-soprano | Bar—Baritone |
| MC—Mezzo-contralto | BBar—Bass-baritone |
| A—Alto | B—Bass |
| C—Contralto | |

### Abduction from the Seraglio, The
See *Entführung aus dem Serail, Die*

### Acis and Galatea
   COMP.: G. F. Handel
   LIBR.: J. Gay

*3 acts*
   London, 28 May 1732
   Stockholm, 1734
   New York (Concert), 1839
   New York (Stage), 1842

Written as a masque in 1719, it may have been performed in that manner in 1721.

### Acis et Galathée
   COMP.: J. B. Lully
   LIBR.: J. G. de Campistron
   Lully's last opera.

*Prologue & 3 acts*
   Anet, France, 6 September 1686
   Hamburg, 1689
   Amsterdam, 1933

## Adam and Eve

COMP.: Everett Helm                          Wiesbaden, 28 October 1951

Adapted from a pre-Shakespearian English mystery play.

## Adone, L'                                  *Prologue & 5 acts*

COMP.: C. Monteverdi                         Venice, 21 December 1639
LIBR.: P. Vendramin

From a poem by Marini

   This was the first opera Monteverdi wrote for the public stage; he was then 72 years old. His previous stage works were performed within the private houses of the nobility.

## Adventures of King Pausole, The

See *Aventures du Roi Pausole, Les*

## Adriana Lecouvreur                         *Tragedy in 4 acts*

COMP.: F. Cilèa                              Milan, 26 November 1902
LIBR.: A. Colautti                           Covent Garden, 1904
From a play by Scribe and Legouvé            Metropolitan, 1907

CAST

| | | | |
|---|---|---|---|
| Maurizio, *Count of Saxony* | T | Adriana Lecouvreur | S |
| Prince de Bouillon | B | Princess de Bouillon | MS |
| L'Abate de Chazeuil | T | Mlle. Jouvenot, *of the Comédie Française* | S |
| Michonnet, *stage director* | Bar | Mlle. Dangeville, *of the Comédie* | |
| Quincault, *of the Comédie Française* | B | *Française* | MS |
| Poisson, *of the Comédie Française* | T | Chamber Maid | |
| Major Domo | T | Ladies, Gentlemen, Servants | |

SYNOPSIS

   I. The Green-room of the Comédie Française. Preparations for a performance are in progress; all is hustle and bustle as the actors and actresses compliment Adriana and go on stage. The Prince, in a quiet moment during the performance, reads a letter he has intercepted in which someone plans a tryst for that night. He thinks it is from the actress Duclos, his mistress, and prepares to expose her. But it is really from his own wife the Princess, and intended for Maurizio.

   II. At the appointed place and time, the Prince and L'Abate find not the Princess, but Maurizio, who has just hidden her away. Maurizio soon realizes that they do not know who the real woman is, and plays along with their mistake. But then Adriana, who has come in answer to an anonymous note of love, makes the double discovery of her lover's true identity as the Count of Saxony and of his insincerity as a lover who already has an unknown mistress.

   III. Adriana wonders who the other woman may be. There is a grand ball at the Prince's house at which she is an honored guest. All during the ball she plies the Princess with veiled questions to confirm her suspicions.

   IV. In the Green-room. It is her birthday, and among the happier gifts she opens one not so happy—a box of poisoned violets, the remains of the ones she had given Maurizio before. When he presents himself, she pleads with him to tell her the truth. Suddenly she feels faint, she becomes delirious and cries that the flowers have affected her. To the horror of Maurizio she dies in his arms, thus satisfying the revenge of the Princess.

## Aegyptische Helena, Die

COMP.: Richard Strauss
LIBR.: H. von Hofmannsthal

2 acts
Dresden, 6 June 1928
Vienna, 1928
Metropolitan, 1928

CAST

| | | | |
|---|---|---|---|
| Helena, *wife of King Menelaus* | S | Da-Ud, *Altair's son* | T |
| Menelaus, *Greek general* | T | Servants of Aithra (2) | S, MS |
| Hermione, *their daughter* | S | Elves (3) | S, S, C |
| Aithra, *a sorceress* | S | The Omniscient Mussel | C |
| Altair, *desert chieftain* | Bar | | |

SYNOPSIS

I. Aithra's magic palace. Aithra wishes to protect those of her own sex from harm, particularly harm from men. In this case, after the Trojan War, she causes a shipwreck and has Menelaus and Helena brought before her before he has a chance to slay his wife (remorsefully) for the ill her beauty had caused Greece. Aithra bewilders Menelaus by nearly convincing him that his suspicions are groundless, that Helena spent all the ten years of the Trojan war in an enchanted sleep right here with the sorceress. Secretly she gives Helena a drink to make them forget their past danger and sends both of them to an enchanted place.

II. In a palmgrove near the desert they live in bliss. Altair visits them. He has a son, Da-Ud, who becomes infatuated with Helena but she pays him no attention. Menelaus pursues him into the desert and kills him. When he returns from the foray, Helena gives him a drink of the antidote for forgetfulness (which Aithra did not intend her to have). Menelaus remembers then that he planned to murder his wife for her sins. In desperation Aithra makes her appearance between them, protecting them from the revenge of the bereaved Altair, and at the same time re-uniting them with Hermione in the hope that their daughter's love will quell their fiercer hate—and this is perfectly successful.

## Africaine, L'

COMP.: G. Meyerbeer
LIBR.: E. Scribe

*Tragedy in 5 acts*
Opéra, 28 April 1865
London, 1865
New York, 1865

CAST

| | | | |
|---|---|---|---|
| Vasco da Gama, *seafarer and discoverer* | T | Sélika, *captured African queen* | S |
| Don Pedro, *councillor to the king* | B | Nélusko, *captured African nobleman* | Bar |
| Don Diego, *councillor to the king* | B | Grand Inquisitor | B |
| Don Alvar, *councillor to the king* | T | High Priest of Brahma | Bar |
| Inès, *Don Diego's daughter* | S | Councillors, Priests, Sailors, Soldiers, | |
| Anna, *her attendant* | C | Ladies, Gentlemen, Attendants, Captives, Inquisitors | |

SYNOPSIS

I. Vasco, having seen the New World, asks backing for an expedition. Because of Don Pedro's intrigues against him, he is turned down. He becomes furious, uttering accusations which land him in prison.

II. Sélika, his captive, takes care of him there. She loves him. But so does Inès. Inès arranges Vasco's freedom by sacrificing herself in marriage to Don Pedro, who has won the right to make the expedition originally proposed by Vasco.

III. Nélusko, taken on as pilot, steers the expedition into dangerous waters. Vasco has found a ship and followed his rival. When he sees the danger he tries to save his countrymen but Pedro has him again put in irons. The ship breaks up on the rocks of Africa's shore, leaving most of the Europeans prey to Nélusko's revenge.

IV. Sélika again saves Vasco. She is Queen in this strange land, and could demand her captive's love. But he cannot forget Inès.

V. Sélika finally relinquishes her claim upon that which she cannot win. Vasco returns to his country on a ship she provides him, taking Inès home. Standing on the shore, watching the ship grow ever smaller on the horizon, Sélika poisons herself.

NOTES

The opera is no longer very popular, chiefly because of its libretto. Sélika, as has been pointed out by others, is supposed to be an African queen, but has Hindu faith. Meyerbeer died during the final preparations of the opening performance.

**Agamemnon**
COMP.: D. Milhaud
LIBR.: P. Claudel (*Translator*)
From Aeschylus

*Tragedy in 1 act*
Paris, 14 April 1927

CAST

Clytemnestra      S     Chorus
This is the first part of the *Orestie* Trilogy.

**Agnes von Hohenstaufen**
COMP.: G. Spontini
LIBR.: E. Raupach

*3 acts*
Berlin, 12 June 1829

**Agrippina**
COMP.: G. F. Handel
LIBR.: V. Grimani

*3 acts*
Venice, 26 December 1709
Hamburg, 1718
Vienna, 1719

**Aida**
COMP.: G. Verdi
LIBR.: Verdi and Ghislanzoni
From a Scenario by du Locle after
a plot by Mariette Bey

*Tragedy in 4 acts (7 scenes)*
Cairo, 24 December 1871
La Scala, 1872
New York, 1873

CAST

| | | | |
|---|---|---|---|
| Aida, *Ethiopian princess, slave of Amneris* | S | Amonasro, *king of Ethiopia, Aida's father* | Bar |
| King of Egypt | B | Ramfis, *High Priest* | B |
| Amneris, *his daughter* | C | Messenger | T |
| Radames, *captain of the guard* | T | Priests, Priestesses, Ministers, Captains, Soldiers, Officials, Ethiopian Slaves, Prisoners, Egyptians | |

MUSICAL HIGHLIGHTS

ACT I. Aria *Celesta Aida* (Heavenly Aida), Radames
Aria *Ritorna vincitor* (Return victorious), Aida
Temple Scene *Nume, custode e vindici* (God, guardian and avenger), Radames, Ramfis, Chorus

ACT II. Triumphal Scene *Gloria all'Egitto* (Glory to Egypt), containing the *Grand March*
ACT III. Aria *O patria mia* (My native land) (*O cieli azzurri*), Aida
ACT IV. Duet *La fatal pietra* (The fatal stone), Aida, Radames
Death Scene, Duet *O terra addio* (O earth farewell), Aida, Radames

### SYNOPSIS

I. The Palace at Memphis. A messenger from Thebes brings the unwelcome news that that city is critically threatened by Amonasro and his armies. The Egyptians need a leader. Radames, who hopes thus to be named, also hopes by victory to win the captive Aida, whom he loves. He does not know that her father is that same Amonasro he must defeat. He is chosen, thus tearing Aida's heart two ways as she cheers with the crowd for victory over her own people. Amneris, seeing the glances between her slave and Radames, suspects the reason for her own lack of success with the general. At the Temple of Vulcan, the Priests consecrate his armor before the battle.

II. When the news of victory reaches the palace Amneris, in order to discover if her suspicions of love between her slave and the general were true, tells Aida that Radames has been slain in battle. Seeing Aida's reaction, she exults in her successful deception and taunts the poor girl with the bitterness of her enslavement. Satisfied that she has no fear of rivalry from her slave, she prepares to welcome Radames.

At the Gate of Thebes the king reviews his victorious armies with his daughter, the court and the slaves gathered around. In highest honor, the king offers Radames anything he wishes. Radames utters no wish at that moment, but has the prisoners brought before the king. Aida sees her father among them, but Amonasro warns her not to give away his identity. In a powerful speech, Amonasro then tells the king that the enemy king was killed in battle. The speech ends with a plea for clemency for the prisoners, in which Radames joins. The king grants it, but the priests demand Amonasro and Aida as hostages. At the end of the act the king, in a burst of gratitude for the victory, promises Radames the hand of his daughter, Amneris.

III. On the moonlit banks of the Nile Aida hides, waiting to meet her lover. But Amonasro appears instead. In words of patriotism he implores her to tell him which way Radames plans next to march, so that Amonasro can effect an ambush against him. In despair of love against the rivalry of Amneris, she waits for Radames. When he comes they speak of their impossible love, their deep emotion. They plan to escape altogether by the road through Napata—and Amonasro hears these words. Radames discovers him but Amneris discovers them all and descends from the temple to prevent their escape. Radames delivers himself as hostage to the High Priest while Amonasro and Aida disappear in the darkness.

IV. While Amneris waits above, torn by love for the man she has betrayed as a traitor, the Priests convict Radames and entomb him alive under the temple. The final scene takes place on two levels—the Temple above and the tomb below. Radames gradually realizes that someone is with him in the tomb. It is Aida who has hidden herself there to die with him while Amneris above prays to her gods for his comfort.

### NOTES

*Aida* was commissioned by the Khedive of Egypt to celebrate the opening of the new Suez Canal in 1869. It was immediately successful, but Verdi refused to allow the Paris Opéra to mount a performance of the work until 1880 because of the ill treatment he had suffered there with *I Vespri Siciliani* and *Don Carlos*. In the end amends were made all around, and France awarded the composer the Legion d'Honneur for *Aida*. As a matter of fact, the first performance of the work anywhere after its European opening at La Scala occurred in Buenos Aires, in October, 1873.

## Aiglon, L'

5 *acts*

COMP.:  A. Honegger  &  J. Ibert
LIBR.:  H. Cain
After Rostand

Monte Carlo, 11 March 1937
Opéra, 1937
Brussels, 1938

## Albert Herring

*Comedy in 3 acts*

COMP.:  B. Britten
LIBR.:  E. Crozier
From a story by Maupassant

Glyndebourne, 20 June 1947
Hanover, 1950
New York, 1952

CAST

| | | | |
|---|---|---|---|
| Lady Billows, *elderly autocrat* | S | Sid, *butcher's assistant* | Bar |
| Florence Pike, *her housekeeper* | C | Albert Herring, *from the greengrocer's* | T |
| Miss Wordsworth, *church school* | | Nancy, *from the bakery* | MS |
| teacher | S | Mrs. Herring, *Albert's mother* | MS |
| Mr. Gedge, *vicar* | Bar | Emmie, *a child* | S |
| Mr. Upfold, *mayor* | T | Cis, *a child* | S |
| Superintendent Budd | B | Harry, *a child* | Treble |

SYNOPSIS

I. On Mayday there must be a May Queen, to be chosen by a committee and approved by Lady Billows. Since there seem to be no more virgins left in town the committee is at a loss to choose one. Supt. Budd makes the excellent suggestion that there be a May King instead. There is only one boy innocent enough to be named—Albert Herring. Albert at that very time has been thinking hard while watching Sid make time with Nancy. Sick of his own innocence, when the committee comes to award him the prize he refuses it.

II. But to no avail. The coronation must take place, willy nilly. Sid pours rum into Albert's glass to help him withstand the ordeal. The new King of the May, Albert the Good, gets drunker and drunker. As soon as he can escape, he decides to let himself go altogether.

III. The town misses its May King; he is nowhere to be found. But little traces turn up here and there, enough to indicate possible foul play. At the height of their grief at their loss he returns to his townspeople, sorry to have caused them worry, but determined to be a man of his own decision from then on.

## Alceste

3 *acts*

COMP.:  C. W. von Gluck
LIBR.:  R. da Calzabigi
From Euripides

Vienna, 26 December 1767
Paris, (*rev.*) 23 April 1776
London, 1795
Metropolitan, 1941

CAST

| | | | |
|---|---|---|---|
| Admetus, *king* | T | Thanatos, *Death* | Bar |
| Alceste, *his wife* | S | Voice of Apollo | Bar |
| High Priest of Apollo | Bar | Herald | Bar |
| Hercules | Bar | Children of Alceste, Spirits of the Under- | |
| Evander | T | world, People, Priests, Priestesses | |

SYNOPSIS

I. In Ancient Greece. The king is mortally ill. The queen Alceste herself leads the prayers for his recovery. Her prayers so move the gods that a cure is granted provided someone else will willingly die in his place. Alceste resolves to sacrifice herself to save her husband.

II. During the celebration of his recovery, the happy king asks how it came about that he was cured. Nobody will tell him who vowed to take his place; therefore he refuses to accept the substitution. Suddenly the sight of his wife's face gives him the secret. But he cannot alter things now; the gods' will is unchangeable.

III. Alceste has died and gone to the underworld. Admetus follows her, leaving his palace desolate. Hercules, their old friend, arrives at their home to find nothing to greet him but sadness. He resolves to save them both. Down he goes to the shadows of Hades and battles Thanatos himself for the lives of his friends. This arouses the admiration of Apollo who intervenes, setting the husband and wife free again and making Hercules himself a god. They return to the upper world amid rejoicing.

NOTES

The score of this opera contains a famous preface written by Gluck in which he explains his concept of the dignity and simplicity of opera, the beauty of drama in music. This preface added fury to the frantic opposition of the "Piccinists"—the defenders of the old style Italian opera who gathered around the name of the quiet and retiring Piccini. The feud had little to do with the composers themselves, but raged in the ranks of the audience and dilettantes like a small civil war.

Du Rollet made changes in the libretto for the French production. Modern performances generally make use of some of these changes, particularly in the lyric of the aria *Divinités du Styx*.

## Alceste ou Le Triomphe d'Alcide

*Prologue & 5 acts*

COMP.: J. B. Lully
LIBR.: P. Quinault
From Euripides

Paris, 19 January 1674

This was the first work of Lully's to be presented at the Palais Royal.

## Alceste

See also *Alkestis*

## Aleko

*1 Act*

COMP.: S. Rachmaninov
LIBR.: V. I. Nemirovitch-Danchenko
From a poem by Pushkin

Moscow, 9 May 1893
London, 1915

## Alessandro

*3 acts*

COMP.: G. F. Handel
LIBR.: P. A. Rolli

London, 16 May 1726
Hamburg, 1726

## Alessandro Stradella

*3 acts*

COMP.: F. von Flotow
LIBR.: W. Friedrich

Paris, 1837
Hamburg (*rev.*), 30 December 1844

Based on the legend of the life of Stradella (q.v.)

SYNOPSIS
Stradella the singer elopes with Leonora, Bassi's mistress. Bassi hires assassins to kill his rival. But when they find him, they are so moved by the beauty of his music they fail to do the job. Bassi takes charge personally, but even he is dissuaded.

NOTE

The story is not in accord with the facts. Stradella did not die of old age, as in the opera, but was murdered.

## Alfonso und Estrella
COMP.: F. Schubert — *3 acts* — Weimar, 24 June 1854
LIBR.: F. von Schober — Vienna, 1882
Composed 1821-22. The opera was first performed under the direction of Franz Liszt.

## Alkestis
COMP.: R. Boughton — *2 acts* — Glastonbury, 26 August 1922
Arranged from Murray's translation — Covent Garden, 1924
of the play of Euripides

## Almira
COMP.: G. F. Handel — *3 acts* — Hamburg, 8 January 1705
LIBR.: F. C. Feustking
From a libretto by Pancieri
Handel's first opera.

## Amahl and the Night Visitors
COMP.: G.-C. Menotti — *Christmas Play in 1 act* — NBC/TV 24 December 1951
LIBR.: by the composer

CAST

| | | | |
|---|---|---|---|
| Amahl, *a crippled boy* | Treble | King Balthazar | B |
| His mother | MS | Page | B |
| King Kaspar, *slightly deaf* | T | Shepherds, Villagers, Dancers | |
| King Melchior | Bar | | |

SYNOPSIS

This is a version of the Christmas story of the Three Kings. The kings, following their star, stop to rest one night at the house of Amahl's mother. All the neighboring shepherds come to see the royal sight. During the evening the kings tell Amahl about the Christ child, and the gifts they have for Him. Amahl piously adds his crutch to the lot—and discovers that he can walk without it. In the morning he goes along with them, on his own two feet, to Bethlehem.

## Amelia Goes to the Ball
COMP.: G.-C. Menotti — *Comedy in 1 act* — Philadelphia, 1 April 1937
LIBR.: by the composer

CAST

| | | | |
|---|---|---|---|
| Amelia | S | Police Commissioner | B |
| Her Husband | Bar | The Maid | MS |
| Her Lover | T | Semda, *the second maid* | MS |
| Her Friend | C | Police, Passersby | |

Amelia, unable to get her husband to take her to the ball, has arranged with her lover to do so. But the husband discovers the lover and engages him in a fight during which he (the husband) is knocked out—by Amelia herself, wielding a vase. Amelia tells the crowd that has gathered that the fight was really an attempted robbery, her lover being the robber. The police chief has the robber carted away, the husband taken care of, and arranges to take Amelia to the ball himself, to her perfect satisfaction.

## Amfiparnaso, L'

| | |
|---|---|
| | Comedy |
| COMP.: O. Vecchi | Modena, 1594 |
| | Published in 1597 |

This work immediately preceded the first operas. It is not itself an opera, but consists of 14 madrigals to illustrate a comedy of masks not intended to be acted. Nowadays, however, it is frequently acted in pantomime with a chorus.

## Amico Fritz, L'

| | |
|---|---|
| | Comedy in 3 acts |
| COMP.: P. Mascagni | Rome, 1 November 1891 |
| LIBR.: P. Suardon (N. Daspuro) | Covent Garden, 1892 |
| From a novel by Erckmann-Chatrian | Philadelphia, 1892 |
| | Metropolitan, 1893 |

CAST

| | | | |
|---|---|---|---|
| Fritz Kobus, *a rich bachelor* | T | Hanezò, *Fritz's friend* | T |
| Suzel, *a farmer's daughter* | S | Federico, *another friend* | B |
| Beppe, *gypsy* | MS | Caterina, *Fritz's housekeeper* | S |
| David, *rabbi* | Bar | | |

SYNOPSIS

I. Fritz and David, old friends, make a bet (to celebrate his fortieth birthday) that Fritz will soon marry. David has been mentioning no names, but Suzel has been in and out during the scene.

II. Fritz begins to be conscious of Suzel's existence, but without result until David drops a hint that Suzel, being young and pretty, has a husband available at her beck. Suddenly Fritz decides he is in love, but that he must restrain himself.

III. David carries on the subtle warfare until Fritz, in distraction, lets slip to Suzel that he loves her. Quite to his surprise, Suzel accepts him, thus allowing David to win the bet.

## Amore dei Tre Re, L'

| | |
|---|---|
| (*The Love of Three Kings*) | Tragedy in 3 acts |
| | La Scala, 10 April 1913 |
| COMP.: I. Montemezzi | Metropolitan, 1914 |
| LIBR.: S. Benelli | Covent Garden, 1914 |
| From a play by Benelli | |

CAST

| | | | |
|---|---|---|---|
| Archibaldo, *king of Altura, Blind* | B | Fiora, *Manfredo's wife* | S |
| Manfredo, *his son* | Bar | Youth, Boy's voice, another voice, Hand- | |
| Avito, *son of the former king* | T | maiden, Young girl, Old woman, | |
| Flaminio, *castle guard* | T | People | |

SYNOPSIS

I. Archibaldo suspects that Fiora, who was married to his son for political reasons, may be seeing her former fiancé Avito. Flaminio, who serves the king for eyes but also protects the intriguers, keeps Archibaldo uninformed. The king very nearly catches

Avito in the castle, but his searchings are interrupted by the tumult of Manfredo's return from war.

II. When war again demands Manfredo, Avito returns to see Fiora. Again Archibaldo nearly traps him, but fails. He questions Fiora, accuses her of infidelity to his son. His fury so overcomes the old king that when Manfredo returns, he finds Fiora strangled by the strong hands of blind Archibaldo.

III. Avito attends the funeral and kisses the corpse. Manfredo confronts him and challenges him, but Avito weakens and dies before his eyes, the victim of poison spread on the lips of the dead princess by Archibaldo. Manfredo, realizing the truth, also kisses her. At the last, the old king feels his way toward the bier to discover the identity of the lover he has been chasing, only to find two bodies, one of which is his son's.

NOTES

Sem Benelli created this story, full of the fury of living people but also symbolic of the political changes in Italy during its unification. Fiora therefore represents not only a woman, but also Italy the nation, loved by two young ideas and one old tradition—and finally strangled by the past.

### Anacréon chez Polycrate

COMP.: A. Grétry
LIBR.: J. H. Guy

3 acts

Opéra, 17 January 1797
Stockholm, 1803

CAST

Anacréon, Greek poet
Olphide, Anaïs' husband
Anaïs, Polycrate's daughter

Lysandre, her child
Polycrate, ruler of Samos
Soldiers

### Andrea Chénier

COMP.: U. Giordano
LIBR.: L. Illica

Tragedy in 4 acts

La Scala, 28 March 1896
New York, 1896
Manchester, 1903
Metropolitan, 1921

CAST

| | | | |
|---|---|---|---|
| Major-domo | Bar | Incredible, spy | T |
| Charles Gérard | Bar | Roucher, Chénier's friend | Bar |
| Madeleine de Coigny | S | Madelon, an old woman | MS |
| Countess de Coigny, her mother | MS | Dumas, presiding judge | B |
| Bersi, Madeleine's maid | MS | Fouquier-Tinville, attorney general | B |
| Fléville, cavalier | Bar | Schmidt, jailer | B |
| Abbé, poet | T | Ladies, Gentlemen, Citizens, Soldiers, | |
| Andrea Chénier, poet | T | Servants, Peasants, Prisoners, Members | |
| Mathieu, waiter ("Populus") | Bar | of the Tribunal, Musicians, Shepherds, | |
| | | etc. | |

SYNOPSIS

I. During the French Revolution, Andrea Chénier, a revolutionary poet, abuses the sensitivities of those who invited him to an aristocratic ball by singing one of his own inflammatory poems against the selfishness of class. The guests are cool. Significantly, a horde of beggars press at the door, but the Major-domo manages to get rid of them.

II. The revolution has come. Chénier should be careful now, but his love for Madeleine overrides caution. The revolutionaries are hunting for her. Trying to protect her, Charles

Gérard himself is wounded. His former friend Gérard warns Chénier that he is being watched.

III. Finally Gérard faces Madeleine, tells her that he loves her and that Chénier is now in prison by his order. She offers herself to him in exchange for Andrea's freedom but the revolutionary tribunal does not listen to Gérard's pleading on the captive's behalf. Andrea Chénier is condemned to die.

IV. At the last, Madeleine changes places with another prisoner so that she may die with her beloved.

**Anna Bolena**         *2 acts*
COMP.: G. Donizetti       Milan, 26 December 1830
LIBR.: F. Romani        London, 1831
                              New Orleans, 1839
                              New York, 1843

**Antar**         *4 acts*
COMP.: G. Dupont       Opéra, 14 March 1921
LIBR.: C. Ganem
Rehearsals were in progress in 1914 when the first World War intervened.

**Antigonae**         *Mourning play in 1 act*
COMP.: C. Orff       Salzburg, 9 August 1949
LIBR.: F. Hölderlin
From Sophocles

CAST

| | | | |
|---|---|---|---|
| Antigonae | S | Hämon | T |
| Ismene, *her sister* | MS | Tiresias, *blind seer* | T |
| Kreon, *their uncle, king* | Bar | Messenger | Bar |
| Watchman | T | | |

NOTES

This is a choral drama with instruments. Orff, never one to make easy use of the accepted forms, has scored his *Antigonae* for six grand pianos (to be played with hands, sticks, etc.), and four harps, nine double basses, six flutes, six oboes, six trumpets with mutes, seven or eight timpani, and ten to fifteen percussion instruments. The effect is of an intense, somewhat primitive, or rather elemental, Greek tragedy. Although it has only one act, it lasts nearly three hours in performance and is intended to be played without interruption.

**Antigone**         *3 acts*
COMP.: A. Honegger       Brussels, 28 December 1927
LIBR.: J. Cocteau       Essen, 1928
From Sophocles       New York, 1930

**Antigone**
COMP.: J. Joubert       BBC, 21 July 1954

**Aphrodite**         *5 acts*
COMP.: C. Erlanger       Paris, 27 March 1906
LIBR.: L. de Gramont       New York, 1920
From a novel by Loüys

## Arabella

| | | 3 acts |
|---|---|---|
| COMP.: R. Strauss | | Dresden, 1 July 1933 |
| LIBR.: H. von Hofmannsthal | | Covent Garden, 1934 |
| | | Salzburg, 1942 |

CAST

| | | | |
|---|---|---|---|
| Graf Waldner | B | Graf Lamoral, *still another suitor* | B |
| Adelaide, *his wife* | MS | Fiakermilli | S |
| Arabella, *his daughter* | S | Fortune Teller | S |
| Zdenka, *his daughter* | S | Welko, *Mandryka's servant* | |
| Mandryka | Bar | Djura, *Mandryka's servant* | |
| Matteo, *officer* | T | Jankel, *Mandryka's servant* | |
| Graf Elemer, *Arabella's suitor* | T | Servant, Duenna, Three Cardplayers, | |
| Graf Dominick, *another suitor* | Bar | Doctor, Groom | |

SYNOPSIS

I. Having lost practically everything in gambling, Waldner sees as his only hope to marry off his daughter to some rich man. One daughter, Zdenka, has been brought up completely as a boy because it is too expensive to maintain two daughters throughout a season in Vienna. This poor girl is in love with Matteo, but Matteo is in love with Arabella who refuses even to speak to him. There is a stranger, however, who occupies her every thought. She has seen him outside her window. Graf Waldner's troubles seem likely to be solved when the suitor calls on Arabella offering money on the side to Waldner to win the father's good will. This is Mandryka.

II. At the Fiaker ball, Arabella falls in love with Mandryka and accepts his proposal of marriage. But Zdenka has plans of her own, beginning with a note she hands to Matteo telling him to come secretly to meet Arabella at night. Coincidently Arabella disappears from the ball, leaving everyone with his private suspicions.

III. People come to the foot of the hotel stairs, led by their search for Arabella. There they find Matteo descending. Mandryka challenges Matteo on the spot. Then Zdenka, with her hair down, dressed in a very feminine negligee, appears at the head of the stairs ready to die for her desperate sin. Graf Waldner repents what he has caused, and gives Zdenka to Matteo. Arabella and Mandryka are both deeply moved by the realization of what has happened.

## Archers, The

| | Ballad Opera in 3 acts |
|---|---|
| COMP.: B. Carr | New York, 18 April 1796 |
| LIBR.: W. Dunlap | Boston, 1797 |
| From the tale of William Tell | |

The first American opera of which parts still exist.

## Ariadne auf Naxos

| | Prologue & 1 act |
|---|---|
| COMP.: R. Strauss | Stuttgart, 25 October 1912 |
| LIBR.: H. von Hofmannsthal | Vienna (*rev.*), 4 October 1916 |
| | Covent Garden, 1925 |
| | Philadelphia, 1928 |

CAST

*Of the Prologue*

| | | | |
|---|---|---|---|
| Major-domo | Spkr | Composer | S |
| Music Master | Bar | Tenor (*plays Bacchus in the Opera*) | T |

| | | | |
|---|---|---|---|
| Officer | T | Lackey | B |
| Dancing Master | T | Zerbinetta | S |
| Wigmaker | B | Prima Donna (*plays Ariadne* | |
| | | *in the Opera*) | S |

*Of the Opera*

| | | | |
|---|---|---|---|
| Ariadne (*plays Prima Donna* | | Naiade, *a nymph* | S |
| *in the prologue*) | S | Dryade, *another nymph* | C |
| Bacchus (*plays Tenor in the* | | Echo, *another nymph* | S |
| *prologue*) | T | | |

*Of the Intermezzo*

| | | | |
|---|---|---|---|
| Zerbinetta | S | Truffaldino | B |
| Harlequin | Bar | Brighella | T |
| Scaramuccio | T | | |

### SYNOPSIS

*Prologue:* Preparations are under way for a private performance of the opera *Ariadne*. To the composer's horror, the Major-domo suddenly announces that his master has decided that there shall be a Harlequinade played intermittently between the scenes of the opera. Nothing can be done about it, the opera begins.

*Opera:* Ariadne languishes, wishing she were dead. Not even the bright Harlequinade can cheer her. Stepping out of the intermezzo, Zerbinetta pleads with her, even tries reasoning. But nothing will rouse her will. Bacchus arrives. She mistakes him for Death, but with him poor Ariadne finds comfort.

### NOTES

The original intention was that the opera would be a *divertissement* during the performance of the play *Le Bourgeois Gentilhomme*, by Molière. The prologue was attached for the Vienna performance, in 1916. There was an amateur performance in New York in 1934. The first professional performance there, however, took place in the City Center in 1946.

**Ariane et Barbe-Bleue**  
(*Ariadne and Blue-Beard*)  
COMP.: P. Dukas  
LIBR.: M. Maeterlinck

3 *acts*  
Comique, 10 May 1907  
Metropolitan, 1911  
Covent Garden, 1937

#### CAST

| | | | |
|---|---|---|---|
| Barbe-Bleue, *Bluebeard* | B | Bellangère, *a fourth* | S |
| Ariane, *Ariadne* | MS | Alladine, *a fifth* | Mime |
| Nourrice, *nurse* | C | Peasant | B |
| Sélysette, *a previous wife* | | Second Peasant | T |
| *of Bluebeard's* | MS | Third Peasant | B |
| Ygraine, *another* | S | Peasants, Crowd | |
| Mélisande, *a third* | S | | |

### SYNOPSIS

1. Ariane, about to be the sixth wife of the notorious Bluebeard, the others presumably murdered, insists on knowing what did happen to them. She opens a secret door and hears their voices. Bluebeard catches her in the act but a violent crowd rushes in to prevent another tragedy.

II. At last alone again, she finds her way into the hidden vault and helps the others get free.

III. The peasants have trapped Bluebeard. They bring their trussed-up prize to the women as a present for their revenge. But his five wives loosen his bonds and wash his wounds. Ariane leaves them at peace.

**Arianna, L'**                         *Prologue & 8 scenes*
   COMP.: C. Monteverdi        Mantua, 28 May 1608
   LIBR.: O. Rinuccini          Florence, 1614
                                   Venice, 1639

Composed to celebrate the wedding of Francesco Gonzaga.

Most of the music is lost. But one melody of great beauty remains both as an aria, and arranged by Monteverdi as a choral piece. This is the famous *Lasciatemi Morire* (O let me die), the *Lamento d'Arianna*. A reconstruction of the opera was presented at Karlsruhe in 1926 and again in Paris in 1931.

**Ariodant**                            *3 acts*
   COMP.: E. Méhul             Comique, 11 October 1799
   LIBR.: F. B. Hoffman         Moscow, 1803
                                   Stockholm, 1808

**Arlecchino**                          *Comedy in 1 act*
   COMP.: F. Busoni            Zurich, 11 May 1917
   LIBR.: by the composer      London BBC, 1939
                                   Venice, 1940

CAST

| | | | |
|---|---|---|---|
| Ser Matteo del Sarto, *tailor* | Bar | Leandro | T |
| Abbate Cospicuo | Bar | Annunziata, *Matteo's wife* | Mute |
| Dr. Bombasto | B | Columbina, *Arlecchino's wife* | MS |
| Arlecchino | Spkr | | |

SYNOPSIS

Arlecchino, almost caught in the act of making love to Annunziata, leaps out the window shouting that the town is invaded by barbarians. Matteo, frightened, runs into his house. The Doctor and the Abbate hide. Arlecchino reappears as a soldier, knocks on the door, drafts Matteo into the army and sends him far, far away. He is about to recommence his amours when Columbina (exempt from any draft) catches him. Gallant Leandro swears to avenge Columbina by duelling Arlecchino. But Arlecchino outduels him with a wooden sword. Columbina, Abbate, and the Doctor find the body. But they are too drunk to do anything about it. Meanwhile, Arlecchino has fetched Matteo's wife and gone off with her.

**Arlesiana, L'**                       *Tragedy in 3 acts*
   COMP.: F. Cilèa            Milan, 27 November 1897
   LIBR.: L. Marenco           Naples, 1912
From the story by Daudet

CAST

| | | | |
|---|---|---|---|
| Rosa Mamai | MS | Metifio, *horse tender* | Bar |
| Federico, *her son* | T | Marco, *Rosa's brother* | B |
| Vivetta, *her god-daughter* | S | L'Innocente, *her second son* | MS |
| Baldassare, *an old shepherd* | Bar | | |

### SYNOPSIS

I. Federico wishes to marry a girl from Arles, but Metifio tells Rosa the girl is a strumpet. For proof he shows her a letter.

II. Vivetta, a home-town girl, loves Federico. Rosa urges her to tell him that she does, to help him get through the loneliness of losing the girl from Arles. Federico proves unwilling, but eventually accepts the girl's affection in order to soothe his mother's misery.

III. Metifio has been having an affair with a girl—the girl from Arles. When Federico hears it, he attacks Metifio and nearly kills him. Unavenged and furious, forgetting Vivetta, Federico goes mad and kills himself.

### NOTES

The opera was originally in four acts, but was reduced to three in 1898.

## Armide
| | 5 acts |
|---|---|
| COMP.: C. W. Gluck | Opéra, 23 September 1777 |
| LIBR.: P. Quinault | London, 1906 |
| From Tasso | New York, 1910 |

## Armide
| | |
|---|---|
| COMP.: J. B. Lully | Opéra, 5 February 1686 |
| LIBR.: P. Quinault | Rome, 1690 |
| From Tasso | Florence, 1911 |

## Ascanio in Alba
| | 2 acts |
|---|---|
| COMP.: W. A. Mozart | Milan, 17 October 1771 |
| LIBR.: G. Parini | |

Performed as half of a double bill for the wedding of the Archduke Ferdinand, with *Ruggiero*, by Hasse. This event has been pointed out as the end of the old style opera and the beginning of the new in a single performance.

## Asrael
| | 4 acts |
|---|---|
| COMP.: A. Franchetti | Reggio Emilia, 11 February 1888 |
| LIBR.: F. Fontana | New York, 1890 |
| | Buenos Aires, 1901 |

## Assassinio nel Cattedrale, L'
| | |
|---|---|
| (*Murder in the Cathedral*) | *Tragedy in 2 acts and an interlude* |
| COMP.: I. Pizzeti | La Scala, 1 March 1958 |
| LIBR.: Msgr. A. Castelli | New York, 1958 |
| From T. S. Eliot's play | |

### CAST

| | | |
|---|---|---|
| Tomasso Becket | B | Four Knights |
| Three Priests | | Two Leaders of the Chorus |
| Four Tempters | | Chorus |

### NOTES

The first American performance had begun at Ellenville, New York, during the summer of 1958, when the tent above collapsed in torrential rain and wind, forcing a halt in the production. Thus the first complete performance occurred in Carnegie Hall in the fall of 1958.

**At the Boar's Head**                                   1 act
    COMP.: G. Holst                  Manchester, 3 April 1925
    From Shakespeare's King Henry IV  London, 1925
                                           New York, 1935

**Atalanta**                                             3 acts
    COMP.: G. F. Handel               Covent Garden, 23 May 1736
    LIBR.: Unknown
    First performed in celebration of the wedding of the Prince of Wales to Princess Auguste of Saxe-Gotha.

**Attaque du Moulin, L'**                                4 acts
    COMP.: A. Bruneau                 Comique, 23 November 1893
    LIBR.: L. Gallet                  London, 1894
    From a story by Zola              New York, 1910

**Attila**                                               *Prologue & 3 acts*
    COMP.: G. Verdi                   Venice, 17 March 1846
    LIBR.: T. Solera                  London, 1848
                                          New York, 1850

**Aus einem Totenhaus**
    See *Z Mrtveho Domu*

**Aventures du Roi Pausole, Les**                        3 acts
    COMP.: A. Honegger                Paris, 12 December 1930
    LIBR.: A. Willemetz               Geneva, 1932
    From a novel by Louÿs

**Azora, the Daughter of Montezuma**                     3 acts
    COMP.: H. Hadley                  Chicago, 26 December 1917
    LIBR.: D. Stevens                 New York, 1918

**Ballad of Baby Doe, The**                              2 acts
    COMP.: D. Moore                   Central City, Colo., 7 July, 1956
    LIBR.: J. Latouche                New York, 1958

CAST

| | | | |
|---|---|---|---|
| Baby Doe, *miner's wife* | S | Old Miner | T |
| Augusta Tabor | MS | Priest | T |
| Horace Tabor, *mining magnate* | Bar | Hotel Clerk | T |
| William Jennings Bryan, *candidate* | | President Chester A. Arthur | T |
|   *for president* | B | Mayor, doorman, bouncer, bellboy, foot- | |
| Mama McCourt, *Baby Doe's mother* | C | man, politician, friends, children | |

SYNOPSIS

Baby Doe, having left her husband, enters the life of the respectable Horace Tabor, thirty years her senior. It means ruin for him in the society of the early West, but her love for him becomes deep and true.

The story is based on the lives of actual people in Leadville, Colorado, in the 1880's.

**Ballad Singer, The**
    See *Gioconda, La*

**Ballo in Maschera, Un**
(*The Masked Ball*)
COMP.: G. Verdi
LIBR.: Somma
From Scribe's libretto for Auber's
*Gustave III*

*Tragedy in 3 acts*
Rome, 17 February 1859
New York, 1861
London, 1861
Metropolitan, 1889

CAST

| | | | |
|---|---|---|---|
| Riccardo, *Count of Warwick, Governor* (*Gustavus III*) | T | Tomaso, *Count Horn, the governor's* enemy | B |
| Amelia, *Renato's wife* | S | Silvano, *a sailor* (*Cristian*) | Bar |
| Renato, *the governor's secretary* (*Anckarstroem*) | Bar | Oscar, *a page* | S |
| Samuele, *Count Ribbing, the governor's enemy* | B | Ulrica, *a fortune teller* (*Arvidson*) Judge, Servant, Populace, Guards, Courtiers | C |

SYNOPSIS

I. Riccardo is delighted to learn that there will be a masked ball at which he will have an opportunity of seeing the fair Amelia, whom he loves. He conceals his identity and pays a visit to Ulrica the fortune teller to find out what the outcome of this romance may be. There he watches Amelia, and overhears her telling Ulrica that she is in love with Riccardo. Ulrica directs her to go to a gallows at midnight to gather a certain herb. When Amelia has gone, Riccardo asks his questions. Ulrica predicts that he will be murdered by a friend.

II. He goes to the gallows to protect Amelia, who is there in veils gathering the herb. Renato follows him to warn him of conspirators who have set up an ambush. Riccardo sends the veiled woman with Renato but takes a different route himself. The conspirators capture Renato and unveil his companion. When Renato sees that the governor's beloved is his own wife, he is enraged.

III. He wants to kill her—but he loves her and cannot. Instead he decides that the governor must die. He and the conspirators draw lots from Amelia's unwilling hand to choose an assassin. It falls to Renato himself. That evening, at the masked ball, Renato ferrets out the governor and stabs him to death.

NOTES

The story is based upon the actual assassination of Gustave III of Sweden, which did take place at a masked ball. The story, however, was uncomfortable for the ruling powers in Italy in the 1850's, so that it became necessary, if there were to be a production, for Verdi to change the names and the locale to some safe place. Of all the available settings, he chose one of the most absurd—Boston. When the opera was about to open in Naples, there was an attempt on the life of Napoleon III. Crowds rioted, using "Viva Verdi" as their slogan. This was only incidentally a public comment on the composer, it was primarily a way of cheering in an acrostic for *Vittorio Emanuele, Re d'Italia* without precisely saying so.

**Barbe-Bleue**
(*Bluebeard*)
COMP.: J. Ibert

Lausanne Radio, 10 October 1943

**Barber of Seville, The**
See *Barbiere di Siviglia, Il*
See also *Nozze di Figaro, Le*

**Barbiere di Siviglia, Il**                    *Comedy in 4 acts*
COMP.: G. Paisiello                            St. Petersburg, 26 September 1782
LIBR.: G. Petrosellini                         New Orleans, 1810
From Beaumarchais' play                        Paris (rev.), 1868

    This opera was at first supplanted by the much more popular work of Rossini. Lately, however, in American opera workshops, the Paisiello is again finding audiences.

**Barbiere di Siviglia, Il**                    *Comedy in 2 acts*
(*The Barber of Seville*)                       Rome, 5 February 1816
COMP.: G. Rossini                              Covent Garden, 1818
LIBR.: Sterbini                                New York, 1819
From the play by Beaumarchais                  Metropolitan, 1883

### CAST

| | | | |
|---|---|---|---|
| Count Almaviva | T | Ambrogio, *the Doctor's servant* | B |
| Doctor Bartolo | B | Rosina, *the Doctor's ward* | S |
| Don Basilio, *a singing teacher* | B | Berta, (*Marcellina*), *Rosina's governess* | S |
| Figaro, *a barber* | Bar | Notary, Constable, Musicians, Soldiers | |
| Fiorello, *the Count's servant* | Bar | | |

### MUSICAL HIGHLIGHTS

ACT I. Serenade *Ecco ridente in cielo* (See in the sky now smiling), Almaviva
    Aria *Largo al factotum* (Room for the factotum), Figaro
    Serenade *Se il mio nome saper* (Shall I then tell you my name?), Almaviva
    Cavatina *Una voce poco fa* (Once a little voice I heard), Rosina
    Aria *La calunnia* (Slander's power), Don Basilio
    Duet *Dunque io son* (Can it therefore be?), Rosina, Figaro

### SYNOPSIS

I. Figaro discovers the Count in the act of serenading Rosina. Being prepared to propose anything, he suggests a way for the Count to meet her. Her guardian, the Doctor, is very watchful, however, so that it becomes necessary for Figaro, who can accomplish anything, to act as a go-between, giving Rosina the notion that the secret lover is his own cousin. This he does, but the Doctor is aware that something is going on. When Almaviva, ridiculously disguised as a soldier, tries to force his way into her presence, the real soldiers unmask him and nearly throw him into prison. Only when he shows them his credentials as a Grandee of the Empire do they let him go.

II. He tries again, this time disguised as her music teacher. Everything seems to be getting along swimmingly, with little love notes tossed in between the others in the music lesson, when the real teacher arrives. He has to be bribed to leave without betraying them. All this takes place while the good Doctor writhes in suspicion, trapped by being shaved by the dexterous barber. Finally he can stand it no longer, and rushes into the lesson room to confront his ward with her lover. Almaviva he denounces as a rake with a mistress. He rushes out to find a notary, but when he returns *sans* that functionary it is too late—Almaviva and Rosina are man and wife, wedded before a notary hastened to the occasion by the fascinating barber of Seville.

### NOTES

    Paisiello's opera on the same play was very popular when Rossini introduced his own. Public feeling was against him, for people were loyal to their favorite work. Rossini had to resort to advertising a letter from the older composer granting him permission to produce his version. At the first performance this strategy was worthless. The audience was hostile;  the actors hardly less so.  The production was full of ludicrous errors, the audience howled it down.  The next night, however, opened in better circumstances, with many changes in the score.  From that time on the Rossini outshone the Paisiello.

On the 29th November, 1825, *The Barber of Seville* opened in New York, the first opera performed in Italian in that city.

**Barbier von Bagdad, Der**
( *The Barber from Bagdad*)
COMP.:  P. Cornelius
LIBR.:  By the composer
From the Arabian Nights

*Comedy in 2 acts*
Weimar, 15 December 1858
Metropolitan, 1890

CAST

| | | | |
|---|---|---|---|
| The Caliph | Bar | Nureddin | T |
| Baba Mustapha, *a Cadi (magistrate)* | T | Abul Hassan Ali Ebn Bekar, *a barber* | B |
| Margiana, *the Cadi's daughter* | S | Servants, Friends, People, Wailing | |
| Bostana, *his servant* | MS | Women, The Caliph's Entourage | |

SYNOPSIS

I. Nureddin, hopelessly dying of love for Margiana, revives slightly when Bostana announces an arrangement for him to go to her.  With all due pomp, he prepares for his assignation, but the Barber, who is the most loquacious man in Bagdad, takes so interminably long in the process of shaving him that Nureddin fears all may be lost.  To prevent the barber from following him, which indeed the Barber seems prepared to do, he has his servants forcefully restrain the man.

II. Safely beneath her windows, the lover woos his love with song.  But backstage another serenade destroys the tenuous beauty of the moment.  It is the Barber.  Then, from somewhere else, come the pitiful cries of some poor slave being beaten.  The Barber rushes in, thinking Nureddin has cried for help from an assassin.  He calls a crowd.  But they find nobody there—Nureddin has hidden in a chest.  The Barber has the people carry out this chest, thinking his patron is dead inside.  At this moment the Cadi enters to see the mob in the act of carrying away his possessions.  All is utter turmoil until the Caliph enters.  In the abject silence of his presence, the people open the chest to find the living Nureddin.  Everything becomes clear, and all the tangles untangle.

NOTES

This work had had no performance until Liszt took interest.  At that time he was carrying on a difference of opinion with the management at Weimar.  When *The Barber of Bagdad* opened, there was an organized demonstration that completely wrecked the performance.  At this Liszt walked out of Weimar altogether.  Finally in 1885, re-orchestrated by Felix Mottl, the opera began to find success.  Not until 1904 was it performed in its original shape.

**Bartered Bride, The**
See *Prodaná Nevěsta*

**Basoche, La**
COMP.:  A. Messager
LIBR.:  A. Carré

*3 acts*
Comique, 30 May 1890
London, 1891
New York, 1893

## Bastien und Bastienne

COMP.: W. A. Mozart
LIBR.: F. A. Weiskern
From Favart's parody on *Le Devin du Village*

*Comedy-Pastoral in 1 act*
Vienna, September 1768
Berlin, 1890
London, 1894
New York, 1916

### CAST

| | |
|---|---|
| Colas, *a would-be sorcerer* | B |
| Bastien, *a lover* | S (or T) |
| Bastienne, *his beloved a shepherdess* | S |

### NOTES

Mozart was twelve when he wrote this. It was first performed in the garden of the famous hypnotist Mesmer.

## Bat, The

See *Fledermaus, Die*

## Béatrice et Bénédict

COMP.: H. Berlioz
LIBR.: By the composer
From Shakespeare's *Much Ado about Nothing*

*Comedy in 2 acts*
Baden-Baden, 9 August 1862
Comique, 1890
Glasgow, 1936
New York (concert), 1960

### CAST

| | | | |
|---|---|---|---|
| Don Pedro, *a general* | B | Claudio, *an officer* | T |
| Leonato, *the governor* | B | Ursula, *Hero's friend* | C |
| Héro, *the governor's daughter* | S | Bénédict, *an officer* | T |
| Béatrice, *his niece* | MS | Somarona, *orchestral conductor* | B |

### SYNOPSIS

I. Bénédict wishes to remain ever a bachelor. But Béatrice, whom he meets on return from battle, is too much for him.

II. Béatrice, on the other hand, used to despise amorous advances until Bénédict turned out to be too much for her. Both try to hide these unfortunate betrayals of weakness. But nothing suffices; they must admit their love and marry.

## Beaucaire, Monsieur

See *Monsieur Beaucaire*

## Beautiful Galatea, The

See *Schöne Galathee, Die*

## Beggar Student, The

See *Bettelstudent, Der*

## Beggar's Opera, The

COMP.: J. Pepusch (*Selected the music*)
LIBR.: J. Gay

*Ballad Opera in 3 acts*
London, 9 February 1728
New York, 1750
Hammersmith, England, 1920
(*it ran 1463 nights*)

### CAST

| | | | |
|---|---|---|---|
| The Beggar | Spkr | Polly Peachum, *their available daughter* | S |
| Mrs. Peachum | MS | Capt. MacHeath, *highwayman* | T |
| Mr. Peachum, *"a fence"* | B | Filch, *Peachum's man, pickpocket* | T |

| | | | |
|---|---|---|---|
| Lockit, *jailer, in league with Peachum* | Bar | Mat of the Mint, *and the* Gentlemen | |
| Lucy Lockit, *the jailer's daughter* | S | of the Road | |
| Diana Trapes, *the tally woman* | MS | Jenny Diver, Sukey Tawdry, *and the* | |
| | | Ladies of the Town | |

### SYNOPSIS

I. Filch lets drop that dear Polly seems to be carrying on with the notorious MacHeath. The Peachums are not sure whether that would imply a rise in station for their family or not, but at least they can turn affairs to their own advantage.

II. MacHeath is indeed involved with dear Polly, but he has other entanglements with the Ladies of the Town. Peachum uses them to trap his quarry in a tavern. To jail the unfortunate hero must go, but this is all in the business. Even Lucy, the jailer's daughter is with child by MacHeath. She lets him out.

III. Again, to save face and fortune, the jailer and the fence join forces to recapture their man. They prepare to hang him to prevent more embarrassments. The two girls vie for recognition as his wife, but four more wives turn up, just as eager to see the slaughter. At the last the beggar intervenes. He thinks all operas should end happily; and this one, being his, does, with a gay chorus of "Lumps of Pudding."

### NOTES

They say that Dean Swift once suggested that "A Newgate Pastoral might be made a pretty thing." Pepusch and Gay took up the idea; Rich produced it. The ballad opera was so remarkably successful that it caused Handel considerable annoyance. It has run intermittently up to the present day. The satire of the corruptions of courtiers and Italian opera carries even to the point of using, for the grand march of the highwaymen to their job, a famous march from *Rinaldo*. There are sixty-nine musical numbers, one of the most beautiful being a variant of "Over the Hills and Far Away."

### Beggar's Opera, The
See also *Dreigroschenoper, Die*

### Belle Hélène, La
    COMP.: J. Offenbach              3 *acts*
    LIBR.: Meilhac & Halevy

                       Paris, 17 December 1864
                       London, 1866
                       New York, 1867

### Belmont und Constanze
    COMP.: J. André                 Berlin, 25 May 1781
    LIBR.: C. F. Bretzner

To Bretzner's unavailing protest, the text of this opera was somewhat altered for use as a libretto for Mozart—*Die Entführung aus dem Serail*.

### Benvenuto Cellini
    COMP.: H. Berlioz            3 *acts*
    LIBR.: du Wailly & Barbier

                       Opera, 10 September 1838
                       Covent Garden, 1853
                       Glasgow, 1939

### CAST

| | | | |
|---|---|---|---|
| Cardinal Salviati | B | Francesco, *an artisan* | T |
| Balducci, *the papal treasurer* | B | Bernadino, *another artisan* | B |
| Teresa, *Balducci's daughter* | S | Fieramosca, *the papal sculptor* | Bar |
| Benvenuto Cellini, *famous goldsmith* | T | Pompeo | Bar |
| Ascanio, *his apprentice* | MS | | |

I. In sixteenth century Rome, the romantic sculptor, Benvenuto Cellini, barely concerned with his work, plans to elope with Teresa during the carnival. This fact is well known to his rival, Fieramosca. But when the suspicious father surprises his daughter in her room, he catches not the right man but Fieramosca.

II. Cellini, as do all artists, needs money. He manages to squeeze a little out of the treasury by promising to finish his *Perseus* by morning. The carnival takes precedence, however. Fieramosca attends in the same disguise that he knows Cellini will wear in order to confuse Teresa and prevent the elopement. There is a fight. One of the disguised ones kills Pompeo. In the confusion again the wrong man is caught—Fieramosca.

III. The *Perseus* is still unfinished. The cardinal threatens to have someone else complete the work. Finally remembering his call to art, Benvenuto rushes to finish the casting. When the moment of his arrest for murder is ripe, he unveils the new statue. Its beauty saves his life.

NOTE

The same subject was used by Franz Lachner, whose opera opened in Munich in 1849, and many others.

## Bettelstudent, Der

| | |
|---|---|
| (*The Beggar Student*) | 3 *acts* |
| COMP.: K. Millöcker | Vienna, 6 December 1882 |
| LIBR.: Zell & Genée | New York, 1883 |
| | London, 1884 |

CAST

| | | | |
|---|---|---|---|
| Palmatica, *the Countess Nowalska* | MS | Col. Ollendorf, *governor of Cracow* | B |
| Countess Laura, *her daughter* | S | Enterich, *prison governor* | Bar |
| Countess Bronislava, *Laura's sister* | S | Richtofen, *Saxon officer* | |
| Simon, *the Beggar Student* | T | Wangenheim, *another* | |
| Jan Janitsky, *his friend* | T | Henrici, *a third* | |

SYNOPSIS

I. In order to avenge his feelings on Palmatica, Ollendorf arranges for two prisoners, one a beggar, to be disguised as nobles and win the hand of her daughters Laura and Bronislava.

II. These two are no ordinary men; they are revolutionists who want to get money to help the Polish insurgents now at the gates of Cracow. Simon tries to tell Laura who he really is, but Ollendorf intercepts the note. When the wedding has been performed, Ollendorf lets his secret out.

III. But Laura is not dismayed, she loves Simon. In another attempt to help the insurrection, Simon has spread the rumor that he is the general of its army. For this he is about to be beheaded when the army breaks in and saves him.

## Billy Budd

| | | |
|---|---|---|
| COMP.: B. Britten | 4 *acts* | |
| LIBR.: Forster & Crozier | Covent Garden, 1 December 1951 | |
| From Herman Melville's novel | Wiesbaden, 1952 | |
| | Paris, 1952 | |

CAST

| | | | |
|---|---|---|---|
| Capt. Vere, *in command* | T | Mr. Redburn, *First Lieutenant* | Bar |
| Billy Budd | Bar | Mr. Flint, *Sailing Master* | Bar |
| Claggert, *Master at Arms* | B | Lt. Ratcliffe | B |

| | | | |
|---|---|---|---|
| Red Whiskers, *an impressed seaman* | T | Maintop | T |
| Donald, *seaman* | Bar | Novice's Friend | Bar |
| Dansker, *an old seaman* | B | Arthur Jones, *an impressed seaman* | Bar |
| Novice | T | Four Midshipmen | Boys |
| Squeak, *ship's corporal* | T | Cabin Boy | Spkr |
| Bosun | Bar | Officers, Sailors, Powder Monkeys, | |
| First *and* Second Mates | Bar (2) | Drummers, Marines | |

SYNOPSIS

I. (*Prologue*) Captain Vere recalls his life:

Once three seamen were thrown aboard, captured from another ship and brought to swell the crew. One of them was the stammerer, Billy Budd. There was hardly time to introduce them to the ship's tasks before the first battle came up.

II. Claggert intends to entrap Billy, his enemy, and embroil him in a framed-up plot for mutiny. Dansker warns the victim, but Billy is a happy-go-lucky sort who pays little attention.

III. Claggert has begun to drop hints to the Captain when the watch aloft sights an enemy sail. The battle lasts but one shot—there is no wind to manoeuvre with. In the doldrums Claggert reinforces his accusations. Being a good sailor, the captain insists that Claggert make the charge to Billy's face. Poor Billy, stifled by stammering, swings at Claggert and accidentally kills the man. By the articles of war he is condemned to be hanged.

IV. Dansker comforts him in the last moments. The yardarm is prepared, the prisoner taken to it. Then the crew boils into mutiny which is quelled—and (*Epilogue*) we see Capt. Vere again alone, contemplating this distant memory.

## Billy Budd
COMP.: G. F. Ghedini                               Venice, 7 September 1949

This work appeared before the Britten version, but has not been as successful.

## Blind King, The
See *Roi Aveugle, Le*
See also *Amore dei Tre Re, L'*

## Blue Forest, The
See *Forêt Bleue, La*
See also *Wald, Der*

## Bluebeard
See *Ritter Blaubart*
See also *Duke Bluebeard's Castle*
See also *Ariane et Barbe-Bleu*
See also *Barbe-Bleu*

## Boar's Head, The
See *At the Boar's Head*

## Boatswain's Mate, The
COMP.: E. Smyth
LIBR.: By the composer
From a story by W. W. Jacobs

*Comedy in* 1 *act,* 2 *parts*
London, 14 January 1916
Old Vic, 1922

CAST

| | | | |
|---|---|---|---|
| Harry Benn, *former boatswain* | T | Policeman | B |
| Ned Travers, *former soldier* | Bar | Farm laborers, Two cats behind | |
| Mrs. Waters, *an eligible landlady* | S | the scenes. | |
| Mary Ann, *her servant* | Spkr | | |

SYNOPSIS

Benn, to impress Mrs. Waters, conspires with Travers to perform a fake hold-up in which Benn may capture Travers, thus saving the lady from imminent danger.

The plan goes awry when Mrs. Waters catches the "thief" herself, pretends to kill him, and scares the wits out of Benn. To top it all, she is so impressed not with Benn but with Travers, she chooses to set her cap for that landsman instead.

NOTE

Dame Ethel Smyth was England's foremost woman composer.

**Bohème, La**           *Tragedy in 4 acts*
COMP.: R. Leoncavallo       Venice, 6 May 1897
LIBR.: By the composer       Hamburg, 1897
From a novel by Murger       Paris, 1899

The fact that Puccini's opera on the same subject came out before Leoncavallo's doomed the work.

**Bohème, La**           *Tragedy in 4 acts*
COMP.: G. Puccini       Turin, 1 February 1896
LIBR.: Giacosa & Illica       Covent Garden, 1897
From a novel by Murger       New York, 1898
      Metropolitan, 1900

CAST

| | | | |
|---|---|---|---|
| Rodolfo, *a poet* | T | Parpignol, *a peddler* | T |
| Marcello, *a painter* | Bar | Customs Official | B |
| Colline, *self-styled philosopher* | B | Musetta | S |
| Schaunard, *musician* | Bar | Mimi, *an embroiderer* | S |
| Benoit, *their landlord* | B | Students, Girls, Citizens, Shopkeepers, | |
| Alcindoro, *State Councillor* | B | Vendors, Soldiers, Waiters, Boys | |

MUSICAL HIGHLIGHTS

ACT I. Narrative *Che gelida manina* (Your tiny hand is frozen), Rodolfo
Aria *Mi chiamano Mimi* (My name is Mimi), Mimi
Duet *O soave fanciulla* (O beautiful maiden), Rodolfo, Mimi
ACT II. Waltz *Quando me'n vo, soletta per la via* (When I go alone along the street), Musetta
ACT III. Duet *Donde lieta usci* (Let us leave here happy) Rodolfo, Mimi
Quartet *Addio dolce svegliare* (Farewell until sweet morning), Mimi, Rodolfo, Musetta, Marcello
ACT IV. Duet *Mimi tu più* (Mimi, you false one), Rodolfo, Marcello
Death Scene *Sono andati* (Have they gone?), Mimi, Rodolfo

SYNOPSIS

I. Christmas Eve. The four artists share a garret on the left bank. There Rodolfo, who is alone for the moment, meets Mimi, who lives across the hall. She is visibly wasting away with "consumption." He falls in love with her immediately.

II. Into the crowded street they go for happiness. They find his room-mates and

Musetta, Marcello's former flame. She quickly drops her latest companion, Alcindoro, and follows her old friends into the evening of pleasures.

III. Later, in February, we find them at the edge of the city, quarreling and tense. Mimi and Rodolfo bitterly decide to separate. Musetta likewise fights with Marcello. But they do not part.

IV. Back to the attic, Musetta brings the now dying Mimi. Too late Rodolfo tries to help, too late they regret their bitterness. She dies in his arms.

## Bolivar

COMP.: D. Milhaud                 Paris, 12 May 1950
LIBR.: M. Milhaud
From Jules Supervielle

## Boris Godunov

| | | |
|---|---|---|
| COMP.: M. Mussorgsky | | *Tragedy in Prologue & 4 acts* |
| LIBR.: By the composer | | St. Petersburg, 8 February 1874 |
| From the play by Pushkin | | Paris, 1908 |
| | | Drury Lane, *&* Metropolitan, 1913 |

CAST

| | | | |
|---|---|---|---|
| Boris Godunov, *Tsar of Russia* | Bar | Rangoni, *a Jesuit in disguise* | B |
| Feodor, *his son* | MS | Varlaam, *a vagrant* | B |
| Xenia, *his daughter* | S | Missail, *another vagrant* | T |
| The Nurse | C | The Innkeeper | MS |
| Prince Shuisky | T | Nikititch, *the constable* | B |
| Shchelkalov, *secretary of the Douma* | | The Simpleton | T |
| (*Parliament*) | Bar | Two Jesuits | B (2) |
| Pimen, *a monk, chronicler* | B | Peasants and Serfs, Members of the | |
| Grigori, *later the pretender* Dmitri | T | Douma, Polish Ladies, Monks, | |
| Marina Mnishek, *Polish princess* | S | Guards, Soldiers, etc. | |

MUSICAL HIGHLIGHTS

PROLOGUE. *Coronation Scene*, Boris, Chorus
ACT I. Pimen's Chronicle *Still one more page*, Pimen, Grigori
     *Song of the duck*, Innkeeper
     *The Siege of Kazan*, Varlaam
ACT II. *Song of the gnat*, Nurse
     *The clapping game*, Feodor, Nurse
     Aria *I have attained the power*, Boris
ACT III. *Chorus of the girls of Sandomir*, Chorus
     Mazurka *Life is dreary*, Marina
     Polacca *No, milord, I scarce believe you*, Marina, Chorus
ACT IV. Pimen's Tale *A peaceful monk*, Pimen
     Death of Boris *Farewell my son*, Boris, Feodor, Chorus
     Simpleton's song *Flow, ah flow my bitter tears*, Simpleton

SYNOPSIS

PROLOGUE: The people, oppressed and weary of oppression, submit to the whips of the Boyards and chant for Boris to accept the crown and be their Tsar. Boris, having committed murder to accomplish this, accepts the office but already his heart is heavy with foreboding.

I. For five years plague rules the land. The peasants are as badly off as ever. Boris must take all the blame. In his quiet cell in the monastery Pimen puts the last words to his chronicle of the history of Russia. He pauses to tell his disciple, Grigori, how the former Tsar and all his family were murdered, the bodies left in the open for the world to see. There is a slight possibility that the Tsarevitch, Dmitri, may have lived. Grigori decides to exploit that possibility. He escapes to Poland to get support for a revolution.

II. Boris, in agony of guilt, hearing of intrigues in Poland, calls Shuisky before him. Shuisky tells him more of the bad news, and insinuates more evil for the Tsar. Alone, Boris becomes hysterical, seeing hostile images even in the mechanical clock in the corner.

III. In Poland, in the color and beauty of the court, Grigori, now called Dmitri, becomes the target of the ambitions of Marina who sees herself as Tsarevna, and of Rangoni, the ecclesiastical enemy of Russia. Rangoni uses Marina to worm his way into Dmitri's future and goads the pretender to return as Tsar.

IV. Boris speaks to the assembled parliament, but in a state of madness. Shuisky has Pimen brought in. Pimen tells all the tale of the murders and the possibility of the survival of Dmitri. Boris collapses. They take the Tsar to privacy, and while he speaks there with his son he hears the funeral chanting of the monks. In terror he dies.

Dmitri, the tool of the Jesuits, marches into Russia. But to the peasants he offers no change, they live like wolves. After all have passed by only the Simpleton is left, weeping in his own way for Russia.

### NOTES

The synopsis follows the original order of scenes. Rimsky-Korsakov, as he did for many musical works that fell into his hands, re-orchestrated and revised the original. The opera was generally performed in that revised form until recently. It is still a matter of hot debate whether the so-called crudities of Mussorgsky's harmony and orchestration may reveal more of the real beauty of the work than the smoothing out of his friend's.

The Imperial Theatre rejected the manuscript in 1869. It was revised and again rejected in 1872. In February of that year a concert performance of the *Coronation Scene* took place, and in April of the *Polonaise* from the Polish scenes. In 1873 three scenes, including that at the inn, were most successful. The first complete performance exhibited the poor vision of the professional critics—they all objected to the work, making it a critical failure in spite of its tremendous popular success.

*Boris Godunov* is without doubt the masterpiece of Russian opera. Its importance is not only in its beauty and its magnificence however; it represents, like the work of Gluck, a great change of style particularly in that it is almost (again like Gluck) a choral drama.

**Brief Life, The**
See *Vida Breve, La*

**Bronwen**
See *Cauldron of Anwyn, The*

**Bronze Horse, The**
See *Cheval de Bronze, Le*

**Brother in Love, The**
See *Frate 'Nnamorato, Lo*

## Butterfly, Madame
See *Madama Butterfly*

## Caïd, Le
COMP.: A. Thomas
LIBR.: T. Sauvage

*2 acts*
Comique, 3 January 1849
New Orleans, 1850
London, 1850
New York, 1852

## Camacho's Wedding
See *Hochzeit des Camacho, Die*

## Campana Sommersa, La
(*The Sunken Bell*)
COMP.: O. Respighi
LIBR.: C. Guastalla
From a play by G. Hauptmann

*4 acts*
Hamburg, 18 November 1927
New York, 1928

## Cantarina, La
(*The Songstress*)
COMP.: J. Haydn
LIBR.: Unknown

*2 acts*
Esterhaz, Austria, 1767
Bielefeld, Germany, 1939

## Canterbury Pilgrims, The
COMP.: R. de Koven
LIBR.: P. W. MacKaye
From Chaucer

Metropolitan, 8 March 1917
Philadelphia, 1917

## Capriccio
COMP.: R. Strauss
LIBR.: C. Krauss

*1 act*
Munich, 28 October 1942
Vienna, 1951
Covent Garden, 1953

CAST

| | | | |
|---|---|---|---|
| Countess | S | M. Taupe | T |
| Clarion, *an actress* | C | Two Italian Singers | S, T |
| Flamand, *a musician* | T | Dancer | Dancer |
| Olivier, *a poet* | Bar | Major-domo | B |
| Count, *the Countess' brother* | Bar | Eight Servants | 4T, 4B |
| La Roche, *a theatrical director* | Bar | Three Musicians | Violin, Cello, Cembalo |

SYNOPSIS

At the time of the war of the Gluckists and Piccinists, the Countess' friends have gathered in her salon. Flamand and Olivier are rivals for her affection. They take up the subject of opera and use it as a means each to win over the other. The opera becomes therefore a discussion of music, words and theater, with each character taking the side of that art with which he is most closely allied—and all for love.

## Capuletti ed i Montecchi, I
COMP.: V. Bellini
LIBR.: F. Romani
From Shakespeare's *Romeo and Juliet*

*Tragedy in 4 parts*
Venice, 11 March 1830
London, 1833
Boston, 1847

## Cardillac

| | | | |
|---|---|---|---|
| COMP.: P. Hindemith | | Dresden, 9 November 1926 | |
| LIBR.: F. Lion | | Zurich (*rev.*), 1952 | |
| From a novel by Hoffman | | London (Concert), 1936 | |

4 *acts*

CAST

| | | | |
|---|---|---|---|
| Cardillac, *a famous goldsmith* | Bar | Klymene, *the Alto of Lully's Opera* | A |
| His Daughter | S | Phaeton, *The Tenor of Lully's Opera* | T |
| His Friend | T | Apollo, *The Bass of Lully's Opera* | B |
| First Singer of the Opera | S | Chorus and Dancers *for Lully's Opera* | |
| Officer | B | Marquis | Mute |
| Cavalier | T | People, Theater Personnel, Night Watch | |

SYNOPSIS

Cardillac the goldsmith has such a fanatic love for the products of his own art that he contrives to murder anyone who manages to buy a piece for himself. The town hates him and fears him, but not until his fiendish revenge misses its mark in an attempt on his own daughter's lover do they become sufficiently aroused to tear him to pieces.

## Carmelites, The

See *Dialogues des Carmélites, Les*

## Carmen

| | | | |
|---|---|---|---|
| COMP.: G. Bizet | | Comique, 1 March 1875 | |
| LIBR.: Meilhac and Halévy | | London, 1878 | |
| From a novel by Mérimée | | New York, 1879 | |

Tragedy in 4 *acts*

CAST

| | | | |
|---|---|---|---|
| Don José, *corporal of the guard* | T | Frasquita, *gypsy friend of Carmen* | S |
| Escamillo, *famous Toreador* | Bar | Mercédès, *gypsy friend of Carmen* | S, MS |
| El Dancairo, *smuggler* | Bar | Carmen, *a gypsy* | S, MS |
| El Remondado, *smuggler* | T | Innkeeper, Guide | |
| Zuniga, *captain of the guard* | B | Officers, Dragoons, Boys, Cigarette Girls, | |
| Morales, *officer of the guard* | B | Gypsies, Smugglers | |
| Micaela, *peasant girl in love with Don José* | S | | |

MUSICAL HIGHLIGHTS

ACT I. March *Avec la garde montant* (Marching with the changing guard), Children and Soldiers

Habañera *L'amour est un oiseau rebelle* (Love is a dangerous bird), Carmen

Seguidilla *Près des ramparts de Séville* (Near the ramparts of Seville), Carmen

ACT II. Aria *Les Tringles des sistres tintaient* (The tingling music of guitars), Carmen

Toreador's Song *Votre toast je peux le rendre* (To your toast I'll give another), Escamillo, chorus

Flower Song *La Fleur que tu m'avais jetée* (The flower that you tossed to me), Don José

ACT III. Aria *Je dis que rien ne m'épouvante* (I say I will not be dismayed), Micaela

Procession of the Toreadors

SYNOPSIS

1. A square in Seville with a cigarette factory on one side. Micaela threads her way through the city crowd. She is looking for someone. Morales offers that he himself is

willing to be found, but Micaela wants to see Don José. She is frightened. She runs away, intending to come back when the guard changes and Don José becomes free. Amid the soldiering of little boys, the guard changes. People tell José his girl was looking for him; he decides to wait for her there. Since he loves her sincerely he pays no attention at all to the cigarette girls as they come out for a break in the sun. Suddenly Carmen is there, the center of all eyes, singing her love-maddening Habañera, tossing her beauty tantalizingly before the unwilling eyes of Don José. At the end of it, leaving her brand upon his heart she tosses a flower to his feet and leaves. The man hardly thinks of the trap as he picks it up, puts it in his tunic and looks up to see Micaela returning.

Carmen gives them no time for love. She causes a fight inside the factory, stabbing another girl. Zuniga orders her arrest, sending Don José in to do the job. But the insulting, attractive girl mocks the soldier so that Zuniga orders her hands to be tied. Don José stands alone with her, guarding the prisoner. She talks to him but he orders her not to talk. She sings to him. He cannot stop her. She sings of love and how to find her later at Lillas Pastia's. This Seguidilla tortures the corporal's soul so much he loosens her hands. When the other guards return to take her away, she frees herself and escapes with a taunting reminder of love lingering behind.

II. At Lillas Pastia's tavern Carmen lives in a kaleidoscope of men and gypsy girls, making love with Captain Zuniga. Escamillo enters her life, the famous Torero, the thrilling image of new possibility of romance. But, work before play; the smugglers call the girls together to plan their next job. Carmen should bring José into their ring, they could use a brave man. She agrees with delight to seduce him. He comes, she caresses him, she tempts him with dance. But he hears the distant bugle calling him to duty. Duty? She hurls the insult back at him, making him plead with her that he loves her. She has his love, but his loyalty to the guard will not waver. Just then Zuniga surprises them, Carmen's latest lover and José's captain. Rank should prevail, Zuniga orders the corporal out. But this straw breaks the back of duty. José draws his sword against his captain, thus committing himself to a criminal life in one gesture.

III. Now the military man has become a smuggler. He has become, also, unhappy. He has learned how brief may be the passion of such a girl as Carmen. Carmen is morose too, and cuts cards with her friends to predict her fate. Spades; death drops its hint. Business stirs them into action. All the smugglers take to the trail leaving Don José alone to guard their camp. When all have gone, a guide brings Micaela to the place. She doesn't find José, although he is nearby in his hiding place as she sings of her forlorn and faithful love. There is another sound in the night—Escamillo climbs to the hideout looking for Carmen. Don José stops him and challenges him on the spot. The fight is fierce until the gypsies return and separate the combatants. Escamillo, the proud bullfighter, invites all of them to see his next fight. Now, in the quiet after his departure, somebody finds Micaela. Don José is blind to her love and deaf to her pleas. Only when she tells him his mother is dying does he decide to go with her.

IV. Crowds gather outside the arena, waiting for the bullfight to begin. The procession enters; bandilleros, picadors, toreros, and finally Escamillo himself, with Carmen on his arm. Everyone goes in to see the fight except Carmen. Just before they leave her, one of her gypsy friends warns that Don José is nearby, with a knife. The glorious noise of the bullfight grows and grows while the two come together again in the square. José begs her once more to come with him. She haughtily refuses. A shout in the arena echos in her own shout for Escamillo's victory in love and fighting. José stabs her. Suddenly it is over, the people pour out of the arena onto the empty stage to find José standing over her body, ready to give himself up as her murderer.

NOTES

This French work symbolizes Spain to every opera audience except, for some reason, the Spanish. Carmen is certainly a masterpiece of the art of welding dramatic event into musical event. The most active moments in the play happen in set pieces of musical form —the Seguidilla in which Carmen effects her escape, the Toast of Escamillo, the contrapuntal mixing of bullfight music and aria in which the sacrificial bull inside the arena and the beautiful woman outside are both stabbed. Perhaps this achievement was one of the reasons the opening night audience seemed to receive the work coldly—the critics again made sure to point out all that was wrong with the work. It was months before people began to realize what a brilliant drama had been brought to them. After the opening performance, Bizet wandered about the city with his friend Guirard, perhaps unhappy at the reception of his greatest work. He died three months later.

There are several innovations of importance. In Carmen, the chorus must not stand still but is required to move and act while singing. They must also smoke cigarettes. These changes of tradition were difficult for singers and provoked a good deal of opposition to the production. The work was cut out of new cloth even to the point of the style of staging and the manner of orchestration. Audiences hardly ever take such changes with goodwill.

One song, the Habañera, was transcribed from an earlier work of Yradier. Bizet was unaware of its authorship while writing the opera.

### Carmina Burana
COMP.: C. Orff        Frankfurt, 8 June 1937
LIBR.: Arranged by the composer from medieval texts

Although this work has been staged in various ways ranging from stylized motion of a chorus to ballet against a choral background it is not so much an opera as it is a collection of choral songs based upon thirteenth century texts in Latin and German vernacular by men who had taken their leave of the monasteries.

### Carriera d'un Libertino
See *Rake's Progress, The*

### Castor et Pollux
COMP.: J. P. Rameau      *Prologue & 5 acts*
LIBR.: P. J. Bernard       Opéra, 24 October 1737
              Glasgow (by amateurs), 1927

### Cauldron of Anwyn      *Trilogy*
COMP.: J. C. Holbrooke
LIBR.: T. E. Ellis

This trilogy consists of the following operas, each first performed as shown:
*Children of Don* London, 15 June 1912
*Dylan*    London, 4 July 1913
*Bronwen*   Huddersfield, 1 February 1929

### Cavalier of the Rose
See *Rosenkavalier, Der*

## Cavalleria Rusticana
(*Rustic Chivalry*)
COMP.: P. Mascagni
LIBR.: Menasci and Targioni-Tozzetti
From a play by Verga

1 *act*
Rome, 17 May 1890
Philadelphia, 1891
Metropolitan, 1891

CAST

| | | | |
|---|---|---|---|
| Turiddu, *young soldier* | T | Mamma Lucia, *Turiddu's mother* | C |
| Alfio, *village teamster* | Bar | Santuzza | S |
| Lola, *Alfio's wife* | MS | Villagers, Peasants, Boys | |

SYNOPSIS

Turiddu loved and betrayed Santuzza. He has left her and returned to his old love, Lola, now Alfio's wife. Santuzza pleads with him to come back to her but he pays no attention. Seeing Lola he follows her into the church. Alfio comes along. Santuzza tells him about his wife and her lover. When Turiddu comes out of church, Alfio challenges him to fight with knives. Turiddu calls across the stage to tell his mother he is going away for a moment. The next thing Santuzza hears is the moan of the women outside saying Turiddu has been murdered.

## Cellini
See *Benvenuto Cellini*

## Cenerentola, La
(*Cinderella*)
COMP.: G. Rossini
LIBR.: J. Ferretti
From a libretto for Isouard's
  opera *Cendrillon*

2 *acts*
Rome, 25 January 1817
London, 1820
New York, 1826
Covent Garden, 1830

CAST

| | | | |
|---|---|---|---|
| Don Ramiro, *Prince of Salerno* | T | Thisbe, *another daughter* | MS |
| Dandini, *his valet* | B | Angelina, *his step-daughter,* | |
| Don Magnifico, *Baron Mountflagon* | B | *called Cinderella* | C |
| Clorinda, *his daughter* | S | Alidoro, *a philosopher* | B |

SYNOPSIS

I. The prince, disguising himself as his own valet, pays a personal visit to the baron's house in order to see the available daughters with his own eyes. Quickly he falls in love with Cinderella. Her sisters have planned to attend the prince's ball, but they will not permit Cinderella, who is little more than a servant to them, to go with them. Alidoro, who represents the fairy godmother, comes to her aid. She prepares to attend as an unknown lady.

II. Dandini, dressed up as the prince, falls in love with Cinderella but she politely refuses him saying she loves his servant, who is really the disguised prince. She identifies herself to him by giving him one of a pair of bracelets.

At home later, the sisters voice their suspicions. Alidoro conjures a storm to drive the unsuspecting prince into their house. During this uncomfortable visit, the prince notices the matching bracelet on Cinderella's arm. They recognize each other. Much to the amazement of the haughty sisters, their underling goes off to the palace with the prince to be married.

31

**Céphale et Procris**
COMP.: A. Grétry
LIBR.: J. Marmontel

3 *acts*
Versailles, 30 December 1773
Brussels, 1930

**Chalet, Le**
COMP.: A. Adam
LIBR.: Scribe and Mélesville

1 *act*
Comique, 25 September 1834
New York, 1836
London, 1845

**Charles the Fifth**
See *Karl V*

**Cheval de Bronze, Le**
COMP.: F. Auber
LIBR.: A. Scribe

3 *acts*
Comique, 23 March 1835
Covent Garden, 1835
New York, 1837

**Children of Don**
See *Cauldron of Anwyn*

**Choëphores**
COMP.: D. Milhaud
LIBR.: P. Claudel
Translated from Aeschylus

*Tragedy in* 1 *act*
Paris (Concert), 15 June 1919
Brussels (Stage), 27 March 1935

CAST

| | | | |
|---|---|---|---|
| Electre, *daughter of Clytemnestre* | S | Solo Leaders *from the chorus* | S, C |
| Oreste, *her brother* | Bar | Chorus | |

NOTE

This is the second part of the *Orestie* Trilogy. The first part is *Agamemnon*, the third is *Eumenides*.

**Christophe Colomb**
COMP.: D. Milhaud
LIBR.: P. Claudel

2 *parts*, 27 *scenes*
Berlin, 5 May 1930
London (Concert), 1937
New York (Concert), 1952

CAST

| | | | |
|---|---|---|---|
| Isabella, *queen of Spain* | S | Master of Ceremonies | T |
| Christopher Columbus I, | | Cook | T |
|   *as an old man* | Bar | King of Spain | B |
| Christopher Columbus II, | | Commandant | B |
|   *as a young man* | Bar | Messenger | Bar |
| Narrator | Spkr | Sultan Miramolin | T |
| Counsel for the Prosecution | Spkr | Officer, Counsel, Creditors, People, and |
| Representative of the Sailors | Spkr |   Cinematic Effects |
| Major-domo | T | |

SYNOPSIS

1. This is the book of the life of Columbus. The Narrator explains this, and shows us in cinema the position of the earth, spinning in space, and a dove. He summons the old man to consider his past life and allow the judgment of posterity upon it.

The young queen was given a dove in a cage by the Sultan Miramolin. She let it go free, and it flew over the seas. (Colombe, in French, is Dove).

Columbus conquers the sea. But his creditors dog him, making his life miserable. He goes to the court for help. The queen arranges to support an expedition for him, urged by the vision (in cinema) of the glories of Spain and of the New World. Columbus fits out three ships, and in spite of the crowd of the evil demons of discovery, sets sail on his voyage.

II. The king listens to hostile advice about his navigator and the new troubles that come with the gold of the New World. Columbus is put in chains aboard ship. The Cook tries to comfort him, but he remembers all the misfortunes he has allowed to happen.

The queen is dead. Columbus is alone now, defenseless against creditors. Suddenly we are in Paradise with the queen and all her past life present. She waits for Columbus to join her, but he cannot. She prays for Columbus.

### Le Cid
COMP.: J. Massenet
LIBR.: d'Ennery, Gallet, Blau
From Corneille's play

4 *acts*
Opéra, 30 November 1885
New Orleans, 1890

### Cinderella
See *Cenerentola, La*

### Clandestine Marriage, The
See *Matrimonio Segreto, Il*

### Clemenza di Tito, La
(*The Clemency of Titus*)
COMP.: W. A. Mozart
LIBR.: C. Mazzolà
From a play by Metastasio

2 *acts*
Prague, 6 September 1791
London, 27 March 1806
Falmouth, England, 1930

CAST

| | | | |
|---|---|---|---|
| Titus, *emperor of Rome* | T | Annius, *young patrician* | MS |
| Vitellia, *daughter of the deposed emperor* | S | Servilia, *Sextus' sister* | S |
| Sextus, *young patrician* | C | Publius, *captain of the guard* | B |

SYNOPSIS

I. To prevent Titus from marrying her rival Berenice, Vitellia conspires with Sextus against him. Titus, however, changes his mind and plans to marry Servilia instead. But she is in love with Annius. The good Titus dislikes breaking up other people's pleasures; he therefore again changes his mind and decides to marry Vitellia. This chain of events prevents the treacherous murder Vitellia had arranged.

II. For his part in the plotting, Sextus has been condemned to death. At the last possible moment Vitellia tells all. Titus, the example of imperial clemency, pardons both.

NOTES

This opera was commissioned for the coronation of Leopold II, as King of Bohemia. It was composed and performed within eighteen days of the commission. The 1806 performance in London was the first production of any Mozart opera in England.

### Cleopatra's Night
COMP.: H. Hadley
LIBR.: A. Pollock
From a story by Th. Gautier

2 *acts*
Metropolitan, 31 June 1920

33

## Cloak, The
See *Tabarro, Il*

## Coachman of Longjumeau, The
See *Postillion de Longjumeau. Le*

## Cock of Gold, The
See *Coq d'Or, Le*

## Columbus
See *Christophe Colomb*
See also *Cristoforo Columbo*

## Combattimento di Tancredi e Clorinda, Il

*Dramatic Cantata*

COMP.: C. Monteverdi　　　　　　　Venice, 1624
From Tasso's *Gerusalemme Liberata*　Published, 1638

NOTES

This work was written for pantomime by actors on the stage while singers sang the roles at one side. For orchestra Monteverdi used a string quartet, double bass and harpsichord.

## Consul, The

3 *acts*

COMP.: G.-C. Menotti　　　　　Philadelphia, 1 March 1950
LIBR.: By the composer　　　　London, 1951
　　　　　　　　　　　　　　　La Scala, 1951

CAST

| John Sorel | Bar | Foreign Woman | S |
| Magda Sorel, *his wife* | S | Anna Gomez | S |
| Mother | C | Vera Boronel | C |
| Secret Police Agent | B | Nika Magadoff, *magician* | T |
| Plainclothes Men (2) | Mute | Assan, *Sorel's friend* | Bar |
| Secretary | MS | Voice on the Record | S |
| Mr. Kofner | BBar | | |

SYNOPSIS

I. Sorel has been wounded while working for the underground. The police find nothing to incriminate him in his house. Magda tries to see the consul for help but an endless chain of bureaucratic delays prevents this.

II. A month later she gets word from her husband that she must get out of the country. At the consulate the wall of bureaucratic delays has cracked enough so that she is just about to see the consul. But the person who has been seeing him just before her is the Secret Police Agent.

III. Back at the apartment, she sends another message to her husband via Assan. She is there but a moment when John bursts in, pursued by the secret police. She leaves for a moment. When she returns, no one is there. The phone is ringing but she does not answer. She turns on the gas and waits for death.

## Contes d'Hoffmann, Les
(*The Tales of Hoffmann*)
COMP.: J. Offenbach
LIBR.: Barbier
From a play by Barbier and Carré

*Prologue, 3 acts, Epilogue*
Comique, 10 February 1881
New York, 1882
London, 1907
Metropolitan, 1913

## CAST

| | | | | |
|---|---|---|---|---|
| Lindorf, *Councillor of Nurnberg** | B | Giulietta, *courtesan* | | S |
| Andrès, *Stella's servant* | T | Schlemil, *her lover* | | B |
| Hermann, *a student* | Bar | Dapertutto, *a sorcerer** | | Bar |
| Nathanael, *a student* | T | Pittichinaccio, *Giulietta's admirer* | | T |
| Luther, *innkeeper* | Bar | Antonia, *singer* | | S |
| Hoffmann, *poet* | T | Crespel, *her father,* | | |
| Nicklausse, *his muse in disguise* | MS | *Councillor of Munich* | | Bar |
| Spalanzani, *inventor of* | | Frantz, *his servant* | | T |
| *strange machines* | T | Dr. Miracle, *doctor** | | Bar |
| Cochenille, *his servant* | T | Antonia's Mother's Voice | | MS |
| Coppelius, *scientist,* | | Stella, *opera singer* | | S |
| *Spalanzani's rival** | Bar | Muse of Poetry | | S |
| Olympia, *a mechanical doll* | S | | | |

* Played by the same man

### MUSICAL HIGHLIGHTS

ACT I. Doll's Song *Les Oiseaux dans la Charmille* (The birds in the bushes), Olympia

ACT II. Barcarolle *Belle nuit, O nuit d'amour* (Beauteous night, O night of love), Giulietta and Nicklausse

Aria *Scintille, Diamant* (Sparkle, Diamond), Dapertutto

### SYNOPSIS

PROLOGUE. Hoffmann has been going through an affair with Stella. Lindorf has been discussing it with the others when the poet enters the tavern. At their insistence, he agrees to tell the stories of his three great loves.

I. *Olympia.* Hoffmann made the mistake of falling in love with a mechanical doll. She nearly danced him to death, and sang his ears off. Only the fury of her creator's rival, Coppelius, smashing the machine to bits, released Hoffmann from his trance.

II. *Giulietta.* Hoffmann was determined not to fall in love, but Dapertutto provided the girl with a magic diamond with which to trap him. She stole his shadow from him with a magic mirror and left him to fight with one Schlemil, who had been likewise bewitched. Hoffmann won, but Giulietta had disappeared.

III. *Antonia.* He loved the consumptive Antonia. He discovered that a Doctor Miracle was treating her for her disease by making her sing, which would most certainly contribute to her death. Hoffmann finds her dead from frantic singing. He wants to call a doctor, but Dr. Miracle answers the call.

EPILOGUE. Hoffmann finishes his story and his wine. He is in love with Stella, but when she comes in he is dead drunk, face on the table. She tosses a flower toward him and leaves with Lindorf.

### NOTES

Offenbach died only four months before the opening. The orchestration was completed by Ernest Guiraud.

## Coq d'Or, Le
(*The Golden Cockerel*)
COMP.: N. Rimsky-Korsakov
LIBR.: V. Bielsky
From Pushkin

3 *acts*
Moscow, 7 October 1907
Drury Lane, 1914
Metropolitan, 1918

CAST

| | | | |
|---|---|---|---|
| King Dodon | B | Amelfa, *royal housekeeper* | C |
| Prince Guidon | T | Astrologer | T |
| Prince Afron | Bar | Queen of Shemakha | S |
| General Polkan | B | The Golden Cockerel | S |

SYNOPSIS

I. To protect the kingdom, the royal astrologer provides his king with a Golden Cockerel which will warn of any danger. With such a safety, the king and all his entourage fall asleep. When the cock crows, the king wakes enough to send out an army, then falls asleep again. It crows again. This time the king wearily puts on his rusty armor.

II. He finds his sons dead. He finds the Queen of Shemakha. The cock crows and crows but the king falls in love with her. Heedless of warning he takes her back to his kingdom.

III. The astrologer demands the Queen of Shemakha as payment for the Golden Cockerel. The king strikes him dead. At this the cock flies through the air and kills the king. Everything goes black. When light returns the queen and the cock have disappeared.

## Corregidor, Der
(*The Magistrate*)
COMP.: H. Wolf
LIBR.: Rosa Mayreder-Obermeyer
From a story by de Alarcon

4 *acts*
Mannheim, 7 June 1896
London, 1934
New York (Concert), 1959

CAST

| | | | |
|---|---|---|---|
| Don Eugenio de Zuniga, *Magistrate* | T | Pedro, *his secretary* | T |
| Doña Mercedes, *his wife* | S | Manuela, *maid* | MS |
| Repela, *his valet* | B | Tonuelo, *court messenger* | B |
| Tio Lucas, *a miller* | Bar | A Neighbour | T |
| Frasquita, *his wife* | MS | Duenna, *to Doña Mercedes* | MS |
| Juan Lopez, *mayor* | B | | |

SYNOPSIS

I. Frasquita, to win favor for her nephew, dances with the magistrate. To his misfortune he falls in love with her. This embarrassment causes him to swear revenge on her husband, Tio Lucas.

II. Tio is arrested. The magistrate appears at Frasquita's door all wet, as if he had fallen in the river. She lets him stay in the house while she goes to find out what happened to her husband. The magistrate hangs up his wet clothes and crawls into bed.

III. Tio escapes his guards and comes home to find the strange clothes hanging there and the magistrate, seen through the keyhole, in his own bed. In revenge he dresses in the now dry clothes and goes after Doña Mercedes. Unaware of this, the magistrate puts on Tio's clothes.

IV. All is soon explained. The miller and the magistrate both receive accidental but significant beatings, and the marriages remain firm as rocks.

## Cosa Rara, Una
COMP.: V. Martin Y Soler
LIBR.: L. da Ponte

2 *acts*
Vienna, 17 November 1786
Halle, 1921
Barcelona, 1936

Mozart quotes from this opera in his own *Don Giovanni*. The work was very popular in its time and is showing some signs of life even now.

**Così fan Tutte**
COMP.: W. A. Mozart
LIBR.: L. da Ponte

*Comedy in 2 acts*
Vienna, 26 January 1790
London, 1811
Metropolitan, 1922

CAST

| | | | |
|---|---|---|---|
| Fiordiligi | S | Guglielmo, *Fiordiligi's fiancé* | B |
| Dorabella, *her sister* | S | Don Alfonso | Bar |
| Ferrando, *Dorabella's fiancé* | T | Despina, *the sisters' maid* | S |

SYNOPSIS

I. The two swains make a bet with Don Alfonso that their fiancées are trustworthy even to the point that they could not be swayed by their own lovers disguised as strangers. To test it, Alfonso announces to the girls that the boys must go off to war. The parting, though full of sentiment, fails to disturb Alfonso in his certainty.

He introduces them to the two "strangers." Wooing begins, but the girls are not moved. The strangers try poison as a demonstration of their devotion. But Despina, disguised as a doctor, brings them back to life with mesmerism. Still the girls remain constant to their departed lovers.

II. Despina, a bit bored perhaps, convinces the girls there's no harm in giving in just a little. The serenading is therefore more successful, and Guglielmo manages to exchange a locket with Dorabella for a medallion containing Ferrando's picture. This astounds Ferrando. They carry their masquerade to the point that the girls finally agree to marry the two strangers. At the last moment, the strangers disclose their real identities. But love has short memory, and all forgive each other the divergences.

**Cricket on the Hearth, The**
See *Heimchen am Herd, Das*

**Cristoforo Columbo**
COMP.: A. Franchetti
LIBR.: L. Illica

*4 acts and Epilogue*
Genoa, 6 October 1892
Buenos Aires, 1902
Philadelphia, 1913

This opera was written to celebrate the 400th anniversary of the discovery of America.

**Cyrano de Bergerac**
COMP.: W. Damrosch
LIBR.: W. J. Henderson
From Rostand's play

*4 acts*
Metropolitan, 27 February 1913

**Czar and Carpenter**
See *Zar und Zimmerman*

**Czar's Bride**
See *Tsar's Bride, The*

**Dafne**
COMP.: M. da Gagliano
LIBR.: O. Rinuccini

Mantua, January 1608
Florence, 1610
Moscow, 1911

**Dafne** *Prologue & 6 scenes*
COMP.: J. Peri Florence, 1597
LIBR.: O. Rinuccini

The first opera. The production may have been a cooperative affair. Caccini and Jacopo Corsi also wrote music for certain parts of the libretto; in fact the only remaining fragments are by Corsi, in whose house this work was first performed.

**Dafne**
COMP.: H. Schütz Torgau, 23 April 1627
LIBR.: Translated by Opitz
From Rinuccini's libretto

This was the first German opera, written to celebrate the wedding of Princess Sophie of Saxony to George, Landgrave of Hesse. The music has been lost.

**Dalibor** *Tragedy in 3 acts*
COMP.: B. Smetana Prague, 16 May 1868
LIBR.: J. Wenzig Vienna, 1892
Berlin, 1940

CAST

| | | | |
|---|---|---|---|
| Vladislav, *king of Bohemia* | Bar | Milada | S |
| Dalibor, *knight* | T | Jitka | S |
| Budivoj, *captain of the guard* | Bar | Zdenek's Ghost | |
| Benes, *jailer* | B | Nobles, Soldiers, Men and Women | |
| Vitek, *Dalibor's squire* | T | | |

SYNOPSIS

I. In revenge for the death of his friend Zdenek, Dalibor killed Milada's brother. His own words of defense impress the bereaved lady, but the king condemns him to life imprisonment.

II. Milada finds her way into the jail, disguised as a boy. She searches for Dalibor and asks his pardon for her accusation which got him into prison.

III. There is an attempt to free Dalibor, but it fails. To prevent further attacks the prisoner is condemned to die. Milada joins the warriors to help in storming the castle, but in the second successful attempt she is wounded. Dalibor himself carries her out, but stabs himself when the king's troops surround him.

**Dame Blanche, La** *3 acts*
COMP.: F. Boieldieu Comique, 10 December 1825
LIBR.: E. Scribe Drury Lane, 1826
From Scott's *Guy Mannering* and New York, 1827
*The Monastery* Metropolitan, 1904

CAST

| | | | |
|---|---|---|---|
| Gaveston | B | Jenny, *his wife* | S |
| Anna, *his ward* | S | Marguerite, *old servant* | S |
| Georges Brown, *an English officer* | T | Gabriel, *Dickson's man* | B |
| Dickson, *tenant* | T | MacIrton, *Justice of the Peace* | B |

SYNOPSIS

I. Poor Dickson has been summoned to appear for judgment before the ghost of the White Lady, who protects innocent females from false-hearted suitors. Georges offers to go in his place.

II. The castle is up for auction. Anna has been acting the part of the White Lady's ghost in order to keep the place out of Gaveston's hands. When Georges appears instead of Dickson she recognizes him as a soldier whose life she once saved. When the auction takes place, Georges bids for the castle, and with Anna's spurring, wins it with a tremendously high bid.

III. It turns out that he is heir of the castle anyway. But to pay the large sum he bid for it, the White Lady conveniently finds a chest full of money.

## Damnation de Faust, La

COMP.: H. Berlioz
LIBR.: Berlioz, Girard, Gandonnière

*Dramatic Legend in 4 parts*
Opéra (Concert), 6 December 1846
Drury Lane (in part), 1847
Manchester (Complete), 1880
New York, 1880

CAST

| | | | |
|---|---|---|---|
| Marguerite | S | Brander | B |
| Faust | T | Students, Soldiers, Citizens, | |
| Méphistophélès | B | Men and Women, Fairies | |

SYNOPSIS

I. Faust contemplates nature and the solitude of intelligence.

II. Faust laments his existence. He considers the church, but Mephisto tempts him to a life of pleasure. Together they visit a beer hall and sing with the students and soldiers, then the banks of the Elbe where all is peace and the air is as perfume.

III. Faust woos Marguerite.

IV. Marguerite has been condemned to death. Faust sees her as in a vision, carried into hell. He gives his own soul to Mephisto for her salvation. In an Epilogue, the spirits of hell seize him while the spirits of heaven gently take her up among the seraphim.

NOTE

The work was first adapted for stage by Raoul Gunsbourg, for a production at Monte Carlo, 18 February 1893. The first production at the Metropolitan was in 1906.

## Danae

See *Liebe der Danae, Die*

## Dantons Tod

(*Danton's Death*)
COMP.: Gottfried von Einem
LIBR.: B. Blacher
From the play by Büchner

*2 acts, 6 scenes*
Salzburg, 6 August 1947

CAST

| | | | |
|---|---|---|---|
| Georg Danton | Bar | Young Man | T |
| Camille Desmoulins | T | Two Hangmen | T |
| Hérault de Séchelles | T | Julie, *Danton's wife* | MS |
| Robespierre | T | Lucile, *Desmoulins' wife* | S |
| St. Just | B | Lady | S |
| Herrmann | Bar | A Wife | C |
| Simon | B | | |

The story of the death of Georges Danton, French revolutionist, and the intrigues of Robespierre.

**Daphne**
See *Dafne*

**Daphne**                                    1 *act*
COMP.: R. Strauss                             Dresden, 15 October 1938
LIBR.: J. Gregor                              La Scala, 1942
                                              Buenos Aires, 1948

CAST

| | | | |
|---|---|---|---|
| Peneios, *fisherman* | B | Apollo | T |
| Gaea, *his wife* | C | Four Shepherds | T, Bar, B, B |
| Daphne, *their daughter* | S | Two maids | S |
| Leukippos, *shepherd* | T | | |

SYNOPSIS

Leukippos loves Daphne, but she loves nature, not Leukippos. Peneios has long been convinced that the gods will once again walk the earth. One day one does; Apollo comes to him dressed as a shepherd.

The people ridicule Peneios for thinking this young man is a god. He calls his daughter to see. She falls in love with Apollo, but tears herself away because she does not want love.

There is a feast at which Leukippos makes advances toward Daphne. Apollo, powerful and jealous, lets fly with a thunderclap, then identifies himself to her. She will have neither of them. Apollo kills Leukippos, but in remorse transforms the girl into a tree—the laurel.

**Dardanus**                                  *Prologue and 5 acts*
COMP.: J. P. Rameau                           Opéra, 19 November 1739
LIBR.: C. L. de la Bruère                     Staged in Algiers, 1934

**Dark Waters**
COMP.: E. Krenek                              University of So. California, 1951

**Daughter of the Regiment, The**
See *Figlia del Reggimento, La*

**David**                                     5 *acts*, 12 *scenes*
COMP.: D. Milhaud                             Jerusalem, 1 June 1954
LIBR.: A. Lunel

NOTES

This huge work was commissioned by the Koussevitzky Foundation and composed for the three thousandth anniversary of Israel.

**Dead City, The**
See *Tote Stadt, Die*

**Debora e Jaele**                            *Tragedy in 3 acts*
COMP.: I. Pizzetti                            La Scala, 16 December 1922
LIBR.: By the composer                        Buenos Aires, 1923

CAST

| | | | |
|---|---|---|---|
| Debora, *prophetess* | MS | Navi, *prince of Nephthali* | Bar |
| Jaele, *Hever's wife* | S | Barak, *Jewish commander* | B |
| Mara | MS | Azriel | T |
| Hever, *the Kenite, spy* | Bar | Shillem | T |

| | | | |
|---|---|---|---|
| Jesser | Bar | Piram | Bar |
| King Sisera | T | Jafia | T |
| Adonisedek | BBar | Enan, *the blind* | B |

SYNOPSIS

I. The people clamor to Debora that Sisera has demolished Israel. They curse Jaele as his consort. Debora satisfies them with a promise of victory over the King through a woman.

II. Jaele goes to Sisera at Debora's bidding to betray the King and to save her own reputation with her people. But Sisera is a man worthy of love rather than hate. She cannot bring herself to stab him.

III. The Jews open the battle and are victorious. Sisera, in flight, goes to Jaele for safety. The Jews follow him there but when they enter her tent they find only his corpse. He has been slain by Jaele to protect him from their vengeance.

### Déserteur, Le

| | |
|---|---|
| COMP.: P. Monsigny | 3 *acts* |
| LIBR.: J. M. Sedaine | Paris, 6 March 1769 |
| | London, 1773 |
| | New York, 1787 |

### Deux Journées, Les
(*The Two Days* or *The Water Carrier*)

| | |
|---|---|
| COMP.: L. Cherubini | 3 *acts* |
| LIBR.: J. N. Bouilly | Paris, 16 January 1800 |
| | Covent Garden, 1801 |
| | New Orleans, 1811 |
| | New York, 1827 |

A favorite of Beethoven, Mendelssohn, and Spohr.

### Devin du Village, Le
(*The Village Soothsayer*)

| | |
|---|---|
| COMP.: J. J. Rousseau | 1 *act* |
| LIBR.: By the composer | Fontainebleau, 18 October 1752 |
| | Drury Lane, 1766 |
| | New York, 1790 |

One of the first operas with spoken dialogue. It uses the same story as *Bastien und Bastienne*.

### Dialogues des Carmélites, Les

| | |
|---|---|
| COMP.: F. Poulenc | 3 *acts*, 12 *scenes* |
| LIBR.: G. Bernanos | La Scala, 26 January 1957 |
| | San Francisco, 1957 |

CAST

| | | | |
|---|---|---|---|
| Blanche | S | S. Mathilde | MS |
| Marquis de la Force, *her father* | Bar | Father Confessor | T |
| Le Chevalier, *his son* | T | First Officer | T |
| Mme. de Croissy, | | Second Officer | Bar |
| *prioress of the Convent* | C | Jailer | Bar |
| Mme. Lidione, *the new prioress* | S | Thierry, *valet* | Bar |
| Mother Marie of the Incarnation | MS | M. Javelinot, *physician* | Bar |
| S. Constance of St. Denis | S | Nuns, Officials, Officers, Police, | |
| Mother Jeanne | C | Prisoners, Guards, Townspeople | |

NOTE

The story recalls the martyrdom of the Carmelite Nuns.

## Dido and Aeneas

| | | *Prologue and 3 acts* |
|---|---|---|
| COMP.: | H. Purcell | Chelsea, London, ca. Christmas, 1689 |
| LIBR.: | N. Tate | New York, 1924 |
| | | Florence, 1940 |

CAST

| | | | |
|---|---|---|---|
| Dido, *queen of Carthage* | MS | Two witches | S |
| Aeneas | T | Spirit | S |
| Belinda, *Dido's lady in waiting* | S | Greek Sailor | T |
| Sorceress | MS | Courtiers, People, Witches, Sailors | |
| Two Women | S, MS | | |

SYNOPSIS

I. Dido laments her grief which she admits is caused by the offer of the love of Aeneas, the Trojan hero. Belinda and the chorus urge her to put away her troubles and accept his love. But there is a sorceress elsewhere in Carthage, plotting the destruction of the city.

II. Dido and Aeneas are enjoying a hunt together when a violent storm sends all but the warrior to shelter. When he is alone, he sees the image of Mercury who warns him to leave Carthage and to go found a great city.

III. The fleet prepares to leave, at which the sorceress rejoices. But the man weakened by love changes his mind and swears he will stay with Dido and risk the vengeance of the gods. This show of indecision is abhorrent to her—if he could have left her before, his promise to remain can be of little worth. He must leave. She turns away from him and prepares to die with the famous lament *When I am Laid in Earth*.

## Dimitri

See *Dmitrij*
See also *Boris Godunov*

## Dinorah

| | | *3 acts* |
|---|---|---|
| COMP.: | G. Meyerbeer | Comique, 4 April 1859 |
| LIBR.: | Barbier and Carré | Covent Garden, 1859 |
| | | New York, 1862 |
| | | Metropolitan, 1892 |

CAST

| | | | |
|---|---|---|---|
| Dinorah, *peasant girl* | S | Huntsman | B |
| Hoël, *goatherd* | Bar | Harvester | T |
| Corentino, *bagpiper* | T | Goatherds (*two*) | S, C |

## Djamileh

| | | *1 act* |
|---|---|---|
| COMP.: | G. Bizet | Comique, 22 May 1872 |
| LIBR.: | L. Gallet | Covent Garden, 1893 |
| From *Namouna*, by de Musset | | Boston, 1913 |

CAST

| | | | |
|---|---|---|---|
| Djamileh, *a slave* | MS | Splendiano, *his secretary* | T |
| Haroun, *prince* | T | A Slave Merchant | |

SYNOPSIS

Djamileh has fallen in love with her master, but he has become tired of her and shows signs of wanting to shop around for another. She arranges with Splendiano to win the prince back or to marry Splendiano instead.

The slave merchant shows the prince his wares. One of them is Djamileh, who in disguise dances and enthralls the prince. He buys her. When he discovers her trick his love is again renewed.

## Dmitrij

| | | 4 *acts* | |
|---|---|---|---|
| COMP.: A. Dvořák | | Prague, 8 October 1882 | |
| LIBR.: M. Červinková-Riegrová | | Vienna, 1892 | |

CAST

| | | | |
|---|---|---|---|
| Dmitrij, *pretender to the throne* | T | Xenia, *daughter of Tsar Boris* | S |
| Marfa, *Tsar Ivan's widow* | | Shuisky, *prince* | |
| Marina | S | | |

NOTE

This is the story of the brief appearance of Dimitri who rode into power at the death of Boris Godunov, and was himself deposed by the accession of Shuisky. The more famous treatment is the opera *Boris Godunov*. Another opera on the same subject (called *Dimitri*) was produced by V. de Joncières in Paris in 1876.

## Doctor Faust

See *Doktor Faust*

## Docteur Miracle, Le

Offenbach offered a prize for an opera to be written to this libretto. Both Georges Bizet and Alexandre Lecocq submitted works in 1857 and shared the prize.

## Doktor Faust

| | | 6 *Tableaux* | |
|---|---|---|---|
| COMP.: F. Busoni | | Dresden, 21 May 1925 | |
| LIBR.: By the Composer | | London (Concert), 1937 | |
| From the ancient puppet play | | Florence, 1942 | |

CAST

| | | | |
|---|---|---|---|
| Doctor Faust | Bar | Jurist | B |
| Wagner, *his attendant* | Bar | Doctor of Natural History | Bar |
| Mephistopheles | T | Four Students from Wittenberg | T(4) |
| Duke of Parma | T | Gravis, *spirit voice* | B |
| Duchess of Parma | S | Levis, *spirit voice* | B |
| Master of Ceremonies | B | Asmodus, *spirit voice* | Bar |
| Brother of the Girl, *a soldier* | Bar | Beelzebub, *spirit voice* | T |
| Lieutenant | T | Megärus, *spirit voice* | T |
| Three students from Krakov | T, B, B | Church goers, Soldiers, Courtiers, | |
| Theologian | B | Hunters, Students, Countrypeople | |

NOTES

This opera was taken not from Goethe but from the more ancient puppet play. Mephisto appears as a Man in Black, Monk, Herald, Chaplain, Courier, Watchman, and a voice. The work was completed by Jarnach.

## Doktor Faust

| | *Tragedy in 4 acts* |
|---|---|
| COMP.: I. Walter | Bremen, 28 December 1797 |
| LIBR.: H. Schmieder | Regensburg (*rev.*), 1819 |
| From Goethe | |

This is the earliest opera on the subject of Faust.

**Doktor und Apotheker**
(*Doctor and Apothecary*)
COMP.: K. von Dittersdorf
LIBR.: G. Stephanie

2 *acts*
Vienna, 11 July 1786
London, 1788
Boston, 1795

**Don Carlos**
COMP.: G. Verdi
LIBR.: Méry and du Locle
From Schiller

*Tragedy in 5 acts*
Opéra, 11 March 1867
Covent Garden, 1867
New York, 1877

CAST

| | | | |
|---|---|---|---|
| Elisabeth de Valois, *queen of Spain* | S | Monk | B |
| Princess Eboli, *her lady-in-waiting* | MS | Tebaldo, *Elisabeth's page* | S |
| Don Carlos, *heir to the throne* | T | Count Lerma | T |
| Rodrigo, *marquis of Poia* | Bar | Royal Herald | T |
| Filippo II, *king of Spain* | B | Heavenly Voice | S |
| Grand Inquisitor | B | | |

SYNOPSIS

I. Don Carlos, betrothed as a condition of peace to Elisabeth of France, falls in love with her. He cannot have her, however, since the king of Spain himself asks her hand to end the war with France.

II. Carlos arranges an interview with her when she has become his new stepmother, but she can no longer accept his vehement love. At this time in the policies of the nation, Rodrigo advises the king it would be wise to ease his repressions in Flanders lest he become infamous. In turn the king warns Rodrigo of his personal liabilities with the Inquisition.

III. Eboli makes an attempt to win Don Carlos' love. When she fails she threatens trouble for him. But he courts trouble himself when at a ceremony of the death of Flemish heretics he openly opposes the king, drawing his sword. Only Rodrigo's intervention prevents serious trouble.

IV. The Grand Inquisitor demands punishment for Rodrigo. The king, at Eboli's suggestion, has searched for and found a picture of Don Carlos in the Queen's possession. Carlos is sent to prison for this. He speaks there with Rodrigo, but an assassin puts an end to Rodrigo's life. Eboli stirs the people to riot to free Carlos.

V. Carlos meets Elisabeth for a short moment in secret before the emperor's tomb. There the king and the Inquisition capture them, but a voice from the tomb stops them and ushers Carlos into the sanctuary.

NOTES

The five act structure of the opera was required by the conditions of its production at the Opéra. Verdi had such differences with the management in Paris that it affected the rest of his relations with that house (see *Aida*).

**Don César de Bazan**
COMP.: J. Massenet
LIBR.: d'Ennery and Chantepie
Massenet's second opera.

3 *acts*
Comique, 30 November 1872
Vienna, 1874

**Don Giovanni**
COMP.: W. A. Mozart
LIBR.: L. da Ponte
From a libretto by Bertati

*Comedy in 2 acts*
Prague, 29 October 1787
London, 1817
Philadelphia, 1818

CAST

| | | | | |
|---|---|---|---|---|
| Leporello, *Don Giovanni's servant* | B | Donna Elvira, *a lady of Burgos* | S | |
| Donna Anna, *Don Ottavio's fiancée* | S | Zerlina, *Masetto's fiancée, peasant* | S | |
| Don Giovanni, *a noble libertine* | Bar | Masetto, *a peasant* | B | |
| Commendatore, *Donna Anna's father* | B | Peasants and Invisible Demons | | |
| Don Ottavio, *Donna Anna's betrothed* | T | | | |

MUSICAL HIGHLIGHTS

ACT I. Aria *Notte e giorno faticar* (That's a servant's life indeed), Leporello

The Catalog *Madamina*, Leporello

Aria *Ho capito, signor sì* (Don't mistake me, signor, don't), Masetto

Duet *Là ci darem la mano* (Do put your hand in my hand), Don Giovanni and Zerlina

Aria *Fuggi il traditore* (Beware that traitor), Donna Elvira

Quartet *Non ti fidar o misera* (Do not trust yourself to him), Donna Elvira, Donna Anna, Don Giovanni, Don Ottavio

Aria *Or sai chi l'onore* (I will have vengeance), Donna Anna

Aria *Dalla sua pace* (She is the measure), Ottavio

Aria *Finch' han dal vino* (Song, women, wine), Don Giovanni

Aria *Batti, batti O bel Masetto* (Scold me, scold me, dear Masetto), Zerlina

The *Menuet*

Trio of the Masks *Protegga il giusto cielo* (Protect us, in the shadows), Elvira, Anna, Don Ottavio

ACT II. Trio *Ah taci, ingiusto core* (Ah, silence, unworthy heart) Donna Elvira, Don Giovanni, Leporello

Serenade *Deh vieni alla finestra* (Look down from your window), Don Giovanni

Aria *Vedrai, carino* (I'm here, my dearest), Zerlina

Aria *Il mio tesoro intanto* (Here is my treasure beloved), Don Ottavio

Aria *Mi tradì quel alma ingrata* (He betrayed me with his attentions), Donna Elvira

Duet *O statua gentillissima* (O Gentlest statue), Leporello and Don Giovanni

Aria *Non mi dir* (Don't tell me), Donna Anna

SYNOPSIS

I. Don Giovanni, who according to Leporello's catalog of affairs has scandalously betrayed some two thousand innocent women, is still busy knocking at the heart of Donna Anna when her father surprises them, challenges the interloper, and is unfortunately killed. Don Ottavio swears to avenge the death of his fiancée's father.

Again on the prowl, Don Giovanni comes upon a band of peasants celebrating a betrothal. He interjects himself here, too, making overtures for the girl's love himself. Masetto threatens revenge but it is Donna Elvira, bitter from her own experience, who comes upon the scene with warning for the innocent Zerlina. Donna Anna, in turn, hearing the noble libertine's voice recognizes her father's murderer.

But Zerlina was not really so completely innocent. She spends a little time in the garden with her lover Masetto, explaining that she loves him and so forth. Then she goes to the ball as she had intended. There three masked ones dance with the others. They are Elvira, Anna, and Ottavio looking for an opportunity for revenge. Don Giovanni manages to remain safe, however, and to woo Zerlina in the bargain.

II. While Don Giovanni, dressed as his own servant, sings a serenade below Zerlina's window, Masetto and his friends come to murder the man. Since they don't recognize him, he sends them off various ways and drubs Masetto privately himself. Leporello, in his master's clothes, very nearly gets the hanging. He escapes, however, and meets Don Giovanni in a convenient churchyard. There they are startled to see the statue of the murdered Commendatore who speaks to them in sepulchral tones. The Don makes Leporello issue the stone image an invitation to visit him. To his horror, during preparations for a supper before Donna Anna's marriage, the statue does appear. Pits of flames open under his feet and Don Giovanni is carried off to hell.

### NOTES

This masterpiece was commissioned by the Prague Opera. They say Mozart was enjoying a party the night before the opening when someone reminded him that there was no overture yet. He thereupon excused himself and wrote, with his wife's company to keep him at it, the whole curtain piece. There is also a fairly probable story that he was unsatisfied with the way the Zerlina screamed during rehearsals. He is said to have sneaked back to the wings and to have pinched her at just the right time, getting precisely the effect he wanted. But this has been told of many others.

The opera first appeared in the United States under the title *The Libertine*.

### Don Juan

Mozart's opera was certainly not the only successful work on the subject. There were plays such as: *El Burlador de Seville* (Tirso de Molina, 1571-1641), *Le Festin de Pierre* (Molière, 1665, introducing Donna Elvira as a character), *The Libertine* (Shadwell, 1676), *Don Giovanni Tenorio* (Goldoni, 1736), and an opera by Gazzanigo with libretto by Bertati, which was the actual source of Mozart's and da Ponte's libretto.

### Don Juan de Mañara

|  |  |
|---|---|
| | 4 *acts* |
| COMP.: E. Goossens, III | Covent Garden, 24 June 1937 |
| LIBR.: A. Bennett | |
| (See also *Ombra di Don Giovanni*) | |

### Don Pasquale

|  |  |
|---|---|
| | *Comedy in 3 acts* |
| COMP.: G. Donizetti | Paris, 3 January 1843 |
| LIBR.: G. Ruffini | London, 1843 |
| From Anelli's *Ser Marcantonio* | New York, 1846 |

### CAST

| | | | |
|---|---|---|---|
| Don Pasquale, *an old bachelor* | B | Norina, *a young widow* | S |
| Doctor Malatesta, *his friend* | Bar | Notary | Bar |
| Ernesto, *his nephew* | T | | |

### SYNOPSIS

I. Don Pasquale has forbidden Ernesto's love for Norina on pain of losing his inheritance. But he himself wishes to be married. His friend, Malatesta, engineers a plan by which a marriage is arranged for him with none other than Norina. Somehow this was to help relieve the bad situation with Ernesto, but Norina doesn't enjoy the idea at all.

II. Playing the shy bride, she does win over the old bachelor. But the moment the false contract has been signed, she changes her colors and suddenly appears as a veritable spitfire to Don Pasquale, demanding every conceivable change in his ways.

III. Finally Pasquale begs for Malatesta to get him off the hook by any possible means. By arranging for Ernesto to take over the difficult bride, everything works out to everyone's complete satisfaction.

**Don Procopio**                                   2 *acts*
COMP.: G. Bizet                         Monte Carlo, 10 March 1906
LIBR.: C. Cambiaggio                    Rome, 1908
   This work, very much in the style of Rossini, was not produced until well after Bizet's death. It was written in 1858.

**Don Quichotte**                                  5 *acts*
(*Don Quixote*)                         Monte Carlo, 19 February 1910
COMP.: J. Massenet                      London, 1912
LIBR.: H. Cain                          New Orleans, 1912
From Cervantes' novel                   Philadelphia, 1913

CAST

| | | | |
|---|---|---|---|
| La Belle Dulcinée | C | Rodriguez, *a third* | T |
| Don Quichotte | B | Juan, *a fourth* | T |
| Sancho Panza, *his squire* | Bar | Two Servants | Bar |
| Pedro, *an admirer of Dulcinée* | S | Tenebrun, the Chief Bandit, Other | |
| Garcias, *another* | S | Bandits, Friends | |

SYNOPSIS

   I. The insane Don serenades his paramour. She agrees to accept him if he will first recover a stolen necklace.
   II. He hunts the bandits. On the way to their hideout he fights the windmills thinking they are giants.
   III. He fights the bandits. They are about to kill him when his politeness wins them over. They give him the necklace he came for.
   IV. He returns victorious, claiming his bride. But she refuses to go along with it.
   V. Now an old man, he dies among his affectionate friends.

**Don Rodrigue**                                   5 *acts*
COMP.: G. Bizet
LIBR.: Gallet and Blau
   Never performed. Only vocal parts and a few sketches remain.

**Don Sebastiano**                                 5 *acts*
COMP.: G. Donizetti                     Opéra, 13 November 1843
LIBR.: A. E. Scribe                     New York, 1864

**Double Trouble**
COMP.: R. Mohaupt                       Louisville, Ky., 4 December 1954
LIBR.: Maren
From Plautus' *Menaechmi*

**Dragons du Villars, Les**                        3 *acts*
(*Villar's Dragoons*)                   Paris, 19 September 1856
COMP.: L. Maillart                      New Orleans, 1859
LIBR.: Lockroy and Corman               London, 1875

**Dream, The**
See *Rêve, Le*

**Dreigroschenoper, Die**
(*The Threepenny Opera*)
COMP.: K. Weill
LIBR.: B. Brecht
From *The Beggar's Opera*, with added
poems by François Villon

*Ballad Opera*
Berlin, 31 August 1928
New York, 1933

This work is not merely a revision of the old *Beggar's Opera*, but a more bitter kind of parody of the same subjects. In an arrangement by Marc Blitzstein it has had a nearly continuous run in New York for several years.

**Due Litiganti**
See *Fra I Due Litiganti*

**Duke Bluebeard's Castle**
COMP.: B. Bartok
LIBR.: B. Balázs

1 *act*
Budapest, 24 May 1918
New York, 1952
London, 1953

CAST

| | | | |
|---|---|---|---|
| Duke Bluebeard | B | Bard, *narrator* | Spkr |
| Judith, *his latest wife* | MS | Three former wives | Mute |

SYNOPSIS

Judith has heard the stories. She wants to know what lies behind the row of closed doors in her husband's castle. She unlocks each one and sees various glorious treasures of his kingdom, all spattered with blood. Behind the sixth door she finds his former wives and lets them free. When they have gone she goes out through the last door, leaving him alone.

**Dumb Girl of Portici, The**
See *Masaniello*

**Dylan**
See *Cauldron of Anwyn*

**Edgar**
COMP.: G. Puccini
LIBR.: F. Fontana
From a story by de Musset

3 *acts*
La Scala, 21 April 1889
Ferrara (*rev.*), 1892
Buenos Aires, 1905

Originally in 4 acts, the opera was reduced to three for the performance in Ferrara.

**Egyptian Helen, The**
See *Aegyptische Helene, Die*

**Elektra**
COMP.: R. Strauss
LIBR.: H. von Hofmannsthal
From Sophocles

*Tragedy in* 1 *act*
Dresden, 25 January 1909
New York, 1910
Covent Garden, 1910
Metropolitan, 1932

CAST

| | | | |
|---|---|---|---|
| Klytemnestra, *Agamemnon's widow* | MS | Aegisth, *Klytemnestra's lover* | T |
| Elektra, *her daughter* | S | Orest, *her son by Agamemnon* | Bar |
| Chrysothemis, *another daughter* | S | Tutor of Orest | B |

| | | | |
|---|---|---|---|
| Klytemnestra's Confidante | S | Old Servant | B |
| Klytemnestra's Trainbearer | S | Overseer | S |
| Young Servant | T | Five Maidservants | C, MS, MS, S, S |

## SYNOPSIS

Elektra lives for only one purpose, to join with their brother in killing their mother and Aegisth for the murder of their father Agamemnon. Chrysothemis fears this as Elektra tells her precisely what she intends to do.

Klytemnestra has heard that her son Orest is dead. But one day while Elektra digs like an animal in the yard a stranger bothers her with many questions. When he is sure of her he identifies himself as her living brother ready to avenge Agamemnon.

Orest goes inside and kills his mother. When Aegisth arrives, Elektra graciously ushers him in to see the corpse. He, too, is murdered. Chrysothemis is bewildered as Elektra, in frenzy, drops dead.

## NOTE

Madame Schumann-Heink laboriously worked her way through the part of Klytemnestra, but after the production had taken place she objected that this wild music was too much for any singer.

## Elisir d'Amore, L'
(*The Elixir of Love*)
COMP.: G. Donizetti
LIBR.: F. Romani

*Comedy in 2 acts*
Milan, 12 May 1832
London, 1836
New York, 1838
Metropolitan, 1904

### CAST

| | | | |
|---|---|---|---|
| Nemorino, *young peasant* | T | Dulcamara, *purveyor of magic potions* | B |
| Adina, *wealthy young landowner* | S | Gianetta, *peasant girl* | S |
| Belcore, *sergeant* | Bar | | |

### SYNOPSIS

I. Nemorino has been courting Adina in such a shy way for so long that she complains there is no elixir of love. In desperation she accepts the proposal of Sergeant Belcore, who at least acts in a military way. One day Dulcamara arrives in town advertising, of all things, an elixir which is really nothing but cheap wine. Nemorino buys some and drinks himself to inebriation, thus making it possible to forget his difficulties in love. The Sergeant has been ordered to move to his next post. He wants an immediate marriage. Poor Nemorino is far too drunk to be able to prevent the preparations.

II. He has enlisted with Belcore to get money. He buys a second bottle of elixir and proceeds to break up the wedding ceremony with loud protestations of his prowess in war. Adina realizes the real cause of all this bombast. Secretly she buys back Nemorino's enlistment papers and then contrives to faint right into his arms. This turns the tables completely. Nemorino comes to his senses. Dulcamara unloads his entire cargo of elixir, and Sergeant Belcore goes off, like a true soldier, to war.

## Emperor Jones, The
COMP.: L. Gruenberg
LIBR.: K. de Jaffa
From Eugene O'Neill's play

*Prologue and 2 acts*
Metropolitan, 7 January 1933
Amsterdam, 1934

CAST

| | | |
|---|---|---|
| Brutus Jones, *emperor* | Bar | Soldiers, Formless Fears, Jeff, Negro |
| Henry Smithers, *cockney trader* | T | Convicts, Prison Guard, Planters, |
| An old native woman | S | Auctioneer, Slaves |
| The Congo witch-doctor | dancer | |

SYNOPSIS

The Negroes suffer under the harsh rule of their self-styled emperor. He has told them that nothing but a silver bullet can kill him. They plan his murder. Only Smithers, the cynical trader who profits from their misery, protects Jones. The boastful emperor professes not to be afraid of the plot, but very gradually, succumbing to the unrecognizable sounds and shadows of the jungle he disintegrates into a frantic animal. He remembers when he was a convict, he recalls slave auctions before the Civil War. Finally, in a paroxysm of fear intensified by the witch doctor, he kills himself with his own, prized, silver bullet.

## Enfant et les Sortilèges, L'
(*The Child and Witchcraft*)
COMP.: M. Ravel
LIBR.: Colette

2 *parts*
Monte Carlo, 21 March 1925
San Francisco, 1930
Buenos Aires, 1944

CAST

| | | | |
|---|---|---|---|
| Child | MS | Pâtre, *shepherd* | C |
| Mother | C | La Fauteuil, *armchair* | B |
| La Bergère, *Louis XV chair* | S | L'Horloge Comtoise, | |
| Chinese Cup | MC | grandfather clock | Bar |
| Fire* | S | La Théière, *tea pot* | T |
| Princess* | S | Arithmetic†, *a little old man* | T |
| Cat | MS | Tom Cat | Bar |
| La Libellule, *dragonfly* | MS | Tree | B |
| La Rossignol, *nightingale** | S | La Rainette†, *frog* | T |
| La Chauve-Souris, *bat* | S | Bench, Sofa, Ottoman, Wicker Chair, | |
| La Chouette, *little owl* | S | Numbers, Shepherds, Frogs, Animals, | |
| L'Écureuil, *squirrel* | MS | Trees | |
| Pastourelle, *shepherdess* | S | | |

* By the same soprano
† By the same tenor

SYNOPSIS

The child, in order that he may do his lessons for school, has been locked in his room. He hates it. Suddenly he gets up and proceeds to tear everything apart. When he has done with it, he sulks.

Then everything becomes alive. First the chairs, then the clock, the fire and so on. Each speaks of the hostility of the child, and its desire for revenge for what he has done. They drive the child to tears.

The tomcat, meanwhile, has met a sleek white cat. They sing a weird cat duet, then leap out the window into the wide outside world. Suddenly the child is out there, in the garden which he tore to shreds the day before. The animals berate him for their past wounds and frights. Finally, when he helps a little squirrel by binding up a wound, they relent and cease the torture.

NOTE

Colette originally intended this to be a ballet. Productions have been mounted in which the cast consists mainly of dancers.

## Enfant Prodigue
See *Prodigal Son, The*

## Engelbrekt
COMP.: N. Berg
LIBR.: By the composer

4 *acts*
Stockholm, 21 September 1929
Brunswick, Germany, 1933

## Enrico Clifford
COMP.: I. Albéniz
LIBR.: Arteaga y Pereira
Translated from an English libretto by Money-Coutts

3 *acts*
Barcelona, 8 May 1895

## Entführung aus dem Serail, Die
(*The Abduction from the Seraglio*)
COMP.: W. A. Mozart
LIBR.: G. Stephanie
C. F. Bretzner's libretto for Johann
André's opera *Belmonte et Constance*

*Singspiel in 3 acts*
Vienna, 16 July 1782
Brooklyn, New York, 1860
Covent Garden, 1827
Metropolitan, 1946

### CAST

| | | | |
|---|---|---|---|
| Constance, *a Spanish lady* | S | Pasha Selim | Spkr |
| Blonde, *her English maid* | S | Osmin, *overseer of the harem* | B |
| Belmonte, *a Spanish nobleman* | T | Turkish Soldiers, Guards, Women | |
| Pedrillo, *his servant* | T | | |

### MUSICAL HIGHLIGHTS

ACT I. Aria *Wer ein Liebchen hat gefunden* (When a maiden takes your fancy), Osmin
Aria *O wie ängstlich* (O such anguish). Belmonte
Trio *Marsch, Marsch, Marsch* (March, March, March), Pedrillo, Belmonte, Osmin
ACT II. Aria *Durch Zärtlichkeit* (With tenderness), Blonde
Duet *Traurigkeit ward mir zum Lose* (Sadness will e'er be my fate), Blonde and
Constance
Aria *Martern aller Arten* (Tortures unabating), Constance
Aria *Welche Wonne, welche Lust* (O what happiness, what joy), Blonde
Duet *Vivat Bacchus* (Long live Bacchus), Osmin, Pedrillo
Serenade *Im Mohrenland* (In Moorish lands), Pedrillo

### SYNOPSIS

I. Belmonte comes to the Pasha's house to rescue Constance, Blonde, and Pedrillo. Constance has managed, during her captivity, to remain faithful to Belmonte. In order to gain admittance, Belmonte has himself introduced to the Pasha as a famous architect.

II. The Pasha presses his love toward Constance, but she remains adamant. Meanwhile Pedrillo persuades Osmin, the Pasha's chief watchdog, to drink himself into a blind stupor so that they may escape.

III. They are on their way out when a wakeful guard catches them and the sobered Osmin confronts them with evident anticipation of revenge. When all are dragged before the Pasha for his judgement he turns out to be a kindly sort, willing to release them all. Before they leave they all join in a chorus in his praise.

### NOTE

In 1779 Mozart worked on a Singspiel, *Zaïde*, which was very much like *Die Entführung aus dem Serail*, but was not finished.

## Ernani

COMP.: G. Verdi
LIBR.: F. Piave
From a play by Victor Hugo

*Tragedy in 4 acts*
Venice, 9 March 1844
London, 1845
New York, 1847
Metropolitan, 1903

CAST

| | | | |
|---|---|---|---|
| Don Carlos, *king of Castile* | Bar | Iago, *di Silva's squire* | B |
| Don Ruy Gomez di Silva, *grandee* | B | Elvira, *related to di Silva* | S |
| Ernani, *or* John of Aragon, | | Giovanna, *her servant* | S |
| *bandit chief* | T | Bandits, Mountaineers, Ladies, Electors, | |
| Don Riccardo, *the king's squire* | T | Pages, Followers of Silva and of Carlos | |

SYNOPSIS

I. Ernani and his men plan to carry off Elvira whom he loves. She is preparing, against her will, to marry the old di Silva. While Ernani is with her, Don Carlos comes to woo her. Silva discovers them all in this situation, but lets them go free when the king reveals who he is.

II. Ernani tries again, disguised as a monk. But when he sees Elvira this time in her bridal gown he throws off his disguise and offers his life to di Silva, since it is now worthless to himself. At this moment the king approaches to capture Ernani. Silva swears that though Ernani is his enemy he is also his guest, and that he must therefore protect him from the king's attack. The king takes Elvira as hostage to force di Silva to give up Ernani. Ernani then swears to give his life to di Silva whenever di Silva shall blow his hunting horn, but that first they should join forces to save the girl.

III. Hidden in the tomb of Charlemagne, the king listens while his enemies formulate their plot against him. The scene is interrupted by the entrance of a procession in the cathedral to proclaim Don Carlos emperor. As his very first imperial act, urged by Elvira, the new monarch pardons the conspirators and allows her marriage to Ernani.

IV. Di Silva gives Ernani brief happiness. As the man and wife stand on a parapet enjoying their peace together they hear the hunting horn. Ernani, remembering his promise, stabs himself to death.

## Esther de Carpentras

COMP.: D. Milhaud
LIBR.: A. Lunel

*Comedy in 2 acts*
Comique, 1 February 1938

CAST

| | | | |
|---|---|---|---|
| Hadassa (Esther) | MS | Vaucluse, *his valet* | T |
| Artaban, *financier* | T | Mask Seller | S |
| Barbacan, *concierge of the synagogue* | B | Jewish Doctor | Bar |
| Cacan, *a theater-lover* | Bar | Disguised Jews, Esther's Friends, | |
| Cardinal, *bishop of Carpentras* | T | Prelates, Children, Guards. | |

## Étoile du Nord, L'

COMP.: G. Meyerbeer
LIBR.: E. Scribe

*3 acts*
Comique, 16 February 1854
New Orleans, 1855
Covent Garden, 1855

In this opera Meyerbeer made use of six pieces of music from an earlier opera *Ein Feldlager in Schlesien*.

## Eugene Onegin

COMP.: P. Tchaikovsky
LIBR.: Tchaikovsky and Shilovsky
From Pushkin's poem

3 *acts*
Moscow, 29 March 1879
London, 1892
Metropolitan, 1920

CAST

| | | | |
|---|---|---|---|
| Madame Larina, *landowner* | MS | Prince Gremin, *a General* | B |
| Tatyana, *her daughter* | S | Captain | B |
| Olga, *another daughter* | C | Zaretsky | B |
| Filipievna, *Tatyana's nurse* | MS | M. Triquet | T |
| Lensky, *Olga's fiancé* | T | Reapers | |
| Eugene Onegin, *his friend* | Bar | | |

SYNOPSIS

I. Tatyana, who thinks it's a secret, is in love with Onegin. She writes him a long letter of love. But he discourages her; he would be a brother to her, not a lover.

II. At a ball he dances with Olga. At this, Lensky becomes jealous enough to challenge his friend. They duel in the dawn and Lensky dies.

III. Years later, Onegin sees Tatyana as the wife of Prince Gremin. He is in love with her at last. She weeps for him, but she leaves him and returns to her husband.

## Eumenides

COMP.: D. Milhaud
LIBR.: P. Claudel
Translated from Aeschylus

*Tragedy*
Antwerp, 27 November 1927

CAST

| | | | |
|---|---|---|---|
| Apollon | Bar | Ghost of Clytemnestra | MS |
| Oreste, *son of Agamemnon* | Bar | Statue of Athena, *triple voice* | S, MS, C |
| La Pythie | S | Erinnyes and People | |

## Euridice

COMP.: J. Peri
LIBR.: O. Rinuccini

*Prologue and 6 Scenes*
Florence, 6 October 1600
Milan, 1916
Munich, 1934

Not the first opera (see *Dafne*) but the earliest of which significant parts still exist. It was composed for the wedding festivities of Henry IV and Maria de Medici at the Pitti Palace in Florence. Peri sang Orpheus, and Corsi played harpsichord. Caccini wrote music for the same libretto at the same time, but his work was not produced until two years later (5 December 1602).

## Euridice

See also *Orfeo*
See also *Orpheus*

## Euryanthe

COMP.: C. M. von Weber
LIBR.: H. von Chézy
From a story of de Nevers

3 *acts*
Vienna, 25 October 1823
Covent Garden, 1833
Metropolitan, 1887

CAST

| | | | |
|---|---|---|---|
| Euryanthe of Savoy | S | Count Lysiart of Forêt | Bar |
| Eglantine of Puiset | MS | Count Adolar of Nevers | T |

| | | | |
|---|---|---|---|
| Louis VI | B | Berthe | S |
| Rudolph, *knight* | T | | |

SYNOPSIS

I. Lysiart and Adolar have made a bet on Euryanthe's constancy. Meanwhile Eglantine, rival for Adolar's love, has discovered that Euryanthe has knowledge of the murder of Adolar's sister.

II. Lysiart, to win his bet, betrays this secret. Adolar sadly takes her into the forest where he intends to kill her and commit suicide.

III. The murder is prevented by a serpent, with whom Adolar fights. The king, hunting, finds Euryanthe there and hears her story. Adolar goes to watch the wedding of Lysiart and Eglantine. Suddenly the bride shouts to all who can hear of her treachery in fathoming Euryanthe's secret and thus causing her death. At this Adolar challenges Lysiart, but the king intervenes. Lysiart kills Eglantine, and is led off as Euryanthe returns to the repentant Adolar.

## Evangeline
COMP.: O. Luening      New York, 5 May 1948

## Fair at Sorotchinsk, The     3 *acts*
COMP.: M. Mussorgsky      St. Petersburg (Concert), 1911
LIBR.: By the composer      St. Petersburg (Stage), 27 October 1917
From Gogol's *Evenings on a Farm*    Metropolitan, 1930

CAST

| | | | |
|---|---|---|---|
| Tcherevik, *old country man* | B | Tcherevik's friend | B |
| Parassia, *his daughter* | S | Gypsy | B |
| Khivria, *his wife* | MS | Young Men and Women, Gypsies, | |
| Gritzko, *young country man* | T |  Merchants, Cossacks, Jews | |
| Son of the Priest | T | | |

SYNOPSIS

I. Parassia, on her first visit to the fair, meets Gritzko who immediately asks for her hand in marriage. An old gypsy offers to help them win over her old parents.

II. The priest's son visits Khivria as her lover and hides while Tcherevik and his friends carouse. Suddenly they have hallucinations, thinking they see the devil disguised as a pig. In their confusion they discover the lover and burst into laughter.

III. Because of the discovery of the priest's son, Tcherevik now has a scandal to hold over his wife. Thus he can now freely give his approval to their daughter's marriage to Gritzko, without the wife's interference.

## Fair Maid of Perth, The
See *Jolie Fille de Perth, La*

## Fairy Queen, The       *Prologue and 5 acts*
COMP.: H. Purcell       London, April 1692
LIBR.: E. Settle        Drury Lane, 1703
Adapted from Shakespeare's    Cambridge, 1920
 *Midsummer Night's Dream*

The score of this opera was lost in 1700, causing the famous advertisement to be published in the London *Gazette* offering a reward of twenty guineas. Evidence that advertising sometimes works may be read from the data of the Drury Lane performance. The first modern stage performance was in Cambridge, England, in 1920.

**Falstaff**
COMP.: G. Verdi
LIBR.: A. Boito
From Shakespeare

*Comedy in 3 acts*
La Scala, 9 February 1893
Covent Garden, 1894
New York, 1895

CAST

| | | | |
|---|---|---|---|
| Sir John Falstaff | Bar | Alice Ford, *Ford's wife* | S |
| Fenton, *young gentleman* | T | Nanetta, *her daughter Anne* | S |
| Ford, *wealthy burgher* | Bar | Mistress Page, *Meg* | MS |
| Doctor Caius | T | Dame Quickly | C |
| Bardolph, *Falstaff's friend* | T | Burghers, Streetfolk, Servants | |
| Pistol, *Falstaff's friend* | B | | |

SYNOPSIS

I. Falstaff is interested in both Mrs. Page and Mrs. Ford. He intends to woo them simultaneously. He sends, therefore, identical letters. Unfortunately the ladies read them to each other and plan to play a trick on him. Also his friends, Bardolph and Pistol, betray his plans to Mr. Ford so that Falstaff's secret is secret no more.

II. Dame Quickly delivers a message to the effect that Falstaff should visit Alice between two and three o'clock. Ford, in disguise, also arranges with Falstaff to have Falstaff woo Alice for him, her "suitor." Then, while the wooing is in progress, Ford comes with friends to surprise the interloper. The women hide Falstaff in a basket so that Ford catches only Nanetta and Fenton kissing behind a screen. When Ford has left the room, the good ladies empty the basket into the Thames.

III. Dame Quickly invites Falstaff to meet Alice a second time, this time disguised as a ghost in the forest. When he makes his appearance in that condition, they surround him with sprites, fairies, and phantasies until the trick finally dawns upon his mind. In a final burst of trickery and disguises, Fenton and Nanetta are blessed in betrothal by Ford who had intended not to do it, and all join in a fugue of the relish of jest.

NOTE

Verdi worked on this opera in privacy, telling his friends that he was not writing for a performance, but for himself. The same subject has been used by Salieri (Vienna, 1798), Balfe (London, 1838), Nicolai (see *Lustigen Weiber von Windsor*), Adam (Paris, 1856, in one act), and Vaughan Williams (see *Sir John in Love*).

**Fanciulla del West, La**
(*The Girl of the West*)
COMP.: G. Puccini
LIBR.: Civinini and Zangarini
From Belasco's play
  *The Girl of the Golden West*

*3 acts*
Metropolitan, 10 December 1910
Covent Garden, 1911
La Scala, 1912

CAST

| | | | |
|---|---|---|---|
| Minnie, *saloon keeper* | S | Sonora, *miner* | Bar |
| Jack Rance, *sheriff* | Bar | Trim, *miner* | T |
| Dick Johnson, *the bandit Ramerrez* | T | Sid, *miner* | Bar |
| Nick, *bartender* | T | Handsome, *miner* | Bar |
| Ashby, *the Wells Fargo man* | B | Harry, *miner* | T |

| | | | |
|---|---|---|---|
| Joe, *miner* | T | Wowkle, *his squaw* | MS |
| Happy, *miner* | Bar | Jake Wallace, *minstrel* | Bar |
| Larkens, *miner* | B | José Castro, *bandit* | B |
| Billy Jackrabbit, *Indian* | B | Courier | T |

SYNOPSIS

I. Rance, on the prowl for Ramerrez, is one of the crowd at the bar when Johnson drops in. Minnie, who used to know Johnson, dances with him. They plan to see each other in private later.

II. While he is with her in her cabin, the sheriff and his men pay her a visit to say that they know quite a bit about Ramerrez now that they have a photograph of the bandit. Unbeknownst to them, their quarry is hiding directly overhead in her loft. They leave. After a suitable time Johnson attempts to leave but a shot from Rance hits him. Johnson hides again in the loft, but Rance, searching, sees drops of blood which lead him to the hiding place. Minnie makes Rance an offer: whoever shall win two of three hands of poker shall have the bandit. In order to win, she cheats.

III. Later, outside, Ramerrez has been caught again and is about to be hanged by the nearest tree when Minnie arrives. With a great speech she convinces the posse that Johnson has sworn to her he will go straight from then on. They are won over and let the man go free.

**Faust**

| | |
|---|---|
| COMP.: C. Gounod | *Tragedy in 5 acts* |
| LIBR.: Barbier and Carré | Paris, 19 March 1859 |
| From part of Goethe's play | London, 1863 |
| | New York, 1863 |
| | Metropolitan's Opening, 1863 |

CAST

| | | | |
|---|---|---|---|
| Faust, *learned doctor* | T | Martha Schwerlein, *Marguérite's* | |
| Méphistophélès | B | *neighbor* | MS |
| Marguérite | S | Students, Soldiers, Villagers, Angels, | |
| Valentin, *soldier, Marguérite's* | | Demons | |
| *brother* | Bar | Cleopatra, Laïs, Helen of Troy, | |
| Siebel, *her lover* | MS | Phryne | Mutes |
| Wagner, *student* | Bar | | |

MUSICAL HIGHLIGHTS

ACT I. Duet *A moi les plaisirs* (All pleasures for me), Faust and Méphistophélès

ACT II. Aria *Avant de quitter ces lieux* (Now before I leave this place), Valentin
   Aria *Le veau d'or* (The golden calf), Méphistophélès
   Waltz, The *Kermesse*

ACT III. Serenade *Faites-lui mes aveux* (Bear her my confession), Siebel
   Cavatina *Salut, demeure chaste et pure* (Hail to the house so chaste and pure), Faust
   Ballad *Il était un roi de Thulé* (There was a king of Thule), Marguérite
   Jewel Song *Ah, je ris* (Ah I laugh), Marguérite

ACT IV. Soldiers' Chorus *Gloire immortelle* (Immortal glory), Chorus
   Serenade *Vous qui faites l'endormie* (You who seem to be sleeping), Méphistophélès

ACT V. Ballet of Walpurgis Night
   Trio *Anges purs, anges radieux* (Angels pure, Angels radiant), Marguérite, Faust, Méphistophélès

# THE OPERAS

I. Faust has failed to solve the riddle of life. He curses life and calls for Satan. Up comes Méphistophélès at his invitation to convert him to a life of pleasures.

II. In a beer hall Méphistophélès taunts the students with more brilliant wit and better wine made magically than they can get by legitimate means. Especially he tortures Valentin. Then he takes Faust to meet Marguérite. Faust falls in love with her beauty while Méphistophélès shudders with laughter by himself.

III. Faust leaves jewels at her door. Then he walks with her in the garden while Méphistophélès escorts her friend Martha conveniently out of the way.

IV. Faust, driven by the devil, deserts Marguérite. Valentin challenges him but the duel is fixed by Méphistophélès and ends with Valentin dead. As he dies he curses his sister.

V. Méphistophélès tries to divert Faust with an exhibition of the famous beauties of antiquity, but Faust sees a vision of Marguérite and insists on seeing her. She is in prison, condemned for killing her child. Delirious with her insanity, she dies in the presence of the man who wronged her. Méphistophélès does not triumph. He gets Faust's soul, but angels come to take Marguérite's to heaven.

NOTE

In Germany, since it uses only the story of Marguérite and Faust, the opera is entitled *Margarethe*.

**Faust**
COMP.: L. Spohr
LIBR.: J. K. Bernard

*Tragedy in 2 acts*
Prague, 1 September 1816
London, 1840

**Faust**
See also *Doktor Faust*
See also *Damnation of Faust*
See also *Mefistofele*

**Favola d'Orfeo, La**
(*The Fable of Orpheus*)
COMP.: C. Monteverdi
LIBR.: A. Striggio

*Tragedy in Prologue and 5 acts*
Mantua, February Carnival, 1607
Breslau, 1913
Smith College, Mass., 1929

SYNOPSIS

I. Shepherds and Nymphs rejoice in the marriage of Orpheus and Euridice.

II. During a tableau of a contest in singing, a messenger brings Orpheus the news that Euridice is dead. Orpheus is transfixed by grief.

III. Orpheus descends into Hades to find her. He wins safe passage with the great beauty of a song.

IV. Pluto releases Euridice to her husband, but on condition that he must not look upon her face until they have reached the outer world. She cannot withstand this avoidance. She makes him look back to be sure she is coming. Immediately she returns to the abode of the dead.

V. Orpheus, alone, laments his lost love until Apollo appoints him to live among the stars whence he can again behold her.

NOTE

This extraordinarily beautiful work has been revived in modern instrumentation by various composers, Malipiero, d'Indy and Orff among them. The performance at Smith was in Malipiero's version with Charles Kullman as Orpheus and Werner Josten conducting.

**Favorita, La**

COMP.: G. Donizetti
LIBR.: Royer and Vaëz
From a play by d'Arnaud

4 *acts*

Opéra, 2 December 1840
Drury Lane, 1843
New York, 1843
Metropolitan, 1895

CAST

| | | | |
|---|---|---|---|
| Alfonso XI, *king of Castile* | Bar | Leonora de Gusman, *the king's* | |
| Ferdinand, *novice (Fernando)* | T | mistress | S |
| Don Gaspar, *the king's minister* | T | Inez, *her confidante* | S |
| Balthasar, *monastery superior* | | Courtiers, Guards, Monks, Ladies, | |
| (*Baldassare*) | B | Attendants | |

SYNOPSIS

I. Ferdinand renounces his novitiate in order to go again to his beloved. She keeps from him the fact of her relationship to the king, and arranges an army commission to keep him busy.

II. He becomes a national hero and the secret of his love is almost out when a Papal Bull is read ordering the king to restore his legitimate wife to the throne and put away his mistress.

III. Alfonso tells the hero to name his own prize for victory. He asks for Leonora's hand, which the king is forced by publicity to grant. Leonora tries to tell Ferdinand about her past by sending a note via Inez, but the note never reaches him. He learns the truth harshly in remarks made in open court. In disgust he renounces his honors and returns to the monastery.

IV. Leonora seeks him out and tells him the whole story. He relents but it is too late; she dies.

**Fedora**

COMP.: U. Giordano
LIBR.: A. Colautti
From a play by Sardou

*Tragedy in 3 acts*

Milan, 17 November 1898
Covent Garden, 1906
Metropolitan, 1906

CAST

| | | | |
|---|---|---|---|
| Princess Fedora Romanov | S | Désiré, *valet* | T |
| Count Loris Ipanov | T | Baron Rouvel | T |
| De Serieux, *diplomat* | Bar | Lorek, *surgeon* | Bar |
| Countess Olga Sukarev | S | Borov, *doctor* | Bar |
| Grech, *policeman* | B | Nicola, *footman* | T |
| Cirillo, *coachman* | Bar | Sergio, *footman* | Bar |
| Dmitri, *groom* | C | Boleslav Lazinski, *pianist* | Mime |
| Savoyard | MS | | |

SYNOPSIS

I. Count Andreievich has been murdered. Grech gathers all the suspects together and narrows the case down to Ipanov, who has escaped.

II. Fedora herself also hunts for the murderer of her fiancé and manages to have him attend her reception in Paris. Loris proves to her that it was a justified murder, that the count had betrayed Loris' wife and caused her death.

III. They live in hiding in Switzerland, but the police search goes on. When Loris hears that it was Fedora who first put the police on his trail, he tries to kill her, but she foils him by taking poison. His sudden rage melts, but it is too late to save her.

**Fedra**                                    *Tragedy in 3 acts*
COMP.: I. Pizzetti                           La Scala, 20 March 1915
LIBR.: G. d'Annunzio                         Buenos Aires, 1920
                                             Opéra, 1923

**Femme Nue, La**                            *4 acts*
COMP.: H. Février                            Monte Carlo, 23 March 1929
LIBR.: L. Payen                              Comique, 1932
From a play by Bataille

**Fennimore und Gerda**
COMP.: F. Delius                             Frankfurt, 21 October 1919
LIBR.: By the composer in German

**Fernando Cortez**                          *Tragedy in 3 acts*
COMP.: G. Spontini                           Opéra, 28 November 1809
LIBR.: Esménard and Jouy                     New York, 1888
From a play by Piron                         Naples (*rev.*), 1951

**Fête Galante**                             *Dance Dream in 1 act*
COMP.: E. Smyth                              Birmingham, 4 June 1923
LIBR.: E. Shanks                             Covent Garden, 1923
From a story by Baring

CAST

| | | | |
|---|---|---|---|
| King | BBar | Columbine | S |
| Lover | T | Four Puppets | S, A, T, B |
| Pierrot | Bar | Pantaloon, Courtiers, Guests, Satyrs, | |
| Harlequin | T | Bacchantes, Guards | |
| Queen | MS | | |

SYNOPSIS

A gala evening in the palace garden. Columbine and the king mistake Pierrot and the queen's lover for each other, causing obvious complications and embarrassments which are finally ironed out only by military force.

**Fêtes de l'Amour et de Bacchus, Les**      *Prologue and 3 acts*
(*Festival of Love and of Bacchus*)          Opéra, 15 November 1672
COMP.: J. B. Lully
LIBR.: P. Quinault
Lully's first opera, using parts of previously successful ballets.

**Feuersnot**                                1 *act*
(*Fire Famine*)                              Dresden, 21 November 1901
COMP.: R. Strauss                            London, 1910
LIBR.: E. von Wolzogen                       Philadelphia, 1927

## Fidelio

COMP.: L. van Beethoven
LIBR.: Joseph and Georg Sonnleithner
From a drama by Bouilly

*Tragedy in 2 acts*
Vienna, 20 November 1805
Covent Garden, 1835
New York, 1839
Metropolitan, 1884

CAST

| | | | | |
|---|---|---|---|---|
| Florestan, *Spanish nobleman* | T | Rocco, *chief jailer* | | B |
| Leonora, *his wife, later Fidelio* | S | Marcellina, *Rocco's daughter* | | S |
| Don Fernando, *king's minister* | B | Jacquino, *Rocco's assistant* | | T |
| Don Pizarro, *prison governor* | B | Soldiers, Prisoners, People | | |

MUSICAL HIGHLIGHTS

*Overture:* Of four composed, one called the *Fidelio Overture* is generally used to open the opera. Another, called the *Leonora Overture, Number 3*, is generally played between the scenes of the second act.

ACT I. Quartet in form of canon *Mir ist so wunderbar* (It seems so wonderful), Leonora, Marcellina, Jacquino, Rocco
Aria *Ha! welch ein Augenblick!* (Ha! in a twinkling!), Pizarro
Scena *Abscheulicher!* (Accursed one!) Leonora
Chorus of Prisoners *O welche Lust* (O such a joy!), chorus

ACT II. Aria *In des Lebens Frühlingstagen* (In my younger spring-like days), Florestan
Duet *O namenlose Freude* (Inexpressible joy), Florestan and Leonora

SYNOPSIS

I. Leonora has disguised herself as a man called Fidelio in order to gain access as a workman to the prison where she believes her husband may be still alive. With some complication by the fact that the jailer's daughter has taken a mistaken fancy toward Fidelio, she finally learns that her suspicions were true, that Florestan is indeed in this place.

At the same time Pizarro has learned that the king's minister is nearby and intends to make an inspection of the prison. It is urgent that Pizarro get rid of Florestan, who is his personal enemy, without the king's minister's knowledge. Pizarro therefore gives orders to dig the prisoner's grave while he prepares to kill him himself.

II. The job falls to Rocco and Fidelio. By this means she actually sees the prisoner and learns that it is her husband. She gives him food and drink. When Pizaro comes with a dagger to do the deed she draws a pistol from her garments and holds him off. At that moment a distant trumpet indicates the minister is at hand. He comes to the dungeon, recognizes Florestan as the king's friend and releases him. Pizarro becomes prisoner in his place.

NOTES

*Fidelio* was originally in three acts, but it lasted only three performances before failing. It was reduced to two acts for 1806. There was to be a new overture for this performance, but it was not ready. Hence the *Ruins of Athens* overture was used in its place. The libretto was then re-written by Treitschke and produced in what is now its final form in 1814. Of the four overtures, the so-called *Leonora Overture number two* was used at the premiere. Number one was intended for Prague, but the production never took place. When the opera was performed at the Park Theater, for the first time in New York, someone must have thought the work insufficient to stand by itself. It was therefore followed by a solo dance, then an extravaganza on the *Deep Deep Sea* in which the Leonora appeared as The Great Sea Monster (Kobbé).

**Fierrebras**
COMP.: F. Schubert
LIBR.: J. Kupelwieser
From a play by Calderón
The opera was written in 1823.

3 *acts*
Karlsruhe, Germany, 9 February 1897
Brussels, 1926

**Fiesta**
COMP:. D. Milhaud
LIBR:. B. Vian

Berlin, 1958
Los Angeles, 1959

**Figlia del Reggimento, La**
(*The Daughter of the Regiment*)
COMP.: G. Donizetti
LIBR.: St. Georges and Bayard

2 *acts*
Comique, 11 February 1840
New York, 1843
London, 1847
Metropolitan, 1902

CAST

| | | | |
|---|---|---|---|
| Marie, *the "daughter" of the regiment* | S | Corporal | B |
| Sulpice, *sergeant of grenadiers* | B | Peasant | T |
| Tonio, *Tyrolean peasant, Marie's lover* | T | Duchesse de Krakenthorp | S |
| Marquise de Birkenfeld | S | Soldiers, Peasants, Friends of the Marquise | |
| Hortensio, *her steward* | B | | |

SYNOPSIS

I. Tonio, caught sneaking around the grenadiers' camp during a battle, is pardoned when Marie, the foundling brought up with the regiment, tells them that he is her rescuer and lover. Tonio decides to join up so that the grenadiers, who want their girl to marry one of their own, will permit him that honor. There is, however, a refugee, the Marquise de Birkenfeld, whose name is soon recognized as one mentioned on papers that were found in Marie's possession when the regiment found her. It turns out that Marie is her niece, and may not therefore marry as planned.

II. The Marquise arranges a fine marriage with a Krakenthorp. To avoid it, Marie and Tonio plan to elope. But when Marie by chance sings a song of her own childhood with the soldiers, the Marquise is deeply touched and allows them to marry.

**Fille de Madame Angot, La**
(*Madame Angot's Daughter*)
COMP.: A. Ch. Lecocq
LIBR.: Clairville, Siraudin and Koning
From a vaudeville by Maillot

3 *acts*
Brussels, 4 December 1872
London, 1873
New York, 1873

**Finta Giardiniera, La**
COMP.: W. A. Mozart
LIBR.: R. Calzabigi

3 *acts*
Munich, 13 January 1775
New York, 1927
London, 1930

**Finta Semplice, La**
COMP.: W. A. Mozart
LIBR.: M. Coltellini
From a libretto by Goldoni

3 *acts*
Salzburg, 1 May 1769
Karlsruhe, 1921
Vienna, 1925

**Fire Famine**
See *Feuersnot*

**Flauto Magico, Il**
See *Zauberflöte, Die*

**Fledermaus, Die**
(*The Bat*)
COMP.: J. Strauss
LIBR.: Haffner and Genée
From a vaudeville by Meilhac
and Halévy

*Comedy in 3 acts*
Vienna, 5 April 1874
London, 1876
New York, 1879
Metropolitan, 1905

CAST

| | | | |
|---|---|---|---|
| Gabriel von Eisenstein | T | Doctor Falke, *Eisenstein's friend* | Bar |
| Rosalinda, *his wife* | S | Doctor Blind, *attorney* | T |
| Frank, *prison governor* | Bar | Adele, *Eisenstein's maid* | S |
| Prince Orlovsky, *a rich Russian* | MS | Frosche, *jailer* | Spkr |
| Alfred, *singer* | T | | |

SYNOPSIS

I. Eisenstein is about to serve eight days in prison. In celebration his wife plans first to send him off with a delicious dinner and second to attend a masquerade ball at Orlovsky's that night. But Eisenstein has decided to celebrate himself, and goes off to the costume ball before the dreary business of going to jail. Thus when the prison governor comes for Eisenstein at the appointed time, he finds Alfred at the house. To prevent gossip, Alfred has to go to jail in his place.

II. At the magnificent Straussian ball Eisenstein makes every attempt to conquer the strange Hungarian Lady who is really his own wife. But promptly at six a.m. he remembers his appointment and goes off to jail.

III. He can't get in; there is someone already there, an impostor, masquerading as Eisenstein. Eisenstein disguises himself therefore as his own attorney and proceeds to cross-examine the prisoner Alfred and his visitor Rosalinda until their liaison is revealed.

At the last, Falke appears and confesses that he has engineered the whole mix-up as revenge for the time when, at another masquerade ball, Eisenstein forced Falke to appear in the streets in daylight in costume as a bat.

**Fliegende Holländer, Der**
(*The Flying Dutchman*)
COMP.: R. Wagner
LIBR.: By the composer
From Heine's *Memoires of Herr von Schnabelewopski*

*Tragedy in 3 acts*
Dresden, 2 January 1843
Drury Lane, 1870
Philadelphia, 1876
Metropolitan, 1889

CAST

| | | | |
|---|---|---|---|
| Daland, *Norwegian sea captain* | B | Steersman | T |
| Senta, *his daughter* | S | The Dutchman | Bar |
| Eric, *huntsman* | T | Sailors, Maidens, Hunters | |
| Mary, *Senta's nurse* | C | | |

SYNOPSIS

Unless the Dutchman can find someone who will love him faithfully, he remains condemned to sail the seas forever. Each seventh year he may come to shore to search for love. On one of these sabbaticals he dropped anchor in Daland's harbor to woo the Norwegian's daughter Senta. She recognized him from the legend which she had always known, but she did not tell him. She swore to love him forever, but once he overheard her former lover, Eric, pleading with her to return to him. The Dutchman misunderstood. Thinking her unfaithful he set sail again. Seeing his ship depart, she cast herself into the seas for his love. In a storm of waves they sailed off to peace and oblivion together.

### NOTE

Wagner intended that the work should be played without division into acts. It is said that he was reminded of Heine's poem while tossed and tormented by a tremendous storm on a voyage from Riga to Paris. He set about the writing soon after.

## Forest, The
See *Wald, Der*

## Forêt Bleue, La
(*The Blue Forest*)
COMP.: L. Aubert
LIBR.: J. Chenevière
From a story by Perrault

3 *acts*
Geneva, 7 January 1913
Boston, 1913
Comique, 1924
London, 1928

## Forza del Destino, La
(*The Power of Destiny*)
COMP.: G. Verdi
LIBR.: F. M. Piave
From a tragedy by The Duke
    of Rivas

*Tragedy in 4 acts*
St. Petersburg, 10 November 1862
New York, 1865
London, 1867
Metropolitan, 1918

### CAST

| | | | |
|---|---|---|---|
| Donna Leonora di Vargas | S | Fra Melitone, *Franciscan* | Bar |
| Preziosilla, *gypsy* | MS | Curra, *Leonora's maid* | MS |
| Don Alvaro, *Leonora's lover* | T | Mayor of Hornachuelos | B |
| Don Carlo di Vargas, *her brother* | Bar | Trabucco, *muleteer* | T |
| Padre Guardiano, *Franciscan* | B | Surgeon | T |
| Marchese di Calatrava, | | | |
|    *Leonora's father* | B | | |

### MUSICAL HIGHLIGHTS

ACT I. Aria *Me pellegrina* (As a wanderer), Leonora
ACT II. Prayer *Madre, pietosa vergine* (Mother, pious virgin), Leonora
ACT III. Duet *Solenne in quest' ora* (In this solemn hour), Don Alvaro, Don Carlo
ACT IV. Prayer, *Pace, pace, mio Dio* (Peace, peace O God), Leonora
    Trio *Non imprecare* (Do not curse me), Leonora, Alvaro, Padre Guardiano

### SYNOPSIS

I. Leonora and Don Alvaro delay so much during their elopement that the Marchese discovers them in the act. In the ensuing argument, Don Alvaro's pistol accidentally discharges, killing the old man.

II. They separate and flee. Leonora sees Don Carlo in disguise. He had been searching for her and for her lover to avenge his father's death. She seeks sanctuary and penance in a cave in a monastery where she intends to live her life in solitude.

III. Both disguised, and unknown to each other, Don Carlo and Don Alvaro meet elsewhere during a severe battle and swear eternal friendship. Don Alvaro, badly wounded, extracts his friend's promise, in case he should die, to burn, unopened, a letter he has in his possession. Don Carlo does not need to read the letter to recognize the portrait of his sister that accompanies it. Don Alvaro revives. Don Carlo tries then to provoke a duel with him, but without success.

IV. Alvaro joins the Franciscans and seeks personal peace as a monk. But Carlo seeks him out and goads him into a duel. They fight near the cell of the hermit, who is really Leonora. There the monk kills his rival. He calls the hermit to administer to the dying man. Leonora rushes out to find her brother dying and her former lover standing over him. Carlo, not willing to forget her part in his father's death, stabs her as he dies.

## Four Saints in Three Acts

| | | | | |
|---|---|---|---|---|
| COMP.: V. Thomson | | Hartford, Conn., 8 February 1934 | | |
| LIBR.: G. Stein | | New York, 1934 | | |
| | | Paris, 1952 | | |

*4 acts*

CAST

| | | | |
|---|---|---|---|
| Compère | B | St. Chavez | T |
| Commère | MS | St. Settlement | S |
| St. Therese I | S | Other Saints in a double choir | |
| St. Therese II | C | Dancers | |
| St. Ignatius Loyola | Bar | | |

SYNOPSIS

Since a saint may be both inside and outside at the same time, there must be two Saints Therese. We participate in visions of the life of St. Therese. We consider the problems of saints, such as how to fly and how to count the windows and doors in the Heavenly Mansion. We think next of the religious thoughts of St. Ignatius. And then; there *should* be four acts. We see the saints in Heaven, at peace and amid glory.

## Fra Diavolo

| | | | | |
|---|---|---|---|---|
| COMP.: D. Auber | | Comique, 28 January 1830 | | |
| LIBR.: E. Scribe | | Drury Lane, 1831 | | |
| | | New York, 1831 | | |

*Tragedy in 3 acts*

CAST

| | | | |
|---|---|---|---|
| Fra Diavolo, *bandit chief* | T | Matteo, *innkeeper* | B |
| Lord Cockburn, *tourist* | T | Zerlina, *his daughter* | S |
| Lady Pamela, *wife to the tourist* | MS | Giacomo, *bandit* | B |
| Lorenzo, *officer* | T | Beppo, *bandit* | T |

SYNOPSIS

I. Cockburn has been waylaid and robbed near Matteo's tavern. He offers a reward to catch the thieves. While he expostulates, Fra Diavolo draws near in disguise and commiserates with the poor fellow. He also, however, passes his time most efficiently by paying compliments to Pamela and extracting from her information of the whereabouts of Cockburn's money.

II. The bandit and his assistants hide in Zerlina's room in order to be near Cockburn's and finish their job. Beppo makes a noise. But Fra Diavolo reveals himself to Cockburn and then to Matteo, telling each he has a rendezvous with the other's feminine relation. This explains everything satisfactorily, except to Lorenzo who challenges him.

III. Lorenzo discovers, before the duel is to take place, who Beppo and Giacomo really are. With this knowledge he entraps Fra Diavolo. The opera then may end either happily or sadly, depending upon whether the producer has Fra Diavolo go free or be shot in ambush.

**Francesca da Rimini**
COMP.: R. Zandonai
LIBR.: T. Ricordi
From d'Annunzio's play

*Tragedy in 4 acts*
Turin, 19 February 1914
Covent Garden, 1914
Metropolitan, 1916

CAST

| | | | |
|---|---|---|---|
| Francesca | S | Garsenda, *Francesca's woman* | S |
| Samaritana, *her sister* | S | Altichiara, *Francesca's woman* | MS |
| Ostasio, *her brother* | Bar | Donella, *Francesca's woman* | MS |
| Giovanni lo Sciancato, | | Slave, *Francesca's slave* | C |
| Malatesta's lame son | Bar | Ser Toldo Berardengo, *lawyer* | T |
| Paolo il Bello, | | Jester | B |
| Malatesta's handsome son | T | Archer | T |
| Malatestino dall-occhio, | | Torchbearer | Bar |
| Malatesta's one-eyed son | T | Archers, Torchbearers, Musicians | |
| Biancofiore, *Francesca's woman* | S | | |

SYNOPSIS

I. For political reasons, Francesca is betrothed to Giovanni. To trick her into it she is introduced to Paolo instead and falls in love with him as he does with her.

II. During a battle between the Guelphs and Ghibellines, Francesca, now married, and Paolo each try to be exposed to death but neither succeeds. The Malatestas win the battle. Paolo is rewarded by becoming a captain and being given a post in Florence.

III. Paolo and Francesca meet again much later. Their love renews.

IV. Again he visits her. But his brothers have been watching. They find him. In the vicious fighting Giovanni makes a thrust at Paolo which kills Francesca instead. With double fury he cuts Paolo down and then breaks his bloody sword over his knee.

**Fra i Due Litiganti il Terzo Gode**
(*Between Two Litigants, a Third Succeeds*)
COMP.: G. Sarti
From Goldoni's *Le Nozze*

3 *acts*
Milan, 14 September 1782
London, 1784

Mozart used an air from this popular work in his own *Don Giovanni*.

**Françoise de Rimini**
COMP.: A. Thomas
LIBR.: Barbier and Carré
See also *Francesca da Rimini*.

*Prologue, 4 acts and Epilogue*
Opéra, 14 April 1882
Antwerp, 1883

**Frate 'nnamorato, Lo**
(*The Brother in Love*)
COMP.: G. Pergolesi
LIBR.: G. A. Federico

*Comedy in 3 acts*
Naples, 23 September 1732

**Frau ohne Schatten, Die**
(*The Woman Without a Shadow*)
COMP.: R. Strauss
LIBR.: H. von Hofmannsthal

3 *acts*
Vienna, 10 October 1919
La Scala, 1940
Buenos Aires, 1949
San Francisco 1959

CAST

| | | | |
|---|---|---|---|
| Emperor | T | Barak, *dyer* | BBar |
| Empress | S | His wife | S |
| Nurse, *die Amme* | MS | One-eye, *his brother* | B |
| Spirit, *messenger* | Bar | One-arm, *his brother* | B |
| Temple Gatekeeper | S or T | Hunchback, *his brother* | T |
| Apparition of a Youth | T | Children's voices | 3S, 3C |
| Voice of the Falcon | S | Nightwatchmen's voices | 3B |
| Voice from Above | C | Servants, Strange Children, Spirits | |

SYNOPSIS

The Empress is a magic person, sprung from a gazelle. She is barren and hence throws no shadow.

I. A messenger tells the nurse that if the Empress cannot find a shadow for herself within three days, she must return to her magic state. In that case the Emperor, likewise, will die. She and the nurse descend to Earth. There they find Barak's wife whom they persuade to give up her shadow, thus remaining childless.

II. When the third day comes, Barak's wife has lost her shadow but the Empress still has none. Barak is about to kill his wife for the loss but the Empress stops him, saying that killing is too high a price to pay. The earth swallows up Barak.

III. In a dark vault the Empress hears the cries of Barak and his wife calling to each other without answer. The Empress stands before her father in judgement. She steadfastly refuses to take the woman's shadow from her at the price they will have to pay. Even the sight of the Emperor slowly turning to stone does not shake her.

Suddenly she has a shadow. The Emperor is saved. As they embrace in their new-found love they see Barak and his wife also restored to each other.

## Freischütz, Der
*(The Freeshooter)*
COMP.: C. M. von Weber
LIBR.: J. F. Kind

3 *acts*
Berlin, 18 June 1821
London, 1824
New York, 1825
Metropolitan, 1884

CAST

| | | | |
|---|---|---|---|
| Prince Ottokar | Bar | Hermit | B |
| Cuno, *head ranger* | B | Samiel, *the wild huntsman* | Spkr |
| Max, *forester* | T | Agathe, *Cuno's daughter* | S |
| Caspar, *forester* | B | Aennchen, *her cousin* | S |
| Kilian, *rich peasant* | T | | |

SYNOPSIS

I. To win Agathe, Max must prove he is the best shot in the district. Unfortunately he is a very bad shot. But Caspar shows him the power of magic bullets. Max agrees to meet Caspar at midnight in the Wolf's Glen to make some of them.

II. Agathe sees Max for a moment. He depresses her by his impatience to leave to go to the Wolf's Glen. She and Aennchen do their best to dissuade him from going to that haunted place.

Caspar shows him the way there and introduces him to the Wild Huntsman who shows him how to make magic bullets. Six will go straight to the mark, the seventh will hit where Samiel directs it. Even the ghost of Max's mother, appearing to him there, cannot change his determination to avail himself of the help of the Devil.

III. Agathe and Aennchen dress for the competition. The shooters arrive. Max has already used up his six predictable bullets in a fabulous hunt beforehand. As Max prepares to shoot his final shot in the competition, Agathe shouts to prevent it. She is too late, Caspar falls dead. Max would have been banished for this accidental murder, but the Hermit wins his reprieve.

### Fremde Erde

(*Strange Land*)
COMP.: K. Rathaus
LIBR.: K. Palffy-Wanieck

5 acts
Berlin, 10 December 1930

### Friedenstag

(*Peace Day*)
COMP.: R. Strauss
LIBR.: J. Gregor

1 act
Munich, 24 July 1938
Berlin, 1939
Venice, 1940

CAST

| | | | |
|---|---|---|---|
| Commander of the Town | Bar | Front Line Officer | Bar |
| Maria, *his wife* | S | Piedmontese | T |
| Sergeant | B | Holsteiner, *commander of the enemy* | B |
| Corporal | Bar | Burgomaster | T |
| Private | T | Bishop | Bar |
| Musketeer | B | Woman | S |
| Bugler | B | Soldiers, Elders, Women, | |
| Officer | Bar | Townspeople | |

SYNOPSIS

The Commander will not allow the town to save itself by surrendering to the besiegers. But under pressure from the townspeople he finally agrees to allow it, on condition that it will not happen until noon and that he will give the signal himself. He plans to signal by blowing up his own garrison.

When the final moment is near, just before the fuse is to be lit, the enemy ceases firing. The Holsteiner comes up to offer peace. This the Commander refuses until again the townspeople and his wife urge him to accept. To the sound of a great hymn to peace the opera ends.

### From a House of the Dead

See *Z Mrtvého Domu*

### Galatea

See *Schöne Galatee*
See also *Acis and Galatea*

### Gazza Ladra, La

COMP.: G. Rossini
LIBR.: G. Gherardini
From a drama by d'Aubigny and
Caigniez

2 acts
La Scala, 31 May 1817
London, 1821
Philadelphia, 1827
New York, 1830

### Genoveva

COMP.: R. Schumann
LIBR.: R. Reineck altered by Schumann
From plays by Ticek and Habbel

4 acts
Leipzig, 25 June 1850
Drury Lane, 1893
Paris (Concert), 1894

## Gianni Schicchi

COMP.: G. Puccini
LIBR.: G. Forzano

*Comedy in 1 act*
Metropolitan, 14 December 1918
Buenos Aires, 1919
Covent Garden, 1920

CAST

| | | | |
|---|---|---|---|
| Gianni Schicchi, 50 | Bar | Simone, *Buoso's cousin*, 70, *heir* | B |
| Lauretta, *his daughter*, 21 | S | Marco, *his son*, 45, *heir* | Bar |
| Zita, *Buoso's cousin*, 60, *heir* | C | La Ciesca, *Marco's wife*, 38, *heir* | MS |
| Rinuccio, *her nephew*, 24, *heir* | T | Maestro Spinellocchio, *doctor* | B |
| Gherardo, *Buoso's nephew*, 40, *heir* | T | Ser Amantio di Nicolao, *lawyer* | Bar |
| Nella, *his wife*, 34, *heir* | S | Pinellino, *cobbler* | B |
| Gherardino, *their son*, 7, *heir* | C | Guccio, *painter* | B |
| Betto di Segna, *Buoso's* | | | |
| *brother-in-law*, *heir* | B | | |

SYNOPSIS

Buoso has just died. His heirs have gathered around his deathbed to pray for his soul and to reap their inheritances. When the will is read, however, they find that all his money went to a monastery. In desperation they turn one and all to Gianni Schicchi in the hope that he can do something about it. He hits upon a plan.

He jumps into the deathbed and draws the curtains. When the doctor comes, Gianni Schicchi mimics the dead man's voice and says he's much better, thank you. That gets rid of the doctor. Gianni then calls for a lawyer.

To the lawyer he dictates a new will, giving little tokens to each relative. But when he comes to a big prize he assigns it—to himself! Not one of those present can utter the slightest protest, since all agreed to the fraud in the first place and witnesses are present. Gianni therefore gives himself the great house, throws all the relatives out and makes his daughter very happy with Rinuccio, whom she loves.

NOTES

This is the third of three one-act operas written for the Metropolitan. The first was *Il Tabarro*, the second *Suor Angelica*. Puccini called the three *Il Trittico*. The subject of the ghoulish Gianni Schicchi is mentioned in a line of the thirteenth canto of Dante's *Inferno* as one who suffers for having counterfeited another's shape.

## Ginevra

COMP.: M. Delannoy

Comique, 1942

## Gioconda, La

(*The Ballad Singer*)
COMP.: A. Ponchielli
LIBR.: A. Boito

*Tragedy in 4 acts*
La Scala, 8 April 1876
Covent Garden, 1883
Metropolitan, 1883

CAST

| | | | |
|---|---|---|---|
| La Gioconda, *ballad singer* | S | Zuane, *boatman* | B |
| La Cieca, *her blind mother* | C | Isèpo, *public scribe* | T |
| Alvise Badoero, *inquisitor* | B | Pilot | B |
| Laura, *his wife* | MS | Monks, Senators, Sailors, Shipwrights, | |
| Enzo Grimaldo, *Genoese nobleman* | T | Ladies, Gentlemen, Populace, | |
| Barnaba, *spy for the inquisition* | Bar | Masquers, Guards | |

SYNOPSIS

I. *The Lion's Mouth*. Barnaba loves Gioconda, but she is in love with Enzo, an enemy to the city, who is in disguise. To win her in spite of this obstacle, Barnaba spreads the rumor that La Cieca is a witch. A riot ensues during which Enzo's men act to protect her. Alvise puts a stop to the uproar and pardons La Cieca at Laura's intercession. Enzo recognizes the inquisitor's wife as the Laura to whom he was once betrothed. Barnaba therefore arranges to have Alvise discover his wife in the act of escaping with Enzo. Gioconda overhears the plot.

II. *The Rosary*. Gioconda goes to the boat to confront Laura, but instead of making trouble, she saves her rival by sending her away when Barnaba appears. Enzo sees her there, and sees the Venetians, his enemies, coming also. He sets fire to his ship.

III. *The House of Gold*. Alvise, made aware of her infidelity, forces his wife to drink poison. But Gioconda has substituted a drug in its place. The inquisitor exhibits her, thinking she is dead, to his guests, among whom is Enzo. Enzo, taken by surprise, reveals himself and is seized by the guards.

IV. *The Orfano Canal*. Gioconda helps Enzo and the revived Laura to escape. Barnaba comes for her, but she thwarts his revenge by stabbing herself before his eyes.

| | | | |
|---|---|---|---|
| **Gioielli della Madonna, I** | | *Tragedy in 3 acts* | |
| (*The Jewels of the Madonna*) | | Berlin, 2 December 1911 | |
| COMP.: E. Wolf-Ferrari | | Chicago and New York, 1912 | |
| LIBR.: Golisciani and Zangarini | | Covent Garden, 1912 | |
| | | Metropolitan, 1925 | |

CAST

| | | | |
|---|---|---|---|
| Gennaro, *blacksmith* | T | Stella | S |
| Maliella, *Carmela's adopted daughter* | S | Concetta | S |
| Rafaele, *Camorrist leader* | Bar | Serena | C |
| Carmela, *Gennaro's mother* | MS | Rocco, *Camorrist* | B |
| Biaso, *scribe* | T | Grazia | Dancer |
| Ciccillo, *Camorrist* | T | Vendors, Monks, People | |

SYNOPSIS

I. Gennaro is finishing a candelabra for the Festival of the Madonna which has already begun. The Camorrists, a band of extortionists, arrive in town. Rafaele seizes Maliella, kisses her laughingly and gives her a flower. He pleads passionate love, and says he would steal even the jewels from the image of the Madonna for her. Gennaro warns her against this man.

II. Gennaro is desperate to protect her from the flamboyant Rafaele. He himself goes off in the night and steals the jewels to foil Rafaele at his own game. Maliella melts with rapture into his arms.

III. For her change of affections Rafaele rejects the girl. The Camorrists shrink from her when they see her wearing the sacred jewels. Finally she is so full of remorse she drowns herself in the sea while Gennaro, full of guilt, stabs himself.

| | |
|---|---|
| **Giorno di Regno, Un** | *Comedy in 2 acts* |
| COMP.: G. Verdi | La Scala, 5 September 1840 |
| LIBR.: F. Romani | Venice, 1845 |
| Verdi's second opera. | |

**Gli Equivoci nel Sembiante**
COMP.: A. Scarlatti
LIBR.: D. F. Contini
Scarlatti's first opera.

3 *acts*
Rome, February 1679
Vienna, 1681

**Girl of the Golden West, The**
See *Fanciulla del West, La*

**Gloriana**
COMP.: B. Britten
LIBR.: W. Plomer

3 *acts*
Covent Garden, 8 June 1953

CAST

| | | | |
|---|---|---|---|
| Queen Elizabeth the First | S | Henry Cuffe, *Essex's satellite* | Bar |
| Robert Devereux, *earl of Essex* | T | Lady-in-Waiting | S |
| Frances, *countess of Essex* | MS | Blind Ballad Singer | B |
| Charles Blount, *Lord Mountjoy* | Bar | Recorder of Norwich | B |
| Penelope, *Lady Rich, sister of Essex* | S | Housewife | MS |
| Sir Robert Cecil, | | Spirit of the Masque | T |
| *secretary of the Council* | Bar | Master of Ceremonies | T |
| Sir Walter Raleigh, | | City Crier | Bar |
| *captain of the guard* | B | Chorus, Dancers, Actors, Musicians | |

SYNOPSIS

I. Essex, jealous of Mountjoy's popularity, provides occasion for a fight and comes away slightly wounded. The queen upbraids them both. She feels herself married to her people, but when Essex sings to her at least it eases her moods. Essex looks upon Raleigh as his rival.

II. The queen witnesses a masque in her honor at Norwich (set for *a capella* voices). She has been delaying the award to Essex of an appointment as Lord Deputy in Ireland. At a ball the queen, rendered ridiculously jealous by the attractiveness of Lady Essex, arranges to steal that unfortunate lady's dress and stalk about in it, badly fitted upon herself. After this demonstration of her feelings, she allows the appointment to go through.

III. Essex is a failure in Ireland. He returns precipitously to England and compounds his ill favor by bursting in upon the queen while she is not yet made-up for the day. After he leaves her she has him put under watch.

Essex is tried and condemned.

In the final scene we see a panorama of the rest of her life, the affairs of England, prayers for the queen and finally her death.

NOTE

*Gloriana* was written to celebrate the coronation of Elizabeth the Second.

**Golden Cockerel, The**
See *Coq d'Or, Le*

**Goldene Kreuz, Das**
(*The Golden Cross*)
COMP.: I. Brüll
LIBR.: S. Mosenthal
From a play by Mélesville and Brazier

2 *acts*
Berlin, 22 December 1875
London, 1878
New York, 1879
Metropolitan, 1886

## Götterdämmerung
(*The Twilight of the Gods*)
COMP.: R. Wagner
LIBR.: By the Composer

*Music Drama in Prologue and 3 acts*
Bayreuth, 17 August 1876
London, 1882
Metropolitan, 1888

CAST

| | | | |
|---|---|---|---|
| Siegfried | T | First Norn | C |
| Gunther | Bar | Second Norn | MS |
| Alberich | BBar | Third Norn | S |
| Hagen | B | Woglinde | S |
| Brünnhilde | S | Wellgunde | S |
| Gutrune | S | Flosshilde | MS |
| Waltraute | MS | Vassals and Women | |

MUSICAL HIGHLIGHTS

PROLOGUE. Siegfried's Rhine Journey
ACT I. Waltraute's Narrative
ACT III. Siegfried's Narrative

SYNOPSIS

PROLOGUE. The three Norns weave the thread of life. The skein breaks and the doom of the gods is foretold.

Siegfried takes leave of Brünnhilde and sets out on a journey down the Rhine.

I. Hagen, of the tribe of Alberich, greets Siegfried, welcomes him to his home, and gives him a potion that makes him forget Brünnhilde and fall in love with Gutrune. Siegfried quickly agrees to bring Brünnhilde to be Gunther's wife; she means nothing to him any more. Therefore he goes back, disguised by the magic Tarnhelm as Gunther, seizes the Ring of the Nibelungs from Brünnhilde's finger and brings her to Hagen's hall.

II. Hagen summons his vassals for the double wedding. But Brünnhilde recognizes the ring on Siegfried's finger and shouts for all to hear that she is already married, to Siegfried. Hagen and Gunther plan to murder the warrior.

III. While Siegfried is resting on a hunt next day, Hagen kills him with a spear in the back. The men carry his body upon his shield to the hall where Brünnhilde directs the construction of a funeral pyre. When the blaze is at its height she rides into it with the ring. At this the Rhine overflows its banks, the Rhinemaidens snatch the ring which was once stolen from them, and Valhalla itself, the abode of the gods, is consumed by the flames.

NOTES

This is the final part of *Der Ring des Nibelungen*. Originally called *Siegfrieds Tod*, it was written in 1848 and orchestrated in 1874.

## Goyescas
COMP.: E. Granados
LIBR.: F. Periquet
From Goya

*3 scenes*
Metropolitan, 28 January 1916
Buenos Aires, 1929
London, 1951

CAST

| | | | |
|---|---|---|---|
| Rosario, *high born young lady* | S | Pepa, *Paquiro's sweetheart* | MS |
| Fernando, *her lover, an officer* | T | Majas, Majos | |
| Paquiro, *toreador* | Bar | | |

SYNOPSIS

I. During a holiday Paquiro sees Rosario and invites her to a candlelight ball. Her lover, Fernando, becomes jealous and formally states that he will escort the lady. Pepa also becomes jealous. She vows to win satisfaction from Rosario.

II. At the ball Fernando's airs amaze everybody. Paquiro challenges him to a duel.

III. While the lady waits, the duel goes on in her garden. She hears Fernando scream. She rushes to him and holds him in her arms as he dies.

NOTE

The composer was on his way home after the opening in New York when his ship was torpedoed at sea by a German submarine and sank with him aboard.

### Grande Duchesse de Gérolstein, La

| | |
|---|---|
| | 3 acts |
| COMP.: J. Offenbach | Paris, 12 April 1867 |
| LIBR.: Meilhac and Halévy | New York, 1867 |
| | Covent Garden, 1867 |

### Guarany, Il

| | |
|---|---|
| | 4 acts |
| COMP.: A. Gomez | La Scala, 19 March 1870 |
| LIBR.: A. Scalvini | Covent Garden, 1872 |
| From a novel by Alencar | New York, 1884 |

### Guillaume Tell

| | |
|---|---|
| (William Tell) | 3 acts (Originally 4) |
| | Opéra, 3 August 1829 |
| COMP.: G. Rossini | Drury Lane, 1830 |
| LIBR.: de Jouy, Bis, | New York, 1831 |
| From Schiller | Metropolitan, 1884 |

CAST

| | | | |
|---|---|---|---|
| Guillaume Tell, Swiss patriot | Bar | Rudolph, captain of the guards | T |
| Hedwige, his wife | S | Walter Furst, Swiss patriot | B |
| Jemmy, his son | S | Leuthold, shepherd | B |
| Arnold, Mathilde's suitor | T | Ruedi, fisherman | T |
| Melcthal, his father | B | Peasants, Knights, Pages, Ladies, Hunters, |  |
| Gessler, tyrant governor | B | Soldiers, Guards, Three Bridal Couples |  |
| Mathilde, his sister | S | | |

SYNOPSIS

I. Tell risks his life to help Leuthold escape the tyrant's guards. In revenge, the guards seize old Melcthal in his place.

II. Arnold, who is in love with Mathilde, learns from Tell that Melcthal has been killed under Gessler's orders. He joins with Tell and Walter to help rid Switzerland of the hated foreign rulers.

III. At the hundredth anniversary of Austrian rule over Switzerland, Gessler has set up his hat on a pole and ordered that all the Swiss bow to it. Tell refuses. Gessler has him seized and commands him to show his prowess by shooting an arrow off his own son's head. Tell takes aim and does this with his first arrow. With his second he kills Gessler as the Swiss, united, arise to throw off the tyrants.

**Gunlöd**
COMP.: P. Cornelius
LIBR.: By the composer

3 *acts*
Weimar, 6 May 1891
Cologne (*rev.*), 1906
Halle, 1918

This work was completed by C. Hoffbauer.

**Gwendoline**
COMP.: E. Chabrier
LIBR.: C. Mendés

2 *acts*
Brussels, 10 April 1886
Dresden, 1890
Opéra, 1893

**Gypsy Baron, The**
See *Zigeunerbaron*

**Habanera, La**
COMP.: R. Laparra
LIBR.: By the composer

3 *acts*
Comique, 26 February 1908
Covent Garden, 1910
Boston, 1910

**Halka**
COMP.: S. Moniuszko
LIBR.: W. Wolski
From a story by Wójcicki

4 *acts*
Vilna, Lithuania, 16 February 1854
New York, 1903
Milwaukee, Wisc., 1923

This opera was originally performed in two acts. There was an amateur production at Vilna in 1847.

**Hamlet**
COMP.: A. Thomas
LIBR.: Barbier and Carré
From Shakespeare

*Tragedy in* 5 *acts*
Opéra, 9 March 1868
Covent Garden, 1870
New York, 1872

Perhaps this is the earliest opera to use a saxophone in the orchestra.

**Hans Heiling**
COMP.: H. Marschner
LIBR.: E. Devrient

*Prologue and* 3 *acts*
Berlin, 24 May 1833
Vienna, 1846

**Hänsel und Gretel**
COMP.: E. Humperdinck
LIBR.: A. Wette (his sister)

3 *acts*
Weimar, 23 December 1893
London, 1894
New York, 1895

CAST

| | | | |
|---|---|---|---|
| Hänsel, *a little boy* | MS | Peter, *their father, a broom maker* | Bar |
| Gretel, *his sister* | S | Sandman | S |
| Witch | MS | Dew Fairy | S |
| Gertrude, *the children's mother* | S, MS | | |

SYNOPSIS

1. Gertrude, in despair to see her children playing when poverty demands labor, sends them out to the woods to look for berries. When Peter comes home quite drunk, carrying a load of sausages and things for supper, she tells him where they have gone. He has heard that there is a wicked witch living in those woods. Both the parents rush off to save their children.

II. Hänsel and Gretel have been eating up their berries as soon as they collect them. Night finds them in the woods. They feel very sleepy. After saying their prayers, they fall asleep together and the Sandman comes to seal their eyes.

III. In the morning they are very hungry. But what do they find? It is a house all made of candy. They break off bits and eat away in joy until the witch catches them at it. She sticks Hänsel into a kennel to fatten him up, and makes Gretel help her with the work. But Gretel is a smart little girl. She manages to free her brother and together they trick the witch into her own oven. When their distracted parents find them the old witch has been baked into a honey cake and all the other little boys and girls who had been caught by the witch have resumed their natural shapes by Gretel's dexterity with the witch's wand.

## Harlequin
See *Arlecchino*

## Harmonie der Welt, Die
(*The Harmony of the World*)
COMP.: Paul Hindemith
LIBR.: By the composer

5 acts
Munich, 11 August 1957

CAST

| | | | |
|---|---|---|---|
| Kaiser Rudolf II/Kaiser Ferdinand II (*The Sun*) | B | Tansur (*Saturn*) | B |
| Johannes Kepler, *astronomer* (*The Earth*) | Bar | Baron Starbemberg | Bar |
| | | Christoph, *Kepler's brother* | T |
| | | Susanna, *later Kepler's wife* (*Venus*) | S |
| Wallenstein, *Commander in Chief* (*Jupiter*) | T | Katharina, *Kepler's mother* (*The Moon*) | C |
| Ulrich Grüsser, *Kepler's assistant, later a soldier* (*Mars*) | T | Little Susanna, *Kepler's daughter by his first wife* | S |
| Daniel Hizler, *Vicar, later vicar of Regensburg* (*Mercury*) | B | Magistrate, Lawyer, People, Soldiers, Stars | |

## Háry János
COMP.: Z. Kodály
LIBR.: Paulini and Harsányi

Fable in 3 acts
Budapest, 16 October 1926
Cologne, 1931
New York (Juilliard), 1960

CAST

| | | |
|---|---|---|
| Háry János | Bar | Kaiser Franz of Austria, Countess Melusine and Countess Estrella, Hungarian Sentry, Russian Sentry, General Blood and Thunder, General Dufla, Two Hussars, Two Artillerymen, Village Elder, Student, Abraham the Innkeeper, Two peasants Spkrs |
| Ilka, *his fiancée* | S | |
| The Empress of Austria | S | |
| Emperor Napoleon | Bar | |
| Marie-Louise, *his wife* | MS | |
| Old Marzci, *her coachman* | Bar | |
| Ritter von Ebelasztin, *her chamberlain* | T | Generals, Soldiers, Peasants, Court Servants |

SYNOPSIS

Háry János is a great teller of tall tales.

First he helps the empress get across the Russian frontier, which is utterly impassable to others. Then he causes the French to declare war on Austria. He takes Napoleon prisoner, turns down Marie-Louise as a wife but takes Ilka instead. And, since she is dead and gone now, who can contradict him?

**Häusliche Krieg, Der**      1 act
(*The Domestic War*)      Frankfort, 29 August 1861
COMP.: F. Schubert      New York, 1877
LIBR.: I. F. Castelli      London (Concert), 1872
From *Lysistrata* by Aristophanes
    Schubert completed this opera in 1823.

**He Who Gets Slapped**
COMP.: R. Ward      New York, 17 May 1956
LIBR.: B. Stambler      (*Columbia University*)
From Andreyev's play      New York (N.Y. City Opera), 1959

CAST

| | | | |
|---|---|---|---|
| Count Mancini | T | Bezano | T |
| Zinida | S | Baron Regnard | Bar |
| Pantaloon | Bar | Tilly | Silent |
| Consuelo | S | Polly | Silent |

NOTE

    In its first production, by Columbia University, the opera was called *Pantaloon*.

**Heimchen am Herd, Das**      3 acts
(*The Cricket on the Hearth*)      Vienna, 21 March 1896
COMP.: K. Goldmark
LIBR.: M. Willner
From the story by Charles Dickens

CAST

| | | | |
|---|---|---|---|
| John | Bar | Edward Plummer | T |
| Dot, *his wife* | S | Tackleton | B |
| May | S | Cricket | S |

**Helen**
See *Belle Hélène, La*

**Helen in Egypt**
See *Aegyptische Helene, Die*

**Helen Retires**      3 acts
COMP.: G. Antheil      New York (Juilliard), 28 February 1934
LIBR.: J. Erskine

**Henry VIII**      4 acts
COMP.: C. Saint-Säens      Opéra, 5 March 1883
LIBR.: Détroyat and Silvestre      Covent Garden, 1898

**Her Foster Daughter**
See *Její Pastorkyňa*

**Hérodiade**      *Tragedy in 4 acts*
COMP.: J. Massenet      Brussels, 19 December 1881
LIBR.: Milliet and Hartmann      New Orleans, 1884
From a story by Flaubert      Covent Garden, 1904
     New York, 1909

**Herodias**
See also *Salome*

**Heure Espagnole, L'**      *Comedy in 1 act*
(*The Spanish Hour*)      Comique, 19 May 1911
COMP.: M. Ravel      Covent Garden, 1919
LIBR.: F. Nohain      Chicago and New York, 1920
     Metropolitan, 1925

CAST

| | | | |
|---|---|---|---|
| Concepcion, *Torquemada's wife* | S | Ramiro, *muleteer* | Bar |
| Gonsalve, *poet* | T | Don Inigo Gomez, *banker* | B |
| Torquemada, *a clockmaker* | T | | |

SYNOPSIS

Torquemada is about to spend the day away from home fixing the clocks in town when Ramiro drops in to have his watch fixed. Torquemada asks him to wait until he returns.

This is the day Concepcion receives her lovers. They are hiding in the clocks, unwilling to be discovered by Ramiro. Concepcion asks the visitor if he'd mind moving some of the heavy clocks for her. Obligingly he carries this one up to her bedroom, that one back downstairs, and so on. Pretty soon he realizes what is going on. He himself is quite taken with Concepcion's beauty. Gradually he woos and wins her.

When Torquemada returns he finds the lovers hidden, each in a clock. He sells each one a clock and sends them away. But he is very glad to have Ramiro stay. Ramiro is such a handy fellow to have around.

**Hin und Zurück**      *1 act*
COMP.: P. Hindemith      Baden-Baden, 17 July 1927
LIBR.: M. Schiffer      Basle, 1928

**Hippolyte et Aricie**      *Prologue and 5 acts*
COMP.: J. P. Rameau      Opéra, 1 October 1733
LIBR.: L'Abbé Pellegrin      Paris, 1908

**Hochzeit des Camacho, Die**      *2 acts*
(*Camacho's Wedding*)      Berlin, 29 April 1827
COMP.: F. Mendelssohn      Boston (Concert), 1885
LIBR.: C. von Lichtenstein      Berlin (Concert), 1886
From *Don Quixote* by Cervantes
     *Camacho's Wedding* has been staged only once.

**Hoffmann**
See *Contes d'Hoffmann, Les*

**Holy Devil, The**
COMP.: N. Nabokov      Louisville, Ky., 18 April 1958
     In Europe this opera is performed as *Rasputin*.

**Hubička**      *Comedy in 2 acts*
(*The Kiss*)      Prague, 7 November 1876
COMP.: B. Smetana      Liverpool, 1948
LIBR.: E. Krasnohorska

CAST

| | | | |
|---|---|---|---|
| Paloucky, *peasant* | BBar | Martinka, *Vendulka's aunt* | C |
| Vendulka, *his daughter* | S | Matous, *smuggler* | B |
| Lukas, *young widower* | T | Barce, *servant* | S |
| Tomes, *his brother-in-law* | Bar | Guard at the Frontier | T |

SYNOPSIS

I. Vendulka is engaged to Lukas. He comes to woo her. He wants to kiss her but no—she refuses. Again and again he makes the attempt but always she refuses. In the end both are furious as he marches away. Outside her window, and in plain sight of everyone in her house including her father who objected to their betrothal anyway, Lukas makes a show of dancing with and kissing every pretty girl he can find.

II. She goes away to escape the humiliation. Their friends arrange for them to meet again. Lukas most formally begs her pardon. Then he kisses her.

## Hugh the Drover

*2 acts*

COMP.: R. Vaughan Williams     London, 4 July 1924
LIBR.: H. Child     Toronto, 1932
    New York, 1952

CAST

| | | | |
|---|---|---|---|
| Showman | Bar | Susan | S |
| Mary, *the constable's daughter* | S | Nancy | C |
| Aunt Jane, *the constable's sister* | C | William | T |
| Turnkey | T | Robert | B |
| Constable | B | Fool | B |
| John the Butcher | BBar | Innkeeper | B |
| Hugh the Drover | T | Sergeant | Bar |
| Cheap Jack | Bar | Stallkeeper, Juggler, Dancing Girl, | |
| Shellfish Seller | B |     Trumpeter | |
| Primrose Seller | C | Townspeople, Toysellers, Boys, Soldiers | |
| Ballad Seller | T | | |

SYNOPSIS

I. When Hugh saw Mary at the fair it was love at first sight. But she had already agreed to marry John on the morrow. What to do? John fought Hugh but Hugh won. John accused him of being a French spy and Hugh was arrested.

II. Mary stole her father's keys to let Hugh out of the stocks, but people came by at the wrong time. She changed her strategy and took the place next to him in the stocks. For this John insulted her and her father disowned her. But when the soldiers came to take Hugh away they discovered that he was certainly not a spy but a famous patriot well known to them. In place of Hugh, therefore, they took John, leaving the lovers free to do as they pleased.

## Huguenots, Les

*Tragedy in 5 acts*

COMP.: G. Meyerbeer     Opéra, 29 February 1836
LIBR.: A. E. Scribe     Covent Garden, 1842
From Deschamps     New York, 1845
    Metropolitan, 1883

CAST

| | | | |
|---|---|---|---|
| Valentine, *betrothed to de Nevers* | S | Tavannes, *Catholic gentleman* | T |
| Marguerite de Valois, *betrothed* | | de Retz | Bar |
| *to Henry IV* | S | Raoul de Nangis, *Huguenot* | |
| Urbain, *her page* | MS | *nobleman* | T |
| Count de St. Bris, *Catholic* | | Marcel, *Huguenot soldier* | B |
| *nobleman* | Bar | Bois-Rosé, *Huguenot soldier* | T |
| Count de Nevers, *Catholic* | | Maurevert, *Catholic nobleman* | B |
| *nobleman* | Bar | Catholic Ladies and Gentlemen, Huguenot | |
| Cossé | T | Ladies and Gentlemen, Soldiers, Pages, | |
| Méru, *Catholic gentleman* | Bar | Citizens, Populace, Night Watch, | |
| Thoré, *Catholic gentleman* | Bar | Monks, Students | |

SYNOPSIS

I. Raoul and Marcel attend a banquet at the house of de Nevers. There Marcel defies the other guests by singing Huguenot hymns. Raoul falls in love with an unknown lady who is there, but she is the count's guest.

II. Marguerite sends for Raoul to bring him and Valentine (the unknown lady) together. She hopes to avert war by uniting a Catholic with a Huguenot. But Raoul thinks Valentine is de Nevers' mistress and refuses her.

III. Valentine then is betrothed to de Nevers. Raoul sends St. Bris his challenge. Valentine hears of a plot to kill Raoul of which she warns him. Not until then does Raoul finally learn that Valentine did love him.

IV. Raoul visits her, even though she is married, and listens as the nobles plan their massacre of the Huguenots. De Nevers refuses to take part in the plot. For that he is imprisoned.

V. During the massacre, de Nevers is killed. Valentine pleads with Raoul to become a Catholic and marry her but he refuses. While they speak St. Bris mounts his attack and kills them without realizing that one of the shadowy figures is his own daughter.

## Idomeneo

| | | |
|---|---|---|
| **Idomeneo** | | 3 *acts* |
| COMP.: W. A. Mozart | | Munich, 29 January 1781 |
| LIBR.: Abbé Varesco | | Glasgow, 1934 |
| From an opera by Campra | | Tanglewood, Mass., 1947 |
| and Danchet | | |

CAST

| | | | |
|---|---|---|---|
| Idomeneo, *king of Crete* | T | High Priest of Neptune | T |
| Idamante, *his son* | S | Voice of Neptune | B |
| Ilia, *Trojan princess* | S | People of Crete, Trojan Prisoners, Sailors, | |
| Elektra, *Greek princess* | S | Soldiers, Priests of Neptune, Dancers | |
| Arbace, *the king's confidant* | T | | |

SYNOPSIS

I. Ilia, a prisoner sent to Crete from the Trojan war, has fallen in love with Idamante. The prisoners are to be set free in celebration of Idomeneo's return but a storm nearly puts a stop to it. As guarantee of his safety Idomeneo has promised to sacrifice the first person he sees after landing. This person turns out to be Idamante.

II. Arbace advises the king to send his son away to avoid the vow. To Ilia's loss, he is to go away with Elektra to Greece. Again, however, Neptune intervenes to prevent the deception.

III. Idamante goes to fight a monster Neptune has sent against Crete. Idomeneo prepares to go ahead with a sacrifice. Ilia pleads to be substituted for Idamante. Finally Neptune relents on condition that Idomeneo relinquish his throne in favor of his son. Thus the tragic opera ends happily.

**Iernin**  
COMP.: G. Lloyd  
LIBR.: W. Lloyd

3 *acts*  
Penzance, England, 6 November 1934  
London, 1935

**Ilsebill**  
COMP.: F. Klose  
LIBR.: H. Hoffman  
From a fairy tale by the brothers Grimm.

5 *scenes*  
Karlsruhe, 7 June 1903  
Munich, 1905  
Basle, 1923

**Immortal Hour, The**  
COMP.: R. Boughton  
LIBR.: By the composer  
From a poem by Fiona MacLeod

2 *acts*  
Glastonbury, England, 26 August 1914  
London, 1922  
New York, 1926

**Impresario, The**  
See *Schauspieldirektor, Der*

**In the Pasha's Garden**  
COMP.: J. L. Seymour  
LIBR.: H. Tracy  
From a story by Dwight

1 *act*  
Metropolitan, 24 January 1935

**Incoronazione di Poppea, L'**  
COMP.: C. Monteverdi  
LIBR.: G. F. Busenello

*Prologue and* 3 *acts*  
Venice, Autumn, 1642  
Naples, 1651

This is Monteverdi's last opera. It was staged in Paris in 1913 and at Smith College, Massachusetts, in 1926. It is perhaps the earliest opera on a historical subject.

**Intermezzo**  
COMP.: R. Strauss  
LIBR.: By the composer

2 *acts*  
Dresden, 4 November 1924  
Berlin, 1925  
Zurich, 1951

CAST

| | | | |
|---|---|---|---|
| Christine | S | His wife | S |
| Little Franz, *her son* | | Kapellmeister Stroh, *Storch's* | |
| Hofkapellmeister Robert Storch, | | *partner* | T |
| *her husband* | Bar | Commercial Councillor, *a partner* | Bar |
| Anna, *chambermaid* | S | Justizrat, *a partner* | Bar |
| Baron Lummer | T | Kammersänger, *a partner* | B |
| Notary | Bar | | |

I. Storch and his wife bicker constantly. He is packing to leave; Christine prepares to go skating. There she meets Lummer and tries to impress him about her husband the composer. Later the young Baron approaches her for money. Still later she intercepts a letter from an unknown woman to her husband. At last everything adds up; she decides to leave Storch immediately.

II. Storch, her telegram in his hand, is bewildered, wondering why his wife should want a divorce. Stroh suggests perhaps the mysterious letter was intended for him, the spelling of their names being similar. Stroh goes to Christine to explain, Storch himself finally arrives home and the reconciliation is complete.

### NOTE

Strauss gave detailed descriptions of his own house as directions to the designer of the sets. The opera is partly autobiographical.

## Iphigénie en Aulide

COMP.: C. von Gluck
LIBR.: Calzabigi
From the tragedy by Racine

3 *acts*
Opéra, 19 April 1774
Oxford, 1933
Philadelphia, 1935

### CAST

| | | | |
|---|---|---|---|
| Agamemnon, *king* | Bar | Achilles, *warrior and general* | T |
| Kalchas, *priest* | B | Patroclus, *his friend* | Bar |
| Clytemnestra, *queen* | MS | Arkas, *messenger* | B |
| Iphigénie, *princess, daughter of* | | Greeks | |
| *Agamemnon* | S | | |

### SYNOPSIS

I. The Gods have demanded that Agamemnon sacrifice his daughter in exchange for a favorable wind to Troy. He cannot worm out of it; she arrives at Aulis ready to marry Achilles in spite of her father's attempt to keep her away by spreading a rumor that Achilles is not worthy of her.

II. Unaware of the sacrifice, Achilles and Iphigénie approach the altar to be wedded. Achilles, hearing of the danger, swears to defend her and defies his general. Agamemnon, torn three ways by this fate, again tries to escape it by sending Iphigénie to Mycenae.

III. The Greeks, whose success in the war depends upon proper observance of the sacrifices required by the gods, force Agamemnon to fulfill his oath. Achilles again defies him, this time with an army. At this the gods declare the sacrifice no longer necessary since Agamemnon has fully demonstrated his intention to comply with it. Thus all is reconciled and the armies depart to make war upon Troy.

## Iphigénie en Tauride

COMP.: C. W. Gluck
LIBR.: F. Guillard
From Euripides

*Tragedy in 4 acts*
Opéra, 18 May 1779
London, 1796
Metropolitan, 1916

### CAST

| | | | |
|---|---|---|---|
| Iphigénie, *Priestess of Diana* | S | Thoas, *King of Scythia* | B |
| Oreste, *her brother* | Bar | Diana, *Goddess* | S |
| Pylade, *his friend* | T | Scythians, Greeks, Priestesses | |

MUSICAL HIGHLIGHTS

ACT I. Aria *De noirs pressentiments* (Such dark presentiments), Thoas
ACT II. The *Mad Scene* of Oreste
Aria *Unis dès la plus tendre enfance* (Together from the tenderest childhood), Pylade
ACT III. Aria *O malheureuse Iphigénie* (O unhappy Iphigénie), Iphigénie
Aria *Je t'implore et je tremble* (I implore you, I tremble), Iphigénie

SYNOPSIS

I. Iphigénie, now the Priestess of Diana, has dreamed that misfortune has befallen her family, whom she has not seen for many years. King Thoas has likewise heard of possible threats to his own safety. He calls for human sacrifice to prevent danger. Two captives are brought to the temple to be victims; they are Oreste and Pylade.

II. Oreste has been driven to the edge of madness by the Furies, his punishment for murdering his own mother. Iphigénie questions him. He tells her that King Agamemnon was murdered by Clytemnestra, and that Oreste slew her. But he does not reveal to Iphigénie that he is Oreste.

III. Iphigénie resolves to send him to Mycenae with a message. This would save him from the sacrifice. But he refuses to leave his friend. Pylade is therefore forced to go in his place.

IV. At the moment of the sacrifice, Iphigénie recognizes Oreste as her own brother. She pleads, but Thoas will not permit him to be relieved of the sacrifice. Pylades arrives at that time with help and saves them.

NOTES

According to Kobbé, Gluck's conducting was interrupted during a rehearsal when some of the orchestra objected that the accompaniment to *Le calme rentre dans mon coeur* (Calm returns to my heart) was too agitated to express the thought. Gluck replied "Go on all the same; he lies, he has killed his mother!"

**Iphigénie en Tauride**                     *Tragedy in 4 acts*
COMP.: N. Piccini                            Opéra, 23 January 1781
LIBR.: A. Dubreuil                           Copenhagen, 1787

This work was written at the instigation of the anti-Gluck faction in the war of the Gluckists and Piccinists. At the opening the prima donna was drunk. The opening was so complete a failure that the Piccinists could no longer carry on their side of the battle, thus letting the war end in favor of the Gluckists. It should be remembered that Gluck and Piccini themselves had very little to do with this partisanship. Piccini's *Iphigénie en Tauride* has been revived several times since.

**Iphigénie en Tauride**
The subject was used by Campra in 1704 and Galuppi in 1768.

**Iris**                                     *3 acts*
COMP.: P. Mascagni                           Rome, 27 November 1898
LIBR.: L. Illica                             Philadelphia, 1902
                                             New York, 1902

CAST

| | | |
|---|---|---|
| Il Cieco, *blind man* | B | Ragpicker, Shopkeepers, Geishas, |
| Iris, *his daughter* | S | Laundry Girls, Samurai, Citizens, |
| Osaka, *rich young man* | T | Strolling Players, Beauty, Death, and a |
| Kyoto | Bar | Vampire |

SYNOPSIS
The story concerns the kidnapping of Iris from her father by people in the pay of Osaka. Her father repudiates her because he thinks she freely chose to become a geisha.

### Isis

COMP.: J. B. Lully  
LIBR.: P. Quinault

*Prologue and 5 acts*  
Paris, 5 January 1677

Quinault was banished for a time for suspected allusions in this libretto to a court scandal revolving around the king's mistress.

### Italiana in Algeri, L'

(*The Italian Girl in Algiers*)  
COMP.: G. Rossini  
LIBR.: A. Anelli

*2 acts*  
Venice, 22 May 1813  
London, 1819  
New York, 1832

CAST

| | | | |
|---|---|---|---|
| Mustafa, *Bey of Algiers* | B | Lindoro, *Isabella's Italian lover* | T |
| Elvira, *his wife* | S | Isabella | C |
| Zulma, *her confidante* | C | Taddeo, *an old Italian* | Bar |
| Haly, *the Bey's captain* | B | Eunuchs of the Harem | |

SYNOPSIS
I. The Bey of Algiers, tired of the same old harem, sends Haly to fetch for him an Italian wife. He has heard that Italian girls are much more interesting. Isabella, who was shipwrecked while hunting for her lost Lindoro, fits the bill perfectly. Haly brings her to the palace. Lindoro, as a matter of fact, is a captive and therefore a slave in the palace. The Bey has been unsuccessful in getting him to marry Elvira, of whom the Bey would gladly wash his hands.

II. Isabella organizes all the Italian captives and they connive to escape by a trick. She announces to the Bey that for him to be a model Italian husband he must be insensitive to all infidelities and must most certainly fall asleep after dinner. They test him. Isabella embraces Lindoro right before his eyes. Finally, in the supreme test of the Bey's after-dinner belief, they all climb into a boat and set sail for home.

NOTE
Rossini wrote this opera, in the style of *Commedia dell'Arte*, in less than a month.

### Ivan Susanin

COMP.: M. Glinka  
LIBR.: G. F. Rozen

*Tragedy in 4 acts and Epilogue*  
St. Petersburg, 9 December 1836  
La Scala, 1874  
Covent Garden, 1887

CAST

| | | | |
|---|---|---|---|
| Antonida, *Susanin's daughter* | S | Polish Commander | Bar |
| Ivan Susanin, *peasant* | B | Soldiers, Polish soldiers, People, | |
| Sobinin, *Antonida's bridegroom* | T | Procession of the Tsar | |
| Vanya, *orphan adopted by Ivan* | C | | |

SYNOPSIS
I. The Polish raiders have been repulsed. Sobinin returns from war to claim his bride. But Ivan delays the preparations until he learns that a Tsar has been proclaimed for Russia.

II. The Poles have learned this also and make plans to kidnap him.

III. Sweeping into the town again they capture Susanin and demand from him directions for reaching the Tsar's home. Ivan plays along with them, but sends Vanya ahead to warn the Tsar.

IV. While Sobinin and his army search for the raiders, Susanin leads the suspicious Poles deep into a forest, far away from the Tsar. When they discover his trick they kill him.

Epilogue. The Tsar's procession enters the capital amid rejoicing, thanks to the peasant Ivan Susanin.

NOTE

Before the communist revolution of 1917 the opera was known as *A Life for the Tsar*. With the revolution came not only a change in title, but certain changes of the text so that what was the personified glory of Russia, its Tsar, became less a reminder of the old days.

## Ivan le Terrible
COMP.: G. Bizet  Bordeaux, 12 October 1951
LIBR.: Leroy and Trianon

## Ivan the Terrible
See also *Pskovityanka*

## Jeanie Deans
4 *acts*
COMP.: H. Maccunn  Edinburgh, 15 November 1894
LIBR.: J. Bennett  London, 1896
From Sir Walter Scott's novel
*The Heart of Midlothian*

## Její Pastorkyňa (Jenufa)
(*Her Foster-Daughter (Jenufa)*)  3 *acts*
COMP.: L. Janáček  Brno, Czechoslovakia, 21 January 1904
LIBR.: By the composer  Metropolitan, 1924
From a story by Preissová  Venice, 1941

CAST

| | | | |
|---|---|---|---|
| Grandmother Buryja, *mill owner* | C | His wife | MS |
| Laca Klemen, *her grandson* | T | Karolka, *their daughter* | MS |
| Steva Buryja, *her grandson* | T | Maid | MS |
| Kostelnicka Buryjovka, | | Barena, *mill servant* | S |
| *her widowed daughter-in-law* | S | Jano, *shepherd boy* | S |
| Jenufa, *her foster daughter* | S | Aunt | C |
| Foreman at the Mill | Bar | Villagers, Musicians, Recruits | |
| Mayor | B | | |

SYNOPSIS

I. Jenufa waits for Steva, by whom she is pregnant. Laca, bitter because Steva is the favored grandson, quarrels with her. In comes the favored one, drunk, rejoicing to be out of the army. But his joy is harshly broken up when Kostelnicka tells him he may not marry Jenufa until he has managed to stay sober for one year. Later Laca, more bitter than ever to hear Jenufa given as prize to the favored brother, slashes her cheek with his knife.

II. The child is born. Kostelnicka confronts Steva with his responsibility, but he tells her he has arranged to marry Karolka. This gives Laca his opportunity. He comes to Kostelnicka to tell her of his love for Jenufa. But when he hears of the baby he draws back. Kostelnicka tells him not to worry, the baby is dead. Then, secretly, she takes it out and kills it.

III. Laca and Jenufa prepare for their wedding. They are interrupted by the shout of someone who has discovered the baby's body. The people accuse Jenufa of the murder, until Kostelnicka confesses publicly to her crime. Jenufa forgives her.

Jenufa withdraws from Laca, but his love for her is sincere. To her his gentleness is a new discovery. They come together now with new devotion.

## Jenufa
See *Jejî Pastorkyňa*

## Jeu de l'Amour et du Hasard, Le
(*The Game of Love and Chance*)       Monte Carlo, 1954
COMP.: H. Rabaud

## Jewels of the Madonna
See *Gioielli della Madonna, I*

## Jewess, The
See *Juive, La*

## Jocelyn
     *4 acts*
COMP.: B. Godard       Brussels, 25 February 1888
LIBR.: Silvestre and Capoul       Paris, 1888
From a poem by Lamartine
    This work contains the famous *Berceuse*.

## Johnny Plays On
See *Jonny Spielt Auf*

## Jolie Fille de Perth, La
     *4 acts*
(*The Fair Maid of Perth*)       Paris, 26 December 1867
COMP.: G. Bizet
LIBR.: St. Georges and Adenis
From Sir Walter Scott

## Jonny Spielt Auf
     *2 parts, 11 scenes*
(*Johnny Plays On*)       Leipzig, 10 February 1927
COMP.: E. Krenek       Metropolitan, 1929
LIBR.: By the composer       Copenhagen, 1930
    A European attempt at jazz opera.

## Jongleur de Notre Dame, Le
     *Tragedy in 3 acts*
(*The Juggler of Notre Dame*)       Monte Carlo, 18 February 1902
COMP.: J. Massenet       Covent Garden, 1906
LIBR.: M. Lena       New York, 1908

CAST

| | | | |
|---|---|---|---|
| Jean, *a tumbler* | T or S | Painter Monk | Bar |
| Boniface, *cook at the monastery* | Bar | Musician Monk | Bar |
| Prior | B | Sculptor Monk | B |
| Poet Monk | T | Two Angels | S, MS |

SYNOPSIS

I. The prior caught Jean singing blasphemous songs outside the monastery. In the course of remonstrating with him he persuaded him to join the monks and dedicate himself to the church.

II. Jean was the only member of the group who had no art. The prior reminded him, however, that even the humblest art can serve religion.

III. All alone before the statue of the virgin, Jean performed his feats of juggling. The monks were scandalized and advanced to stop him, but stopped in wonder as the statue's arm rose to bless the boy. Then the prior and the others went forward to him as he collapsed in death.

**Joseph**
COMP.: E. Méhul
LIBR.: A. Duval

3 *acts*
Comique, 17 February 1807
Birmingham, England (Concert), 1826
New York, 1857

**Jota, La**
COMP.: R. Laparra
LIBR.: By the composer

2 *acts*
Comique, 26 April 1911

**Juan, Don**
See *Don Juan*
See also *Don Giovanni*
See also *Ombra di Don Giovanni, L'*

**Judith**
COMP.: E. Goossens, III
LIBR.: A. Bennett

1 *act*
Covent Garden, 25 June 1929
Philadelphia, 1929

**Judith**
COMP.: A. Honegger
LIBR.: R. Morax

3 *acts*
Monte Carlo, 13 February 1926
Boston, 1927

**Judith**
COMP.: A. Serov
LIBR.: Serov and Maikov
From a play by Giacometti

5 *acts*
St. Petersburg, 28 May 1863
Paris, 1909

**Juggler of our Lady, The**
See *Jongleur de Notre Dame, Le*

**Juif Polonais, Le**
(*The Polish Jew*)
Comp.: C. Erlanger
LIBR.: Cain and Gheusi
From a novel by Erckmann-Chatrain

3 *acts*
Comique, 11 April 1900
St. Petersburg, 1904
Vienna, 1906

**Juive, La**
(*The Jewess*)
COMP.: J. Halévy
LIBR.: A. E. Scribe

*Tragedy in 5 acts*
Opéra, 23 February 1835
New York, 1845
Drury Lane, 1846

CAST

| | | | |
|---|---|---|---|
| Princess Eudoxia, *the emperor's niece* | S | Ruggiero, *provost* | Bar |
| Rachel, *Eléazer's daughter* | S | Albert, *sergeant* | B |
| Eléazer, *Jewish goldsmith* | T | Cardinal de Brogni | B |
| Leopold, *prince employed by Eléazer as Samuel* | T | Soldiers, Populace | |

SYNOPSIS

I. During a great Christian festival the Jew Eléazer is dragged up before Ruggiero for working in his shop when everything else is closed. Ruggiero is harsh, but the Cardinal, recognizing Eléazer, pardons him. Later his apprentice Samuel, really the prince Leopold, serenades Rachel whom he loves.

II. During the Passover ceremony at the shop Rachel notices that Leopold does not take part. Her thoughts are interrupted however by the entrance of the princess Eudoxia who wants to buy a gold chain for her husband. Leopold is very careful not to be discovered. Later Eléazer finds out that although Samuel is in love with his daughter he cannot marry her. This enrages the father.

III. At the palace Rachel has traced prince Leopold to find that he is rumored to be in love with a Jewess, herself.

IV. The Cardinal tries to make Eléazar become a Christian in order to save Leopold. This the Jew refuses to do.

V. The Jewish father and daughter are thereupon executed. As Rachel is thrown into the flames ahead of her father, Eléazar turns to the Cardinal whom he has known all his life and informs him, "Your daughter dies there."

**Julien**
COMP.: G. Charpentier
LIBR.: By the composer
A sequel to *Louise*.

*Prologue and 4 acts*
Comique, 4 June 1913
Metropolitan, 1914
Prague, 1914

**Jürg Jenatsch**
COMP.: H. Kaminski
LIBR.: By the composer
From a novel by Meyer

*6 scenes*
Dresden, 27 April 1929
Nuremburg, 1937

**Kamyenny Gost**
(*The Stone Guest*)
COMP.: A. Dargomizhsky
LIBR.: Pushkin
On the subject of Don Juan. Score completed by Cui and Rimsky-Korsakov.

*3 acts*
St. Petersburg, 28 February 1872
Salzburg, 1928
Prague, 1935

**Karl V**
COMP.: E. Krenek
LIBR.: By the composer

*2 parts*
Barcelona (in part), 18 April 1936
Prague, 15 June 1938

**Kata Kabanova**
COMP.: L. Janáček
LIBR.: Cervinka
From Ostrovsky's *The Storm*

*Tragedy in 3 acts*
Brno, Czechoslovakia, 23 October 1921
Sadlers Wells, 1951
New York, 1960

CAST

| | | | |
|---|---|---|---|
| Vanya Kudrjas, *Dikoy's clerk* | T | Tichon Ivanovitch Kabanov, *her son* | T |
| Glashka, *servant* | MS | Barbara, *foster child* | MS |
| Dikoy, *merchant* | B | Katerina Kabanova (Káta), | |
| Boris Grigorievitch, *his nephew* | T | Tichon's wife | S |
| Feklusha, *servant* | MS | Kuligin, *Vanya's friend* | Bar |
| Marfa Kabanova, *widow, Kabanička* | C | | |

## SYNOPSIS

I. Boris is in love with the married Káta. The lovers live under the constant oppression of Dikoy and Kabanička. Only the confidence of Barbara helps Káta through the ordeal. To protect herself from temptation she tries to make her husband order her to remain faithful to him while he is away. He cannot understand why he should do such a thing.

II. He is gone. The lovers meet at night. Resistance to each other becomes impossible.

III. There is a terrible storm. The people are driven all into the same shelter by the rain. There, for all to hear, Káta screams to her returned husband of the terrible sin she has committed. She runs away. In the forest she meets Boris for a moment, then leaves him in sadness. She throws herself into the river and drowns.

### Kenilworth

*Prologue and 3 acts*

COMP.: B. O. Klein  
LIBR.: W. Müller  
From Scott's novel

Hamburg, 13 February 1895

### Khovantschina

*5 acts*

COMP.: M. Mussorgsky  
LIBR.: Mussorgsky and Stassov

St. Petersburg, 21 February 1886  
Drury Lane, 1913  
Philadelphia, 1928

### CAST

| | | | |
|---|---|---|---|
| Prince Ivan Khovansky | B | Varsonofiev, *Vassily's attendant* | Bar |
| Prince Andrey Khovansky, *his son* | T | Kuzka, *archer* | Bar |
| Prince Vassily Galitsin | T | Three Archers | T, B, B |
| The Boyar Shaklovity | Bar | Streshniev, *an Old Believer* | T |
| Dositheus, *leader of the Old Believers* | B | Susanna, *an Old Believer* | S |
| Martha, *widow, an Old Believer* | MS | Archers, Old Believers, Maids in Waiting, |
| Scrivener | T | Slaves, Bodyguards, Populace |
| Emma, *young girl* | S | | |

### SYNOPSIS

I. Shaklovity sends a message, via the Scrivener, to the Tsar to warn him against the Khovanskys. The Princes have allied themselves with the Old Believers to capture the throne. Meanwhile the young Prince, Andrey, has ceased his affair with Martha in order to woo Emma. Martha meets him in public and upbraids him for this. The prince would have killed her had not his father arrived on the scene and had Emma arrested for his own whimsical pleasure.

II. Dositheus wields subtle power among the various intrigues in the city. He repairs the torn relations between the old prince and Galitsin in time to protect their revolutionary interest before the Tsar suddenly arrives to suppress them.

III. The people are disturbed by the ravages of the Tsar's troops near the city. The archers range here and there in anarchic uncertainty. The people would rise against the Tsar but prince Khovansky counsels them to submit.

IV. As the old prince relaxes amid his pleasures Varsonofiev tries to warn him of his impending murder. He pays no attention. Shaklovity stabs him and kills him there. The murderer is banished and the archers are condemned for their opposition to the Tsar.

V. The Old Believers have lost their case; now they live under official persecution. With Martha and Andrey, who has followed her into this exile, the remaining ones mount a huge pyre on which they have decided to perish rather than to submit to the troops sent to capture them.

NOTE

The official premiere of *Khovantschina* took place in St. Petersburg, 7 November 1911. It opened in the Metropolitan in 1950. Like other magnificent works of Mussorgsky, it was completed and re-orchestrated by Nicolai Rimsky-Korsakov.

**King Arthur, or The British Worthy**     *Prologue, 5 acts, Epilogue*
COMP.: H. Purcell     London, May or June 1691
LIBR.: J. Dryden     New York, 1800
    Cambridge, England, 1928

**King in Spite of Himself**
See *Roi Malgré Lui, Le*

**King's Henchman, The**     *3 acts*
COMP.: D. Taylor     Metropolitan, 17 February 1927
LIBR.: E. St. Vincent Millay

**King of Lahore, The**
See *Roi de Lahore, Le*

**Kiss, The**
See *Hubička*
See also *Poisoned Kiss, The*

**Kitezh**     *4 acts*
COMP.: N. Rimsky-Korsakov     St. Petersburg, 20 February 1907
LIBR.: V. Bielsky     Covent Garden, 1926
    Ann Arbor, Mich. (Concert), 1932
Full title: *The Legend of the Invisible City of Kitezh and the Maiden Fevronia.*

**Kluge, Die**
(*The Wise Maiden*)     Frankfurt, 20 February 1943
COMP.: C. Orff
LIBR.: By the composer

CAST

| | | | |
|---|---|---|---|
| King | Bar | Man with a Donkey | T |
| Farmer | B | Man with a Mule | Bar |
| Farmer's Daughter | S | Three Tramps | T, Bar, B |
| Jailer | B | | |

NOTE

Called *The Story of the King and the Wise Maiden*, the opera takes place in a simultaneous staging, with little stages in front of and above the main acting area. The costumes and masks, Orff stipulates, must be fantastic in their coloring and expression. *Die Kluge* provided an excellent show for the Marionette Theater in Munich.

**Knight Bluebeard**
See *Ritter Blaubart*

**Knight of the Rose, The**
See *Rosenkavalier, Der*

**Koanga**
COMP.: F. Delius
LIBR.: C. F. Keary
From a novel by Cable

*3 acts and Epilogue*
Elberfeld, Germany, 30 March 1904
Covent Garden, 1935

**König Manfred**
COMP.: C. Reinecke
LIBR.: F. Roeber

*5 acts*
Wiesbaden, 26 July 1867
Leipzig, 1868

**Königin von Saba, Die**
(*The Queen of Sheba*)
COMP.: K. Goldmark
LIBR.: H. von Mosenthal

*Tragedy in 4 acts*
Vienna, 10 March 1875
Metropolitan, 1885
Manchester, England, 1910

CAST

| | | | |
|---|---|---|---|
| King Solomon | Bar | Sulamith, *his daughter* | S |
| Baal Hanan, *palace overseer* | Bar | Queen of Sheba | MS |
| Assad | T | Astaroth, *her slave* | S |
| High Priest | B | Voice of the Temple Watchman | B |

SYNOPSIS

I. Assad, who was sent by the king to bring back the queen of Sheba, returns confused and in love because of the sight of a beautiful woman in a grove of the cedars of Lebanon. When the queen arrives Assad recognizes her as that woman, but she shows no recognition of him.

II. Assad marries Sulamith. At the wedding ceremony the queen interrupts, feigning to bring a wedding gift for the bride. But Assad throws his ring upon the floor thus desecrating the temple. For this he is condemned to death.

III. The queen intercedes with Solomon to win a reprieve for Assad. This the king will not grant. Instead, he allows the condemned man to be banished into the desert.

IV. There, banished, Assad formally refuses the queen's love, the cause of his losing Sulamith. Sulamith finds him, repentant, dying of exposure. She forgives him.

**Königskinder, Die**
(*The King's Children*)
COMP.: E. Humperdinck
LIBR.: E. Rosmer

*3 acts*
Metropolitan, 28 December 1910
Covent Garden, 1911
Boston, 1912

This was originally no more than music for a play, produced in Munich in 1897. Humperdinck expanded and developed it later.

**Kovantchina**
See *Khovantschina*

**Lady Macbeth of Minsk**
COMP.: D. Shostakovitch
LIBR.: Shostakovitch and Preis
From a novel by Lyeskov

*4 acts*
Leningrad, 22 January 1922
Cleveland, 1935
New York, 1935

**Lakmé**
COMP.: L. Délibes
LIBR.: Gondinet and Gille
From *Le Mariage de Loti*

*Tragedy in 3 acts*
Comique, 14 April 1883
London, 1885
New York, 1886

CAST

| | | | | |
|---|---|---|---|---|
| Lakmé, *Nilakantha's daughter* | S | Gérald, *English officer* | | T |
| Mallika, her slave | MS | Nilakantha, *Brahmin priest* | | BBar |
| Ellen, English lady | S | Frédéric, *English officer* | | Bar |
| Rose, English lady | S | Hadji, *Nilakantha's servant* | | T |
| Mistress Bentson, *their governess* | MS | Soldiers, Sailors, Tourists | | |

MUSICAL HIGHLIGHTS

ACT I. Invocation *Blanche Dourga Pâle Silva* (Fair Durga, Pale Silva), Lakmé
  Barcarole *Dôme épais* (O Jasmine), Lakmé and Mallika
ACT II. Bell Song *Où va la jeune Hindoue?* (Where goes the Hindu maiden?), Lakmé

SYNOPSIS

I. Brahminism has been forbidden by the British governor, but Nilakantha keeps up his religion undismayed. Some English tourists have broken into his temple garden to see the sights. When they leave, one of their escorts, Gérald, stays behind to sketch some jewels. There Lakmé discovers him. It is love at first sight for Gérald. Lakmé makes him leave just before her father comes to kill the intruder.

II. Nilakantha does not know who it was that desecrated his temple. He sets Lakmé as bait for a trap. She is to sing a song in the crowd at the bazaar until Nilakantha spots the passerby who notices her. She sings the famous Bell Song. Suddenly, at the sight of Gérald, she faints and Nilakantha has the information he wants. During a procession that night Gérald falls from a stab wound, but Lakmé manages to spirit him away where she can nurse him back to health.

III. Gérald and Lakmé pledge eternal love for each other. In a while Frédéric finds them and reminds Gérald of his duty as a soldier. Lakmé, realizing that Gérald will now leave her, eats a poisonous plant that grows nearby and dies in his arms in the sight of Nilakantha who has come to kill the Englishman.

## Lalla Roukh

|   |   |
|---|---|
| | 2 *acts* |
| COMP.: F. David | Comique, 12 May 1862 |
| LIBR.: Lucas and Carré | Vienna, 1863 |
| From the poem by Thomas Moore | Budapest, 1863 |

  This almost forgotten work won the State Prize of twenty thousand francs.

## Leap Over the Shadow, The

See *Sprung über den Schatten*

## Leonora

|   |   |
|---|---|
| | 3 *acts* |
| COMP.: W. H. Fry | Philadelphia, 4 June 1845 |
| LIBR.: J. R. Fry (his brother) | New York, 1857 |
| From Bulwer-Lytton's novel | New York (in part), 1929 |

  Probably the first "grand" opera by an American.

## Leonora

See also *Fidelio*

## Leonore 40/45

|   |   |
|---|---|
| COMP.: R. Liebermann | Basel, 25 March 1952 |
| LIBR.: H. Strobel | Berlin, 1953 |

## Let's Make an Opera

COMP.: B. Britten
LIBR.: E. Crozier

*Entertainment for Young People in 2 parts,*
3 *acts*
Aldeburgh, England, 14 June 1949

CAST

| | | | |
|---|---|---|---|
| Gladys Parworthy, *later* Miss Baggot, *housekeeper* | C | Anne Dougall, *later* Juliet Brook, 14 | S |
| Norman Chaffinch, *later* Black Bob, *sweepmaster, and later* | | Mr. Harper, *later* conductor | |
| | | John, *later* Sam, *sweep boy*, 8 | Treble |
| Tom, *the coachman* | B | Bruce, *later* Gay Brook, 13 | Treble |
| Max Westleton, *later* Clem, *Bob's* | | Monica, *later* Sophie Brook, 10 | S |
| *assistant, and later* Alfred, *gardener* | T | Peter, *later* John Crome, 15 | Treble |
| Pamela Wilton, *later* Rowan, *maid* | S | Mavis, *later* Tina Crome, 8 | S |
| | | Ralph, *later* Hugh Crome, 8 | Treble |

SYNOPSIS

I. Miss Parworthy tells everybody a story. The children decide to make an opera of it.

II. They rehearse, with the help of the audience.

III. This is the opera: A little chimneysweep named Sam is saved from the horrible Black Bob and Clem by the children and Rowan who hide him until it is safe for him to leave.

## Libuša

COMP.: B. Smetana
LIBR.: J. Wenzig (Translated by Spindler)

3 *acts*
Prague, 11 June 1881
Vienna, 1924
Zagreb, 1933

## Liebe der Danae, Die

(*The Love of Danae*)
COMP.: R. Strauss
LIBR.: J. Gregor

*Comedy in 3 acts*
Salzburg, 14 August 1952
La Scala, 1953
Covent Garden, 1953

CAST

| | | | |
|---|---|---|---|
| Jupiter | Bar | Semele, *Queen* | S |
| Mercury | T | Europa, *Queen* | S |
| Pollux, *King of Eos* | T | Alcmene, *Queen* | MS |
| Danae, *his daughter* | S | Leda, *Queen* | C |
| Xanthe, *her servant* | S | Four Watchmen | 4B |
| Midas, *King of Lydia* | T | Creditors, Servants, Followers, People | |
| Four Kings, *nephews to Pollux* | 2T, 2B | | |

SYNOPSIS

I. Poor Pollux has seen bad times. His creditors hound him; everything seems awry. In a last effort to stave them off he tells them that rich King Midas is on his way to marry Danae. At this the girl dreams of a rain of gold and pearls. Midas does come, but in disguise. Then Jupiter, seizing the opportunity to woo a mortal beauty, comes made up as Midas, making a grand entrance.

II. The four queens recognize the absurd god. They are very jealous. But Jupiter prevents Midas from giving him away by threatening to withdraw the gift of the touch of gold. Midas then, dressed as himself, approaches Danae. She does not quite understand just who he is, but when she allows his embrace she turns immediately to gold. Jupiter and Midas defy each other, but the voice of Danae chooses the mortal king.

III. Midas renounces gold and returns to comfortable poverty. Quite willingly Danae goes along. Jupiter causes a rain of gold to get Pollux out of his financial mess and once again tries for Danae but to no avail; she will not betray her husband.

NOTE

The opera was in the final stages of rehearsal in 1944 when Hitler ordered all theaters closed. The production was held up eight years. Actually the work was written in 1940.

## Life for the Tsar, A
See *Ivan Susanin*

## Life of Orestes
COMP.: E. Krenek

## Life of Orestes
See *Orestie*

## Linda di Chamounix
COMP.: G. Donizetti
LIBR.: G. Rossi

3 acts
Vienna, 19 May 1842
London, 1843
New York, 1847

CAST

| | | | |
|---|---|---|---|
| Marquis de Boisfleury | Bar | Antonio | Bar |
| Charles, *Vicomte de Sirval* | T | Maddalena | S |
| Prefect | B | Intendant | T |
| Pierrotto | C | Peasants, Savoyards | |
| Linda | S | | |

## Lobetanz, Der
COMP.: L. Thuille
LIBR.: O. Bierbaum

3 acts
Karlsruhe, 6 February 1898
Vienna, 1901
New York, 1911

## Lodoiska
COMP.: L. Cherubini
LIBR.: C. F. Loraux

3 acts
Paris, 18 July 1791
Berlin, 1797
New York, 1826

## Lodoletta
COMP.: P. Mascagni
LIBR.: G. Forzano
From Ovida—*Two Little Wooden Shoes*

3 acts
Rome, 30 April 1917
Metropolitan, 1918
Vienna, 1920

## Lohengrin
COMP.: R. Wagner
LIBR.: By the composer

3 acts
Weimar, 28 August 1850
Covent Garden, 1875
New York, 1871
Metropolitan, 1885

CAST

| | | | |
|---|---|---|---|
| Henry the Fowler, *king of Germany* | B | Elsa of Brabant | S |
| Lohengrin, *knight of the Grail* | T | Duke Godfrey, *her brother* | Bar |

| | | |
|---|---|---|
| Frederick of Telramund, *count of* | | King's Herald | B |
| Brabant | Bar | Counts, Nobles, Ladies of Honor, |
| Ortrud, *his wife* | MS | Pages, Attendants |

MUSICAL HIGHLIGHTS

ACT I. Elsa's Dream
ACT II. Aria *Euch Lüften* (Fair Breezes), Elsa
ACT III. Prelude
    Bridal Chorus
    Narrative *Im fernen Land* (In distant lands), Lohengrin
    Lohengrin's Farewell (The Swan Song).

SYNOPSIS

I. Before the king, Frederick accuses Elsa of having murdered her brother Godfrey. For that reason, he explains, he married Ortrud instead of Elsa. The king demands a trial by battle between Frederick and Elsa's champion. Elsa says a knight of her dream will be her champion. The king commands trumpets to sound to the four directions, and Lohengrin appears in a boat drawn by a white swan. He exacts one promise from Elsa, that she will never ask his name. When she has agreed, he challenges Frederick and wins.

II. Ortrud conspires with her banished Frederick to sow the seed of curiosity in Elsa's mind and thus to regain their position. At the wedding of the strange knight and Elsa, Ortrud shouts that the bride does not know who her bridegroom may be.

III. After the wedding, in the privacy of night, Elsa asks the forbidden question. There is a moment of danger when Frederick breaks in to murder Lohengrin, but the White Knight kills the intruder.

Lohengrin takes her to the spot where he first appeared, where the knights have gathered. There he tells her that he is the son of Parsifal. His swan reappears. He is about to depart when Ortrud shouts that the swan is really the bewitched brother Godfrey, changed by Ortrud's evil magic. Silently Lohengrin prays and the swan changes to a man, Godfrey brought back to life. With this act Lohengrin departs in his boat, drawn by a dove.

NOTES

Wagner wrote *Lohengrin* backwards—first the last act, then the second, finally the first. It was finished in 1847 but the composer's complicity in the revolt of 1849 prevented its production until the mighty Liszt used his influence to mount it at Weimar. Wagner did not hear the opera until he was allowed to return to Germany in 1861.

**Lombardi, I**          *4 acts*
   COMP.: G. Verdi          La Scala, 11 February 1843
   LIBR.: T. Solera          London, 1846
   From a poem by Crossi      New York, 1847
    *I Lombardi* was the first of Verdi's operas to be heard in New York.

**Louise**          *Romance in 4 acts*
   COMP.: G. Charpentier     Comique, 2 February 1900
   LIBR.: By the composer      New York, 1908
                         Covent Garden, 1909
                         Metropolitan, 1921

CAST

| | | | |
|---|---|---|---|
| Louise | S | Julien, *artist* | T |
| Her Mother | C | Louise's father | B |
| Irma | S | Noctambulist | T |
| Camille | S | Ragman | B |
| Gertrude | C | Bohemian | Bar |
| Errand Girl | S | Song Writer | Bar |
| Elise | S | Junkman | B |
| Blanche | S | Painter | B |
| Suzanne | C | Two Philosophers | T, B |
| Street sweeper | MS | Poet | Bar |
| Ragpicker | MS | Student | T |
| Forewoman | MS | Two Policemen | 2Bar |
| Milk Woman | S | Street Arab | S |
| Newspaper Girl | S | Sculptor | Bar |
| Coalgatherer | MS | Old Clothes Man | T |
| Marguérite | S | Apprentice | Bar |
| Madeleine | C | King of Fools | T |
| Dancer | | Pedlars, Workmen, People | |

SYNOPSIS

I. Louise insists that Julien go through the formality of writing to her parents to ask for her hand in marriage. Her tyrannical mother hates Julien, but at least her father seems more considerate.

II. She is at work in a dressmaking factory when Julien serenades her outside the factory window, driving her to tears. She has to go to him.

III. They run off to live together in raptures of bohemian joy until her mother intervenes to tell her that her father has become seriously ill and needs his daughter.

IV. When her father has recovered, the parents refuse to let Louise return to the former life of love she led with Julien. Finally, however, she defies them and runs away.

NOTE

In act III occurs the celebrated romance *Depuis le Jour* (E'er since the day), which concert audiences still enjoy although the opera is losing its popularity.

## Love for Three Oranges, The

Prologue and 4 *acts*

COMP.: S. Prokofiev
LIBR.: By the composer
From a comedy by Gozzi

Chicago, 30 December 1921
New York, 1922
La Scala, 1947

CAST

| | | | |
|---|---|---|---|
| King of Clubs, *ruler* | B | Lineta, *princess in an orange* | C |
| Prince, *his son* | T | Nicoletta, *princess in an orange* | MS |
| Princess Clarissa, *his niece* | C | Ninetta, *princess in an orange* | S |
| Leandro, *the Prime Minister and King of Spades* | Bar | Cook | B |
| | | Farfarello, *devil* | B |
| Truffaldino, *the king's jester* | T | Smeraldina, *Fata Morgana's servant* | MS |
| Pantaloon, *the king's adviser* | Bar | Master of Ceremonies | T |
| Celio, *magician, the king's protector* | B | Herald | B |
| Fata Morgana, *witch, Leandro's protector* | S | Trumpeter | Bass Trombone |
| | | Ten Reasonable Spectators | 5T, 5B |

THE OPERAS

Monsters, Drunkards, Gluttons, Guards,    Wits, Romantics, Lowbrows, Little
Servants, Soldiers, Jokers, Highbrows,    Devils, Doctors, Courtiers

SYNOPSIS

I. The prince, unfortunately, is a hypochondriac. Only if he laughs may he be cured. Pantaloon and the king make a valiant attempt, but Leandro intends to prevent their success. With Clarissa ready to marry him, he plans to fill the prince with gloomy poetry, thus enhancing his own chances to win the throne.

II. Truffaldino puts on his funniest shows, but the prince will not laugh. Only when Fata Morgana accidentally trips over something does he burst into paroxysms. The embarrassed and enraged witch curses him saying he will fall in love with three oranges.

III. The prince and Truffaldino are wafted away to a castle guarded by the Cook. They snatch three oranges from this worthy and run away into the desert. Truffaldino slits one open. Out steps a princess, dying of thirst. There being no water handy she does die. Another orange, another princess. Again a death of thirst. The prince opens the third, and this princess would die also but for the Ten Reasonable Spectators who quickly provide her with a bucket of water. This is only a temporary triumph. Fata Morgana turns the girl into a rat and substitutes Smeraldina.

IV. The princess being very ugly as a rat, Celio works to restore her original appearance. When he has succeeded the king condemns all the prince's enemies, filling the stage with a great rout.

### Love in a Village
    COMP.: T. Arne
    LIBR.: I. Bickerstaffe

3 acts
Covent Garden, 8 December 1762
Philadelphia, 1767
New York, 1768

This opera was partly written by Arne and partly selected by him from pieces by fifteen composers. It was performed in Kingston, Jamaica, in 1779, Calcutta in 1791, and in modern times in London, 1923.

### Love of Danae
See *Liebe der Danae*

### Love of Three Kings
See *Amore dei tre Re, L'*

### Lowlands
See *Tiefland*

### Lucia di Lammermoor
    COMP.: G. Donizetti
    LIBR.: S. Cammarano
    From Scott's novel

*Tragedy in 3 acts*
Naples, 26 September 1835
London, 1838
New York, 1843
Metropolitan, 1883

CAST

| | | | |
|---|---|---|---|
| Lord Henry Ashton of Lammermoor (*Enrico*) | Bar | Raymond, *chaplain of Lammermoor* (*Raimondo*) | B |
| Lucy, *his sister* (*Lucia*) | S | Alice, *Lucy's companion* (*Alisa*) | MS |
| Edgar, *master of Ravenswood* (*Edgardo*) | T | Norman, *follower of Ashton* (*Normando*) | T |
| Lord Arthur Bucklaw (*Arturo*) | B | Relatives, Retainers, Friends | |

ACT I. Legend *Regnava nel silenzio* (The night was all in silence), Lucia
Aria *Quando rapita* (With such speed), Lucia
Duet *Verranno a te sull'aure* (My sighs will reach you), Lucia, Edgardo
ACT II. Sextet *Chi mi fena* (What restrains me?), Lucia, Alisa, Edgardo, Enrico, Arturo, Raimondo
ACT III. Mad Scene, Lucia
Aria *Tu che a Doi* (You who to heaven), Edgardo

SYNOPSIS

I. The last of his hereditary enemies remains a trouble to Henry when he learns that Edgar and Lucy have been seeing each other. He swears to kill Edgar. But Lucy loves him, and sees him before he leaves for France.

II. Henry arranges for her to marry Bucklaw and at the same time contrives to undermine her faith in Edgar by means of a forged letter hinting that he has betrayed her. But at the moment of signing the marriage compact, Edgar reappears.

III. Henry challenges Edgar to a duel. Meanwhile Lucy has become insane and has killed her new husband. When the time for the duel arrives, Edgar sees not his antagonist but a funeral procession for Lucy, who has died. Full of remorse, realizing that her madness must have been caused by his misunderstanding of her marriage, he stabs himself to death.

## Lucio Silla

COMP.: W. A. Mozart
LIBR.: G. de Gamerra (altered by Metastasio)

3 *acts*
Milan, 26 December 1772
Prague, 1929

## Lucretia

See *Rape of Lucretia, The*

## Lucrezia Borgia

COMP.: G. Donizetti
LIBR.: F. Romani
From Victor Hugo

*Prologue and 2 acts*
La Scala, 26 December 1833
London, 1839
New York, 1844

CAST

| | | | |
|---|---|---|---|
| Alfonso d'Este, *duke of Ferrara* | Bar | Rustighello, *follower of Don Alfonso* | T |
| Lucrezia Borgia | S | Gubetta, *Lucrezia's servant* | B |
| Maffio Orsini | C | Astolfo | B |
| Gennaro, *Venetian nobleman* | T | Gentlemen-at-Arms, Officers, Nobles of | |
| Liverotto, *Venetian nobleman* | T | the Venetian Republic, Ladies-in-Wait- | |
| Vitellozzo, *Venetian nobleman* | B | ing, Capuchin Monks, etc. | |
| Gazello | B | | |

SYNOPSIS

PROLOGUE. At a festival Lucrezia, in disguise, discovers Gennaro asleep on a bench. He wakes and they speak together until his friends arrive. Among them is Maffio Orsini who tears off Lucrezia's mask and reveals to Gennaro that she is a murderess.

I. Alfonso has condemned Gennaro to death for having insulted him. The duke insists that Lucrezia poison him, since he believes that Gennaro is her secret lover. She gives Gennaro an antidote, however, and helps him to escape.

II. At a banquet in Ferrara Lucrezia poisons all the guests, thinking they are all her enemies. But one of them is Gennaro. In horror she tells him that he is her own illegitimate son. She tries to give him an antidote which he refuses; he would rather die with his friends.

### NOTE

This opera, unfortunately, perpetuates the myth that Lucrezia Borgia was a ruthless murdress. In reality, she was one of the great women of a violent era, whose biography (by Bellonci) is well worth reading. The famous poisonings and other murders were accomplished by men, some of them by Lucrezia's brother Cesare.

| Luisa Miller | *Tragedy in 3 acts* |
|---|---|
| COMP.: G. Verdi | Naples, 8 December 1849 |
| LIBR.: S. Cammarano | New York, 1852 |
| From Schiller's play *Kabale und Liebe* | London, 1858 |

### CAST

| | | | |
|---|---|---|---|
| Count Walter | B | Laura, *peasant girl* | C |
| Rodolfo, *his son* | T | Wurm | B |
| Miller, *old soldier* | Bar | Ladies, Pages, Servants, Archers, | |
| Luisa, *his daughter* | S | Villagers | |
| Federica, *Duchess of Ostheim,* | | | |
| *Walter's niece* | C | | |

### SYNOPSIS

I. Wurm, rival for Luisa's love, tells Miller that her suitor is really Rodolfo, his master's son. But the count has promised a marriage between Rodolfo and the widow Federica. Rodolfo prevents the imprisonment of the Millers by threatening to reveal how Walter gained his title by means of murder.

II. Miller is put in prison anyway. To save him, Luisa agrees to write a letter saying her love for Rodolfo was faked. When Rodolfo is confronted with this evidence, he agrees to the arranged marriage, but swears also to kill Luisa and himself.

III. He seeks her out and hears her admit that she wrote the letter. He produces poison which they both drink. Only then does she tell him how Wurm compelled her to do it, though it was a lie. Just before their deaths, Rodolfo avenges them both by killing their traitor.

| Lulu | *Tragedy in 3 acts* |
|---|---|
| COMP.: A. Berg | Zürich (in part), 2 June 1937 |
| LIBR.: By the composer | Venice (Complete), 1949 |
| From Wedekind | Essen, 1953 |

### CAST

| | | | |
|---|---|---|---|
| Lulu | S | Alwa, *his son, writer* | T |
| Gräfin Geschwitz | MS | Animal Tamer (*in Prologue*) | B |
| Wardrobe Mistress | C | Rodrig, *athlete* (Act II) | |
| Schoolboy, *gymnasiast* (*the same singer as above*) | | (*same singer as above*) | |
| | | Schigolch, *old man* | B |
| Doctor | Spkr | Prince, *traveller in Africa* | T |
| Painter | T | Theater Director | B |
| Dr. Schön, *editor* | Bar | | |

In the Prologue we are introduced to the Animal Trainer's troupe, which includes, significantly, Lulu.

I. Lulu is a dangerously attractive girl. The painter cannot paint for lust for her. While he is struggling to win a kiss from her, her husband breaks in and sees the event. The shock of it kills him. When the painter has become her husband, the whole sequence occurs again, this time involving Dr. Schön. She forces Schön to break off his engagement to another in favor of herself.

II. Now Schön is the husband. But the new suitor is the Gräfin Geschwitz, which gives a different sort of bitter twist to Lulu's progress. Schön discovers that there are several other lovers including even Alwa. Schön loses his reserve, drives the others away and tries to get Lulu to shoot herself. In this he fails; she takes the revolver and shoots him instead. In a filmed interlude she is brought to trial and condemned, but makes her escape with the help of the Gräfin.

III. Her past chases her to Paris, and from there to London. Finally she reaches the depths of walking the streets. Her last pickup is Jack the Ripper who murders her.

NOTE

Unlike *Wozzeck*, which was written in an extension of ordinary tonality, *Lulu* entirely conforms to the dodecaphonic system of harmony. The entire opera, like *Wozzeck*, is composed in formal periods so that parts are in sonata form, parts in rondo. Berg had not completed the last act before he died, but the remainder was fully sketched.

## Lurline

| | |
|---|---|
| COMP.: W. Wallace | 3 *acts* |
| LIBR.: E. Fitzball | Covent Garden, 23 February 1860 |
| | Cambridge, Mass., 1863 |
| | New York, 1869 |

## Lustigen Weiber von Windsor, Die

| | |
|---|---|
| COMP.: O. Nicolai | *Comedy in 3 acts* |
| LIBR.: H. von Mosenthal | Berlin, 9 March 1849 |
| From Shakespeare's *The Merry Wives* | Philadelphia, 1863 |
| *of Windsor* | London, 1864 |
| | Metropolitan, 1900 |

CAST

| | | | |
|---|---|---|---|
| Sir John Falstaff | B | Dr. Caius | B |
| Herr Fluth (*Mr. Ford*) | Bar | Frau Fluth (*Mistress Ford*) | S |
| Herr Reich (*Mr. Page*) | B | Frau Reich (*Mistress Page*) | MS |
| Fenton | T | Jungfer Anna Reich (*Anne Page*) | S |
| Junker Spärlich (*Slender*) | T | Erster Burger (*First Citizen*) | T |

SYNOPSIS

I. We listen as Mrs. Ford and Mrs. Page compare love letters they have each received from Falstaff. Then we listen to Mr. Page telling his daughter's suitors that he wishes her to marry Slender. He does not like either Caius or Fenton.

Falstaff comes to court Mrs. Ford but must hide in a laundry basket when the husband surprises them, as the women had secretly planned.

II. Ford, calling himself Bach, seeks out Falstaff in his favorite tavern and extracts what he can of the knight's affair with his wife. Meanwhile all three young suitors serenade Anne in her garden. Home again, Ford hunts for traces of Falstaff's presence but the culprit, dressed as an old, deaf woman escapes handily.

III. In Windsor Forest poor Falstaff is surrounded by strange beings disguised as sprites and phantoms, completing the ladies' plan for his chastisement.

## Lustigen Weiber von Windsor, Die
See also *Falstaff*
See also *Sir John in Love*

| **Macbeth** | *Tragedy in Prologue and 3 acts* |
|---|---|
| COMP.: E. Bloch | Comique, 30 November 1910 |
| LIBR.: E. Fleg | Naples, 1938 |
| From Shakespeare | |

| **Macbeth** | *Tragedy in 3 acts* |
|---|---|
| COMP.: L. Collingwood | Sadler's Wells, 12 April 1934 |
| LIBR.: By the composer | |
| From Shakespeare | |

| **Macbeth** | *Tragedy in 4 acts* |
|---|---|
| COMP.: G. Verdi | Florence, 14 March 1847 |
| LIBR.: F. M. Piave | New York, 1850 |
| From Shakespeare | Dublin, 1859 |
| | Metropolitan, 1959 |

### CAST

| | | | |
|---|---|---|---|
| Lady Macbeth | S | Malcolm, *Duncan's son* | T |
| Macbeth, *a general* | Bar | Fleance, *Banquo's son* | Mute |
| Banquo, *a general* | B | Doctor | B |
| Macduff, *Scottish noble* | T | Three Witches | |
| Duncan, *King of Scotland* | Mute | Hecate, *witch* | |
| Lady in Waiting, to Lady Macbeth | S | | |

### SYNOPSIS

I. Three witches tell Macbeth he will become powerful. But the king lives, occupying the ultimate power Macbeth could aspire to. Therefore, goaded by wife, he plans to murder the king while the royal entourage stay as guests at his house. The deed is done while the king sleeps. Banquo and Macduff discover the body.

II. To insure the final steps toward power, Banquo must be murdered too. Macbeth has this done by hired assassins. But they fail to complete their work. Fleance escapes them. That evening Macbeth holds a festive banquet. It turns sour when Banquo's ghost attends, visible only to Macbeth's tortured mind.

III. Again the witches prophesy for Macbeth. This time they foretell his death at Dunsinane, and of the future kings who will spring from Banquo's line. Lady Macbeth urges him, being now so powerful, to overlook these grim forebodings.

IV. There is a battle at Dunsinane, between Malcolm's army and Macbeth's. During the height of it, news reaches Macbeth that his wife is dead. He fights with renewed vigor. But Macduff finds him alone and in single combat slays him.

### NOTES

This opera was a favorite of Verdi's. He began with a scenario and worked from it. When time came for rehearsals he become most particular that each detail should be perfect. This made it necessary to rehearse the duet after the murder more than one hundred and fifty times, and to go over the sleepwalking scene constantly for a period of three months. Nevertheless the work has its difficulties with audiences, not the least of which is a certain ludicrous quality about the witches.

## Macbeth
See also *Lady Macbeth*

## Madama Butterfly

COMP.: G. Puccini
LIBR.: Giacosa and Illica
From Belasco's play

*Tragedy in 2 acts*
La Scala, 17 February 1904
Covent Garden, 1905
New York, 1906

CAST

| | | | |
|---|---|---|---|
| Cio-Cio San, *Madame Butterfly* | S | Prince Yamadori | Bar |
| Suzuki, *her servant* | MS | The Bonze, *priest, Cio-Cio San's uncle* | B |
| Kate Pinkerton, *Pinkerton's* | | Imperial Commissioner | B |
| *American wife* | MS | Official Registrar | Bar |
| Lieutenant B. F. Pinkerton, *USN* | T | Trouble, *Cio-Cio San's child* | |
| Sharpless, *U.S. Consul at Nagasaki* | Bar | Relatives of Cio-Cio San, Friends, | |
| Goro, *marriage broker* | T | Servants | |

MUSICAL HIGHLIGHTS

ACT I. Love duet *Viene la sera* (Evening is falling), Cio-Cio San and Pinkerton
ACT II. Aria *Un bel dì vedremo* (One fine day he'll come home), Cio-Cio San
Aria *Sai cos'ebbe cuore* (Do you hear what he's saying?), Cio-Cio San

SYNOPSIS

I. Pinkerton, far from home, had arranged to entertain himself by having a Japanese wife and home while he was there. Sharpless tried to dissuade him, especially after he met the bride and found out that she was seriously in love with the American. She had even renounced her religion. When The Bonze heard about this, he called down the curses of her family and her ancestors upon her.

II. The marriage lasted not at all. Pinkerton was called away from Japan and stayed three years. During all that time Cio-Cio San kept herself faithful to him in spite of every attempt Sharpless could make to tell her that Pinkerton was married in America. Sharpless tried to get her to understand a letter from Pinkerton explaining that he was about to arrive with his American wife, but Cio-Cio San was too thrilled to see his ship coming to understand the facts.

When Pinkerton came to the house, Suzuki had managed to put Cio-Cio San to sleep upstairs. Pinkerton could not stand the thought of telling her the truth; he left abruptly so that when Cio-Cio San descended she found Sharpless and Kate waiting for her. Quietly she sent them with a message asking Pinkerton to come for his son in half an hour. Then she stabbed herself with a ceremonial sword.

NOTES

Puccini went from Italy to London to see the play, of which he could not have understood very much, his English being not remarkable. He was moved by it, however, and set to work on the opera, taking three years for the job. The first performance was a notorious fiasco, but with a few revisions it was successfully revived two months later at Brescia.

## Madame Angot's Daughter
See *Fille de Madame Angot, La*

**Madame Chrysanthème**
COMP.: A. Messager
LIBR.: Hartmann and Alexandre
From a novel by Loti

*Prologue, 4 acts and Epilogue*
Paris, 30 January 1893
Montreal, 1912
New York, 1920

**Madame Sans-gêne**
COMP.: U. Giordano
LIBR.: R. Simoni
From a play by Sardou and Moreau

*3 acts*
Metropolitan, 25 January 1915
Turin, 1915
Comique, 1916
Breslau, 1931

**Madonna Imperia**
COMP.: F. Alfano
LIBR.: A. Rossato
From a story by Balzac

*1 act*
Turin, 5 May 1927
Metropolitan, 1928
Vienna, 1928

**Madrisa**
COMP.: H. Haug
LIBR.: J. Jegerlehner

*3 acts*
Basel, 15 January 1934

**Maestro di Musica, Il**
COMP.: *Unknown*

*2 acts*
1731

Although this work is commonly attributed to Pergolesi, its author is unknown.

**Magic Flute**
See *Zauberflöte, Die*

**Magistrate, The**
See *Corregidor, Der*

**Maid Marian**
See *Robin Hood*

**Maid Mistress**
See *Serva Padrona, La*

**Maid of Arles, The**
See *L'Arlesiana*

**Maid of Pskov, The**
See *Pskovityanka*

**Mala Vita**
COMP.: U. Giordano
LIBR.: N. Daspuro

*3 parts*
Rome, 21 February 1892
Berlin, 1892

**Malheurs d'Orphée, Les**
(*The Griefs of Orpheus*)
COMP.: D. Milhaud
LIBR.: A. Lunel

*3 scenes*
Brussels, 7 May 1926
Paris, 1927
Buenos Aires, 1927

CAST

| | | | |
|---|---|---|---|
| Orphée | Bar | Four Animals | S, C, T, B |
| Euridice | S | Three Bohemians | S, MS, C |

## Man Without a Country, The
COMP.: W. Damrosch
LIBR.: A. Guiterman
From the story by Hale

2 acts
Metropolitan, 12 May 1937

## Manfred
See *König Manfred*

## Manon
COMP.: J. Massenet
LIBR.: Meilhac and Gille
From the novel by Prévost

*Tragedy in 5 acts*
Comique, 19 January 1884
Liverpool, 1885
New York, 1885

CAST

| | | | |
|---|---|---|---|
| Chevalier des Grieux | T | Javotte, *actress* | S |
| Count des Grieux, *his father* | B | Rosette, *actress* | S |
| Lescaut, *Manon's cousin* | Bar | Innkeeper, Sergeant, Soldier, Students, | |
| Guillot de Morfontaine, *old roué* | T | Gamblers, Merchants, Wives, Croup- | |
| de Bretigny, *nobleman* | Bar | iers, Sharpers, Guards, Travellers, | |
| Manon Lescaut | S | Ladies, Gentlemen, Porters, Postillions, | |
| Pousette, *actress* | S | People | |

MUSICAL HIGHLIGHTS

ACT II. Aria *Adieu, notre petite table* (Goodby, our little table), Manon
The Dream *En fermant les yeux* (On closing my eyes), des Grieux
ACT III. Gavotte *Obéissons quand leur voix appelle* (O listen when the voice of youth), Manon
Aria *Ah! Fuyez douce image* (Ah! leave me, sweetest dream), des Grieux

SYNOPSIS

I. At very first sight, des Grieux and Manon fall in love. Commandeering a carriage reserved for Guillot they fly to Paris.

II. There her cynical cousin Lescaut, with de Bretigny, finds them living together but unmarried. They arrange to have des Grieux taken away from her, leaving her free to take up with de Bretigny.

III. She does, and leads a life of richness and pleasure. But one day she hears that des Grieux has decided to enter a monastery. She goes there to see him. The interview weakens his determination to take the orders.

IV. Together again they go gambling at the casino. Luck is with the indecisive des Grieux. He wins so much so quickly that Guillot calls the police to arrest him as a cheat and her as a prostitute.

V. Des Grieux goes free but Manon is condemned to be deported to the new colony of Louisiana. Des Grieux intercepts the march of the prisoners to the harbor and bribes the guard to let Manon go free. She is so weakened that she sees visions of brilliant jewels as she dies in his arms.

## Manon
See also *Portrait de Manon*

## Manon Lescaut
COMP.: F. Auber
LIBR.: A. E. Scribe
From the novel by Prévost

Comique, 23 February 1856
Liège, 1875

## Manon Lescaut

| | | | |
|---|---|---|---|
| COMP.: G. Puccini | | *Tragedy in 4 acts* | |
| | | Turin, 1 February 1893 | |
| LIBR.: Praga, Oliva and Illica | | Covent Garden, 1894 | |
| From the novel by Prévost | | Philadelphia, 1894 | |
| | | Metropolitan, 1907 | |

CAST

| | | | |
|---|---|---|---|
| Manon Lescaut | S | Music Master | T |
| Lescaut, *her brother* | Bar | Musician | MS |
| Chevalier des Grieux | T | Lamplighter | T |
| Geronte de Ravoir, *Treasurer General* | B | Naval Captain | B |
| Edmondo, *student* | T | Wig maker | Mime |
| Innkeeper | B | Sergeant of Archers | B |

SYNOPSIS

I. Manon and des Grieux fall in love at first sight and elope to Paris.

II. Geronte, whom she jilted for des Grieux, manages to retrieve her and keep her amid magnificence. Des Grieux sees her once but she will not run away with him and give up her new jewels. This delay in their second elopement causes them to be caught.

As an abandoned woman she is tried and condemned to be sent to Louisiana.

III. Des Grieux pleads to be allowed to go with her. The captain of the ship warns him against it, but takes him along.

IV. In the harshness of the new world she dies.

## Maria di Rudenz

COMP.: G. Donizetti  *3 acts*
Venice, 30 January 1838
LIBR.: S. Cammarano  Rio de Janeiro, 1851

## Maria Golovin

COMP.: G.-C. Menotti  Brussels, 20 August 1958
LIBR.: By the composer  New York, 1958

## Marie Galante

COMP.: K. Weill

## Maritana

COMP.: V. Wallace  *3 acts*
Drury Lane, 15 November 1845
LIBR.: E. Fitzball  Philadelphia, 1846
From the play *Don César de Bazan*  New York, 1848

CAST

| | | | |
|---|---|---|---|
| Maritana, *gypsy* | S | Captain of the guard | Bar |
| Don César de Bazan | T | Marquis of Montefiore | B |
| Don José de Santarem, *courtier* | Bar | King | B |
| Lazarillo, *poor boy* | MS | Alcade | B |
| Marchioness of Montefiore | MS | Soldiers, Gypsies, Populace | |

## Marouf

COMP.: H. Rabaud  *5 acts*
Comique, 15 May 1914
LIBR.: L. Népoty  Metropolitan, 1917

CAST

| | | | |
|---|---|---|---|
| Princess Saamcheddine | S | Two Merchants | T, B |
| Fatimah, *Marouf's wife* | S | Chief Sailor | T |
| Marouf, *cobbler* | T or Bar | Two Muezzins | T |
| Sultan of Khaitan | B | Ahmad, *pastry cook* | B |
| Vizier | Bar | Cadi | B |
| Ali | Bar | Two Mamaliks | B |
| Fellah | T | | |

SYNOPSIS

I. Marouf is unhappy. His wife is a bad one. She runs to the Cadi to complain that Marouf beats her. For this the Cadi has him whipped. All in all there is only one thing to do; he goes away with the sailors.

II. He is shipwrecked but found by Ali. Ali sets him up in style as a rich merchant. His reputation becomes such that even the Sultan wishes to see him.

III. The Sultan offers Marouf a princess for a bride. Of course he accepts.

IV. When the princess discovers that her husband is really not rich at all she shows how intelligent she is by disguising herself as a boy and getting him to fly with her away from the city.

V. Just before the Sultan's army catches up with them they discover a magic ring. By proper manipulation of this object they produce a genie who produces riches, thus giving body to their deception and saving their lives.

## Marriage, The
See *Zhenitba*

## Marriage of Figaro, The
See *Nozze di Figaro, Le*

## Martha

COMP.: F. von Flotow
LIBR.: W. Friedrich
From a Ballet-Pantomime

5 acts
Vienna, 25 November 1847
Drury Lane, 1849
New York, 1852

CAST

| | | | |
|---|---|---|---|
| Lady Harriet Durham, *Maid of Honor to the Queen* | S | Nancy, *Lady Harriet's waiting maid* | C |
| | | Sheriff | B |
| Lord Tristan de Mikleford, *her cousin* | B | Three Man Servants | T, B, B |
| | | Three Maid Servants | S, S, MS |
| Plunkett, *young farmer* | B | Courtiers, Pages, Ladies, Hunters, | |
| Lionel, *his foster brother* | T | Huntresses, Farmers, Servants | |

## Masaniello

COMP.: F. Auber
LIBR.: Scribe and Delavigne

Tragedy in 5 acts
Opéra, 29 February 1828
Drury Lane, 1829
New York, 1831

CAST

| | | | |
|---|---|---|---|
| Alfonso d'Arcos, *son of the Viceroy* | T | Fenella, *Masaniello's sister* | Dancer |
| Lorenzo, *his confidant* | T | Borella, *fisherman* | B |
| Selva, *officer in the guard* | B | Moreno, *fisherman* | B |
| Masaniello, *fisherman* | T | Elvira, *Princess* | S |
| Pietro, *his friend* | Bar | Maid of Honor to the Princess | MS |

I. Alfonso has cast off the mute Fenella in order to marry the Princess. The Princess, however, hears of the dumb girl's plight and is able to learn from her in pantomime that Alfonso has betrayed her.

II. By the same means, Fenella tells Masaniello and Pietro of her trouble. The men swear to depose the tyrants who oppress them.

III. Alfonso sends soldiers to find Fenella. This is enough provocation for Masaniello to call his revolt into being.

IV. Having won, Masaniello is now the strong man. To him come Alfonso and Elvira, begging protection from the mobs. For his seeming change of heart Pietro swears revenge against the revolutionary leader.

V. He poisons Masaniello, but the poisoned man is still able to go out with his soldiers once more. Masaniello dies protecting Elvira and Fenella kills herself in remorse.

NOTES

Masaniello is a milestone in operatic history, being one of the earliest realistic tragedies. It had its effect on history also, when at Brussels, 25 August 1830, its performance triggered the outbreak of the Belgian revolution.

## Masked Ball, The
See *Ballo in Maschera, Un*

## Massimilla Doni
COMP.: O. Schoeck
LIBR.: A. Rueger
From a novel by Balzac

3 *acts*
Dresden, 2 March 1937
Zürich, 1937

## Master Peter's Puppet Show
See *Retablo de Maese Pietro, El*

## Mastersingers, The
See *Meistersinger, Die*

## Mathis der Maler
(*Mathias the Painter*)
COMP.: P. Hindemith
LIBR.: By the composer

7 *scenes*
Zürich, 28 May 1938
London (Concert), 1939
Edinburgh, 1952

CAST

| | | | |
|---|---|---|---|
| Albrecht von Brandenburg, *Archbishop of Mainz* | T | Truchsess von Waldburg, *confederate leader* | B |
| Mathis (Grünewald), *Painter* | Bar | Sylvester von Schaumberg, *his officer* | T |
| Lorenz von Pommersfelden, *dean of Mainz* | B | Graf von Helfenstein | Mute |
| Wolfgang Capito, *Cardinal's councillor* | T | Gräfin von Helfenstein, *his wife* | C |
| | | Ursula, *Riedinger's daughter* | S |
| Riedinger, *rich Lutheran* | B | Regina, *Schwalb's daughter* | S |
| Hans Schwalb, *peasant leader* | T | | |

SYNOPSIS

I. Mathis, at work on a fresco, interrupts himself to help the rebel Schwalb and his daughter to escape pursuit.

II. Before the Cardinal von Brandenburg the painter defends the peasants' rebellion. The Cardinal cannot disobey his church and help them. He gives Mathis permission, however, to withdraw from his service.

III. For a year he is gone. When he returns he meets Ursula, whom he loves. She is unaware that there is a political plan to marry her to the Cardinal as a means of helping the cause of Lutheranism.

III. There is a battle between peasants and soldiers. It teaches one fact of importance to Mathis—he is no warrior. He does help to save the life of Regina, after her father is killed, however.

V. The Cardinal refuses to break his vow of celibacy, but he grants the Lutherans permission to meet publicly.

VI. Mathis and Regina make their escape together. During the course of it they rest for a while. He dreams of his temptations: wealth, luxury, and so forth. The vision tortures him. He seems to see the Cardinal, as St. Paul, advising and comforting him.

VII. Regina dies. At the end, Ursula and Mathis are with her. Feeling his own mortality, Mathis slowly puts away his tools and his various works.

NOTES

This is Hindemith's fifth opera, famous enough in performance but made more famous by the orchestral suite he made from it. The sixth scene is based upon Grünewald's great painting over the altar at Isenheim.

| | | |
|---|---|---|
| **Matrimonio Segreto, Il** | | *Comedy in 2 acts* |
| (*The Secret Marriage*) | | Vienna, 7 February 1792 |
| COMP.: D. Cimarosa | | La Scala, 1793 |
| LIBR.: G. Bertati | | London, 1794 |
| From Colman *The Clandestine* | | Metropolitan, 1934 |
| *Marriage* | | |

CAST

| | | | |
|---|---|---|---|
| Geronimo | B | Fidalma, *his sister* | MS |
| Elisetta, *his daughter* | S | Count Robinson, *English nobleman* | B |
| Carolina, *his daughter* | S | Paolino | T |

SYNOPSIS

I. Paolino and Carolina have become secretly wed. She wants to reveal it. She pleads with him to let the secret out. Meanwhile the Count has sent overtures to her father mentioning his interest in Elisetta but Elisetta is in love with Paolino. When this becomes clear to the Count, he graciously changes his affections to favor her sister Carolina. Poor Geronimo cannot fathom it all.

II. Geronimo and the Count finally agree it shall be Carolina. Desperately Paolino works to prevent a terrible situation, but Elisetta and Fidalma make matters worse by intriguing to have Carolina sent to a convent.

Finally Elisetta hears love-making going on behind Carolina's door. Thinking to catch the Count, she rouses the whole house. Fortunately it was not the Count, but the properly though secretly married Paolino and Carolina. Geronimo forgives them, the Count marries Elisetta after all and everybody is happy.

NOTE

Leopold II so enjoyed hearing this comedy that he invited the entire company to a late supper after opening night, then requested they repeat the opera, which they did with gusto.

**Mavra**
COMP.: I. Stravinsky
LIBR.: By the composer
From a folktale

1 *act*
Opéra, 2 June 1922
New York, 1923
BBC, 1935

*Mavra* was privately performed at the house of Princess Polignac in Paris, 1922.

**Maximilien**
COMP.: D. Milhaud
LIBR.: A. Lunel

3 *acts*
Opéra, 4 January 1932

From a German libretto by Hoffman and Franz Werfel's *Juarez and Maximilian*.

**Maximilien**
See also *Massimilla*

**Medée**
COMP.: D. Milhaud
LIBR.: M. Milhaud (his wife)
From Euripides, Seneca, and Corneille.
Commissioned by the Government of France.

1 *act, 3 scenes*
Antwerp, 7 October 1939
Opéra, 1940

**Medea**
The subject has been used also by Marc Antoine Charpentier (1693), Luigi Cherubini (1797), Giovanni Pacini (1843), and Lehman Engel (1935).

**Medium, The**
COMP.: G.-C. Menotti
LIBR.: By the composer

2 *acts*
New York, 8 May 1946
London, 1948

CAST

| | | | |
|---|---|---|---|
| Monica, *Flora's daughter* | S | Mrs. Gobineau, *her client* | S |
| Toby, *mute* | Dancer | Mr. Gobineau, *her husband, client* | Bar |
| Madame Flora (*Baba*), *the Medium* | C | Mrs. Nolan, *their friend, client* | MS |

SYNOPSIS

I. While in the process of deceiving her clients with the sepulchral imitations of her accomplices, Madame Flora feels something touch her. She sends the clients away and tries to discover who has played a trick on her. She is terribly frightened.

II. When the clients return she tries to tell them that she has been a fraud, but they refuse to believe it. She throws them all out. Later, intoxicated, she takes a gun and shoots wildly about the room at what she thinks is a ghost. Blood appears on the floor as Toby falls dead behind a curtain.

**Mefistofele**
COMP.: A. Boito
LIBR.: By the composer

*Prologue, 4 acts, Epilogue*
La Scala, 5 March 1868
London, 1880
New York, 1880
Metropolitan, 1883

CAST

| | | | |
|---|---|---|---|
| Mefistofele | B | Wagner | T |
| Faust | T | Elena | S |
| Margherita | S | Pantalis | C |
| Martha | C | Nereo | T |

Mystic Choir, Celestial Phalanxes, Cherubs, Penitents, Wayfarers, Men at arms, Huntsmen, Students, Citizens, Populace, Townsmen, Witches, Wizards, Greek Chorus, Sirens, Naiads, Dancers, Warriors

## SYNOPSIS

PROLOGUE. Mefistofele wagers that he can turn the good Faust to evil.

I. He reveals himself to Faust and agrees to provide him with one hour of untroubled peace in exchange for his soul.

II. Mefistofele takes Faust and Margherita to a witches' sabbath. Faust sees there a vision of Margherita in chains. But she has fallen in love with him and he with her.

III. Bereft of her lover, Margherita languishes in prison, insane. Faust returns to help her, but she dies.

IV. In the Vale of Tempe Faust meets Helen of Troy and again falls in love.

EPILOGUE. The old Faust rejects all transient pleasures, finding salvation only in the Scriptures. Mefistofele fails to ensnare him. Faust dies in salvation.

## Meistersinger von Nürnberg, Die
(*The Mastersingers of Nürnberg*)
COMP.: R. Wagner
LIBR.: By the composer

3 *acts*
Munich, 21 June 1868
Drury Lane, 1882
Metropolitan, 1886

### CAST

| | | | |
|---|---|---|---|
| Hans Sachs, *cobbler* | Bar | Hans Schwarz, *stocking weaver* | B |
| Veit Pogner, *goldsmith* | B | Hans Foltz, *coppersmith* | B |
| Kunz Vogelgesang, *furrier* | T | Walther von Stolzing, | |
| Conrad Nachtigall, *buckle maker* | B | Franconian knight | T |
| Sixtus Beckmesser, *town clerk* | B | David, *Sachs' apprentice* | T |
| Fritz Kothner, *baker* | Bar | Night Watchman | B |
| Balthazar Zorn, *pewterer* | T | Eva, *Pogner's daughter* | S |
| Ulrich Eisslinger, *grocer* | T | Magdalena, *her nurse* | MS |
| Augustin Moser, *tailor* | T | Burghers, Journeymen, Apprentices, | |
| Hermann Ortel, *soap boiler* | B | Girls | |

### MUSICAL HIGHLIGHTS

The Overture

ACT I. Pogner's Address
Aria *Am stillen Herd* (By silent hearth), Walther

ACT II. Sach's Monologue *Wie duftet doch der Flieder* (How sweet the scent of Elder), Sachs
*Cobbler's Song*, Sachs

ACT III. Monologue, *Wahn, Wahn, überall, Wahn!* (Mad, mad, everyone's mad!), Sachs
Dance of the Apprentices
*Prize Song*, Walther

### SYNOPSIS

I. In church Walther and Eva exchange silent signallings and messages of love during the end of the service. The congregation is hustled out in order to make room for the contest of the Mastersingers which is to take place there later. Pogner speaks with his daughter to propose that he announce that her hand will be the prize this year. She agrees to it and Walther immediately becomes a candidate. The trials come. Beckmesser, who is, as Sachs points out, a rival for the girl's hand, marks every error of accepted style that Walther makes in his song, thus winning the first round.

II. In the evening Sachs learns of Eva's love for Walther. The good man decides to help. When Beckmesser comes to serenade her, Sachs turns the tables on him by marking each of his mistakes with a resounding bang of the hammer on his last. The constant interruptions, the constant crescendo required of Beckmesser, everything combines to raise the whole neighborhood screaming for silence in the night time.

III. Walther shows Sachs the words of a song he has composed for the contest. Sachs allows the manuscript to fall into Beckmesser's hands on the correct assumption that Beckmesser will make an ass of himself trying to reproduce someone else's inspiration. When the contest opens this succeeds magnificently. Sachs proposes that Walther sing his own song and all the town rejoices in its beauty. All honor goes to Sachs after congratulations to Walther and his new fiancée.

## Mephistopheles
See *Faust*
See also *Mefistofele*
See also *Doktor Faust*

## Mermaid, The
See *Russalka*

## Merrie England
2 acts
COMP.: E. German
London, 2 April 1902
LIBR.: B. Hood

## Merry Mount
3 acts
COMP.: H. Hanson
Metropolitan, 10 February 1934
LIBR.: R. Stokes
From a story by Hawthorne
*Merry Mount* was first performed in concert in Ann Arbor, Michigan, 1933.

## Merry Wives of Windsor, The
See *Lustigen Weiber von Windsor, Die*
See also *Falstaff*
See also *Sir John in Love*

## Midsummer Night's Dream
See *Songe d'une Nuit d'Été, Le*

## Mignon
3 acts
COMP.: A Thomas
Comique, 17 November 1866
LIBR.: Barbier and Carré
Drury Lane, 1870
From Goethe's *Wilhelm Meister*
New York, 1871
Metropolitan, 1883

CAST

| | | | |
|---|---|---|---|
| Mignon, *kidnapped in childhood* | MS | Lothario, *wandering minstrel* | B |
| Philine, *actress* | S | Giarno, *gypsy* | B |
| Frédéric, *nobleman* | T or C | Antonio, *servant* | B |
| Wilhelm Meister, *travelling student* | T | Townspeople, Gypsies, Actors, Actresses, | |
| Laertes, *actor* | T | Servants | |

# THE OPERAS

ACT I. Aria *Connais-tu le pays?* (Knowest thou the land?), Mignon
Entr'acte *Gavotte*
ACT II. Aria *Adieu Mignon* (Goodby, Mignon), Wilhelm
Duet *As-tu souffert?* (Have you suffered?), Mignon, Lothario
Polonaise *Je suis Titania* (I am Titania), Philine
ACT III. Aria *Elle ne croyait pa*s (Ah, don't believe it), Wilhelm

SYNOPSIS

I. Seeing her about to be beaten by the gypsy, Wilhelm saves Mignon by buying her from him. She falls in love with him.

II. But Philine loves him too, which makes Mignon jealous. Wilhelm finally decides Mignon must go and bids her farewell. Distracted by this she wanders near the conservatory while Philine is inside acting in Shakespeare. There she meets Lothario who, in his cloudiness of mind, thinks to do her a favor by setting fire to the place. By accident, Mignon is the only one inside at the time. Wilhelm saves her from the flames.

III. Wilhelm buys an old derelict castle for the girl. They all go to see it, including Lothario. Strange memories stir in the old minstrel's heart as he begins to recognize it as his former home, left when his daughter was kidnapped long ago. Certain tokens they both remember bring out the identity of Mignon as the missing daughter.

## Mireille

COMP.: C. Gounod
LIBR.: Carré
From Mistral's poem *Mireio*

3 *acts (Originally* 5)
Paris, 19 March 1864
London, 1864
Metropolitan, 1919

CAST

| | | | | |
|---|---|---|---|---|
| Mireille | S | Taven, *old woman* | | MS |
| Vincent, *her lover* | T | Andreloux, *shepherd* | | MS |
| Ourrias, *bull tender* | Bar | Maître Ambroise, *Vincent's father* | | B |
| Maître Ramon, *Mireille's father* | B | Clémence | | S |

SYNOPSIS

I. Against the approval of her parents, Mireille has fallen in love with Vincent.

II. Ourrias asks for her hand, but is refused. Ambroise asks for it for his son but he is likewise turned down.

III. Ourrias makes an attempt on the life of Vincent. The lovers meet in the sanctuary. There her father finds them and relents, blessing her union with the man she loves.

## Mitridate re di Ponto

(*Mithridates, King of Ponto*)
COMP.: W. A. Mozart
LIBR.: V. Cigna-Santi
From the tragedy by Racine

3 *acts*
Milan, 26 December 1770

## Mona

COMP.: H. Parker
LIBR.: B. Hooker

3 *acts*
Metropolitan, 14 March 1912

This work won the ten thousand dollar Metropolitan prize.

**Mond, Der**
(*The Moon*)                          Munich, 5 February 1939
COMP.: C. Orff
LIBR.: By the composer

CAST

Narrator                              Another Mayor
Four youths, *who steal the moon*     Three groups of people
Farmer                                Old man
Village Mayor                         Little Child
Landlord

**Monna Vanna**                       4 *acts*
COMP.: H. Février                     Opéra, 13 January 1909
LIBR.: M. Maeterlinck                 Boston, 1913
From Maeterlinck's play               New York, 1914

**Monsieur Beaucaire**                *Prologue and* 3 *acts*
COMP.: A. Messager                    Birmingham, England, 7 April 1919
LIBR.: Rivoire and Veber              London, 1919
From the story by Tarkington          New York, 1919

**Montezuma's Daughter**
See *Azora*

**Mörder, Hoffnung der Frauen**
COMP.: P. Hindemith                   Stuttgart, 4 June 1921
LIBR.: O. Kokoschka                   Prague, 1923

**Mother, The**
COMP.: S. Hollingworth                1954

**Mother of Us All, The**             *Pageant in* 2 *acts,* 8 *scenes*
COMP.: V. Thomson                     New York, 7 May 1947
LIBR.: G. Stein

CAST

| | | | |
|---|---|---|---|
| Susan B. Anthony | S | Constance Fletcher | S |
| Anne | S | Gloster Heming | MS |
| Gertrude S. | MS | Isabel Wentworth | MS |
| Virgil T. | Bar | Anna Hope | MS |
| Daniel Webster | Bar | Lillian Russell | S |
| Jo the Loiterer | T | Jenny Reefer | S |
| Chris the Citizen | Bar | Ulysses S. Grant | Bar |
| Indiana Elliott | MS | Herman Atlan | Bar |
| Angel More | S | Donald Gallup | T |
| Henrietta M. | S | A.A. and T.T. | |
| Henry B. | T | Andrew J. | T |
| Anthony Comstock | | Negro Man and Woman | |
| John Adams | T | Indiana Elliott's Brother | |
| Thaddeus Stevens | T | | |

The authors call *The Mother of Us All* a Pageant. Its theme is the winning in the United States of political rights for women. People enter the pageant from all periods in history to remark upon the event.

### Muette de Portici, La
(*The Dumb Girl of Portici*)
See *Masaniello*

### Murder in the Cathedral
See *Assassinio nel Cattedrale, L'*

### Mute Wife, The
See *Schweigsame, Frau, die*

### Mutter, Die
COMP.: A. Hába
LIBR.: By the composer

10 *scenes*
Munich, 17 May 1931

*Die Mutter* won the Czech State Prize in 1931. It is one of the foremost examples of opera written with microtones.

### Nabucco
COMP.: G. Verdi
LIBR.: T. Solera

4 *acts*
La Scala, 9 March 1842
London, 1846
New York, 1848

CAST

| | | | |
|---|---|---|---|
| Abigaille, *slave,* | | Nabucco, *king of Babylon* | |
| *supposed daughter of Nabucco* | S | (*Nebuchadnezzer*) | Bar |
| Fenena, *Nabucco's daughter* | S | Zaccaria, *high priest of Jerusalem* | B |
| Ismaele, *nephew of the* | | High Priest of Babylon | B |
| *King of Jerusalem* | T | Abdallo, *Nabucco's officer* | T |
| | | Anna, *Zaccaria's sister* | S |

SYNOPSIS

I. Nabucco's army advances toward Jerusalem where Fenena is being held hostage in the temple by Ismaele who loves her. Abigaille, leading some of the troops, invades the temple and threatens Ismaele with death unless he will renounce Fenena for her. In a moment, however, Nabucco himself arrives. Zaccaria attempts to kill the hostage, but Ismaele stops him while Nabucco ravages the place.

II. Back in Babylon, Fenena, who rules during her father's absence, grants a general amnesty to the captive Hebrews. Abigaille lays claim to the crown, but Nabucco returns and puts a stop to all pretensions by proclaiming that he is not only king, but god. In a clap of thunder the crown is wrested from him and the king is reduced to madness.

III. Abigaille becomes regent. Her first act is to arrange to wipe out the Jews. Zaccaria prophesies the fall of Babylon, but the Jews have nearly given up hope.

IV. With the help of Abdallo, Nabucco breaks out of his imprisonment in time to save Fenena from the trumped-up execution ordered by Abigaille. He has prayed to Jehovah for pardon, causing the idols to be destroyed as if by magic, a triumph for Zaccaria. There is general rejoicing but for Abigaille who poisons herself and dies.

**Nadeshda**
COMP.: A. Thomas
LIBR.: J. R. Sturgis

4 *acts*
Drury Lane, 16 April 1885
Dublin, 1885

**Naïla**
COMP.: P. Gaubert
LIBR.: M. Léna

3 *acts*
Opéra, 7 April 1927

**Natoma**
COMP.: V. Herbert
LIBR.: J. Redding

3 *acts*
Philadelphia, 25 February 1911
New York, 1911

**Navarraise, La**
COMP.: J. Massenet
LIBR.: Claretie and Cain

2 *acts*
Covent Garden, 20 June 1894
Metropolitan, 1895
Saigon, 1900

**Nebuchadnezzer**
See *Nabucco*

**Nerone**
COMP.: P. Mascagni
LIBR.: Targioni-Tozzetti
From a comedy by Cossa

*Comedy in* 3 *acts*
La Scala, 16 January 1935
Zürich, 1937

**Nerone**
COMP.: A. Boito
LIBR.: By the composer

*Tragedy in* 4 *acts*
La Scala, 1 May 1924
Rome, 1928
Buenos Aires, 1926

CAST

| | | | |
|---|---|---|---|
| Nerone, *emperor of Rome* (Nero) | T | Tigellino, *follower of Nerone* | B |
| Simon Mago, *sorcerer* | Bar | Gobrias, *follower of Mago* | T |
| Fanuèl, *Christian* | Bar | Dositeo, *Roman* | Bar |
| Asteria | S | Perside, *Christian* | S |
| Rubria, *Vestal Virgin,* | | Cerinto | C |
| *secretly a Christian* | MS | | |

SYNOPSIS

I. Nero, full of guilt for murdering his mother, buries her ashes. Suddenly a figure seems to rise from the grave and threaten him. Nero flies from it. Simon Mago stays to find that it is Asteria, whom he can use in his future evil workings. Two Christians meet nearby to speak of love together. They are Rubria and Fanuèl. In Mago they see their worst enemy.

II. Simon produces a prodigious but wholly false ritual including oracles, visions of goddesses, and so forth, with which to charm Nero. Nero recognizes Asteria playing goddess and destroys the illusion. He condemns Simon to be thrown from a tower and fly—if he can.

III. Simon manages to escape and hunt out the Christians in their secret meeting. He betrays them to the guards. Meekly but with fortitude the Christians submit to capture.

IV. Nero orders magnificent games to amuse himself and the people of Rome. Rubria, as Vestal Virgin, pleads to him to save the Christians but the thought is so abhorrent to him that he has her thrown in with them as another victim. He settles back with the audience to watch the sport as flames rise in the background, burning Rome in a fire set by Simon Mago for revenge. In the pit where the torn bodies of victims are heaped together, Rubria and Fanuèl confess to each other their love and their resignation.

### NOTE

Boito spent most of his mature life working on this opera, which was produced posthumously.

**Neues vom Tage**
*(News of the Day)*
COMP.: P. Hindemith
LIBR.: M. Schiffer

3 *parts*
Berlin, 8 June 1929

**Nibelungenlied**
See *Ring des Nibelungen, Der*

**Nightdancers**
COMP.: E. Loder
LIBR.: G. Soane

2 *acts*
London, 28 October 1846
New York, 1847

**Night Flight**
See *Volo di Notte*

**Nightingale, The**
See *Rossignol, Le*

**Noël**
COMP.: F. d'Erlanger
LIBR.: J. and P. Ferrier

3 *acts*
Comique, 28 December 1910
Chicago, 1913

**Norma**
COMP.: V. Bellini
LIBR.: F. Romani
From a tragedy by Soumet

*Tragedy in 2 acts*
La Scala, 26 December 1831
London, 1833
New York, 1841

### CAST

| | | | |
|---|---|---|---|
| Pollione, *roman pro-consul in Gaul* | T | Clotilda, *Norma's friend* | S |
| Oroveso, *archdruid, Norma's father* | B | Flavio, *centurion* | T |
| Norma, *druid high priestess* | S | Priests, Gauls, Priestesses, Temple Virgins, | |
| Adalgisa, *temple virgin* | S | Norma's children | |

### MUSICAL HIGHLIGHTS

ACT I. Aria *Casta diva* (Chaste goddess), Norma
ACT II. Duet *Mira, O Norma* (Hear me, O Norma), Adalgisa, Norma
   Duet *Qual cor tradisti* (How you have betrayed), Norma, Pollione

### SYNOPSIS

I. Once long ago, while Pollione and Norma were in love, she bore him a child. But the love is past now, and Pollione is interested rather in Adalgisa whom he asks to go with him to Rome. Adalgisa is a faithful friend to the forlorn Norma. She tells her of her love and Norma finds out who the man is.

II. It would be better if Adalgisa would go with him; it would free Norma of a dangerous entanglement with a national enemy. Since she will not go, however, Norma incites the Gauls to war against the Romans. Meanwhile Pollione, who has been looking for Adalgisa, breaks into the temple and is caught there by the Gauls. To save him Norma tells them there is a worse traitor present, herself. They build a pyre upon which the traitor must be sacrificed. When it is in flames, Pollione leaps upon it to join her in death.

## North Star, The
See *Étoile du Nord, L'*

## Notre Dame de Paris
COMP.: W. Fry    Philadelphia, 3 May 1864

## Nozze di Figaro, Le
(*The Marriage of Figaro*)
COMP.: W. A. Mozart
LIBR.: L. da Ponte
From Beaumarchais *La Folle Journée ou
Le Mariage de Figaro*

*Comedy in 4 acts*
Vienna, 1 May 1786
London, 1812
Covent Garden, 1819
New York, 1824

### CAST

| | | | |
|---|---|---|---|
| Figaro, *valet to the count* | Bar | Don Basilio, *music master* | T |
| Susanna, *maid to the countess* | S | Countess Almaviva | S |
| Dr. Bartolo | B | Antonio, *gardener, Susanna's uncle* | B |
| Marcellina, *duenna* | S | Don Curzio, *lawyer* | T |
| Cherubino, *former page to the countess* | S | Barbarina, *Antonio's niece* | S |
| Count Almaviva | Bar | Chorus of Villagers | |

### MUSICAL HIGHLIGHTS

The Overture

ACT I. Aria *Se a caso Madama* (If my lady should call you), Figaro
Aria *Se vuol ballare* (If you'd go dancing), Figaro
Aria *La vendetta* (Now comes vengeance), Dr. Bartolo
Aria *Non so più cosa son, cosa faccio* (I don't know if it's pain or pleasure), Cherubino
Aria *Non più andrai* (No more play), Figaro

ACT II. Aria *Porgi Amor* (God of love), Countess
Cavatina *Voi che sapete* (You who have seen him), Cherubino
Aria *Cognoscete, signor Figaro* (You must tell me, Mr. Figaro), Almaviva

ACT III. Duet *Crudel, perchè finora* (O why are you so cruel), Susanna and the Count
Aria *Vedrò mentr'io sospiro* (Must I withhold my breathing), Count
Aria *Dove sono?* (O where are they?), Countess
Letter Duet *Che soave zeffiretto* (How soft the evening breezes), Susanna and the Countess

ACT IV. Aria *Aprite un po' quegli occhi* (Open your eyes just a little), Figaro
Cavatina *Deh vieni non tardar* (O come and don't delay), Susanna

### SYNOPSIS

I. Figaro and Susanna are about to be married. There are complications, however. The count is interested in her; Cherubino cannot be trusted in that respect; and Marcellina intends to blackmail the groom into marrying her instead.

II. Too, the countess has long languished for attention and love from her own husband. She agrees quite easily to an intrigue by which Cherubino will dress as Susanna and keep a rendezvous with the count. While they dress the boy for the part, the count surprises them, nearly catching the young page. The count is completely bewildered but he suspects the plot, even though each person manages to cover up for the other.

III. The plot takes shape as Susanna delivers the treacherous letter, asking for the assignation with the count during the preparations for the marriage.

IV. At the appointed time and place Figaro happens to see the countess dressed as Susanna and vice versa and believes the worst as he sees first Cherubino and then the count have their supposedly secret meetings with what he thinks is his own bride. When Figaro sees the supposed countess, however, he recognizes who is who and woos Susanna so that the count, who is obviously watching, believes his wife unfaithful. As the unfortunate count approaches the height of his fury the real countess reveals herself and intercedes for the servants. All ends happily and all marriages become sublime.

NOTES

This fascinating masterpiece was not so well received at its opening in Vienna. Not until a subsequent production at Prague did it meet with the success we take now for granted. It is said that Mozart wrote the music very quickly, perhaps in less than a month. He had a good libretto to work with, shaped by da Ponte from the complex and funny play by Beaumarchais.

**Nusch-Nuschi**                                  1 *act*
COMP.: P. Hindemith                      Stuttgart, 4 June 1921
LIBR.: F. Blei                                     Prague, 1923

**Oberon**                                          3 *acts*
COMP.: C. M. von Weber                 Covent Garden, 12 April 1826
LIBR.: J. R. Planché                         New York, 1828
From the poem *Oberon* by Wieland   Metropolitan, 1918
   from the story *Huon de Bordeaux*

CAST

| | | | |
|---|---|---|---|
| Sir Huon of Bordeaux | T | A Sea Nymph | S |
| Sherasmin, *his squire* | Bar | Charlemagne, Haroun al Rashid, | |
| Oberon, *king of the fairies* | T | Babekan, Almanzor, Abdullah, | |
| Puck | S | Titania, Roshana, Namouna, | |
| Reiza, *daughter of Haroun al Rashid* | S | Nadina | Spkrs |
| Fatima, *her attendant* | MS | | |

SYNOPSIS

I. Oberon in a fury vows never to be reconciled with Titania until he shall find two lovers who remain faithful throughout every trouble. His trusty Puck tells him of Huon who has been sentenced, for an affront to Charlemagne, to go alone into Bagdad to kill the Caliph's right-hand man and marry his daughter. Oberon has the knight and his squire brought before him in a charmed sleep, and presents Huon with a vision of Reiza, thus adding fire to the warrior's duty. Off go Huon and Sherasmin to Bagdad. On the way they come across Babekan whom they rescue, but who in turn betrays them since he claims priority to Reiza's hand.

II. Using the magic horn given to him by Oberon, Huon invades the very court of Haroun al Rashid and carries off Reiza and Fatima. Now begins the trial of love that Oberon requires. Puck causes the returning knight to be shipwrecked and attacked by pirates. The pirates carry off Reiza, leaving Huon a castaway on the barren shore.

III. Rumors whisper to Huon that Reiza is captive of the kindly Emir of Tunis. When he goes to rescue her he finds that the Emir's wife Roshana wishes to have help in killing her husband to assuage her jealousy over Reiza. Huon will not help her. She tries to do it herself but fails. The Emir has them captured and condemns Huon to be put to death for complicity. A blast on the magic horn, however, brings Oberon to the rescue. All are transported back to the court of Charlemagne with a chorus of thanksgiving.

NOTES

The libretto for this very influential opera was written in English. In the original work there were extensive scenes without musical accompaniment for which Mahler later composed musical connections and a few accompaniments which were to go with a new German translation by Brecher.

### Oberto, Conte di S. Bonifacio

(*Oberto, Count of St. Boniface*)
COMP.: G. Verdi
LIBR.: A. Piazza (altered by Morelli and Solera)
Verdi's first opera.

2 *acts*
La Scala, 17 November 1839
Barcelona, 1842
Chicago (Concert), 1903

### Oedipus

COMP.: G. Enesco
LIBR.: E. Fleg
This work made some use of microtones.

*Tragedy in 4 acts*
Opéra, 10 March 1936

### Oedipus Rex

COMP.: I. Stravinsky
LIBR.: J. Cocteau (Translated into Latin by Danielou)
From Sophocles

*Opera-Oratorio in 2 acts*
Paris (Oratorio), 30 May 1927
Vienna (Opera), 1928
New York (Opera), 1931
London (Oratorio), 1936

CAST

| | | | |
|---|---|---|---|
| Narrator | | Tiresias, *soothsayer* | B |
| Oedipus, *King of Thebes* | T | Shepherd | T |
| Jocasta, *his wife* | MS | Messenger | BBar |
| Creon, *her brother* | BBar | Chorus of the Old Men of Thebes | |

SYNOPSIS

I. There has been a terrible plague in the city of Thebes. Creon, returning from a visit to the oracle, announces to the king and to the people that the cause of the plague is the presence within the city of the murderer of the former king. Oedipus curses the unknown murderer and orders that he be found. To him, under duress, comes the blind Tiresias who tells him only one fact: the king's murderer is himself a king.

II. Jocasta, deriding the oracle, accidentally reveals that the old king, her former husband, was killed at a certain meeting of three roads. On such a morning Oedipus, travelling from his home, had once killed a man. Suspicions are still dim in his mind when a Shepherd comes to tell him that his father, Polybus, is dead. This is a shock to the king, for long ago the oracle had declared that he would slay his own father. That indeed was his reason for travelling away from home. Thus Polybus could not have been his father, but the circumstances incriminate Oedipus as the murderer of the former king of Thebes who must have been his father. The truth is exposed. At the news that Jocasta has hanged herself, Oedipus goes and tears out his own eyes.

### Oedipus Tyrannus

COMP.: C. Orff

Stuttgart, 1959

**Oca del Cairo, L'**  
COMP.: W. A. Mozart  
LIBR.: G. Varesco  

2 *acts*  
Paris, 6 June 1867  
London, 1870  
Salzburg, 1936  

Actually the opera Mozart wrote under this name was not finished. The performances at Paris and elsewhere were made up of the unfinished work plus additions from *Lo Sposo Deluso* and others.

**Old Maid and the Thief, The**  
COMP.: G.-C. Menotti  
LIBR.: By the composer  

1 *act*, 14 *scenes*  
NBC radio, 22 April 1939  
Philadelphia, 11 February 1941  

CAST

| Laetitia | S | Miss Pinkerton | S |
| Miss Todd | C | Bob, *a tramp* | Bar |

SYNOPSIS

The two sweet old maids are busy having tea together when there is a knock at the door. They open it to find a poor tramp, Bob, who asks them for a little food. Delighted with his handsomeness they take him in and feed him. Further delighted at the presence of a man in the house, they prevail upon him to stay over for a while.

News reaches them that there has been a jailbreak nearby. Thinking Bob may be the escapee, they keep him hidden away while they resort to sneaking and even stealing in order to keep him both happy and safe.

When he finally explains that he is not an escapee at all, they are horrorstricken at what they have done. Miss Todd, in a grand huff, goes off to call the police. But while she is away Laetitia invites the young man to run off with her, in Miss Todd's car and with Miss Todd's little trinkets to sell. This he reluctantly accepts.

**Olympia**  
COMP.: G. Spontini  
LIBR.: Dieulafoy and Brifaut  
From a tragedy of Voltaire  

*Tragedy in* 3 *acts*  
Opéra, 22 December 1819  
Berlin, 1821  
Rome, 1885  

**Ombra di Don Giovanni, L'**  
(*The Shade of Don Juan*)  
COMP.: F. Alfano  
LIBR.: E. Moschino  

3 *acts*  
La Scala, 2 April 1914  
Florence, 1941  

The performance at Florence was billed under the title: *Don Giovanni di Manara*.

**Operas-Minutes**  
COMP.: D. Milhaud  
LIBR.: H. Hoppenot  
*L'Enlèvement d'Europe*  
*L'Abandon d'Ariane*  
*La Délivrance de Thésée*  

Wiesbaden, 20 April 1928  

8 *scenes*  
1 *Act*  
1 *Act*  

The first of these tiny works was produced separately at Baden-Baden on 17 July 1927.

**Oracolo, L'**  
COMP.: F. Leoni  
LIBR.: C. Zanoni  
From a story by Fernald  

1 *act*  
Covent Garden, 28 June 1905  
New York, 1915  
Metropolitan, 1926

**Orestes**
  See *Orestie*
  See also *Life of Orestes*
  See also *Elektra*

| | |
|---|---|
| **Orestes** | *Trilogy* |
| COMP.: S. Taneief | |

| | |
|---|---|
| **Orestes** | *Tragedy, in 3 parts* |
| COMP.: F. Weingartner | Leipzig, 15 February 1902 |
| LIBR.: By the composer | Berlin, 1902 |
| From Aeschylus | Prague, 1909 |

| | |
|---|---|
| **Orestie** | *Trilogy* |

This consists of three operas by Milhaud:
  *Agamemnon*
  *Choëphores*
  *Eumenides*

| | |
|---|---|
| **Orfeo** | |
| Composer unknown | Mantua, 1472 |
| LIBR.: A. Poliziano | |

This play with musical numbers is known to have been produced with sets by Raphael.

**Orfeo**
  See *Favola d'Orfeo*
  See also *Euridice*
  See also *Orpheus*

| | |
|---|---|
| **Orfeo ed Euridice** | *Tragedy in 3 acts* |
| COMP.: C. W. Gluck | Vienna, 5 October 1762 |
| LIBR.: R. da Calzabigi | London, 1770 |
| | New York, 1863 |
| | Metropolitan, 1891 |

CAST

| | | | |
|---|---|---|---|
| Orfeo | C | Shepherds and Shepherdesses, Furies | |
| Euridice | S | and Demons | |
| Amor, *god of love* | S | Heroes and Heroines in Hades | |
| A Happy Shade | S | | |

MUSICAL HIGHLIGHTS

ACT I. Aria *Chiamo il mio ben* (Hear me, O my love), Orfeo and chorus

ACT II. Scene *Chi mai dell'Erebo* (Who dares to enter hell), Orfeo and Chorus
    Aria *È quest' asilo ameno e grato* (In this tranquil and lovely abode), Euridice and chorus
    Aria *Che puro ciel* (What heavenly light), Orfeo

ACT III. Duet, *Su, e con me vieni, o cara* (Trust me and come with me O dear one), Orfeo and Euridice
    Duet *Che fiero momento* (How proud the moment), Orfeo and Euridice
    Aria *Che farò senza Euridice* (I have lost my Euridice), Orfeo.

I. Orfeo weeps for the death of his wife. Called by the lamentation, the god of love appears and tells Orfeo that he may go if he wishes into Hades and bring her back, provided that he avoids looking upon her until they shall have reached the outside world. After the easy promise, Orfeo goes to find her.

II. Confronted by the furies of hell who bar his way, Orfeo sings. Their ferocity abates and they let him enter the abode of the dead. There, in the valley of the blest, the shades bring Euridice to him. Without looking at her he takes her hand and leads her back toward the living world.

III. She cannot understand his avoidance. She pleads with him to look upon her face. She weeps for his love. Unable to resist at last, he clasps her in his arms. Hardly has the thought taken action before she is snatched from him and taken back into death. Forlorn he sings again of his lost love, again so beautifully that Amor restores her to him without conditions.

NOTES

This is the earliest of the classic operas to remain steadily in repertory in modern times. Gluck makes remarkable use of the chorus both musically and dramatically throughout the work. In this respect, together with a few modern operas, it stands as one of the great achievements in the search for a dramatic and musical successor to the classic Greek drama as sought by the Florentine group in 1600 (See *Euridice* by Peri). Gluck wrote the part of Orfeo for the male contralto Guadagni. In French productions he added tenor arias for Legros, who played that role. Berlioz, however, restored the original voice distribution.

**Orphée aux Enfers**
(*Orpheus in Hades*)
COMP.: J. Offenbach
LIBR.: Halévy and Crémieux

*Comedy in 2 acts*
Paris, 21 October 1858
New York, 1861
London, 1865

CAST

| | | | | |
|---|---|---|---|---|
| Pluton, *god of the underworld,* | | Morphée, *god of sleep* | | T |
| called *Aristée* | T | Euridice, *Orphée's wife* | | S |
| Jupiter, *king of the gods* | Bar | Diane, *goddess of the hunt* | | S |
| Orphée, *violinist* | T | L'Opinion Publique, *public opinion* | | MS |
| John Styx, *fool* | Bar | Vénus, *goddess of love* | | C |
| Mercure, *messenger of the gods* | T | Cupidon, *Cupid* | | S |
| Bacchus, *god of wine* | Spkr | Junon, *goddess, Jupiter's wife* | | MS |
| Mars, *god of war* | B | Minerve | | S |

SYNOPSIS

I. Orpheus and his wife do not get along with any notable harmony. She is heartily sick of him and his violin playing. When an opportunity for love presents itself to her in the person of Aristée she is quick to snap it up. Since Aristée is Pluton, however, he requires her to go to the underworld with him. What an adventure! Leaving Orphée a little note saying she is dead, off she goes. Orpheus is delighted to be free, but Public Opinion insists that he go to Hades and fetch her up again. The fact that he is unwilling makes the deed even more heroic in Opinion's eyes. Orpheus, thus goaded, makes his half-hearted appeal to Jupiter on Olympus and is granted permission to retrieve the errant wife. All the gods and goddesses decide to go down with him to take a look for themselves.

II. Jupiter finds her first. He does his reputation as a lover no damage by assuming the form of a fly and buzzing a little love-duet with her, wooing her for himself. The gods love Euridice and she loves them. Everyone is marvelously happy. They all break into a can-can to celebrate the initiation of such a lively girl into their midst.

Then Orpheus with his prim companion arrives. Jupiter lays down a condition to the bargain: Orpheus must take her out without looking back at her. That agreed, the reluctant husband begins his journey. Everything is going well, much too well to satisfy Jupiter who sees his latest amour being led away by her husband. To prevent such an irreparable loss the god hurls a thunderbolt at Orpheé's heels. The poor man, startled for a moment, glances back, sees his wife and loses his bargain. With joy she trips back into the circle of deliriously happy gods and her relieved spouse goes back where he would rather be.

Not once was he able to sing his famous song to open the gates of Hades. The gods had known the tune all along and sang it to him before he had a chance to clear his throat.

### NOTES

Offenbach was trying to make ends meet at his theater *Les Bouffes Parisiennes* when he brought out his Orpheus. It was an astounding success.

**Orpheus und Euridike**  
COMP.: E. Krenek  
LIBR.: O. Kokoschka

3 *acts*  
Kassel, Germany, 27 November 1926

**Orpheus and Euridice**  
See also *Orfeo ed Euridice*  
See also *Favola d'Orfeo*

**Orpheus in Hades**  
See *Orphée aux Enfers*

**Otello**  
COMP.: O. Rossini  
LIBR.: B. di Salsa  
From Shakespeare

*Tragedy in 3 acts*  
Naples, 4 December 1816  
London, 1822  
New York, 1826

**Otello**  
COMP.: G. Verdi  
LIBR.: A. Boito  
From Shakespeare

*Tragedy in 4 acts*  
La Scala, 5 February 1887  
New York, 1888  
London, 1889  
Metropolitan, 1891

### CAST

| | | | | |
|---|---|---|---|---|
| Otello, *a moor, Venetian governor of Cyprus* | T | Montano, *Otello's predecessor* | B | |
| Iago, *his ensign* | Bar | Herald | B | |
| Cassio, *his lieutenant* | T | Desdemona, *Otello's wife* | S | |
| Roderigo, *Venetian gentleman* | T | Emilia, *her lady, Iago's wife* | MS | |
| Lodovico, *Venetian ambassador* | B | Soldiers, Sailors, Ladies and Gentlemen, Cypriotes | | |

### MUSICAL HIGHLIGHTS

ACT I. Scena *Esultate!* (Rejoice!), Otello and Chorus  
　　　Duet *Già nella notte* (Here in the night), Otello and Desdemona  
ACT II. Aria *Credo in un dio crudel* (I believe in a cruel god), Iago  
　　　Aria *Ora e per sempre addio* (Now and forever, goodbye), Otello

ACT IV. Willow Song *Piangea cantando* (With weeping and in song), Desdemona
*Ave Maria*, Desdemona

SYNOPSIS

I. Triumphant after defeating the enemies of Cyprus, Otello returns to the island. His ensign in his absence has conceived a deep hatred for him because Cassio was made lieutenant instead of himself. Therefore Iago plans to use Cassio in an intrigue to destroy Otello.

II. He sends Cassio to Desdemona to plead for her intercession with the governor to restore Cassio to the favor which was lost through Iago's machinations. Advertising their meeting in the most cunning way, Iago makes sure that the Moor interprets it as a tryst behind his back. At the height of Otello's jealousy Iago speaks openly to him of Desdemona's "faithlessness" saying that Cassio has even her handkerchief, given to her by Otello.

III. Otello demands the handkerchief from her, but she cannot find it. Iago arranges for Otello to see it in Cassio's hand. At this the Moor swears to kill his wife. The last straw breaks when Venetian ambassadors arrive to inform the governor that he has been recalled to Venice and that Cassio has been appointed governor in his place.

IV. At night Desdemona sings a little song to herself as she prepares for bed. When Emilia is about to leave her, Desdemona suddenly cries farewell to her, in tears. Then Otello comes. She cannot admit any crime against him; she knows of none. But he cannot believe her against such mounting, visible evidence. He strangles her with his bare hands. Emilia discovers them; then Cassio rushes in to tell him that he has discovered Iago's plot. In remorse Otello kills himself in their presence, beside his murdered wife.

**Our Lady's Juggler**
See *Jongleur de Notre Dame, Le*

| **Pagliacci, I** | *Tragedy in Prologue and 2 acts* |
|---|---|
| (*The Players*) | Milan, 17 May 1892 |
| COMP.: R. Leoncavallo | New York, 1893 |
| LIBR.: By the composer | Metropolitan, 1893 |
| | Covent Garden, 1893 |

CAST

| | | | | |
|---|---|---|---|---|
| Canio, *chief player,* "*Pagliaccio*" | T | Beppe, *a player,* "*Harlequin*" | T |
| Nedda, *his wife* "*Columbine*" | S | Silvio, *villager* | Bar |
| Tonio, *clown* "*Taddeo*" | Bar | Villagers | |

MUSICAL HIGHLIGHTS

PROLOGUE. *Si può? signore, signori* (By your leave, ladies and gentlemen), Tonio
ACT I. Balatella *O, che volo d'augelli* (O how beautifully birds sing), Nedda
Aria *Vesti la giubba* (On with the play), Canio
ACT II. Serenade *O Colombina*, Harlequin
Scena *No!, Pagliaccio non son* (No, I'm no longer playing), Canio

SYNOPSIS

Tonio steps before the curtain and sings the prologue, introducing the play.

I. To the delight of everybody, the players arrive in a new village amid shouting and drumming, marching down the street. Soon the citizens notice a rivalry between Tonio and Canio, and someone suggests perhaps Tonio intends to make a play for Canio's wife, just as he does in character in the Harlequinade. Canio darkly refuses to believe it. But the clown does love Nedda, and tries to win her. With disgust she drives him away with a whip, stirring a thirst in his heart for revenge. He overhears her planning an elopement with a villager, Silvio. This information he takes immediately to Canio who comes to witness the betrayal with his own eyes. Canio tries to catch him, but Silvio gets away clean. In vain Canio tries to beat the name of her lover from Nedda.

II. The play begins. It is the old story in which Harlequin and Columbine plan to elope, leaving her husband forlorn. Pagliaccio suspects them, but Harlequin escapes. Pagliaccio tries to frighten Columbine into telling him who the lover is—but at this point Canio can no longer contain his personal feelings. He demands to know the name of Nedda's lover. The villagers in the audience at first think he is a marvelously gifted actor. But soon they begin to realize that something serious is going on as he takes out a dagger and chases the frightened actress off the stage. As he stabs her to death Silvio rushes upon him, only to be stabbed by her side. Thus the comedy is finished.

## NOTES

Leoncavallo was sued for plagiarism by another author. Although there have been many plays on similar subjects, he defended himself by pointing out that he had heard of a real case of such a murder in a travelling theatrical troupe, his own father being judge at the trial. He had used his memory of the event for his source. The suit was withdrawn.

## Palestrina

| | |
|---|---|
| COMP.: H. Pfitzner | Munich, 12 June 1917 |
| LIBR.: By the composer | Vienna, 1919 |

3 acts

### CAST

| | | | |
|---|---|---|---|
| Pope Pius IV | B | Silla, *his pupil* | MS |
| Giovanni Morone, *papal legate* | Bar | Bishop Ercole Severolus | BBar |
| Bernardo Novagerio | T | Five singers of Santa Maria | |
| Cardinal Christoph Madruscht | B | Maggiore | 2T, 3B |
| Carlo Borromeo, *Cardinal* | Bar | Two Papal Nuncios, Jesuits, Massarelli | |
| Cardinal of Lorraine | B | the Bishop of Thelesia, Secretary of | |
| Abdisu, *patriarch of Assyria* | T | the Council, Giuseppe, an old | |
| Anton Brus von Müglitz, | | Servant | Mutes |
| *archbishop of Prague* | B | Lucretia, *Palestrina's dead wife* | C |
| Count Luna, *envoy from Spain* | Bar | Nine dead composers | 3T, 3Bar, 3B |
| Bishop of Budoja, *Italian bishop* | T | Three Angelic Voices | S |
| Theophilis of Imola, *Italian bishop* | T | Singers of the Papal Chapel, | |
| Avosmediano, *bishop of Cadiz* | BBar | Archbishops, Bishops, Abbots, | |
| Giovanni Pierluigi da Palestrina | T | Ambassadors, Envoys, Theologians, | |
| Ighino, *his son* | S | Servants, Soldiers, People, Angels | |

### SYNOPSIS

The story concerns the composition of the *Missa Papae Marcelli* and its companion works which Palestrina wrote in demonstration of the worth of polyphonic music in the church. By the great beauty of this music the Pope was convinced that polyphony would not destroy the ritual continuity and texture of the service, and that it would be unnecessary for him to issue his orders requiring the church to revert to the ancient Gregorian plainsong.

## Paolo and Francesca

See *Francesca da Rimini*

**Pantaloon**
See *He Who Gets Slapped*

**Pardon de Ploërmel, Le**
See *Dinorah*

**Parsifal**

COMP.: Richard Wagner
LIBR.: By the composer
From traditional legends

*Stage Dedication Festival Play in 3 acts*
Bayreuth, 26 July 1882
Metropolitan, 1903
Covent Garden, 1914

CAST

| | | | |
|---|---|---|---|
| Amfortas, *ruler of the kingdom of the Grail* | BBar | Kundry | S |
| Titurel, *his father* | B | Two Knights | T, B |
| Gurnemanz, *knight of the Grail* | B | Four Esquires | 2S, 2T |
| Klingsor, *magician* | B | Six Flower Maidens | S |
| Parsifal | T | Knights of the Grail, Youths, Boys, Two choirs of Flower Maidens | |

SYNOPSIS

Amfortas, contesting against Klingsor, lost to him the sacred spear with which Klingsor thereupon dealt him an unhealing wound. Only a guileless innocent may retrieve the spear from Klingsor and heal Amfortas.

I. Gurnemanz waits in the forest while the king tries to salve his wound in the lake. Speaking with youths, he tells them of the wound and the spear that made it. Kundry comes to him, bringing an Arabian ointment to soothe the king. Suddenly the knights bring in a stranger who has shot a sacred swan. He is so unconscious of any guilt and so guileless that he seems to be the proper candidate for saving the spear. His name is Parsifal. Gurnemanz takes him to see the unveiling of the Holy Grail in the castle, but the fool understands nothing of the ceremony and is thrown out.

II. The bewitched Kundry lures Parsifal into Klingsor's magic garden and there kisses him. But rather than enslaving him, the kiss reveals to him his mission. Kundry shouts to warn Klingsor, who hurls the sacred spear at Parsifal. But instead of killing him it comes to rest in his unharmed hand. Parsifal makes the sign of the cross and the magic castle is destroyed.

III. After many wanderings Parsifal returns on Good Friday to the forest of the Grail. Here the aged Gurnemanz opposes him. But when Parsifal shows him the sacred spear Gurnemanz greets him as the new King of the Grail. As king, Parsifal's first act is to baptize Kundry, thus freeing her from her ancient curse. They enter the castle where Parsifal heals Amfortas with the touch of the spear that wounded him. Then he leads the knights in their sacrament.

NOTES

At the opening of *Parsifal* there were three casts, alternating from night to night. The story was based upon legends of the Grail; *Percival le Galois*, or *Contes de Grail*, Chrétien de Troyes (1190), *Parsifal*, by Wolfram von Eschenbach, and the so-called *Mabinogion manuscript* of the 14th century. One of the most memorable motives from the opera is taken from the Dresden Fourfold Amen.

**Partenope**

COMP.: G. F. Handel
LIBR.: S. Stampiglia

3 *acts*
London, 7 March 1730
Covent Garden, 1737
Göttingen, 1935

**Pastor Fido, Il**
(*The Faithful Shepherd*)
COMP.: G. F. Handel
LIBR.: G. Rossi
From a play by Guarini
    Handel composed two versions of the opera, the first performed in London on 3 December 1712, the second on 29 May 1734.

**Paul Bunyan**
COMP.: B. Britten          New York, 5 May 1941

**Paul et Virginie**          3 *acts*
COMP.: V. Massé          Paris, 15 November 1876
LIBR.: Barbier and Carré      Covent Garden, 1878
From a story by St. Pierre     New Orleans, 1879

**Pauvre Matelot, Le**       *Tragedy in 3 acts*
(*The Poor Sailor*)        Comique, 16 December 1927
COMP.: D. Milhaud       Philadelphia, 1937
LIBR.: J. Cocteau        London, 1950

CAST

| Wife | S | Father in law | B |
|------|---|---------------|---|
| Sailor | T | Friend | Bar |

SYNOPSIS

I. After years of absence, during which his good wife remains faithful and sure that he will return to her, the sailor returns unrecognized. Instead of going directly home he proposes to spend the night at his friend's house.

II. Next morning he knocks at his wife's door and tells her he has news of her husband. Unrecognizing, she hears that her husband will return in a couple of weeks, but that he is now very, very poor. He even suggests that she should debase herself to earn money to get her poor husband out of debt. She rejects this, she loves her husband whether he be rich or poor. Saying that he needs a safe place to spend the night with his gold on his person, the sailor requests permission to sleep that night at her house. This she grants. As he drops off to sleep she remarks on how this rich man resembles her own poor husband.

III. That night, desperate to get money to get her husband out of debt, the wife takes a hammer and kills the poor sailor, really her husband, as he sleeps unrecognized in his own house.

**Peace Day**
See *Friedenstag*

**Pearl Fishers, The**
See *Pêcheurs de Perles, Les*

**Pearl of Brazil, The**
See *Perle du Brésil, La*

**Pêcheurs de Perles, Les**     *Tragedy in 3 acts*
(*The Pearl Fishers*)       Paris, 30 September 1863
COMP.: G. Bizet         Covent Garden, 1887
LIBR.: Cormon and Carré    Philadelphia, 1893
                       Metropolitan (2 acts only), 1896

CAST

| | | | | |
|---|---|---|---|---|
| Leïla, *priestess of Brahma* | S | Zurga, *king of the fishermen* | | Bar |
| Nadir, *fisherman* | T | Nourabad, *high priest of Brahma* | | B |

SYNOPSIS

I. Nadir and Zurga, who once had been rivals for the hand of Leïla, have sworn eternal friendship. There is an invisible goddess who has been protecting the fishermen at sea. It turns out that Leïla is this person. Nadir recognizes her and tells her privately of his continuing love.

II. As they had sworn their friendship, she has vowed to remain alone as protectress of the fishermen. Love, however, overwhelms her reservation so that Nourabad is able to surprise and trap her together with Nadir. Thus the fishermen are imperilled without their protectress. Zurga swears vengeance for all and for himself.

III. At the last moment, however, Zurga saves them from the death Nourabad had intended for them. While they escape, Nourabad makes sure that Zurga is stabbed to death.

### Peer Gynt
COMP.: W. Egk        Berlin, 24 November 1938
LIBR.: By the composer
From Ibsen's play

### Pelléas et Mélisande
COMP.: C. Debussy
LIBR.: M. Maeterlinck
From Maeterlinck's play

*Tragedy in 5 acts*
Comique, 30 April 1902
New York, 1908
Covent Garden, 1909
Metropolitan, 1925

CAST

| | | | | |
|---|---|---|---|---|
| Arkel, *king of Allemonde* | B | Golaud, *Arkel's grandson* | | Bar |
| Geneviève, *mother of Pelléas* | | Mélisande | | S |
| *and Golaud* | C | Yniold, *Golaud's son* | | S |
| Pelléas, *Arkel's grandson* | T | Physician | | B |

SYNOPSIS

I. Golaud brings to his grandfather's castle a strange, mysterious and beautiful girl, Mélisande. In this gloomy place she meets Pelléas.

II. They walk together secretly in the groves, slowly falling in love. In a fountain near a pool she lost her ring. Golaud sends her back there to find it.

III. Pelléas must leave. Tender with love is their leave-taking until Golaud interrupts. Full of suspicion he searches for some hint of intrigue in their glances.

IV. He is tormented by his suspicions. Finding them together saying goodbye, he slays Pelléas.

V. Later Mélisande dies with Golaud weeping beside her, haunted without any proof of his suspicions.

### Pénélope
COMP.: G. Fauré
LIBR.: R. Fauchois

*3 acts*
Monte Carlo, 4 March 1913
Antwerp, 1924

### Pepita Jiménez
COMP.: I. Albéniz
LIBR.: F. Money-Coutts
From a story by Valera

*1 act, 2 scenes*
Barcelona, 5 January 1896
Prague, 1897
Comique, 1923

**Pepys, Samuel**
See *Samuel Pepys*

**Perfect Fool, The**  1 *act*
COMP.: G. Holst   Covent Garden, 14 May 1923
LIBR.: By the composer

**Périchole, La**  2 *acts*
COMP.: J. Offenbach   Paris, 6 October 1868
LIBR.: Meilhac and Halévy   New York, 1869
   London, 1870
There was a production of *Périchole* in New York, 1887, in Yiddish.

**Perle du Brésil, La**  3 *acts*
(*The Pearl of Brazil*)   Paris, 22 November 1851
COMP.: F. David   Brussels, 1852
LIBR.: Gabriel and St. Étienne   Rouen, 1889

**Peter Grimes**  *Tragedy in Prologue, 3 acts, and Epilogue*
COMP.: B. Britten   Sadlers Wells, 7 June 1945
LIBR.: M. Slater   Berkshire Festival, Mass., 1946
From the poem *The Borough* by   Metropolitan, 1948
George Crabbe

CAST

| | | | |
|---|---|---|---|
| Peter Grimes, *fisherman* | T | Swallow, *lawyer* | B |
| John, *his apprentice* | Mute | Mrs. Sedley | MS |
| Ellen Orford, *widow, schoolmistress* | S | Rev. Horace Adams, *rector* | T |
| Captain Balstrode, *retired skipper* | Bar | Ned Keene, *apothecary and quack* | Bar |
| Auntie, *tavernkeeper* | C | Dr. Thorp | Mute |
| Two Nieces, *main attractions* | | Hobson, *carrier* | B |
| at the tavern | S | Townspeople, Fisherfolk | |
| Bob Boles, *fisherman, Methodist* | T | | |

SYNOPSIS

There is an inquest into the cause of the death at sea of Peter Grimes' apprentice. Although the townspeople are convinced that Peter Grimes is guilty, the court acquits him.

I. Now the fisherman needs a new apprentice. With the reputation so vividly described in the prologue, he seems hard put to keep one, but Ellen Orford offers to help by taking care of the new boy. A storm is raging as the new boy is brought to Peter, who takes him home.

II. On Sunday, for others a day of rest, Grimes puts his new apprentice to his first day's work. The congregation at church, stirred to action by the inflammatory speeches of Bob Boles, go in a body to Peter's hut to see for themselves what is going on there. Grimes tells the boy to hide, but in hiding the lad falls off the cliff upon the rocks and dies.

III. The enraged people, extremely suspicious at finding neither the boy nor his harsh master there, find the boy's shirt in the water. Captain Balstrode and Ellen, his only defenders, finally convince Peter to quiet the town by sinking his boat in the sea. Next morning someone sights the overturned craft drifting in the waves, but nobody cares much about it any more.

**Peter Ibbetson**
COMP.: D. Taylor
LIBR.: Taylor and Collins
From the novel by du Maurier

3 *acts*
Metropolitan, 7 February 1931

**Peter the Shipwright**
See *Zar und Zimmerman*

**Phèdre**
See *Fedra*

**Philémon et Baucis**
COMP.: C. Gounod
LIBR.: Barbier and Carré

3 *acts*
Paris, 18 February 1860
Liverpool (Amateurs), 1888
Metropolitan, 1893

**Pickwick**
COMP.: A. Coates
LIBR.: By the composer
From Dickens

3 *acts*
Covent Garden, 20 November 1936

**Pierrot and Pierette**
COMP.: J. Holbrooke
LIBR.: W. Grogan

2 *scenes*
London, 11 November 1909

**Pilgrim's Progress, The**
COMP.: R. Vaughan Williams
LIBR.: By the composer
From Bunyan's allegory

*Morality in Prologue, 4 acts and Epilogue*
Covent Garden, 26 April 1951

CAST

| | | | |
|---|---|---|---|
| John Bunyan, *writer* | BBar | Madam Wanton | S |
| Pilgrim | Bar | Madam Bubble | MS |
| Evangelist | B | Pontius Pilate | B |
| Pliable, *neighbor* | T | Usher | T |
| Obstinate, *neighbor* | B | Lord Hate-Good | B |
| Mistrust, *neighbor* | Bar | Malice | S |
| Timorous, *neighbor* | T | Pickthank | C |
| Three Shining Ones | S, MS, C | Superstition | T |
| Interpreter | T | Envy | B |
| Watchful, *porter* | Bar | Woodcutter's boy | S |
| Herald | Bar | Mr. By-Ends | T |
| Apollyon | B | Madam By-Ends | C |
| Two Heavenly Beings | S, C | Three Shepherds | T, Bar, B |
| Lord Lechery | T | Voice of a bird | S |
| Jester | dancer | Celestial Messenger | T |
| Demas | Bar | Men, Women, Certain Persons clothed |
| Simon Magus | B | in gold, Doleful Creatures, Traders, |
| Worldly Glory | Bar | Angels |

SYNOPSIS

Bunyan reads his story to us:

1. Pilgrim sets out to discover the secret of eternal life. Reaching the House Beautiful he lays his burden aside.

II. Traveling by way of the straight road through the Valley of Humiliation he conquers Apollyon.

III. By dint of much struggle he threads his way through Vanity Fair and resists its temptations. But Lord Hate-Good imprisons him. Using the Key of Promise he effects his escape.

IV. He approaches the Delectable Mountains. There, crossing the River of Death he finally enters the Celestial City.

Thus Bunyan has finished his tale.

## Pipe of Desire, The      I *act*
COMP.: F. Converse      Boston, 31 January 1906
LIBR.: G. Barton      Metropolitan, 1910
    The first American opera performed at the Metropolitan.

## Pique-Dame      *Tragedy in 3 acts*
(*The Queen of Spades*)      St. Petersburg, 19 December 1890
COMP.: P. Tchaikovsky      La Scala, 1906
LIBR.: M. Tchaikovsky (his brother)      Metropolitan, 1910
From Pushkin      London, 1915

CAST

| | | | |
|---|---|---|---|
| Tchekalinsky, *officer* | T | Governess | MS |
| Sourin, *officer* | B | Mascha, *Lisa's maid* | S |
| Herman, *young officer* | T | Master of Ceremonies | T |
| Count Tomsky (Plutus) | Bar | Tchaplitsky, *gambler* | T |
| Prince Yeletsky | Bar | Narumoff, *gambler* | B |
| Countess | MS | Chloë | S |
| Lisa, *her granddaughter* | S | Servants, Guests, Gamblers, Children, |
| Pauline, *Lisa's friend* (Daphnis) | C | Nurses, Governesses |

SYNOPSIS

I. Herman has fallen in love with Lisa; prince Yeletsky has become engaged to Lisa. The countess was once a very successful gambler, said to have had a magic combination. Herman, aware of this rumor, sets out to discover its secret. Also secretly he visits Lisa to declare his love.

II. At a ball, after a masque of Daphnis and Chloë, Lisa gives her lover a key with which he may visit her. On the way there he hides in the countess' room and surprises her with a pistol, threatening to shoot her if she will not tell him her gambling secret. The countess faints away and dies.

III. Her ghost pays Herman a visit and tells him the secret, naming three cards by which he may win, on condition that he marry Lisa.

He goes to Lisa, but his desire to gamble is too strong to be delayed. When she hears of his complicity in the death of the countess, and sees his thirst to gamble, Lisa throws herself in despair into the canal and drowns. Herman gambles everything on the three fateful cards. By accident he turns up the Queen of Spades and sees in it the face of the ghost. At the sight he stabs himself to death.

## Pirata, Il      2 *acts*
(*The Pirate*)      La Scala, 27 October 1827
COMP.: V. Bellini      London, 1830
LIBR.: F. Romani      New York, 1832

**Poacher, The**
See *Wildschütz, Der*

**Poia**
COMP.: E. Nevin
LIBR.: R. Hartley
From legend

3 *acts*
Pittsburgh, Pa. (Concert), January 1907
Berlin, 23 April 1910

**Poirier de Misère, Le**
COMP.: M. Delannoy
LIBR.: Limozin and de la Tourrasse

3 *acts*
Comique, 21 February 1927

**Poisoned Kiss, The**
COMP.: R. Vaughan Williams
LIBR.: E. Sharpe
From stories by Garnett and
Hawthorne

*Romantic Extravaganza in 3 acts*
Cambridge, 12 May 1936
Sadlers Wells, 1936
New York, 1937

CAST

| | | | |
|---|---|---|---|
| Dipsacus, *magician* | B | Three Mediums, *assistants to the* | |
| Tormentilla, *his daughter* | S | *empress* | |
| Angelica, *her maid* | S | Empress Persicaria | C |
| Amaryllus, *the Empress' son* | T | Hob, *assistant to Dipsacus* | |
| Gallanthus, *his jester* | Bar | Gob, *assistant to Dipsacus* | |
| | | Lob, *assistant to Dipsacus* | |

SYNOPSIS

I. Tormentilla, who has been reared from birth on various poisons, does not understand when her new acquaintance Amaryllus kills a snake, her pet, in the woods. She was brought up in this virulent manner by Dipsacus to win revenge for him by poisoning with a kiss the son of the Empress, who had once refused Dipsacus. Tormentilla abhors the idea of being a murder-tool. Her father therefore banishes her.

II. The empress, on the other hand, protects herself from the loss of her son's affections by poisoning any girls who get too near. Of course, Tormentilla is immune to this. But the assistants of Dipsacus, Hob, Gob, and Lob, have more success. They bring the two young people together and the poisoned lips seem to do their job well.

III. But he isn't dead, the Empress has stuffed him with antidotes since birth. Nor is he completely cured, however, until Tormentilla can be present to cheer him. When Dipsacus comes to boast to the empress that he has won revenge, his boasting dwindles and they, the parents, fall in love all over again. Marriages are subsequently arranged for all.

**Polish Jew, The**
See *Juif Polonais, Le*

**Polly**
COMP.: J. Pepusch and Arnold
LIBR.: J. Gay

*Ballad Opera in 3 acts*
London, 19 June 1777
New York, 1925

Called *An Opera, being the Second Part of the Beggar's Opera*, this second product of the collaboration of Pepusch and Gay was composed in 1729 but forbidden performance until certain alterations had been made in 1777. Even then, being less a spontaneous creation than an attempt to ride the ragged coattails of the *Beggar*, it did not have notable success.

**Pomone**  *Prologue and 5 acts*
COMP.: R. Cambert   Opéra, 3 March 1671
LIBR.: P. Perrin   London, 1674
   This, the first French opera, was the first presented at the Académie Royal de Musique.

**Poor Sailor, The**
See *Pauvre Matelot, Le*

**Porgy and Bess**  *Tragedy in 3 acts*
COMP.: G. Gershwin   Boston, 30 September 1935
LIBR.: I. Gershwin and DuBose Heyward   Zürich, 1945
From a play by DuBose Heyward   Copenhagen, 1946

CAST

| | | | |
|---|---|---|---|
| Porgy, *cripple* | BBar | Annie | MS |
| Bess, *Crown's girl* | S | Lily, *strawberry woman* | MS |
| Crown, *stevedore* | Bar | Jim, *cottonpicker* | Bar |
| Serena, *Robbins' wife* | S | Undertaker | Bar |
| Clara, *Jake's wife* | S | Nelson | T |
| Maria, *cookshopkeeper* | C | Crab Man | T |
| Jake, *fisherman* | Bar | Mr. Archdale, *white man* | Spkr |
| Sportin' Life, *dope peddler* | T | Detective, *white man* | Spkr |
| Mingo | T | Policeman, *white man* | Spkr |
| Robbins | T | Coroner, *white man* | Spkr |
| Peter, *the honeyman* | T | Scipio, *small boy* | Spkr |
| Frazier, *"lawyer"* | Bar | | |

MUSICAL HIGHLIGHTS

ACT I. Lullaby *Summertime*, Clara and Chorus
   Burial Scene *My man's gone now*, Serena and Chorus
ACT II. Song *O I got plenty o' nuttin*, Porgy
   Duet *Bess, you is my woman now*, Porgy and Bess
   Sermon *It ain't necessarily so*, Sportin' Life and Chorus
   Song *A red headed woman*, Crown
ACT III. Song *There's a boat that's leaving soon for New York*, Sportin' Life
   Finale *O Lord, I'm on my way*, Porgy and Chorus

SYNOPSIS

   I. Catfish row, Charleston, South Carolina. Porgy gets around by means of a little cart, a lonely man. He likes Bess, but she's Crown's girl. During a crap game one night there is an altercation in which Crown kills Robbins with his bale hook. Crown has to leave. He tells Bess to take care of herself, but to remember he'll be back to renew his claim on her when the search dies down. But nobody will take her in after he goes, except Porgy. At the burial, during which everybody puts what coins he can spare into a plate to help pay the cost of the service, the police interrupt to find out who the murderer may be. Since no one says a word, the police haul away Peter as an example of their intentions.

   II. Porgy is happy now; Bess stays with him. Sportin' Life can't entice her away—not from Porgy, who is the first person who ever treated her with tenderness. Everybody's going to a picnic on Kittiwah Island. Bess wants to go, but of course she hates to leave Porgy behind. Porgy makes her go along, however, rather than let her feel left out of things.

At the picnic Crown appears, snatches Bess away from the returning people and forces her to stay with him in hiding. Two days later she returns to Porgy, sick and broken-hearted. She's afraid of Crown, but she loves Porgy and he loves her.

There is a terrible hurricane sweeping in from the sea. Jake and his men are out fishing when it hits. Crown comes out of hiding, boasting that he is the only one there man enough to go out and fight the Lord to save Jake.

III. That night, in the quiet after the storm, Crown struggles back to Catfish row, weary and nearly drowned. As he passes by Porgy's door, the crippled man's strong arm reaches out and stabs the stevedore to death. Again the police come; this time everybody swears that Crown was the murderer they were after before, but nobody knows who murdered him. In the turmoil Sportin' Life has finally won Bess over to the temptations of New York, and of dope. She has left her man. Porgy, unconcerned that New York is a great distance away, starts pushing his little cart to follow her and bring her back home.

NOTES

There are many American operas, written and not yet written, that may claim a deeper musical conception, but *Porgy and Bess* remains the most brilliant and deeply moving operatic work in its field. The music is not really Negro, but it sounds Negro. The songs are not really folk music, but they have that same quality of unquestionable accuracy that folk music is supposed to have. The rhythmic texture throughout the work is commonly called jazz, and yet actually it is Gershwin rhythm, Gershwin texture which has influenced jazz composition so strongly that the two are hard to distinguish. Although the two works are hardly comparable in other ways, both *Porgy* and *Boris Godunov* celebrate the people in magnificent choral scenes which make action move in the play.

There are one or two interesting stories about productions of *Porgy* which are worth retelling here. One concerns the opening in Boston. There was, the story goes, a res-taurateur whose business near the theater where rehearsals were in progress was about to fold up for lack of trade. When *Porgy* opened, business picked up. *Porgy* stayed so long that business mounted to the point where the man could open a branch restaurant, then another, and another, and so on. *Porgy* later moved, but the restaurateur was able with such a boost to develop a nationwide chain of roadside restaurants with business in the millions of dollars.

The second story was heard by this author in conversation with some of the cast who had recently returned from a triumphal tour of Europe and Asia (which began, incidentally, against the judgment of the State Department which thought the play might harm foreign relations). The troupe had found it difficult to work with the musicians who made up the various orchestras in Europe. The musicians did not seem to feel free with the jazz rhythms, and the improvisatory quality of the score. Someone thought of the ideal remedy. Some members of the cast could play instruments. It was decided that during certain scenes, notably the picnic, these actors would produce their horns from under their jackets and improvise in jazz fashion while the orchestra and chorus went through the scene. However, the effect, at least to one well versed in jazz, was not entirely desirable.

**Portrait de Manon, Le**           I *act*
COMP.: J. Massenet           Comique, 8 May 1894
LIBR.: G. Boyer           New York, 1897

A sequel to *Manon* in which des Grieux, now old, sees a girl in New Orleans who bears a remarkable resemblance to the portrait of Manon, who was the girl's mother.

## Postillon de Longjumeau, Le

COMP.: A. Adam
LIBR.: Brunswick and de Leuven

*Comedy in 3 acts*
Comique, 13 October 1836
London, 1837
New York, 1840

CAST

| | | | |
|---|---|---|---|
| Madeleine, *Chappelou's wife* | S | Marquis de Corcy, *chief of the Opéra* | T |
| Rose | S | Bijou, *Chappelou's friend* | Bar |
| Chappelou, *postillion* | T | Bourdon | B |

SYNOPSIS

I. Unfortunately Chappelou made the mistake of singing at his own wedding. His voice was heard by the Marquis, who happened to be passing by at that moment, causing this impresario to hire Chappelou on the spot and demand that he leave his new wife immediately and join the Opéra.

II. Ten years later the faithful Madeleine, who has inherited a fortune, travels to Paris to find her husband. As a rich but unknown lady, she entraps him into a love affair and marriage without his once catching on.

III. The Marquis, who also has conceived a passion for the rich lady, has Chappelou arrested as a bigamist. But at that juncture Madeleine reveals her identity and saves the day.

## Power of Evil, The

COMP.: A. Serov
Serov died before finishing this opera. It was completed by N. T. Solovyev.

*5 acts*
St. Petersburg, 1 May 1871

## Pré aux Clercs, Le

COMP.: L. Hérold
LIBR.: F. de Planard

*3 acts*
Comique, 15 December 1832
London, 1833
New York, 1843

## Prigioniero, Il

COMP.: L. Dallapiccola

Florence, 20 May 1950
New York (Juilliard), 1951
New York City Opera, 1960

## Prince Igor

COMP.: A. Borodin
LIBR.: By the composer
From a medieval Russian chronicle,
Arranged by Stassov.

*Tragedy in Prologue and 4 acts*
St. Petersburg, 4 November 1890
Drury Lane, 1914
Metropolitan, 1915

CAST

| | | | |
|---|---|---|---|
| Igor Sviatoslavovitch, *Prince* | Bar | Skoula, *gudok player* | B |
| Yaroslavna, *his wife* | S | Eroshka, *gudok player* | T |
| Vladimir Igorevitch, *his son* | T | Yaroslavna's Nurse | S |
| Vladimir Galitsky, | | Maiden, *Polovtsian* | S |
| *Yaroslavna's brother* | B | Princes and Princesses, Boyars and | |
| Kontchak, *Polovtsian Khan* | B | their wives, Old Men, Warriors, | |
| Gzak, *Polovtsian Khan* | B | Young Women, People, Polovtsian | |
| Kontchakovna, *Kontchak's daughter* | MS | Chiefs, Slaves, Prisoners, Soldiers. | |
| Ovlour, *Polovtsian* | T | | |

## SYNOPSIS

PROLOGUE. In medieval Russia, Prince Igor departs with his army to pursue the Polovtsi (Mongols).

I. Galitsky has been left in charge of things at home, but Yaroslavna keeps him under control, thus winning the goodwill of the people. News comes that the prince has been defeated and is taken prisoner.

II. The Khan promises Igor his freedom if the prince will give his word not to make war on the Polovtsi again. This Igor refuses, knowing it is impossible.

III. The other prisoners urge Igor to escape, even though it is against his pledge. Vladimir tries to go with him, but because his love for Kontchakovna delays him he is caught.

IV. Igor returns to his home and to Yaroslavna, giving Russia again the hope of winning against the Mongols.

**Prodaná Nevěsta**
( *The Bartered Bride* )
COMP.: B. Smetana
LIBR.: K. Sabina

*Comedy in 3 acts*
Prague, 30 May 1866
Chicago, 1893
Drury Lane, 1895
Metropolitan, 1909

### CAST

| | | | |
|---|---|---|---|
| Kruschina, *peasant* | Bar | Jenik, *Micha's first wife's son* | T |
| Katinka, *his wife* | S | Kecal, *marriage broker* | B |
| Marenka, *his daughter* | S | Springer, *manager of actors* | T |
| Micha, *landlord* | B | Esmeralda, *dancer* | S |
| Agnes, *his wife* | MS | Muff, *comedian* | T |
| Vasek, *his son* | T | Clowns, Dancers | |

### SYNOPSIS

I. Marenka loves Jenik, but her parents have promised her instead to Micha's son. To prevent their going through with the formalities, she tells them that she and Jenik are engaged.

II. The timid Vasek goes to woo Marenka under his parents' orders, but she shunts him off to another girl. Kecal tries to bargain with Jenik to get him to relinquish his claim, which Jenik finally does but only in favor of Micha's eldest son. Only he knows that the eldest son is himself.

III. Marenka, of course, is hurt and furious to discover that her affections have been sold for money. But when the strangely worded contract is publicly announced Micha recognizes Jenik and acknowledges him as the eldest.

**Prodigal Son, The**
Three works have appeared under this name as follows:
by A. Ponchielli, Milan, 1880
by F. Jacobi, (1944)
by G. Malipiero, Florence, 1957

**Prométhée**
( *Prometheus* )
COMP.: G. Fauré
LIBR.: Lorrain and Hérold

*Lyric Tragedy in 3 acts*
Béziers, France, 27 August 1900
Paris, 1907

**Prophète, Le**
COMP.: G. Meyerbeer
LIBR.: A. E. Scribe

*Tragedy in 5 acts*
Opéra, 16 April, 1849
Covent Garden, 1849
New Orleans, 1850
Metropolitan, 1884

CAST

| | | | |
|---|---|---|---|
| John of Leyden | T | Zacharias, *Anabaptist* | B |
| Fides, *his mother* | MS | Count Oberthal | Bar |
| Bertha, *his bride* | S | Nobles, Citizens, Anabaptists, Peasants, | |
| Jonas, *Anabaptist* | T | Soldiers, Prisoners, Children | |
| Matthisen, *Anabaptist* | B | | |

SYNOPSIS

I. Oberthal, coming across three Anabaptists, orders them beaten by his soldiers. Seeing Bertha, who is betrothed to John, the count has her sent to his castle for his own pleasure.

II. She escapes, but John, in order to save his mother's life, turns Bertha back to Oberthal. With mounting hatred, the Anabaptists urge John to join their cause and to fight this oppressor.

III. John is proclaimed prophet. Leading a siege of Münster he captures the Count.

IV. To prevent his identification, the Anabaptists have spread the rumor that John of Leyden was killed by the prophet, but when his coronation as emperor takes place, Fides cries out that he is her son. By a ruse he makes her deny the fact.

V. Bertha, unaware of the masquerade, plots to blow up the castle he now occupies. The Anabaptists have revolted from him; thus she learns that the prophet is indeed John. Powerless to prevent the explosion she herself planted, she kills herself. John, so that they may all die at once, gathers all his enemies together in the banquet room in time for the catastrophe.

NOTES

Meyerbeer worked thirteen years on this megalithic tragedy. For his story he used the true history of Jan Beukelszoon.

**Protagonist, Der**
COMP.: K. Weill
LIBR.: G. Kaiser

I *act*
Dresden, 27 March 1926
Berlin, 1928

**Prozess, Der**
(*The Trial*)
Comp.: G. von Einem
Libr.: Blacher and von Cramer
From Kafka's novel

2 *acts*, 9 *scenes*
17 August 1953

CAST

| | | | |
|---|---|---|---|
| Josef K. | T | Franz | B |
| Student | T | Thrasher | B |
| Lawyer | Bar | Court Attendant | B |
| Titorelli | T | Manufacturer | Bar |
| Examining Judge | Bar | Director/Representative | B |
| Overseer | Bar | Government Director | B |
| Albert K. | B | Passer-by | Bar |
| Willem | Bar | Youth | T |

| Three Young People | T, Bar, B | Frau Grubach | MS |
| Fräulein Bürstner | S | An Obsequious Girl | S |
| Wife of the Court Attendant | S | Mute Crowds, Soldiers, Maidens. | |
| Leni | S | | |

**Pskovityanka** · *Tragedy in 4 acts*

(*The Maid of Pskov*) · St. Petersburg, 13 January 1873

COMP.: N. Rimsky-Korsakov · Paris, 1909

LIBR.: By the composer · Drury Lane, 1913

From a play by Mei

CAST

| Tsar Ivan the Terrible | B | Princess Olga Yourievna Tokmakova | S |
| Prince Youry Ivanovitch Tokmakov, | | Boyardin Stepanida Matuta, | |
| *mayor of Pskov* | B | *her friend* | S |
| Boyard Nikita Matuta | T | Vlassievna, *nurse* | C |
| Prince Afanasy Viazemsky | T | Perfilievna, *nurse* | MS |
| Bomely | B | Sentry | T |
| Michael Andreievitch Tutcha | T | Officers, Judges, Boyars, Burgher's Sons | |
| Youshko Velebin, *messenger* | B | Bodyguards, Pages, Archers, Maidens, | |
| | | Boys, People, Huntsmen | |

SYNOPSIS

I. Ivan the Terrible approaches Pskov to deal punishment to the town. Tokmakov argues that the people should meet him humbly, but Michael goes out to offer a fight.

II. Ivan arrives. Meeting Olga he inquires her identity and learns that she is of an unknown father. This news moves him so deeply that he grants Pskov a reprieve from punishment, because he is her father.

III. Matuta brings Olga to the Tsar as a kind of offering. The Tsar throws him out, but keeps Olga there to tell her that he, Ivan, is her real father. At that moment Michael makes his attack. As her lover approaches the tent to kill Ivan, Olga rushes out to stop him. The bullet meant for Michael kills her instead.

**Puritani, I** · *3 acts*

(*The Puritans*) · Paris, 25 January 1835

COMP.: V. Bellini · London, 1835

LIBR.: Count Pepoli · Philadelphia, 1843

From a play by Ancelot and Saintine · Metropolitan, 1883

CAST

| Lord Gaultiers Walton, *Puritan* | B | Sir Benno Robertson, *Puritan* | T |
| Sir George Walton, his brother, | | Henrietta, *widow of Charles I* | |
| *Puritan* (Giorgio) | B | *of France* (Enrichetta) | S |
| Lord Arthur Talbot, *Cavalier* | | Elvira, *Lord Walton's daughter* | S |
| (Arturo) | T | Puritans, Soldiers of the Commonwealth, | |
| Sir Richard Forth, *Puritan* | | Men-at-Arms, Women, Pages | |
| (Riccardo) | Bar | | |

SYNOPSIS

I. Elvira prepares for her marriage to Arthur with, in spite of the partisan warfare between Puritans and Cavaliers, her father's permission. Arthur, in an attempt to save

Henrietta, who has been sentenced to death, conducts her away in Elvira's bridal gown. When this deed is discovered, Elvira goes mad, thinking her lover unfaithful.

II. To avenge her madness, Richard and George prepare to meet Arthur in battle.

III. Arthur pays Elvira a visit in secret, but this fails to relieve her insanity. The Puritans capture him and are about to kill him when news comes that the war has been settled. Elvira revives and happily accepts her lover again.

**Quattro Rusteghi, I**
(*The Four Rustics*)
COMP.: E. Wolf-Ferrari
LIBR.: G. Pizzola
From a comedy by Goldoni

*Comedy in 3 acts*
Munich, 19 March 1906
Milan, 1914
London, 1946
New York, 1951

CAST

| | | | |
|---|---|---|---|
| Lunardo, *Mr. Crusty, Venetian merchant* | B | Simon, *Mr. Gruff, her husband* | BBar |
| Margarita, *Margery, his second wife* | MS | Canciano, *Sir James Pinchbeck, wealthy merchant* | B |
| Lucieta, *Lucinda, his daughter by his first wife* | S | Felice, *Felicia, his wife* | S |
| Maurizio, *Mr. Hardstone, merchant* | BBar | Count Riccardo Arcolai, *visitor to Venice* | T |
| Filipeto, *Peter, his son* | T | Young Maid | |
| Marina, *Maria, his aunt* | S | | |

SYNOPSIS

I. Without a thought of consulting the pair who have not even met, the two fathers arrange a marriage between Lucieta and Filipeto, paying great attention to detail.

II. The bridegroom, who insists upon seeing his bride before he becomes attached for life, disguises himself as a girl to effect, with Riccardo's help, a meeting. When this insubordination comes to the attention of Canciano and Lunardo, their anger puts a stop to the wedding preparations.

III. The indomitable Felice upbraids the fathers for such high-handed conduct and proves to them that it can be a good thing if the young couple take a liking to each other, as they have. Thus all ends happily.

**Queen of Cornwall, The**
COMP.: R. Boughton
LIBR.: T. Hardy
From a play by Hardy

*2 acts*
Glastonbury, 21 August 1924
Liverpool, 1927

**Queen of Sheba, The**
See *Königin von Saba, Die*
See also *Reine de Saba, La*

**Queen of Spades, The**
See *Pique-Dame*

**Rake's Progress, The**
COMP.: I. Stravinsky
LIBR.: W. H. Auden and C. Kallman

*Tragedy in 3 acts and Epilogue*
Venice, 11 September 1951
Edinburgh, 1953
Metropolitan, 1953

CAST

| | | | |
|---|---|---|---|
| Truelove | B | Baba the Turk, *a bearded lady* | MS |
| Anne, *his daughter* | S | Sellem, *auctioneer* | T |
| Tom Rakewell | T | Keeper of the madhouse | B |
| Nick Shadow | Bar | Whores and Roaring Boys, Servants, | |
| Mother Goose, *proprietress of a* | | Citizens, Madmen | |
| *brothel* | MS | | |

SYNOPSIS

I. Nick, appearing just after the good Tom has professed his love for (1) Anne, and (2) idleness, takes the innocent in hand and leads him into the hell of London. There he is snatched up into the whirl of the world of Mother Goose. Anne, left lamenting at home, decides to go find him.

II. Tom, in spite of all the pleasures of vice, becomes unhappy. Nick prescribes marriage as a cure, suggesting the bearded Baba. Tom agrees. After the wedding Tom catches a brief glimpse of Anne who urges him to return to her; London is no place for him. But, being married, he is no longer free. Soon the marriage begins to pall on him. Baba's incessant chatter having ground away his patience, he wishes for release. Nick, ever resourceful, provides him with a machine which will make bread from stones, or so he convinces Tom.

III. Tom, still unhappy, challenges Nick to a game of cards to win back his soul. He wins, but Nick curses him with insanity. The next we see of poor Tom he is an idiot in Bedlam. There Anne goes to find him. Taking his sick head in her arms she sings him to soothing sleep and leaves him dying.

**Rape of Lucretia, The**
COMP.: B. Britten
LIBR.: R. Duncan
From the play by Obey

*Tragedy in 2 acts*
Glyndebourne, 12 July 1946
Basle, 1947
New York, 1949

CAST

| | | | |
|---|---|---|---|
| Male Chorus | T | Lucia, *her attendant* | S |
| Female Chorus | S | Bianca, *her nurse* | C |
| Lucretia | C | Tarquinius, *prince of Rome* | Bar |
| Collatinus, *her husband* | B | Junius, *general* | Bar |

SYNOPSIS

I. Tarquinius the arrogant rules Rome. One evening during a lull in battle away from the city the soldiers wonder what their wives may be doing at home. Each is unsure whether his own wife is more trustworthy than any other's, but Collatinus has faith in his Lucretia's chastity. By this Tarquinius' lust is aroused. He resolves, secretly, to make Collatinus a cuckold with the rest.

At home all is quiet as Lucretia and her girls prepare for the night's sleep. In the streets one may hear the approaching hoofbeats of the horse bearing her betrayer.

II. Tarquinius attacks Lucretia in her bed. Next morning she sends urgently for Collatinus. When he arrives she greets her husband in robes of mourning. Unable to bear her guilt she stabs herself and falls into his arms.

**Rappresentazione dell' Anima e del Corpo, Il.**
COMP.: E. de'Cavalieri                    Rome, 1600

A morality play set to simple music, with hymns between the episodes and stage directions in the score. This work, not quite an opera, immediately preceded the first actual operas.

**Raymond**
3 *acts*
COMP.: A. Thomas
Comique, 5 June 1851
LIBR.: de Leuven and Rosier
Vienna, 1857
Prague, 1862

**Regina**
*Prologue and* 3 *acts*
COMP.: M. Blitzstein
New York, 31 October 1949
LIBR.: By the composer
From the play *The Little Foxes*, by Lillian Hellman

**Reine de Saba, La**
4 *acts*
COMP.: C. Gounod
Opéra, 28 February 1862
LIBR.: Barbier and Carré
New Orleans, 1889
London, 1865

**Reine de Saba, La**
See also *Königin von Saba, Die*

**Resurrection**
See *Risurrezione*

**Retablo de Maese Pedro, El**
1 *act*
(*Master Peter's Puppet Show*)
Sevilla, 23 March 1923
COMP.: M. de Falla
New York, 1925
LIBR.: By the composer
London, 1928
From an episode in *Don Quixote* by Cervantes

**Return of Ulysses, The**
See *Ritorno d'Ulisse in Patria, Il*

**Rêve, Le**
4 *acts*
(*The Dream*)
Comique, 18 June 1891
COMP.: A. Bruneau
Covent Garden, 1891
LIBR.: L. Gallet
Königsberg, 1892
From Emile Zola

**Rheingold, Das**
*Prologue to Der Ring des Nibelungen,* 4 *scenes*
COMP.: R. Wagner
Munich, 22 September 1869
LIBR.: By the composer
London, 1882
Metropolitan, 1889

CAST

| | | | |
|---|---|---|---|
| Wotan, *chief of the gods* | BBar | Mime, *Nibelung dwarf* | T |
| Donner | BBar | Fricka, *goddess* | MS |
| Froh | T | Freia, *goddess of youth* | S |
| Loge | T | Erda, *goddess* | MS |
| Fasolt, *a giant* | BBar | Woglinde, *daughter of the Rhine* | S |
| Fafner, *a giant* | B | Wellgunde, *daughter of the Rhine* | S |
| Alberich, *Nibelung dwarf* | BBar | Flosshilde, *daughter of the Rhine* | MS |

I. Alberich watches bitterly as the beautiful Rhine Maidens swim. Suddenly he sees their hidden gold that cannot be stolen except by him who renounces love. Quickly making his decision, Alberich makes the renunciation and rushes off with his prize.

II. The giants have built Valhalla for the abode of the gods. In payment they demand Freia from Wotan, but the god is unwilling to keep his promise. Loge describes to them the ring that he knows Alberich has made from the Rhine gold. They propose that Wotan should get them that magic ring as ransom for the goddess.

III. Alberich has made more than the ring, however. He has also fashioned a magic helmet, the Tarnhelm, which will render its wearer invisible to others, or provide him another shape. Loge, who came with Wotan to negotiate with the dwarf, tricks him into assuming the shape of a toad. While Alberich is in that small condition, Loge snatches away the Tarnhelm, binds up the toad and takes him up to the outside world.

IV. There they carry on their negotiations with more with which to bargain. Alberich agrees to give them the Rhine gold and the ring he made from it to win his freedom. With the ransom, however, goes his curse. With the gold, the Tarnhelm and finally the ring, Wotan saves Freia from the giants. But the giants, heir now to the curse of Alberich, fall to fighting immediately, and Fasolt is slain. In vain do the Rhine Maidens cry to have their ring as Wotan and the gods ascend a rainbow bridge toward Valhalla.

**Richard Coeur de Lion**
(*Richard the Lion-Hearted*)
COMP.: A. Grétry
LIBR.: J. Sedaine

3 *acts*
Paris, 21 October 1784
London, 1786
Boston, 1797

**Riders to the Sea**
COMP.: R. Vaughan Williams
LIBR.: J. M. Synge
From the play by Synge

1 *act*
London, 1 December 1937
Cambridge, Mass. 1938

**Rienzi**
COMP.: R. Wagner
LIBR.: By the composer
From the novel by Bulwer-Lytton

5 *acts*
Dresden, 20 October 1842
New York, 1878
London, 1879
Metropolitan, 1886

CAST

| | | | |
|---|---|---|---|
| Cola Rienzi, *Roman tribune* | T | Baroncelli, *Roman citizen* | T |
| Irene, *his sister* | S | Cecco del Vecchia, *Roman citizen* | B |
| Steffano Colonna | B | Messenger of Peace | S |
| Adriano, *his son* | MS | Ambassadors, Nobles, Priests, Monks, | |
| Paolo Orsini | B | Soldiers, Messengers, People | |
| Raimondo, *Papal Legate* | B | | |

SYNOPSIS

Colonna fights to protect Irene from abduction by Orsini. In the battle Rienzi becomes enraged and urges the people to revolt against the nobles. His revolution succeeds, but the nobles lay a plot to kill him.

When the people hear that their new leader plans to enter a league with Germany they turn against him. The church excommunicates him, and finally he is burned to death in the flames of the capitol.

# Rigoletto

COMP.: G. Verdi
LIBR.: F. Piave
From Victor Hugo's play
*Le Roi s'Amuse*

*Tragedy in 3 acts*
Venice, 11 March 1851
Covent Garden, 1853
New York, 1857

## CAST

| | | | |
|---|---|---|---|
| Duke of Mantua | T | Cavaliere Marullo, *courtier* | Bar |
| Rigoletto, *his jester* | Bar | Countess Ceprano | MS |
| Count Ceprano | Bar | Gilda, *Rigoletto's daughter* | S |
| Count Monterone | B | Giovanna, *her duenna* | MS |
| Sparafucile, *an assassin by profession* | B | Maddalena, *Sparafucile's sister* | C |
| Matteo Borsa, *courtier* | T | Courtiers, Nobles, Pages, Servants | |

## MUSICAL HIGHLIGHTS

ACT I. Aria *Questa o quella* (This or that one), Duke
Soliloquy *Pari siamo* (How alike we are), Rigoletto
Aria *Caro nome* (Dearest name), Gilda
ACT II. Duet *Piangi, fanciulla* (Weep my dearest), Rigoletto and Gilda
ACT III. Aria *La donna è mobile* (A woman is changeable), Duke
Quartet *Bella figlia dell'amore* (Fairest daughter of the graces), Maddalena, Gilda, Duke, Rigoletto

## SYNOPSIS

I. The Duke is intrigued by the memory of an unknown girl he has seen. But meanwhile, making hay while the sun shines, he woos the Countess Ceprano who is among the guests at his ball. Rigoletto tortures the Count about his wife's infidelity. At this the Count decides to be repaid for such damage by means of the girl he believes is the jester's mistress. Suddenly old Count Monterone breaks into the party to denounce the Duke for dishonoring his daughter. Rigoletto mocks the old man. Monterone curses the jester with a father's curse, leaving Rigoletto visibly shaken.

In disguise, the Duke meets Gilda in her garden and pledges his love. Then Ceprano and his friends, using Rigoletto as their unsuspecting dupe, kidnap the girl who is really the jester's daughter although they think she is his mistress. When they are gone Rigoletto realizes the validity of Monterone's curse.

II. Rigoletto finds Gilda in the Duke's palace, where she was taken. Together they weep.

III. He hires Sparafucile to kill the Duke. Maddalena will be bait for the trap. She lures him, but she begins to fall in love with him herself. At the assassin's place she urges Sparafucile to murder someone else, to let the Duke go free. Finally it is agreed that the next man who enters the door will be the victim. It is Gilda who enters, in man's clothes in order to escape from Mantua in secret. The murderers kill her and stuff her body into a sack which they give to Rigoletto as evidence of having done what he paid them for. While the fool hauls the sack toward the river to get rid of it, he hears the Duke singing in the night. Tearing open the sack he finds his own daughter, still breathing, but dying in fulfillment of the old count's curse.

## NOTES

*Rigoletto* is said to have been written in forty days. The censors made it necessary for the locale to be shifted from France to avoid political complications. The play itself had been banned in 1832 as immoral.

**Rinaldo**
COMP.: G. F. Handel
LIBR.: G. Rossi
From Tasso

3 *acts*
London, 7 March 1711
Dublin, 1711
Naples, 1718

The celebrated *March* from *Rinaldo* was brilliantly satirized as the march of the thieves in the *Beggar's Opera*. *Rinaldo* was the first opera Handel wrote for London.

**Ring des Nibelungen, Der**
(*The Ring of the Nibelungs*)
A Stage Festival play for Three Days and an Evening.

The first performance of the entire tetralogy was mounted in Bayreuth, in August 1876, twenty-eight years after Wagner had begun the work. The first complete performances in London and at the Metropolitan were in May 1882 and March 1889 respectively. Wagner wrote the libretti of the four parts in reverse order. For casts and individual synopses see the individual parts:

Rheingold, Das
Walküre, Die
Siegfried
Götterdämmerung

SYNOPSIS OF THE CYCLE

Alberich lusts for wealth and power. To rob the Rhine Maidens of the gold he renounces love. From the gold he forges a magic ring, but Wotan tricks him out of it and gives it to the giants Fafner and Fasolt as ransom for Freia, the goddess of youth and beauty. But a curse goes with the ring, first destroying Fasolt.

To restore the ring to the Rhine Maidens and thus avoid the curse is the burden of the three remaining operas. This cannot be accomplished except by one whose motives are unselfish. Wotan fathers Siegmund and Sieglinde, human beings, to do it. Their illicit child, Siegfried, slays Fafner with Siegmund's sword and gives the magic ring to Brünnhilde, whom he has saved from a ring of fire put around her by Wotan in punishment for having shielded Siegmund from his wrath.

Siegfried is treacherously slain by Hagen, Alberich's son. Brünnhilde, taking the ring with her, plunges into his funeral pyre. Now the Rhine Maidens can retrieve their gold, because of Brünnhilde's unselfish act. But Valhalla, the abode of the gods, is destroyed in the flames.

**Rip van Winkle**
COMP.: R. de Koven
LIBR.: P. MacKaye
From the story by Washington Irving

3 *acts*
Chicago, 2 January 1920
New York, 1920

**Risurrezione**
(*Resurrection*)
COMP.: F. Alfano
LIBR.: C. Hanau
From the novel by Tolstoi

4 *acts*
Turin, 30 November 1904
Chicago, 1925
Santiago, Chile, 1928

**Ritorno d'Ulisse in Patria, Il**
COMP.: C. Monteverdi
LIBR.: G. Badoaro

*Prologue and 5 acts*
Venice, February 1641
Paris, 1925
Florence, 1942

CAST

| | | | |
|---|---|---|---|
| Giove (*Jove, Jupiter*) | T | Pisandro, *Penelope's suitor* | T |
| Nettuno (*Neptune*) | B | Anfinomo, *Penelope's suitor* | T |
| Minerva | S | Eurimaco | T |
| Ulisse (*Ulysses, Odysseus*) *Greek hero* | T | Melanto | MS |
| Penelope, *his wife* | C | Eumete | T |
| Telemaco, *his son* | MS | Iro, *jester* | T |
| Antinoo, *Penelope's suitor* | B | Ericlea, *old nurse* | MS |

(*Note: Voicing according to Dallapiccola's arrangement*)

SYNOPSIS

I. Penelope laments for Ulysses, absent for twenty years now, ten in the Trojan war, and ten on the way home. Giove and Nettuno discuss the sins of men as Minerva finds Ulysses cast up on a foreign shore.

II. Ulysses, with the help of that goddess, arrives home in disguise. Telemaco, who has been searching for his father, returns also and discovers him outside their palace. Inside, Penelope, who has been plagued for years with suitors she does not want, puts them off yet a little longer in the hope that her husband may actually be returning.

III. As a beggar, Ulysses, the hero, takes part in an arrow-shooting contest among the suitors. After his astoundingly accurate display he turns on the suitors themselves and kills them all. But Penelope will not believe even yet that it is really her husband until Ericlea identifies him by marks she remembered from his boyhood.

NOTES

Today *Ulysses* is performed in modern arrangements of the ancient score by Dallapiccola and by d'Indy. The original version was not published until nearly three hundred years after its composition, when it was printed in Vienna in 1923.

## Ritter Blaubart

(*Knight Bluebeard*)
COMP.: E. von Rezniček
LIBR.: H. Eulenberg

3 *acts*
Darmstadt, 29 January 1920
Berlin, 1920
Prague, 1922

## Robert le Diable

(*Robert the Devil*)
COMP.: G. Meyerbeer
LIBR.: Scribe and Delavigne

5 *acts*
Paris, 22 November 1831
Drury Lane, 1832
New York, 1834
Metropolitan, 1883

CAST

| | | | |
|---|---|---|---|
| Alice, *Robert's foster sister* | S | Robert, *duke of Normandy* | T |
| Isabella, *princess of Sicily* | S | Bertram, *the unknown* | B |
| Abbess | Dancer | Raimbaut, *minstrel* | T |

SYNOPSIS

In reality Bertram is the Devil and Robert's father. He attempts by every means within his power to drive Robert to evil but Alice fights and succeeds in preserving the good in him. In the end Robert marries Isabella.

## Robin Hood

COMP.: R. de Koven
LIBR.: H. Smith

3 *acts*
Chicago, 9 June 1890
Boston, 1890
London, 1890

**Rognyeda**
COMP.: A. Serov
LIBR.: D. Averkiev

5 acts
St. Petersburg, 8 November 1865
Moscow, 1868

**Roi de Lahore, Le**
(*The King of Lahore*)
COMP.: J. Massenet
LIBR.: L. Gallet

5 acts
Opéra, 27 April 1877
Covent Garden, 1879
New Orleans, 1883

**Roi d'Ys, Le**
(*The King of Ys*)
COMP.: E. Lalo
LIBR.: Lalo and Blau
From a Breton legend

*Tragedy in 3 acts*
Comique, 7 May 1888
Covent Garden, 1901
Metropolitan, 1922

CAST

| The King of Ys | B | Karnac | Bar |
| Margared, *his daughter* | S | St. Corentin | B |
| Rozenn, *his daughter* | S | Jahel | Bar |
| Mylio | T | Nobles, Warriors, Soldiers, People | |

SYNOPSIS

I. Margared is in love with Mylio, but unfortunately she is engaged for political reasons to Karnac. Rozenn also loves Mylio although she is unaware that he is the same man whom Margared loves. Mylio pays Rozenn a secret visit. When the king comes to take Margared to meet her future husband, Rozenn tells her that she has reason to believe that Margared's lover is nearby. Therefore Margared bravely refuses to marry Karnac, and the war which might have come to an end continues.

II. There is to be a battle. The lines are drawn, all is ready for the blood to be shed when Margared, realizing that Rozenn meant that same Mylio that she loves, curses his name. Mylio is victorious, but Margared finds Karnac and betrays the city by revealing to him how he can let loose a flood of waters upon it.

III. Rozenn marries Mylio. The floods come. The people climb to the highest point in the city to avoid drowning. There Margared thinks it over and regrets her thirst for revenge at such a cost. Knowing that nothing will save the city until the waters have claimed a victim for her curse, she leaps to her death.

**Roi d'Yvetot, Le**
(*The King of Yvetot*)
COMP.: C. Adam
LIBR.: de Leuven and Brunswick
From a poem by Béranger

3 acts
Comique, 13 October 1842
Leipzig, 1843
London, 1850

**Roi d'Yvetot, Le**
(*The King of Yvetot*)
COMP.: J. Ibert
LIBR.: Limozin and de la Tourasse

4 acts
Comique, 15 June 1930
Düsseldorf, 1936
Prague, 1937

**Roi l'a Dit, Le**
(*The King Said So*)
COMP.: L. Delibes
LIBR.: E. Gondinet

3 acts
Comique, 24 May 1873
Prague, 1874
London, 1894

**Roi Malgré Lui, Le**
(*King in Spite of Himself*)
COMP.: E. Chabrier
LIBR.: Burani and de Najac
From a comedy by Ancelot

*Comedy in 3 acts*
Comique, 18 May 1887
Karlsruhe, 1890
Prague, 1931

**Roi Pausole, Le**
See *Aventures du Roi Pausole, Les*

**Romeo and Juliet**
See also *Village Romeo and Juliet, The*
and *Capuletti ed I Montecchi, I*

**Roméo et Juliette**
COMP.: C. Gounod
LIBR.: Barbier and Carré
From Shakespeare

*Tragedy in 5 acts*
Paris, 27 April 1867
Covent Garden, 1867
New York, 1867
Metropolitan, 1891

CAST

| | | | |
|---|---|---|---|
| Duke of Verona | B | Stephano, *Romeo's page* | S |
| Count Paris | Bar | Gregory, *Capulet's retainer* | Bar |
| Count Capulet | B | Friar Lawrence | B |
| Juliette, *his daughter* | S | Benvolio, *Montagues' retainer* | T |
| Gertrude, *her nurse* | MS | Friar Jean | B |
| Tybalt, *Capulet's nephew* | T | Nobles, Ladies, Citizens, Soldiers, | |
| Romeo, *a Montague* | T | Monks, Pages | |
| Mercutio | Bar | | |

SYNOPSIS

I. Romeo, hidden behind a mask at his enemy's ball, falls in love with Juliette at first sight, as does she with him. Tybalt hears of it, but old Capulet will not allow his party to be broken up by murder.

II. Romeo visits her at night by climbing to her balcony.

III. In secret they marry in Friar Lawrence's cell. Near the Capulet House, Stephano sings an insulting song and sparks a street battle during which Mercutio and Tybalt are killed. For this Romeo is banished from Verona.

IV. Again the lovers meet by night. When Romeo has gone, Capulet comes with Friar Lawrence to arrange Juliette's marriage with Paris. But the good Friar provides the girl with a drink with which she may escape this fate by seeming to be dead.

V. Hearing that Juliette has died, Romeo breaks into her tomb and kills himself there. She awakes from the potion only to find her husband dying at her side. Rather than live without him, she stabs herself and dies with him.

**Rondine, La**
(*The Swallow*)
COMP.: G. Puccini
LIBR.: G. Adami
From a libretto by Willner and Reichert

*Comedy in 3 acts*
Monte Carlo, 27 March 1917
Bologna, 1917
Rome, 1918
Metropolitan, 1928

CAST

| | | | |
|---|---|---|---|
| Magda, *Rambaldo's mistress* | S | Crébillon, *his friend* | BBar |
| Lisette, *her maid* | S | Yvette, *Magda's friend* | S |
| Ruggero, *young man* | T | Bianca, *Magda's friend* | S |
| Prunier, *poet* | T | Suzy, *Magda's friend* | MS |
| Rambaldo, *wealthy Parisian* | Bar | Steward | B |
| Périchaud, | BBar | Ladies and Gentlemen, Citizens, Students, |  |
| Gobin, *his friend* | T | Artists, Demi-mondaines, Dancers |  |

SYNOPSIS

I. Magda wishes she could relive the good old days on the left bank. Ruggero helpfully suggests that the best Bohemian place to go, in Paris, is Boullier's.

II. There they all meet. Magda, dressed as in the old days, enters into a little affair with Ruggero. Rambaldo finds her in this condition.

III. She and Ruggero, having gone off together, find they cannot live happily. She feels out of place in the innocence of his life. She therefore leaves him, and ceases the attempt to recapture her past, to return to Rambaldo.

**Rosamond**  3 *acts*
COMP.: T. Arne  London, 18 March 1733
LIBR.: J. Addison  Dublin, 1743
Only six songs and a duet remain of this opera.

**Rose et Colas**  1 *act*
COMP.: P. Monsigny  Paris, 8 March 1764
LIBR.: J. Sedaine  Warsaw, 1765
From a tale of La Fontaine  Vienna, 1776

**Rosenkavalier, Der**  Comedy in 3 acts
(*The Knight of the Rose*)  Dresden, 26 January 1911
COMP.: R. Strauss  Covent Garden, 1913
LIBR.: H. von Hofmannsthal  Metropolitan, 1913

CAST

| | | | |
|---|---|---|---|
| Princess von Werdenberg, | . | Notary | B |
| the Marschallin | S | Innkeeper | T |
| Baron Ochs von Lerchenau | B | Singer | T |
| Octavian | MS | Three Orphans | S, MS, C |
| Herr von Faninal, *wealthy parvenu* | Bar | Dressmaker | S |
| Sophie, *his daughter* | S | Animal Tamer | T |
| Marianne, *her duenna* | S | Four Servants of the Marschallin | 2T, 2B |
| Valzacchi, *scandalmonger* | T | Four Waiters | T, 3B |
| Annina, *his partner* | C | Flute Player, Hairdresser, Scholar, |  |
| Police Commissioner | B | Widow | Mutes |
| Major-Domo to the Marschallin | T | Mahomet and other pages | Mutes |
| Major-Domo to von Faninal | T | | |

MUSICAL HIGHLIGHTS

ACT I. Italian Aria *Di rigori armato il seno*, Singer
ACT II. Waltzes
ACT III. Trio *Hab' mir's gelobt* (This is my vow), Marschallin, Sophie, Octavian
Duet *Ist ein Traum* (It's a dream), Octavian and Sophie

I. Ochs interrupts a very romantic moment between Octavian and the Princess to ask her to appoint an intermediary, a knight of the Rose, to take a symbolic rose to Sophie as token of his proposal of an engagement to that girl. He leaves; the Marschallin dallies about it but then sends Octavian away. Suddenly making up her mind she sends the rose after him.

II. In pomp and with gracious ritual Octavian completes his mission. Seeing Sophie, he falls in love with her. When the famous Baron Ochs comes to stake his claim after sending his token, Sophie is repelled by him and knows that she loves Octavian. This is a godsend for the evil Valzacchi and his accomplice. They tell the baron; the baron challenges Octavian to a duel and in a very delicate fight receives a very slight wound. Lying alone, reduced to utter pain, he receives a note by the hand of Annina who has been hired for the occasion by Octavian. The note invites Ochs to an assignation.

III. Dressed as a girl, his young rival receives Baron Ochs in a special room at an inn. There he is subjected to all the tortures and tricks of Valzacchi and Octavian until somebody calls for the police. But he can hardly explain the situation without getting his own name muddy. The Marschallin, hearing of the whole affair, arrives in time to set everything straight with the Commissioner, to subdue Ochs, and to forgive Octavian, for whom she was certainly not young enough anyway. With magnaminity the Princess gives the boy to Sophie for a lover.

## Rosiera, La

| | 3 *acts* |
|---|---|
| COMP.: V. Gnecchi | Gera, Germany, 12 February 1927 |
| LIBR.: Gnecchi and Zangarini | Vienna, 1928 |
| From a story by de Musset | Pilsen, 1927 |

This opera is one of the few which makes use of microtones.

## Rossignol, Le

| | 3 *acts* |
|---|---|
| (*The Nightingale*) | Opéra, 26 May 1914 |
| COMP.: I. Stravinsky | London, 1914 |
| LIBR.: Stravinsky and Mitousoff | Metropolitan, 1926 |
| From a fairy tale by Andersen | Buenos Aires, 1927 |

CAST

| | | | |
|---|---|---|---|
| Fisherman | T | Three Japanese Envoys | 2T, Bar |
| Nightingale | S | Emperor of China | Bar |
| Cook | MS | Death | C |
| Chamberlain | B | Courtiers, Ghosts | |
| Bonze | B | | |

SYNOPSIS

I. The nightingale is formally invited to sing before the emperor.

II. The envoys of Japan offer the emperor a mechanical bird which they claim is superior to the natural variety. In shame and grief the real nightingale flies away. This insubordination is insulting to the emperor who banishes it forever from his empire.

III. When the emperor lies dying, the nightingale returns. So beautiful is her song that the emperor does not die but becomes well again, proving that live music is always better than the canned substitute. NOTES

This delicious work lasts only fifty minutes. It is best known to American audiences through recordings of a suite made from it.

**Royal Palace, The**
COMP.: K. Weill
LIBR.: I. Goll

1 *act*
Berlin, 2 March 1927

**Rusalka**
(*The Mermaid*)
COMP.: A. Dargomizhsky
LIBR.: By the composer
From a poem by Pushkin

4 *acts*
St. Petersburg, 16 May 1856
New York, 1922
London, 1931

**Rusalka**
COMP.: A. Dvořák
LIBR.: J. Kvapil

3 *acts*
Prague, 31 March 1901
Vienna, 1910
Stuttgart, 1929

**Russlan and Ludmilla**
COMP.: M. Glinka
LIBR.: Composer, Shirkov, Bakhturin, and others
From Pushkin

5 *acts*
St. Petersburg, 9 December 1842
London, 1931
Berlin, 1951

CAST

| | | | | |
|---|---|---|---|---|
| Svictosar, *prince of Kiev* | B | Gorislava, *Ratmir's slave* | | S |
| Ludmilla, *his daughter* | S | Finn, *benevolent wizard* | | T |
| Russlan, *a knight, suitor* | Bar | Naina, *malevolent witch* | | MS |
| Ratmir, *oriental prince, suitor* | C | Bayan, *bard* | | T |
| Farlaf, *warrior, suitor* | B | Tchernomor, *evil dwarf* | | |

SYNOPSIS

I. In the midst of festivities, Ludmilla disappears. Svietosar offers her hand in marriage to him who can rescue her.

II. Russlan, one who could win her, finds a lance, a sword, and a shield all with magic properties, and learns where to find the girl's captor.

III. He passes through an enchanted palace.

IV. He finds Tchernomor and fights him. But having won, he is unable to waken Ludmilla from her enchanted sleep.

V. Finn gives him a magic ring with which he breaks the spell; Ludmilla awakens and becomes his prize.

NOTE

Because of Pushkin's death in a duel, Shirkov and Bakhturin were called in to complete the libretto.

**Rustic Chivalry**
See *Cavalleria Rusticana*

**Sacrifice, The**
COMP.: F. Converse
LIBR.: Converse and Macy

3 *acts*
Boston, 3 March 1911

**Sadko**
COMP.: N. Rimsky-Korsakov
LIBR.: Rimsky-Korsakov and Bielsky

7 *scenes*
Moscow, 7 January 1898
Metropolitan, 1930
London, 1931

CAST

| King of the Ocean | B | Viking Merchant | B |
| Volkhova, *his daughter* | S | Hindu Merchant | T |
| Sadko, *singer* | T | Venetian Merchant | Bar |
| Lubava, *his wife* | MS | Four Buffoons | 2MS, T, B |
| Nezhata, *musician* | MS | Two Elders of Novgorod | T, B |

SYNOPSIS

I. The people of Novgorod listen as Sadko sings. He sings wistfully that if only Novgorod were at the sea, everyone would become rich.

II. The sea princess Volkhova falls in love with Sadko.

III. Lubava grieves to have lost him.

IV. Sadko catches three golden fish and becomes rich. He decides to go to Venice.

V. After twelve years Sadko is becalmed on the way home. He frees his ship only by disembarking from it himself.

VI. At the bottom of the sea Sadko marries Volkhova in a fury of celebration.

VII. Volkhova takes her temporary husband back in his sleep to Novgorod. Leaving him there she transforms herself into a great river connecting the city with the sea.

NOTE

Sadko contains one of the most famous of Rimsky-Korsakov's songs, the *Song of India*, sung by the Hindu Merchant.

## Safié
1 *act*
COMP.: H. Hadley      Mainz, 4 April 1909
LIBR.: E. Oxenford

## Saint of Bleecker Street, The
3 *acts, 5 scenes*
COMP.: G.-C. Menotti      New York, 27 December 1954
LIBR.: By the composer      La Scala, 1955

## Sakuntala
This subject was used for operas by Ignace Paderewski, Louis Coerne (1904), and Franco Alfano (1922).

## Salammbô
5 *acts*
COMP.: L. Reyer      Brussels, 10 February 1890
LIBR.: C. du Locle      New Orleans, 1900
From a novel by Flaubert      New York, 1901

## Salome
1 *act*
COMP.: R. Strauss      Dresden, 9 December 1905
LIBR.: H. Lachmann      Metropolitan, 1907 once only, revived 1933
From Oscar Wilde      Covent Garden, 1910

CAST

| Herod Antipas | T | Five Jews | 4T, B |
| Herodias, *his wife* | MS | Two Nazarenes | T, B |
| Salome, *her daughter* | S | Two Soldiers | B |
| Jokanaan, *John the Baptist* | Bar | Cappadocian | B |
| Narraboth, *Syrian captain of the guard* | T | Slave | |
| Page | C | | |

*The Dance of the seven veils*

Finale—*Scene of Salome with the head of John the Baptist*

SYNOPSIS

For a moment the powerful voice of the captive Jokanaan casts fear into the hearts of the soldiers of Herod's guard. But Salome, hearing it, is filled with a voracious lust for the man. When he stands before her she is consumed with hot desire. She bends to him, tempts him, but he will not listen. Herod covets her, himself thirsting with lust but she has no eyes but for the prisoner. Herod asks her to dance for him, he promises to give her anything she wants.

Salome dances before Herod, wearing seven veils, one of which she removes, then another and another. In payment she demands the head of Jokanaan who would not kiss her alive, but who cannot withhold his lips when dead. Herod offers her anything else, but she wants only the head.

It is brought to her, bleeding, upon a silver tray. Seizing it in her claws she kisses its mouth. Herod, utterly sickened by the sight of her depravity, orders the soldiers to crush her to death.

NOTE

Sometimes the *Dance of the Seven Veils* is performed by a dancer in substitution for the singer. Once a prima donna tried to do the dance herself, but they say Strauss was taken so aback by the gyrations she produced that he insisted she desist.

The board of directors of the Metropolitan had the opera taken off after a dress rehearsal and one performance. It has since, nevertheless, become a standard exhibition piece for great singing actresses in the more seriously progressive companies, not excluding the Metropolitan.

**Salome**

See also *Herodiade*

**Samson et Dalila**          *Tragedy in 3 acts*

COMP.: C. Saint-Saëns          Weimar, 2 December 1877

LIBR.: F. Lemaire          Covent Garden (concert), 1893

Metropolitan, 1895

CAST

| | | | |
|---|---|---|---|
| Dalila, *a Philistine* | MS | Old Hebrew | B |
| Samson, *warrior* | T | Messenger of the Philistines | T |
| High Priest of Dagon | Bar | Hebrews, Philistines | |
| Abimelech, *satrap of Gaza* | B | | |

MUSICAL HIGHLIGHTS

ACT I. Scena *Je viens célébrer la victoire* (I come to celebrate your victory), Dalila and chorus

ACT II. Aria *Amour, viens aider ma faiblesse* (O love, come aid me in my weakness), Dalila

Aria *Mon Coeur s'ouvre à ta voix* (My heart opens at thy voice), Dalila

ACT III. *Baccanale*

SYNOPSIS

1. Samson, in a desperate effort to provide the weary Hebrews with some deed of encouragement, slays their enemy Abimelech with his own sword. In the flush of such a victory he is unaware of the sinister undertones of the suppliant ovation of the Philistine maidens with Dalila at their head.

II. She is determined, he is uncertain. She worms from Samson the secret of his tremendous strength, his hair. While he relaxes his vigil against treachery she cuts it off so that he is easily defeated by the resurgent Philistine host.

III. Blinded and imprisoned Samson is the toy of his enemies. They drag him out to be exhibited at the dedication of a new temple to Dagon. There, in chains, the hero prays to Jehovah for strength. Seizing the pillars of the temple he brings it down on all their heads, sacrificing himself.

### Samuel Pepys
1 act
COMP.: A. Coates      Munich, 21 December 1929
LIBR.: Drury and Pryce
From the diary of Samuel Pepys

### Sancta Susanna
1 act
COMP.: P. Hindemith      Frankfurt, 26 March 1922
LIBR.: A. Stramm      Prague, 1923

### Sapho
3 acts
COMP.: C. Gounod      Opéra, 16 April 1851
LIBR.: E. Augier      Covent Garden, 1851
     Antwerp, 1894

Gounod's first opera.

### Sapho
5 acts
COMP.: J. Massenet      Comique, 27 November 1897
LIBR.: Cain and Bernède      New York, 1909
From the novel by Daudet      New Orleans, 1913

### Šarka
3 acts
COMP.: Z. Fibich      Prague, 28 December 1897
LIBR.: A. Schulzová

### Šarka
3 acts
COMP.: L. Janáček      Brno, 11 November 1925
LIBR.: J. Zeyer
Janáček's first opera. The date of the first performance is uncertain.

### Savitri
1 act
COMP.: G. Holst      London, 5 December 1916
LIBR.: By the composer      Cincinnati, 1939
From the *Maha Bharata*      Covent Garden, 1923

CAST

| | | | |
|---|---|---|---|
| Satyavan, *woodman* | T | Death | B |
| Savitri, *his wife* | S | Hidden Female Chorus | |

SYNOPSIS

Death comes for Satyavan. Savitri pleads with Death and wins his life back.

NOTE

Savitri is intended for performance in the open air.

**Scala di Seta, La**
*(The Silken Ladder)*
COMP.: G. Rossini
LIBR.: G. Rossi
From a French libretto by Planard

1 *act*
Venice, 9 May 1812
Barcelona, 1823
Lisbon, 1825

**Scarecrow, The**
COMP.: N. Lockwood

New York, 19 May 1945

**Scarlet Letter, The**
COMP.: W. Damrosch
LIBR.: G. Lathrop
From the story by Hawthorne, who
was Lathrop's father-in-law

3 *acts*
Boston, 10 February 1896
New York, 1896

**Scarlet Letter, The**
COMP.: V. Giannini

Hamburg, 2 June 1938

**Schauspieldirektor, Der**
*(The Impresario)*
COMP.: W. A. Mozart
LIBR.: G. Stephanie

*Comedy in* 1 *act*
Vienna, 7 February 1786
London, 1857
New York, 1870

This parody of the opera business was written for a garden party at Schönbrunn. It consists of an overture, 2 airs, trio and finale, plus dialogue. The story deals with the troubles of an unfortunate impresario with his prima donna, or the story of Mozart, Schikaneder and Madame Hofer.

**Schöne Galathea, Die**
*(The Beautiful Galatea)*
COMP.: F. von Suppé
LIBR.: L. von Kohlenegg

1 *act*
Berlin, 30 June 1865
New York, 1867
London, 1872

**School for Fathers, The**
See *Quattro Rusteghi, I*

**Schwanda the Bagpiper**
See *Švanda Dudák*

**Schweigsame Frau, Die**
*(The Silent Woman)*
COMP.: R. Strauss
LIBR.: S. Zweig
From the play *Epicoene* by Ben Jonson

*Comedy in* 3 *acts*
Dresden, 24 June 1935
La Scala, 1936
Zurich, 1936
New York, 1958

CAST

| | | | |
|---|---|---|---|
| Sir Morosus Blunt | B | Carlotta, *actress* | MS |
| Housekeeper | C | Morbio, *actor* | Bar |
| Schneidebart, *barber* | Bar | Vanuzzi, *actor* | B |
| Henry Morosus Blunt, *actor* | T | Farfallo, *actor* | B |
| Aminta, *his wife, actress* | S | Actors, Neighbors | |
| Isotta, *actress* | S | | |

I. His housekeeper is very interested in Sir Morosus. She engages the barber in a plot to get him to marry her. The old man hates any kind of noise in the house and until now has managed to keep the place in a state somewhat akin to that of a mausoleum. Back, as if from the dead, comes his nephew Henry with a wife and a troupe of actors. This is too much for Sir Morosus. He begs the barber to find him a wife, a silent wife. Thus the housekeeper's pot begins to boil.

II. From three candidates whisked before the old man, Sir Morosus chooses to marry Aminta. She plays her part very silently; the other actors conspire as priests and notary to perform the mock ceremony in the most delicate quiet. When all is said and done Aminta suddenly breaks into a veritable torrent of words at the top of her voice, nagging and noisy, calculated to make Sir Morosus wish he had never been married to such a woman.

III. The hoax goes on. Aminta orders carpenters to make all kinds of alterations in the house, which the actors seem about to carry out. Finally another actor arrives, in the character of chief justice. Sir Morosus pleads with him for a divorce, but it is refused. The old man is nearly mad when finally the actors reveal themselves to him and tell him of their hoax. With relief he relaxes, and there seems to be hope for an easier future in the house.

**Secret Marriage, The**
See *Matrimonio Segreto, Il*

**Segreto di Susanna, Il**　　　　　　　　*Comedy in 1 act*
(*The Secret of Susanna*)　　　　　　　Munich, 4 December 1909
COMP.: E. Wolf-Ferrari　　　　　　　New York, 1911
LIBR.: E. Golisciani　　　　　　　　　Covent Garden, 1911
　　　　　　　　　　　　　　　　　Metropolitan, 1912

CAST

Count Gil, 30　　　　　Bar　　Santi, *their servant*, 50　　　　Mute
Countess Susanna, 20　　S

SYNOPSIS

In the house where smoking is forbidden, Gil smells the tell-tale odor of cigarettes. He meets, he greets, he kisses his wife and smells tobacco. In the depths of his dark suspicion he begins to wonder who may be the lover with whom she has taken up secret meetings, a lover who smokes. In fury and grief he separates from her.

Santi picks things up around the room.

Gil storms out. Susanna, alone at last, lights a forlorn but comforting cigarette. Gil returns, she hides it. But he smells it again and believes the secret lover must be present. His jealousy knows no bounds. While he shouts at her he wonders what secret she is hiding from him behind her back. He snatches at it, then jumps back, slightly burned. It was not a lover at all, but his own wife who smoked. With relief he forgives her.

**Selva Incantada, La**
(*The Enchanted Forest*)　　　　　　Berlin, 17 January 1803
COMP.: V. Righini　　　　　　　　Stockholm, 1831
LIBR.: A. da Caramondani
From Tasso's *Gerusalemme Liberata*

## Semiramide

| | |
|---|---|
| COMP.: G. Rossini | 2 acts |
| LIBR.: G. Rossi | Venice, 3 February 1823 |
| From Voltaire | London, 1824 |
| | New York, 1845 |
| | Metropolitan, 1893 |

### CAST

| | | | |
|---|---|---|---|
| Semiramide, *queen of Babylon* | S | Azema, *princess* | S |
| Arsace, *general of the Assyrians* | C | Idreno, *Indian prince* | T |
| Ghost of Nino | B | Mitrane, *captain of the guard* | T |
| Oroe, *high priest of the Magi* | B | Magi, Guards, Satraps, Slaves | |
| Assur, *prince* | Bar | | |

### SYNOPSIS

Semiramide, who with the help of Assur, murdered her husband Nino, has conceived a love for Arsace. Arsace, however, is her own unrecognized son. The ghost of Nino rises to name Arsace as the rightful king of Babylon, and orders him to visit the tomb of his father to learn of the assassination. Assur goes there also, to kill Arsace. But in the fighting Semiramide intervenes and loses her life. Arsace is victorious.

### NOTE

Semiramide, a most Italian sounding piece which was once censured as being too "German," was written in three weeks.

## Semiramide Riconosciuta

| | |
|---|---|
| (*Semiramide Rewarded*) | 3 acts |
| COMP.: C. von Gluck | Vienna, 14 May 1748 |
| LIBR.: Metastasio | Hamburg, 1936 |

Composed in honor of the birthday of Maria Theresa.

## Serse

| | |
|---|---|
| (*Xerxes*) | 2 acts |
| COMP.: G. F. Handel | London, 26 April 1738 |
| LIBR.: N. Minato (with alterations) | Northampton, Mass., 1928 |
| | London, 1935 |

This most serious work is based upon a comic plot. It contains the celebrated "Largo from Xerxes," *Ombra mai fu.*

## Serva Padrona, La

| | |
|---|---|
| (*The Servant-Mistress*) | *Intermezzo in 2 parts* |
| COMP.: G. Pergolesi | Naples, 28 August 1733 |
| LIBR.: G. Federico | London, 1750 |
| | New York, 1858 |

### CAST

| | | | |
|---|---|---|---|
| Uberto | B | Vespone, *another servant* | Mute |
| Serpina, *his servant* | S | | |

### SYNOPSIS

I. Uberto, tyrannized by his servant Serpina, complains that he has to wait three hours for his chocolate. But Serpina so overwhelms him with words that he pleads with Vespone to go find him a wife for his protection. Serpina jumps at the chance to fight for that coveted position.

II. To win him she plots a complex trick with Vespone as her ferocious lover. Her sweet demeanor and sad pleas evoke pity from her master, thus trapping him into uncertainty whether he may perhaps be in love with his own servant. When Vespone plays his part, Uberto falls straight into the trap, but he cannot escape even when he sees how it was sprung.

NOTES

This famous work first appeared between the acts of *Il Prigioniero Superbo*. The subject was also used by Giovanni Paisiello.

**Servante Maîtresse, La**
See *Serva Padrona, La*

**Shade of Don Juan, The**
See *Ombra di Don Giovanni, L'*

**Shamus O'Brien**
COMP.: C. Stanford
LIBR.: G. Jessop
From a poem by Le Fanu

2 *acts*
London, 2 March 1896
New York, 1897
Dublin, 1924

**Shanewis**
COMP.: C. W. Cadman
LIBR.: N. Eberhardt

2 *acts*
Metropolitan, 23 March 1918
Denver, 1924

CAST

| | |
|---|---|
| Shanewis | Philippe Harjo |
| Lionel | Mrs. Everton |
| Amy | |

**Siberia**
COMP.: U. Giordano
LIBR.: L. Illica

3 *acts*
La Scala, 19 December 1903
New Orleans, 1906
New York, 1908

**Sicilian Vespers, The**
See *Vespri Siciliani, I*

**Siege of Rhodes, The**
COMP.: M. Locke (in part)
LIBR.: W. d'Avenant

*Opera in 5 entries*
London, September 1656

The music of this first opera in English is lost. The vocal parts were by Matthew Locke (4th entry), Henry Lawes (1st and 5th entries), and Henry Cook (2nd and 3rd entries). The instrumental sections were by Charles Coleman and George Hudson.

**Siegfried**
COMP.: R. Wagner
LIBR.: By the composer

*Music Drama in 3 acts*
Bayreuth, 16 August 1876
London, 1882
Metropolitan, 1887

CAST

| | | | |
|---|---|---|---|
| Siegfried, *son of Siegmund and Sieglinde* | T | Fafner, *giant* | B |
| Mime, *Nibelung dwarf* | T | Erda | C |
| Wotan, *disguised as The Wanderer* | BBar | Forest Bird | S |
| Alberich | BBar | Brünnhilde | S |

155

# THE OPERAS

SYNOPSIS

I. The foundling Siegfried has been reared by Mime in the hope that he may be useful in retrieving the Ring of the Nibelungs from Fafner. Mime has been trying to weld the broken sword of Siegmund into useful shape, but he has had no success. Wotan, who also wants the ring back, comes in disguise to Mime and drops the hint that only Siegfried can repair the sword. Siegfried seizes the fragments of his father's sword and welds them together masterfully. To test it he splits the anvil in two.

II. Mime conducts his foundling to the mouth of Fafner's cave. There the giant, in the shape of a dragon, faces him. But Siegfried soon slays him with the invincible sword. When the victor touches the blood of the giant to his lips suddenly he understands the songs of birds. One of them tells him of the magic ring, the Tarnhelm and the Rhine Gold. These he takes for himself, killing Mime when he comes to claim them. The bird speaks to Siegfried and leads him away.

III. As the Wanderer, Wotan bars the way but Siegfried shatters the god's spear and goes on into the circle of fire. Within it he finds Brünnhilde. The goddess awakens to see the handsome man standing over her and they immediately fall in love with each other. As the curtains close Siegfried seals their marriage with the ring of the Nibelungs.

**Sigurd**
COMP.: L. Reyer
LIBR.: Blau and du Locle

4 acts
Brussels, 7 January 1884
New Orleans, 1891
Covent Garden, 1884

**Silent Woman, The**
See *Schweigsame Frau, Die*

**Silken Ladder, The**
See *Scala di Seta, La*

**Simon Boccanegra**
COMP.: G. Verdi
LIBR.: F. M. Piave
From a play by Gutierrez

Prologue and 3 acts
Venice, 12 March 1857
La Scala, 1881
New York, 1932

CAST

| | | | |
|---|---|---|---|
| Amelia Boccanegra, *alias Maria, and* | | Jacopo Fiesco, *patrician,* | |
| *in Act I called Amelia Grimaldi* | S | *former Doge (Duke)* | B |
| Gabriele Adorno, *patrician* | T | Paolo Albiani, *plebian* | B |
| Simon Boccanegra, *plebian,* | | Captain | T |
| *the Doge (Duke)* | Bar | Pietro, *plebian* | B |

SYNOPSIS

Simon Boccanegra becomes Doge (Duke) by favor of the plebian majority. But an old scandal in his life comes to plague him to add to the difficulties of the patrician's plots against him. His natural daughter Amelia is in love with his enemy Gabriele. Adorno would have killed the Doge, but the news that Amelia is his daughter dissuades him. His older enemy, Paolo, has poisoned the Doge with a slow poison. When the revolt has been crushed, Fiesco is to be hanged for his part in it. The two ancient enemies face each other at the last instant and make atonement. Adorno is appointed successor to Boccanegra as the Doge dies.

# THE OPERAS

The opera was unsuccessful at first, but after extensive revisions by Boito and Verdi, principally in the finale of Act I, it became more popular.

**Simon Bolivar**
See *Bolivar*

**Simplicius Simplicississimus Jugend, Der**
COMP.: K. Hartmann                    Cologne, 23 October 1948

**Sir John in Love**                  *4 acts*
COMP.: R. Vaughan Williams            London, 21 March 1929
LIBR.: From Shakespeare's *Merry*     London, 1939
*Wives of Windsor*

**Sister Angelica**
See *Suor Angelica*

**Sleepwalker, The**
See *Sonnambula, La*

**Snow Maiden, The**
See *Snyegurotchka*

**Snyegurotchka**                     *Prologue and 4 acts*
(*Snow-Maiden*)                       St. Petersburg, 10 February 1882
COMP.: N. Rimsky-Korsakov             New York, 1922
LIBR.: By the composer                Sadlers Wells, 1933
From a play by Ostrovsky

CAST

| | | | |
|---|---|---|---|
| Snyegurotchka, *the Snow Maiden* | S | Page | MS |
| Shepherd Lehl | C | Tsar Berendey | T |
| Koupava | S | Mizgir | Bar |
| Fairy Spring | MS | King Frost | B |
| Bobilicka | MS | Bobil | T |
| Spirit of the Forest | T | Bermiata | |

SYNOPSIS

PROLOGUE. Spring entrusts her daughter, the Snow Maiden, to the Spirit of the Forest for safe keeping. She is immediately adopted by Bobil and Bobilicka.

I. Mizgir falls in love with her, but she will not have him.

II. Koupava claims damages for the loss of Mizgir's love. In court, when the Snow Maiden pleads her case and states that she has no lover, the Tsar orders her to go get one.

III. Lehl offers, but she is shy. Mizgir tries, but she will not have him.

IV. Her mother helps her; then she falls in love with Mizgir after all. But because of love there is sunshine in the Snow Maiden's heart, and she must die.

**Socrate**                           *3 parts*
COMP.: E. Satie                       Paris, (Concert), 14 February 1920
LIBR.: V. Cousins
Translated from the *Dialogues of Plato*

157

# THE OPERAS

Satie, never willing to fit his works into stereotype molds, called this a *Drame Symphonique avec Voix*.

**Songe d'une Nuit d'Été, Le**  
(*The Midsummer Night's Dream*)  
COMP.: A. Thomas  
LIBR.: Rosier and de Leuven  

3 *acts*  
Comique, 20 April 1850  
New Orleans, 1851  
New York, 1852  

This is *not* the play by Shakespeare, but a play *about* Shakespeare.

**Songstress, The**  
See *Cantarina, La*

**Sonnambula, La**  
COMP.: V. Bellini  
LIBR.: F. Romani  

2 *acts*  
Milan, 6 March 1831  
London, 1831  
New York, 1835  

CAST

| | | | |
|---|---|---|---|
| Count Rodolpho, *Lord of the Castle* | B | Elvino, *farmer* | T |
| Teresa, *miller* | S | Alessio, *villager* | B |
| Amina, *her foster daughter* | S | Notary, Villagers | |
| Lisa, *innkeeper* | S | | |

MUSICAL HIGHLIGHTS

ACT I. Aria *Vi ravviso o luogho ameni* (As I view the scenes of childhood), Rodolpho  
Duet *D'un pensiero* (Not a single thought), Amina and Elvino  
ACT II. Sleepwalking scene *Ah, non credea* (Ah, do not believe), Amina  
Aria, *Ah, non giunge*, Amina  

SYNOPSIS

I. In spite of the jealousy of Lisa, Amina and Elvino have mutually pledged their troth. A stranger, really Rodolpho in disguise, has come to town to recall his carefree childhood and is in his room at the inn when Amina, walking in her sleep, climbs into his window and into bed. Lisa takes Elvino to witness what looks like his bride's infidelity.

II. Elvino takes back the ring he had given her, and promises to marry Lisa instead. He cannot understand what Rodolpho is talking about in his explanation of Amina's somnambulism. But finally the unnerving exhibition of the frail girl, again sound asleep, walking over a dangerous bridge above the millwheel and then singing a sleepy narration of her difficulty with Elvino brings the man back to his senses and makes him again her bridegroom.

NOTE

The role of Amina was long a favorite for sopranos who wished to make striking debuts. The most famous of these was Malibran, who first appeared in the role in the first performance of it in English at Drury Lane in 1833.

**Sophie Arnould**  
COMP.: G. Pierné  

Comique, 21 February 1927  

**Spanish Hour, The**  
See *Heure Espagnole, L'*

**Sposo Deluso, Lo**  
COMP.: W. A. Mozart  
For details of the use of this unfinished work, see *Oca del Cairo*.

**Sprung über den Schatten, Der**
(*The Leap over the Shadow*)
COMP.: E. Krenek
LIBR.: By the composer

3 *acts*
Frankfurt, 9 June 1924
Leningrad, 1927

**Star of the North, The**
See *Étoile du Nord, L'*

**Statue, The**
COMP.: L. Reyer
LIBR.: Barbier and Carré

3 *acts*
Paris, 11 April 1861
Weimar, 1864

**Stone Guest, The**
See *Kamyenny Gost*
See also *Don Juan*

**Stradella**
See *Alessandro Stradella*

**Strange World**
See *Fremde Erde*

**Street Scene**
COMP.: K. Weill
LIBR.: E. Rice, L. Hughes
From the play by Elmer Rice

2 *acts*
New York, 9 January 1947

"An American Opera," according to the heading on the score. The work consists in part of songs in the popular tradition, and yet it has so much orchestral music that it cannot be called a ballad opera.

**Sunken Bell, The**
See *Campana Sommersa, La*

**Suor Angelica**
(*Sister Angelica*)
COMP.: G. Puccini
LIBR.: G. Forzano

1 *act*
Metropolitan, 14 December 1918
Rome, 1919
Covent Garden, 1920

CAST

| | | | |
|---|---|---|---|
| Suor Angelica | S | Suor Osmina | S |
| Princess, *her aunt* | C | Suor Dulcina | MS |
| Abbess | MS | Aspirant Sisters | MS |
| Alms Collector | S | Nursing Sister | S |
| Mistress of Novices | MS | Novices, Sisters | |
| Suor Genoveva | S | | |

SYNOPSIS

Angelica, repenting for illegitimate motherhood, has been in the convent for seven long years. When her aunt visits on other business Angelica asks about her child only to learn that it has been dead for two years. From flowers the nun concocts a poison and drinks it, begging forgiveness for this suicide.

NOTE

This short work is one of a trilogy containing *Il Tabarro* and *Gianni Schicchi*. The first performance listed above included, as *Il Trittico*, all three.

**Susannah**
COMP.: C. Floyd
LIBR.: By the composer

2 *acts*
Tallahassee, Florida, 24 February 1955
New York, 1956

**Susanna's Secret**
See *Segreto di Susanna, Il*

**Susanna**
See also *Sancta Susanna*

**Švanda Dudák**
(*Schwanda the Bagpiper*)
COMP.: J. Weinberger
LIBR.: M. Kares

2 *acts*
Prague, 27 April 1927
Metropolitan, 1931
Covent Garden, 1934

CAST

| | | | |
|---|---|---|---|
| Švanda the Bagpiper | Bar | Executioner | T |
| Dorotka, *his wife* | S | Devil | B |
| Babinsky, *romantic bandit* | T | Devil's Familiar Spirit | T |
| Queen Iceheart | MS | Captain of Hell's Guard | T |
| Magician | B | Two Forest Rangers | T, B |
| Judge | T | | |

SYNOPSIS

I. Hiding from the pursuit of the rangers, Babinsky meets Švanda and his wife. His talk of the world entrances the poor bagpiper until he decides to leave home behind and go travelling with the romantic wanderer.

First he meets the queen, who falls in love with him. They marry and share the throne. Dorotka sweeps him off that seat, however, and the queen condemns both of them to death. Babinsky gets them away from the guards, and Švanda's energetic bagpiping keeps everyone dancing until they effect their escape. At Dorotka's insistence, Švanda swears by the devil that he never kissed the queen. For this boldfaced lie the devil takes him.

II. The devil makes Švanda play. He has the musician's soul, but only for a moment; Babinsky wins it back for Švanda in a game of cards. Back goes the Bagpiper to the arms of his dear wife, never again to venture forth.

**Swallow, The**
See *Rondine, La*

**Tabarro, Il**
(*The Cloak*)
COMP.: G. Puccini
LIBR.: G. Adami
From a play by Didier Gold

*Tragedy in 1 act*
Metropolitan, 14 December 1918
Buenos Aires, 1919
Covent Garden, 1920
La Scala, 1922

CAST

| | | | |
|---|---|---|---|
| Michele, *bargeman*, 50 | Bar | Talpa, *stevedore*, 55 | B |
| Luigi, *stevedore*, 20 | T | Giorgetta, *Michele's wife*, 25 | S |
| Tinca, *stevedore*, 35 | T | Frugola, *Talpa's wife*, 50 | MS |

SYNOPSIS

Luigi and Giorgetta are lovers. Giorgetta's husband Michele suspects the fact. He is on deck one evening quietly smoking when Luigi sees the flick of his match and mistakes it for a signal from Giorgetta for their midnight meeting. When Luigi appears, Michele springs on him and strangles him to death. Giorgetta discovers the body hidden under a cloak when she rushes on deck to see what is the matter.

NOTES

This melodrama is the first part of *Il Trittico*, a trilogy containing also *Suor Angelica* and *Gianni Schicchi*. The first performance listed above was actually the first performance of the entire series.

**Tableau Parlant, Le**
(*The Talking Table*)
COMP.: A. Grétry
LIBR.: L. Anseaume

1 act
Paris, 20 September 1769
Charleston, S.C., 1794
Philadelphia, 1796

**Tale of the Invisible City of Kitezh, The**
See *Kitezh*

**Tales of Hoffmann, The**
See *Contes d'Hoffmann, Les*

**Taming of the Shrew, The**
COMP.: V. Giannini
From Shakespeare

Cincinnati (Concert), 31 January 1953
New York (TV), 1954

**Taming of the Shrew, The**
See also *Widerspenstigen Zähmung, Der*

**Tammany**
COMP.: J. Hewitt
LIBR.: A. J. Hatton

3 acts
New York, 3 March 1794
Philadelphia, 1794
Boston, 1796

This opera, also called *America Rediscovered*, was sponsored by the Tammany Society of New York. The music has been lost.

**Tancred**
See *Combattimento di Tancredi e Clorinda, Il*

**Tancredi**
COMP.: G. Rossini
LIBR.: G. Rossi
From Tasso's *Gerusalemme Liberata*

2 acts
Venice, 6 February 1813
London, 1820
New York, 1825

This was the first Italian opera to be presented at Boston, where it was produced in 1829.

**Tannhäuser und der Sängerkrieg auf dem Wartburg**
(*Tannhäuser, and the Singing Contest at the Wartburg*)
COMP.: R. Wagner
LIBR.: By the composer

3 acts
Dresden, 19 October 1845
New York, 1859
Covent Garden, 1876

CAST

| | | | |
|---|---|---|---|
| Hermann, *Landgrave of Thuringia* | B | Walter von der Vogelweide, | |
| Tannhäuser, *knight and minnesinger* | T | *minnesinger* | T |
| Wolfram von Eschenbach, | | Biterolf, *minnesinger* | B |
| *knight and minnesinger* | Bar | Heinrich der Schreiber, *minnesinger* | T |

Reinmar von Zweter, *minnesinger*    B    Four Noble Pages    2S, 2A
Elisabeth, *Herman's niece*    S    Nobles, Knights, Ladies, Pilgrims, Sirens,
Venus    S    Naiads, Nymphs, Bacchantes
Young Shepherd    S

MUSICAL HIGHLIGHTS

ACT I. *Venusberg Music*
    *Dich Teure Halle* (Hail hall of song), Elisabeth
ACT II. Hymn to Venus, *Dir Göttin der Liebe* (Thou goddess of love), Tannhäuser
ACT III. Song to the Evening Star, *O du mein holder Abendstern* (O thou bright shining
    Evening Star), Wolfram
    Pilgrims' Chorus

SYNOPSIS

I. Trapped by the soporific beauties of the enchanted palace of Venus, Tannhäuser longs
to return to the outside world. Uttering a Christian prayer, he suddenly finds himself alone
on a mountainside, listening to a band of pilgrims on their way to Rome. He starts to go
with them, but the sight of a troop of minnesingers and the recognition of his friend
Wolfram who tells him of Elisabeth's continuing love for him leads Tannhäuser back to
the Wartburg.

II. There he takes part in a singing contest for which the prize is to be Elisabeth's hand
in marriage. The Landgrave is sure of Tannhäuser's victory as is everyone else present.
But after all the others have had their songs, Tannhäuser bursts unwillingly into such a
praise of pagan Venus that all draw their swords against him. Only Elisabeth's intervention prevents his death. The Landgrave sends him out with the pilgrims to Rome,
there to beg forgiveness.

III. He fails to return. Elisabeth, watching for him in vain finally gives up and goes
home to die in sorrow. Wolfram stands alone, singing to himself of the beauteous evening
star, when Tannhäuser stumbles up the path, worn and dejected, unforgiven. He is about to
throw himself again into the oblivion of the Venusberg when a procession comes by,
with the corpse of Elisabeth. Tannhäuser falls upon the bier, dying just as more pilgrims
arrive from Rome bearing the Pope's staff, which has borne leaves in sign of his redemption.

NOTES

For the production at Paris in 1861 Wagner made extensive changes in the score,
considerably enlarging some of the scenes and generally rendering the work more dramatic.

**Tender Land, The**     1 *act*
COMP.: A. Copland     New York, 1 April 1954
LIBR.: H. Everett

CAST

Laurie    S    Top, *a drifter*
Beth, *a child*    S    Splinters, *postman*
Ma Moss      Mrs. Splinters
Grandpa Moss      Mrs. Jenks
Martin, *a drifter*      Mr. Jenks

**Tempest, The**     3 *acts*
COMP.: N. Gatty     London, 17 April 1920
LIBR.: R. Gatty (his brother)
From Shakespeare
This subject has been used also by Frank Martin and by Alois Haba.

**Templar und die Judin, Der**
(*The Knight and the Jewess*)
COMP.: H. Marschner
LIBR.: W. Wohlbrück
From *Ivanhoe*, by Scott

3 *acts*
Leipzig, 22 December 1829
London, 1840
New York, 1872

**Testament de la Tante Caroline, La**
(*Aunt Caroline's Will*)
COMP.: A. Roussel
LIBR.: Nino

*Comedy in* 3 *acts*
Olomouc, Czechoslovakia, 14 November
1936
Comique, 1937

**Thaïs**
COMP.: J. Massenet
LIBR.: L. Gallet
From the novel by Anatole France

*Tragedy in* 3 *acts*
Opéra, 16 February 1894
New York, 1907
Covent Garden, 1911

CAST

| | | | |
|---|---|---|---|
| Athanaël, *young monk* | Bar | Thaïs, *courtesan* | S |
| Nicias, *young Alexandrian* | T | Crobyle, *slave* | S |
| Palémon, *old Cenobite* | B | Myrtale, *slave* | MS |
| Servant of Nicias | Bar | Albine, *abbess* | C |

SYNOPSIS

Athanaël returns to his convent scandalized at the temptings of Thaïs which he has witnessed in Alexandria. He resolves to take her out of her life of sin. Persuasion fails, but later, of her own accord, she comes to him ready to enter the novitiate. But the poor theologian is in love with her. This terrible magic works within him. At the same time the separation of convent life stifles her so that, in spite of his ardent wish to save her, she dies.

**Thieving Magpie, The**
See *Gazza Ladra, La*

**Three Penny Opera, The**
See *Dreigroschenoper, Die*
See also *Beggar's Opera*

**Tiefland**
(*The Lowlands*)
COMP.: E. d'Albert
LIBR.: R. Lothar
From the play *Terra Baixa*
  by Guimerá

*Tragedy in Prologue and* 2 *acts*
Prague, 15 November 1903
Berlin, 1907
Vienna, 1908
Metropolitan, 1908
Covent Garden, 1910

CAST

| | | | |
|---|---|---|---|
| Sebastiano, *rich landowner* | Bar | Rosalia | C |
| Tommaso, *village elder* | B | Nuri, *little girl* | S |
| Moruccio, *miller* | Bar | Pedro, *shepherd* | T |
| Marta, *Sebastiano's mistress* | S | Nandro, *shepherd* | T |
| Pepa | S | Priest | Mute |
| Antonia | S | | |

# THE OPERAS

PROLOGUE. In order to provide a shield for his affair with his mistress, Marta, Sebastiano has decided upon Pedro as a husband for her. Pedro, therefore, must leave the mountains and live in the village.

I. The marriage is performed as intended, but Pedro does not know about the relationship that exists between Marta and Sebastiano. When the bride insists upon going into her room without her legal husband, Pedro refuses to leave her side or to let her leave his. They settle down for the night on the floor.

II. Pedro is in love with the girl. She is beside herself trying to get the true facts across to him. When it finally penetrates his romantic disbelief, his fury and suspicions give way to despair at the loss of her love. But she begins to love him. They decide to go away together. As they get ready to depart Sebastiano stops them and has Pedro taken away. Later Pedro escapes, finds Sebastiano and strangles him with his bare hands.

## Till Eulenspiegel

COMP.: O. Jeremiaš

Prague, 13 May 1949

## Tosca

COMP.: G. Puccini
LIBR.: Giacosa and Illica
From a play by Sardou

*Tragedy in 3 acts*
Rome, 14 January 1900
Covent Garden, 1900
Metropolitan, 1901

### CAST

| | | | |
|---|---|---|---|
| Floria Tosca, *celebrated singer* | S | Jailer | B |
| Mario Cavaradossi, *painter, her lover* | T | Shepherd Boy | C |
| Baron Scarpia, *chief of police* | Bar | Roberti, *executioner* | |
| Cesare Angelotti, *political prisoner* | B | Cardinal, Judge, Scribe, Officer, Sergeant | |
| Sacristan | Bar | Soldiers, Police, Ladies, Nobles, Citizens, | |
| Spoletta, *police agent* | T | Artisans | |
| Sciarrone, *gendarme* | B | | |

### MUSICAL HIGHLIGHTS

ACT I. Aria *Recondita armonia* (Strange harmony), Mario
Duet *Non la sospiri la nostra casa* (Not the sweet hope of our home), Tosca and Mario
ACT II. Cantabile *Già mi dicon venal* (Some may call me venal), Scarpia
Aria *Vissi d'arte, vissi d'amore* (I have lived for art and love), Tosca
ACT III. Aria *È lucevan le stelle* (The stars were brightly shining), Mario

### SYNOPSIS

I. Cavaradossi is painting in the chapel when the prisoner Angelotti escapes jail and asks his help in hiding. The fugitive is out of sight when Tosca comes to see her lover. She suspects him of being unfaithful because of his preoccupation and what she sees in the portrait he has begun. She leaves in time for Mario to help Angelotti get away just before the police come. Scarpia searches the chapel and voices his suspicions of Cavaradossi. Then he sees Tosca to tell her, as a goad to further his own ends, that Mario has another lover.

II. Scarpia captures Cavaradossi and has him tortured in the next room while he questions Tosca for information. Finally, when the prisoner's cries become too unbearable to her, she reveals Angelotti's hiding place.

Scarpia bargains with her for her love, saying he can save Mario from execution if she will give in to him. She agrees, but while he is writing out her safe-conduct she steals a knife from the table and stabs him. In terrible formality she puts candles near his body and a crucifix upon his breast before leaving.

III. Believing Scarpia's promise, that the execution by firing squad of her lover Cavaradossi, upon the high roof of the fortress tomb of Hadrian in Rome, is to be only a mock for the sake of appearances, she goes to watch it. But Scarpia's tricks outlive the man. As the rifles crack, Mario falls dead. Tosca leaps over the edge of the roof to her own death.

NOTE

Sardou's play was a favorite of Sarah Bernhardt.

## Tote Stadt, Die

3 acts

(*The Dead City*)
COMP.: E. Korngold
LIBR.: P. Schott
From a play by Rodenbach

Hamburg and Cologne, 4 December 1920
Metropolitan, 1921
Prague, 1922

## Transatlantic

3 acts

COMP.: G. Antheil
LIBR.: By the composer
This was originally called *The People's Choice*

Frankfurt, 25 May 1930

## Traviata, La

*Tragedy in 3 acts*

(*The Frail One*)
COMP.: G. Verdi
LIBR.: F. M. Piave
From *La Dame aux Camélias*, by
A. Dumas

Venice, 6 March 1853
London, 1856
New York, 1856
Metropolitan, 1883

CAST

| | | | |
|---|---|---|---|
| Alfredo Germont, *Violetta's lover* | T | Giuseppe, *Violetta's servant* | T |
| Giorgio Germont, *his father* | Bar | Violetta Valery, *courtesan* | S |
| Gastone de Letorières | T | Flora Bervoix, *her friend* | MS |
| Baron Douphol, *Alfredo's rival* | Bar | Annina, *her confidante* | S |
| Marchese d'Obigny | B | Ladies and Gentlemen, Servants, Masks, | |
| Doctor Grenvil | B | Dancers, Guests | |

MUSICAL HIGHLIGHTS

ACT I. Brindisi *Libiamo, libiamo* (Let's drink, let's drink), Alfredo, Violetta and chorus
  Duet *Un dì felice* (Some fine day), Alfredo and Violetta
  Aria *Ah! fors' è lui* (Ah, but for love), Violetta
  Aria *Sempre libera* (Always freely), Violetta

ACT II. Aria *De' miei bollenti spiriti* (So wild my dream of ecstasy), Alfredo
  Aria *Dite alla giovine* (Tell it to me, young as I am), Violetta
  Aria *Imponete* (You command me), Violetta
  Aria *Di provenza il mar* (In our home land by the sea), Giorgio

ACT III. *Prelude*
  Aria *Addio del passato* (Goodbye to my happiness), Violetta
  Duet *Parigi, o cara* (We must leave Paris), Alfredo and Violetta

SYNOPSIS

I. The courtesan, Violetta, already aware that she is increasingly sick, is deeply touched that Alfredo professes his undying love for her. On the surface, however, she seems to brush it off quite lightly.

II. They take up a new life together, in poverty in Paris. Their happiness is complete until Alfredo's father visits her to plead with her to leave his son because of her past. She does, and returns to her former life. Believing that she left him out of unfaithfulness, Alfredo follows her and publicly insults her.

III. Later, alone and forlorn, Violetta lies dying in her room. The elder Germont has told his son the true cause of her separation from him. Alfredo returns to her to hold her in his arms during her last moments.    NOTES

It was the misfortune of *La Traviata* to have one of the most ill-fated debuts of any famous and successful opera. The tenor had a cold; the baritone in a fit of pique walked most languidly through the entire role. It was a failure, a poor beginning for one of the most melodious and most famous works of the Italian stage. It is said that Verdi wrote the entire score in four weeks, immediately after the opening of *Il Trovatore*.

### Trial of Lucullus

COMP.: R. Sessions                Berkeley, Calif., 18 April 1947
LIBR.: B. Brecht

### Triomphe de l'Amour sur Bergers    1 act
### et Bergères, La                    The Louvre, 22 January 1655
*The Triumph of love over Shepherds
and Shepherdesses)*
COMP.: M. la Guerre
LIBR.: C. de Beys
Perhaps the first French opera. The music is lost.

### Tristan und Isolde

|  |  |  |  |
|---|---|---|---|
| COMP.: R. Wagner | | Tragedy in 3 acts | |
| LIBR.: By the composer | | Munich, 10 June 1865 | |
| From legends | | Drury Lane, 1882 | |
| | | Metropolitan, 1886 | |

CAST

| | | | |
|---|---|---|---|
| Tristan, *knight of Cornwall* | T | Brangäne, *Isolde's maid* | MS |
| King Marke of Cornwall, | | Shepherd | T |
| *Tristan's uncle* | B | Sailor | T |
| Isolde, *Irish princess* | S | Helmsman | Bar |
| Kurwenal, *Tristan's retainer* | Bar | Sailors, Knights, Men at Arms, Esquires | |
| Melot, *courtier* | Bar | | |

MUSICAL HIGHLIGHTS

ACT II. Duet (The Love Duet) *Isolde, Tristan geliebter* (Isolde, Tristan my lover), Tristan and Isolde

ACT III. Liebestod (The Love Death) *Mild und leise* (Mildly, softly), Isolde

SYNOPSIS

I. Tristan, deeply in love with Isolde who also loves him, brings her from Ireland to be the king's bride. Full of the idea, however, that her knight does not love her and that she is to be wedded to someone else, she intends to kill herself and him by poison. Brangäne thwarts her wish by substituting a magic love-potion for the poison so that Tristan and Isolde embrace in raptures of love before the ship reaches Cornwall.

II. In darkness they meet while the king is away hunting. High in a tower, Brangäne watches for his return. Suddenly hunters appear and Brangäne warns them in time for

Tristan to make sure Isolde is hidden for the moment. But Melot, his enemy, draws his sword and wounds Tristan.

III. Near death in his own home, Tristan waits for Isolde's coming. She arrives and he dies in her arms. King Marke and his knights have followed her but Kurnewal battles with them, slaying Melot but being himself slain. The king had come, however, not as an enemy but with forgiveness. He was too late: Isolde has cast herself upon the corpse of her lover and dies before his arrival.

NOTES

Wagner made note of the story of Tristan and Isolde in *Die Meistersinger von Nürnberg* wherein Hans Sachs says that he will have no such fate for himself as a lover as did Tristan. The opera *L'Elisir d'Amore* also makes oblique reference to the story, this opera being a satire on the subject of love potions.

### Trittico, Il
See *Suor Angelica; Tabarro, Il; Gianni Schicchi.*

### Triumph of St. Joan, The
COMP.: N. Dello Joio            Bronxville, N.Y., 9 May 1950
LIBR.: Dello Joio and Machlis

### Troilus and Cressida
| | |
|---|---|
| | 3 *acts* |
| COMP.: W. Walton | Covent Garden, 3 December 1954 |
| LIBR.: Chr. Hassall | San Francisco, 1955 |
| From Chaucer | |

CAST

| | | | | |
|---|---|---|---|---|
| Calkas, *High Priet of Pallas* | B | Evadne, *her servant* | | MS |
| Antenor, *Captain of Trojan Spears* | Bar | Horaste, *a friend of Pandarus* | | Bar |
| Troilus, *Prince of Troy* | T | Diomede, *Prince of Argos* | | Bar |
| Pandarus, *Brother of Calkas* | T | Priests, Priestesses of Pallas, Trojans, | | |
| Cressida, *Daughter of Calkas, a widow* | S | Greeks | | |

Commissioned originally for a BBC broadcast, the opera was actually first performed, with BBC permission, on the stage.

### Trojans, The
See *Troyens, Les*

### Trompeter von Säkkingen, Der
(*The Trumpeter from Säkkingen*)     4 *acts*
COMP.: V. Nessler            Leipzig, 4 May 1884
LIBR.: R. Bunge             Metropolitan, 1887
From a poem by von Scheffel    London, 1892

### Troubadour, The
See *Trovatore, Il*

### Trovatore, Il
(*The Troubadour*)         *Tragedy in 4 acts*
COMP.: G. Verdi          Rome, 19 January 1853
LIBR.: S. Cammarano      New York, 1855
From a play by Gutierrez    Covent Garden, 1855
                           Metropolitan, 1883

CAST

| | | | |
|---|---|---|---|
| Count di Luna, *of Aragon* | Bar | Duchess Leonora | S |
| Ferrando, *his captain of guard* | B | Inez, *her confidante* | S |
| Manrico, *troubadour,* | | Azucena, *gypsy woman of Biscay* | MS |
| *supposed son of Azucena* | T | Followers of di Luna and Manrico, | |
| Ruiz, *one of his soldiers* | T | Messengers, Jailers, Soldiers, Nuns, | |
| Old Gypsy | Bar | Gypsies | |

MUSICAL HIGHLIGHTS

ACT I. Aria *Tacea la notte* (Calmly the evening), Leonora
Romance, *Deserto sulla terra* (In this deserted land), Manrico
ACT II. The Anvil Chorus, Gypsies
Aria *Stride la vampa* (Upward the flames roll), Azucena
Aria *Mal reggendo all'aspiro assalto* (At my mercy I hold my enemy), Manrico
Aria *Il balen del suo sorriso* (How glowingly her smile), Count
Aria *Per me ora fatale* (For me the fatal hour), Count
Chorus of Nuns *Ah se l'error t'ingombra* (Ah, in the shadow of error)
ACT III. Aria *Ah si, ben mio coll'essere* (Ah yes, beloved, I'm here with you), Manrico
Scena *Di quella pira* (The fatal fire), Manrico and Chorus
ACT IV. Miserere *Ah! che la morta ognora* (Ah, how death delays me), Manrico
Duet *Ai nostri monti* (Back to our mountains), Manrico and Azucena

SYNOPSIS

In revenge for the death of her mother, Azucena the gypsy stole one of two babies from the castle years ago. This child she brought up as Manrico, the troubadour.

I. *Il Duello* (The Duel). Ferrando, hoping to capture the unknown troubadour who serenades Leonora, waits for him one evening and narrates the story of the kidnapping to pass the time. When the troubadour makes his appearance, he finds not only Leonora but the count ready for him. The count challenges him to a duel.

II. *La Zingara* (The Gypsy). Having spared the count, Manrico, back at the camp of the gypsies, ponders his reasons. Ruiz interrupts his introspection to urge him to the defense of Biscay, telling him incidentally that Leonora has planned to enter a convent. Manrico goes to the convent to prevent her, but finds the count there for the same purpose. Manrico takes her away.

III. *Il Figlio della Zingara* (The son of the gypsy). The count and his men lay siege to Manrico, capturing Azucena whom he recognizes and throws into prison. The news of the gypsy woman's impending death reaches Manrico just as he and Leonora are about to be married. He rushes to her aid.

IV. *Il Supplizio* (The torture). He fails in his mission and is imprisoned with her. Leonora visits him and then wins his freedom by promising to marry the count. But she takes poison instead, and dies in Manrico's arms. The count orders Manrico to be killed, making Azucena witness the execution. But as she watches, she turns and informs the count that Manrico was his own brother, kidnapped by her when he was a baby.

**Troyens, Les**
(*The Trojans*)
COMP.: H. Berlioz
LIBR.: By the composer
From the *Aeneid* of Virgil

*In two parts 5 acts*
First complete performance,
Karlsruhe, 5 and 6 December 1890

# THE OPERAS

PART ONE, LA PRISE DE TROIE (*The Fall of Troy*)

### CAST

| | | | |
|---|---|---|---|
| Cassandre, *prophetess* | S | Priam, *king of Troy* | B |
| Ascagne, *son of Aeneas* | S | Soldier of Troy | Bar |
| Hécube, *Priam's wife* | MS | Captain of the Greeks | B |
| Polyxène, *Priam's daughter* | S | Helenus, *Priam's son* | T |
| Enée (Aeneas), *Trojan hero* | T | Andromaque, *Hector's widow* | Mime |
| Chorèbe, *Cassandre's lover* | Bar | Astynax, *her son* | Mime |
| Panthée, *priest* | B | Greek Soldiers, Trojan Soldiers, Citizens, |
| Hector's Ghost | B | Women, Children, Shepherds |

### SYNOPSIS

I. Cassandre has been cursed by Apollo. She can foresee the truth, but no one will believe her. All the Trojans rush off to see the fabulous wooden horse left by the Greeks on the shore as they seemingly beat a retreat. Aeneas has seen a terrifying vision. He suggests that they bring the horse within the city to placate the goddess it represents. The people comply with his request, tearing a breach in their own walls to bring the huge object in.

II. Hector's ghost warns Aeneas to take his son and leave the city, to sail westward and found a new empire on the Italian peninsula. Meanwhile the Greek warriors, hidden by the wily Odysseus within the huge wooden horse, burst out of it and sack the city from inside.

Aeneas leaves his doomed homeland. The Greek forces enter and find Cassandre who stabs herself as an example to the other Trojan women.

PART TWO, LES TROYENS À CARTHAGE (*The Trojans at Carthage*)

### CAST

| | | | |
|---|---|---|---|
| Didon (Dido), *Queen of Carthage* | MS | Cassandre's ghost | MS |
| Anna, *her sister* | C | Chorèbe's ghost | Bar |
| Ascagne | S | Hector's ghost | B |
| Enée (Aeneas) | T | Priam's ghost | B |
| Iopas, *poet* | T | Mercury | B |
| Hylas, *Trojan sailor* | T | Trojan Captains, Courtiers, Hunters, |
| Narbal, *Dido's minister* | B | Carthaginians, Invisible Ghosts, |
| Panthée | B | Workmen, Sailors, Laborers, Naiads, |
| Two Soldiers | Bar, B | Fairies, Satyrs, Wood Nymphs |
| Two Trojan Captains | Bar, B | |

### SYNOPSIS

III. The Trojan fleet, headed by Aeneas, lands at Carthage to find the city threatened by invasion by its enemies. The Trojan general offers his help, and leading the Carthaginian army he beats off the hostile forces.

In a dream of magic in an enchanted forest, Dido and Aeneas realize their love for each other.

IV. After the battle Aeneas returns to Carthage and to Dido. Having experienced the same delicious dream, they approach each other with love. But over the Trojan warrior hovers the remembrance of the voice of Hector's ghost which sent him westward to found a city.

v. Aeneas decides to leave. Dido begs him to stay but he will not. After he has left she causes a ceremonial pyre to be raised. When the flames are high enough she kills herself.

NOTES

This huge double opera has been performed most frequently in separate parts. Part One was first shown in Nice (1891), and Paris (1899). Part Two appeared in Paris, 4 November 1863, then in Liverpool (1897), and so on. The two parts together were performed as noted above, with Part One being heard then for the first time. There was another complete performance in Glasgow in 1935.

## Trumpeter of Säkkingen, The
See *Trompeter von Säkkingen, Der*

## Tsar's Bride
See *Tsarskaya Nyevesta*

| **Tsarskaya Nyevesta** | 3 *acts* |
|---|---|
| (*The Tsar's Bride*) | Moscow, 3 November 1899 |
| COMP.: N. Rimsky-Korsakov | Seattle, Wash., 1922 |
| LIBR.: L. Mey | London, 1931 |

| **Turandot** | *Chinese Fable in 2 acts* |
|---|---|
| COMP.: F. Busoni | Zürich, 11 May 1917 |
| LIBR.: By the composer | Frankfurt, 1918 |
| From a play by Gozzi | Venice, 1940 |

CAST

| | | | |
|---|---|---|---|
| Emperor Altoum | B | Tartaglia, *minister* | B |
| Turandot, *his daughter* | S | Pantaleone *minister* | B |
| Adelma, *her confidante* | MS | Eight Doctors | T, B |
| Calaf, *young unknown prince* | T | Singer | MS |
| Barak, *his servant* | Bar | Slaves, Weeping Women, Eunuchs, | |
| Queen Mother of Samarkand, *Negress* | S | Soldiers, Dancers, a Priest | |
| Truffaldino, *chief eunuch* | T | | |

SYNOPSIS

I. In spite of the evident risk of losing his life as had all the contestants before him, Calaf answers the riddles propounded by the royal mind and wins the hand of Turandot.

II. The tables are turned. Turandot must guess the name of her betrothed in order to get herself out of the bargain of marriage. This is not so difficult, however, when Adelma, who knew Calaf before, gives him away. The princess, in a triumph of virginal revenge, reveals her ill-gotten knowledge to the prince, but then she relents and marries him anyway.

NOTE

The opera was developed from incidental music written for the play, produced by Max Reinhardt.

| **Turandot** | *Romance in 3 acts* |
|---|---|
| COMP.: G. Puccini | La Scala, 25 April 1926 |
| LIBR.: Adami and Simoni | Metropolitan, 1926 |
| From a fable by Gozzi | Covent Garden, 1927 |

CAST

| | | | |
|---|---|---|---|
| Princess Turandot | S | Ping, *Grand Chancellor of China* | Bar |
| Emperor Altoum, *her father* | T | Pang, *Supreme Lord of Provisions* | T |
| Timur, *exiled Tartar King, blind* | B | Pong, *Supreme Lord of the* | |
| Calaf, *his son* | T | *Imperial Kitchen* | T |
| Liù, *slave* | S | Mandarin | Bar |

SYNOPSIS

I. Turandot's beauty inspires love in the hearts of all young men who see her, but to win her hand one must answer three difficult riddles. To fail is death. Calaf sees her, falls in love, and in spite of his father's objections makes the proper arrangements for the test.

II. He answers the riddles perfectly. But the princess does not want to keep her part of the bargain. He agrees that if she can discover who he is, he will submit to death.

III. No torture can extract his name. Turandot tries with Timur, but Liù cries that only she can reveal it. She refuses to do so, however, because of her own love for Calaf. To prevent being tortured, Liù stabs herself to death.

Calaf forcibly kisses Turandot, and suddenly she melts into a real woman. In the court she announces that she has discovered his name: it is Love.

NOTE

Act III was completed by Franco Alfano.

**Turco in Italia, Il**
(*The Turk in Italy*)
COMP.: G. Rossini
LIBR.: F. Romani

2 *acts, 7 scenes*
La Scala, 14 August 1814
London, 1821
New York, 1826

**Turn of the Screw, The**
COMP.: B. Britten
LIBR.: M. Piper
From the story by Henry James

2 *acts and Epilogue*
Venice, 14 September 1954
Sadlers Wells, 1954
Stratford, Conn., 1958
New York, 1958

CAST

| | | | |
|---|---|---|---|
| Governess | | Mrs. Grose | S |
| Miles, *a boy* | | Miss Jessel | MS |
| Quint's Ghost | T | Flora | S |

**Twelfth Night**
COMP.: C. A. Gibbs
From Shakespeare

1947

**Twilight of the Gods, The**
See *Götterdämmerung*

**Un Ballo in Maschera**
See *Ballo in Maschera, Un*

**Un Giorno di Regno**
See *Giorno di Regno, Un*

**Undine**
COMP.: E. Hoffmann
LIBR.: F. Fouqué

3 *acts*
Berlin, 3 August 1816
Aachen, 1922

**Undine**
COMP.: A. Lortzing
LIBR.: By the Composer
From the story by Fouqué

4 *acts*
Magdeburg, 21 April 1845
New York, 1856
Brussels, 1867

**Valkyr, The**
See *Walküre, Die*

**Vampyr, Der**
(*The Vampire*)
COMP.: H. Marschner
LIBR.: W. Wohlbrück

2 *acts*
Leipzig, 29 March 1828
London, 1829
Liège, 1845

**Vanessa**
COMP.: S. Barber
LIBR.: G-C. Menotti

4 *acts*
Metropolitan, 15 January 1958
Salzburg, 1958

CAST

| | | | |
|---|---|---|---|
| Vanessa | S | Anatol | T |
| Erika, *her niece* | MS | Baroness | C |
| Doctor | B | Major-Domo | B |

SYNOPSIS

Vanessa was once, long ago, in love with a man named Anatol, and has kept herself and her house shut off from the world ever since losing him. A guest arrives, named Anatol, who is actually the son of her lover. In his first night he seduces Erika, but later he takes up with Vanessa, giving that older woman a new breath of youth. Erika is pregnant and tries to kill herself, but fails in the attempt. As Vanessa and her lover go off gaily to their honeymoon, Erika orders the house closed up again, in token of her having lost her lover as her aunt had before.

**Venus**
COMP.: O. Schoeck
LIBR.: A. Rüeger
From a story by Mérimée

3 *acts*
Zürich, 10 May 1922
Berne, 1934

**Veronique**
COMP.: A. Messager
LIBR.: Vanloo and Duval

3 *acts*
Paris, 10 December 1898
London, 1903
New York, 1905

**Vespri Siciliani, I**
(*The Sicilian Vespers*)
COMP.: G. Verdi
LIBR.: Scribe and Duveyier

*Tragedy in 5 acts*
Opéra, 13 January 1855
La Scala, 1856
Drury Lane, 1859
New York, 1859

CAST

| | | | |
|---|---|---|---|
| Duchess Elena | S | Count Vaudermont, *French officer* | B |
| Arrigo, *young Sicilian* | T | Ninetta, *Elena's attendant* | S |
| Guido di Monforte, *governor of Sicily* | Bar | Danieli, *young Sicilian* | T |
| | | Tebaldo, *French soldier* | T |
| Giovanni da Procida, *Sicilian doctor* | B | Roberto, *French soldier* | B |
| di Béthune, *French officer* | B | Manfredo, *Sicilian* | T |

SYNOPSIS

SYNOPSIS

I. There is a good deal of friction in Sicily, known always for the quick passions of its people, because of the occupation by French troops. Elena makes her contribution to unrest by publicly singing an inflammatory song of patriotism. Only the appearance of Manfredo prevents the incipient riot.

II. Procida returns from exile to rouse the Sicilians against the oppressive French. In order to stir the people to overt action, he effects what appears to be a mass kidnapping of Sicilian girls by the soldiers.

III. The revolutionary leader arranges for his partisans to attend a masked ball to be given at Monforte's palace. But there Arrigo, who has discovered that he is the long lost son of Monforte, notices the conspirators in the crowd. He is torn between his revolutionary sentiments and love for his newly discovered father. But at the last moment, when the assassination is about to take place, Arrigo steps in to betray his friends,

IV. The assassins are tried and condemned. Arrigo demands that he be executed along with them, since he was fully in accord with their aims. Monforte offers them pardon if he will acknowledge him as father. At last he does, and the prisoners are freed. Elena and Arrigo thereupon become publicly betrothed.

V. The wedding bells were to be a signal for a new insurrection against the French. Elena tries to prevent this, but Monforte, unaware of the plans, causes the bells to ring and the havoc to commence.

NOTES

*I Vespri Siciliani* was commissioned for the Great Exposition of 1855. Verdi disliked the libretto. But that was not all that made the production difficult: Cruvelli, who was was assigned the part of Elena, disappeared during the preparations without explanation. One month later she returned, also without explanation, but quite evidently she had spent the time most romantically with a man she later married.

**Vestale, La**                              3 *acts*
COMP.: G. Spontini                           Opéra, 16 December 1807
LIBR.: Étienne de Jouy                       Philadelphia, 1828
                                             London, 1826

**Vida Breve, La**                           *Tragedy in 2 acts*
(*The Brief Life*)                           Nice, 1 April 1913
COMP.: M. da Falla                           Buenos Aires, 1923
LIBR.: C. F. Shaw                            Metropolitan, 1926

CAST

| | | | |
|---|---|---|---|
| Salud, *gypsy* | S | Singer | Bar |
| Grandmother | MS | Manuel, *Carmela's brother* | Bar |
| Carmela | MS | Voice in the Forge, Voice of a | |
| Paco | T | Street-Seller, Distant Voice | T |
| Uncle Sarvaor | B | | |

SYNOPSIS

I. Uncle Sarvaor knows that Paco plans to wed someone, not Salud, the next day. He would have revenge, for Salud loves Paco very much.

II. Salud interrupts the festivities of the announcement of Paco's betrothal to Carmela. She tells him of her love, then drops dead at his feet.

NOTE

This famous Spanish work was composed in 1904–05.

## Village Romeo and Juliet, A

COMP.: F. Delius
LIBR.: By the composer
From a story by Keller

*Prologue and 3 acts*
Berlin, 21 February 1907
Covent Garden, 1910

CAST

| | | | |
|---|---|---|---|
| Manz, *rich farmer* | Bar | | |
| Marti, *rich farmer* | Bar | Wheel of Fortune Woman | S |
| Sali, *son of Manz, as a child* | S | Cheap Jewelry Woman | MS |
| *as a man* | T | Showman | T |
| Vreli, *Marti's daughter* | S | Merry-go-round Man | Bar |
| Dark Fiddler | Bar | Slim Girl | S |
| Two Peasants | Bar | Wild Girl | MS |
| Three Women | S, MS | Poor Hornplayer | T |
| Gingerbread Woman | S | Hunchbacked Bass Fiddler | B |

SYNOPSIS

A feud develops between Marti and Manz over the boundaries between their lands. But their children are in love. This love tears them from their unyielding parents. They go off together to join a band of vagabonds, never to return.

## Villar's Dragoons

See *Dragons de Villars, Les*

## Villi, Le

COMP.: G. Puccini
LIBR.: F. Fontana

*4 acts*
Milan, 31 May 1884
Manchester, England 1897
New York, 1908

Puccini's first opera.

## Vintage, The

COMP.: M. Pelissier
LIBR.: Dunlap

New York, 1799

According to Ritter, this is one of the earliest operas to be composed in New York.

## Volo di Notte

COMP.: L. Dallapiccola
From *Night Flight*, by St. Exupéry

Florence, 18 May 1940

## Wald, Der

(*The Forest*)
COMP.: E. Smyth
LIBR.: By the composer

*Prologue, 1 act and Epilogue*
Berlin, 9 April 1902
Covent Garden, 1902
Metropolitan, 1903

## Walküre, Die

(*The Valkyr*)
COMP.: R. Wagner
LIBR.: By the composer

*Music Drama in 3 acts*
Munich, 26 June 1870
New York, 1877
Covent Garden, 1892

CAST

| | | | |
|---|---|---|---|
| Siegmund, *the Wälsung* | T | Fricka | MS |
| Hunding | B | Gerhilde, Orlinde, Waltraute, | |
| Wotan | BBar | Schwertleite, Helmwige, Siegrune, | |
| Sieglinde | S | Grimgerde, Rossweisse, *Valkyrs* | S, MS |
| Brünnhilde | S | | |

I. Siegmund staggers, wounded, into the hall of Hunding who is away from home. Sieglinde, Siegmund's sister and Hunding's unwilling wife, without recognizing the warrior, gives him water. They fall in love. When Hunding returns, Siegmund relates the story of his fight to protect his sister. By this Hunding recognizes him as his enemy and determines to kill him the next day. Buried in the ash tree which grows through the center of the hall is a sword which none but Siegmund may wield. When Sieglinde tells him of its story he understands who she is and takes the sword.

II. Fricka demands of Wotan that the two humans be punished for their incestuous love for each other, an insult to her as the goddess of marriage. Wotan sends Brünnhilde to see that Hunding succeeds in killing Siegmund, but Brünnhilde tries to save the warrior instead. It is necessary for Wotan himself to intervene, helping Hunding while the disobedient Valkyr takes up Sieglinde and rides out of reach of the god's wrath.

III. Safely hidden in Fafner's forest, Brünnhilde tells Siegmund that she will bear a son, Siegfried, by him. Their escape is short-lived. Wotan finds her and places her in isolation, circled by magic fire which none but a hero may penetrate. Wotan had attempted to end the curse of the Nibelungs by the destruction of Siegmund, but the birth of Siegfried carries the battle onward.

**Wallenstein**
COMP.: J. Weinberger
LIBR.: M. Kares
From Schiller

*6 scenes*
Vienna, 18 November 1937

**Wally, La**
COMP.: A. Catalani
LIBR.: L. Illica

*Tragedy in 4 acts*
La Scala, 20 January 1892
Metropolitan, 1909
Manchester, England, 1919

CAST

| | | | |
|---|---|---|---|
| Wally | S | Giuseppe Hagenbach, *of Sölden* | T |
| Stromminger, *her father* | B | Vincenzo Gellner, *of Hochstoff* | Bar |
| Afra, *landlady* | C | Messenger, *of Schnals* | T |
| Walter, *strolling minstrel* | S | | |

SYNOPSIS

I. Stromminger hopes that his daughter will marry Gellner, but she wishes otherwise. She is in love with Hagenbach. She threatens to leave her father if he insists she marry Gellner, but she keeps secret the fact of her love.

II. When her father dies, Wally inherits his fortune. But still she cannot get rid of Gellner. Gellner tries intrigue, telling her that Hagenbach is engaged to Afra. At this news Wally is infuriated and insults her rival. Hagenbach swears to avenge the insult. They dance together, and Hagenbach is so entranced as to fall in love with Wally. But she does not know his change of heart; she promises herself in despair to Gellner.

III. Gellner tries to murder Hagenbach by pushing him off a precipice. He fails; the man is brought up alive and given over, to Wally's mortification, to Afra to be nursed back to health.

IV. Wally has made up her mind to commit suicide when Hagenbach comes to her to confess that he does love her. They are fully reconciled. He leaves her, and after a moment she calls out to him. Hearing no response she rushes out the door to die with him in an avalanche.

**Warrior, The**
COMP.: B. Rogers
LIBR.: N. Corwin

*1 act, 4 scenes*
Metropolitan, 11 January 1947

CAST

| | | | |
|---|---|---|---|
| Samson | Bar | Three Captains | 2T, Bar |
| Delilah | S or MS | Officer | Bar |
| Four Lords | 2T, Bar, B | Boy | S or MS |

**Water Nymph, The**
See *Rusalka*

**War and Peace**
COMP.: S. Prokofiev
From Tolstoy's novel

Leningrad, 12 June 1946

**Werther**
COMP.: J. Massenet
LIBR.: Blau, Milliet and Hartmann
From the novel by Goethe

*Tragedy in 4 acts*
Vienna, 16 February 1892
Metropolitan, 1894
Covent Garden, 1894

CAST

| | | | |
|---|---|---|---|
| Werther, *poet*, 23 | T | Johann, *Le Bailli's friend* | B |
| Albert, *young man*, 25 | Bar | Charlotte, *Le Bailli's daughter*, 20 | MS |
| Le Bailli, 50 | B | Sophie, *her sister*, 15 | S |
| Schmidt, *Le Bailli's friend* | T | Children, Neighbors | |

SYNOPSIS

I. Charlotte loves Werther, and he loves her. But her father is intent on marrying her to Albert.

II. After her marriage, the unsuccessful Werther cannot keep himself away from her.

III. She still loves him; they see each other again and again and sing of their passion. Then, dejected, he leaves her. A moment after that he sends Albert a message asking to to borrow some pistols.

IV. Realizing the significance of his message, Charlotte rushes to his room but finds him dying. He will not let her leave him to get help, but dies confident in her love.

**White Lady, The**
See *Dame Blanche, La*

**Widerspenstigen Zähmung, Der**
(*The Taming of the Shrew*)
COMP.: H. Goetz
LIBR.: J. Widman
From Shakespeare

*Comedy in 4 acts*
Mannheim, 11 October 1874
Drury Lane, 1878
New York, 1886

**Wife of Martin Guerre, The**
COMP.: W. Bergsma
LIBR.: Janet Lewis

New York, 15 February 1956

## Wildschütz, Der
(*The Poacher*)
COMP.: A. Lortzing
LIBR.: By the composer
From a play by Kotzebue

3 *acts*
Leipzig, 31 December 1842
Drury Lane, 1895

CAST

| | | | |
|---|---|---|---|
| Count of Eberbach | Bar | Baculus, *schoolmaster* | B |
| Countess, *his wife* | C | Gretchen, *his fiancée* | S |
| Baron Kronthal, *her brother* | T | Pancratius, *major-domo to the count* | Spkr |
| Baroness Freimann, *the count's* | | Servants, Huntsmen, Peasants, | |
| *widowed sister* | S | Schoolboys | |
| Nanette, *her maid* | S | | |

SYNOPSIS

I. Quite accidentally Baculus shot a buck on the grounds of the count's estate. He is summoned to defend himself against the charge of poaching. The good baroness arranges with Gretchen to exchange clothes with her and make an appearance before the count in behalf of the poor schoolmaster. Thus she may surreptitiously see her betrothed, Kronthal.

II. At the castle everybody falls in love with the intercessor. The baron offers the schoolmaster a fortune, instead of a lawsuit, if he will give up his claim to his "betrothed".

III. Baculus does his best, trying to persuade her who he thinks is Gretchen to transfer her affections from him to the count. But in this embarrassing act he discovers that the girl is not Gretchen at all. This leads to obvious complications on all sides until the false Gretchen's identity is finally revealed. Then everyone is happy again, and the schoolmaster, who never intended to hit anything anyway, is pardoned for his accidental shot.

## William Tell
See *Guillaume Tell*

## Wir Bauen eine Stadt
(*We Build a City*)
COMP.: P. Hindemith

*Children's Opera*
Berlin, 21 June 1930

## Wise Maiden, The
See *Kluge, Die*

## Witch of Salem, A
COMP.: C. W. Cadman
LIBR.: N. R. Eberhadt

2 *acts*
Chicago, 8 December 1926

## Woman Without a Shadow, The
See *Frau ohne Schatten, Die*

## Wozzeck
COMP.: A. Berg
LIBR.: By the composer
From the play by Büchner

*Tragedy in 3 acts, 15 scenes*
Berlin, 14 December 1925
Philadelphia and New York, 1931
London (Concert), 1931
N.Y. City Opera, 1952

CAST

| | | | |
|---|---|---|---|
| Wozzeck, *a soldier* | Bar | Fool | T |
| Drum Major | T | Marie | S |
| Andres | T | Margret | C |
| Captain | T | Marie's Child | Treble |
| Doctor | B | Soldiers, Maids, Servants, Children | |
| Two Workmen | Bar, B | | |

MUSICAL ANALYSIS (Berg)

ACT I. *Five Character Pieces*

Scene 1. *Suite* (Wozzeck and the Captain)
    2. *Rhapsody* (Wozzeck and Andres)
    3. *Military March and Lullaby* (Marie and Wozzeck)
    4. *Passacaglia* (Wozzeck and the Doctor)
    5. *Andante Affetuoso* (*quasi Rondo*)(Marie and the Drum Major)

ACT II. *Symphony in five movements*

Scene 1. *Sonata* (Marie, the Child, Wozzeck)
    2. *Fantasy and Fugue* (Captain, Doctor, Wozzeck)
    3. *Largo* (Marie and Wozzeck)
    4. *Scherzo* (In the Beer Garden)
    5. *Rondo con introduzione* (In the Barracks)

ACT III. *Six Inventions*

Scene 1. *Invention on a theme* (Marie and the Child)
    2. *Invention on one note* (Marie and Wozzeck)
    3. *Invention on a rhythm* (At the Inn)
    4. *Invention on a chord of six notes* (Wozzeck's death)
       *Interlude, Invention on a key*
    5. *Invention on a quaver figure* (Children at play)

SYNOPSIS

I. The lowly Wozzeck shaves the captain while the latter enjoys himself by interfering in the underling's life with unwanted advice. Later, while Wozzeck and Andres are cutting wood, Wozzeck worries about ghosts and sorcerers. For a moment, before going back to the barracks, he sees Marie. But she is frightened by his weird vagaries. The doctor uses Wozzeck as a sort of inexpensive guinea pig for his experiments, and indulges, as did the captain, in lofty hints. Marie, in the meanwhile, takes in the drum major.

II. Wozzeck gives all his money to Marie as a matter of course. But the captain and the doctor continue to torment him about supporting a prostitute. When Wozzeck sees Marie, he can hardly talk. His anger mounts as he watches her dancing with the drum major. In the barracks his rival roughs him up a little.

III. Marie weeps over the Bible. Then Wozzeck takes her out in the soft night air, into the woods, and stabs her to death. Back at the dance hall he dances with Margret until Margret sees blood on him. He returns to the woods to hide the knife and drowns himself in a pond. The children stop their play to run to see the body of the dead woman, while Marie's son, unknowing, hops and hops in his little game.

NOTES

This remarkable work was completed in 1921. It has never entered the repertory of any company without a good deal of controversy. Its music, as may be guessed from the above analysis, is extremely tightly composed in tenuous tonalities. The vocal lines are mostly in what one usually calls *Sprechstimme*—speechlike but musical intonation. The work might be called atonal in that it is based upon the most ephemeral relations of tonalities rather than, as for instance in classic music, upon simple relationships of keys. The relationships between the parts of *Wozzeck* are more differentiated by their form than by their tonal levels. The composer did not, however, make use of the dodecaphonic system (based upon the twelve equally-tuned notes of the piano keyboard) as he did in his later work, *Lulu*. Whereas *Der Rosenkavalier* once held the spotlight for having a very large orchestra of 112, *Wozzeck* has edged into it by having, at the performance in 1959 at the Metropolitan, 113.

Berg found it necessary, after making the musical analysis of the work and after many explanations of the complexity of its melodic structure, to remind listeners that it is a work of music, not of mathematics. And indeed when one listens to a performance, the beautiful experience of the harsh story and its musical expression should never be disturbed by an awareness of the technicalities.

**Wreckers, The**
COMP.: E. Smyth
LIBR.: H. Brewster

*Tragedy in 1 act*
Leipzig, 11 November 1906
Prague (Concert), 1906
London (Concert), 1906

CAST

| | | | |
|---|---|---|---|
| Pascoe, *headman and preacher*, 55 | BBar | Mark, *fisherman* | T |
| Lawrence, *lighthouse keeper* | Bar | Thirza, *Pascoe's wife*, 22 | MS |
| Harvey, *his brother in law* | B | Avis, *Lawrence's daughter*, 17 | S |
| Tallan | T | Fishermen, Shepherds, Miners, Women, | |
| Jack, *his son*, 15 | MS | Wreckers, Pietists | |

SYNOPSIS

The wreckers make their living by looting the cargoes of ships wrecked on their coasts. The ships are directed to doom by the placement of false signals in the night. But Thirza has been setting a beacon to counteract the false ones. The people search for the traitor and capture her. They condemn her, along with her lover Mark, to be locked in a tidal cave while the tide rises.

**Wuthering Heights**
COMP.: C. Floyd
LIBR.: By the composer
From the novel by Brontë

*Prologue and 3 acts*
Santa Fe, N.M., 16 July 1958
New York, 1959

**Xerxes**
See *Serse*

**Z Mrtvého Domu**
(*From the House of the Dead*)
COMP.: L. Janáček
LIBR.: By the composer
From Dostoyevsky

*Tragedy in 3 acts*
Brno, 12 April 1930
Prague, 1931
Mannheim, 1930

The text was completed by O. Zitek, the music by B. Bakala.

**Zaïda**
COMP.: W. A. Mozart
LIBR.: J. Schachter (rewritten by
Gollmick)

*Singspiel in 2 acts*
Frankfort, 27 January 1866
Vienna, 1902
Monte Carlo, 1930

Mozart left this work unfinished. It is very similar, in some respects, to *Die Entführung aus dem Serail*.

**Zagmuk**

COMP.: A. Krein

Moscow, 29 May 1930

**Zampa**

COMP.: L. Hérold
LIBR.: A. Mélesville

3 *acts*
Comique, 3 May 1831
London, 1833
New York, 1833

**Zar und Zimmermann**
(*Tsar and Carpenter*)
COMP.: A. Lortzing
LIBR.: By the composer
From the French play by Merle

*Comedy in 3 acts*
Leipzig, 22 December 1837
New York, 1857
London, 1871

CAST

| | | | |
|---|---|---|---|
| Peter I, *Tsar of Russia* | Bar | Lord Sydenham, *English ambassador* | B |
| Peter Ivanov, *runaway soldier* | T | Marquis de Chateauneuf, | |
| van Bett, *burgomaster* | B | *French ambassador* | T |
| Marie, *his niece* | S | Witwe Browe | C |
| Admiral Lefort, *Russian ambassador* | B | | |

SYNOPSIS

I. The Tsar, incognito, works as a shipwright in Holland in order to learn Dutch techniques. The ambassadors of England and France have some slight suspicion of this, and hire van Bett to locate him for them. Van Bett, quite mistakenly, introduces them to Ivanov. But the French ambassador, without telling anyone, recognizes the real Tsar.

II. Van Bett, much impressed with the importance of his position, entertains the ambassadors and the others at dinner. But when he feels the fire of the drinks within him, he incautiously demands to know who the various worthies may be. This leads to an open altercation between the parties who do not wish to be known to each other. The real Tsar defends himself in the mêlée with a sword.

III. Van Bett, still happy in his mistake, prepares a gallant send-off for Ivanov. But in the midst of the speeches, the salutes of cannon announce the departure of the real Tsar elsewhere, in all pomp and festivity.

NOTE

The English title of the work is usually *Peter the Shipwright*.

**Zauberflöte, Die**
(*The Magic Flute*)
COMP.: W. A. Mozart
LIBR.: E. Schikaneder

*Comedy in 2 acts*
Vienna, 30 September 1791
London, 1811
New York, 1833

CAST

| | | | |
|---|---|---|---|
| Tamino, *Egyptian prince* | T | Monostatos, *Sarastro's* | |
| Three Ladies, *attendants to the* | | *brutish servant* | T |
| *Queen of the Night* | 2S, MS | Pamina, *daughter of the* | |
| Papageno, *a bird catcher* | Bar | *Queen of the Night* | S |
| Queen of the Night | S | Three Genii | 2S, MS |

| Orator | B | Papagena | S |
|---|---|---|---|
| Sarastro, *high priest of Isis* | | Two men in armor | T, B |
| and *Osiris* | B | Slaves, Priests, People | |
| Two Priests | T, B | | |

## MUSICAL HIGHLIGHTS

ACT I. Aria *Der Vogelfänger bin ich ja* (I am a happy bird catcher), Papageno
Aria *Dies Bildnis ist bezaubernd schön* (This picture has a beauteous look), Tamino
Scena *O zittre nicht* (O do not fear), Queen of the Night
Recitative *O ew'ge Nacht* (O endless night), Tamino and Chorus

ACT II. Prayer *O Isis und Osiris*, Sarastro
Aria *Alles fühlt der Liebe* (Now in the heat of love), Monostatos
Aria *Der Hölle Rache* (To my revenge), Queen of the Night
Aria *In diesen heil'gen Hallen* (In this most holy temple), Sarastro
Aria *Ach, ich fühl's* (Ah, 'tis gone), Pamina

## SYNOPSIS

I. Tamino, in battle with a serpent, stumbles into the magic realm of the Queen of the Night. Three ladies with magic swords kill the serpent, saving the handsome prince, and then disappear in the shadows. Along comes Papageno, a birdcatcher singing his song. Tamino mistakes him for the one who saved him. Papageno graciously accepts the prince's praise until the three ladies seal his lips to cut off such lying. They tell Tamino that he is in the realm of the Queen of the Night, and that he may be the one to save the princess, who is ensnared by danger in the palace of Sarastro. To clinch his determination the three ladies show him a picture of the girl, who is ravishingly beautiful. Thereupon the queen herself appears to plead with him to make the attempt to save her daughter. Fired with love and duty he undertakes the task, fore-armed with a magic flute and with the help of Papageno who carries magic bells to add to his birdcatcher's pan-pipes. Papageno is the first to find Pamina, trapped by the lustful Monostatos who runs away mistaking Papageno for some devil. Papageno takes her with him back to Tamino. Tamino, meanwhile, has heard that Sarastro is no evil person, but a magnanimous priest of Isis and Osiris. The reason behind the kidnapping is withheld from him. When Papageno brings Pamina to him Monostatos comes in pursuit to capture all three. But the prompt appearance of his master Sarastro protects all.

II. In a grand and mystic ceremony the priests decide to permit Tamino to undergo the ordeal of the search for truth. He and Papageno are commanded to keep silence, then sent on their way. They pass the first tests fairly easily. Monostatos has meanwhile recaptured Pamina, whom he found sleeping. He is about to attack her when the Queen of the Night stops him with her magic and a warning. She wakes Pamina and gives her a dagger, ordering her to kill Sarastro. The priest, when he hears of it, promises Pamina he will not harm her mother. Papageno's particular torture is an old woman who bothers him by saying she'll be his wife. Tamino's is Pamina, who cannot understand why he keeps silent in her presence. When Papageno finally agrees to his marriage, the old woman becomes the delightful Papagena. For Tamino, however, the ordeal goes almost to the point of Pamina's suicide before they have safely passed all the trials and arrived at the temple of success. Now the light of day triumphs over darkness, the Queen of the Night and all her shadowy cohorts dissolve in the golden flood of sunlight and Sarastro blesses the lovers with his benediction.

NOTES

Freemasonry was outlawed in Austria when Schikeneder (of *Schauspieldirektor* fame) and Mozart took up the subject of *The Magic Flute*. They were both Masons, and saw in the circumstances a chance to use some of the ritual in opera. Originally Schikeneder had been working on a puppet show, but another producer anticipated him. He therefore made extensive alterations in the story (*Lulu*, by Liebeskind), turning it into the libretto for *Zauberflöte*. The aria of the Queen of the Night *Der Hölle Rache* is one of the most brilliant showpieces in the soprano repertory, written, some say, to provide a challenge to the first Queen of the Night who was the composer's sister in law.

**Zazà**

COMP.: R. Leoncavallo
LIBR.: By the composer

4 *acts*

Milan, 10 November 1900
London, 1909
Metropolitan, 1920

CAST

| | | | |
|---|---|---|---|
| Zazà, *music hall singer* | S | Lartigon, *monologist* | B |
| Anaide, *her mother* | C | Duclou, *stage manager* | Bar |
| Floriana, *music hall singer* | S | Michelin, *journalist* | Bar |
| Natalia, *Zazà's maid* | MS | Courtois | B |
| Mme. Dufresne | MS | Mario, *Dufresne's butler* | T |
| Milio Dufresne, *man about town* | T | Toto, *Dufresne's child* | S |
| Cascart, *music hall performer* | Bar | Auguste | T |
| Bussy, *journalist* | Bar | Claretta | S |
| Marlardot, *proprietor of the music hall* | T | Simona | S |

SYNOPSIS

I. Zazà boasts that she'll win the love of Milio. When Bussy goes to see Milio she finds that the boast has already come true.

II. Everything goes along nicely until Cascart hints that Milio is untrue to her.

III. Zazà discovers that the rival is really Milio's legal wife.

IV. Lying, she tells Milio she has revealed the scandal to his wife. For this treachery he beats her, ends the affair and goes home.

**Zémire et Azor**

COMP.: A. Grétry
LIBR.: J. Marmontel
From a comedy by La Chaussée

*Comedy in 4 acts*

Fontainebleau, 9 November 1771
London, 1776
New York, 1787

**Zenobia**

COMP.: L. Coerne
LIBR.: O. Stein

3 *acts*

Bremen, 1 December 1907

The first American opera to be performed in Europe.

**Zhenitba**

(*The Marriage*)
COMP.: M. Mussorgsky
LIBR.: By the composer
From a comedy by Gogol

St. Petersburg, 1 April 1909 (with piano accompaniment)
Paris, 1923
Essen, 1937

This opera was composed in 1868. It was edited for the Paris performance by Ravel, and for Essen by Alexander Tcherepnin.

**Zigeunerbaron**
(*The Gypsy Baron*)
COMP.: J. Strauss
LIBR.: J. Schnitzer
From a libretto by Jokai

*Operetta in 3 acts*
Vienna, 24 October 1885
New York, 1886
London, 1935

### CAST

| | | | |
|---|---|---|---|
| Graf Peter Homonay | Bar | Mirabella, *her governess* | C |
| Conte Carnero | Bar | Ottokar | T |
| Sandor Barinkay | T | Czipra, *gypsy leader* | MS |
| Kalman Zsupan, *pig farmer* | Bar | Saffi, *her foster daughter* | S |
| Arsena, *his daughter* | S | Pali, *gypsy* | B |

### MUSICAL HIGHLIGHTS

The Overture
ACT I. Waltz *Als flotter Geist*, Barinkay
ACT II. Trio *Mein Aug'bewacht* (My eyes are wide), Saffi, Barinkay, Czipra
Treasure Waltz *Ha, seht es winkt'* (Ha, see it beckon), Saffi, Barinkay, Czipra
Duet *Wer uns getraut?* (Who married us?), Saffi and Barinkay

### SYNOPSIS

I. Barinkay has inherited a castle in which, Czipra says, there is a treasure which he may find only through a faithful wife. At first he courts Arsena for this project, but she will not have less than a noble husband. As soon as he meets Saffi, however, he forgets the difficulty and joins the gypsies, being made their baron.

II. He, his love and Czipra find the treasure just as it was predicted. He is happy until Czipra tells him that Saffi is really a princess and is therefore higher in station than he. Dejected he goes off to the wars with his friends.

III. Barinkay and Ottokar return from war each rewarded for heroism by a grant of nobility, thus paving the way toward renewed happiness with Saffi as is indicated by the grand waltz of the finale.

# THE PEOPLE IN OPERA

This section lists the best-known singers, authors, conductors, and other persons in opera. After each singer's name appears a list of some of the roles he or she has sung; after each composer, a list of some of the most significant operas he wrote.

An index to this section, arranged according to voice (soprano, contralto, etc.) or function (conductor, librettist, etc.) will be found at the end of the book.

Beneath a few of the names in this list no birth dates appear. In most cases, particularly of singers, the information is not available.

**Ackté, Aïno**                        *Soprano*
b. Helsinki, 1876: d. there, 1944
Debut as Marguérite at Opéra, 1897; at Metropolitan, 1904.
Elisabeth, Elsa, Gilda, Juliette, Nedda, Ophélie, Salome, Sieglinde.

**Adam, Adolphe Charles**        *Composer*
b. Paris, 1803: d. there, 1856
Called one of the creators of opéra-comique, Adam composed fifty-three works for the stage. He was also an organist and composer of nonoperatic music such as the famous *Cantique de Noël*, and the ballet *Giselle*. In 1847 he organized and managed the Théâtre Nationale, but soon went heavily into debt. His most famous works were:

| | | |
|---|---|---|
| Pierre et Catherine | Opéra-Comique | 1829 |
| Le Chalet | ,, | 1834 |
| Le Postillon de Longjumeau | ,, | 1836 |
| Le Fidèle Berger | ,, | 1838 |
| Le Brasseur de Preston | ,, | 1838 |
| Régine, ou Les Deux Nuits | ,, | 1839 |
| La Reine d'un Jour | ,, | 1839 |
| Le Roi d'Yvetot | ,, | 1842 |
| Cagliostro | ,, | 1844 |

| | | |
|---|---|---|
| Si j'étais Roi | Lyrique | 1844 |
| Richard en Palestine | Opéra | 1854 |

**Adam de la Halle**                *Composer*
b. Arras, France circa 1230: d. Naples, 1287
A *trouvère*, he wrote the famous *Jeu de Robin et de Marion* for the court of Aragon at Naples, in 1285. The work has been re-orchestrated and edited by Darius Milhaud for modern performance.

**Adamberger, Valentin**                *Tenor*
b. Munich, 1743: d. Vienna, 1804
Called Adamonti in Italy. He sang the first Belmonte (*Die Entführung aus dem Serail*), the part being written for him. He played a part also in *Der Schauspieldirektor*.

**Adams, Suzanne**                        *Soprano*
b. Cambridge, Mass., 1872: d. London, 1953
She made her debut at the Opéra in 1895 as Juliette. In 1899 she did the same role in her Metropolitan debut.
Cherubino, Elvira, Euridice, Gilda, Marguérite (trained by Gounod), Micaela, Zerlina.

**Adler, Kurt**                        *Conductor*
b. Neuhaus, Czechoslovakia, 1907:
Pianist and conductor in Berlin, Prague

and Kiev before coming to the United States. Chorusmaster and conductor at the Metropolitan since 1943.

**Adler, Kurt Herbert**  *Conductor*
b. Vienna, 1905:
Conductor at Salzburg, then at Chicago. In 1943 he became conductor, then artistic director at San Francisco.

**Adler, Peter Herman**  *Conductor*
b. Jablonec, Czechoslovakia, 1899:
Conductor at Bremen, Kiev and New York. Music Director of NBC Opera Theater since 1949.

**Agthé, Rosa**  *Soprano*
b. Weimar, 1827: d. there, 1906
First Elsa in *Lohengrin*. Married the baritone von Milde.

**Albanese, Licia**  *Soprano*
b. Bari, Italy, 1913:
Debut at Parma in 1935, at Metropolitan, 1940, as Cio-cio San.
Concepcion, Giorgetta, Inez, Lauretta, Liù, Margherita (*Mefistofele*), Mimi, Tosca, Violetta.

**Albani, Emma**  *Soprano*
(*Really* Marie Louise Cécilie Emma Lajeunesse)
b. Chambly, Montreal, 1847: d. London, 1930
Having made her professional beginning singing in church in Albany, N.Y., she took her stage name from the name of the city. She made her operatic debut as Aminta at Messina in 1870, then Covent Garden, 1872, and the New York Academy of Music in 1874. She married Ernest Gye in 1878, retired from the stage to sing in concerts after 1896, and was made a Dame of the British Empire in 1925.
Antonida, Desdemona, Elisabeth, Elsa, Eva, Isolde, Lucia, Marguérite, Mignon, Ophélie.

**Albéniz, Isaac**  *Composer*
b. Camprodón, Spain, 1860: d. Cambo-Les-Bains, Pyrénées, 1909
At thirteen he ran away from home and traveled throughout Spain, making his living as a pianist. Thence he went to Puerto Rico, Cuba and the United States, living by the same means until 1875. He lived mostly in Paris after 1893.

| | | |
|---|---|---|
| The Magic Opal | London | 1893 |
| San Antonio de la Florida | Madrid | 1894 |
| Merlin (*part of a trilogy*) | | |
| Enrico Clifford | Barcelona | 1895 |
| Pepita Jiménez | „ | 1896 |

**Albert, Eugene, Francis Charles d'**  *Composer*
b. Glasgow, 1864: d. Riga, 1932
He led a troubled life, married and divorced six times. He was a pianist and a conductor, and studied with Franz Liszt.

| | | |
|---|---|---|
| Der Rubin | Karlsruhe | 1893 |
| Ghismonda | Dresden | 1895 |
| Tiefland | Prague | 1903 |
| Flauto Solo | „ | 1905 |
| Die Toten Augen | Dresden | 1916 |
| Der Golem | Frankfurt | 1926 |
| Mr. Wu | Dresden | 1932 |

(*The last was completed by Blech.*)

**Alboni, Marietta**  *Contralto*
b. Cesena, Italy, 1823: d. Ville d'Avray, France, 1894
She was a pupil of Rossini in preparing roles in his works. Her debut was as Saffo (Pacini), in 1842.
1st Zerlina (*Fra Diavolo*), Fidés, Maffio Orsini, Rosina (*Il Barbiere di Siviglia*), Semiramide.

**Alda, Frances**  *Soprano*
(*Really* Frances Davies)
b. Christchurch, New Zealand, 1883: d. Venice, 1952
She made her debut at the Opéra-Comique in 1904 as Manon, and as Gilda in 1908 at the Metropolitan,

opposite Caruso. In 1910 she married
Giulio Gatti-Casazza, and became, in
1939, a citizen of the United States.

Aida, Desdemona, Francesca, Harriet
(*Martha*), Juliette, Louise, Manon Lescaut,
Margherita (*Mefistofele*), Marguérite
(*Faust*), Micaela, Mimi, Princess (*Marouf*),
Rozenn (*Roi d'Ys*), Violetta.

**Alessandro, Victor**                         *Conductor*
b. Waco, Tex. 1915:
   Conductor at Oklahoma City, then at
San Antonio.

**Alfano, Franco**                               *Composer*
b. near Naples, 1876: d. San Remo, 1954
   Besides his own works, he completed
Puccini's *Turandot*.

| Miranda | Leipzig | 1896 |
| La Fonte di Enscir | Breslau | 1898 |
| Risurrezione | Turin | 1904 |
| Madonna Imperia | ,, | 1927 |

**Allin, Norman**                                    *Bass*
b. Ashton-on-Lyne, England, 1885:
   After establishing himself as a singer, he
became director of the British National
Opera Company.
   Aged Hebrew (*Samson et Dalila*),
Bartolo (*Le Nozze di Figaro*), Dositheus,
Falstaff (*Die Lustigen Weiber von Windsor*),
Gurnemanz, Parsifal, Ragman (*Louise*).

**Althouse, Paul**                                  *Tenor*
b. Reading, Penna., 1889: d. New York,
1954
   Cola Rienzi, Dmitrij, Erik (*Der Fliegende
Holländer*), Huon, Lohengrin, Max (*Der
Freischütz*), Parsifal, Tannhäuser, Tristan,
Siegfried, Siegmund, Walther.

**Alvarez, Albert Raymond**              *Tenor*
(*Really* Albert Gourron)
b. Bordeaux, 1860: d. Nice, 1933
   He began as Faust, in Paris in 1892,
then as Roméo at the Metropolitan in
1899. Eventually he built up his repertory
to nearly sixty roles.

1st Nicias (*Thaïs*), Faust (*La Damnation
de Faust*), Don José, Otello, John of
Leyden, Tannhäuser, Walther.

**Alvary, Lorenzo**                                  *Bass*
b. Debrecen, Hungary, 20 February 1909:
   Don Alfonso (*Così fan Tutte*), Angelotti,
Arkel, Le Bailli (*Werther*), Bonze (*Butter-
fly*), Foltz, Hortensius, Masetto, Baron
Ochs, Pimen, Samuele (*Un Ballo in
Maschera*), Simone (*Gianni Schicchi*), Truf-
faldino (*Ariadne auf Naxos*), Zuniga
(*Carmen*).

**Alvary, Max**                                      *Tenor*
(*Really* Max Achenbach)
b. Düsseldorf, 1856: d. Thuringia, 1898
   He made his debut at the Metropolitan
in 1885 as Don José. Later he made
himself a specialist in Wagnerian roles.
   Adolar (*Euryanthe*), Cola Rienzi, Lohengrin, Parsifal, Siegfried, Siegmund, Tannhäuser, Tristan, Walther.

**Amara, Lucine**                                 *Soprano*
b.
   Antonia, Countess Almaviva, Countess
Ceprano (*Rigoletto*), Helmwige, Micaela,
Mimi, Nedda, Tatyana,

**Amato, Pasquale**                              *Baritone*
b. Naples, 1878: d. New York, 1942
   Amato made his debut at Naples in
1900 as Germont, and in the same role
in 1918 at the Metropolitan.
   1st Rance, Amfortas, Escamillo, Giovanni (*Francesca da Rimini*), Golaud,
Manfredo, Napoleone (*Madame Sans-
Gêne*).

**Ancona, Mario**                                *Baritone*
b. Livorno, Italy, 1870: d. Florence, 1931
   He made his debut as Scindia in *Le
Roi de Lahore*. He played the first Tonio
in London and in New York.
   1st Silvio, Alfonso (*La Favorita*),
Amonasro, Figaro (*Il Barbiere di Siviglia*),
Hans Sachs, Nelusko, de Nevers, Telramund, Zurga (*Les Pêcheurs de Perles*).

**Anderson, Marian** *Contralto*
b. Philadelphia, 1902:
Marian Anderson, made famous by her concert career, became the first Negro on the principal staff of the Metropolitan. In February, 1939, she was denied an appearance at the hall of the Daughters of the American Revolution in Washington, D.C., because of her race. A committee headed by the wife of the President was immediately formed and found a chance for her to sing in the open, on the steps of the Lincoln Memorial, to an immense crowd of grateful Washingtonians. She frequently has sung Ulrica at the Metropolitan.

**Angeles, Victoria de los** *Soprano*
b. Barcelona, 1923:
Having made her debut in opera at Madrid in 1944, she first appeared in the United States at Carnegie Hall in 1950 and at the Metropolitan the same year.
Cio-cio San, Elisabeth (*Tannhäuser*), Eva, Manon, Marguérite, Mélisande, Micaela, Mimi, Rosina (*Il Barbiere di Siviglia*), Salud.

**Angelo, Louis d'** *Bass*
b. Naples, 1888: d. Jersey City, N.J., 1958
He first sang at the Metropolitan in 1917 and stayed nearly thirty years, leaving in 1946 after having sung almost three hundred roles.
Bartolo (*Il Barbiere di Siviglia*), Uberto (*La Serva Padrona*).

**Ansseau, Fernand** *Tenor*
b. near Mons, France, 1890:
Faust, des Grieux (*Manon*), Don José, Julien, Orfeo (as originally written for male voice), Romeo.

**Antheil, George** *Composer*
b. Trenton, N.J., 1900: d. New York, 1959
Antheil was famous in Europe for flamboyant modernism, to accomplish which he went to extreme lengths, using even airplane engines to make new sounds. This became the subject of a most remarkable little book on the creation of music by Ezra Pound.

| | | |
|---|---|---|
| Transatlantic (*to his own libretto using jazz rhythms*) | | 1930 |
| Helen Retires | | 1934 |

**Arditi, Luigi** *Composer*
b. Crescentino, Italy, 1822: d. near Brighton, England, 1903
Famous not only as a composer, but also as a conductor. He supplied recitatives for the production of *Die Entführung aus dem Serail* in London, 1866. He is the composer of a famous vocal waltz, *Il Bacio*.

| | | |
|---|---|---|
| I Briganti | Milan | 1841 |
| Il Corsaro | Havana | 1846 |
| La Spia | New York | 1856 |

**Arensky, Antony Stepanovich** *Composer*
b. Novgorod, 1861: d. Finland, 1906

| | | |
|---|---|---|
| Voyevoda (*A Dream on the Volga*) | Moscow | 1891 |
| Raphael | ,, | 1894 |
| Nal and Damayanti | ,, | 1904 |

**Ariosti, Attilio** *Composer*
b. Bologna, 1666: d. (place unknown) circa 1740
An accomplished organist and player upon the viola d'amore, Ariosti was a co-director, with Handel and Bononcini, of the Royal Academy of Music at London in 1720. For a short time he lived as a Dominican friar.

| | | |
|---|---|---|
| Tirsi | Venice | 1686 |
| Morte Placado | Vienna | 1707 |
| Mars und Irene | Berlin | 1703 |
| Artaserse | London | 1724 |

**Arne, Thomas Augustine** *Composer*
b. London, 1710: d. there, 1778
It is said that as a boy Arne, forbidden to study music, used to borrow servants' clothes in order to stand in the shadows of the mighty and watch operas. Later, before making the definite break

with parental authority, he tried being a solicitor for a while.

Rosamund London 1733
Tom Thumb „ 1733
Alfred (*masque, with* Rule
Britannia *as its finale*) Clivedon, 1740
The Temple of Dullness
Drury Lane, 1745
Artaxerxes (*his first in the*
*Italian manner*) 1762
Love in a Village
(*ballad opera*) Drury Lane, 1762

**Arnould, Madeleine Sophie** *Soprano*
b. Paris, 1740: d. there, 1802
Sophie Arnould commenced a most notorious career with a debut at the Opéra in 1757. She lives on as the subject of a one-act comedy by Gabriel Pierné. She sang the first Iphigénie (*Iphigénie en Aulide*), and the first Euridice.

**Auber, Daniel François Esprit**
*Composer*
b. Caen, 1782: d. Paris, 1871
Auber was director of the Paris Conservatoire from 1842 to 1871.

Le Séjour Militaire Paris 1813
Le Testament et les
Billets-Doux Comique 1819
La Bergère Châtelaine „ 1820
Masaniello Opéra 1828
Fra Diavolo Comique 1830
Le Cheval de Bronze „ 1835
Les Diamants de la
Couronne Comique 1841
Manon Lescaut „ 1856

**Aubert, Louis François** *Composer*
b. Paramé, Belgium, 1877:
La Forêt Bleue Boston 1913

**Audran, Edmund** *Composer*
b. Lyons, 1840: d. Tierceville, France, 1901
A writer of comic operas such as:
La Mascotte 1880
L'Oeuf rouge 1890
M. Lohengrin 1896

**Austin, Frederick** *Bass*
b. London, 1872: d. there, 1952
Austin was not only a singer but a successful arranger and composer of operatic and orchestral works. He edited and arranged the production of the revived *Beggar's Opera* for Hammersmith (London).
Guglielmo (*Cosi fan Tutte*), Gunther, Peachum.

**Austin, Sumner** *Baritone*
b. London, 1888:
A member of the Carl Rosa Opera Company, famous for his Gianni Schicchi.

**Autori, Federico** *Bass*
b.
Archibaldo, Matteo (*Fra Diavolo*).

**Baccaloni, Salvatore** *Bass*
b. Rome, 1900:
Beginning as a student of architecture, Baccaloni switched to opera and made his debut under Toscanini at La Scala in 1926. He first played at the Metropolitan as Bartolo in 1940.
Alcindoro, Bartolo (*Le Nozze di Figaro* and *Il Barbiere di Siviglia*), Benoit, Dulcamara, Falstaff (*Falstaff*), Gianni Schicchi, Leporello, Don Pasquale, Sacristan (*Tosca*), Sulpice, Uberto.

**Bach, Johann Christian** *Composer*
b. Leipzig, 1735: d. London, 1782
The eleventh son of Johann Sebastian Bach and an organist like his father, Johann Christian wrote thirteen operas, much chamber music and many concertos. He is called the London Bach.
Artaserse (*Metastasio*) 1761
Catone in Utica
(*Metastasio*) 1761
Orione(*first opera to use*
*clarinets in the orchestra*
*in England*) 1763
Alessandro nell'Indie Naples 1762
Lucio Silla Mannheim 1776

**Baklanov, George** *Baritone*
b. St. Petersburg, 1882: d. Basel, 1938
He made his debut in St. Petersburg in 1905. In 1935 he sang the first Agamemnon (*Iphigénie en Aulide*) in the United States, at Philadelphia.
Boris, Rigoletto, Scarpia.

**Balaban, Emanuel** *Conductor*
b. New York, 1895:
Conductor at Dresden, then in the Opera Department of the Eastman School of Music in Rochester, N.Y., 1927–1953. Afterwards he conducted in New York City. He is presently on the faculty of Juilliard School of Music.

**Balfe, Michael William** *Composer*
b. Dublin, 1808: d. Hertfordshire, 1870
Balfe was not only a composer but also a violinist and a baritone. He played in the orchestra at Drury Lane in 1824. He sang Figaro (*Il Barbiere di Siviglia*) for Rossini at Paris, and Papageno for the first production in England of *Die Zauberflöte*.

| | | |
|---|---|---|
| The Siege of | | |
| Rochelle | Drury Lane | 1835 |
| The Maid of Artois | London | 1836 |
| Falstaff | ,, | 1838 |
| The Bohemian | | |
| Girl | Drury Lane | 1843 |
| The Rose of Castile | London | 1857 |

**Bamberger, Carl** *Conductor*
b. Vienna, 1902:
After conducting opera in Danzig, Darmstadt, Russia and Egypt he came to the United States. Here he conducted for NBC and CBS, and was head of the opera department of the Mannes College of Music from 1939.

**Bamboschek, Giuseppe** *Conductor*
b. Trieste, 1890:
After making his conducting debut at Trieste in 1908 he became accompanist to Pasquale Amato, traveling throughout the United States in 1913. From 1916 to 1926 he was conductor at the Metropolitan. He then directed opera at Philadelphia.

**Bampton, Rose** *Soprano*
b. Cleveland, 1909:
Rose Bampton made her first debut as a mezzo-soprano at the Metropolitan in 1932, playing Gioconda. In 1937 she came out a second time at the same place, singing the soprano role of Leonora (*Il Trovatore*).
Aida, Amneris, Donna Anna, Daphne, Laura (*Gioconda*), Gioconda, Leonora (*Il Trovatore*), Norma, Sieglinde.

**Bantock, Sir Granville** *Composer*
b. London, 1868: d. there, 1946
He was known not only as composer, but as a conductor and teacher. From 1907 to 1934 he was professor of music at Birmingham. He was knighted in 1930.

| | | |
|---|---|---|
| Caedmar | London | 1892 |
| The Pearl of Iran | | 1894 |
| The Seal Woman | Birmingham | 1924 |
| (*all on Celtic subjects*) | | |

**Barber, Samuel** *Composer*
b. West Chester, Pa., 1910:
A nephew of Louise Homer and a singer himself. Not a prolific composer, but a very sure one. He is a close associate of Menotti, who wrote the libretto for Barber's only full-scale opera. In 1960 the pair brought out a tiny, nine-minute scene, *A Hand of Bridge*.

| | | |
|---|---|---|
| Vanessa | New York | 1958 |

**Barbier, Jules Paul** *Librettist*
b. Paris, 1822: d. there, 1910
An associate of Carré, with whom he wrote libretti for *Dinorah*, *Faust*, *Roméo et Juliette*, *Mignon*, *Les Contes d'Hoffmann*. With du Wailly he turned out *Benvenuto Cellini*.

**Barbieri, Fedora** *Contralto*
Adalgisa, Amneris, Azucena, Carmen, Dalila, Princess Eboli, Laura (*La Gioconda*), Orfeo (*La Favola d'Orfeo*), Santuzza.

**Barbot, Joseph Théodore Désiré** *Tenor*
b. Toulouse, 1824: d. Paris, 1897
The first Faust. Studied with Manuel
Garcia.

**Bardi, Giovanni** *Patron*
b. Florence, 1534: d. Rome, 1612
The Count of Vernio, a patron of music
and an amateur composer. In his house,
about 1600, were held the meetings that
led to the invention of opera. The new
art, stemming from a desire to re-create
the beauty of Greek drama, was the
outcome of many conversations between
his friends, among whom were Vincenzo
Galilei (Galileo's father), Bernardo Strozzi,
Girolamo Mei, Ottavio Rinuccini, Giulio
Caccini (his secretary), Jacopo Peri,
Giacomo Corsi, and Emilio dei Cavalieri.
These, constituted as the *Camerata*, were
the inventors of modern opera. Bardi
himself, besides taking part in the productions, wrote madrigals and prose
works.

**Barrientos, Maria** *Soprano*
b. Barcelona, 1884: d. Ciboure, France,
1946
A famous Lucia, having made her debut
in that role at the Metropolitan in 1916.
Her first role in opera was that of Selika,
in Barcelona in 1899, when she was only
fifteen. She was also a pianist, violinist,
and composer; she wrote a symphony
when she was still a child.
Dinorah, Gilda, Lakmé, Linda di
Chamounix, Martha, Philine, Mireille,
Ophélie, Urbain.

**Bartók, Béla** *Composer*
b. Nagy-szent-miklós, Hungary, 1881:
d. New York, 1945
One of the greatest composers of the
twentieth century, and one whose style
had very deep influence upon practically
all the composers of the following
generation. He is famous also as a collector
of thousands of Hungarian folk songs and

dances which he, in association with
Kodály, analyzed in great detail. His six
string quartets are generally considered to
be masterworks in the form; they are also
revolutionary in their rhythmic and
harmonic style. Among the most popular
of his larger works are such extended
pieces for small groups of instruments as
the *Sonata for Two Pianos and Percussion*,
and his *Music for Strings, Percussion and
Celesta*.
Duke Bluebeard's
    Castle      Budapest  1918

**Bassani, Giovanni Battista** *Composer*
b. Padova, 1657: d. Bergamo, 1716
A composer of oratorios, masses,
suites, sonatas and operas. He was also
a violinist and organist.
Amorosa Preda di
    Paride      Bologna  1683
    Alarico, Re de Goti  Ferrara  1685
Falaride, Tiranno
    d'Agrigento          1684

**Bassi, Luigi** *Baritone*
b. Pesaro, 1766: d. Dresden, 1825
He made his debut in the town of his
birth in 1779, at thirteen. Mozart wrote
the part of Don Giovanni for him when
he was only twenty-two, and listened
to the singer's advice on technical details.
1st Don Giovanni, Almaviva (*Le Nozze
di Figaro*), Barnaba, Gennaro.

**Baum, Kurt** *Tenor*
b. Prague, Czechoslovakia, 15 March 1908:
Don Alvaro, Drum Major (*Wozzeck*),
Enzo, Grigorij, Don José, Mario, Radames,
Singer (*Der Rosenkavalier*), Turiddu.

**Beard, John** *Tenor*
b. circa 1717: d. 1791
A singer in Handel's operas in London.
He was the first Captain MacHeath.

**Beaumarchais, Pierre Augustin Caron de**
*Playwright*
b. Paris, 1732: d. there, 1799

This most famous French playwright also made a name for himself as a flutist and harpist. He wrote the trilogy for which Mozart, Paisiello and Rossini composed three of the most famous operas in the history of the comic stage. The plays were:

Le Barbier de Seville
Le Mariage de Figaro
La Mère Coupable

**Beck, Johann Nepomuk**          Baritone
b. Budapest, 1827: d. Pressburg, 1904

Almaviva (Le Nozze di Figaro), Amonasro, Don Giovanni, Guillaume Tell, Hamlet, Hans Heiling, Nelusko, Orestes, Richard (I Puritani).

**Beck, Karl**          Tenor
b. Austria, 1814: d. Vienna, 1879

The first Lohengrin.

**Beecham, Sir Thomas**          Conductor
b. near Liverpool, 1879: d. London, 1961

Born wealthy, he made use of his money and his talent, as did Mendelssohn, to bring out great works of music, especially operas. He conducted the first performances in England of Elektra, Salomé, Der Rosenkavalier, Ariadne auf Naxos, A Village Romeo and Juliet, The Wreckers, Tiefland, Dylan and The Critic. In 1928 he toured the United States. He conducted at Seattle from 1941 through 1943, then at the Metropolitan from 1942 to 1944. He organized the Royal Philharmonic Orchestra of London in 1947. Among musicians he was noted for his acid but accurate criticisms and his uncompromising attention to obtaining the maximum effort from the players.

**Beethoven, Ludvig van**          Composer
b. Bonn, 1770: d. Vienna, 1827

This celebrated creator of nine symphonies was not a child prodigy as were many of his contemporaries, but was, nevertheless, a professional musician early in his life, playing the organ and other keyboard instruments in the orchestra of the Elector of Bonn, for whom his father worked. His duties included not only the usual organ playing for religious occasions, but also the accompaniment and conducting of private performances of operas. Thus, quite early, he became acquainted both with the keyboard works of Johann Sebastian Bach, and the stage works of Gluck, Paisiello and others.

In 1787 he is said to have visited Vienna where he played before the famous Mozart and took a few lessons. The following year the new Elector established a national theater at Bonn, in the orchestra of which young Beethoven played viola and learned more about music for the stage. In 1792 Haydn visited the court, and Beethoven was able to show him some of his works. Encouraged by the great man's approval, and supported financially by the Elector, Beethoven went to study with Haydn in Vienna in his twenty-first year. Bonn, meanwhile, was taken over by the advancing French armies, and the composer was never again required to go home.

By 1803, Beethoven was famous as a composer and performer. He agreed to compose an opera to be produced by the impresario Schikaneder. It was not, however, until the idea had mulled for some time and the request had been repeated that he finally, in the early months of 1805, began to work on the piece. After very intense labor the score was finished that summer and shown to friends, the composer roaring the vocal lines as he played the piano. It was first performed in November.

At that time Vienna was occupied by the French, but Beethoven's concentration upon his music was not materially distracted. After the first production of his opera he withdrew it and began to make changes. It was brought out briefly in 1806, but withdrawn again and extensively repaired and altered. In 1814 it finally appeared in the form we know it, with a revised libretto and many changes in the score.

After *Fidelio*, Beethoven wanted to compose another opera. He read libretto after libretto but was never quite satisfied. He tried *Melusine* by Grillparzer, but ceased working when he heard of a ballet on the same subject. According to friends, he had always searched for a noble and "elevating" subject, rather than a scandalous one such as might have pleased Mozart. He never found one to his liking.

While *Fidelio* was being composed, Beethoven's deafness had just begun to bother him. By 1816 he was forced to use an ear-trumpet, and by 1820 was totally deaf.

| | | |
|---|---|---|
| Fidelio | Vienna | 1805 |

**Bellincioni, Gemma** *Soprano*
b. Monza, Italy, 1864: d. Naples, 1950
She made her debut in Naples in 1881; the same year she married Robert Stagno. She was the first Fedora, Santuzza and Sapho.
Carmen, Fedora, Santuzza, Sapho, Violetta.

**Bellini, Vincenzo** *Composer*
b. Catania, Sicily, 1801: d. near Paris, 1835
This very famous composer of many operas lived only thirty-four years, but wrote works which are still in repertory throughout the world. Perhaps some of his success came from luck. A performance of an opera while he was still in school led to his first commission, for the San Carlo theater at Naples, in 1826. One success led to another, and his career was launched. Bellini's importance stretches beyond his own stage works. He is greatly admired by many for the simplicity of his melodic line, and this has influenced the work of composers as

different from Bellini's tradition as, for instance, Stravinsky.

| | | |
|---|---|---|
| Il Pirata | La Scala | 1827 |
| La Straniera | „ | 1829 |
| I Capuletti ed I Montecchi | Venice | 1830 |
| La Sonnambula | Milan | 1831 |
| Norma | La Scala | 1831 |
| I Puritani | Paris | 1835 |

**Bemberg, Herman** *Composer*
b. Paris, 1859: d. Bern, 1931
Bemberg won the Rossini prize in 1885. He composed operas, cantatas and songs.

| | | |
|---|---|---|
| Le Baiser de Suzon | Paris | 1888 |
| Elaine | Covent Garden | 1892 |

**Bender, Paul** *Bass*
b. Westerwald, Germany, 1875: d. Munich, 1947
He made his Metropolitan debut in 1922.
Amfortas, Gurnemanz, Hans Sachs, Baron Ochs, Pizarro, Sarastro, Wotan.

**Bennett, Robert Russell** *Composer*
b. Kansas City, Kan., 1894:
Best known for his arrangements in the Broadway style, his largest and most successful venture was the arrangement of *Carmen Jones* in 1943.

| | | |
|---|---|---|
| Maria Malibran | New York | 1935 |
| The Enchanted Kiss | „ | 1944 |

**Benoist, François** *Composer*
b. Nantes, 1794: d. Paris, 1878

| | |
|---|---|
| Léonore et Félix | 1821 |
| L'Apparition | 1848 |

**Benoist, Peter** *Composer*
b. Harlebeke, Belgium, 1834: d. Antwerp, 1901
He was a composer of oratorios and cantatas. He founded a school of music which, in 1898, became the Royal Flemish Conservatory.

| | | |
|---|---|---|
| Het Dorp in 't gebergte (*A Mountain Village*) | Brussels | 1856 |
| Roi des Aulnes | „ | 1859 |
| Isa (*in Flemish*) | „ | 1867 |

**Bentonelli, Joseph**    *Tenor*
(*Really* Benton)
b. Sayre, Okla., 1900:
The first American Achilles, in *Iphigénie en Aulide* at Philadelphia in 1935. He studied with Jean de Reszke and made his Metropolitan debut in 1936, singing des Grieux.

**Berg, Alban**    *Composer*
b. Vienna, 1885: d. there, 1935
One of the most advanced composers of the twelve-tone school, a follower of Schönberg, whom he excels in many ways. He wrote several well-known works for orchestra and for various smaller combinations of instruments.

| | | |
|---|---|---|
| Wozzeck | Berlin | 1925 |
| Lulu (*unfinished*) | Zürich | 1937 |

**Berg, Natanael**    *Composer*
b. Stockholm, 1879:
He began as a student of medicine. He composed works for ballet and orchestra and the following operas:

| | | |
|---|---|---|
| Lelia | Stockholm | 1912 |
| Engelbrekt | „ | 1929 |
| Judith | „ | 1936 |
| Birgitta | „ | 1942 |
| Genoveva | „ | 1947 |

**Berger, Erna**    *Soprano*
b. Dresden, 1900:
Her Metropolitan debut took place in 1949.
Anne (*Rake's Progress*), Constanze, Leila, Pamina, Sophie, Zerlina (*Fra Diavolo*).

**Berger, Rudolph**    *Baritone/Tenor*
b. Moravia, 1874: d. New York, 1915
He made his debut as a baritone in 1891 at Brünn. Changing to tenor, he came out at Berlin in 1909 as Lohengrin. In 1913 he married Marie Rappold. His repertory is said to have included ninety-six baritone and eighteen tenor roles.
Eric (*Der Fliegende Holländer*), Jokanaan (*seventy-nine times*), Lohengrin, Parsifal, Siegfried, Siegmund, Tannhäuser, Tristan, Walther.

**Bergsma, William**    *Composer*
b. Oakland, Calif., 1921:

| | | |
|---|---|---|
| The Wife of Martin Guerre | New York | 1956 |

**Berkeley, Lennox**    *Composer*
b. near Oxford, 1903:

| | |
|---|---|
| Nelson | London |

(*Preview*, 1953; *complete*, 1954.)

| | | |
|---|---|---|
| A Dinner Engagement | Aldeburgh, England | 1954 |

**Berlioz, Hector**    *Composer*
b. La Côte Saint-André, 1803: d. Paris, 1869
A great innovator of instrumentation, and a great critic of music. From 1852 to his death he held the sinecure of librarian of the Paris Conservatory. He restored Gluck's *Orfeo* to its original shape and prepared recitatives for *Der Freischütz* for Paris in 1841. His most famous works are *The Fantastic Symphony* and *The Requieme*.

| | | |
|---|---|---|
| Benvenuto Cellini | Opéra | 1838 |
| Béatrice et Bénédict | Baden-Baden | 1862 |
| Les Troyens | | |
|   Part Two | Paris | 1863 |
|   Entire | Karlsruhe | 1890 |
| La Damnation de Faust | | |
|   (concert) | Opéra-Comique | 1846 |
|   (staged) | Monte-Carlo | 1893 |

**Bernstein, Leonard**    *Composer*
b. Lawrence, Mass., 1918:
Most famous as a pianist and conductor (of the New York Philharmonic), Bernstein has also written much music for the theater including the musical shows *On the Town*, *Wonderful Town*, *West Side Story* and the ballet *Fancy Free*. He was the first American to conduct a regular performance of opera at La Scala.

| | | |
|---|---|---|
| Trouble in Tahiti | Waltham, Mass. | 1952 |

**Berwald, Franz Adolf**     *Composer*
b. Stockholm, 1796: d. there, 1868
He wrote six symphonies, five cantatas, and other works.

| | | |
|---|---|---|
| Estrella di Soria | Stockholm | 1862 |
| Drottningen af | | |
| Golconda | ,, | 1864 |

**Betz, Franz**     *Tenor, Baritone*
b. Mainz, 1835: d. Berlin, 1900
The first Siegfried, Walther and Wotan.
He made his debut as Don Carlos (*Ernani*), in Berlin in 1859.
Don Carlos, Falstaff, Hans Sachs, Siegfried, Walther, Wotan.

**Bible, Frances**     *Mezzo-soprano*
b.
Amneris, Angelina, Cherubino, Hansel, Lola, Mrs. Nolan (*The Medium*), Octavian, Page (*Salomé*), Siebel, Smeraldina, Suzuki.

**Billington, Elizabeth**     *Soprano*
(*Née* Weichsel)
b. London, circa 1765: d. near Venice, 1818
She made her debut in Dublin as Euridice in 1784, and as Rosetta in *Love in a Village* at Covent Garden in 1786. In 1809 she retired.

**Bing, Rudolf**     *Manager*
b. Vienna, 1902:
Manager of the Darmstadt State Theater from 1928 to 1930, the opera at Charlottenberg, 1930–1933, at Glyndebourne, 1935–1939 and again from 1946 to 1949, and director of the Edinburgh Festival from 1947 to 1949. Since 1949 he has been general manager of the Metropolitan, making many long-overdue improvements in the house and the company.

**Bishop, Henry Rowley**     *Composer*
b. London, 1786: d. there, 1855
He wrote nearly one hundred thirty works for the stage. He was also a conductor and became a knight in 1809. The Circassian Bride

| | | |
|---|---|---|
| | Drury Lane | 1809 |
| Cortez | | 1823 |
| Clari, or the Maid of | | |
| Milan (*containing* Home Sweet | | |
| Home) | Covent Garden | 1823 |
| The Fall of Algiers | | 1825 |
| Aladdin | | 1826 |
| The Fortunate Isles | | 1841 |

**Bispham, David Scull**     *Baritone*
b. Philadelphia, 1857: d. New York, 1921
He made his debut in London in 1891. In 1896 he sang for the first time at the Metropolitan, as Beckmesser. He organized a Society of American Singers to stimulate opera in English, and established the Bispham prize for it.
Alberich, Colas, (*Bastien und Bastienne*), Dutchman, Escamillo, Falstaff (*Falstaff*), Iago, Kurnewal, Masetto, Peter (*Hänsel und Gretel*), Pizarro, Schikaneder, Telramund, Wolfram, Wotan.

**Bittner, Julius**     *Composer*
b. Vienna, 1874: d. there, 1939
Bittner practiced law until 1920. Besides operas, he wrote ballets, orchestral music, etc.

| | | |
|---|---|---|
| Die Rote Gret | Frankfurt | 1907 |
| Der Musikant | Vienna | 1910 |
| Der Bergsee | ,, | 1911 |
| Der Abenteurer | Cologne | 1913 |
| Das Höllisch Gold | Darmstadt | 1920 |
| Das Rosegärtlein | Mannheim | 1923 |
| Mondnacht | Berlin | 1928 |
| Das Vielchen | Vienna | 1934 |

**Bizet, Georges**     *Composer*
(*Really* Alexander César Léopold)
b. Paris, 1838: d. there, 1875
Bizet won the Prix de Rome and wrote a good deal of music to which the world paid practically no attention. With the exception of his music for *L'Arlésienne* he had no public success until the scandalous "critical failure" of *Carmen*. When Bizet

died, three months after the opening of that most famous work, he was unaware that it had begun to be recognized as a masterpiece. In 1857, he shared with Lecocq the Offenbach prize for his music to the libretto *Le Docteur Miracle*. In 1869 he married Geneviève Halévy, the daughter of his teacher. Otherwise his life was one of interminable labor on his music and unrelieved difficulties with the arbiters of taste in Paris in his time.

| | |
|---|---|
| La Prêtresse | 1854 |
| Le Docteur Miracle | 1857 |
| Don Procopio | 1906 |
| La Guzla de l'Emir | |
| Les Pêcheurs de Perles | 1863 |
| La Jolie Fille de Perth | 1867 |
| Numa | 1871 |
| Djamileh | 1872 |
| Carmen | 1875 |
| Ivan le Terrible | 1951 |

(*The above list shows the order of composition of the operas. The dates indicate the actual first performances which, in the cases of* Don Procopio *and* Ivan le Terrible *were long after Bizet's death.*)

**Bjoerling, Jussi**                *Tenor*
b. Stora, Sweden, 1907: d. near Stockholm, 1960
Born to a singing family, Jussi Bjoerling first appeared in the United States as a member of his family's male quartet, singing Swedish folk songs at community gatherings. He made his operatic debut in Stockholm in 1930 as Don Ottavio. Again he toured the United States as a concert singer in 1937, before making his debut as Rodolfo at the Metropolitan in 1938. Bjoerling was especially remarkable as one of the few singers from the north who excelled in Italian roles.
Calaf, des Grieux, Duke (*Rigoletto*), Faust (by Gounod), Manrico, Don Ottavio, Rhadames, Riccardo (*Un Ballo in Maschera*), Rodolfo, Romeo, Turiddu.

**Blacher, Boris**                *Composer*
b. Newchang, China, 1903:
A composer of ballets, orchestral music and opera, and also a librettist. Blacher wrote the texts of *Dantons Tod* and *Der Prozess*. In 1953 he became director of the Hochschule für Musik in West Berlin.

| | | |
|---|---|---|
| Fürstin Tarakanova | Dresden | 1941 |
| Die Flut | „ | 1947 |
| Die Nachtschwalbe | Leipzig | 1948 |
| Das preussisches Märchen | | |
| (*ballet opera*) | Berlin | 1952 |
| Abstract Opera No. 1 | Frankfurt | 1953 |

**Blauvelt, Lillian Evans**                *Soprano*
b. Brooklyn, N.Y., 1874: d. Chicago, 1947
The first Xenia in the opera of that name by her husband, Savine. She made her debut in Brussels in 1893 singing Mireille.

**Blech, Leo**                *Composer*
b. Aachen, 1871: d. Berlin, 1958
A pupil of Humperdinck. He was also a conductor at Prague, Berlin, Riga and Stockholm.

| | | |
|---|---|---|
| Aglaja | | 1893 |
| Cherubina | | 1894 |
| Das war ich | Dresden | 1902 |
| Rappelkopf | Berlin | 1917 |
| Aschenbrödel | Prague | 1905 |
| Versiegelt | Hamburg | 1908 |

**Blitzstein, Marc**                *Composer*
b. Philadelphia, 1905:
In 1960 he was commissioned to compose an opera on the subject of Sacco and Vanzetti for the Metropolitan.

| | | |
|---|---|---|
| The Harpies | New York | 1931 |
| The Cradle Will Rock | „ | 1937 |
| No for an Answer | „ | 1941 |
| Regina | Boston | 1949 |

**Bliss, Arthur**                *Composer*
(*Really* Edward Drummond)
b. London, 1891:
A composer of much ballet, orchestral music and music for films. He was knighted in 1950.

| | | |
|---|---|---|
| The Olympians | London | 1949 |

**Bloch, Ernst** *Composer*
b. Geneva, 1880: d. Portland, Oregon, 1959

Bloch's fame rests upon his orchestral works, particularly the rhapsody *Schelomo*, and upon his liturgical music for the synagogue. He was Director of the Cleveland Conservatory of Music and the San Francisco Conservatory before joining the staff of the University of California in 1944. He then went to live in Oregon.

| | | |
|---|---|---|
| Macbeth | Opéra-Comique | 1910 |
| Jézabel | (unfinished; begun 1918) | |

**Blockx, Jan** *Composer*
b. Antwerp, Belgium, 1851: d. there, 1912

| | | |
|---|---|---|
| Jets Vergeten | Antwerp | 1877 |
| Herbergprinses | „ | 1896 |
| Maître Martin | Brussels | 1892 |
| Thyl Eulenspiegel | „ | 1900 |
| De Bruid der Zee | Antwerp | 1901 |
| De Kapel | „ | 1903 |
| Chanson d'Amour | „ | 1912 |

**Bockelmann, Rudolf** *Baritone*
b. Bodenteich, Germany, 1892:

A member of the Chicago Opera for a brief period in the thirties, he is famous for his three major Wagnerian roles: Dutchman, Hans Sachs, Wotan.

**Bodansky, Artur** *Conductor*
b. Vienna, 1877: d. New York, 1939

Assistant Conductor at Vienna, Berlin, Prague, Mannheim and at the Metropolitan from 1915. He also composed recitatives for the production of *Oberon* at the Metropolitan in 1918.

**Böhm, Karl** *Conductor*
b. Graz, Austria, 1894:

Conductor at Dresden, Vienna, Chicago, and the Metropolitan.

**Bohnen, Michael** *Bass*
b. Keulen, Germany, 1886:

He made his debut in Düsseldorf in 1910, and as Francesco (*Mona Lisa*), at the Metropolitan in 1923.
Gurnemanz, King Marke.

**Boïeldieu, François Adrien** *Composer*
b. Rouen, 1775: d. Jarcy, 1834

His career began with an opera on a libretto by his father and ended with painting, which he took up late in his life. From 1803 to 1811 he tried the life of Court Composer at St. Petersburg, but returned to Paris for his greatest successes.

| | | |
|---|---|---|
| La Fille Coupable | Rouen | 1793 |
| La Famille Suisse | Paris | 1797 |
| Le Caliphe de Bagdad | „ | 1801 |
| La Dame Blanche | „ | 1825 |

**Boito, Arrigo** *Composer*
b. Padua, 1842: d. Milan, 1918

One of the great poets of opera, Boito wrote the magnificent libretti for *Otello* and *Falstaff* and revised *Simon Boccanegra* to make it dramatically practical. He wrote words for *La Gioconda* too, and composed his own operas. To add to his trades, he conducted the opening of his own *Mefistofele*.

| | | |
|---|---|---|
| Mefistofele | La Scala | 1868 |
| Nerone | Milan | 1924 |

**Bonci, Alessandro** *Tenor*
b. Cesena, Italy, 1870: d. near Rimini, 1940

Bonci made his debut at Parma in 1896, singing Fenton. *I Puritani* was revived for him at the Manhattan Opera in 1906 for his American debut, in which he sang the role of Arturo.

Fra Diavolo, Duke ( *Rigoletto*), Faust, Riccardo (*Un Ballo in Maschera*), Rodolfo (*La Bohème*).

**Bonelli, Richard** *Baritone*
( *Really* Bunn)
b. Port Byron, N.Y. 1894:

Bonelli first sang as Valentin in Brooklyn, 1915. He studied with Jean de Reszke and appeared for the first time at the Metropolitan, singing Germont, in 1932.

In 1945 he retired, but was soon heard again, singing Giorgio as late as 1952.
Barnaba, Giorgio, Germont, Manfredo, Tonio.

**Bononcini, Giovanni**  *Composer*
b. Modena, 1670: d. Vienna, 1747
Bononcini, or Buononcini, was associated with Handel in the establishment of the Royal Academy of Music in London. He also wrote his part of one of those multi-composer works for the stage that were favorite but soon forgotten devices of the time, *Muzio Scevola*, London, 1721. He returned to the Continent and invested his money in an alchemist's scheme to make gold. Having lost everything, he died in poverty.

| | | |
|---|---|---|
| Serse | Rome | 1694 |
| Tullio Ostilio | ,, | 1694 |
| Arstarto | London | 1720 |

**Borgatti, Giuseppe**  *Tenor*
b. Cento, Italy, 1871: d. Lago Maggiore, 1950
The first Andrea Chenier.
Andrea Chenier, Herod, Mario Cavaradossi, Tristan.

**Borghi-Mamo, Adelaide**  *Mezzo-soprano*
b. Bologna, 1829: d. there, 1901
She made her debut in 1846 at Urbino.
Leonora (*Favorita*), Marguérite (*Faust*).

**Borgiolo, Dino**  *Tenor*
b. Florence, 1891: d. there, 1960
Borgioli made his debut in Milan in 1918, singing in *La Favorita*. He made his name there under Toscanini at La Scala, then toured to Rome, Madrid, Portugal, Vienna, London, Paris, and Argentina. His American debut took place at the opening of the San Francisco War Memorial Opera House in 1932. He first appeared in New York as Rodolfo in *La Bohème* at the Metropolitan.
Duke ( *Rigoletto*), Fritz (*L'Amico Fritz*), Mario Cavaradossi, Don Ottavio, Riccardo (*Un Ballo in Maschera*), Rodolfo.

**Bori, Lucrezia**  *Soprano*
( *Really* Lucrezia Borja y Gonzalez de Riancho)
b. Valencia, 1887: d. New York, 1960
She made her debut as Micaela in Rome, 1908. Four years later she appeared for the first time at the Metropolitan, singing Manon Lescaut.
She was one of the most popular members of the Metropolitan company, famous not only for her singing and acting, but also for her lack of the normal vanity and insecurity of prima donnas. She was a member of the board of directors. She left the stage, intentionally quitting while still in command of her great technique, in 1936.
Antonia (*Les Contes d'Hoffman*), Concepcion, Fiora, Iris, Juliette, Louise, Magda (*La Rondine*), Manon, Mary (*Peter Ibbetson*), Mélisande, Mignon, Mimi, Norina, Snyegurotchka, Susanna (*Il Segreto di Susanna*), Suzel, Violetta.

**Borkh, Inge**  *Soprano*
b. Mannheim, 1921:
She made her debut at Lucerne in 1940 singing Agathe.
Aida, Eglantine, Elektra, Freia, Lady Macbeth, Leonora (*Fidelio*), Magda (*The Consul*), Marie (*Wozzeck*), Mona Lisa, Salome, Senta, Sieglinde, Tosca, Turandot.

**Borodin, Alexander**  *Composer*
b. St. Petersburg, 1833: d. there, 1887
Borodin was famous as a chemist, and taught that subject at a school of medicine for women in St. Petersburg, besides writing treatises. He is one of the "Mighty Five" of nineteenth-century Russian music, and is best known for his "Polovtzian Dances" from *Prince Igor*.
Bogatyri ( *The Valiant Knights*)
Moscow 1867
Prince Igor St. Petersburg 1890

**Bottesini, Giovanni**  *Composer*
b. Lombardy, 1821: d. Parma, 1889

Bottesini was the first real virtuoso of the double bass. He conducted opera in Italy, New Orleans, and at Paris. It was he who conducted the première of *Aida* in Cairo.

| | | |
|---|---|---|
| Cristoforo Colombo | Havana | 1847 |
| L'Assedio di Firenze | Paris | 1856 |
| Ali Baba | London | 1871 |
| Il Diavolo della Notte | Milan | 1858 |
| Marion Delorme | Palermo | 1862 |
| Vinciguerra | Paris | 1870 |
| Ero e Leandro | Turin | 1879 |
| La Regina di Nepal | ,, | 1880 |

**Boughton, Rutland** *Composer*
b. Aylesbury, England, 1878:
An advocate of choral drama.

| | | |
|---|---|---|
| The Birth of Arthur | Glastonbury | 1915 |
| The Immortal Hour | ,, | 1914 |
| Snow White | | 1914 |
| The Round Table | | 1916 |
| Bethlehem | ,, | 1915 |
| Alkestis | ,, | 1922 |
| The Queen of Cornwall | | |
| | ,, | 1924 |
| The Ever Young | | 1928 |
| The Lily Maid | | 1934 |
| Galahad | | 1944 |
| Avalon | | 1946 |

**Bouhy, Jacques Joseph André** *Baritone*
b. Pepinster, Belgium, 1848: d. Paris, 1929
The first Escamillo and the first Don César de Bazan. He was director of the New York Conservatory from 1885 to 1889. He made his operatic debut at the Opéra in 1871 singing Méphistophélès in *Faust*.

**Boulanger, Marie Julie** *Mezzo-soprano*
(*Née* Hallinger)
b. 1786: d. 1850
The first Pamela (*Fra Diavolo*). Not to be confused with Lili Boulanger, the composer, nor with Nadia, the conductor and teacher.

**Bovy, Vina** *Soprano*
b. Ghent, 1900:
After a debut as Violetta at the Metropolitan in 1936, she sang in various opera houses. In 1948 she became manager of the opera at Ghent. She is also a pianist.

**Bouvier, Hélène** *Soprano*
b.
Jocasta (*Oedipus Rex*).

**Bower, Minnia** *Soprano*
b.
One of the Nieces in the first production of *Peter Grimes*, in 1945.

**Bowles, Paul Frederick** *Composer*
b. New York, 1910:
A composer of ballet, orchestral music and little pieces for the piano. He is better known for his work in the novel.

| | |
|---|---|
| Denmark Vesey | 1937 |
| The Wind Remains | 1943 |

**Braham, John** *Tenor*
(*Really* Abraham)
b. London, 1774: d. there, 1856
The first Sir Huon. He made his debut in Covent Garden in 1787. His voice was phenomenal, having a compass of three octaves. Not only did he sing, however; he also composed his own parts in several operas.
Don Giovanni, Masaniello, Max, Guillaume Tell.

**Braithwaite, Warwick** *Conductor*
b. Dunedin, New Zealand., 1898:
Has conducted the National Orchestra of Wales, and at Sadlers Wells and Covent Garden.

**Brand, Max** *Composer*
b. Lwow, Poland, 1896:
Formerly a dodecaphonist, his one opera had a spectacular success during the early 1930's.
Maschinist Hopkins
Duisberg, Germany 1929

**Brandt, Marianne**   *Soprano and Contralto*
(*Really* Marie Bischoff)
b. Vienna, 1842: d. there, 1921
The second person to appear as Kundry, there being three to share the opening three performances. She made her debut as Rachel in *La Juive* at Graz in 1867.

Amneris, Azucena, Brangäne, Eglantine, Elsa, Elvira, Eva, Fidès, Gerhilde, Hedwige (*Guillaume Tell*), Irene, Kundry, Leonora (*Fidelio*), Margarethe (*Genoveva*), Rachel, Selika.

**Braun, Karl**   *Bass*
b. Meisenheim, Prussia, 1885:
Famous as Gurnemanz, he made his debut at the Metropolitan in 1913, retiring in 1939.
Gurnemanz, Rocco, Thoas.

**Braunfels, Walter**   *Composer*
b. Frankfort, 1882: d. Cologne, 1954

| Princess Bambilla | Stuttgart | 1909 |
| Till Eulenspiegel | „ | 1913 |
| Die Vögel (Aristophanes' *The Birds*) | Munich | 1920 |
| Don Gil von den Grünen Hosen | Munich | 1924 |
| Der Gläserne Berg | Cologne | 1928 |
| Ein Traum, ein Leben | „ | 1929 |
| Galathea | „ | 1930 |
| Die Heilige Johanna | | 1942 |

**Brema, Marie**   *Mezzo-soprano*
(*Really* Minny Fehrman)
b. Liverpool, 1856: d. Manchester, 1925
She made her debut at Oxford in 1891 as Adriana Lecouvreur.

Adriana Lecouvreur, Amneris, Brangäne, Brünnhilde, Dalila, Fricka, Kundry, Lola Marcellina (*L'Attaque du Moulin*), Orfeo, Ortrud.

**Britten, Benjamin**   *Composer*
b. Lowestoft, 1913:
The foremost opera composer of present-day England. He has also taken an active part in the establishment of grass-roots opera in that country. He arranged *Dido and Aeneas* for a production at Hammersmith, and *The Beggar's Opera* for Cambridge and for film.

| Paul Bunyan | New York | 1941 |
| Peter Grimes | London | 1945 |
| Rape of Lucretia | Glyndebourne | 1946 |
| Albert Herring | „ | 1947 |
| Let's Make an Opera | Aldeburgh | 1949 |
| Billy Budd | London | 1951 |
| Gloriana | Covent Garden | 1953 |
| The Turn of the Screw | Venice | 1954 |
| Midsummer Night's Dream | | 1960 |

**Brouwenstijn, Gré**   *Soprano*
b. Holland, 1915:
Debut at Covent Garden, 1951 as Aida.

Aida, Amelia (*Un Ballo in Maschera*), Countess Almaviva, Desdemona, Elizabeth, Elisabeth de Valois, Iphigénie (*Iphigénie en Aulide*), Yaroslavna, Jenufa, Leonora (*Fidelio* and *Trovatore*), Rezia, Rusalka, Santuzza, Tatyana, Tosca.

**Brownlee, John Donald Mackenzie**
*Baritone*
b. Geelong, Australia, 1900:
Melba discovered this young singer. He went on to a debut as Rigoletto at Covent Garden in 1926 and at the Metropolitan in 1937. From 1956 he was director of the Manhattan School of Music in New York.

Don Alfonso, Almaviva (*Le Nozze di Figaro*), Dr. Falke, Don Giovanni, Kothner, Don Ottavio, Papageno, Rigoletto, Sharpless, von Faninal.

**Brüll, Ignaz**   *Composer*
b. Prossnitz, Moravia, 1846: d. Vienna, 1907

| Die Bettler von Samarkand | | 1864 |
| Das Goldene Kreuz | Berlin | 1875 |
| Der Landfriede | Vienna | 1877 |
| Bianca | Dresden | 1879 |
| Königin Marietta | Munich | 1883 |
| Gloria | Hamburg | 1886 |

Das Steinerne Herz    Vienna    1888
Gringoire             Munich    1892
Shach dem Könige      „         1893
Der Husar             Vienna    1898

**Bruneau, Alfred**    *Composer*
b. Paris, 1857: d. there, 1934
Kerim                  Opéra-
                       Comique   1887
Le Rêve                „         1891
L'Attaque du Moulin    „         1893
Messidor               „         1897
L'Ouragan              „         1901
L'Enfant Roi           „         1905
Naïs Micoulin     Monte Carlo    1907
La Faute de L'Abbé
  Mouret          Opéra Comique  1907
Les Quatre Journées    „         1916
Le Roi Candaule        „         1920
Angelo, Tyran de
  Padove               „         1928
Virginie               „         1931

**Bülow, Hans Guido von**    *Conductor*
b. Dresden, 1830: d. Cairo, 1894
An advocate of Wagner and Brahms, he gave to the former not only his best efforts as a conductor but also his wife Cosima, whom he had married in 1857; she left him and married Wagner in 1869. He conducted the first *Tristan und Isolde* and the first *Die Meistersinger von Nürnberg*.

**Bunn, Alfred**    *Librettist*
b. 1796: d. Bologne, 1860
Bunn wrote the libretto for *The Bohemian Girl*, among others. He was manager and director of Drury Lane for a time.

**Burgstaller, Alois**    *Tenor*
b. Holzkirchen, Germany, 1871: d. Gmund, 1945
Cosima Wagner urged him to take up singing professionally. He made his Metropolitan debut in 1903 in *Die Walküre*. He sang Siegfried and the first Parsifal in America.

**Burian, Karel**    *Tenor*
(*Sometimes* Burrian)
b. Rousinow, Czechoslovakia, 1870: d. near Prague, 1924
Burian made his debut at Brno in 1891, at Bayreuth as Parsifal in 1898, and as Tannhäuser at the Metropolitan in 1906. He was also the first Herod in *Salome*. One evening after a final curtain, while removing his make-up, Burian picked up a glass of what he thought was a drink prepared for him. The disinfectant in the glass irreparably burned his throat.

**Burke, Edmund Arbrickle**    *Bass*
b. Toronto, 1876:
Abimelech, Amfortas, Prince Igor, Méphistophélès, Nilakantha, Nourabad, Pogner.

**Busch, Fritz**    *Conductor*
b. Westphalia, 1890: d. London, 1951
Conducted at Stuttgart, Dresden, Glyndebourne, the Metropolitan and in South America.

**Busoni, Ferruccio Benvenuto**    *Composer*
b. Empoli, Italy, 1866: d. Berlin, 1924
Busoni was most famous as a pianist and a composer of music for that instrument. His *Doktor Faust* was completed by his pupil, Jarnach.
Die Brautwahl     Hamburg    1912
Turandot          Zurich     1917
Arlecchino        „          1917
Doktor Faust      Dresden    1925

**Butt, Clara**    *Contralto*
b. Sussex, 1873: d. Oxford, 1936
She made her debut as Ursula in *The Golden Legend*. In 1920 she was made a Dame of the British Empire.

**Caccini, Giulio**    *Composer*
b. Rome, circa 1546: d. Florence, 1618
Caccini was one of the inventors of opera. Parts of his music for *Euridice* were performed in the first production of that first opera by Peri. In 1602 his

entire work on the theme came out. He was not only a composer, but a singer and lutenist as well. His wife composed, and even their daughter was both composer and singer. Caccini contributed to the understanding of the new principle of monodic music—the single voice accompanied—with the publication in 1602 of his collected songs, *Nuove Musiche.*

Il Rapimento di Cefalo
Florence 1600
Euridice „ 1602

**Cadman, Charles Wakefield** *Composer*
b. Johnstown, Pa., 1881: d. Los Angeles, 1946
A founder of the Hollywood Bowl Concerts, and a fairly well known composer of songs including *At Dawning.*

Shanewis Metropolitan 1918
The Sunset Trail Denver 1922
The Garden of Mystery
New York 1925
A Witch of Salem Chicago 1926
The Willow Tree NBC 1933

**Cahier, Madame Charles** *Contralto*
(*Née* Sara Jane Layton-Walker)
b. Nashville, Tenn., 1870: d. Manhattan Beach, Calif., 1951
A pupil of Jean de Reszke, she made her debut in Nice in 1904.

Carmen, Brangäne, Fricka, Ortrud

**Caldara, Antonio** *Composer*
b. Venice, 1670: d. Vienna, 1738
Caldara wrote the first of his eighty-seven operas in 1688.

**Callas, Maria Meneghini** *Soprano*
(*Née* Calogeropoulos)
b. New York, 1923:
This famous prima donna made her debut in Verona, 1947, singing Laura in *La Gioconda.* In 1956 she made her first appearance at the Metropolitan singing Norma, which she had sung in Chicago in 1954 and Covent Garden, 1952. She became a journalistic treasure in 1957 and

1958 with her pyrotechnic public relations and her vociferous battle with Rudolf Bing about the priority and privilege of her position as prima donna. Bing won, but Callas remained newsworthy. In her defense she pointed with pride to her record of having a large repertory in which were many roles not usually known by other sopranos.

Aida, Amelia, Amina, Armida, Cio-cio San, Elena, Elvira (*I Puritani*), Fiorilla (*Il Turco in Italia*), Gilda, Lady Macbeth, Laura (*La Gioconda*), Leonora (*La Forza del Destino*), Leonora (*Il Trovatore*), Medea (Cherubini), Mimi, Nedda, Norma, Rosina (*Il Barbiere di Siviglia*), Santuzza, Tosca, Turandot, Violetta.

**Calvé, Emma** *Soprano*
(*Really* Emma Calvet)
b. Aveyron, France, 1858: d. Millau, 1942
The first Anita (*La Navarraise*), and the first Sapho. Calvé made her debut at Brussels in 1882 as Marguerite, and at the Metropolitan as Santuzza in 1893. When she first sang Ophélie at La Scala in 1887 her performance was roundly hissed. But later performances wrested cheers from the audience.

Carmen, Leïla, Margherita (*Mefistofele*), Marguerite (*La Damnation de Faust*), Ophélie, Santuzza.

**Calzabigi, Raniero** *Librettist*
b. Livorno, Italy, 1714: d. Naples 1795
Calzabigi was creator of the famous libretti for Gluck's operas: *Alceste, Orfeo ed Euridice, Iphigénie en Aulide,* and *Paride ed Elena.* He was also a public supporter of the Gluckists in their war against the Piccinists.

**Cambert, Robert** *Composer*
b. Paris, circa 1628: d. London, 1677
The first French composer of opera. In association with Perrin, Cambert brought out the first opera at the Académie Royale de Musique (L'Opéra) in 1671. Later

Lully managed to snatch away the royal patent and took over the Académie for himself.

La Pastorale en Musique (*lost*) 1659
Ariane, ou le Mariage de
Bacchus (*lost*) 1661
Pomone (*the first*
*French Opera*) Paris 1671
Les Peines et les Plaisirs
de l'Amour Paris 1671

**Cammarano, Salvatore** *Librettist*
b. Naples, 1801: d. there, 1852
He was a pupil of Gabriele Rossetti. He wrote the libretti of *Lucia di Lammermoor*, *Don Pasquale*, *Luisa Miller*, *Il Trovatore* and many others.

**Campanari, Giuseppe** *Baritone*
b. Venice, 1855: d. Milan, 1927
He came to the United States not as a singer but as a cellist. He sang, however, the first performance in this country of *Pagliacci*, taking the part of Tonio. Escamillo was another of his favorite roles.

**Campanini, Cleofonte** *Conductor*
b. Parma, 1860: d. Chicago, 1919
His brother, the tenor Italo Campanini, helped him to make the right acquaintances to become a conductor in the United States. Here he brought out many works never heard in this country before. These included *Thaïs*, *Hérodiade*, *Louise*, *Il Segreto di Susanna*, *Sapho*, *Pelléas et Mélisande*, and the first Chicago performance of *La Favola d'Orfeo*. He conducted the first American performance of Verdi's *Otello* and was principal conductor and general director at Chicago from 1910 until his death.

**Campanini, Italo** *Tenor*
b. Parma, 1845: d. near there, 1896
Brother of Cleofonte Campanini. He fought for Garibaldi in the war for the unification of Italy, and was wounded in battle. In 1869 he made his debut in opera, singing the part of Manrico at Odessa. In

1872 in London, and in 1873 in New York, he appeared as Gennaro, in *LucreziaBorgia*. One episode of his career established him as a typical Italian in his treatment of Wagner's roles, when he appeared as Lohengrin with a great blue plumed hat on his head.

Edgardo, Faust (*La Damnation de Faust*), Faust (in the opening performance of the Metropolitan, 1883), Faust (*Mefistofele*), Gennaro (*Lucrezia Borgia*), Ferdinand (*La Favorita*), Don José, Lohengrin, Manrico, Otello, Radames, Raoul.

**Campenhout, François von** *Composer*
b. Brussels, 1779: d. there, 1848
Composer of six operas, many cantatas and other works. Best known for his song *La Brabançonne*, which became the Belgian national anthem.
Grotius 1808
Le Passe-partout 1815

**Camporese, Violante** *Soprano*
b. Rome, 1785: d. there, 1839
Donna Anna, Desdemona, Penelope (by Cimarosa), Sesto (*La Clemenza di Tito*), Susanna (*Le Nozze di Figaro*).

**Camprá André** *Composer*
b. Aix en Provence, 1660: d. Versailles, 1744
L'Europe Galante Paris 1697
Le Carnival de Venise ,, 1699
Tancrède ,, 1702
Iphigénie en Tauride ,, 1704
Idomenée ,, 1712

**Caniglia, Maria** *Soprano*
b.
Adriana Lecouvreur, Aida, Amelia, Desdemona, Elisabetta (*Don Carlos*), Fedora, Francesca, Iphigénie (*Iphigénie en Tauride*), Madeleine (*Andrea Chénier*), Manon Lescaut, Margherita (*Mefistofele*), Minnie, Selika, Tosca, Wally.

**Capoul, Joseph Amédée Victor** *Tenor*
b. Toulouse, 1839: d. Pujaudron du Gers, 1924

In 1861 he made his debut as a singer in the role of Daniel (*Le Chalet*), at the Opéra-Comique. In 1897 he became a stage manager.

Almaviva (*Il Barbiere di Siviglia*), Daniel (*Le Chalet*), Faust, Romeo, Wilhelm (*Mignon*).

**Carey, Francis Clive Savill**  *Baritone*
b. Essex, 1883:
Carey produced the operas and sang these roles:
Figaro (*Le Nozze di Figaro*), Don Giovanni, Papageno (*Die Zauberflöte*).

**Carey, Henry**  *Composer*
b. Yorkshire(?), circa 1690: d. London, 1743
Henry Carey wrote nine ballad operas and the words of the song *Sally in our Alley*. His son claimed he wrote *God Save the King*, but this has been refuted. Carey died a suicide.

The Contrivances  1729
A Wonder, or the Honest
Yorkshireman  1735

**Carissimi, Giacomo**  *Composer*
b. near Rome, 1605: d. Rome, 1674
Carissimi wrote no operas, but his development of the techniques of recitative in his oratorios were influential to the composers who did.

**Caron, Rose**  *Soprano*
b. Monerville, France, 1857: d. Paris, 1930
In 1884 at Brussels she made her debut singing Alice in *Robert le Diable*. She was the first Lorance (*Jocelyn*).
Alice (*Robert le Diable*), Desdemona, Leonore (*Fidelio*), Lorance (*Jocelyn*), Sieglinde.

**Carr, Benjamin**  *Composer*
b. London, 1768: d. Philadelphia, 1831
Benjamin Carr established the first music store in America, at Philadelphia, and published the first American music,

including the forever famous *Yankee Doodle*. Only fragments of his own opera survive.

The Archers  New York and
Boston  1796

**Carroll, Joan**  *Soprano*
b.
The first in the United States to sing Aminta (*Die Schweigsame Frau*).

**Caruso, Enrico**  *Tenor*
b. Naples, 1873: d. there, 1921
Certainly one of the greatest tenors of modern times. He was the eighteenth child in a family of twenty. The seventeen who preceded him did not survive. In 1894 he made his debut in Naples. He sang for the first time in London in 1902 and at the Metropolitan in 1903 as the Duke in *Rigoletto*, one of his most famous roles. He was at work in San Francisco when the earthquake struck that city in 1906. There was a scandal in New York when his fiancée's father refused to allow him to marry Dorothy Benjamin, which event took place anyway in 1918. There was another scandal when a New York woman haled him into court for making advances to her in Central Park. This was soon quashed. He sang for the last time in New York in 1920. One of the few failures in his singing career was with Lohengrin, which he sang only three times, in Buenos Aires. He was the first Johnson (*La Fanciulla del West*), the first Loris (*Fedora*), Federico (*L'Arlesiana*), and Maurizio (*Adriana Lecouvreur*).

Don Alvaro, Canio, The Duke (*Rigoletto*), Edgardo, Eleazar, Enzo, Faust (in *Faust* and in *Mefistofele*), Federico, Ferdinand (*La Favorita*), des Grieux (*Manon*), des Grieux (*Manon Lescaut*), John of Leyden, Johnson (*La Fanciulla del West*), Don José, Lionel, Lohengrin, Loris (*Fedora*), Manrico, Mario Cavaradossi, Maurizio, Nadir (*Les Pêcheurs de Perles*), Nemerino (*L'Elisir d'Amore*), Osaka (*Iris*),

Pinkerton, Radames, Raoul, Riccardo (*Un Ballo in Maschera*), Rodolfo, Samson.

**Carvalho, Eleazar de** *Composer*
b. Iquato, Brazil, 1912:
He is not only a composer, but a conductor. He also once played tuba in the Brazilian Navy Band.

| | | |
|---|---|---|
| Descoberta do Brasil | Rio da Janeiro | 1939 |
| Tiradentes | „ | 1941 |

**Carvalho, Marie Caroline Félix**
*Soprano*
b. Marseilles, 1827: d. near Dieppe, 1895
The first Marguérite (*Faust*), the first Mireille and Juliette. She made her debut as Lucia at the Opéra-Comique in 1849. In 1885 she retired.

Cherubino, Countess Almaviva, Dinorah, Donna Elvira, Isabella (*Le Pré aux Clercs*), Juliette, Lucia, Mathilde, Marguérite, Mireille, Pamina, Oscar (*Un Ballo in Maschera*), Rosina (*Il Barbiere di Siviglia*), Zerlina (*Fra Diavolo*), Zerlina (*Don Giovanni*).

**Cary, Anna Louise** *Contralto*
b. Wayne, Maine, 1841: d. Norwalk, Conn., 1921
She studied with Viardot-Garcia and made her debut in Copenhagen as Azucena. In 1874 she became the first American to sing Ortrud, at New York.

Amneris, Azucena, Elena (*Mefistofele*), Leonora (*La Favorita*), Ortrud, Urbain.

**Casa, Lisa Della** *Soprano*
b. near Berne, 1919:
The first Fräulein Burstner and the first Leni. She made her debut as Cio-cio San.

Donna Anna, Antonia, Arabella, Countess (*Capriccio*), Countess Almaviva, Donna Elvira, The Marschallin, Marzellina, Mimi, Nedda, Octavian, Pamina, Sophie, Zdenka (*Arabella*), Zerlina.

**Cassell, Walter** *Baritone*
b.
Almaviva, Escamillo, Ford, Giorgio Germont, Don Giovanni, Jokanaan, Ramiro (*L'Heure Espagnole*), Scarpia.

**Castagna, Bruna** *Mezzo-soprano*
b. Bari, 1908:
Her debut was in Mantua, singing Marina Mnishek in 1927. In 1936 she sang for the first time at the Metropolitan as Amneris.

Amneris, Carmen, Laura, Marina Mnishek.

**Castelnuovo-Tedesco, Mario** *Composer*
b. Florence, 1895:
A composer of oratorios, orchestral and chamber music and of music for Hollywood films.

La Mandragola (*his own libretto*) 1926

**Catalani, Alfredo** *Composer*
b. Lucca, 1854: d. Milan, 1893

| | | |
|---|---|---|
| Elda | Turin | 1880 |
| Dejanice | Milan | 1883 |
| Edmea | „ | 1886 |
| La Wally | „ | 1892 |

**Catalani, Angelica** *Soprano*
b. Sinigaglia, 1780: d. Paris, 1849
She made her debut as a singer at Venice, 1795, then at La Scala in 1801. But in 1814 she took over the management of the *Théâtre des Italiens* in Paris, a job she held until 1817.

**Cavalieri, Emilio del** *Composer*
b. circa 1550: d. Rome, 1602
Composer of the first known oratorio, and one of the first to use the "figured bass" notation, one of the steps toward monody and opera. He was a member of the *Camerata* in Florence. His most famous work is *La Rappresentazione dell'-Anima e del Corpo*, "A Morality with simple music, with hymns between the episodes; meant to be acted."

Il Satiro 1590

La Disperazione di Fileno     1595
Il Giuoco della Cieca     1595
(*These three are approaches to opera.*)
La Rappresentazione
   dell'Anima e del Corpo
            Rome    1600(?)

**Cavalieri, Katharina**     *Soprano*
b. Währing, near Vienna, 1760: d.
Vienna, 1801
She was the first Constanze in *Die
Entführung aus dem Serail*, and the first
Madame Silberklang in *Der Schauspieldirektor*. Mozart wrote the aria *Mi Tradi*
for her voice. Never once did she sing
outside Vienna.

**Cavalli, Pier Francesco**     *Composer*
b. Crema, Italy, 1602: d. Venice, 1676
He got his training in the new art of
monody partly by singing under Monteverdi at San Marco in Venice.

Le Nozze di Teti     Venice    1639
Giasone               ,,       1649
Serse                 ,,       1654
   *and thirty nine more.*

**Cavan, Marie**     *Soprano*
b. New York, 1889:
She made her debut in Chicago in 1910,
singing Irma in *Louise*. She sang Mimi
opposite Caruso.

**Cebotari, Maria**     *Soprano*
b. Bessarabia, 1910: d. Vienna, 1949
The first Aminta (*Die Schweigsame Frau*),
she made her debut as Mimi in Dresden.
Aminta, Antonida (*Ivan Susanin*), Cio-
cio San, Countess (*Capriccio*), Daphne,
Mimi, Salome.

**Cehanovsky, George**     *Baritone*
b.
Betto (*Gianni Schicchi*), Corporal (*La
Figlia del Reggimento*), Dancaire, Douphol
(*La Traviata*), Fiorello (*Il Barbiere di
Siviglia*), Johann (*Werther*), Marullo,
Melot, Schaunard, Sciarrone, Silvano (*Un
Ballo in Maschera*), Silvio, Surgeon (*La

*Forza del Destino*), Tchelkalov (*Boris
Godunov*), Watchman (*Die Meistersinger*),
Yamadori, Zuane (*La Gioconda*).

**Cesti, Marcantonio**     *Composer*
b. Arezzo, 1623: d. Florence, 1669
A Franciscan monk who not only
composed, but sang tenor.

L'Orontea     Venice    1649
Cesare Amante        ,,    1651
Argia     Innsbrück   1655
Semiramide     Vienna    1667
La Schiava Fortunata     ,,    1674

**Chabrier, Emanuel**     *Composer*
b. Ambert, France, 1841: d. Paris, 1894
Chabrier was a government clerk until
1862, when he was finally able to free
himself for music. He is best known
for his orchestral rhapsody *España*.

L'Étoile     Paris    1877
L'Éducation Manquée     ,,    1879
Gwendoline     Brussels   1886
Le Roi Malgré Lui     Opéra-
               Comique   1887
Briseïs     (*unfinished*)

**Chadwick, George Whitefield**     *Composer*
b. Lowell, Mass., 1854: d. Boston, 1931
A composer for the organ, the piano,
the voice and of chamber music.

The Quiet Lodging     Boston   1894
Tabasco (*burlesque*)     ,,    1894
Judith     Worcester, Mass.   1901
The Padrone     1915
Love's Sacrifice     1917

**Chaliapin, Feodor Ivanovitch**     *Bass*
b. Kazan, Russia, 1873: d. Paris, 1938
One of the most famous basses of
modern times, and certainly the most
famous to sing the role of Boris Godunov.
He was the first Don Quichotte, both on
stage and on film. He made his Metropolitan debut as Mefistofele in 1907.
Don Basilio (*Il Barbiere di Siviglia*),
Boris Godunov, Don Quichotte, Ivan
(*Pskovityanka*), Leporello, Melnik

(*Rusalka*), Mefistofele, Méphistophélès (*Faust*).

**Charpentier, Gustave**                    *Composer*
b. Dieuze, France, 1860: d. Paris, 1956
Charpentier had an abiding interest in the alleviation of poverty around him, and especially in the plight of young girls working in factories. In 1900 he founded a society to help them out. He wrote the libretti for his own operas.

| Louise | Opéra | 1900 |
| Julien | ,, | 1913 |

**Charpentier, Marc Antoine**    *Composer*
b. Paris, 1634: d. there, 1704
One of Lully's many enemies, made so by Lully's successful intrigues with the Dauphin for Charpentier's job.

| Medée | 1693 |
| Les Amours d'Acis et Galatée | 1678 |
| Endimion | 1681 |
| Philomèle | |

**Charton-Demeur, Ann Arsène**
                                        *Mezzo-soprano*
b. Sanjon, France, 1824: d. Paris, 1892
The first Didon (*Les Troyens*), and the first Béatrice (*Béatrice et Bénédict*). She made her debut as Lucia.
Amina, Béatrice, Desdemona, Lucia, Madeleine (*Le Postillion de Longjumeau*).

**Chausson, Ernest**                    *Composer*
b. Paris, 1855: d. Mentes sur Seine, 1899

| Hélène | 1885 |
| Les Caprices de Marianne | 1880 |
| Le Roi Arthus (*his own libretto*) | Brussels 1903 |

**Cherubini, Luigi**                    *Composer*
(*Full name* Maria Luigi Carlo Zenobia Salvatore Cherubini)
b. Florence, 1760: d. Paris, 1842
He wrote a mass at thirteen, and his first successful opera, *Armida*, in 1782.

| Démophon | Opéra | 1788 |
| Marguerite d'Anjou | | 1790 |

| Lodoïska | Paris | 1791 |
| Elisa | ,, | 1794 |
| Medée | ,, | 1797 |
| L'Hotellerie Portugaise | ,, | 1798 |
| La Punition | ,, | 1799 |
| Les Deux Journées | ,, | 1800 |
| Faniska | Vienna | 1807 |
| Ali Baba | Opéra | 1833 |

**Chollet, Jean Baptiste Marie**          *Tenor*
b. Paris, 1798: d. Nemours, 1892
The first Fra Diavolo and the first Chappelou (*Le Postillion de Longjumeau*).

**Christoff, Boris**                         *Bass*
b. Sofia, 1918:
Famous for his recording of *Boris Godunov* in France. He made his debut in Rome in 1946 and in San Francisco as Boris in 1956.
Boris, Méphistophélès (*Faust*), Mosè (*by Rossini*)

**Cibber, Susanna Maria**             *Soprano*
b. 1714: d. 1766
Handel composed the part of Micah in his oratorio *Samson* for her. She was famous as a great actress among singers. To Handel's chagrin she sang Polly in *The Beggar's Opera*.

**Cigna, Gina**                         *Soprano*
b. Paris, 1904:
After her debut in La Scala in 1929 she appeared for the first time at the Metropolitan as Aida in 1937.
Alceste, Aida, Amelia, Asteria (*Nerone*), Daphné, Elisabeth (*Don Carlos*), Francesca, Gioconda, Leonora (*La Forza del Destino*), Marguerite (*La Damnation de Faust*), Tosca, Turandot, Wally.

**Cilèa, Francesco**                    *Composer*
b. Calabria, 1866: d. Varazze, 1950

| Gina | Naples | 1889 |
| La Tilda | Florence | 1892 |
| L'Arlesiana | Milan | 1897 |
| Adriana Lecouvreur | ,, | 1902 |
| Gloria | La Scala | 1907 |

**Cimarosa, Domenico**  *Composer*
b. near Naples, 1749: d. Venice, 1801
A most prolific composer. During the single year 1781 he brought out five new works. From 1787 to 1791 he stayed in St. Petersburg. In 1798 he was imprisoned in Naples for a short term because of his part in a revolutionary uprising. In all he turned out seventy-six operas.

La Finta Parigiana    Naples   1773
L'Italiana in Londra    Rome   1778
Il Matrimonio Segreto    Vienna   1792

**Cleva, Fausto**  *Conductor*
b.
Conducted at the Metropolitan and other houses.

**Coates, Albert**  *Composer*
b. St. Petersburg, 1882: d. near Cape Town, 1953
He made a name as a conductor at Eberfeld, Dresden, Mannheim, in Russia and in England. He taught at the Eastman School of Music, Rochester, N.Y.,

Assurbanipal    1919
Samuel Pepys    Munich   1929
Pickwick    London   1936
Tafelberg se Kleed
  (*Van Hanks and the
  Devil*)    Cape Town   1952

**Coates, Edith**  *Contralto*
b.
The first Auntie in *Peter Grimes*, 1945. She has also sung Carmen.

**Cobelli, Giuseppina**  *Soprano*
b.
Adriana Lecouvreur, Fiora (*L'Amore dei Tre Re*), Isolde, Marguerite (*La Damnation de Faust*), Minnie, Tosca.

**Coerne, Louis Adolphe**  *Composer*
b. Newark, N.J., 1870: d. Boston, 1922
Coerne received the first Ph.D. in music in America from Harvard University. His *Zenobia* was also the first opera by an American to be performed in Europe.

Sakuntala    1907
Zenobia    Bremen   1907

**Cole, Blanche**  *Soprano*
b. Portsmouth, England, 1851: d. London, 1888
Amina, Marie (*Zar und Zimmerman*).

**Collingwood, Lawrance Arthur**
  *Composer*
b. London, 1887:
Macbeth    Sadlers Wells   1944
The Death of Tintagiles (*concert*)   1950

**Colzani, Anselmo**  *Baritone*
b.
Made his debut at the Metropolitan as Simon Boccanegra in 1960.
Barnaba, Nabucco, Simon Boccanegra

**Conley, Eugene**  *Tenor*
b.
Alfredo, Duke (*Rigoletto*), Don Ottavio, Mario, Pinkerton, Rinuccio (*Gianni Schicchi*), Rodolfo, Tom Rakewell, Turiddu, Werther.

**Conner, Nadine**  *Soprano*
b.
Mélisande, Micaela, Mimi, Sophie, Zerlina (*Le Nozze di Figaro*).

**Converse, Frederick Shepherd**
  *Composer*
b. Newton, Mass., 1871: d. Boston, 1940
Dean of the New England Conservatory of Music from 1930 to 1938. He wrote four operas, oratorios, cantatas and other works.

The Pipe of Desire    Boston   1906
  (*The first American
  Opera to be performed
  at the Metropolitan, in
  1909.*)
The Sacrifice    „   1911

**Cooper, Emil**  *Conductor*
b. Kherson, Russia, 1877: d. New York 1960
Conductor at the Metropolitan from 1940–1950.

**Copland, Aaron**    *Composer*
b. Brooklyn, N.Y., 1900:
One of the best-known modern composers in the United States, and famous for his diatonic style, which seems to give an open-air American atmosphere to most of his orchestral works. The most renowned are *El Salon Mexico* and *Appalachian Spring*.

The Tender Land    New York    1954
The Second Hurricane    ,,    1961

**Corena, Fernando**    *Bass*
b. Geneva, 1917:
Corena made his Metropolitan debut as Gianni Schicchi in 1954.
Dr. Bartolo (*Le Nozze di Figaro*), Fra Melitone, Gianni, Schicchi, Leporello, Don Pasquale, Sacristan (*Tosca*).

**Cornelius, Peter**    *Composer*
b. Mainz, 1824: d. there, 1874
Cornelius began professional life as an actor, but he failed. As a composer he was much better, but political intrigues among directors cost him performances. When Liszt conducted his *Barber* at Weimar, a planned demonstration against him in the audience caused the great conductor to quit his position.

The Barber of Bagdad    Weimar    1858
Der Cid    ,,    1865
Gunlöd    ,,    1874

**Corsi, Jacopo**    *Patron*
b. circa 1560: d. Florence, 1604
At his house in Florence the first opera, *Dafne*, was performed. It was by Peri, but it contained some parts written by Corsi, who also played harpsichord. Corsi was a member, with Bardi, of the famous *Camerata*, the group of Florentines who first conceived opera.

**Cowell, Henry Dixon**    *Composer*
b. Menlo Park, Calif., 1897:
A spectacular modernist famous for using his elbows and wooden boards to make "tone-clusters" on the keyboard.

He has written more than a thousand works of all kinds.
O'Higgins of Chile    1949

**Crivelli, Gaetano**    *Tenor*
b. Bergamo, 1774: d. Brescia, 1836
Don Ottavio, Fiorello (*Il Barbiere di Siviglia*).

**Crooks, Richard Alexander**    *Tenor*
b. Trenton, N.J., 1900:
He made his debut in Philadelphia in 1930 as Mario Cavaradossi. In 1933 he sang des Grieux in his first appearance at the Metropolitan. He has also sung Romeo.

**Cross, Joan**    *Soprano*
b. London, 1900:
The first Ellen Orford, the first Queen Elizabeth in *Gloriana*, the first Mrs. Billows and Mrs. Goose (*The Turn of the Screw*).
Aida, Amelia, Mrs. Billows, Carmen, Cherubino, Cio-cio San, Desdemona, Dido (*Dido and Aeneas*), Elisabeth, Ellen Orford, Elsa, Donna Elvira, Frasquita, Mrs. Goose (*The Turn of the Screw*), Lady Macbeth (*by Collingwood*), Marenka (*Prodaná Nevěsta*), The Marschallin, Mary (*Hugh the Drover*), Mercedes, Micaela, Mimi, Pamina, Queen Elisabeth (*Gloriana*), Tatyana, Violetta.

**Cruvelli, Jeanne Sophie Charlotte**
    *Soprano*
b. Westphalia, 1826: d. Monte Carlo, 1907
The first Duchess Elena in *I Vespri Siciliani*.
Countess Almaviva, Duchess Elena, Leonora (*Fidelio*), Valentine (*Les Huguenots*).

**Cuenod, Hugues**    *Tenor*
b.
The first Sellem (*The Rake's Progress*).

**Cui, César**    *Composer*
b. Vilna, Russia, 1835: d. Petrograd, 1918

A government worker, as were the other members of "The Mighty Five," Cui worked in a technical capacity as topographer and expert on fortification. He was tutor in military engineering to Tsar Nicholas the second. Not only did he write many operas, but he also completed *The Fair at Sorotchinsk.*

| | | |
|---|---|---|
| The Mandarin's Son | | |
| | St. Petersburg | 1859 |
| The Captive in the | | |
| Caucasus | St. Petersburg | 1883 |
| William Ratcliffe | „ | 1869 |
| Angelo | „ | 1876 |
| Le Flibustier | „ | 1889 |
| The Saracen | Comique | 1899 |
| The Captain's | | |
| Daughter | „ | 1911 |
| Mam'zelle Fifi | Moscow | 1903 |
| Matteo Falcone | „ | 1908 |
| A Feast in Time | | |
| of Plague | „ | 1901 |

**Curtin, Phyllis**                              *Soprano*
b.

Alice Ford, Fräulein Burstner, Catherine (*Wuthering Heights*), Leni, Salomé, Susanna Polk, Wife of the Court Attendant.

**Dallapiccola, Luigi**                       *Composer*
b. Pisino, Istria, 1904:

Perhaps the foremost Italian composer of the twelve-tone school. He has written a great deal of music for ballet, orchestra and so forth. For the production in Florence in 1942 he transcribed *Il Ritorno d'Ulisse in Patria.*

| | | |
|---|---|---|
| Volo di Notte | Florence | 1940 |
| Il Prigioniero | „ | 1950 |
| (*Previously broadcast,* 1949.) | | |

**Dalmorès, Charles**                            *Tenor*
b. Nancy, 1871: d. Hollywood, 1939

A famous tenor, teacher of singing and virtuoso of the French horn, Dalmorès made his operatic debut in Rouen, 1899, and in New York, as Faust, in 1906. He was the first to sing Parsifal in Chicago.

Faust (*La Damnation de Faust*), John (*Salomé*), Don José, Julien, Lohengrin, Parsifal, Pedro (*La Habanera*), Tristan.

**Damrosch, Leopold**                      *Conductor*
b. Posen, 1832: d. New York, 1895

Damrosch was a most successful orchestral conductor in New York when the Metropolitan Opera slumped toward disaster after its first season. He offered to take over the artistic direction and supply singers and orchestra for a season provided that the management would allow him a certain freedom in the matter of repertory. His offer was accepted and the Metropolitan thereupon embarked on a season so German in its texture as to give the company a Teutonic reputation for years. He did save it from collapse, and he provided New York with brilliant productions of *Fidelio*, the first *Ring des Nibelungen*, *Die Meistersinger*, etc. He is certainly one of the fathers of music in New York, responsible for the Symphony Society which later became the New York Philharmonic Society, and for the opera itself. It is interesting to note that he won the degree of M.D. in Berlin in 1854, although his medical practice was limited, probably, to sick musical organizations.

**Damrosch, Walter Johannes**    *Composer*
b. Breslau, 1862: d. New York, 1950

The son of Leopold Damrosch carried on in his father's tradition. He conducted the first American performances of *Samson et Dalila*, *Eugene Onegin*, and *Parsifal*. He was the first to conduct a network symphonic broadcast, in 1926. From 1894 to 1899 he led his own opera company on a nationwide tour. Most listeners who were in grammar school in the 1930's remember Walter Damrosch as the voice who told them all about Wagner, Brahms and Bach over the air.

The Scarlet Letter Boston 1896
The Dove of Peace „ 1912
Cyrano de
Bergerac Metropolitan 1913
The Man Without
a Country „ 1937
The Opera Cloak New York 1942

**Danco, Suzanne** *Soprano*
b. Brussels, 1911:
She made her American debut in 1950.
Donna Anna, Cherubino, Ellen Orford,
Fiordiligi, Jocasta, Marie (*Wozzeck*).

**Dargomyzhsky,**
**Alexander Sergeyevitch** *Composer*
b. Tula, Russia, 1813: d. St. Petersburg,
1869
As did his younger contemporaries, the
"Mighty Five," Dargomyzhsky worked
for the government until 1835. He was a
great champion and influence for "The
Five."
Esmeralda Moscow 1847
Russalka St. Petersburg 1856
Kamennyi Gost
(*The Stone Guest*)
(*Completed by*
*Cui and Rimsky-*
*Korsakov*.) St. Petersburg 1872

**Davenant, William** *Librettist*
b. 1606: d. 1668
Davenant was the earliest English opera
manager.

**David, Félicien César** *Composer*
b. Vaucluse, France, 1810: d. St. Germaine-en-Laye, 1876
Successor to Berlioz in the sinecure of
librarian of the Conservatoire. He
composed many works for piano, voice
and orchestra. Although the Théatre
Lyrique rejected his *Herculaneum*, it was
accepted by the Opéra and won the state
prize of twenty thousand francs.
La Perle du Brésil Paris 1851
Herculaneum Opéra 1859
Lalla Roukh Opéra-Comique 1862
Le Saphir „ 1865

**Davies, Tudor** *Tenor*
b.
The first Hugh (*Hugh the Drover*.)
Jenik (*Prodaná Nevěsta*), Rinuccio, Florestan, Wilhelm (*Mignon*).

**Davis, John David** *Composer*
b. Birmingham, 1867: d. Portugal, 1942
The Zaporogues
(*The Cossacks*) Antwerp 1903

**Debussy, Achille Claude** *Composer*
b. St. Germaine-en-Laye, 1862: d. Paris,
1918
A revolutionary composer, closely
allied with the impressionist poets of his
day. Debussy wrote much for the piano
and concert orchestra including his very
famous *Clair de Lune* and his *L'Après-midi
d'un Faune*. He planned two operas
beyond *Pelléas et Mélisande*, but never
worked on them. His death, attributed
to cancer, occurred during a bombard-
ment of the city during the First World
War.
Pelléas et Mélisande Paris 1902

**Delannoy, Marcel** *Composer*
b. Ferté Alais, France, 1898:
Le Poirier de Misère Paris 1927
Arlequin Radiophile Paris 1946
Ginevra Comique 1942
Puck Strasbourg 1949

**Delibes, Clément Philibert Léo**
*Composer*
b. St. Germaine du Val, France, 1836: d.
Paris, 1891
Besides *Lakmé*, Delibes is best known
for his two ballet scores *Coppelia* and
*Sylvia*.
La Roi l'a Dit Opéra-Comique 1873
Jean de Nivelle „ 1880
Lakmé 1883
Kassya (*completed by Massenet*) 1893

**Delius, Frederick** *Composer*
b. Bradford, Engl., 1862: d. Grez-sur-
Loing, France, 1934

Delius wrote some of the calmest music imaginable. One of his best-known works is the *Walk to the Paradise Garden* which occurs in his *A Village Romeo and Juliet.* Another is his rhapsody on *Over the Hills and Far Away.* In 1922 he became paralyzed, then blind.

| | | |
|---|---|---|
| Irmelin (*written* 1892) | Oxford | 1953 |
| The Magic Fountain | | 1893 |
| Margot la Rouge | | 1902 |
| A Village Romeo and | | |
| Juliet | Berlin | 1907 |
| Fennimore and Gerda | Frankfurt | 1919 |
| Koanga | Elberfeld | 1904 |

**Delmas, Jean François**  *Bass*
b. Lyons, 1861: d. St. Alban de Monthel, 1933
The first Athanaël (*Thaïs*). He made his debut as St. Bris at the Opéra in 1886.
Gurnemanz, Hans Sachs, King (*Lohengrin*), Méphistophélès (*Faust*), Nadir, St. Bris, Wotan.

**Delna, Marie**  *Contralto*
(*Really* Marie Ledan)
b. Meudon, France, 1875: d. Paris, 1932
She made her debut singing Didon in *Les Troyens* at the Opéra-Comique in 1892.
Orfeo, Charlotte (*Werther*), Didon, Françoise (*L'Attaque du Moulin*).

**Destinn, Emmy**  *Soprano*
(*Née* Kittl)
b. Prague, 1878: d. Budejovice, Czechoslovakia, 1930
This celebrated singer claimed a repertory of eighty roles. She took her stage name from her teacher's. When she sang in her native land she called herself Destinnová. Her debut occurred in Berlin in 1898 as Santuzza. In 1904 she sang for the first time at Covent Garden as Donna Anna, and in 1908 at the Metropolitan as Aida. She was the first Minnie (*La Fanciulla del West*).
Amelia, Aida, Donna Anna, Cio-cio San, Diemut (*Feuersnot*), Elsa, Gioconda, Lisa

(*Pique-Dame*), Louise, Marenka (*Prodaná Nevěsta*), Marta (*Tiefland*), Nedda, Salomé, Santuzza, Senta, Tatyana, Tosca, Valentine (*Les Huguenots*), Wally.

**Dickons, Maria**  *Soprano*
b. London, 1770: d. there, 1833
Countess Almaviva, Polly Peachum, Rosina (*Il Barbiere di Siviglia*).

**Didur, Adamo**  *Bass*
b. Galicia, 1874: d. Katowice, Poland, 1946
This famous basso made his debut in Rio de Janeiro in 1894. His debut at the Metropolitan in 1908 was as Mefistofele. He was the first Michele (*Il Tabarro*), and the first Boris in America.
Archibaldo, Boris Godunov, Geronte, Guglielmo (*Così fan Tutte*), Gremin, Mefistofele, Oberthal, Ramfis.

**Dippel, Johann Andreas**  *Tenor*
b. Cassell, 1866: d. Hollywood, 1932
Dippel made his debut in Bremen in 1887 and at the Metropolitan in 1890. Once in New York he was spending the evening peacefully at home. The leading tenor at that night's performance was taken sick just before curtain time. The trusty Dippel, who could always be counted upon in an emergency, was rushed to the dressing room just as the messenger found him—in his bathrobe. His career included not only singing but management. He was administrative manager of the Metropolitan from 1908 to 1910, and general manager at Chicago after that. In 1913 he founded an independent company to tour with light operas.
Fenton, Parsifal, Raoul, Steuerman, Tannhäuser, Walther.

**Dittersdorf, Karl Ditters von**  *Composer*
b. Vienna, 1739: d. near Neuhaus, 1799
Beethoven wrote a set of variations on a theme by his friend von Dittersdorf.

His operas total twenty-eight, but he also wrote chamber music and choruses.

| | | |
|---|---|---|
| Doktor und Apotheker | Vienna | 1786 |
| Hieronymous Knicker | | 1787 |
| Die Lustigen Weiber von Windsor | | 1797 |

**Dobbs, Mattiwilda**      *Soprano*
b.
Gilda, Olympia (*Les Contes d'Hoffmann*), Queen of Shemakha (*Le Coq d'or*).

**Dönch, Karl**      *Baritone*
b.
Beckmesser, Doctor (*Wozzeck*).

**Donizetti, Gaetano**      *Composer*
b. Bergamo, 1797: d. there, 1848
Donizetti was one of the most prolific and successful of all opera composers. He lived to be only fifty-one, yet he turned out sixty-six operas, choral music and songs.

| | | |
|---|---|---|
| Anna Bolena | Milan | 1830 |
| L'Elisir d'Amore | ,, | 1832 |
| Lucrezia Borgia | La Scala | 1833 |
| Lucia di Lammermoor | Naples | 1835 |
| La Figlia del Reggimento | Opéra-Comique | 1840 |
| La Favorita | Opéra | 1840 |
| Linda di Chamounix | Vienna | 1842 |
| Don Pasquale | Paris | 1843 |
| Don Sebastiano | ,, | 1843 |
| Maria di Rohan | Vienna | 1843 |

**Dorus-Gras, Julie Aimée Josèphe**
     *Soprano*
b. Valenciennes, 1805: d. Paris, 1896
The first Alice (*Robert le Diable*), the first Marguerite (*Les Huguenots*), and the first Teresa (*Benvenuto Cellini*).

**Dow, Dorothy**      *Soprano*
b. Houston, Texas, 1920:
She made her debut at Buffalo, N.Y., in 1946.
Danae (*Die Liebe der Danae*), Gioconda, Lady Macbeth, Marie (*Wozzeck*).

**Draghi, Antonio**      *Composer*
b. Rimini, 1635: d. Vienna, 1700
One of the more prolific composers of the early years of opera. He wrote sixty-seven, plus many musical plays, oratorios, etc. He spent the last thirty years of his life in Vienna.
La Monarchia Latina Trionfante.

**Ducloux, Walter**      *Conductor*
b. Kriens, Switzerland, 1913:
Assistant conductor at the Festival of Lucerne, 1938 and 1939. In New York during the Second World War; he made broadcasts for the Voice of America from 1949 to 1952, and afterwards was engaged as opera director at the University of Southern California.

**Dufranne, Hector**      *Baritone*
b. Mons, Belgium, 1870: d. Paris, 1951
The first Golaud. He made his debut as Valentin (*Faust*) at Brussels in 1896. His first appearance in New York was at the Manhattan Opera in 1908.

**Dukas, Paul**      *Composer*
b. Paris, 1865: d. there, 1935
Dukas is most famous for his programmatic orchestral scherzo *L'Apprenti-Sorcier* (The Sorcerer's Apprentice).

| | | |
|---|---|---|
| Ariane et Barbe-Bleue | Comique | 1907 |

**Duncan, Todd**      *Baritone*
b. Danville, Kentucky, 1903:
The first Porgy (*Porgy and Bess*).

**Dupont, Gabriel**      *Composer*
b. Caen, France, 1878: d. Vésinet, 1914

| | | |
|---|---|---|
| La Cabrera | Milan | 1904 |
| La Glu | Nice | 1910 |
| La Farce du Cuvier | Brussels | 1912 |
| Antar | Opéra | 1921 |

**Duprez, Gilbert**      *Tenor*
b. Paris, 1806: d. Passy, 1896
The first Benvenuto Cellini, the first Edgardo. He was the thirteenth of twenty-two children (*see* Caruso). Not

only did he sing, he also composed eight operas and wrote treatises on the art of singing. He made his debut in Paris, 1825, singing Almaviva.

**Duval, Denise** *Soprano*
b.
Blanche (*Les Dialogues des Carmélites*)

**Duval, Franca** *Soprano*
b.
The first Maria Golovin in New York. Concepcion (*L'Heure Espagnole*).

**Dux, Claire** *Soprano*
b. Poland, 1885:
She made her debut in Cologne, 1906.
Eva, Pamina, Sophie.

**Dvořák, Anton** *Composer*
b. Mulhausen (near Prague), 1841: d. there, 1904
Dvořák made a famous visit to the United States during which he listened and looked with great care. The outcome of this was his celebrated *New World Symphony*. His chief inspiration, however, was the folk music of his Bohemian homeland.

| | | |
|---|---|---|
| King and Collier | Prague | 1874 |
| Vanda | „ | 1876 |
| The Peasant and the Rogue | „ | 1878 |
| Dimitrij | „ | 1882 |
| The Jacobin | „ | 1889 |
| The Devil and Kate | „ | 1899 |
| Rusalka | „ | 1901 |
| Armida | „ | 1904 |

**Dyke, Ernest van** *Tenor*
b. Antwerp, 1861: d. Berlaer-lez-Lievre, 1923
He made his debut as Lohengrin in Paris, 1887.
Lohengrin, Parsifal, Tannhäuser.

**Eames, Emma** *Soprano*
b. Shanghai, China, 1867: d. New York, 1952
Emma Eames was brought up in Bath,

Maine. She made her debut at the Opéra as Juliette in 1889 and at Covent Garden as Marguérite in 1891. She sang the first Colombe in *Ascanio*.
Aida, Alice Ford, Charlotte, Colombe (*Ascanio*), Countess Almaviva, Desdemona, Elisabeth, Elsa, Eva, Iris, Juliette, Margherita (*Mefistofele*), Marguérite (*Faust*), Micaela, Pamina, Santuzza, Sieglinde, Tosca.

**Easton, Florence Gertrude** *Soprano*
b. Middlesbrough, England, 1884: d. New York, 1955
The first Lauretta (*Gianni Schicchi*). She made her debut in Covent Garden, 1903, as Cio-cio San, and at the Metropolitan in 1917 as Santuzza. She is sometimes known by her married name; MacLennan.
Aida, Brünnhilde, Carmen, Cio-cio San, Dulcinée, Elektra, Elena (*Mefistofele*), Elsa, Lauretta (*Gianni Schicchi*), The Marschallin, Rachel, Salome, Santuzza, Serpina, Sieglinde, Turandot.

**Edvina, Marie Louise Lucienne** *Soprano*
(*Née* Martin)
b. Montreal, circa 1885: d. London, 1948
The first Francesca da Rimini. She made her debut as Marguérite in *Faust*.
Du Barry, Fiora (*L'Amore dei Tre Re*), Francesca da Rimini, Louise, Maliella, Manon, Marguérite, Mélisande, Thaïs, Tosca.

**Egk, Werner** *Composer*
b. Bavaria, 1901:

| | | |
|---|---|---|
| Die Zaubergeige | Frankfurt | 1935 |
| Columbus | „ | 1942 |
| (*Previously heard in radio, 1933.*) | | |
| Peer Gynt | Berlin | 1938 |
| Circe | „ | 1948 |
| Irische Legende | Salzburg | 1955 |
| Der Revisor | Schwetzingen | 1957 |

**Einem, Gottfried von** *Composer*
b. Bern, 1918:
A pupil of Boris Blacher, who wrote for him the libretti of his operas. For

four months in 1938 von Einem was imprisoned by the Gestapo.

| | |
|---|---|
| Dantons Tod | 1947 |
| Der Prozess | 1953 |

**Elias, Rosalind** *Mezzo-soprano*
b.
Giulietta (*Les Contes d'Hoffmann*), Grimgerde, Marina Mnishek, Olga (*Eugene Onegin*).

**Elmo, Cloe** *Contralto*
b. Lecce, Italy:
Azucena, Nancy (*Martha*), Penelope (*Il Ritorno d'Ulisse in Patria*), Pepa (*Goyescas*), Princess de Bouillon.

**Enesco, Georges** *Composer*
b. Rumania, 1881: d. Paris, 1955
Georges Enesco, well known as a composer for his second *Rumanian Rhapsody*, was famous also as a violinist and as a conductor. His native town was renamed Enescu (the Rumanian form of Enesco) in his honor. The opera, *Oedipus*, is a grandiose opera in a modern manner using a few quarter-tones in one section.
Oedipus            Paris 1932

**Engel, A. Lehman** *Composer*
b. Jackson, Miss., 1910:
He is known for his scores for stage plays, and as a conductor.

| | | |
|---|---|---|
| Pierrot of the Minute | | |
| | Cincinnati | 1928 |
| Medea | | 1935 |
| The Soldier | New York | 1956 |

**Erede, Alberto** *Conductor*
b. Genoa, 1908:
Conducted in England in the thirties and after the Second World War. He conducted in New York, NBC, 1939, and joined the Metropolitan in 1954.

**Erlanger, Camille** *Composer*
b. Paris, 1863: d. there, 1919

| | | |
|---|---|---|
| St. Jean l'Hospitalier | | 1896 |
| Kermaria | Paris | 1897 |
| Le Juif Polonais | ,, | 1900 |

| | | |
|---|---|---|
| Le Fils de L'Étoile | ,, | 1904 |
| Aphrodité | ,, | 1906 |
| Bacchus Triomphant | Bordeaux | 1909 |
| L'Aube Rouge | Rouen | 1911 |
| La Sorcière | Paris | 1912 |
| Le Barbier de Deauville | | 1917 |
| Forfaiture | Comique | 1921 |

**Erlanger, Frederic d'** *Composer*
b. Paris, 1868: d. London, 1943
The Baron d'Erlanger frequently wrote under the pseudonym Frédéric Regnal.

| | | |
|---|---|---|
| Jehan de Saintré | Aix (Aachen) | 1893 |
| Inez Mendo | London | 1897 |
| Tess of the d'Urbervilles | | |
| | Naples | 1906 |
| Noël | Paris | 1910 |

**Erskine, John** *Librettist*
b. New York, 1879: d. there, 1951
President of the Juilliard School from 1928 to 1937. A pianist and a novelist, with *The Private Life of Helen of Troy* to his credit. He wrote the libretti for *Helen Retires*, and *Jack and the Beanstalk*.

**Esplá, Oscar** *Composer*
b. Alicante, 1886:
Like other late nineteenth-century Russians, Esplá was a technical man besides being a composer. He was a civil engineer.

| | | |
|---|---|---|
| La Bella Dormiente | Vienna | 1909 |
| La Balteira | | 1939 |

**Evans, Edith** *Mezzo-soprano*
b.
Annina, Cherubino, Flora (*La Traviata*), Frau Grubach, Lola, Margret (*Wozzeck*), Mercedes, Mrs. Nolan (*The Medium*), Octavian, Shepherd (*Tosca*), Smeraldina (*The Love for Three Oranges*), Suzuki, Tisbe (*La Cenerentola*).

**Falcon, Marie Cornélie** *Soprano*
b. Paris, 1814: d. there, 1897
The list of her firsts includes: Rachel, Valentine (*Les Huguenots*), Mrs. Anckarström (*Gustave III*), Morgiana (Cherubini's

*Ali Baba*), and Leonora (*Alessandro Stradella*). She made her debut in 1832 at the Opéra singing Alice (*Robert le Diable*). In 1838 she lost her voice and in 1840 had to leave the stage altogether. She was also famous for her Donna Anna and her Julie (*La Vestale*).

**Falk, Richard**  *Conductor*
b. Moringen, Germany, 1879: d. New York, 1949
He conducted in the United States after 1939.

**Falla, Manuel de**  *Composer*
b. Cádiz, 1876: d. Córdoba, Argentina, 1946
One of the great modern Spanish composers. He is best known for his ballet music *El Amor Brujo* and *The Three-Cornered Hat*.

| El Retablo de Maese | | |
| Pedro | Paris | 1923 |
| La Vida Breve | Nice | 1913 |

**Farrar, Geraldine**  *Soprano*
b. Melrose, Mass., 1882:
This almost legendary singer made her debut as Marguérite in *Faust* at Berlin, 1901. In 1906 she appeared as Juliette at the Metropolitan. She was the first Suor Angelica.

Ariane (*Ariane et Barbe-Bleue*), Carmen (*both stage and film*), Charlotte, Caterina (*Madame Sans-Gêne*), Cherubino, Cio-cio San (*first time in United States*), Desdemona, Elisabeth, Elsa, Donna Elvira, Eva, Gilda, Juliette, Manon, Marguérite (*Faust*), Marguerita (*La Damnation de Faust*), Marguerite (*Mefistofele*), Micaela, Mignon, Mimi, Suor Anglica, Susanna (*Le Nozze di Figaro*), Susanna (*Il Segreto di Susanna*), Thaïs, Tosca, Violetta, Zara, Zerlina (*Don Giovanni*).

**Farrell, Eileen**  *Soprano*
b. Willimantic, Conn., 1920:
Famous as a concert and radio singer, particularly in her interpretations of the arias and cantatas of J. S. Bach. She made her operatic debut in a concert performance of *Medea* (Cherubini), in 1955.

Alcestis, Ariadne (*Ariadne auf Naxos*), La Gioconda, Leonora (*Il Trovatore*), Medea (*Cherubini*).

**Faull, Ellen**  *Soprano*
b.
Donna Anna, Birdie (*Regina*), Chrysothemis (*Elektra*), Cio-cio San, Countess Almaviva, Fata Morgana, Helmwige, Miss Pinkerton (*The Old Maid and the Thief*).

**Fauré, Gabriel Urbain**  *Composer*
b. Pamiers, France, 1845: d. Paris, 1924
A pupil of Saint-Saëns, Fauré carried along the great classical tradition of France by teaching Ravel, Enesco, Nadia Boulanger and others. He was director of the Paris Conservatoire from 1905 to 1920. Most music-lovers know him best by his *Requiem*.

| Promethée | Béziers | 1900 |
| Pénélope | Monte Carlo | 1913 |

**Faure, Jean Baptiste**  *Baritone*
b. Moulins, 1830: d. Paris, 1914
The first Rodrigo (*Don Carlos*). He made his debut at the Opéra-Comique, 1852. He is also known as a great teacher of singing and the composer of the song *Les Rameaux*.

Alfonso (*Lucrezia Borgia*), Assur, Cacique (*Il Guarany*), Caspar, De Nevers, Fernando (*La Gazza Ladra*), Figaro, Don Giovanni, Guillaume Tell, Hamlet, Hoël, Iago (Rossini's *Otello*), Lotario (*Mignon*), Marquis (*Manon Lescaut*), Méphistophélès (*Faust*), Nelusko, Peter (*Zar und Zimmerman*), Pietro (*Masaniello*), Rodrigo (*Don Carlos*), Rudolph (*La Sonnambula*), St. Bris.

**Favart, Charles Simon**  *Librettist*
b. Paris, 1710: d. there, 1792
He is said to have written nearly one hundred and fifty libretti. Some of them

were used by such composers as Gluck and Grétry. The first version of *Bastien and Bastienne* is Favart's. He became stage manager of the Opéra-Comique in 1758, then director.

**Favero, Mafalda** *Soprano*
b.

Adriana Lecouvreur, Cio-cio San, Harriet (*Martha*), Liù, Louise, Magda (*La Rondine*), Manon, Manon Lescaut, Mimi, Suzel (*L'Amico Fritz*), Thaïs, Wife (*Le Pauvre Matelot*), Zaza.

**Fenn, Jean** *Soprano*
b.
She made her debut in San Francisco as Elena in *Mefistofele* in 1952. Her first appearance in New York was as Musetta in 1953.
Nedda, Rosalinda (*Die Fledermaus*), Violetta.

**Fenton, Lavinia** *Soprano*
(*Really* Beswick)
b. London, 1708: d. Greenwich, 1760
She was the first Polly Peachum. Her fame from that brilliant, long-run masterpiece led her to a marriage by which she became Duchess of Bolton.

**Ferrari, Benedetto** *Composer*
b. Reggio, Italy, 1597: d. Modena, 1681
He wrote the libretto for *Andromeda*, by Manelli, the first opera ever performed for the public, 1637. He also wrote the libretti for his own works.

| | | |
|---|---|---|
| Armida | Venice | 1639 |
| Il Pastor Regio | ,, | 1640 |
| La Ninfa Avara | ,, | 1641 |
| Il Principe Giardiniero | ,, | 1643 |
| Erosilde | Modena | 1658 |

**Ferrari-Fontana, Edoardo** *Tenor*
b. Rome, 1878: d. Toronto, 1936
The first Avito (*L'amore dei Tre Re*).
Avito (*L'Amore dei Tre Re*), Canio, Don José, Wagner (*Faust*).

**Ferrier, Kathleen** *Contralto*
b. Lancashire, England, 1912: d. London, 1953
The first Lucretia (*The Rape of Lucretia*). She was famous for her singing of Orfeo at Glyndebourne and at Covent Garden. Cancer hastened her death.

**Fevrier, Henri** *Composer*
b. Paris, 1875: d. there, 1957
A pupil of Fauré, Massenet and others.

| | | |
|---|---|---|
| Le Roi Aveugle | Paris | 1906 |
| Monna Vanna | Paris | 1909 |
| Ghismonda | Chicago | 1919 |
| La Damnation de Blanche-Fleur | Monte-Carlo | 1920 |
| La Femme Nue | ,, | 1929 |

**Fibich, Zdenko** *Composer*
b. Všeboriče, Czechoslovakia, 1850: d. Prague, 1900
A prolific composer not only of opera but also of music for stage plays, orchestra, chorus and chamber music.

| | | |
|---|---|---|
| Bukovín | Prague | 1871 |
| Blaník | ,, | 1881 |
| Nevěsta Messinska (*The Bride of Messina*) | ,, | 1884 |
| Bouře (*The Tempest*) | ,, | 1895 |
| Hédy | ,, | 1896 |
| Sárka | ,, | 1897 |
| Pad Arkuna (*The Fall of Arkun*) | ,, | 1900 |

**Figner, Nicolay Nicolayevitch** *Tenor*
b. St. Petersburg, 1857: d. Kiev, 1919
He made his debut in St. Petersburg in 1887. He took part in the first performance of *Pique-Dame*, and was famous for his Lensky.

**Fischer, Emil** *Bass*
b. Brunswick, 1838: d. Hamburg, 1914
This famous Wagnerian basso made his debut at Graz in 1857, and at the Metropolitan in 1885.
Daland, Hans Sachs, Henry the Fowler, King Marke, Louis VI (*Euryanthe*), Steffano Colonna.

**Fischer, Ludwig**                    *Bass*
b. Mainz, 1745: d. Berlin, 1825
The first Osmin in *Die Entführung aus dem Serail.*

**Fischer-Dieskau, Dietrich**    *Baritone*
b. Berlin, 1925:
He made his debut in Berlin in 1948 and in New York, 1955.
Kurnewal, Orfeo, Papageno.

**Fisher, Sylvia**                   *Soprano*
b. Melbourne, Australia
Agathe, Donna Anna, Brünnhilde, Elisabeth, Ellen Orford, Elsa, Isolde, Kostelnika (*Jejì Pastorkyňa,*) Leonore (*Fidelio*), The Marschallin, Ortrud, Sieglinde.

**Flagstad, Kirsten**                *Soprano*
b. Hamar, Norway, 1895:
The great Flagstad made her debut as Nuri (*Tiefland*) in 1913. She first sang at Bayreuth as Brünnhilde in 1934 and at the Metropolitan as Sieglinde in 1935. Her reputation for Wagnerian roles is unsurpassed. Her husband was accused of being a Quisling during the Second World War. After the war, she felt that the Americans were somewhat less pleased with her and retired to her homeland.
Aida, Alceste, Anne Page, Brünnhilde, Dido (*Dido and Aeneas*), Elisabeth, Elsa, Euryanthe, Gutrune, Isolde, Leonore (*Fidelio*), Kundry, Mimi, Minnie, Nuri (*Tiefland*), Ortlinde, Rezia, Senta, Sieglinde.

**Fleischer, Editha**                *Soprano*
b. Falkenstein, Germany, 1898:
A pupil of Lilli Lehman, she made her debut at Berlin in 1919 and at the Metropolitan in 1926.
Aithra, Lisette (*La Rondine*), Serpina, Zerlina (*Don Giovanni*).

**Flem, Paul Le**                   *Composer*
b. Lézardieux, France, 1881:
Le Rossignol de St.
    Malo                 Comique   1942

La Clairière des Fées            1943
La Magicienne de la Mer   Paris   1954

**Flotow, Friedrich von**          *Composer*
b. Teutendorf, Germany, 1812:  d. Darmstadt, 1883
La Naufrage de Méduse    Paris   1839
Alessandro Stradella   Hamburg   1844
Martha                   Vienna   1847

**Floyd, Carlisle**                *Composer*
b. Latta, S.C., 1926:
The Fugitives                    1951
Susanna                          1955
Wuthering Heights
            Santa Fe, N.M.   1958

**Fodor-Mainvielle, Joséphine**    *Soprano*
b. Paris, 1789: d. Lyons, 1870
Desdemona (*Otello*, by Rossini). Ninetta (*Il Barbiere di Siviglia*), Rosina (*Il Barbiere di Siviglia*), Semiramide (Rossini), Zelmira, Zerlina (*Don Giovanni*).

**Foerster, Joseph Bohuslav**      *Composer*
b. Prague, 1859: d. Novy Vestec, 1951
Deborah              Prague   1898
Eva                       „      1899
Jessica                   „      1905
Nepřemoženi
    (*The Conquerors*)    „      1906
Srdce (*The Heart*)       „      1923
Bloud                     „      1936

**Foli, Allen James**                 *Bass*
(*Really* Foley)
b. Tipperary, 1835: d. Southport, 1899
Assur, Don Basilio, Bertram, Caspar, Commedatore, Daland, Elmiro, Hermit (*Der Freischütz*), Marcel, Méphistophélès (*Faust*), Oroe (*Semiramide*), Priest (*Die Zauberflöte*), Rodolfo (*La Sonnambula*), Sarastro, St. Bris, Sparafucile.

**Formes, Karl Johann**               *Bass*
b. Mulheim am Rhein, 1815: d. San Francisco, 1889
He made his debut at Cologne in 1841.
Don Basilio (*Il Barbiere di Siviglia*),

Bertram, Caspar, Leporello, Marcel, Rocco, Sarastro.

**Formichi, Cesare**　　　　　　*Baritone*
b. Rome, 1887:
Amonasro, Gerard (*Andrea Chénier*), Iago, Méphistophélès (*La Damnation de Faust*), Rigoletto, Scarpia, Tonio.

**Fornia-Labey, Rita**　　　*Mezzo-soprano*
(*Née* Neumann).
b. San Francisco, 1878: d. Paris, 1922
A pupil of Jean de Reszke, she began as a soprano, then changed to mezzo. She joined the Metropolitan in 1908 and stayed until 1922. Her stage name was constructed from the last letters of the name of her native state.
Amneris, Carmen, Elisabeth, Gutrune, Leonora (*Fidelio*), Nedda, Ortrud, Rosina (*Il Barbiere di Siviglia*), Sieglinde, Venus, Woglinde.

**Forrest, Hamilton**　　　　　*Composer*
b. Chicago, 1901:
　Yzdra　　　　　　　　　　1925
　Camille (for Mary Garden)　　1930

**Forsyth, Cecil**　　　　　　*Composer*
b. Greenwich, England, 1870: d. New York, 1941
Best known as the author of a treatise on orchestration.
　Westward Ho!　　　　　　London
　Cinderella　　　　　　　　　　,,

**Forti, Anton**　　　　　　　*Baritone*
b. Vienna, 1790: d. there, 1859
Figaro (*Il Barbiere di Siviglia*), Figaro (*Le Nozze di Figaro*), Don Giovanni, Pizzaro (*Fidelio*), Telasco (*Fernando Cortez*).

**Foss, Lucas**　　　　　　　*Composer*
(*Really* Fuchs)
b. Berlin, 1922:
　Griffelkin　　　　　　NBC TV 1955

**Franchetti, Alberto**　　　　*Composer*
b. Turin, 1860: d. Viareggio, 1942
　Asraël　　　　　　Reggio 1888

| | | |
|---|---|---|
| Cristoforo Colombo | Genoa | 1892 |
| Fior d'Alpe | Milan | 1894 |
| Il Signor di Pourceaugnac | ,, | 1897 |
| Germania | La Scala | 1902 |
| La Figlia di Jorio | Milan | 1906 |
| Notte di Leggenda | ,, | 1915 |
| Giove a Pompeii (*with Giordano*) | Rome | 1921 |
| Glauco | Naples | 1922 |

**Franci, Benvenuto**　　　　　*Baritone*
b.
Alfio, Barnaba, Fanuel (*Nerone*), Gerard, High Priest (*Alceste*), Marcello (*La Bohème*), Michele (*Il Tabarro*), Orfeo (*La Favola d'Orfeo*), Rance, Rigoletto, Scarpia.

**Franck, César Auguste**　　　*Composer*
b. Liège, 1822: d. Paris, 1890
Famous as an organist and a teacher. He is best known for his *Symphony in D minor*.
| | | |
|---|---|---|
| Le Valet de Ferme | | 1852 |
| Hulda | Monte Carlo | 1894 |
| Ghisèle (*completed by his pupils*) | ,, | 1896 |

**Franke, Paul**　　　　　　　*Tenor*
b.
Dr. Blind, Borsa, Captain (*Wozzeck*), Count Lerma, David (*Die Meistersinger*), Flavio (*Norma*), Goro, Major Domo to von Faninal (*Der Rosenkavalier*), Messenger (*Aida*), Parpignol, Sellem (*The Rake's Progress*), Shepherd (*Tristan und Isolde*), Schuisky (*Boris Godunov*), Simpleton (*Boris Godunov*).

**Fremstad, Olive**　　*Soprano and Contralto*
b. Stockholm, 1871: d. Irvington on Hudson, N.Y., 1951
A pupil of Lilli Lehman, she made her debut in Cologne, 1895, as Azucena. At her Metropolitan debut, 1903, she sang Sieglinde. She was the first in Paris and the first in the United States to sing Salome. She also sang the first Iolanthe (*Der Wald*).

Armida, Azucena, Brangäne, Brünnhilde, Carmen, Elisabeth, Elsa, Fricka, Isolde, Kundry, Salome, Santuzza, Selika, Sieglinde, Tosca, Venus.

**Fricsay, Ferenc**  *Conductor*
b. Budapest, 1914:
Conducted at Budapest, throughout Europe and the United States, and over the Berlin radio (RIAS).

**Fry, William Henry**  *Composer*
b. Philadelphia, 1813: d. Santa Cruz, W.I., 1864
His *Leonora* was the first opera by a native American to be performed here. He also wrote four symphonies and other orchestral music. But beyond that he ranged very far: he was a politically active professional journalist and a lecturer.

Leonora     Philadelphia   1845
Notre Dame de Paris    „     1864
The Bride of Dunure
Aurelia the Vestal

**Fuchs, Marta**  *Soprano*
b.
Brünnhilde,   Isolde,   Kostelnicka, Kundry.

**Fursch-Madi, Emma**  *Soprano*
b. Bayonne, France, 1847: d. Warrenville, N.Y., 1894
She made her debut in Paris as Marguérite.
Aida, Donna Anna, Laura, Lucrezia Borgia, Marguérite (*Faust*), Ortrud.

**Furtwängler, Wilhelm**  *Conductor*
b. Berlin, 1886: d. Baden-Baden, 1954
Conductor of opera in Switzerland and Germany, Music Director of the Berlin State Opera in 1919. He was also a composer of orchestral and choral music and a writer of essays.

**Gadski, Johanna**  *Soprano*
b. Prussia, 1873: d. Berlin, 1932

The first Hester Prynne (*The Scarlet Letter*, by Damrosch). She made her debut in Berlin in 1889 as Undine (by Lortzing). In 1895 she appeared for the first time in New York, singing Elsa. From 1898 to 1917 she sang, intermittently, at the Metropolitan.
Agathe, Aida, Anna (*La Dame Blanche*), Brünnhilde, Elisabeth, Elsa, Euridice, Eva, Isolde, Sieglinde, Undine.

**Gagliano, Marco da**  *Composer*
b. Gagliano, Italy, 1575: d. Florence, 1642
A member of the Florentine Camerata (*see* Bardi). Gagliano wrote masses and cantatas in polyphonic form as well as operas.
Dafne          Mantua   1608
La Flora (*with Peri*)   Florence   1628

**Gál, Hans**  *Composer*
b. Brunn, Austria, 1890:
Der Arzt der Sobeide    Breslau   1919
Die Heilige Ente     Düsseldorf   1923
Das Lied der Nacht    Breslau   1926
Der Zauberspiegel     „     1930
Die Beiden Klaas     „     1933

**Galassi, Antonio**  *Baritone*
b. Lovetto, Italy, 1845: d. 1904
One of the most famous singers at the old New York Academy of Music.
Enrico (*Lucia di Lammermoor*), Escamillo, Iago, Riccardo (*I Puritani*), Rigoletto.

**Galeffi, Carlo**  *Baritone*
The first Fanuél (*Nerone*), and the first Manfredo (*L'Amore dei Tre Re*).
Fanuél (*Nerone*), Gianni Schicchi, Manfredo (*L'Amore dei Tre Re*), Méphistophélès (*La Damnation de Faust*), Michele (*Il Tabarro*), Orfeo (*La Favola d'Orfeo*), Rance, Scarpia.

**Galilei, Vincenzo**  *Composer*
b. Florence, 1533: d. there, 1591
Father of Galileo Galilei, the astronomer and physicist. Vincenzo was one of the most influential members of the Florentine

*Camerata* (*see* Bardi) that conceived opera as an approach to the great Greek drama. He may have been the first to compose music in monodic form (i.e., single-voice with accompaniment). He also composed madrigals and cantilenas, some of which are published.

**Galli, Amintore**                 *Composer*
b. Talamello, Italy, 1845: d. Rimini, 1919

| Il Como d'Oro | Turin | 1876 |
| David | Milan | 1904 |

**Galli, Filippo**                 *Baritone*
b. Rome, 1783: d. there, 1853
   The first Fernando (*La Gazza Ladra*), and the first Maometto (Rossini's opera). He began his career as a tenor, but later became a baritone.

**Galli-Curci, Amelita**                 *Soprano*
b. Milan, 1889:
   At first this famous prima donna studied to be a pianist. She instructed herself in singing. Her debut came in 1909 in Rome where she sang Gilda. She sang for the first time in Chicago in 1916 in the same role, and at the Metropolitan as Violetta in 1920.
   Amina, Dinorah, Donna Elvira, Gilda, Juliette, Lakmé, Leila, Lucia, Rosina (*Il Barbiere di Siviglia*), Violetta.

**Galli-Marie, Marie Célestine Laurence**
                 *Mezzo-soprano*
b. Paris, 1840: d. near Nice, 1905
   The first Carmen, the first Mignon. She made her debut in Strasbourg in 1859 and as Serpina at the Comique in 1862.

**Galuppi, Baldassare**                 *Composer*
b. Burano, Italy, 1706: d. Venice, 1785
   Called the father of Opera Buffa, Galuppi wrote one hundred twelve operas, twenty oratorios, music for the harpsichord, and so on.

| Dorinda | 1729 |
| Didone Abbandonata | 1752 |
| Il Re Pastore | 1762 |
| Ifigenia in Tauride | 1768 |

**García, Eugénie**                 *Soprano*
(*Née* Mayer)
b. Paris, 1818: d. there, 1880
   The wife of Manuel Patricio García. She made her debut at the Opéra-Comique in 1842.

**García, Gustave**                 *Baritone*
b. Milan, 1837: d. London, 1925
   The son of Manuel Patricio García. He sang Don Giovanni, among other roles.

**García, Manuel del Pópolo Vicente**
                 *Tenor*
b. Seville, 1775: d. Paris, 1832
   The first Almaviva; one might also refer to him as the first García, in honor of the family he founded. Two of his daughters, Maria Malibran and Viardot-García became internationally famous. His son Manuel Patricio was one of the great teachers of singing. Manuel himself produced the first Italian opera in America, opening in New York with *Il Barbiere di Siviglia* on 29 November 1825. When he first sang Almaviva in that opera's Italian premiere, he appeared with a guitar to sing a Spanish song of his own suggestion. The guitar had lost a string, and thus began a chain of events that culminated with a demonstration in the audience against the whole opera. Rossini quickly replaced the Spanish song with the famous *Ecco Ridente in Cielo*, in time to save his reputation.
   García also composed many an opera for his troupe.

**García, Manuel Patricio Rodriguez**
                 *Bass*
b. Madrid, 1805: d. London, 1906
   Inventor of the laryngoscope, and a famous teacher of singing. He taught at the Royal Academy of Music in London from 1848 to 1895. Among his pupils was the celebrated Jenny Lind. He was the son of Manuel del Pópolo Vicente García and sang in his father's company for

a short while, singing Leporello and Figaro (*Il Barbiere di Siviglia*).

**Garden, Mary**       *Soprano*
b. Aberdeen, Scotland, 1877:
The first Camille in an opera by Hamilton Forrest commissioned by her. The first Mélisande. In the latter role her appearance caused Maeterlinck, the author of the play, to break with Debussy. Maeterlinck had expected his mistress to be the star. Mary Garden made her debut on particularly short notice as Louise at the Opéra-Comique in 1900, substituting for Rioton. She made her Manhattan debut, as Thaïs, in 1907 and in Chicago in 1910. She was manager of the Chicago Opera from 1921 to 1922.

Camille, Carmen, Dulcinée, Jean (*Le Jongleur de Notre Dame*), Louise, Manon, Marguérite (*Faust*), Mélisande, Salome, Sapho, Thaïs.

**Garrison, Mabel**       *Soprano*
b. Baltimore, 1886:
She made her debut in Boston in 1912, playing Philine in *Mignon*. She joined the Metropolitan in 1914 and sang there until 1922.

**Gassier, Édouard**       *Baritone*
b. 1820: d. Havana, 1872
Ambrose (*Mireille*), Assur, Figaro (*Il Barbiere di Siviglia*), Figaro (*Le Nozze di Figaro*), Don Beltrano (*L'Oca del Cairo*), Ferrando (*Il Trovatore*), Laertes (*Mignon*), Malatesta (*Don Pasquale*), Fra Melitone, Méphistophélès (*Faust*), Page (*Die Lustigen Weiber von Windsor*), Pirro (*I Lombardi*), Count Rodolpho, Thoas (*Iphigénie en Tauride*).

**Gatti, Gabriele**       *Soprano*
b.
Euridice (*La Favola d'Orfeo*), Marguérite (*La Damnation de Faust*), Marie (*Wozzeck*).

**Gatti-Casazza, Guilio**       *Manager*
b. Udine, Italy, 1868: d. Ferrara, 1940

Director of La Scala from 1898 to 1908, General Manager of the Metropolitan from 1908 until 1935. He was instrumental in bringing out new works and operas not before heard in the United States. It was he who brought Toscanini to the Metropolitan. In 1910 he married Frances Alda, but they were divorced in 1929.

**Gatty, Nicholas Comyn**     *Composer*
b. Bradford, England, 1874: d. London, 1946

| | | |
|---|---|---|
| Greysteel | London | 1906 |
| Duke or Devil | ,, | 1909 |
| Prince Ferelon | ,, | 1919 |
| The Tempest | ,, | 1920 |
| Macbeth | | |

**Gaubert, Philippe**       *Composer*
b. Cahors, France, 1879:
Best known for his music for the flute, of which he is an accomplished player. He has also conducted opera, notably *Alceste* at Covent Garden in 1937.

| | | |
|---|---|---|
| Sonia | Nantes | 1913 |
| Naïla | Paris | 1927 |

**Gavazzeni, Gianandrea**     *Conductor*
b. Bergamo, 1909:
A composer of music for orchestra, chamber orchestra and so forth. He has conducted at La Scala and Chicago.

**Gay, John**       *Librettist*
b. Devon, England, 1685: d. London, 1732
His association with Rich, in the production of *The Beggar's Opera*, led to the famous remark that the work made "Gay rich and Rich gay." His attempt, again with the composer/editor Pepusch, to ride the crest of the wave with a sequel, *Polly*, was unsuccessful.

| | | |
|---|---|---|
| The Beggar's Opera | London | 1728 |
| Black Eyed Susan | | |
| Polly | London | 1777 |

**Gay, Maria**       *Contralto*
b. Barcelona, 1879: d. New York, 1943

While in prison for her part in a political demonstration, she took up the study of the violin. This led to a general study of music and finally to singing, which she learned by herself. She made her debut in Brussels in 1902 as Carmen, and at the Metropolitan in 1908 in the same role. She sang in Boston, 1910 to 1912, and in Chicago until 1927. In 1913 she married Giovanni Zenatello.

Azucena, Brangäne, Carmela (*I Gioielli della Madonna*), Carmen, Charlotte, Dalila, Geneviève (*Pelléas et Mélisande*), Maddalena (*Rigoletto*), Mother (*Louise*), Orfeo, Suzuki.

**Gazzaniga, Giuseppe** *Composer*
b. Verona, 1743: d. Crema, 1818
He wrote a total of fifty operas. *Il Finto Cieco* was to a libretto by Lorenzo da Ponte.

| | | |
|---|---|---|
| Il Finto Cieco | Vienna | 1770 |
| Il Convietato di Pietro | | 1787 |

**Gedda, Nicolai** *Tenor*
b.
Flamand (*Capriccio*), Hoffmann, Don Narciso (*Il Turco in Italia*), Don Ottavio, Pinkerton, Tamino.

**Genée, Franz Richard** *Composer*
b. Danzig, 1823: d. Vienna, 1895
A composer of operettas. Together with Haffner he wrote the libretto for *Die Fledermaus*.

| | |
|---|---|
| Der Geiger aus Tirol | 1857 |
| Der Musikfiend | 1862 |

**German, Edward** *Composer*
(*Originally* Edward German Jones)
b. Whitechurch, 1862: d. 1936

| | | |
|---|---|---|
| The Rival Poets | London | 1886 |
| The Emerald Isle (*with Arthur Sullivan*) | „ | 1901 |
| Merrie England | „ | 1902 |
| A Princess of Kensington | „ | 1903 |
| Tom Jones | „ | 1907 |

**Gershwin, George** *Composer*
b. Brooklyn, N.Y., 1898: d. Beverly Hills, Calif., 1937
A songwriter of spectacular success, the composer of *Embraceable You, Of Thee I Sing, Rhapsody in Blue*, and so forth. He wrote a large number of Broadway shows such as *Lady Be Good, Funny Face, Girl Crazy*. His style was so thoroughly developed that it became the Broadway style. His single opera has achieved a tremendous success throughout the world, although Europeans tend to see it as a tour de force; and some Americans as too simple an imitation of Negro music.

| | | |
|---|---|---|
| Porgy and Bess | Boston | 1935 |

**Gerster, Etelka** *Soprano*
b. Kschau, Hungary, 1855: d. near Bologna, 1920
She made her debut as Gilda in Venice, 1876. In 1877 she sang for the first time in London, as Amina, and in 1878 in New York in the same role.

Amina, Elvira (*I Puritani*), Gilda, Lucia, Ophélie.

**Gerster, Ottmar** *Composer*
b. Braunfels, 1897:

| | | |
|---|---|---|
| Liselotte | Essen | 1933 |
| Enoch Arden | Düsseldorf | 1936 |
| Die Hexe von Passau | „ | 1941 |
| Das Verzauberte Ich | „ | 1949 |

**Gerville-Réache, Jeanne** *Contralto*
b. Orthez, France, 1882: d. New York, 1915
A pupil of Viardot-Garcia, she made her debut as Orfeo at the Comique in 1900. She was the first Geneviève (*Pelléas et Mélisande*), and the first Katherine (*Le Juif Polonais*).

**Gevaert, François Auguste** *Composer*
b. Huysse, Belgium, 1828: d. Brussels, 1908
Not only a composer of orchestral

music, choral music and opera, but also the author of books of history of music and of orchestration.

| | |
|---|---|
| Georgette | 1852 |
| Le Billet de Marguerite | 1854 |
| Quentin Durward | 1858 |
| Le Diable au Moulin | 1859 |
| Les Deux Amours | 1861 |
| Le Capitaine Henriot | 1861 |

**Ghedini, Giorgio Federico** *Composer*
b. Cuneo, Italy, 1892:

| | | |
|---|---|---|
| Maria d'Alessandria | Bergamo | 1937 |
| Re Hassan | Venice | 1939 |
| La Pulce d'Oro | Genoa | 1940 |
| La Baccanti | Milan | 1948 |
| Billy Budd | Venice | 1949 |
| L'Ipocrita Felice | Milan | 1956 |

**Ghislanzoni, Antonio** *Librettist*
b. Lecco, Italy, 1824: d. Caprino, 1893
Besides *Aida*, he wrote nearly sixty libretti. But he was also a baritone, and made his debut in Lodi, 1846.

**Giannini, Dusolina** *Soprano*
b. Philadelphia, 1902:
The sister of Vittorio Giannini, she studied with Sembrich and made her debut at Carnegie Hall in New York in 1925. In 1927 she sang in her first opera, at Hamburg, Germany, and in 1936 at the Metropolitan as Aida.
Aida, Carmen, Cio-cio San, Hester Prynne (*The Scarlet Letter* by her brother), Maliella (*I Gioielli della Madonna*).

**Giannini, Vittorio** *Composer*
b. Philadelphia, 1903:
Brother of Dusolina Giannini, and a composer of much music for orchestra and for voice.

| | | |
|---|---|---|
| Lucedia | Munich | 1934 |
| Flora | | 1937 |
| The Scarlet Letter | Hamburg | 1938 |
| Beauty and the Beast | (radio) | 1938 |
| Blennerhasset | ,, | 1939 |
| The Taming of the Shrew | TV | 1954 |

**Gibbs, Cecil Armstrong** *Composer*
b. near Chelmsford, England, 1889:

| | |
|---|---|
| The Blue Peter | 1924 |
| Twelfth Night | 1947 |
| The Great Bell of Burley (*for children*) | 1949 |

**Gigli, Beniamino** *Tenor*
b. Recanati, Italy, 1890: d. Rome, 1957
Well known in the United States not only for his operatic roles on the stage, but also for his appearances in films. He made his debut at the Metropolitan as Faust in *Mefistofele* in 1920, and stayed until 1932.
Alfredo (*La Traviata*), Don Alvaro, Andrea Chénier, Avito (*L'Amore dei Tre Re*), Canio, Duke (*Rigoletto*), des Grieux (*Manon*), des Grieux (*Manon Lescaut*), Lionel, Lohengrin, Milio (*Zaza*), Mylio (*Le Roi d'Ys*), Nemerino, Osaka (*Iris*), Riccardo (*Un Ballo in Maschera*), Rodolfo, Romeo, Ruggero (*La Rondine*), Vasco da Gama, Wilhelm (*Mignon*).

**Gilardi, Gilardo** *Composer*
b. San Fernando, Argentina, 1889:

| | | |
|---|---|---|
| Ilse | Buenos Aires | 1923 |
| La Legenda de Urutaú | ,, | 1934 |

**Gilbert, William Schwenck** *Librettist*
b. London, 1836: d. Middlesex, 1911
In twenty years' association with Arthur Sullivan (*q.v.*), Sir William Gilbert produced some of the most famous operetta libretti ever played. He was knighted in 1907.

**Giordano, Umberto** *Composer*
b. Foggia, 1867: d. Milan, 1948

| | | |
|---|---|---|
| Mala Vita | Rome | 1892 |
| Regina Diaz | ,, | 1894 |
| Andrea Chénier | La Scala | 1896 |
| Fedora | Milan | 1898 |
| Siberia | La Scala | 1903 |
| Marcella | Milan | 1907 |
| Mese Mariano | Palermo | 1910 |
| Madame Sans-Gêne | Metropolitan | 1915 |

| Giove a Pompeii | Rome | 1921 |
| La Cena delle Beffe | La Scala | 1924 |
| Il Re | La Scala | 1929 |

**Giraldoni, Eugenio** *Baritone*
b. Marseilles, 1871: d. Helsinki, 1924
The first Scarpia. He made his debut in Barcelona as Don José in 1891.

**Giraudet, Alfred Auguste** *Bass*
b. Étampes, Belgium, 1845: d. New York, 1911
A teacher of opera in New York. He made his debut as Méphistophélès (*Faust*) at Paris in 1868.

**Glanville-Hicks, Peggy** *Composer*
b. Melbourne, 1912:
A pupil of Vaughan Williams.
Caedmon
The Transposed Heads
Louisville, Ky. 1954

**Glaz, Herta** *Contralto*
b. Vienna, 1914:
She made her debut at Breslau and appeared for the first time at the Metropolitan in 1942 as Amneris.
Annina (*Der Rosenkavalier*), Maddalena, Magdalene (*Die Meistersinger*), Mercedes (*Carmen*), Shepherd (*Tosca*), Siegrune.

**Glazunov, Alexander Constantinovitch** *Composer*
b. St. Petersburg, 1865: d. Paris, 1936
Although he wrote no operas of his own, Glazunov helped complete *Prince Igor* after Borodin's death.

**Glière, Reinhold Moritzovitch** *Composer*
b. Kiev, 1875: d. Moscow, 1956
He is best known in the United States for selections, particularly the *Sailors' Dance*, from his ballet *The Red Poppy*.
Shah Senem  Baku  1927

**Glinka, Mikhail Ivanovitch** *Composer*
b. Smolensk, 1803: d. Berlin, 1857

| Ivan Susanin (*A Life for the Tsar*) | St. Petersburg | 1836 |
| Russlan and Ludmilla | „ | 1842 |

**Gluck, Alma** *Soprano*
(*Really* Reba Fiersohn)
b. Bucharest, 1886: d. New York, 1938
Alma Gluck sang in opera from 1909, when she made her debut at the Metropolitan as Sophie (*Werther*), until 1912 when she retired. She had also sung Armide and Mimi.

**Gluck, Christoph Willibald Ritter von** *Composer*
b. Bavaria, 1714: d. Vienna, 1787
One of the greatest composers of opera and a continuing influence upon other composers. Gluck had written for years in the accepted Italian style before, with *Orfeo*, he rebelled against it and produced a kind of choral opera which he considered nearer to what musical drama should be. He outlined his ideas in the preface to his next work, *Alceste*, and then moved to Paris where his arrival and his ideas stirred up a war between those who agreed with him and those who did not. The dissenters rallied around the name of the unfortunate Piccini and thus the battle of the Gluckists and Piccinists was joined. It ended in a resounding triumph for Gluck when Piccini was prevailed upon to write an *Iphigénie en Tauride* to replace Gluck's. Because of a number of ludicrous troubles at the opening and the inebriation of the prima donna, the replacement was howled down. Gluck changed the face of opera by deleting the harpsichord, adding clarinets, trombones, harps and percussion, throwing out so-called *secco recitatif*, simplifying the aria and using the chorus as characters with legitimately choral music.

| Artaserse | Milan | 1741 |
| Orfeo ed Euridice | Vienna | 1762 |
| Alcestis | „ | 1767 |
| Paride ed Elena | „ | 1770 |

| Iphigénie en Aulide | Paris | 1774 |
|---|---|---|
| Armide | ,, | 1777 |
| Iphigénie en Tauride | ,, | 1779 |

**Gnecchi, Vittorio** *Composer*
b. Milan, 1876: d. there, 1954

| Virtù d'Amore | | 1896 |
|---|---|---|
| Cassandra | Bologna | 1905 |
| La Rosiera (*written* 1910) | | 1927 |

**Gobbi, Tito** *Baritone*
b. Bassano del Grappo, Italy, 1915:
Gobbi made his debut at Rome in 1938, then in San Francisco in 1948 and at the Metropolitan as Scarpia in 1956.

Amonasro, Falstaff (*Falstaff*), Figaro (*Il Barbiere di Siviglia*), Giorgio Germont, Méphistophélès (*La Damnation de Faust*), Pimen, Renato (*Un Ballo in Maschera*), Rigoletto, Scarpia, Simon Boccanegra, Tonio, Wozzeck.

**Godard, Benjamin Louis Paul**
*Composer*
b. Paris, 1849: d. Cannes, 1895
Godard is chiefly remembered for the *Berceuse* from *Jocelyn*.

| Les Bijoux de Jeannette | | 1878 |
|---|---|---|
| Pedro de Zalamea | Antwerp | 1884 |
| Jocelyn | Brussels | 1888 |
| Dante | Comique | 1890 |
| La Vivandière | Paris | 1895 |
| Les Guelphs | Rouen | 1902 |

**Goedicke, Alexander Fedorovitch**
*Composer*
b. Moscow, 1877: d. there, 1957

| At the Crossing | | 1933 |
|---|---|---|
| Jacquerie | | 1937 |

**Goetz, Hermann** *Composer*
b. Königsberg, 1840: d. near Zürich, 1876

| Der Widerspenstigen Zähmung (*The Taming of the Shrew*) | Mannheim | 1874 |
|---|---|---|
| Francesca da Rimini (*Completed by Ernest Frank.*) | ,, | 1877 |

**Goldberg, Theo** *Composer*
b. Chemnitz, Germany, 1921:

| Minotauros | | |
|---|---|---|
| Schwere Zeiten für Engel | Berlin | 1952 |

**Goldmark, Karl** *Composer*
b. Készthely, Hungary, 1830: d. Vienna, 1915
Goldmark worked on his only opera that is still remembered, *The Queen of Sheba*, for ten years.

| Die Königin von Saba | Vienna | 1875 |
|---|---|---|
| Merlin | ,, | 1886 |
| Das Heimchen am Herd (*The Cricket on the Hearth*) | ,, | 1896 |
| Die Kriegsgefangene | ,, | 1899 |
| Götz von Berlichingen | Budapest | 1902 |
| Ein Wintermärchen (*A Winter's Tale*) | Vienna | 1908 |

**Goldovsky, Boris** *Conductor*
b. Moscow, 1908:
Founder and director of the New England Opera Theater in 1946, and of the opera workshop at Tanglewood, Lenox, Massachusetts.

**Goltz, Christel** *Soprano*
b. Dortmund, Germany:
The first Penelope in Liebermann's opera in Salzburg, 1954.

Agathe, Aida, Amelia, Antigonae (*Antigonae*, by Carl Orff), Ariadne (*Ariadne auf Naxos*), Desdemona, Elisabeth, Eva, Fiordiligi, Jenufa, Leonora (*Fidelio*), Marie (*Wozzeck*), Musetta, Octavian, Penelope (Liebermann), Rezia, Salome, Santuzza, Tosca.

**Gomez, Antonio Carlos** *Composer*
b. Compinas, Brazil, 1836: d. Parà, Belém, 1896

| Noite do Castillo | Rio de Janeiro | 1861 |
|---|---|---|
| Joanna de Flandres | ,, | 1863 |
| Il Guarany | La Scala | 1870 |

| | | |
|---|---|---|
| Salvator Rosa | Genoa | 1874 |
| Maria Tudor | La Scala | 1879 |
| Lo Schiavo | Rio de Janeiro | 1889 |
| Condor | La Scala | 1891 |

**Goossens, Eugene III** *Composer*
b. London, 1893:
Conducted the Rochester Philharmonic Orchestra from 1923 to 1930, the Cincinnati Symphony from 1931 to 1946 and in Sydney, Australia, 1947–1956.

| | | |
|---|---|---|
| Judith | Covent Garden | 1929 |
| Don Juan | ,, | 1937 |

**Gorin, Igor** *Baritone*
b. Ukraine, 1908:
Not only a singer, but a composer of songs.

**Goritz, Otto** *Baritone*
b. Berlin, 1873: d. Hamburg, 1929
He made his debut as Matteo in Neustrelitz, 1895, and at the Metropolitan as Klingsor in 1903.

**Gotovac, Jakov** *Composer*
b. Split, Yugoslavia, 1895:

| | | |
|---|---|---|
| Morana | Brno | 1930 |
| Ero s onoga Svijeta | Zagreb | 1935 |
| Kámenik | ,, | 1946 |
| Mila Gojsalica | ,, | 1952 |

**Gounod, Charles François** *Composer*
b. Paris, 1818: d. there, 1893
One of his most widely known works is the vocal line he added to the first Prelude of Bach's *Well-Tempered Clavichord*, making an *Ave Maria*.

| | | |
|---|---|---|
| Sapho | Opéra | 1851 |
| Faust | Paris | 1859 |
| Mireille | ,, | 1864 |
| Philémon et Baucis | ,, | 1860 |
| La Reine de Saba | ,, | 1862 |
| Roméo et Juliette | ,, | 1867 |

**Grad, Gabriel** *Composer*
b. near Kovno, Lithuania, 1890:
Living in Tel Aviv since 1924.
Judith and Holofernes

**Graener, Paul** *Composer*
b. Berlin, 1872: d. Salzburg, 1944
Don Juans Letztes

| | | |
|---|---|---|
| Abenteuer | Leipzig | 1914 |
| Theophano | Munich | 1918 |
| Schirrin und Gertaude | Dresden | 1920 |
| Hanneles Himmelfahrt | ,, | 1927 |
| Friedemann Bach | Schwerin | 1931 |
| Der Prinz von Hamburg | Berlin | 1935 |
| Schwanhild | Cologne | 1941 |

**Graf, Herbert** *Stage Director*
b. Vienna, 1904:
Directed at the Philadelphia Grand Opera from 1934 to 1935, then at the Metropolitan. In 1949 he became head of the opera department of the Curtis Institute in Philadelphia.

**Granados, Enrique** *Composer*
b. Lérida, Catalonia, 1867: d. at sea, 1916
Granados had attended the opening of his *Goyescas* at the Metropolitan and was en route to Europe when his ship was torpedoed by a German submarine in the English Channel.

| | | |
|---|---|---|
| María del Carmen | Madrid | 1898 |
| Picarol | Barcelona | 1901 |
| Follet | ,, | 1903 |
| Gaziel | ,, | 1906 |
| Liliana | ,, | 1911 |
| Goyescas | Metropolitan | 1916 |

**Grandi, Margherita** *Soprano*
b.
Elisabeth (*Don Carlos*), Lady Macbeth, Maria (*Friedenstag*), Oscar, Tosca.

**Grau, Maurice** *Manager*
b. Brünn, Austria, 1849: d. Paris, 1907
Manager at the Metropolitan from 1883 to 1884, then 1891 to 1903 (intermittently).

**Graziani, Lodovico** *Tenor*
b. Fermo, Italy, 1823: d. there, 1855
The first Alfredo (*Traviata*); it is worth noting that he was hoarse at the opening.
Don Carlos, Radames.

**Grétry, André Ernest Modeste**
*Composer*
b. Liège, 1741: d. Montmorency, 1813
One of the great composers of opera and religious music. Even his daughter Lucille composed two operas.

| | | |
|---|---|---|
| Zémire et Azor | Fontainebleau | 1771 |
| Céphale et Procris | Versailles | 1773 |
| Richard Coeur de Lion | Paris | 1784 |
| Anacréon chez Polycrate | ,, | 1793 |
| La Rosière Républicaine | ,, | 1794 |

**Grisi, Giuditta** *Mezzo-soprano*
b. Milan, 1805: d. near Cremona, 1840
The first Romeo (*I Capuletti ed I Montecchi*). She made her debut in Vienna in 1823.

**Grisi, Giulia** *Soprano*
b. Milan, 1811: d. Berlin, 1869
The first Elvira (*I Puritani*), the first Norina (*Don Pasquale*), Adalgisa (*Norma*) and Juliette (*I Capuletti ed I Montecchi*). She made her debut as Emma in Rossini's *Zelmira* in 1828. In 1832 she appeared as Semiramide in Paris, and in 1834 as Ninetta (*La Gazza Ladra*) in London. She married the tenor Mario in 1844.

**Griswold, Putnam** *Bass*
b. Minneapolis, 1875: d. New York, 1914
He made his debut in Berlin in 1904 and at the Metropolitan, singing Hagen, in 1911.
Beckmesser, Daland, Gurnemanz, Hagan, Hans Sachs, Henry the Fowler, Hermann (*Tannhäuser*), Hunding, King Marke, Paolo Orsini, Pogner, Wotan.

**Grob-Prandl, Gertrude** *Soprano*
b.
Amelia, Brünnhilde, Isolde, Turandot.

**Gruenberg, Louis** *Composer*
b. near Brest-Litovsk, Poland, 1884:
A pupil of Busoni, he also wrote orchestral and vocal music.

| | |
|---|---|
| The Witch of Brocken | 1912 |
| The Bride of the Gods | 1913 |
| The Mute Wife | 1921 |
| Jack and the Beanstalk New York | 1931 |
| The Emperor Jones ,, | 1933 |
| Queen Helena | 1936 |
| Green Mansions CBS radio | 1937 |
| Volpone | 1937 |

**Gruhn, Nora** *Soprano*
b. London, 1908:
She made her debut at Covent Garden in 1931 and at Sadlers Wells, 1946.

**Guadagni, Gaetano** *(Male) Contralto*
b. Lodi, 1725: d. 1785 (?)
The first Orfeo, and a very famous singer. Gluck wrote the part for him, as did Handel in writing Samson. Guadagni also composed arias.

**Guarnieri, Carmago** *Conductor*
b. São Paulo, Brazil, 1907:
A conductor of opera and a composer of songs, piano music and music for the orchestra.

**Guarrera, Frank** *Baritone*
b.
Escamillo, Figaro (*Il Barbiere di Siviglia*), Guglielmo (*Così fan Tutte*), Lescaut (*Manon Lescaut*), Manfredo (*L'Amore dei Tre Re*), Marcello, Tonio.

**Gudehus, Heinrich** *Tenor*
b. Hanover, 1845: d. Dresden, 1909
The second person to sing Parsifal, there being three who alternated in the opening performances. He made his debut in Berlin in 1871.
Parsifal, Tamino, Tristan, Walther.

**Gueden, Hilde** *Soprano*
b. Vienna, 1917:
She made her debut in Munich as Zerlina (*Don Giovanni*), in 1939, and at the Metropolitan as Gilda in 1951.
Amor, Anne Trulove, Cherubino, Despina, Fiordiligi, Gilda, Ilia (*Idomeneo*), Lucretia (*The Rape of Lucretia*), Micaela, Mimi, Musetta, Norina (*Don Pasquale*),

Rosalinda (*Die Fledermaus*), Sophie (*Der Rosenkavalier*), Susanna (*Le Nozze di Figaro*), Zerlina (*Don Giovanni*).

**Guerre, Michel La**                   *Composer*
b. Paris, 1605: d. there 1679
Composer of what is probably the earliest French opera.

| Le Triomphe de l'Amour sur Bergers et Bergères | The Louvre | 1655 |
|---|---|---|

**Guerrini, Guido**                   *Composer*
b. Faenza, 1890:

| Zalebi |  | 1915 |
|---|---|---|
| Nemici | Bologna | 1921 |
| La Vigna | Rome | 1935 |
| Enea | ,, | 1953 |

**Gui, Vittorio**                   *Conductor*
b. Rome, 1885:
He conducted memorable performances at Florence and Edinburgh. He is also a composer.

| Fata Malerba | Turin | 1927 |
|---|---|---|

**Guiraud, Ernst**                   *Composer*
b. New Orleans, 1837: d. Paris, 1892
A friend of Bizet, he composed the recitatives for *Carmen*'s performances outside the Opéra-Comique. He also completed the orchestration of *Les Contes d'Hoffmann*. Saint-Saëns completed Guiraud's *Frédégonde*.

| En Prison | Paris | 1869 |
|---|---|---|
| Le Kobold | ,, | 1870 |
| Madame Turlepin | ,, | 1872 |
| Piccolino | ,, | 1876 |
| Galante Aventure | ,, | 1882 |
| Frédégonde | ,, | 1895 |

**Gulbranson, Ellen**                   *Soprano*
(*Née* Norgren)
b. Stockholm, 1863: d. Oslo, 1947
She made her debut at Stockholm in 1889. She was famous in the following roles:
Amneris, Brünnhilde, Kundry.

**Gundry, Inglis**                   *Composer*
b. London, 1905:
A pupil of Ralph Vaughan Williams.

| Naaman | 1938 |
|---|---|
| The Return of Odysseus | 1941 |
| The Partisans | 1946 |
| Aron | 1949 |

**Gura, Eugen**                   *Bass-baritone*
b. Bohemia, 1842: d. Bavaria, 1906
He made his debut in Munich in 1865. Amfortas, Barber (*Der Barbier von Bagdad*), Donnor, Gunther, Hans Sachs, King Marke, Lysiart (*Euryanthe*), Minister (*Fidelio*).

**Guridi, Jesús**                   *Composer*
b. Vittoria, Spain, 1886:

| Mirentxu |  |  |
|---|---|---|
| Amaya | Bilbao | 1920 |
| La Meiga | Madrid | 1928 |

**Gurlitt, Manfred**                   *Composer*
b. Berlin, 1890:
A pupil of Humperdinck, a composer of opera, orchestral and chamber music and a conductor.

| Die Heilige | Bremen | 1920 |
|---|---|---|
| Wozzeck (*see also* Berg, Alban) | ,, | 1926 |
| Soldaten |  | 1929 |
| Nana |  | 1933 |
| Seguidilla Bolero |  | 1937 |

**Gutheil-Schoder, Marie**   *Mezzo-soprano*
b. Weimar, 1874: d. there, 1935
She made her debut at Weimar in 1891. In 1926 she was appointed stage manager at Vienna.
Carmen, Elektra, Louise, Octavian, Salome.

**Gyrowetz, Adalbert**                   *Composer*
b. Bohemia, 1763: d. Vienna, 1850
He wrote about thirty operas.

| Agnes Sorel | 1806 |
|---|---|
| Der Augenarzt | 1811 |
| Helene | 1816 |

**Haas, Joseph** *Composer*
b. Maihingen, Germany, 1879:
Tobias Wunderlich    Kassel   1937
Die Hochzeit des Jobs   Dresden   1944

**Hába, Alois** *Composer*
b. Moravia, 1893:
Hába is one of the foremost proponents of microtones, and all his operas have been written in that system, as have his works for special pianos and chamber groups.
Die Mutter     Munich   1931
Nová Země             1935
Thy Kingdom Come       1940

**Hába, Karel** *Composer*
b. Moravia, 1898:
Brother of Alois Hába, but although interested in microtones, he has written his major works in conventional scales.
Janošík       Prague   1934

**Hackett, Charles** *Tenor*
b. Worcester, Mass., 1889: d. New York, 1942
He made his debut in Genoa, then appeared in 1919 as the Count in *Il Barbiere di Siviglia* at the Metropolitan.

**Hadley, Henry Kimball** *Composer*
b. Somerville, Mass., 1871: d. New York, 1937
A pupil of G. W. Chadwick. He was also a conductor at Seattle in 1909, in San Francisco from 1911 to 1915, with the New York Philharmonic until 1922, and with the Manhattan Symphony from 1929 to 1932.
Safie       Mainz   1909
The Atonement
   of Pan    San Francisco   1912
Azora       Chicago   1917
Nancy Brown
Bianca       New York   1918
Cleopatra's Night   Metropolitan   1918
A Night in Old Paris       1925

**Hageman, Richard** *Composer*
b. Leeuwarden, Netherlands, 1882:

A writer of songs and conductor at the Metropolitan from 1908 to 1926.
Caponsacchi    Freiburg   1932
The Crucible    Los Angeles   1943

**Hahn, Reynaldo** *Composer*
b. Caracas, 1875: d. Paris, 1947
A pupil of Massenet.
L'île du Rêve      Comique   1898
La Carmelite        ,,      1902
Fête Triomphante    Opéra   1919
Nausicaa    Monte Carlo   1919
La Colombe de Buddha   Cannes   1921
Ciboulette        Paris   1923
Le Marchand de Venise   Opéra   1935
Malvina         Paris   1935

**Halász, László** *Conductor*
b. Debrecen, Hungary, 1905:
Conductor at Budapest, Prague, Vienna, and beginning in 1939 at St. Louis. From 1943 to 1951 he conducted the New York City Opera Company.

**Halévy, Jacques François Fromental Elie** *Composer*
(*Originally* Lévy)
b. Paris, 1799: d. Nice, 1862
Gounod was his pupil. Bizet was his pupil also, and became his son-in-law.
La Juive       Opéra   1835
L'Éclair       Opéra   1835

**Halévy, Ludovic** *Librettist*
b. Paris, 1834: d. there, 1908
With Meilhac he wrote the libretti of *Carmen*, *La Belle Hélène*, *La Vie Parisienne*, and *La Grande Duchesse de Gérolstein*. With Crémieux he wrote *Les Contes d'Hoffmann*.

**Hamerik, Asger** *Composer*
b. Copenhagen, 1843: d. Fredericksborg, 1923
A pupil of Berlioz and himself a teacher. From 1872 to 1898 he was director of the Peabody Conservatory in Baltimore.
Tovelille       Paris   1865
Hjalmar und Ingeborg

| La Vendetta | Milan | 1870 |
| Der Reisende | | |

**Hamerik, Ebbe**                    *Composer*
b. Copenhagen, 1898:
Son of Asger Hamerik. A writer of
orchestral and piano music and songs.

| Stepan | Mainz | 1924 |
| Leonardo da Vinci | Antwerp | 1939 |
| Marie Grubbe | Copenhagen | 1940 |
| Rejsekammeraten | „ | 1946 |

**Hamlin, George**                    *Tenor*
b. Elgin, Ill., 1868: d. New York, 1923
He made his debut in Philadelphia in
1911.
Don José, Mario.

**Hammerstein, Oscar**            *Manager*
b. Stettin, Germany, 1846: d. New York,
1919
Hammerstein made his money in the
cigar-making business. He invented a
machine for the process in 1868. In 1906
he established the Manhattan Opera
House, which became a very serious rival
of the Metropolitan. In 1908 he did the
same thing in Philadelphia. In 1910 the
Metropolitan got rid of the threat by
buying him out.

**Handel, Georg Friedrich**        *Composer*
b. Halle, Germany, 1685: d. London,
1759
The great German composer of oratorios and operas, a contemporary of
J. S. Bach. He studied in Italy and settled
in England, becoming famous there in the
reign of George the First, who had been
his patron as the Elector of Hannover in
Germany. Handel wrote in all forms.
Oratorio was his favorite. Perhaps it
eventually served him as a substitute for
opera. His style was uproariously satirized in *The Beggar's Opera* by the un-
authorized use of a march from *Rinaldo*
as the March of the Thieves.

| Almira (*his first*) | Hamburg | 1705 |
| Agrippina | „ | 1709 |

| Rinaldo | London | 1711 |
| Il Pastor Fido (*first version*) | „ | 1712 |
| Scipione | „ | 1726 |
| Partenope | „ | 1730 |
| Il Pastor Fido (*second version*) | „ | 1734 |
| Serse | „ | 1738 |
| Deidamia (*his last*) | „ | 1741 |

**Hanson, Howard Harold**        *Composer*
b. Wahoo, Nebr., 1896:
An advocate of American music,
founder of the National Association of
American Composers and Conductors.
He was director of the Eastman School of
Music from 1924.

| Merry Mount | Metropolitan | 1934 |

(*Commissioned by the Metropolitan*)

**Harling, William Franke**        *Composer*
b. London, 1887: d. Sierra Madre, Calif.,
1958
A Light from St. Agnes

| | Chicago | 1925 |
| Deep River | New York | 1926 |

**Harman, Carter**                    *Composer*
b. Brooklyn, 1918:
Charms for the Savage

**Harrell, Mack**                    *Baritone*
b. Celeste, Tex., 1909: d. Dallas, Tex.,
1960
He made his debut at the Metropolitan
in 1939 but later became a teacher at
Southern Methodist University. He also
taught at the Juilliard School of Music.
Nick Shadow, Kothner, Samson

**Harrison, Lou**                    *Composer*
b. Portland, Oregon, 1917:
A pupil of Henry Cowell and Arnold
Schönberg.

| Rapunzel | New York | 1959 |

**Harsányi, Tibor**                    *Composer*
b. Magyarkanizsa, Hungary, 1898: d.
Paris, 1954

| Illusion | Paris (Radio) | 1949 |
| Les Invités | Gera, Ger. | 1930 |

**Harshaw, Margaret**  *Contralto, then Soprano*
b. Narbeth, Penna, 1912:
At first a contralto, she made her debut at the Metropolitan in 1942. In 1950 she came out as a soprano.
Amneris, Donna Anna, Azucena, Brünnhilde, Elisabeth, Isolde, Kundry, Ortrud.

**Hart, Frederick Patton**  *Composer*
b. Aberdeen, Wash. 1898:
| The Wheel of Fortune | 1934 |
| The Romance of the Robot | 1937 |

**Hartmann, Carl**  *Tenor*
b. Solingen, 1895:
He made his debut as Tannhäuser at Elberfeld in 1928. His first appearance at the Metropolitan was in 1937, as Siegfried. He has also sung Tristan.

**Hartmann, John Peder Emilius**  *Composer*
b. Copenhagen, 1805: d. there, 1900
| The Raven | Copenhagen | 1832 |
| The Corsairs | „ | 1835 |
| Little Christina | „ | 1846 |

**Hartmann, Karl Amadeus**  *Composer*
b. Munich, 1905:
Des Simplicius Simplicissimus Jugend  Cologne  1949

**Hastreiter, Helene**  *Contralto*
b. Louisville, Ky. 1858: d. Varese, Italy, 1922
Dalila, Euridice, Orfeo, Ortrud, Senta

**Hauer, Josef Matthias**  *Composer*
b. Vienna, 1883: d. there, 1959
A theorist of the dodecaphonic school.
| Salammbo | 1930 |
| Die Schwarze Spinne | 1931 |

**Haug, Hans**  *Composer*
b. Basel, 1900:
A pupil of Ernst Lévy.
Don Juan in der Freunde  Basel  1930

| Madrisa | Basel | 1934 |
| Tartuffe | „ | 1937 |
| Der Spiegel del Agrippina | | 1944 |
| Le Malade Imaginaire | Zürich | 1947 |

**Hauk, Minnie**  *Mezzo-soprano*
(*Née* Hauck)
b. New York, 1852: d. near Lucerne, Switzerland, 1929
Said to have had a repertory of one hundred roles, she made her debut as Amina in Brooklyn in 1866. It was she who produced the first *Cavalleria Rusticana* in Chicago.
Aida, Amina, Carmen, Inez (*L'Africaine*), Juliette, Lucia, Manon, Marguérite (*Faust*), Norma, Zerlina.

**Haydn, Franz Joseph**  *Composer*
b. Rohrau, Austria, 1732: d. Vienna, 1809
The "father of the symphony," Haydn was one of the most prolific of the great composers. He wrote about one hundred fifty symphonies, some of which his wife chose to burn up, leaving one hundred four. He also, however, turned out one singspiel, four Italian comedies, fourteen buffe, five musical plays for marionettes, pieces for mechanical clocks (one of which machines he is known to have built himself), and many, many more. Haydn had the benefit of a complete musical and theatrical establishment under his direction at the magnificient court of Esterház. This included even a marionette theater, of which he was especially fond. Some of his operas were:
| L'Infedeltà Delusa | Esterház | 1773 |
| Philémon et Baucis | „ | 1773 |
| La Vera Costanza | „ | 1776 |
| La Fedeltà Premiata | „ | 1780 |
| Ritter Roland | „ | 1782 |
| Armida | „ | 1783 |
| L'Isola Disabitata | „ | 1785 |
| Orfeo | „ | 1791 |

**Heger, Robert** *Composer*
b. Strasbourg, 1886:
He composed in many forms. He also conducted at Strasbourg, Nuremberg, Vienna, Berlin, and Munich.
Ein Fest auf Haderslev
                          Nuremberg   1919
Der Bettler Namelos    Munich       1932
Der Verlorene Sohn     Dresden       1936
Lady Hamilton          Nuremberg   1951

**Helm, Everett** *Composer*
b. Minneapolis, 1913:
A pupil of Malipiero and Vaughan Williams.
Adam and Eve          Wiesbaden   1951
The Siege of Tottenburg
                       Radio (Germany)   1956

**Hempel, Frieda** *Soprano*
b. Leipzig, 1885: d. Berlin, 1955
She made her debut in Berlin in 1905 and appeared at the Metropolitan for the first time in 1912 as the Queen in *Les Huguenots*.
Amelia, Antonia, Constanze, Countess Almaviva, Euryanthe, Eva, Fiordiligi, Gilda, Giulietta (*Les Contes d'Hoffmann*), Leila, Lucia, Martha, Mimi, Olympia, Pamina, Queen (*Les Huguenots*) Rosina, Violetta.

**Henneberg, Albert** *Composer*
b. Stockholm, 1901:
Inka
Bolla och Badin
I Madonnas Skugga

**Henriques, Fini Valdemar** *Composer*
b. Copenhagen, 1867: d. there, 1940
A violinist and composer of ballets, orchestral and chamber music.
Staerstikkeren   Copenhagen   1922

**Hensel, Heinrich** *Tenor*
b. Neustadt, 1874: d. Hamburg, 1935
He made his debut at the Metropolitan in 1911 singing Lohengrin.

**Henze, Hans Werner** *Composer*
b. Güttersloh, Germany, 1926:
Das Wundertheater
                       Heidelberg   1949
Boulevard Solitude     Hanover      1952
König Hirsch           Berlin       1956

**Herbert, Victor** *Composer*
b. Dublin, 1859: d. New York, 1924
Composer of many famous shows and operettas, such as *The Red Mill, Babes in Toyland*.
Natoma         Philadelphia   1911
Madeleine      Metropolitan   1913

**Hérold, Louis Joseph Ferdinand**
*Composer*
b. Paris, 1791: d. Les Ternes, 1833
Zampa          Comique   1831
Le Pré aux Clercs   „        1832

**Herrmann, Josef** *Baritone*
b.
Wozzeck

**Herrmann, Bernard** *Composer*
b. New York, 1911:
Wuthering Heights                1950

**Herrmann, Hugo** *Composer*
b. Ravensburg, Germany, 1896:
Gazellenhorn
Picknick
Vasantasena
Das Wunder
Paracelsus
Der Rekord
Der Überfall
Die Heinzelmännchen

**Hertog, Johannes Den** *Conductor*
b. Amsterdam, 1904:
Assistant conductor at the Concertgebouw, 1938 to 1941. Conductor of the Flemish Opera since 1948.

**Hertz, Alfred** *Conductor*
b. Frankfort, 1872: d. San Francisco, 1942
He conducted the first American performance of *Parsifal*. From 1915 to

1930 he was in San Francisco. It was he who organized the summer concerts at the Hollywood Bowl.

**Hertzog, Emilie**                    *Soprano*
b. Diessenhofen, Germany, 1859: d. Aarburg, Switzerland, 1923:
She made her debut in Munich in 1880.

**Hess, Ludwig**                    *Composer*
b. Marburg, Germany, 1877: d. Berlin, 1944

| | | |
|---|---|---|
| Abu und Nu | Danzig | 1919 |
| Vor Edens Pforte | | |
| Kranion | Erfurt, | 1933 |

**Hewitt, James**                    *Composer*
b. Dartmoor, England, 1770: d. Boston, 1827

| | | |
|---|---|---|
| Tammany | New York | 1794 |
| The Patriot | ,, | 1794 |
| Columbus | ,, | 1799 |

**Hidalgo, Huan**                    *Composer*
b. circa 1600, d. Madrid, 1685
The earliest known Spanish opera composer.

| | | |
|---|---|---|
| Celos aún del Aire Matan | | |
| | Madrid | 1660 |
| La Púrpura de la Rosa | ,, | 1660 |

**Hillis, Margaret**                    *Conductor*
b. Kokomo, Ind., 1921:
Although she specializes in choral conducting, she has made a point of helping to bring out the more ancient operas.

**Hinckley, Allen Carter**                    *Bass*
b. Gloucester, Mass., 1877: d. Yonkers, N.Y., 1954
He made his debut as Henry the Fowler at Hamburg, 1903.

**Hindemith, Paul**                    *Composer*
b. Hanau, 1895:
Certainly one of the great modernists and a very prolific composer of music in every conceivable form.

| | | |
|---|---|---|
| Mörder, Hoffnung der Frauen | Stuttgart | 1921 |
| Das Nusch-Nuschi | ,, | 1921 |
| Sancta Susanna | Frankfurt | 1922 |
| Cardillac | Dresden, | 1926 |
| Hin und Zurück | Baden Baden | 1927 |
| Neues vom Tage | Berlin | 1929 |
| Wir Bauen eine Stadt | ,, | 1930 |
| Mathis der Maler | Zürich | 1938 |
| Die Harmonie der Welt | | |
| | Munich | 1957 |

**Hines, Jerome**                    *Bass*
b.
His Metropolitan debut took place in 1947.
Arkel, Banquo, Don Basilio (*Il Barbiere di Siviglia*), Grand Inquisitor, Padre Guardiano, Gurnemanz, Hermann, Nick Shadow, Philip the Second, Pimen, Sparafucile.

**Hinshaw, William**                    *Baritone*
b. Union, Iowa, 1867: d. Washington, D.C., 1947
Famous as a teacher. He made his debut at St. Louis in 1899 singing Méphistophélès (*Faust*). In 1910 he appeared at the Metropolitan. He founded a school of opera in Chicago which merged with the Chicago Conservatory with Hinshaw as its president. From 1920 to 1926 he managed his own opera company.

**Hislop, Joseph**                    *Tenor*
b. Edinburg, 1887:
Alfredo, Duke (*Rigoletto*), Faust (*Faust*), Rodolfo, Romeo.

**Höffding, Finn**                    *Composer*
b. Copenhagen, 1899:

| | | |
|---|---|---|
| Kejserens nye Klaeder (*The Emperor's New Clothes*) | Copenhagen | 1928 |
| Kilderejsen | ,, | 1942 |

**Höffer, Paul**                    *Composer*
b. Barmen, Germany, 1895: d. Berlin, 1949

| | |
|---|---|
| Borgia | 1931 |
| Der Falsche Waldemar | 1934 |

**Hofman, Ludwig**         *Baritone*
b. Frankfurt, 1895:
He made his debut at the Metropolitan in 1932, singing Hagen.

**Hofmannsthal, Hugo von**     *Librettist*
b. 1874: d. 1929
One of the great librettists. *Elektra, Ariadne auf Naxos, Die Aegyptische Helene, Arabella, Der Rosenkavalier*, all were his products.

**Holbrooke, Joseph Charles**   *Composer*
b. London, 1878: d. London, 1958

| | | |
|---|---|---|
| Pierrot and Pierrette | London | 1909 |
| The Cauldron of Anwyn, | | |
| *consisting of* | | |
| The Children of Don | | |
| | London | 1912 |
| Dylan | ,, | 1913 |
| Bronwen | Huddersfield | 1929 |
| The Wizard | | 1915 |
| The Stranger | | 1924 |
| The Enchanter | Chicago | 1915 |

**Hollingsworth, Stanley**     *Composer*
b. Berkeley, Calif., 1924:
A pupil of Milhaud.

| | | |
|---|---|---|
| The Mother | | 1954 |
| La Grande Bretèche | NBC | 1957 |

**Holoubek, Ladislav**       *Composer*
b. Prague, 1913:

| | | |
|---|---|---|
| Stella | Bratislava | 1939 |
| Svitanie | ,, | 1941 |
| Túžba (*Desire*) | ,, | 1944 |

**Holst, Gustav Theodore**     *Composer*
(*Originally* von Holst)
b. Cheltenham, England, 1874: d. London, 1934

| | | |
|---|---|---|
| Savitri | London | 1916 |
| The Perfect Fool | | |
| | Covent Garden | 1923 |
| At the Boar's Head | | |
| | Manchester | 1925 |
| The Wandering Scholar | | 1929 |

**Homer, Louise Beatty**   *Mezzo-soprano*
b. Pittsburg, 1871: d. Winter Park, Fla., 1947

She made her debut at Vichy in 1898 singing Leonora (*La Favorita*). She first appeared with the Metropolitan on tour in San Francisco in 1900 as Amneris.

Amneris, Azucena, Brangäne, Dalila, Dame Quickly, Erda, Fidés, Fricka, Laura, Leonora (*La Favorita*), Lola, Magdalene (*Die Meistersinger*), Orfeo, Ortrud, Suzuki, Waltraute, The Witch (*Hänsel und Gretel*).

**Honegger, Arthur**       *Composer*
b. Le Havre, 1892: d. Paris, 1955
One of "*Les Six*" known for his realistic orchestral movement, *Pacific 231*.

| | | |
|---|---|---|
| Judith | Monte Carlo | 1926 |
| Antigone | Brussels | 1927 |
| Les Aventures du Roi | | |
| Pausole | Paris | 1930 |
| Amphion | Paris | 1931 |
| L'Aiglon (*with Ibert*) | | |
| | Monte Carlo | 1937 |
| Charles le Téméraire | Mezières | 1944 |

**Hoose, Ellison van**       *Tenor*
b. Murfreesboro, Tenn., 1868: d. Houston, Texas, 1936
A pupil of Jean de Reszke. He made his debut as Tannhäuser in Philadelphia in 1897.

**Hopf, Hans**           *Tenor*
b.
Lohengrin, Walther.

**Hotter, Hans**         *Baritone*
b. Offenbach, Germany, 1909:
The first Commandant (*Friedenstag*), the first Jupiter (*Liebe der Danae*). He made his debut in Prague in 1922.

Altair, Commandant, Dutchman, Hans Sachs, Jupiter, King Henry (*Lohengrin*), Hunding, Jokanaan, Kurnewal, King Marke, Pogner, La Roche (*Capriccio*), Wotan.

**Howard, Kathleen**       *Contralto*
b. Clifton, Ontario, 1884: d. Hollywood, 1936

A pupil of Jean de Reszke. For the period from 1928 to 1933 she was fashion editor of *Harper's Bazaar*. She made her debut at Metz in 1907 and in New York in 1914. She joined the Metropolitan in 1916 and stayed twelve years. She is said to have known eighty roles.

**Hubay, Jenö (Eugen)**      *Composer*
b. Budapest, 1858: d. there, 1937
Luthier de Crémone
           Budapest   1894

**Huber, Hans**      *Composer*
b. Eppenberg, Switzerland, 1852: d. Locarno, 1921
Weltfrühling      Basel   1894
Die Schöne Bellinda      Bern   1916

**Huehn, Julius**      *Baritone*
b. Revere, Mass., 1910:
He made his debut at the Metropolitan in 1935 singing the Herald in *Lohengrin*.

**Hugo, John Alden**      *Composer*
b. Bridgeport, Conn., 1873: d. there, 1945
The Temple Dancer
           Metropolitan   1919
The Hero of Byzanz

**Humperdinck, Engelbert**    *Composer*
b. near Bonn, 1854: d. Neustrelitz, 1921
Wagner's assistant and close friend. Humperdinck's sister wrote the libretto of *Hänsel und Gretel*.
Hänsel und Gretel    Weimar  1893
Dornröschen    Frankfurt  1902
Die Heirath wider willen
           Berlin   1905
Königskinder    Metropolitan   1910
Die Marketenderin    Cologne   1914
Gaudeamus    Darmstadt   1919

**Hurley, Laurel**      *Soprano*
b. Allentown, Penn., 1927:
She made her debut in New York in 1952 as Zerlina at the City Center of Music and Drama. In 1955 she sang for the first time at the Metropolitan.

Clorinda (*La Cenerentola*), Gretel, Laetitia (*The Old Maid and the Thief*), Micaela, Princess Ninetta (*The Love for Three Oranges*), Oscar, Rosalinda (*Die Fledermaus*), Susanna (*Le Nozze di Figaro*), Zerlina.

**Hyde, Walter**      *Tenor*
b. Birmingham, 1875: d. London, 1957
He studied with Gustave Garcia.
Parsifal, Pinkerton, Siegmund, Walther.

**Ibert, Jacques**      *Composer*
b. Paris, 1890:
Ibert was a pupil of Fauré. He became director of the French Academy at Rome in 1937, and director of the Paris Opéra and of the Opéra-Comique in 1955. He has written much for the ballet, for voice, orchestra and small groups.
Angélique    Paris   1927
Persée et Andromède    Paris   1929
Le Roi d'Yvetot    ,,   1930
Gonzague    Monte Carlo   1935
L'Aiglon
  (*with Honegger*)    ,,   1937
Les Petites Cardinal
  (*with Honegger*)    Paris   1938
Barbe-Bleue    Lausanne (radio)   1943

**Ilitsch, Daniza**      *Soprano*
b. Belgrade, 1919:
She made her debut as Nedda at Berlin in 1936. Her first appearance at the Metropolitan was in 1947, as Desdemona. In 1944 she was imprisoned by the Nazi regime in Vienna for four months.

**Illica, Luigi**      *Librettist*
b. near Piacenza, 1857: d. there, 1919
This most prolific librettist was responsible for *La Wally, Andrea Chénier, Iris*, and (with Giacosa) *La Bohème, Tosca, Madama Butterfly*. With Praga and Oliva he wrote *Manon Lescaut*.

**Incledon, Charles Benjamin**    *Tenor*
b. Cornwall, England, 1763: d. London, 1826

235

One of the famous portrayers of Captain MacHeath, and a very famous tenor in many roles in England.

**Indy, d', Paul Marie Theodore Vincent** *Composer*
b. Paris, 1851: d. there, 1931
One of the great composers of romantic symphonic works of nineteenth-century France, D'Indy made a very significant contribution to opera not only with his own works but with his practical re-orchestrations and arrangements of *La Favola d'Orfeo* and *Il Ritorno d'Ulisse in Patria* by Monteverdi, making these stage masterpieces again available for performance in modern times. He was a pupil of César Franck and carried on the traditions of French style by teaching many modern French composers himself.

| | | |
|---|---|---|
| Fervaal | Brussels | 1897 |
| L'Étranger | „ | 1903 |
| La Legende de St. | | |
| Christophe | Opéra | 1920 |
| Le Rêve de Cynias | Paris | 1927 |

**Inghelbrecht, Désiré Émile** *Composer*
b. Paris, 1880:
This composer was also a conductor and director of the Opéra-Comique from 1924 to 1933. He conducted at the Opéra after 1945.

| | |
|---|---|
| La Nuit Vénitienne | 1908 |

**Inghilleri, Giovanni** *Baritone*
b.
Barnaba, Father (*Le Pauvre Matelot*), Gerard, Iago, Manfredo (*L'Amore dei Tre Re*).

**Ippolitov-Ivanov, Michael Mikhailo-vitch** *Composer*
b. Gatchina, Russia, 1859: d. Moscow, 1935
It was he who completed Mussorgsky's unfinished opera *Zhenitba* (The Marriage).

| | | |
|---|---|---|
| Ruth | Tiflis | 1887 |
| Asra | „ | 1890 |
| Asva | Moscow | 1900 |

| | | |
|---|---|---|
| Treason | | 1909 |
| The Spy | | 1912 |
| Ole from Nordland | Moscow | 1916 |
| The Last Barricade | | 1934 |

**Ivogün, Maria** *Soprano*
(*Really* Inge von Gunther)
b. Budapest, 1891:
The first Ighino (*Palestrina*), and the first Laura (*Der Ring des Polycrates*). She made her debut in Munich, 1913.
Gilda, Ighino, Laura, Zerbinetta.

**Jachino, Carlo** *Composer*
b. San Remo, 1889:

| | | |
|---|---|---|
| Giocondo e il suo Re | Milan | 1924 |

**Jackson, William** *Composer*
b. Exeter, England, 1730: d. there, 1803
Jackson's claim to historic fame rests partly on the fact that his opera *The Lord of the Manor* had a libretto by General Burgoyne, who had previously led the British redcoats into the unfortunate (for him) Battle of Bennington in the American Revolution.

| | | |
|---|---|---|
| The Lord of the Manor | | |
| | London | 1780 |
| The Metamorphosis | „ | 1783 |

**Jacobi, Frederick** *Composer*
b. San Francisco, 1891: d. New York, 1952

| | |
|---|---|
| The Prodigal Son | 1944 |

**Jadlowker, Herrmann** *Tenor*
b. Riga, Lithuania, 1878: d. Tel Aviv, 1953
He made his debut at Cologne in 1889, and sang Faust in his first appearance at the Metropolitan in 1910.

**Jagel, Frederick** *Tenor*
b. Brooklyn, N.Y., 1897:
He made his debut as Rodolfo in 1924 at Leghorn, Italy. In 1927 he sang for the first time at the Metropolitan, as Radames.
Avito, Gennaro, Gérald (*Lakmé*), Luigi (*Il Tabarro*), Rodolfo, Radames.

**Janáček, Leoš** *Composer*
b. Moravia, 1854: d. there, 1928
One of the great Czech composers,
mostly known for his opera, *Její
Pastorkyňa* (performed often under the
title *Jenufa*).

| | | |
|---|---|---|
| Počátek Románu | Brno | 1894 |
| Její Pastorkyňa | „ | 1904 |
| Káta Kabanová (*in* | | |
| German, Katia Kabanowa) | „ | 1921 |
| Šarka (*written* 1887) | „ | 1925 |
| Věc Makropulos | „ | 1926 |
| Příhody Lišky Bystroušky | „ | 1928 |
| Z mrtvého Domu (*From* | | |
| a House of the Dead) | „ | 1930 |
| Osud (*written* 1904) | | |
| | Brno (radio) | 1934 |

**Janssen, Herbert** *Baritone*
b. Cologne, 1895:
Famous as Amfortas, he made his
debut with the Metropolitan as Wotan
while on tour in Philadelphia, 1934.
Amfortas, Dutchman, Orest (*Elektra*),
Wotan.

**Jaques-Dalcroze, Émile** *Pedagogue*
b. Vienna, 1865: d. Geneva, 1950
The founder of the Dalcroze Schools of
Eurythmics, of particular value to opera
singers and composers. He composed in
all forms, and has written many French
songs that are sometimes mistaken for
folk songs.

| | | |
|---|---|---|
| Le Violon Maudit | Geneva | 1893 |
| Sancho Panza | „ | 1897 |
| Fête de la Jeunesse et | | |
| de la Joie | „ | 1932 |

**Jarno, Georg** *Composer*
b. Budapest, 1868: d. Breslau, 1920

| | | |
|---|---|---|
| Die Schwarze Kaschka | Breslau | 1895 |
| Der Richter von Zalamea | „ | 1899 |
| Der Goldfisch | „ | 1907 |
| Die Förster-Christel | Vienna | 1907 |
| Das Musikantenmädel | „ | 1910 |
| Die Marine-Gustel | „ | 1912 |
| Das Farmermädchen | Berlin | 1913 |

**Jenkins, David** *Composer*
b. Trecastle, Wales, 1848: d. Aberstwyth,
1915
The Enchanted Island

**Jensen, Ludwig Irgens** *Composer*
b. Oslo, 1894:
Heimferd　　　　　　Oslo　1947

**Jepson, Helen** *Soprano*
b. Titusville, Pa., 1905:
A pupil of Mary Garden's. She made
her debut at the Metropolitan in 1935.
Fiora (*L'Amore dei Tre Re*), Mélisande,
Thaïs.

**Jeremiáš, Jaroslav** *Composer*
b. Pisek, Czechoslovakia, 1889: d. Budě-
jovice, 1919
Starý Král (*The
Old King*)　　　　Prague　1919

**Jeremiáš, Otakar** *Composer*
b. Pisek, Czechoslovakia, 1892:
Brother of Jaroslav Jeremiáš. Director
of the Prague Opera since 1945, and a
composer of orchestral and chamber
music for concert and for film.
The Brothers Karamazov
　　　　　　　　Prague　1928
Till Eulenspiegel　　„　1949

**Jeritza, Maria** *Soprano*
(*Really* Jedlitzka)
b. Brünn, Austria, 1887:
The first Ariadne (*Ariadne auf Naxos*),
and the first Nurse in *Die Frau ohne
Schatten*. She made her debut as Elsa in
1910 at Olmütz, and appeared for the
first time at the Metropolitan in 1921
singing Mariette in *Die Tote Stadt*.
Ariadne, Carmen, Elisabeth, Elsa, Fedora, Helena (*Aegyptische Helene*), Jenufa,
Maliella (*I Gioielli della Madonna*), Marguérite, Mariette (*Die Tote Stadt*), Minnie,
Salome, Santuzza, Sieglinde, Thaïs, Tosca,
Turandot, Violetta.

**Jirák, Karel Boleslav** *Composer*
b. Prague, 1891:

Apollonius of Tyana
Woman and the God      Brno   1928

**Jochum, Eugen**                    *Conductor*
b. Babenhausen, Germany, 1902:
Beginning at Munich, in 1927, he has
conducted opera at Mannheim, Duisberg,
Berlin (*radio*), Hamburg and Munich
(*radio*).

**Jochum, Georg Ludwig**        *Conductor*
b. Babenhausen, Germany, 1909:
Like his older brother, he conducted
opera at Frankfurt, beginning in 1937, and
in Linz.

**Johnson, Edward**                     *Tenor*
b. Guelph, Ontario, 1878: d. there, 1959
Called "di Giovanni" in Italy, he made
his debut at the Metropolitan in 1922.
But his reputation rests chiefly on his
general management of that organization
from 1935 to 1950.
Luigi (*Il Tabarro*), Peter Ibbetson,
Rinuccio (*Gianni Schicchi*).

**Joio, Norman Dello**               *Composer*
b. New York, 1913:
A very successful composer in New
York.
The Triumph of St. Joan          1950
The Ruby                                  1955
The Trial at Rouen                    1956

**Jolivet, André**                    *Composer*
b. Paris, 1905:
Dolores                Paris (radio)   1947

**Joncières, Victorin de**           *Composer*
(*Originally* Félix Ludger Rossignol)
b. Paris, 1839: d. there, 1903
He was a painter at first.
Sardanapale               Paris   1867
Le Dernier Jour de
  Pompeii                      „      1869
Dimitri                          „      1876
La Reine Berthe            „      1878
Le Chevalier Jean          „      1885
Lancelot du Lac             „      1900

**Jones, Rowland**                       *Tenor*
b.
Boris (*Kata Kabanova*), Lensky (*Eugene
Onegin*), Werther.

**Jones, Sidney**                      *Composer*
b. London, 1861: d. there, 1946
He wrote thirteen operas in all.
Geisha                     London   1896

**Josten, Werner**                   *Conductor*
b. Elberfeld, Germany, 1885:
He composed orchestral and chamber
music. In the 1920's he went to the United
States and taught at Smith College for
many years. It was there that he conducted the first American stage performance of *La Favola d'Orfeo*, in 1929.

**Joubert, John**                      *Composer*
b. Capetown, S. Africa, 1927:
Antigone                      BBC   1954

**Journet, Marcel**                       *Bass*
b. Grasse, France, 1867: d. Vittel, 1933
The first Simon Mago. He made his
debut at Montpellier in 1893, and sang
for the first time at the Metropolitan in
1908.
Escamillo, Langrave (*Tannhäuser*), Méphistophélès (*Faust*), Simon Mago (*Nerone*).

**Juch, Emma**                          *Soprano*
b. Vienna, 1863: d. New York, 1939
She made her debut in London in 1883.
In 1888 she toured Mexico and the United
States with her own company, which
managed to last for three years.
Aida, Elisabeth, Elsa, Isabella (*Robert le
Diable*), Marguérite (*Faust*), Martha, Mig-
non, Queen (*Les Huguenots*), Queen of the
Night, Senta, Sieglinde, Valentine (*Les
Huguenots*), Violetta.

**Jurinac, Sena**                       *Soprano*
b. Yugoslavia, 1921:
Antonia (*Les Contes d'Hoffmann*), Ariadne (*Ariadne auf Naxos*), Cherubino, Composer (*Ariadne auf Naxos*), Countess
Almaviva (*Le Nozze di Figaro*), Dorabella,

Donna Elvira, Eva, Fiordiligi, Freia, Giulietta (*Les Contes d'Hoffmann*), Ighino, Ilia (*Idomeneo*), Lisa (*Pique-Dame*), Manon, Marenka, Marguérite (*Faust*), Mimi, Octavian, Pamina.

**Kabalevsky, Dmitri Borisovitch**
*Composer*
b. St. Petersburg, 1904:

| | | |
|---|---|---|
| Colas Breugnon | Leningrad | 1938 |
| Before Moscow | „ | 1942 |
| The Family of Taras | Moscow | 1947 |
| Nikita Vershinin | „ | 1955 |

**Kadosa, Paul** *Composer*
b. Leva, Hungary, 1903:
A pupil of Kodály.

| | |
|---|---|
| Adventure at Hoszt | 1950 |

**Kalisch, Paul** *Tenor*
b. Berlin, 1855: d. St. Lorenz, Austria, 1946
A famous Tristan, he made his debut in *Der Fliegende Holländer* at the Metropolitan in 1889. He had married Lilli Lehmann the year before.

**Kalnins, Alfred** *Composer*
b. Zehsis, Latvia, 1879: d. Riga, 1951
A composer in all forms, he is especially noted for his works for chorus.

| | | |
|---|---|---|
| Banuta | Riga | 1920 |
| Salinieki (*The Islanders*) | „ | 1925 |
| Dzimtenes Atmoda | | |
| (*The Nations Awakening*) | „ | 1933 |

**Kalnins, Janis** *Composer*
b. Riga, 1904:
Son of Alfred Kalnins. He settled in Canada in 1944, and was engaged as conductor of the conservatory orchestra at Fredericton, New Brunswick, in 1952.

| | | |
|---|---|---|
| Hamlet | Riga | 1936 |

**Kalomiris, Manolis** *Composer*
b. Smyrna, 1883:
Founder of the National Conservatory of Athens.

| | | |
|---|---|---|
| Protomastoras | Athens | 1916 |
| L'Anneau de la Mère | „ | 1917 |

**Kamienski, Lucian** *Composer*
b. Gniezno, Poland, 1885:

| | | |
|---|---|---|
| Tabu | Königsberg | 1917 |
| Dami i Huzary | Poznan | 1938 |

**Kaminski, Heinrich** *Composer*
b. Baden, 1886: d. Bavaria, 1946

| | | |
|---|---|---|
| Jürg Jenatsch | Dresden | 1929 |

**Kapp, Ergen** *Composer*
b. Astrakhan, 1908:
Twice a winner of the Stalin Prize.

| | | |
|---|---|---|
| Flames of Vengeance | Tallinn | 1945 |
| Freedom's Singer | „ | 1950 |

**Kappel, Gertrude** *Soprano*
b. Halle, 1884:
A famous Isolde, she made her debut at Hannover in 1903 and at San Francisco in 1933.
Brünnhilde, Isolde, Elektra.

**Karajan, Herbert von** *Conductor*
b. Salzburg, 1908:
Conductor of the opera at Berlin from 1938 to 1945, and in Vienna since 1956.

**Karel, Rudolf** *Composer*
b. Pilsen, Czechoslovakia, 1880: d. Teresin, 1945
His death occurred in a concentration camp at the end of the Second World War.

| | | |
|---|---|---|
| Ilseino Srdce | | |
| (*Ilsea's Heart*) | Prague | 1924 |
| Smrt Kmotřička | | |
| (*Godmother Death*) | „ | 1933 |

**Karyotakis, Theodore** *Composer*
b. Argos, Greece, 1903:

| | |
|---|---|
| Moon's Flower | 1953 |

**Kassern, Tadeusz Zygfried** *Composer*
b. Lvov, Poland, 1904: d. New York, 1957

| | |
|---|---|
| The Anointed | 1951 |
| Sun Up | 1952 |

**Kastalsky, Alexander** *Composer*
b. Moscow, 1856: d. there, 1926

A pupil of Tchaikovsky, and a composer of orchestral, choral and piano music.

Clara Milich      Moscow   1916

**Kastle, Leonard**      *Composer*
b. New York, 1929:
The Swing      NBC-TV   1956
Deseret      NBC-TV   1961

**Kauffman, Leo Justinus**    *Composer*
b. Alsace, 1901: d. Strasbourg, 1944:
Kauffman died during an air raid near the end of the Second World War.
Die Geschichte vom
   Schönen Annerl    Strasbourg   1942

**Kaufmann, Walter**      *Composer*
b. Karlsbad, 1907:
Der Himmel Bringt es
   an den Tag      1934
Anasuya    Bombay Radio   1938
Parfait for Irène      1952
Bashmashkin      1952

**Kaun, Hugo**      *Composer*
b. Berlin, 1863: d. there, 1932
Sappho      Leipzig   1917
Der Fremde      Dresden   1920
Menandra      Kiel   1925

**Keilberth, Joseph**      *Conductor*
b. Karlsruhe, 1908:
Conductor of the opera at his birthplace from 1935 to 1940, at Dresden from 1945 to 1951, and subsequently at Bayreuth.

**Keldorfer, Robert**      *Composer*
b. Vienna, 1901:
Verena      Klagenfurt   1951

**Kellogg, Clara Louise**      *Soprano*
b. Sumpterville, S.C., 1842: d. New Hartford, Conn., 1916
A pupil of E. Muzio, she made her debut at New York in 1861, and later as Marguérite at London in 1867. From 1873 to 1875 she managed her own "English Opera Company."

Aida, Gilda, Linda, Lucia, Marguérite (*Faust*), Martha, Philine, Violetta, Zerlina (*Don Giovanni*).

**Kelly, Michael**      *Tenor*
b. Dublin, 1762: d. Margate, 1826
Michael Kelly is famous for his reminiscences of Mozart and his times. He sang the first Don Basilio and the first Don Curzio in *Le Nozze di Figaro*. Beside all that, he was a composer himself, and wrote music to accompany the performances of sixty-two plays.

**Kelley, Norman**      *Tenor*
b.
The first to sing Doctor Zuckertanz in Menotti's *Maria Golovin*.
Eugenio (*Der Corregidor*), Gonsalve (*L'Heure Espagnole*), Nika Magadoff, Doctor Zuckertanz.

**Kemp, Barbara**      *Soprano*
b. Kochenn, Germany, 1886: d. Berlin, 1959
She was famous as Kundry. In 1923 she married Max Schillings, the composer of *Mona Lisa*.
Arline (*The Bohemian Girl*), Empress (*Die Frau ohne Schatten*), Kundry, Mona (*Mona Lisa*, by Schillings).

**Kempe, Rudolf**      *Conductor*
b. near Dresden, 1910:
Conductor of the Munich Opera from 1952 to 1954.

**Kenessy, Jenö**      *Composer*
b. Budapest, 1906:
Gold and the Woman
     Budapest   1943

**Kerll, Johann Caspar**      *Composer*
b. Saxony, 1627: d. Munich, 1693
Famous as composer and as organist.
Oronte      1657
Erinto      1661

**Kienzl, Wilhelm**      *Composer*
b. Austria, 1857: d. Vienna, 1941
A pupil of Franz Liszt.

Heilmar, der Narr    Munich   1892
Der Evangelimann
(*The Apostle*)      Berlin   1895
Don Quixote       „    1898
Der Kuhreigen     Vienna   1911
Das Testament      „    1916
Hassan, der Schwärmer
               Chemnitz   1925
Sanctissimum      Vienna   1925

**Kiepura, Jan**          *Tenor*
b. Sosnowiec, Poland, 1902:
Kiepura made his debut in Warsaw in 1923, and sang Rodolfo (*La Boheme*) in his first appearance at the Metropolitan in 1938.

**Kind, Johann Friedrich**    *Librettist*
b. Leipzig, 1768: d. Dresden, 1843
Among his many libretti, *Der Freischütz* is the most famous.

**Kindermann, August**     *Baritone*
b. Berlin, 1817: d. Munich, 1891
The first Wotan
Figaro, Titurel, Wotan.

**Kipnis, Alexander**        *Bass*
b. Zhitomir, Russia, 1891:
One of the most famous bassos. He made his debut at Wiesbaden in 1917. In 1923 he sang Pogner for his first appearance in the United States. He came out at the Metropolitan in 1940 as Gurnemanz.
Boris Godunov, Gurnemanz, King Marke, Baron Ochs, Pogner, Rocco (*Fidelio*), Sarastro.

**Kirkby-Lunn, Louise**   *Mezzo-soprano*
b. Manchester, England, 1873: d. London, 1930
She made her Metropolitan debut in 1902.
Amneris, Brangäne, Dalila, Kundry, Laura, Ortrud.

**Kirsten, Dorothy**      *Soprano*
b. Montclair, N.J., 1917:
Her debut was in Chicago in 1940. In 1942 she appeared for the first time in New York City, singing Mimi. Her Metropolitan debut, in 1945, was in the same role.
Blanche (*Dialogues des Carmélites*), Ciocio San, Fiora (*L'Amore dei Tre Re*), Louise, Manon Lescaut, Mimi, Tosca, Violetta.

**Klafsky, Katharina**      *Soprano*
b. Hungary, 1855: d. Hamburg, 1896
She made her debut in Salzburg in 1875. In 1895 she married Otto Lohse.
Brünnhilde, Sieglinde.

**Klebe, Giselher**       *Composer*
b. Mannheim, 1925:
Die Räuber     Düsseldorf   1957

**Kleiber, Erich**        *Conductor*
b. Vienna, 1890: d. Zürich, 1956
Beginning at Darmstadt in 1912, he conducted at Elberfeld, Mannheim and elsewhere in Germany before becoming Musical Director of the Berlin Opera from 1923 to 1935. From 1936 to 1949 he directed the opera at Buenos Aires, and afterwards conducted the State Opera in Vienna.

**Klein, Bruno Oscar**     *Composer*
b. Osnabrück, 1858: d. New York, 1911
Kenilworth     Hamburg   1895

**Klemperer, Otto**      *Conductor*
b. Breslau, 1885:
Conductor of the Berlin Opera from 1927 to 1933, and in Budapest from 1947 to 1950.

**Klenau, Paul August von**   *Composer*
b. Copenhagen, 1883: d. there, 1946
Kjarten und Gudrun   Mannheim   1918
Die Lästerschule   Frankfurt   1926
Michael Kohlhaas   Stuttgart   1933
Rembrandt von Rijn   Berlin   1937
Elisabeth von England   Kassel   1939

**Klose, Friedrich**       *Composer*
b. Karlsruhe, 1862: d. Lugano, 1942
Ilsebill      Munich   1905

**Klose, Margarete** *Mezzo-soprano*
b.
Brangäne, Fricka, Klytemnestra (*Elektra*), Ulrica (*Un Ballo in Maschera*).

**Knappertsbusch, Hans** *Conductor*
b. Elberfeld, Germany, 1888:
Conductor of the Munich Opera from 1922 to 1938, and since then at Vienna.

**Knoch, Ernst** *Conductor*
b. Karlsruhe, 1875: d. New York, 1959
Conductor at Strasbourg in 1901, then Bayreuth, Essen and Cologne, etc.

**Knote, Heinrich** *Tenor*
b. Munich, 1870: d. Garmisch, 1953
He made his debut at Munich in 1892 and at the Metropolitan ten years later.

**Kobart, Ruth** *Contralto*
b.
The first Agata in Menotti's *Maria Golovin*, and the first to sing the Housekeeper (*Die Schweigsame Frau*) in New York.

**Koch, Erland von** *Composer*
b. Stockholm, 1910:
Lasse Lucidor 1943

**Kodály, Zoltán** *Composer*
b. Kecskemét, Hungary, 1882:
An associate of Bartók in a far-reaching study of Hungarian folk music.
Háry János Budapest 1926
Czinka Panna „ 1948

**Kondracki, Michal** *Composer*
b. Ukraine, 1902:
Popieliny Warsaw 1934

**Konetzni, Anni** *Soprano*
b.
Elektra, Duchess Elena (*I Vespri Siciliani*) Marschallin, Reiza (*Oberon*), Selika.

**Konetzni, Hilde** *Soprano*
b.
Chrysothemis (*Elektra*), Empress (*Die Frau ohne Schatten*), Lisa, Marenka, Milada (*Dalibor*).

**Konjović, Petar** *Composer*
b. Poland, 1882:
Vilin Vee (*The Wedding of Milos*) Zagreb 1917
Koštana „ 1931
Knez od Zete (*The Duke of Zeta*) Belgrade 1939
Sel Jaci (*The Peasants*) „ 1952

**Korngold, Erich Wolfgang** *Composer*
b. Brno, Czechoslovakia, 1897: d. Hollywood, 1957
Der Ring des Polycrates Munich 1916
Violanta „ 1916
Die Tote Stadt Hamburg 1920
Die Wunder der Heliane „ 1927
Kathrin Stockholm 1937
Die Stumme Serenade Dortmund 1954

**Kósa, Gyorgy** *Composer*
b. Budapest, 1897:
A pupil of Bartók.
The King's Robe 1927
The Two Knights Budapest 1936
Cenodoxus 1942
Anselmus 1945
The Bees 1946

**Koussevitzky, Sergey** *Conductor*
b. Russia, 1874: d. Boston, 1951
Celebrated conductor and virtuoso of the double bass. He left Russia in 1920 after a successful career in both fields, conducted in Paris for a while, then became the conductor of the Boston Symphony Orchestra at which post he stayed until 1950. He established a foundation in memory of his wife with the principal object of stimulating the composition of new works, including operas, by commissioning them.

**Koven, Reginald de** *Composer*
b. Middletown, Conn., 1859: d. Chicago, 1920

| Robin Hood | | 1890 |
|---|---|---|
| The Canterbury | | |
| Pilgrims | Metropolitan | 1917 |
| Rip van Winkle | | |
| Chicago and New York | | 1920 |
| Rob Roy | | 1894 |

**Krasa, Hans**     *Composer*
b. Prague, 1899: d. Oswiecim, 1944

| Betrothed in a Dream | 1933 |
|---|---|
| Brundibar | 1940 |

**Krauss, Ernst**     *Tenor*
b. Erlangen, Germany, 1863: d. Wörthsee, 1941
He made his debut as Tamino at Mannheim in 1893.

**Kraus, Felix von**     *Bass*
b. Vienna, 1870: d. Munich, 1937
This famous Gurnemanz made his debut as Hagen at Bayreuth in 1899. In the same year he married Adrienne Osborne.

**Kraus, Otakar**     *Baritone*
b.
The first Nick Shadow (*The Rake's Progress*).

**Krauss, Clemens**     *Conductor*
b. Vienna, 1893: d. Mexico City, 1954
Strauss dedicated his *Friedenstag* to Krauss and Ursuleac. Krauss conducted its premiere. He was conductor at Frankfurt, Berlin, Munich, Salzburg and Vienna.

**Krauss, Marie Gabrielle**     *Soprano*
b. Vienna, 1842: d. Paris, 1906
In 1860 she made her debut in Vienna singing Mathilde in *Guillaume Tell*.
Aida, Anna (*La Dame Blanche*), Donna Anna, Elsa, Gilda, Katherine (*Henry VIII*), Leonore (*Fidelio*), Leonora (*Trovatore*), Lucia, Lucrezia Borgia, Mathilde (*Guillaume Tell*), Norma, Rachel, Sapho, Semiramide, Valentine (*Les Huguenots*).

**Krein, Alexander**     *Composer*
b. Nizhni-Novgorod, 1883: d. Moscow, 1951

| Zagmuk | Moscow | 1930 |
|---|---|---|
| Daughter of the People | | 1949 |

**Krejčí, Iša**     *Composer*
b. Prague, 1904:

| The Revolt of | | |
|---|---|---|
| Ephesus | Prague | 1946 |

**Krejči, Miroslav**     *Composer*
b. Czechoslovakia, 1891:

| Léto (*Summer*) | Prague | 1940 |
|---|---|---|
| Posledni Hejtman (*The Last Captain*) | „ | 1948 |

**Krenek, Ernst**     *Composer*
b. Vienna, 1900:

| Zwingburg | Berlin | 1924 |
|---|---|---|
| Der Sprung über den Schatten | Frankfurt | 1924 |
| Orpheus und Eurydike | Kassel | 1926 |
| Jonny Spielt Auf | Leipzig | 1927 |
| Leben des Orest | „ | 1930 |
| Charles V | Prague | 1938 |
| Tarquin | Poughkeepsie, N.Y. | 1941 |

**Kreutzer, Rodolphe**     *Composer*
b. Versailles, 1766: d. Geneva, 1831
This is the famous violinist to whom Beethoven dedicated his *Kreutzer Sonata*. He wrote forty operas.

| Jeanne d'Arc | Paris | 1790 |
|---|---|---|
| Paul et Virginie | „ | 1791 |
| Lodoïska | „ | 1791 |

**Křička, Jaroslav**     *Composer*
b. Moravia, 1882:

| Hipolyta | Prague | 1917 |
|---|---|---|
| Ogaři | | 1919 |
| Bilý Pán (*White Ghost*) | Brno | 1929 |
| Král Lávra (*King Lawrence*) | Prague | 1940 |
| Jachym a Juliana | | 1948 |

**Krips, Joseph**     *Conductor*
b. Vienna, 1902:
Conductor at Vienna and at Salzburg.

**Kronold, Selma** *Soprano*
b. Krakov, 1866: d. New York, 1920
In 1882 she came out as Agatha (*Der Freischütz*), in Leipzig. Her Metropolitan debut was in 1896. In 1904 she retired.
Agatha, Nedda, Santuzza.

**Krueger, Karl** *Conductor*
b. Atchison, Kansas, 1894:
Assistant conductor at Vienna from 1919 to 1924. Conductor of the Detroit Symphony from 1943 to 1949.

**Kubelík, Rafael** *Conductor*
b. Near Kolín, Czechoslovakia, 1914:
Although best known as a conductor on both sides of the Atlantic, he also composed an opera:
Veronika  Brno  1947

**Kullman, Charles** *Tenor*
b. New Haven, Conn., 1903:
He made his debut as Pinkerton in Berlin, 1931. In 1935 he sang for the first time at the Metropolitan, as Faust.
Avito (*L'Amore dei Tre Re*), Belmonte, Eisenstein (*Die Fledermaus*), Faust, Sir Huon, Jenik (*Prodaná Nevěsta*), Orfeo (in the first American stage performance of *La Favola d'Orfeo*), Pinkerton, Schuisky (*Boris Godunov*), Tannhäuser.

**Kunz, Eric** *Bass*
b.
Beckmesser, Figaro (*Le Nozze di Figaro*), Leporello, Papageno.

**Kurka, Robert** *Composer*
b. 1922: d. New York, 1957
The Good Soldier
Schweik (*posthumous*)
New York  1957

**Kurt, Melanie** *Soprano*
b. Vienna, 1880: d. New York, 1941
She was not only an opera singer, but also a pianist, winning the Liszt Prize. Her opera debut came in Lübeck, in 1902, when she sang Elisabeth. She sang

Isolde in her first appearance at the Metropolitan in 1915.
Elisabeth, Iphigénie (*Iphigénie en Tauride*), Isolde, Kundry.

**Kurz, Selma** *Soprano*
b. Silesia, 1875: d. Vienna, 1933
She made her debut at Covent Garden in 1904 singing Gilda.
Gilda, Oscar, Violetta, Zerbinetta (*Ariadne auf Naxos*).

**Labia, Maria** *Soprano*
b. Verona, Italy, 1880:
She made her debut in Stockholm, in 1905, singing Mimi. Her first appearance at New York occurred in 1908, when she sang Tosca.
Carmen, Giorgetta (*Il Tabarro*), Mimi, Nedda, Tosca, Violetta.

**Lablache, Luigi** *Bass*
b. Naples, 1794: d. there, 1858
Lablache has been called the greatest of all Leporellos. He made his debut at Naples in 1812. He sang the first Giorgio (*I Puritani*) and the first Don Pasquale.
Assur (*Semiramide*), Dandini (*Cenerentola*), Geronimo (*Il Matrimonio Segreto*), Giorgio (*I Puritani*), Don Giovanni, Henry VIII (*Anna Bolena*), Leporello, Méphistophélès (*Faust*), Oroveso, Don Pasquale, Podestà (*La Gazza Ladra*).

**Labroca, Mario** *Composer*
b. Rome, 1896:
A pupil of Malipiero, and a composer of orchestral and chamber music.
La Principessa di Perepepè
Rome  1927
Le Tre Figliuole di
Pinco Pallino  „  1928

**Lachner, Franz** *Composer*
b. Rain am Lech, Germany, 1803: d. Munich, 1890
Brother of Ignaz Lachner.
Die Bürgschaft  Pest  1828
Alidia  Munich  1839

Catarina Cornaro    „    1841
Benvenuto Cellini    „    1849

**Lachner, Ignaz**      *Composer*
b. Rain am Lech, Germany, 1807: d.
Hanover, 1895
Brother of Franz Lachner.

| Der Geisterturm | Stuttgart | 1837 |
| Die Regenbrüder | „ | 1839 |
| Loreley | Munich | 1846 |

**Lacombe, Louis Brouillon**    *Composer*
b. Bourges, 1818: d. St-Vaast-la-Hougue,
1884

| L'Amour | Paris | 1859 |
| La Madone | „ | 1861 |
| Winkelried | Geneva | 1892 |
| Le Tonnelier | Coblenz | 1897 |

**Lail, Lorri**      *Mezzo-soprano*
b. Oslo, 1904:

**Lajtha, László**      *Composer*
b. Budapest, 1891:
A composer of music for ballet, for
orchestra, and for chorus.

Chapeau Bleu      1952

**Lalo, Édouard**      *Composer*
(*Full name*: Victor Antoine Édouard)
b. Lille, 1823: d. Paris, 1892
Lalo wrote music in all forms, but is
best known for his *Symphonie espagnole*.

Le Roi d'Ys    Opéra-Comique   1888

**Lamoureux, Charles**      *Conductor*
b. Bordeaux, 1834: d. Paris, 1899
An advocate of Wagner, conductor of
the Paris Opéra from 1877 to 1879,
Lamoureux was the founder of the
concert series which bears his name.

**Langendorff, Frieda**      *Contralto*
b. Breslau, 1868: d. New York, 1947
She made her debut in Strasbourg in
1901 and at the Metropolitan in 1907:
Amneris, Azucena, Dalila, Fricka,
Ortrud.

**Laparra, Raoul**      *Composer*
b. Bordeaux, 1876: d. near Paris, 1943

A pupil of Fauré and Massenet, and a
composer of music for piano and for
orchestra. He was killed in an air raid
during World War II.

| Peau d'âne | Bordeaux | 1899 |
| La Habanera | Comique | 1908 |
| La Jota | „ | 1911 |
| Le Joueur de Viole | Paris | 1925 |
| Las Toreras | Lille | 1929 |
| L'Illustre Fregona | Paris | 1931 |

**Larsén-Todsen, Nanny**      *Soprano*
b. Kalmar län, Sweden, 1884:
She made her debut in Stockholm as
Agathe in 1906, and at the Metropolitan
in 1925 as Brünnhilde.
Agathe, Brünnhilde, Fricka, Isolde,
Leonore (*Fidelio*).

**Larsson, Lars Erik**      *Composer*
b. Akarp, Sweden, 1908:
Prinsessan av Cypern
                 Stockholm   1937

**Lassalle, Jean Louis**      *Baritone*
b. Lyons, 1847: d. Paris, 1909
He made his debut at the Opéra in
1872 and at the Metropolitan, singing
Nelusko, twenty years later. He was the
first to sing Scindia (*Le Roi de Lahore*),
and the first High Priest (*Samson et
Dalila*).
Ashton (*Lucia di Lammermoor*), Esca-
millo, Don Giovanni, Hans Sachs, High
Priest (*Samson et Dalila*), Nelusko, De
Nevers, Rigoletto, Scindia, St. Bris,
Guillaume Tell, Telramund.

**Lassen, Eduard**      *Composer*
b. Copenhagen, 1830: d. Weimar, 1904
It was Lassen who conducted the
première of *Samson et Dalila*. He also
made a living writing music for stage
plays.

| Landgraf Ludwigs | | |
| Brautfahrt | Weimar | 1857 |
| Frauenlob | „ | 1860 |
| Le Captif | Brussels | 1865 |

**Lattuada, Felice** *Composer*
b. near Milan, 1882:

| | | |
|---|---|---|
| La Tempestà | Milan | 1922 |
| Sandha | Genoa | 1924 |
| Le Preziose Ridicole | Milan | 1929 |
| Don Giovanni | Naples | 1929 |
| La Caverna di Salamanca | | |
| | Genoa | 1938 |

**Launis, Armas Emanuel** *Composer*
(*Really* Lindberg)
b. Hämeenlinna, Finland, 1884:
A pupil of Jan Sibelius.

| | | |
|---|---|---|
| Seitsemän Veljestä (*The* | | |
| *Seven Brothers*) | Helsingfors | 1913 |
| Kullervo | „ | 1917 |
| Aslak-Hetta | Nice | 1938 |

**Lauri-Volpi, Giacomo** *Tenor*
b. near Rome, 1892:
He made his debut in Rome in 1920 and at the Metropolitan, singing the Duke (*Rigoletto*), in 1923.
Andrea Chénier, Calaf, Duke, Johnson, Manrico, Nerone, Otello, Radames, Raoul, Rodolfo.

**Lawrence, Marjorie** *Soprano*
b. near Melbourne, 1909:
This famous singer became paralyzed at the height of her career. Nevertheless she endeavored to keep singing, and appeared as Venus, in *Tannhäuser*, being able in that role to remain seated upon a couch.
Alceste, Brünnhilde, Salome, Venus.

**Lazarus, Daniel** *Composer*
b. Paris, 1898:

| | | |
|---|---|---|
| Trumpeldor | Paris (concert) | 1946 |

**Lazzari, Sylvio** *Composer*
b. Bozen, 1857: d. Paris, 1944

| | | |
|---|---|---|
| Armor | Prague | 1898 |
| La Lépreuse | Paris | 1912 |
| Le Sautériot | Chicago | 1918 |
| Melaenis | Mulhouse | 1927 |
| La Tour de Feu | Paris | 1928 |

**Leblanc, Georgette** *Soprano*
b. c. 1880: d. Cannes, 1941
The first Ariane (*Ariane et Barbe-Bleue*). She was to have been the first Mélisande, or so her lover Maeterlinck thought, but to his mortification Mary Garden got the part.

**Lecocq, Alexandre Charles** *Composer*
b. Paris, 1832: d. there, 1918
Lecocq shared the Offenbach prize with Bizet in 1857 when both wrote acceptable operas to the libretto of *Le Docteur Miracle*.

| | | |
|---|---|---|
| Le Docteur Miracle | Paris | 1857 |
| Fleur de Thé | „ | 1868 |
| La Fille de Mme. | | |
| Angot | Brussels | 1872 |
| Giroflé-Girofla | „ | 1874 |

**Lee, Dai-Keong** *Composer*
b. Honolulu, 1915:
A pupil of Roger Sessions and of Aaron Copland.

| | |
|---|---|
| The Poet's Dilemma | 1940 |

**Lefebvre, Charles Édouard** *Composer*
b. Paris, 1843: d. Aix-les-Bains, 1917

| | | |
|---|---|---|
| Zaïre | Lille | 1887 |
| Djelma | Paris | 1894 |
| Le Trésor | Angers | 1883 |

**Leffler-Burckard, Martha** *Soprano*
b. Berlin, 1865: d. Wiesbaden, 1954
She made her debut at Strasbourg in 1890, and at the Metropolitan in 1908.
Brünnhilde, Elisabeth, Elsa, Eva, Isolde, Leonora (*Fidelio*).

**Leginska, Ethel** *Composer*
(*Really* Liggins)
b. Hull, England, 1886:

| | | |
|---|---|---|
| Gale | Chicago | 1935 |
| The Rose and the | | |
| Ring | Los Angeles | 1957 |

**Legros, Joseph** *Tenor*
b. Laon, 1730: d. La Rochelle, 1793
The first French Orfeo (*Orfeo ed Euridice*), the first Achilles (*Iphigénie en*

*Aulide*), and the first Pylade (*Iphigénie en Tauride*). He also composed a little.

**Lehár, Franz**                          *Composer*
b. Komorn, Hungary, 1870: d. Bad
Ischl, 1948
Kukuschka (*or* Tatjana) Leipzig 1896
Die Lustige Witwe
(*The Merry Widow*)      Vienna  1905
Der Graf von
  Luxembourg                 „     1909
Zigeunerliebe                „     1910

**Lehmann, Lilli**                        *Soprano*
b. Würzburg, 1848: d. Berlin, 1929
Stories about Lilli Lehmann's frugality
and modesty would fill a small book.
One of the best describes how, when
singing as prima donna at the Metropolitan, she rode a horse car to work
instead of taking a more ostentatious
vehicle. She made her debut in Prague in
1865, and sang for the first time at the
Metropolitan in 1885 as Carmen. She
was the teacher of Farrar and Fremstad.
It is said she knew one hundred and
seventy roles. In 1888 she married Paul
Kalisch. Her recording of *Casta Diva*,
made when she was in her late fifties, is
perhaps unequaled.
   Aida, Amelia, Donna Anna, Bertha
(*Le Prophète*), Brünnhilde, Carmen, Desdemona, Euryanthe, Irene (*Rienzi*), Isolde,
Leonore (*Fidelio*), Margherita (*Mefistofele*),
Norma, Ortrud, Philine, Queen of
Sheba, Rachel, Sieglinde, Sulamith, Wog-
linde (*coached by Wagner*), Violetta.

**Lehmann, Lotte**                        *Soprano*
b. Perleberg, Germany, 1888:
   The first Empress (*Die Frau ohne
Schatten*), the first Christine (*Intermezzo*),
and the first Composer (*Ariadne auf
Naxos*). She made her United States
debut at Chicago in 1930, and at the
Metropolitan in 1934.
   Christine, Composer (*Ariadne auf Naxos*),
Empress (*Die Frau ohne Schatten*), Leonore

(*Fidelio*), Marschallin, Octavian, Sieglinde,
Tatyana, Tosca.

**Leider, Frida**                         *Soprano*
b. Berlin, 1888:
   Like Lotte Lehman, Frida Leider made
her first United States appearance in
Chicago, in 1928, singing Brünnhilde.
She made her Metropolitan debut as
Isolde, in 1933.
   Brünnhilde, Isolde, Kundry, Marsch-
allin, Senta.

**Leigh, Walter**                         *Composer*
b. Wimbledon, England, 1905: d. To-
bruk, Libya, 1942
   He was a composer of film, stage and
chamber music. He died in action during
the African campaign against Rommel in
the Second World War.
   The Jolly Roger        London  1933
   The Pride of the
     Regiment             „       1932

**Leinsdorf, Erich**                      *Conductor*
b. Vienna, 1912:
   Assistant conductor at Salzburg in 1934,
he went to the Metropolitan in 1938. In
1947 he became conductor of the
Rochester Philharmonic.

**Lemnitz, Tiana**                        *Soprano*
b. Metz, 1897:
   She made her debut at Frankfurt in
1922.
   Eva, Jenufa, Marschallin, Milada (*Dalibor*), Pamina, Sieglinde, Tatyana.

**Leo, Leonardo**                         *Composer*
b. near Brindisi, Italy, 1694: d. Naples,
1744
   Pisistrato               Naples  1714
   L'Imbroglio Scoperto              1723
   Demofoonte                        1735
   Amor Vuol Sofferenze              1739

**Leoncavallo, Ruggiero**                 *Composer*
b. Naples, 1858: d. Montecatini, 1919
   I Pagliacci              Milan   1892
   Tommaso Chatterton               1896

| La Bohème | Venice | 1897 |
| Zaza | Milan | 1900 |
| Maia | Rome | 1910 |
| Malbruk (*within four* | | |
| *days of Maia*) | ,, | 1910 |
| La Reginetta delle Rose | | |
| | Rome and Naples | 1912 |
| Gli Zingari | London | 1912 |

**Leonova, Darya**　　　　　　*Contralto*
b. Tver, Russia, 1829: d. St. Petersburg, 1896
A friend of Mussorgsky.

**Lesueur, Jean François**　　　*Composer*
b. near Abbeville, France, 1760: d. Paris, 1837

| La Caverne | Paris | 1793 |
| Paul et Virginie | ,, | 1794 |
| Télémaque | ,, | 1796 |
| Les Bardes | ,, | 1804 |
| La Mort d'Adam | ,, | 1809 |

**Levasseur, Marie Claude Josèphe**
(*Called* Rosalie)　　　　　　*Soprano*
b. Valenciennes, France, 1749: d. Neuwied am Rhein, Germany, 1826
The first Armide, the first Alceste in Paris, the first Iphigénie (*Iphigénie en Tauride*), and one of the first to sing that role in the *Iphigénie en Aulide*.

**Levasseur, Nicholas Prosper**　　*Bass*
b. Bresles, France, 1791: d. Paris, 1871
The first Bertram (*Robert le Diable*), the first Cardinal (*La Juive*). He made his debut at the Opéra in 1813.
Bertram, Cardinal (*La Juive*), St. Bris, Figaro (*Il Barbiere di Siviglia*), Mosè (by Rossini).

**Levi, Hermann**　　　　　　*Conductor*
b. Giessen, Germany, 1839: d. Munich, 1900
Although Wagner was afflicted with some degree of anti-Semitism, Levi was the only conductor he would trust with the premiere of *Parsifal*.

**Lewis, Brenda**　　　　　　*Soprano*
b.
Donna Elvira, Giorgetta (*Il Tabarro*), Lion Tamer (*He Who Gets Slapped*), Marschallin, Musetta, Regina.

**Lewis, Richard**　　　　　　*Tenor*
b.
Bacchus (*Ariadne auf Naxos*), Ferrando, Idomeneo, Tom Rakewell.

**Lhotka, Fran**　　　　　　*Composer*
b. Czechoslovakia, 1883:
Lhotka studied with Dvořák, Janáček, and Klička.

| Minka | Zagreb | 1918 |
| The Sea | ,, | 1920 |

**Lhotka-Kalinski, Ivo**　　　　*Composer*
b. Zagreb, 1913:
The son of Fran Lhotka.

| Pomet | | 1944 |
| Matija Gubec | | 1948 |

**Liatoshinsky, Boris**　　　　*Composer*
b. Zhitomir, Russia, 1895:
A pupil of Glière.

| The Golden Hoop | | 1931 |
| Shehors | Kiev | 1938 |

**Liebermann, Rolf**　　　　　*Composer*
b. Zürich, 1910:

| Leonore 40/45 | Basel | 1952 |
| The School for Wives | | |
| | Louisville, Ky. | 1955 |
| Penelope | Salzburg | 1954 |

**Liebling, Estelle**　　　　　*Soprano*
b. New York, 1884:
Best known in New York as a teacher of singing.

**Liljefors, Ingemar**　　　　　*Composer*
b. Göteborg, Sweden, 1906:

| Hyrkusken | | 1951 |

**Lind, Jenny**　　　　　　　*Soprano*
b. Stockholm, 1820: d. Malvern Wells, England, 1887
The Swedish Nightingale. She studied with Manuel García and made her debut

at Stockholm in 1838 as Agathe. Her London debut, as Alice in *Robert le Diable*, occurred in 1847. She was brought to the United States by P. T. Barnum and exhibited as a kind of supernatural being to awe-struck multitudes. She was the first Amalia (*I Masnadieri*, by Verdi).

Adina (*L'Elisir d'Amore*), Agathe, Alice, Amalia (*I Masnadieri*), Amina, Donna Anna, Euryanthe, Giulia (*La Vestale*), Lucia, Marie (*La Figlia del Reggimento*), Susanna (*Le Nozze di Figaro*), Valentine (*Les Huguenots*).

**Lindberg, Oskar Fredrik**          *Composer*
b. Gagnef, Sweden, 1887: d. Stockholm, 1955
Fredlos                Stockholm    1943

**Linley, George**          *Composer*
b. Leeds, 1798: d. London, 1865
Francesca Doria                      1849
La Poupée de Nurenberg               1861

**Linstead, George Frederick**          *Composer*
b. Melrose, Massachusetts, 1908:
Eastward of Eden                     1935

**Lipovska, Lydia Yakolevna**          *Soprano*
b. Bessarabia, 1884: d. Beirut, 1955
She made her debut at St. Petersburg in 1909, and sang Lakmé in Boston and Violetta at the Metropolitan that same year.

Gilda, Juliette, Lakmé, Manon Lescaut, Mimi, Susanna (*Il Segreto di Susanna*), Tatyana, Violetta.

**Lipton, Martha**          *Mezzo-soprano*
b.
Annina (*Der Rosenkavalier*), Brangäne, Frasquita (*Der Corregidor*), Innkeeper (*Boris Gudonov*), Maddalena (*Rigoletto*), Mother Goose (*The Rake's Progress*).

**List, Emanuel**          *Bass*
b. Vienna, 1891:
He made his debut at Vienna in 1922 singing Méphistophélès in *Faust*. The following year he sang the Landgraf (*Tannhäuser*) in his first appearance at the Metropolitan.

Fafner, Landgraf (*Tannhäuser*), Méphistophélès (*Faust*), Baron Ochs.

**Liszt, Franz**          *Composer*
b. Raiding, Hungary, 1811: d. Bayreuth, 1886
Famous as pianist, composer and teacher, he was also a conductor. When *Lohengrin* was prohibited in Germany, Liszt, with all the prestige his name carried, produced and conducted its première at Dresden in 1850. His activity at Weimar made that city a center of opera. His daughter Cosima became the wife first of von Bülow, then of Richard Wagner.

**Litvinne, Félia**          *Soprano*
b. St. Petersburg, 1861: d. Paris, 1936
She made her debut at Paris in 1885.
Aida, Donna Anna, Brünnhilde, La Gioconda, Isolde, Leonora (*Il Trovatore*).

**Ljungberg, Göta**          *Soprano*
b. Sundsval, Sweden, 1893: d. near Stockholm, 1955
The first Lady Marigold (*Merry Mount*). She made her Metropolitan debut in 1932. Her first professional appearance occurred in Stockholm, in 1920, as Elsa.
Elsa, Judith (*by Goossens*), Lady Marigold (*Merry Mount*).

**Lloyd, David**          *Tenor*
b.
Gonsalve (*L'Heure Espagnole*), Pedrillo, Pinkerton, Prince of Tartaglia (*The Love for Three Oranges*), Prince Ramiro (*Cenerentola*.

**Lloyd, George**          *Composer*
b. St. Ives, England, 1913:
Iernin                Penzance    1934
The Serf              London      1938
John Socman                       1951

**Locke, Matthew**          *Composer*
b. Exeter, England, 1630: d. London, 1677

He wrote part of the first English opera, *The Siege of Rhodes* (1656). He also sang in the production.

**Lockwood, Normand** *Composer*
b. New York, 1906:
Scarecrow      New York      1945

**Locle, Camille de** *Librettist*
b. Vaucluse, 1832: d. Capri, 1903
Du Locle wrote the scenario for *Aida*, and with Méry the libretto for *Don Carlos*. He was at one time director of the Opéra-Comique.

**London, George** *Baritone*
(*Really* Burnstein)
b. Montreal, 1920:
George London began his singing career in Los Angeles, singing in the chorus of the local opera. He first sang in New York as a member of the cast of the show *Desert Song*. This led to a concert series. He went to Europe on his own in order to find acceptance as an opera singer, then returned to make his debut as Amonasro at the Metropolitan in 1951. In 1960 he became the first American to sing Boris at the Bolshoi Theater in Moscow, for which he received a tremendous ovation.
Amfortas, Amonasro, Boris Godunov, Coppelius, Dapertutto, Escamillo, Eugene Onegin, Don Giovanni, Lindorf, Mandryka, Méphistophélès (*Faust*), Docteur Miracle, Parsifal, Scarpia, Graf Waldner (*Arabella*), Wolfram.

**Loomis, Clarence** *Composer*
b. Sioux Falls, S.D, 1889:
A Night in Avignon
Castle of Gold
Yolande of Cyprus
                London, Ontario   1929
David
The Fall of the House of Usher

**Loomis, Harvey Worthington** *Composer*
b. Brooklyn, N.Y., 1865: d. Boston, 1930
A pupil of Dvořák.

The Traitor Mandolin
The Maid of Athens
Going Up?

**Lorenz, Max** *Tenor*
b. Düsseldorf, 1901:
He made his Metropolitan debut in 1931 as Walther.
Aegisth (*Elektra*), Cola Rienzi, Herod (*Salome*), Siegfried, Siegmund, Tristan, Walther.

**Lortzing, Gustav Albert** *Composer*
b. Berlin, 1801: d. there, 1851
For his first two operas, Lortzing wrote his own libretti.

| | | |
|---|---|---|
| Zar und Zimmerman | Leipzig | 1837 |
| Die Beiden Schützen | ,, | 1837 |
| Der Wildschütz | | 1842 |
| Undine | Magdeburg | 1845 |
| Der Waffenschmied | Vienna | 1846 |

**Lotti, Antonio** *Composer*
b. Venice, 1667: d. there, 1740

| | | |
|---|---|---|
| Giove in Argo | Dresden | 1717 |
| Ascanio | | 1718 |
| Teofane | Dresden | 1719 |

**Løveberg, Aase** *Soprano*
(*Née* Nordmo)
b. Målselv, Norway, 1923:
She made her debut in Oslo in 1948 and at the Metropolitan in 1959.

**Lualdi, Adriano** *Composer*
b. Larino, Italy, 1885:
A pupil of Wolf-Ferrari.

| | | |
|---|---|---|
| Guerrin Meschino | Rome | 1920 |
| La Figlia del Re | Turin | 1922 |
| Le Furie d'Arlecchino | | |
| | Buenos Aires | 1924 |
| Il Diavolo ne Campanile | | |
| | La Scala | 1925 |
| La Granceola | Venice | 1932 |
| Lumavig e la Saetta | Rome | 1937 |

**Lubin, Germaine** *Soprano*
b. Paris, 1890:

250

She made her debut at the Opéra-Comique in 1912.
Alceste, Isolde, Kundry.

**Luca, Giuseppe de** *Baritone*
b. Rome, 1876: d. New York, 1950
The first Prince (*Adriana Lecouvreur*), the first Sharpless, the first Gianni Schicchi, and the first Paquiro (*Goyescas*). He made his debut as Valentin (*Faust*) in Piacenza in 1897. He first appeared at the Metropolitan as Figaro (*Il Barbiere di Siviglia*), in 1915.
Don Carlo (*La Forza del Destino*), Eugene Onegin, Figaro (*Il Barbiere di Siviglia*), Gianni Schicchi, Hoël (*Dinorah*), Don Pasquale, Paquiro (*Goyescas*), Plunkett (*Martha*), Prince (*Adriana Lecouvreur*), Rigoletto, Rodrigo (*Don Carlos*), Sancho Panza, Sharpless, Zurga (*Les Pêcheurs de Perles*), Valentin (*Faust*).

**Lucca, Pauline** *Soprano*
b. Vienna, 1841: d. there, 1908
She made her debut at Olmütz in 1859, singing Elvira (*Ernani*).
Carmen, Cherubino, Elisabetta (*Don Carlos*), Elvira (*Ernani*), Leonora (*La Favorita*), Lucia, Marguérite (*Faust*), Marie (*La Figlia del Reggimento*), Norma, Selika, Valentine (*Les Huguenots*), Zerlina (*Fra Diavolo*).

**Lucia, Fernando de** *Tenor*
b. Naples, 1860: d. there, 1925
Canio, Mario Cavaradossi, Don Ottavio.

**Ludikar, Pavel** *Bass*
b. Prague, 1882:
He made his debut at Prague, 1904, in Boston, 1913, and at the Metropolitan in 1926. He sang the first Karl (*Karl V*).
Figaro (*Il Barbiere di Siviglia*), Karl V.

**Ludwig, William** *Baritone*
(*Really* Ledwidge)
b. Dublin, 1847: d. London, 1923
Hans Sachs, Telramund, Vanderdecken

(*Der Fliegende Holländer*), Wolfram, Wotan.

**Luening, Otto** *Composer*
b. Milwaukee, Wisc., 1900:
In association with Vladimir Ussachevsky, Luening is experimenting with electronic music.
Evangeline    New York    1948

**Lully, Jean Baptiste** *Composer*
b. Florence, 1632: d. Paris, 1687
At first a dancer in ballets, Lully became in 1672 the producer at the Académie Royale de Musique (Opéra), replacing Perrin and Cambert, and gaining thereby the monopoly for opera production in the nation. He was not known for his friendliness and goodwill. The cause of his death was occupational: he died of gangrene caused by a bruise on his foot which happened when the cane with which he beat time struck it during a performance.
Les Fêtes de L'Amour
    et de Bacchus    Opéra    1672
Alceste    „    1674
Thesée    „    1675

**Lussan, Zélie de** *Soprano*
b. Brooklyn, 1863: d. London, 1949
She made her debut in Boston in 1885.
Anne (*Falstaff*), Arline (*The Bohemian Girl*), Carmen, Desdemona, Juliette, Mignon, Musetta, Nedda, Zerlina (*Don Giovanni*).

**Lyford, Ralph** *Composer*
b. Worcester, Mass., 1882: d. Cincinnati, 1927
Castle Agrazant    Cincinnati    1926

**Lyne, Felice** *Soprano*
b. Slater, Missouri, 1887: d. Allentown, Pa., 1935
She made her debut in London in 1911, singing Gilda.

**Maas, Joseph** *Tenor*
b. Dartford, England, 1847: d. London, 1886

Don César de Bazan, des Grieux (*Manon*), Faust (*Faust*), Lohengrin, Radames, Raoul, Cola Rienzi, Thaddeus (*The Bohemian Girl*).

**Macbeth, Florence**　　　　*Soprano*
b. Mankato, Minn., 1891:
Called, perhaps in imitation of Jenny Lind, "The Minnesota Nightingale," she made her debut at Chicago as Rosina (*Il Barbiere di Siviglia*), 1914, and stayed with that company until 1935. For one year she toured the United States with her own company.

**Maccunn, Hamish**　　　　*Composer*
b. Greenock, Scotland, 1868: d. London, 1916
Not only a composer, he was conductor of the Carl Rosa company from 1898 to 1900, and assistant conductor at Covent Garden from 1910.

| | | |
|---|---|---|
| Jeanie Deans | Edinburgh | 1894 |
| Diarmid | London | 1897 |
| The Masque of | | |
| War and Peace | ,, | 1900 |

**Mackenzie, Alexander Campbell**
　　　　　　　　　　　　*Composer*
b. Edinburgh, 1847: d. London, 1935
A composer, conductor, violinist. He wrote for his own instrument and for chorus, orchestra and chamber groups.

| | | |
|---|---|---|
| Colomba | London | 1883 |
| The Troubador | ,, | 1886 |
| His Majesty | ,, | 1897 |
| The Knight of the Road | ,, | 1905 |
| The Cricket | | |
| on the Hearth | ,, | 1914 |

**Mackerras, Charles**　　　　*Conductor*
b. Schenectady, N.Y., 1925:

**Maclean, Alexander Morvaren**
　　　　　　　　　　　　*Composer*
b. Eton, England, 1872: d. London, 1936
Quentin Durward (*Composed* 1892)

| | | |
|---|---|---|
| | Newcastle on Tyne | 1920 |
| Petruccio | London | 1895 |
| The King's Price | ,, | 1904 |
| Maître Seiler | ,, | 1909 |

**Maclennan, Francis**　　　　*Tenor*
b. Bay City, Mich., 1879: d. Port Jefferson, N.Y., 1935
After his debut as Faust at Covent Garden in 1902 he became the first foreigner to sing Tristan in Germany. In 1904 he married Florence Easton.
Faust, Parsifal, Tristan.

**Madetoja, Leevi**　　　　*Composer*
b. Uleaborg, Finland, 1887: d. Helsinki, 1947

| | | |
|---|---|---|
| Pohjalaisia | Helsinki | 1924 |
| Juha | ,, | 1935 |

**Madeira, Jean**　　　　*Contralto*
b.
Amneris, Baba the Turk (*The Rake's Progress*), Berta (*Il Barbiere di Siviglia*), Carmen, La Cieca, Maddalena, Mother Goose (*The Rake's Progress*), Nurse (*Boris Godunov*), Schwertleite, Ulrica.

**Manganini, Quinto**　　　　*Composer*
b. Fairfield, Conn., 1897:

| | | |
|---|---|---|
| Tennessee's Partner | | |
| | New York (radio) | 1942 |

**Magnard, Albéric**　　　　*Composer*
b. Paris, 1865: d. Oise, 1914
Magnard was more successful as a composer for instruments than as an opera composer. He was killed while defending his home from the Germans during the First World War.

| | | |
|---|---|---|
| Yolande | Brussels | 1892 |
| Guercoeur (*partly lost*) | | 1910 |
| Bérénice | Opéra-Comique | 1911 |

**Mahler, Gustav**　　　　*Conductor*
b. Kalischt, Poland, 1860: d. Vienna, 1911
He was music director of the Budapest opera from 1888, then at Hamburg, 1891 to 1897, then Vienna. In 1908–1909 he conducted a season at the Metropolitan. He is famous as a symphonist. But in opera his only original work remains unfinished. For a production of *Oberon* he

made an extensive addition of musical accompaniment for the spoken scenes.

Der Herzog von Schwabe  (*Unfinished*)

**Maillart, Louis** (*or* **Aimé**)  *Composer*
b. Montpellier, France, 1817:  d. Moulins, 1871

| | | |
|---|---|---|
| Gastibelza | Paris | 1847 |
| Le Moulin des Tilleuls | „ | 1849 |
| La Croix de Marie | „ | 1852 |
| Les Dragons de Villars | „ | 1856 |
| Les Pêcheurs de Catane | „ | 1860 |
| Lara | „ | 1864 |

**Maison, René**  *Tenor*
b. Frameries, Belgium, 1895:
He made his debut at Monte Carlo in 1921, then at Chicago in 1927 where he stayed five years. In 1936 he first appeared at the Metropolitan as Walther.
Admetus, Herod, Don José, Julien, Walther.

**Makarova, Nina Vladimirovna**
*Composer*
b. Yurin, Russia, 1908:
The wife of Aram Khatchaturian.

| | |
|---|---|
| Courage | 1942 |

**Malherbe, Edmund Paul Henri**
*Composer*
b. Paris, 1870:
A pupil of Fauré and Massenet.

| | | |
|---|---|---|
| Madame Pierre | Paris | 1912 |
| L'Émeute | „ | 1912 |

**Malibran**  *Contralto*
(*Née* Marietta Felicita García)
b. Paris, 1808:  d. Manchester, England, 1836
The celebrated daughter of Manuel del Popolo Vicente García, and her father's most famous pupil. In 1826 she married the elderly Malibran, a businessman in New York. Later she married the violinist Bériot. She made her debut as Rosina (*Il Barbiere di Siviglia*) in London, 1825. She was the first Felicia (*Il Crociato in Egitto* by Meyerbeer).

Amina, Angelina (*Cenerentola*), Desdemona, Felicia (*Il Crociato in Egitto*), Juliette, Leonora (*Fidelio*), Rosina (*Il Barbiere di Siviglia*), Zerlina (*Don Giovanni*).

**Malipiero, Gian Francesco**  *Composer*
b. Venice, 1882:
A great modern contributor to the revival of ancient opera, and a composer of some twenty-five operas of his own. He made one of the two standard arrangements of *La Favola d'Orfeo*.

| | | |
|---|---|---|
| Canossa | Rome | 1914 |
| Sogno d'Un Tramonto d'Autunno | | 1914 |
| L'Orfeide (*trilogy*) | Düsseldorf | 1925 |
| La Morte delle Maschere | | |
| Sette Canzone | | |
| Orfeo | | |
| (*All of these are in revolutionary form, using pantomime, film, multiple stages, etc.*) | | |
| Il Mistero di Venezia (*trilogy*) | Coburg | 1932 |
| Le Aquile di Aquileia | | |
| Il Finto Arlecchino | | |
| I Corvi di San Marco | | |
| Il Figliuol Prodigo | Florence | 1957 |
| Venere Prigioniera | „ | 1957 |

**Malipiero, Riccardo**  *Composer*
b. Milan, 1914:
Nephew of Gian Francesco Malipiero.

| | | |
|---|---|---|
| Minnie La Candida | Parma | 1942 |
| La Donna è Mobile | | 1954 |

**Maliszewski, Witold**  *Composer*
b. Poland, 1873:  d. Warsaw, 1939

| | | |
|---|---|---|
| The Mermaid | Warsaw | 1939 |
| Boruta | | 1930 |

**Mallinger, Mathilde**  *Soprano*
(*Née* Lichtenegger)
b. Croatia, 1847:  d. Berlin, 1920
The first Eva. She made her debut as Norma at Munich, 1866.
Elsa, Eva, Norma.

**Malten, Thérèse** *Soprano*
(*Really* Müller)
b. Prussia, 1855: d. near Dresden, 1930
The third to sing Kundry, there being three who shared in the opening performances of Parsifal. She made her debut in Dresden, 1873.

Agatha, Armida, Brünnhilde, Elisabeth, Genoveva, Iphigénie (*Iphigénie en Tauride*), Isolde, Jessonda, Kundry, Leonore (*Fidelio*), Leonora (*Il Trovatore*), Marguérite (*Faust*), Pamina, Queen of Sheba.

**Mancinelli, Luigi** *Composer*
b. Orvieto, Italy, 1848: d. Rome, 1921
A conductor and a cellist. He led performances at Buenos Aires, Covent Garden and the Metropolitan.

| | | |
|---|---|---|
| Isora di Provenza | Bologna | 1884 |
| Tizianello | Rome | 1895 |
| Ero e Leandro | Madrid | 1897 |
| Sogno di una Notte d'Estate | | |
| Paolo e Francesca | Bologna | 1907 |

**Manén, Joan** *Composer*
b. Barcelona, 1883:

| | | |
|---|---|---|
| Giovanna di Napoli | Barcelona | 1902 |
| Der Fackeltanz | Frankfurt | 1909 |
| Nero und Akté | Karlsruhe | 1928 |
| Soledad | Barcelona | 1952 |

**Manners, Charles** *Bass*
b. London, 1857: d. Dublin, 1935
Founder of the Moody-Manners Opera Company. He made his debut with the d'Oyly Carte company in 1882, and married Fanny Moody in 1890.

**Manning, Kathleen Lockhart** *Composer*
b. near Hollywood, 1890: d. Los Angeles, 1951
She was also a singer, and a member of the Hammerstein Opera Company in London.
Mr. Wu
For the Soul of Rafael

**Manski, Dorothée** *Soprano*
b. New York, 1895:

As an actress she had appeared in productions of Max Reinhardt's before she made her debut in opera singing the Witch (*Hänsel und Gretel*), at the Metropolitan in 1927.

**Mapleson, James Henry** *Manager*
b. London, 1830: d. there, 1901
Under the name Enrico Mariani he sang opera in Italy before becoming a manager at Her Majesty's in London, 1862. He subsequently held the same position at Drury Lane, Covent Garden and the New York Academy of Music.

**Mapleson, Lionel S.** *Librarian*
b. London, 1865: d. New York, 1937
The nephew of James Henry Mapleson. He was librarian of the Metropolitan for forty-five years. In that position he was able to make the first recordings of actual performances of the de Reszkes, Calvé, etc.

**Marcel, Lucille** *Soprano*
(*Really* Wasself)
b. New York, 1887: d. Vienna, 1921
She made her debut at Vienna in 1908 singing Elektra, and at Boston singing Tosca in 1912. She married Felix Weingartner in 1911.

**Marchesi, Blanche** *Soprano*
b. Paris, 1863: d. London, 1940
She made her debut in Berlin, 1895, and in London the following year.
Brünnhilde, Elisabeth, Elsa, Eva, Isolde, Kundry, Senta, Sieglinde.

**Marcoux, Vanni** *Baritone*
(*Full name* Jean Émile Diogène Marcoux).
b. Turin, 1877:
The first Colonna (*Monna Vanna*). He made his debut as Friar Laurence in Bayonne, 1900. He claimed a repertory of two hundred forty roles.
Boris, Colonna, Friar Laurence, Méphistophélès (*Faust*).

**Marinuzzi, Gino (Giuseppe)** *Composer*
b. Palermo, 1882: d. (*murdered*) Milan, 1945
He was director of the Chicago Opera in 1920–1921, at Rome 1928–1934, and at La Scala from 1934 to 1945.

| Barberina | Palermo | 1903 |
| Jacquerie | Buenos Aires | 1918 |
| Palla de' Mozzi | La Scala | 1932 |

**Marinuzzi, Gino** *Conductor*
b. New York, 1920:
Son of Gino Marinuzzi (above), and a conductor at Rome since 1946.

**Mario** *Tenor*
(*Really* Giovanni Matteo Mario Cavaliere di Candia)
b. Cagliari, 1810: d. Rome, 1883
To avoid family embarrassment (for it was improper for members of the nobility to act on the stage), he used the plain "Mario" for his stage name. In 1836 he quit the army and eloped with a ballerina, but later he made a more serious marriage with Grisi. He made his debut at the Paris Opéra as Robert le Diable in 1838, and was the first Ernesto (*Don Pasquale*).
Alfredo (*La Traviata*), Count Almaviva (*Il Barbiere di Siviglia*), Duke, Ernesto (*Don Pasquale*), Gennaro, Lionel (*Martha*), Don Ottavio, Raoul, Robert le Diable.

**Mario, Queena** *Soprano*
(*Really* Tillotson)
b. Akron, Ohio, 1896: d. New York, 1951
She made her Metropolitan debut as Micaela in 1922. From 1931 she was a teacher at the Curtis Institute in Philadelphia. From 1925 to 1936 she was Wilfred Pelletier's wife.

**Mariz, Vasco** *Baritone*
b. Rio de Janeiro, 1921:
He was a Doctor of Jurisprudence at Rio de Janeiro before making his debut at Porto Allegre in 1945 as Doctor Bartolo in *Le Nozze di Figaro*. Then he devoted himself to music criticism.

**Marschner, Heinrich August** *Composer*
b. Saxony, 1795: d. Hanover, 1861
He wrote fourteen operas in all.

| Der Vampyr | Leipzig | 1828 |
| Der Templar und Die Judin (*from Ivanhoe*) | „ | 1829 |
| Hans Heiling | Berlin | 1833 |

**Marsick, Armand** *Composer*
b. Liège, 1877: d. Brussels, 1959

| Lara | | 1913 |
| L'Anneau Nuptial | | 1920 |
| La Jane | Liège | 1921 |

**Marteau, Henri** *Composer*
b. Reims, 1874: d. Lichtenberg, 1934

| Meister Schwalbe | Plauen | 1921 |

**Martelli, Henri** *Composer*
b. Corsica, 1895:

| La Chanson de Roland | | 1923 |

**Martin, Frank** *Composer*
b. Geneva, 1890:
Well known in Europe for his music for plays, orchestral and chamber works.

| The Tempest | Vienna | 1956 |

**Martin, Riccardo** *Tenor*
(*Really* Hugh Whitfield Martin)
b. Hopkinsville, Ky., 1881: d. New York, 1952
He made his debut as Faust in Nantes, 1904. In 1906 he appeared as Canio in his United States debut at New Orleans. A year later he came out at the Metropolitan.
Avito, Canio, Enzo, Faust, Hagenbach (*La Wally*), Mario Cavaradossi, Manrico, Pinkerton, Rodolfo.

**Martin, Vincente** *Composer*
(*Really* Martin y Soler)
b. Valencia, 1754: d. St. Petersburg, 1806
Although it receives performances now and then, his best known opera, *Una Cosa Rara*, owes its fame to a quotation in Don Giovanni. Perhaps this happened partly because the librettist was da Ponte in each case.

| Una Cosa Rara | Vienna | 1786 |

**Martinelli, Giovanni**      *Tenor*
b. Montagnana, Italy, 1885:
He sang his operatic debut in *Ernani* at
Milan, 1911. Martinelli was a member
of the company of the Metropolitan from
1913 to 1946. His debut there was as
Rodolfo. He sang the first Paolo (*Paolo e
Francesca*), and the first Fernando (*Goy-
escas*).
Calaf, Canio, Don Carlos, Eléazar,
Enzo, Fernando (*Goyescas*), Gennaro,
Gérald, John (*Le Prophète*), Johnson, Don
José, Lensky, Loris (*Fedora*), Manrico,
Oberon, Otello, Paolo (*Paolo e Francesca*),
Radames, Raoul, Riccardo (*Un Ballo in
Maschera*), Rodolfo, Samson, Tristan,
Vasco de Gama.

**Martini, Nino**      *Tenor*
b. Verona, Italy, 1905:
He made his debut in Philadelphia in
1931 before appearing for the first time at
the Metropolitan two years later as the
Duke in *Rigoletto*.

**Martinon, Jean**      *Composer*
b. Lyons, 1910:
Hécube      1954

**Martinu, Bohuslav**      *Composer*
b. Czechoslovakia, 1890: d. Liestal, Switzerland, 1959

| | | |
|---|---|---|
| The Soldier and the Ballerina | Brno | 1928 |
| Les Lames du Couteau | Paris | 1928 |
| Hry o Marii | Brno | 1934 |
| Juliette | Prague | 1938 |
| The Marriage | NBC/TV | 1953 |

**Marty, Eugène Georges**      *Composer*
b. Paris, 1860: d. there, 1908

| | | |
|---|---|---|
| Le Duc de Ferrare | Paris | 1899 |
| Daria | ,, | 1905 |

**Mascagni, Pietro**      *Composer*
b. Leghorn, Italy, 1863: d. Rome, 1945
The protagonist of the Italian "Verismo," producing realistic music drama.
His short opera *Cavalleria Rusticana* which

won the prize of the publisher Sonzogno,
created a sensation and established a trend.

| Pinotta | | |
|---|---|---|
| (*composed* 1880) | San Remo | 1932 |
| Cavalleria Rusticana | Rome | 1890 |
| L'Amico Fritz | ,, | 1891 |
| Guglielmo Ratcliff | Milan | 1895 |
| Iris | Rome | 1898 |
| Le Maschera | ,, | 1901 |
| (*Simultaneously produced in six cities.*) | | |
| Nerone | Milan | 1935 |

**Massa, Juan Bautista**      *Composer*
b. Buenos Aires, 1865: d. Rosario, 1938

| | | |
|---|---|---|
| Zoraide | Buenos Aires | 1909 |
| L'Eraso | Rosario | 1922 |
| La Magdalena | Buenos Aires | 1929 |

**Massé, Victor**      *Composer*
b. Lorient, France, 1822: d. Paris, 1884
Les Noces de Jeannette    Paris   1853

**Massenet, Jules Émile Fréderic**
     *Composer*
b. near St. Étienne, 1842: d. Paris, 1912
A pupil of Ambroise Thomas and himself a teacher of many opera composers.

| | | |
|---|---|---|
| Don César de Bazan | Paris | 1872 |
| Le Roi de Lahore | ,, | 1877 |
| Hérodiade (Salomé) | Brussels | 1881 |
| Manon | Paris | 1884 |
| Le Cid | ,, | 1885 |
| Werther | Vienna | 1892 |
| Thaïs | Paris | 1894 |
| Le Portrait de Manon | ,, | 1894 |
| La Navarraise | London | 1894 |
| Sapho | Paris | 1897 |
| Le Jongleur de Notre Dame | Monte Carlo | 1902 |
| Don Quichotte | ,, | 1910 |

**Materna, Amalie**      *Soprano*
b. Styria, 1845: d. Vienna, 1918
She was the very first among the three
sopranos who shared the role of Kundry
at the opening of *Parsifal*. She was also
the first Brünnhilde in *Siegfried*. Her debut
was in 1864, and her first appearance at the
Metropolitan, as Elisabeth, in 1885.

Brünnhilde, Elisabeth, Kundry, Rachel, Selika, Valentine (*Les Huguenots*).

**Matzenauer, Margarete**
       *Soprano and Mezzo-soprano*
b. Hungary, 1881:
    She made her debut in Strasbourg in 1901 and at the Metropolitan, as Amneris, in 1911. The following year she married the singer Ferrari-Fontana.

    Aida, Amelia, Amneris, Donna Anna, Azucena, Brünnhilde, Carmen, Dalila, Donna Elvira, Erde, Fatima (*Oberon*), Gioconda, Kostelnika (*Její Pastorkyňa*), Kundry, Leonore (*Fidelio*), Mignon, Norma, Ortrud, Santuzza, Selika, Ulrica, Venus.

**Maurel, Victor**       *Baritone*
b. Marseilles, 1848: d. New York, 1923
    The first Iago, the first Tonio, and the first Falstaff. He made his debut at the Opéra in 1868 singing de Nevers.

    Count Almaviva (*Le Nozze di Figaro*), Amonasro, Cacique (*Il Guarany*), Domingo (*Paul et Virginie*, by Massé), Dutchman, Falstaff, Don Giovanni, Guillaume Tell, Hamlet, Hoël, Iago, Conte di Luna, de Nevers, Peter the Great, Renato, Telramund, Tonio, Valentin (*Faust*), Wolfram.

**Mayr, Richard**       *Bass*
b. near Salzburg, 1877: d. Vienna, 1935
    He made his debut as Hagen at Bayreuth in 1902, and as Pogner at the Metropolitan in 1927.

    Gurnemanz, Don Gomez (*Ernani*), Hagen, Idomeneo, King Marke, Baron Ochs, Pogner, Wotan.

**McArthur, Edwin**       *Conductor*
b. Denver, Colo., 1907:
    He began his operatic career as pianist for Flagstad, Jeritza and Pinza. He subsequently conducted at Chicago, San Francisco and St. Louis.

**McCormack, John**       *Tenor*
b. Athlone, Ireland, 1884: d. near Dublin, 1945

    The story goes that the novelist James Joyce once contemplated singing as a career, but decided against it when he heard John McCormack singing opposing him in a contest. McCormack made his debut in Covent Garden as Turiddu in 1907, and at New York as Alfredo Germont in 1909.

    Alfredo Germont, Duke, Faust (*Faust*), Faust (*Mefistofele*), Gérald, Gritzko (*The Fair at Sorotchinsk*), Mario Cavaradossi, Pinkerton, Don Ottavio, Rodolfo, Tonio, Turiddu.

**McCoy, William J.**       *Composer*
b. Crestline, Ohio, 1848: d. Oakland, Calif. 1920

    Egypt       Berkeley, Calif.  1921

**McCracken, James**       *Tenor*
b.
    Alvaro, Bacchus, Otello.

**Mediņš, Janis**       *Composer*
b. Riga, Lithuania, 1890:
    Uguns un Nakts
      (*Fire and Night*)     Riga  1921
    Deevi un Cilveki       „  1922

**Méhul, Étienne Nicolas**       *Composer*
b. Givet, France, 1763: d. Paris, 1867
    Ariodant     Opéra-Comique  1799
    Joseph           „       1807
    Les Amazones     Opéra  1811

**Meisle, Kathryn**       *Contralto*
b. Philadelphia, 1899:
    She made her debut as Erda at Chicago and as Amneris at the Metropolitan, 1935.

**Melba, Nellie**       *Soprano*
(*Really* Helen Porter Armstrong, *nèe* Mitchell)
b. near Melbourne, 1861: d. Sydney, Australia, 1931

    A famous Lucia, the first Hélène (*Saint-Saëns*), she made her stage name from the name of her home town. She first sang at Brussels as Gilda in 1887 and at the Metropolitan as Lucia in 1893. Melba toast is named for her.

Brünnhilde, Elsa, Gilda, Juliette, Lucia, Margherite (*La Damnation de Faust*), Marguérite (*Faust*), Maguerite de Valois, Micaela, Mimi, Nedda, Ophélie, Rosina (*Il Barbiere di Siviglia*), Violetta.

**Melchior, Lauritz**                 *Tenor*
b. Copenhagen, 1890:
This famous heroic tenor made his debut at his birthplace as Canio in 1913, then at the Metropolitan in 1926 as Tannhäuser.
Canio, Otello, Parsifal, Siegfried, Siegmund, Tannhäuser, Tristan.

**Melis, Carmen**                 *Soprano*
b. Cagliari, Sardinia, 1885:
A pupil of Jean de Reszke and herself the teacher of Renata Tebaldi. She made her debut at Naples in 1906 and at the Metropolitan as Tosca in 1909.

**Mellers, Wilfrid Howard**     *Composer*
b. Leamington, England, 1914:
The Tragical History of
  Christopher Marlowe            1952

**Melnikov, Ivan Alexandrovitch**     *Bass*
b. St. Petersburg, 1832: d. there, 1906
The first to sing Boris Godunov in a complete performance.

**Melton, James**                 *Tenor*
b. Moultrie, Ga., 1904:
A pupil of Giuseppe de Luca. He made his debut at Cincinnati in 1938 and sang at the Metropolitan from 1942 to 1950. He is fairly well known outside opera as a collector of antique automobiles.

**Mendelssohn-Bartholdy, Felix** *Composer*
(*Full name* Jakob Ludwig Felix Mendelssohn-Bartholdy)
b. Hamburg, 1809: d. Leipzig, 1847
Famous as a symphonist and for his delicious music to the *Midsummer Night's Dream* of Shakespeare, Mendelssohn is also notable for having brought out in 1829 the *St. Matthew Passion* of Bach

which had lain unheard since its composer's death.
Loreley (*unfinished*)
Die Hochzeit des
  Camacho                 Berlin    1827

**Menotti, Gian-Carlo**         *Composer*
b. Cadegliano, Italy, 1911:
Menotti is celebrated for his excellent staging—he frequently directs productions of his own works. He is a pioneer in the field of television opera. Besides libretto's for his own works, Menotti wrote the libretto for and staged Barber's *Vanessa*.
Amelia Goes to the
  Ball                 Philadelphia  1937
The Old Maid and the
  Thief                        NBC    1939
The Island God      Metropolitan   1942
The Medium          New York      1946
The Consul                 „        1950
Amahl and the Night
  Visitors              NBC/TV     1951
The Saint of
  Bleecker Street   New York      1954
Maria Golovin        Brussels      1958

**Mercadante, Giuseppe Saverio Raffaele**
                          *Composer*
b. Altamura, 1795: d. Naples, 1870
L'Apoteosi d'Ercole      Naples    1819
Elisa e Claudio          La Scala  1821
Il Giuramento             Milan    1837

**Merikanto, Oskar**            *Composer*
b. Helsinki, 1868: d. Hausjarvi-Oiti, 1924
Pohjan Neiti             Viborg    1908
Elinan Surma            Helsinki   1910
Regina von Emmeritz        „       1920

**Merrill, Robert**             *Baritone*
b. Brooklyn, N.Y., 1917:
He made his debut at the Metropolitan in 1945 as Germont.
Escamillo, Count di Luna, Figaro (*Il Barbiere di Siviglia*), Germont, Renato (*Un Ballo in Maschera*), Rigoletto, Rodrigo, Tonio.

**Messager, André Charles Prosper**
*Composer*
b. Montlucon, France, 1853: d. Paris, 1929
A conductor too, he led the first performance of *Pelléas et Mélisande*.

| | | |
|---|---|---|
| La Basoche | Paris | 1890 |
| Madame Chrysanthème | „ | 1893 |
| Mirette | London | 1894 |
| Véronique | Paris | 1898 |
| Monsieur Beaucaire | Birmingham | 1919 |

**Messner, Joseph**
*Composer*
b. Tyrol, 1893:

| | | |
|---|---|---|
| Hadassa | Aachen | 1925 |
| Das Letzte Recht | | 1932 |
| Ines | | 1933 |
| Agnes Bernauer | | 1935 |

**Metastasio, Abbé**
*Librettist*
(*Really* Pietro Trapassi)
b. Rome, 1698: d. Vienna, 1782
He made his stage name by an anagram of his original name plus the Greek word for change—*meta*, "beyond." He composed music, played the harpsichord and sang. He wrote twenty-nine dramas, eight oratorios, and many other works. Among his dramas are *Semiramide* (used by Gluck, Meyerbeer and others), *Artaserse* (by the same, forty-one times), *La Clemenza di Tito* (used by Gluck, Mozart, etc.), *Il Re Pastore* (Gluck, Mozart, etc.).

**Meyerbeer, Giacomo**
*Composer*
(*Really* Jakob Liebmann Beer)
b. Berlin, 1791: d. Paris, 1864
Meyerbeer's operas are the prototypes of that style called "grand opera." They are distinguished not so much for size of cast or production, but for a formality and richness of style plus, usually, a choice of subject of grand proportions.

| | | |
|---|---|---|
| Robert le Diable | Opéra | 1831 |
| Les Huguenots | „ | 1836 |
| Le Prophète | „ | 1849 |

| | | |
|---|---|---|
| L'Étoile du Nord | Opéra-Comique | 1854 |
| Dinorah | „ | 1859 |
| L'Africaine | Opéra | 1865 |

**Meyerowitz, Jan**
*Composer*
b. Breslau, 1913:

| | | |
|---|---|---|
| Simoon | Tanglewood, Mass. | 1949 |
| The Barrier | New York | 1950 |
| Eastward in Eden | Detroit | 1951 |
| Bad Boys in School | Tanglewood | 1953 |
| Esther | Urbana, Ill. | 1957 |

**Michaelides, Solon**
*Composer*
b. Nicosia, Cyprus, 1905:
Ulysses (*Libretto by the composer.*)

**Mignone, Francisco**
*Composer*
b. São Paulo, Brazil, 1897:

| | | |
|---|---|---|
| O Contractador dos Diamantes | Rio de Janeiro | 1924 |
| L'Innocente | „ | 1928 |

**Mihalovici, Marcel**
*Composer*
b. Bucharest, 1898:

| | | |
|---|---|---|
| L'Intransigeant Pluton Phèdre | | 1948 |
| Die Heimkehr | Frankfurt Radio | 1954 |

**Milanov, Zinka**
*Soprano*
b. Zagreb, 1906:
A pupil of Ternina, she made her debut in Zagreb in 1927 as Leonora (*Il Trovatore*), and at the Metropolitan in 1937 in the same role. She is famous for her high pianissimi.

Aida, Amelia, Donna Anna, Desdemona, Elvira (*Ernani*), Gioconda, Leonora (*La Forza del Destino*), Leonora (*Il Trovatore*), Maddalena, Maria (*Simon Boccanegra*), Norma, Reiza, Santuzza, Tosca.

**Milde, Hans Feodor von**
*Baritone*
b. near Vienna, 1821: d. Weimar, 1899
The first Telramund, the first High Priest (*Samson et Dalila*). He was a pupil of Manuel García the younger, and the husband of Rosa Agthé.

**Mildenburg, Anna von**  *Soprano*
b. Vienna, 1872: d. there 1947
Amneris, Brünnhilde, Iphigénie (*Iphigénie en Aulide*), Isolde, Klytemnestra, Kundry.

**Milder, Anna**  *Soprano*
(*Really* Pauline Anne Milder-Hauptmann)
b. Constantinople, 1785: d. Berlin, 1838
The first Leonore (*Fidelio*). When Haydn heard her sing, as a child, he said "My dear, you have a voice like a house." She made her debut in Vienna in 1803.
Alcestis, Armida (*Gluck*), Donna Elvira, Iphigénie (*Iphigénie en Tauride*), Leonore (*Fidelio*), Susanna (*Le Nozze di Figaro*).

**Miles, Philip Napier**  *Composer*
b. Gloucestershire, England, 1865: d. Bristol, 1935

| | | |
|---|---|---|
| Westward Ho! | London | 1913 |
| Markheim | | 1926 |
| Queen Rosamund | | |

**Milhaud, Darius**  *Composer*
b. Aix-en-Provence, 1892:
A very prolific composer of music in all forms; one of "Les Six." His three *Minute Operas* are little gems.

| | | |
|---|---|---|
| Les Choëphores | Paris | 1919 |
| La Brebis Égarée | „ | 1923 |
| Les Malheurs | | |
| d'Orphée | Brussels | 1926 |
| Agamemnon | Paris | 1927 |
| Le Pauvre Matelot | „ | 1927 |
| Les Euménides | Antwerp | 1927 |
| Christophe Colomb | Berlin | 1930 |
| Maximilien | Paris | 1932 |
| Esther de Carpentras | „ | 1938 |
| Medée | Antwerp | 1939 |
| Bolivar | „ | 1950 |
| David | Jerusalem | 1954 |

**Miller, Mildred**  *Mezzo-Soprano*
b. Cleveland, Ohio, 1924:
She had her debut at Stuttgart in 1949. In 1951 she sang for the first time at the Metropolitan as Cherubino.

Carmen, Cherubino, Dorabella, Fyodor (*Boris Godunov*), Octavian, Orlovsky, Preziosilla (*La Forza del Destina*), Suzuki.

**Millöcker, Karl**  *Composer*
b. Vienna, 1842: d. there, 1899
Der Bettelstudent  Vienna  1882

**Mitropoulos, Dmitri**  *Conductor*
b. Athens, 1896: d. Milan, 1960
A famous symphony conductor who also conducted opera at the Metropolitan and elsewhere.

**Mitterwurzer, Anton**  *Baritone*
b. Sterzing, Germany, 1818: d. near Vienna, 1876
The first Wolfram, the first Kurnewal.

**Mödl, Martha**  *Soprano*
b. Nürnberg, 1912:
She made her debut as Dorabella in Düsseldorf in 1944.
Brünnhilde, Carmen, Composer (*Ariadne auf Naxos*), Dorabella, Princess Eboli, Isolde, Klytemnestra, Jocasta, Kundry, Lady Macbeth, Leonore (*Fidelio*), Magda (*The Consul*), Marie (*Wozzeck*), Octavian, Ortrud.

**Mohaupt, Richard**  *Composer*
b. Breslau, 1904: d. Reichenau, Austria, 1957

| | | |
|---|---|---|
| Die Wirtin von Pinsk | Dresden | 1938 |
| Die Bremer | | |
| Stadtmusikanten | Bremen | 1949 |
| Double Trouble | Louisville, Ky. | 1954 |

**Monaco, Mario Del**  *Tenor*
b. Florence, 1915:
He made his debut as Pinkerton in Milan in 1941, and as des Grieux at the Metropolitan in 1950.
Don Alvaro, Andrea Chénier, Canio, Dick Johnson, Enzo, Faust (*Mefistofele*), des Grieux, Don José, Luigi (*Il Tabarro*), Manrico, Mario Cavaradossi, Otello, Pinkerton, Radames, Samson.

**Mondonville, Jean Joseph Cassanea de**
*Composer*
b. Narbonne, France, 1711: d. Paris, 1772

| | | |
|---|---|---|
| Isbé | Paris | 1742 |
| Le Carnaval du Parnasse | „ | 1749 |

**Moniusko, Stanislaus** *Composer*
b. Minsk, 1820: d. Warsaw, 1872
Moniuszko wrote twenty operas.

| | | |
|---|---|---|
| Halka | Vilna | 1848 |
| Flis | Warsaw | 1858 |
| Der Paria | „ | 1869 |

**Monsigny, Pierre Alexandre** *Composer*
b. near St. Omer, France, 1729: d. Paris, 1817

| | | |
|---|---|---|
| Le Déserteur | Paris | 1769 |
| Rose et Colas | „ | 1764 |
| Le Faucon | „ | 1772 |
| La Belle Arsène | „ | 1775 |

**Montéclair, Michel Pinolet de**
*Composer*
b. Andelot, France, circa 1666: d. near Paris, 1737
A composer and a very early double-bass player.

| | | |
|---|---|---|
| Jephté | Opéra | 1732 |

**Monti, Toti dal** *Soprano*
(*Really* Antonietta Meneghal)
b. Treviso, Italy, 1893:
Cio-cio San, Gilda.

**Montemezzi, Italo** *Composer*
b. near Verona, 1875: d. 1952

| | | |
|---|---|---|
| Giovanni Gallurese | Turin | 1905 |
| Hellera | „ | 1909 |
| L'Amore dei Tre Re | La Scala | 1913 |
| La Nave | Milan | 1918 |
| La Notte di Zoraima | „ | 1931 |
| L'Incantesimo | NBC | 1943 |

**Monteux, Pierre** *Conductor*
b. Paris, 1875:
Celebrated conductor of symphony and opera; continued an active career in his eighties.

**Monteverdi, Claudio** *Composer*
b. Cremona, 1567: d. Venice, 1643

One of the greatest of opera composers. He spent the most productive part of his career in Venice. He is credited, with the invention of the pizzicato and the tremolo (not the vibrato) as orchestral techniques. Of his *Arianna*, only one *Lamento* remains, and it is one of the most beautiful melodies in all opera.

| | | |
|---|---|---|
| La Favola d'Orfeo | Mantua | 1607 |
| Arianna | „ | 1608 |
| Il Ballo delle Ingrate | „ | 1608 |
| Il Combattimento di Tancredi e Clorinda | Venice | 1624 |
| Proserpina Rapita | „ | 1630 |
| Il Ritorno d'Ulisse in Patria | „ | 1641 |
| Le Nozze di Enea con Lavinia | „ | 1641 |
| L'Incoronazione di Poppea | „ | 1642 |

**Moody, Fanny** *Soprano*
b. Redruth, Cornwall, 1866: d. near Dublin, 1945
Co-founder with her husband of the Moody-Manners Opera Company. She had married him in 1890.
Elisabeth, Elsa, Eva, Irene (*Rienzi*), Isolde, Kundry, Senta, Sieglinde.

**Moor, Emanuel** *Composer*
b. Hungary, 1862: d. 1931

| | | |
|---|---|---|
| Die Pompadour | Cologne | 1902 |
| Andreas Hofer | „ | 1902 |
| Hochzeitsglocken | Kassel | 1908 |

**Moore, Douglas** *Composer*
b. Cutchogue, N.Y., 1893:

| | | |
|---|---|---|
| The Headless Horseman | | 1936 |
| The Devil and Daniel Webster | New York | 1939 |
| The Emperor's New Clothes | „ | 1949 |
| Giants in the Earth | „ | 1951 |
| The Ballad of Baby Doe | Central City, Colo. | 1956 |

**Moore, Frank Ledlie** *Composer*
b. Cambridge, Mass., 1923:

A composer of dramas in music to his own libretti, and of music in all forms.

| The Anarchists | 1955 |
| John Brown | 1957 |
| Ryan | 1958 |
| Mine Host | 1960 |

**Moore, Grace** *Soprano*
b. Jellico, Tenn., 1901: d. Copenhagen, 1947
She made her debut at the Metropolitan as Mimi in 1928. She sang in many films.
Fiora, Louise, Manon, Mimi.

**Morel, Jean** *Conductor*
b. Abbeville, France, 1903:
He has been with the Metropolitan since 1956.

**Morelli, Carlo** *Baritone*
(*Really* Zanelli)
b. Valparaiso, Chile, 1897:
He sang at the Metropolitan from 1935 to 1940.
Barnaba, Manfredo (*L'Amore dei Tre Re*), Wolfram.

**Morena, Berta** *Soprano*
(*Really* Meyer)
b. Mannheim, 1878: d. Rottach Eggern, 1952
She made her debut as Agathe in Munich, 1898, and as Sieglinde at the Metropolitan in 1908.
Agathe, Brünnhilde, Elisabeth, Elsa, Eva, Isolde, Sieglinde.

**Mortari, Virgilio** *Composer*
b. near Milan, 1902:
He completed the unfinished opera L'Oca del Cairo, by Mozart, for performance in Salzburg, 1936.

| Secchi e Sberlecchi | Udine | 1927 |
| La Scuola delle Moglie | | 1930 |
| La Figlia del Diavolo | Milan | 1954 |

**Moscona, Nicola** *Bass*
b. Athens, 1907:
He made his debut at the Metropolitan in 1937 singing Ramfis.

Alvise, Arkel, Colline, Ferrando (*Il Trovatore*), Old Hebrew (*Samson et Dalila*), Oroveso, Ramfis, Sparafucile, Il Talpa (*Il Tabarro*).

**Moszkowski, Moritz** *Composer*
b. Breslau, 1854: d. Paris, 1925
He was famous as a pianist and a composer for the piano.

| Boabdil | Berlin | 1892 |

**Mottl, Felix** *Composer*
b. near Vienna, 1856: d. Munich, 1911
He put *Der Barbier von Bagdad* into its present form, and conducted the premiere of the first complete production of *Les Troyens*.

| Agnes Bernauer | Weimar | 1880 |
| Fürst und Sänger | Karlsruhe | 1893 |

**Mouret, Jean Joseph** *Composer*
b. Avignon, France, 1682: d. Charenton, 1738

| Ariane | Paris | 1717 |

**Moussorgsky**
See Mussorgsky

**Mozart, Wolfgang Amadeus**
*Composer*
b. Salzburg, Austria, 1756: d. Vienna, 1791
One of the most famous composers in every form of music in use in Europe, Mozart made changes in the technique of opera that are still basic today, and which infuse his own work with an excitement throughout every scene. Although he continued the practice of dry recitative, his sense of dramatic flow maintains our interest on a high level even in these passages. His arias almost always carry on the action of the play, rather than stopping it for the sake of the voice, and their musical character is always closely in tune with their dramatic purpose. He had studied with Haydn, and had himself given Beethoven a few lessons. In composing *Don Giovanni* Mozart worked very closely

with his librettist, and even spent a few days at cafes working out dramatic ideas with the famous Casanova. This, however, could hardly have been as instructive to Mozart, who was himself an experienced enchanter of court ladies, as it must have been pleasurable.

Although he was remarkably successful in opera and in concerts, Mozart died, at the age of thirty-five, penniless.

| | | |
|---|---|---|
| La Finta Semplice | Salzburg | 1769 |
| Bastien et Bastienne | Vienna | 1768 |
| L'Oca del Cairo | (Unfinished) | |
| Lo Sposo Deluso | " | |
| Mitridate | Milan | 1770 |
| Ascanio in Alba | " | 1771 |
| Il Sogno di Scipione | Salzburg | 1772 |
| Lucio Silla | Milan | 1772 |
| La Finta Giardiniera | Munich | 1775 |
| Il Re Pastore | Salzburg | 1775 |
| Zaïda | (Unfinished) | |
| Idomeneo | Munich | 1781 |
| Die Entführung aus dem Serail | Vienna | 1782 |
| Der Schauspieldirektor | Schönbrunn | 1786 |
| Le Nozze di Figaro | Vienna | 1786 |
| Don Giovanni | Prague | 1787 |
| Così fan Tutte | Vienna | 1790 |
| La Clemenza di Tito | Prague | 1791 |
| Die Zauberflöte | Vienna | 1791 |

**Muck, Karl**　　　　　　　*Conductor*
b. Darmstadt, 1859: d. Stuttgart, 1940
　Conductor of the Boston Symphony and of the Berlin Opera.

**Mugnone, Leopoldo**　　　*Conductor*
b. Naples, 1858: d. there, 1941
　He conducted the first performance of *Cavalleria Rusticana*.

**Müller, Maria**　　　　　　*Soprano*
b. Leitmoritz, Austria, 1898: d. Bayreuth, 1958
　She made her Metropolitan debut as Sieglinde in 1925.
　Helena (*Die Aegyptische Helena*),

Iphigénie (*Iphigénie en Tauride*), Jenufa, Marenka (*Prodaná Nevěsta*), Rezia, Senta, Sieglinde.

**Mullings, Frank**　　　　　　*Tenor*
b. Walsall, England, 1881:
　The first Apollo (*Alkestis* by Boughton).
　Apollo (*Alkestis*), Otello, Parsifal, Radames, Siegfried, Tannhäuser, Tristan.

**Munsel, Patrice**　　　　　*Soprano*
b. Spokane, Wash., 1925:
　She made her debut at the Metropolitan in 1943, the youngest debutante the Metropolitan ever had.
　Adele (*Die Fledermaus*), Gilda, Juliette, Lakmé, Lucia, Musetta, Rosina (*Il Barbiere di Siviglia*), Violetta, Zerlina (*Don Giovanni*).

**Muratore, Lucien**　　　　　*Tenor*
b. Marseilles, 1876: d. Paris, 1954
　He made his debut at the Opéra-Comique, in 1902, and at the Metropolitan in 1913.
　Faust (*Faust*), Don José, Rinaldo (*Armide*), Romeo.

**Murska, Ilma di**　　　　　*Soprano*
b. Croatia, 1836: d. Munich (*suicide*), 1889
　She made her debut at Florence in 1862.
　Amina, Astrifiamante, Constanze, Dinorah, Inez, Linda, Lucia, Martha, Senta.

**Mussorgsky, Modest**　　　*Composer*
b. near Pskov, 1839: d. St. Petersburg, 1881
　The greatest of the Russian composers of opera, one of the "Mighty Five." He is well known also in concerts for his piano piece, *Pictures at an Exhibition*.

| | | |
|---|---|---|
| Boris Godunov | St. Petersburg | 1874 |
| Khovantchina | " | 1885 |
| The Fair at Sorotchinsk | " | 1911 |
| Zhenitba | " | 1917 |

**Muzio, Claudia**　　　　　*Soprano*
b. Pavia, Italy, 1889: d. Rome, 1936

She had her debut at Arezzo in 1912 as Manon, and at the Metropolitan in 1916 as Tosca. She was the first Giorgetta (*Il Tabarro*).

Aida, Bertha (*Le Prophète*), Fiora, Giorgetta, Leonora (*La Forza del Destino*), Maddalena, Manon, Marguerite (*Mefistofele*), Norma, Tatyana, Tosca, Turandot, Violetta.

**Nabokov, Nicolas** *Composer*
b. near Minsk, R., 1903:
The Holy Devil   Louisville, Ky.   1958

**Nachbaur, Franz** *Tenor*
b. Giessen, Germany, 1830: d. Munich, 1902
The first Walther.
Adolar, Lohengrin, Mime, Walther.

**Napoli, Jacopo** *Composer*
b. Naples, 1911:

| | | |
|---|---|---|
| Il Malato Immaginario | Naples | 1939 |
| Miseria e Nobilità | „ | 1945 |
| Un Curioso Accidente | Bergamo | 1950 |
| Masaniello | La Scala | 1951 |

**Napravnik, Eduard F.** *Composer*
b. Bohemia, 1839: d. St. Petersburg, 1916
In St. Petersburg he became the chief conductor of the Imperial Opera where he led over three thousand performances.

| | | |
|---|---|---|
| Nizhegorotzy | St. Petersburg | 1869 |
| Harold | „ | 1886 |
| Dubrovsky | „ | 1895 |
| Francesca da Rimini | „ | 1902 |

**Nardini, Emilio** *Tenor*
b. Parma, 1823: d. Boulogne sur Mer, 1890
The first Vasco da Gama.

**Naumann, Johann Gottlieb** *Composer*
b. near Dresden, 1741: d. Dresden, 1801
He wrote twenty-four operas.

| | |
|---|---|
| La Clemenza di Tito | 1769 |
| Armida | 1773 |
| Amphion (*in Swedish*) | 1776 |
| Cora | 1780 |

**Nessler, Victor E.** *Composer*
b. Baldenheim, Alsace, 1841: d. Strasbourg, 1890

| | | |
|---|---|---|
| Der Rattenfänger von Hameln | Leipzig | 1879 |
| Der Trompeter von Säkkingen | „ | 1884 |
| Die Rose von Strassburg | Munich | 1890 |

**Neumann, František** *Composer*
b. Moravia, 1874: d. Brno, 1929
He not only wrote his own operas, but conducted most of the first performances of those by Janáček. From 1925 to 1929 he was director of the Czech National Opera.

| | | |
|---|---|---|
| Leyer und Schwert | | 1901 |
| Die Brautwerbung | Linz | 1901 |
| Liebelei | Frankfurt | 1910 |
| Herbststurm | Berlin | 1919 |
| Beatrice Caracci | Brno | 1922 |

**Nevada, Emma** *Soprano*
(*Née* Wixom)
b. Alpha, Calif., 1859: d. Liverpool, 1940
She made her debut as Amina in London in 1880.
Amina, Lucia, Mireille, Zora (*La Perle du Brésil*).

**Nevada, Mignon Marie** *Soprano*
b. Paris, 1886:
Daughter of Emma Nevada. She made her debut as Rosina in *Il Barbiere di Siviglia* in 1907.

**Nevin, Arthur Finley** *Composer*
b. Edgeworth, Pa., 1871: d. Sewickley, Pa., 1943
Nevin's best known work, *Poia*, survived only four performances.

| | | |
|---|---|---|
| Poia | Berlin | 1910 |
| A Daughter of the Forest | Chicago | 1918 |

**Neway, Patricia** *Soprano*
b.
The first Magda (*The Consul*). Always an organizer, in 1960 she formed her own opera company in New York.

Magda (*The Consul*), Marie (*Wozzeck*), Mother (*Amahl and the Night Visitors*), Mother (*Maria Golovin*), Nelly (*Wuthering Heights*), Santuzza.

**Nicholls, Agnes**　　　　*Soprano*
b. Cheltenham, England, 1877:
She made her debut in London as Dido (*Dido and Aeneas*), in 1895.

**Nicolai, Karl Otto Ehrenfried**
　　　　　　　　　　*Composer*
b. Königsberg, 1810: d. Berlin, 1849
The founder of the Berlin Philharmonic. He was organist of the Prussian Embassy at Rome, Kapellmeister in Vienna, and head of the Berlin Opera.

| | | |
|---|---|---|
| Rosmonda d'Inghilterra | Turin | 1838 |
| Il Templario | „ | 1840 |
| Odoardo e Gildippe | „ | 1841 |
| Il Proscrito | Milan | 1841 |
| Die Lustigen Weiber von Windsor | Berlin | 1849 |

**Nicolini**　　　　　　　*Tenor*
(*Originally* Ernest Nicolas)
b. Saint-Malo, France, 1834: d. Pau, 1898
He made his debut at the Opéra-Comique in 1857. In 1886 he married Patti.
Edgardo, Faust (*Faust*), Lohengrin, Raoul.

**Nielsen, Carl August**　　*Composer*
b. Funen, Denmark, 1865: d. Copenhagen, 1931
The most celebrated composer of Denmark, his symphonies are popular.

| | | |
|---|---|---|
| Saul and David | Copenhagen | 1902 |
| Maskarade | „ | 1906 |

**Nielsen, Ludolf**　　　　*Composer*
b. Nørre-Tvede, Denmark, 1876: d. Copenhagen, 1939

| | | |
|---|---|---|
| Isabella | Copenhagen | 1915 |
| Uhret (*The Clock*) | „ | 1920 |
| Lola | „ | 1920 |

**Niemann, Albert**　　　　*Tenor*
b. near Magdeburg, Germany, 1831: d. Berlin, 1917

He made his debut at Hanover in 1860 and at the Metropolitan, singing Siegmund, in 1886.
Florestan, John of Leyden, Joseph, Lohengrin, Parsifal, Raoul, Siegfried, Siegmund, Tannhäuser, Walther.

**Nikolaidi, Elena**　　　*Contralto*
b. Smyrna, Greece, 1914:
She made her debut in Vienna in 1936.

**Nilsson, Birgit**　　　　*Soprano*
b. Västra Karup, Sweden, 1921:
Brünhilde, Elektra, Elisabeth (*Tannhäuser*), Salome, Turandot (Puccini).

**Nilsson, Christine**　　　*Soprano*
b. near Vexiö, Sweden, 1843: d. Stockholm, 1921
She made her debut as Violetta in Paris, 1864. Her first appearance at the Metropolitan was the night that theater opened; she sang Marguérite. She sang the first Myrrha (*Sardanapale*).
Astrifiamante, Cherubino, Countess Almaviva (*Le Nozze di Figaro*), Desdemona, Elsa, Donna Elvira, Gioconda, Helen (*Mefistofele*), Lucia, Marguérite (*Faust*), Mignon, Myrrha (*Sardanapale*), Ophélie, Violetta.

**Nissen, Hans Hermann**　　*Baritone*
b. near Danzig, 1896:
Father (*Le Pauvre Matelot*), Hans Sachs, Orest (*Elektra*), Wotan.

**Nordica, Lillian**　　　　*Soprano*
(*Née* Norton-Gower)
b. Farmington, Maine, 1857: d. Java, 1914
She came out first in Milan as Donna Elvira, 1879. She first sang in New York in 1883 as Marguérite. Her Metropolitan debut was in 1890.
Aida, Amelia, Donna Anna, Brünnhilde, Elsa, Donna Elvira, Gilda, Gioconda, Isolde, Lucia, Marguérite (*Faust*), Ophélie, Philine, Selika, Susanna (*Le Nozze di Figaro*), Valentine (*Les Huguenots*), Violetta.

**Norena, Eide**       *Soprano*
(*Really* Kaja Hansen Eide)
b. Horten, Norway, 1884:
She made her debut at the Metropolitan
in 1933 as Mimi.
Desdemona, Gilda, Liù, Mimi.

**Noskowsky, Sigismund**    *Composer*
b. Warsaw, 1846: d. Wiesbaden, 1909

Livia Quintilla    Lemberg   1898
Wyrok          Warsaw   1907

**Nouguès, Jean**       *Composer*
b. Bordeaux, 1875: d. Auteil, 1932
His opera *Quo Vadis* had a spectacular
success.

Quo Vadis       Nice   1909

**Nourrit, Adolphe**       *Tenor*
b. Paris, 1802: d. Naples (*suicide*), 1839
After a debut as Pylade (*Iphigénie en
Tauride*) at the Opéra in 1821, Nourrit
sang the following roles for their first
performances:
Arnold (*Guillaume Tell*), Douglas (*Macbeth*), Eléazar, Masaniello, Raoul, Robert
le Diable, Stradella (by Niedermayer).

**Nourrit, Louis**       *Tenor*
b. Montpellier, 1780: d. Brunoy, 1831
The father of Adolphe Nourrit, and
famous as a singer himself. But he never
gave up his trade as a diamond merchant.

**Novák, Vitezslav**     *Composer*
b. Bohemia, 1870: d. Slovakia, 1949

Burgkobold      Prague   1915
A Night at Karlstein    „    1916
Lucerna           „    1923
Deduv Odkaz (*The
Grandfather's Heritage*)   Brno   1926

**Novello, Clara**       *Soprano*
b. London, 1818: d. Rome, 1908
A famous singer in concert and opera.
She made her debut in Padua in 1841, but
spent the greater part of her professional
career in England.

**Novotna, Jarmila**      *Soprano*
b. Prague, 1903:

A pupil of Destinn. She made her
debut in *La Traviata* at Prague, 1926. Her
first appearance in this country was at San
Francisco, 1939, when she sang Suzuki.
Cherubino, Euridice, Frasquita (*Der
Corregidor*), Freia, Marenka, Octavian,
Orlovsky, Pamina, Suzuki, Wife (*Le
Pauvre Matelot*).

**Ober, Margarete**
     *Soprano and Mezzo-soprano*
b. Berlin, 1885:
She made her debut at Frankfurt in 1906
singing Azucena, and at the Metropolitan
in 1913 as Ortrud.
Amneris, Azucena, Brangäne, Dalila,
Eglantine, Erda, Fidès, Fricka, Klytem-
nestra (*Iphigénie en Aulide*), Laura, Marina
Mnishek, Octavian, Ortrud, Waltraute,
Witch (*Hänsel and Gretel*).

**Oboussier, Robert**     *Composer*
b. Antwerp, 1900: d. Zürich (*murdered*),
1957
Amphitryon      Berlin   1951

**Offenbach, Jacques**    *Composer*
(*Really* Jacob Eberst)
b. Cologne, 1819: d. Paris, 1880
From 1855 to 1866 Offenbach was
manager of his own theater *Les Bouffes
Parisiens*. Things did not go well until
he brought out his hilarious *Orphée aux
Enfers* and became a success for life. His
most famous, but not his best, work, *Les
Contes d'Hoffmann*, was completed by
Bizet's friend Guiraud.

Orphée aux Enfers   Paris   1858
Geneviève de Brabant   „   1859
La Belle Hélène     „   1864
La Vie parisienne    „   1866
La Grande Duchesse de
Gérolstein       „   1867
La Périchole      „   1868
Les Contes
d'Hoffmann Opéra-Comique 1881

**Olczewska, Maria**     *Contralto*
b. near Augsburg, Germany, 1892:

She made her debut in Leipzig in 1920 and at the Metropolitan, singing Brangäne, thirteen years later.
Brangäne, Carmen, Herodias (*Salome*), Octavian.

**Ollone, Max d'**                    *Composer*
b. Besançon, France, 1875: d. Paris, 1959
A pupil of Massenet.

| | | |
|---|---|---|
| Le Retour | Angers | 1913 |
| Les Uns et les Autres | Paris | 1922 |
| L'Arlequin | „ | 1924 |
| Georges Dandin | „ | 1930 |
| La Samaritaine | „ | 1937 |

**Olsen, Ole**                    *Composer*
b. Hammerfest, Norway, 1850: d. Oslo, 1927
He wrote his own libretti. .

| | | |
|---|---|---|
| Stig Hvide | | 1876 |
| Stallo | | 1902 |
| Klippeøerne | | 1905 |
| Lajla | Oslo | 1908 |

**Onégin, Sigrid**                    *Contralto*
b. Stockholm, 1889: d. Magliaso, Switzerland, 1943
She made her debut as Carmen in Stuttgart in 1912, and as Amneris at the Metropolitan ten years later.
Amneris, Carmen, Dalila, Lady Macbeth.

**Orefice, Giacomo**                    *Composer*
b. Vicenza, 1865: d. Milan, 1922
Besides his original works, he arranged *La Favola d'Orfeo* for a production in Milan, 1909.

| | | |
|---|---|---|
| Mariska | Turin | 1889 |
| Consuelo | Bologna | 1895 |
| Il Gladiatore | Madrid | 1898 |
| Chopin | Milan | 1901 |
| Cecilia | Vicenza | 1902 |
| Mosè | Genoa | 1905 |
| Il Pane d'Altrui | Venice | 1907 |
| Radda | Milan | 1912 |

**Orff, Carl**                    *Composer*
b. Munich, 1895:

Orff has startled a good many audiences with his primitive-sounding music. He prefers harmonic simplicity to contrapuntal complexity. He is best known for his cycle of choral songs, *Carmina Burana*, to medieval texts.

| | | |
|---|---|---|
| Der Mond | Munich | 1939 |
| Die Kluge | Frankfurt | 1943 |
| Antigonae | Salzburg | 1949 |
| Oedipus Tyrannus | Stuttgart | 1959 |

**Osborn, Jane**                    *Soprano*
(*Really* Osborn-Hannah)
b. Wilmington, Ohio, 1873: d. New York, 1943
She made her debut at Leipzig in 1904 and sang Elisabeth in her Metropolitan debut in 1910.
Brünnhilde, Elisabeth, Elsa, Eva, Irene, Isolde, Senta.

**Ostrčil, Ottokar**                    *Composer*
b. near Prague, 1879: d. there, 1935

| | | |
|---|---|---|
| Vlasty Skon (*Vlasta's death*) | Prague | 1904 |
| Kunálovy Oči (*Kunala's eyes*) | „ | 1908 |
| Poupě (*The Bud*) | „ | 1911 |
| Legenda z Erinu (*Legend of Erin*) | Brno | 1921 |
| Honzovo Královstvi (*Johnny's Kingdom*) | „ | 1934 |

**Pacini, Giovanni**                    *Composer*
b. Catania, Italy, 1796: d. Pescia, 1867
He wrote nearly ninety operas. (*See* Piccini). *Saffo* was composed in twenty-eight days.

| | | |
|---|---|---|
| Saffo | Naples | 1840 |
| Medea | Palermo | 1843 |
| La Regina di Cipro | Turin | 1846 |

**Pacini, Leonardo**                    *Composer*
b. near Pistoia, Italy, 1885: d. Viareggio, 1937

| | | |
|---|---|---|
| Alla Muda | Viareggio | 1925 |
| Mirta | | |

**Pacius, Fredrik**                    *Composer*
b. Hamburg, 1809: d. Helsinki, 1891

He wrote the first Finnish opera.

| Kung Karlsjakt | Helsinki | 1852 |
| Lorelei | ,, | 1887 |

**Paderewski, Ignacy Jan**  *Composer*
b. Podolia, Poland, 1860: d. New York, 1941
A very famous pianist, and also a very famous Polish patriot. He became the first prime minister of the Polish Republic after World War I.

| Manru | Dresden | 1901 |

**Paër, Ferdinand**  *Composer*
b. Parma, 1771: d. Paris, 1839
He wrote over forty operas. His Leonora is on the same subject as Beethoven's *Fidelio*

| Camilla | Vienna | 1799 |
| Leonora | Dresden | 1804 |
| Le Maître de chapelle | Paris | 1821 |

**Pahissa, Jaime**  *Composer*
b. Barcelona, 1880:

| La Presó de Lleida | Barcelona | 1906 |
| Gala Plácida | ,, | 1913 |
| Marianella | ,, | 1925 |

**Paisiello, Giovanni**  *Composer*
b. Taranto, 1740: d. Naples, 1816
His operas were the mainstays of the Italian tradition until Rossini came along. His *Barbiere* is beginning to find a public again.

| Il Barbiere di Siviglia | St. Petersburg | 1782 |
| Il Re Teodoro | Vienna | 1784 |
| Nina, o La Pazza per Amore | Naples | 1788 |

**Palester, Roman**  *Composer*
b. Poland, 1907:

| The Living Stones | | 1944 |

**Palma, Athos**  *Composer*
b. Buenos Aires, 1891: d. Miramar, Argentina, 1951

| Nazdah | Buenos Aires | 1924 |
| Los Hijos del Sol | ,, | 1928 |

**Palmgren, Selim**  *Composer*
b. Björneborg, Finland, 1878: d. Helsinki, 1951
Best known for his piano pieces, Palmgren was also a conductor.

| Daniel Hjort | Åbo | 1910 |

**Panizza, Ettore**  *Composer*
b. Buenos Aires, 1875:
Famous as a conductor, he began at Covent Garden in 1907 and led performances there, at La Scala, at the Metropolitan and in Berlin.

| Il Fidanzato del Mare | Buenos Aires | 1897 |
| Medio evo Latino | Genoa | 1900 |
| Aurora | Buenos Aires | 1908 |
| Bisanzio | ,, | 1939 |

**Paolis, Alessio de**  *Tenor*
b.
The first to play the Philistine in *Samson et Dalila*.
Don Basilio (*Le Nozze di Figaro*), Borsa, Emperor Altoum, Figaro (*Il Barbiere di Siviglia*), Fool (*Wozzeck*), Gastone, Gherardo, Goro, Isèpo, Philistine (*Samson et Dalila*), Remondado, Schuisky, Spoletta, Valzacchi, Zorn.

**Papandopulo, Boris**  *Composer*
b. Honef am Rhein, Germany, 1906:

| Amphytrion | 1940 |
| Sunflower | 1942 |

**Parepa-Rosa, Euphrosyne**  *Soprano*
b. Edinburgh, 1836: d. London, 1874
She made her debut as Amina at Malta, 1853. In 1867 she married Carl Rosa.
Amina, Donna Anna, Camilla, Elsa, Elvira (*I Puritani*), Norma, Zerlina (*Fra Diavolo*), Zerlina (*Don Giovanni*).

**Parker, Horatio William**  *Composer*
b. Auburndale, Mass., 1863: d. Cedarhurst, N.Y., 1919
Parker won ten thousand dollars for each of his two operas, both of which are now nearly forgotten. The Metropolitan awarded him a prize for *Mona*;

the National Federation of Women's Clubs one for *Fairyland*.

| Mona | Metropolitan | 1912 |
| Fairyland | Los Angeles | 1915 |

**Parry, Joseph** *Composer*
b. Wales, 1841: d. Penarth, 1903

| Blodwen | Aberdare | 1878 |
| Virginia | „ | 1883 |
| Arianwen | Cardiff | 1890 |
| Sylvia | „ | 1895 |
| King Arthur | | 1897 |

**Pasquini, Bernardo** *Composer*
b. Tuscany, 1637: d. Rome, 1710
La Forza d'Amore
Dov' è Amore e Pietà                    1679

**Pasta, Giuditta** *Soprano*
b. near Milan, 1798: d. Blavio, near Como, 1865
The first Amina, the first Norma, Anna Bolena, and Niobe.

**Paton, Mary Anne** *Soprano*
b. Edinburgh, 1802: d. Chapelthorpe, 1864
The first Rezia. She was a harpist, pianist, and a violinist. In addition she also composed religious music. She made her operatic debut in London as Susanna (*Le Nozze di Figaro*), in 1822.
Agathe, Alice (*Robert le Diable*), Rezia, Susanna (*Le Nozze di Figaro*).

**Patti, Adelina** *Soprano*
b. Madrid, 1843: d. Brecknock, Wales, 1919
A most celebrated soprano. She made her debut as Amina in London, 1861, and as Lucia in New York, 1859. By 1882 she commonly received five thousand dollars (minimum) per performance.
Aida, Amina, Carmen, Dinorah, Gilda, Juliette, Lakmé, Lucia, Marguérite (*Faust*), Marie (*La Figlia del Reggimento*), Martha, Mireille, Ophélie, Rosina (*Il Barbiere di Siviglia*), Violetta, Zerlina (*Fra Diavolo*), Zerlina (*Don Giovanni*).

**Patzak, Julius** *Tenor*
b. Vienna, 1898:
He made his debut in Reichenberg, 1927, and in the United States at Cincinnati in 1954. He was the first Burgomeister in *Friedenstag*.
Burgomeister (*Friedenstag*), Florestan, Herod (*Salomé*), Midas (*Die Liebe der Danae*), Palestrina, Titus (*La Clemenza di Tito*).

**Pauly, Rosa** *Soprano*
b. Eperjes, Hungary, 1895:
She made her debut in Hamburg as Aida.
Aida, Elektra, Empress (*Die Frau ohne Schatten*), Káta Kabanová, Leonore (*Fidelio*), Marie (*Wozzeck*).

**Paumgartner, Bernhard** *Composer*
b. Vienna, 1887:
For the Salzburg performance in 1949 he arranged *La Clemenza di Tito*.
Rossini in Neapel          Zürich     1936

**Paur, Emil** *Conductor*
b. Bukovina, 1855: d. Mistek, Czechoslovakia, 1932
A conductor at the Metropolitan from 1900 to 1904.

**Pears, Peter** *Tenor*
b. Farnham, England, 1910:
He is generally associated with the operas of Benjamin Britten, having created the following roles: Peter Grimes, Male Chorus (*Rape of Lucretia*), Vere (*Billy Budd*), and Essex (*Gloriana*).
Male Chorus (*Rape of Lucretia*), Essex (*Gloriana*), Ferrando (*Così fan tutte*), Jenik (*Prodaná Nevěsta*), MacHeath (*The Beggar's Opera*), Oedipus, Peter Grimes, Vere (*Billy Budd*).

**Pederzini, Gianna** *Mezzo-Soprano*
b. Avio, 1908
Baba (*The Medium*), Carmen, Charlotte, Dido, Fedora, Kostelnicka (*Její Pastorkyňa*) Lady Macbeth (by Bloch), Mignon,

269

Princess (*Adriana Lecouvreur*), Rezia, Rosa (*L'Arlesiana*).

**Pedrell, Carlos** *Composer*
b. Minas, Uruguay, 1878: d. near Paris, 1941
The nephew of Felipe Pedrell.

| | | |
|---|---|---|
| Ardid de Amor | Buenos Aires | 1917 |
| Cuento de Abril | Madrid | 1924 |
| La Guitare | ,, | 1924 |

**Pedrell, Felipe** *Composer*
b. Tortosa, Spain, 1841: d. Barcelona, 1922

| | | |
|---|---|---|
| El último Abencerrage | Barcelona | 1874 |
| Quasimodo | ,, | 1875 |
| Los Pirineos (*trilogy*) | ,, | 1902 |
| La Celestina | | 1903 |

**Pedrollo, Arrigo** *Composer*
b. Near Vicenza, Italy, 1878:

| | | |
|---|---|---|
| Terra Promessa | Cremona | 1908 |
| Juana | | 1914 |
| La Veglia | Milan | 1920 |
| L'Uomo che Ride | Rome | 1920 |
| L'Amante in Trappola | Verona | 1936 |

**Peerce, Jan** *Tenor*
(*Really* Jacob Perelmuth)
b. New York, 1904:
He made his debut as the Duke in *Rigoletto*, Philadelphia, 1938. He first appeared at the Metropolitan as Alfredo in 1941.
Alfredo, Duke, Edgardo, Faust (*Mefistofele*), Mario Cavaradossi, Don Ottavio, Riccardo (*Un Ballo in Maschera*), Rodolfo, Turiddu.

**Pelemans, Willem** *Composer*
b. Antwerp, 1901:

| | |
|---|---|
| Le Juif Errant (*choral*) | 1932 |
| Flores et Blanchefleur (*choral*) | 1939 |
| Le Petit Soldat de Plomb | 1945 |

**Pelissier, Victor** *Composer*
b. (unknown)

Pelissier was a virtuoso of the horn and a composer for the theater.

| | | |
|---|---|---|
| Edwin and Angelina | New York | 1796 |
| Ariadne Abandoned by Theseus on the Isle of Naxos | ,, | 1797 |
| The Vintage | | 1799 |

**Pelletier, Wilfred** *Conductor*
b. Montreal, 1896:
Conductor at the Metropolitan since 1932, and conductor at San Francisco from 1921 to 1931. In 1925 he married Queena Mario, but divorced her in 1936 and married Rose Bampton a year later.

**Pepusch, Doctor John Christopher** *Composer*
b. Berlin, 1667: d. London, 1752
It was he who collected and (partly) composed the music for the perdurable *Beggar's Opera* in 1728, *The Wedding* (1729), and *Polly* (1729). He also founded, in those ancient times, an Academy of Ancient Music. He was a thorn in the side of his fellow German, Handel, whose operas had to compete against *The Beggar's Opera*.

**Peragallo, Mario** *Composer*
b. Rome, 1910:

| | | |
|---|---|---|
| Ginevra degli Almieri | Rome | 1937 |
| Lo Stendardo di S. Giorgio | | 1941 |
| La Gita in Campagna | Milan | 1954 |

**Pergolesi, Giovanni Battista** *Composer*
b. near Ancona, Italy, 1710: d. Pozzuoli, 1736
At least one opera commonly attributed to Pergolesi, *Il Maestro di Musica*, is now considered to be the work of someone else. His most famous work is the *Stabat Mater*.

| | | |
|---|---|---|
| Lo Frate innamorato | Naples | 1732 |
| Il Prigioniero Superbo | ,, | 1733 |
| La Serva Padrona (*intermezzo to the above*) | ,, | 1733 |
| Adriano in Siria | ,, | 1734 |

Livietta e Tracollo
(*intermezzo to the above,*
*also called* La Finta
Polacca)      Naples   1734
L'Olimpiade      Rome   1735

**Peri, Jacopo**      *Composer*
b. Florence, 1561: d. there, 1633
A member of the Florentine Camerata
(*see* Bardi and Corsi). It was his *Dafne*
which was chosen for performance as its
first opera. His *Euridice* was performed
for the marriage of Maria de' Medici to
Henri IV of France. Peri also composed
the recitatives for Monteverdi's lost
*Arianna*.

| | | |
|---|---|---|
| Dafne | Florence | 1597 |
| Euridice | „ | 1600 |
| Adone | | 1620 |
| La Precedenza delle | | |
| Dame | Florence | 1625 |
| La Flora (*with* | | |
| Gagliano) | „ | 1628 |

**Périer, Jean**      *Tenor*
b. Paris, 1869: d. there, 1954
The first Pelléas.

**Perini, Flora**      *Contralto*
b. Rome, 1887:
The first Princess (*Suor Angelica*), the
first Pepa (*Goyescas*). She made her debut
at La Scala in 1908 and at the Metropolitan in 1915.

**Perlea, Jonel**      *Conductor*
b. Ograda, Rumania, 1900:
Conductor of the Bucharest Opera
from 1934 to 1944, of the Metropolitan
from 1949, and of the Connecticut
Symphony Orchestra since 1955.

**Perrin, Pierre**      *Librettist*
(*Called* L'Abbé Perrin.)
b. Lyons, 1616: d. Paris, 1675
With Cambert he won the first patent
to establish the Académie Royale de
Musique (Opéra) in 1668, but lost it to
Lully in 1672. Perrin wrote the libretto to

the first French Opera, *La Pastorale*, and to
*Pomone* and *Ariane* (all by Cambert).

**Perron, Karl**      *Baritone*
b. Palatinate, 1858: d. Dresden, 1928
A famous Amfortas, he sang the first
Jokanaan, the first Orest (*Elektra*), and the
first Baron Ochs.

**Pertile, Aureliano**      *Tenor*
b. Montagnana, 1885: d. 1952
The first Nerone (*by Mascagni*).
Fra Diavolo, Faust (*Mefistofele*), des
Grieux (*Manon*), Julien, Lionel, Loris,
Mario Cavaradossi, Maurizio, Nerone (*by
Mascagni*), Osaka (*Iris*), Otello, Paolo,
Pinkerton, Radames, Rodolfo.

**Peschka-Leutner, Minna**      *Soprano*
(*Née* Leutner)
b. Vienna, 1839: d. Wiesbaden, 1890
Agathe, Aida, Alice (*Robert le Diable*),
Almira (*Almira*, by Handel), Eglantine,
Isabel, Marguerite of Valois.

**Peters, Roberta**      *Soprano*
b. New York, 1930:
On very short notice she made her
debut at the Metropolitan in 1950 as
Zerlina in *Don Giovanni*. She married
Robert Merrill in 1952 but was later
divorced.
Adele (*Die Fledermaus*), Arline, Despina,
Gilda, Queen of the Night, Rosina (*Il
Barbiere di Siviglia*), Shepherd (*Tann-
häuser*), Sophie (*Der Rosenkavalier*), Su-
sanna (*Le Nozze di Figaro*), Zerlina (*Don
Giovanni*).

**Petersen, Wilhelm**      *Composer*
b. Athens, 1890: d. Darmstadt, 1957
Der Goldne Topf    Darmstadt   1941

**Petrassi, Goffredo**      *Composer*
b. near Rome, 1904:

| | | |
|---|---|---|
| Il Cordovano | La Scala | 1949 |
| La Morte dell' Aria | Rome | 1950 |

**Petrella, Enrico**      *Compose*
b. Palermo, 1813: d. Genoa, 1877

| Marco Visconti | Naples | 1854 |
| Ione (*after* The Last Days | | |
| of Pompeii) | Milan | 1858 |
| La Contessa d'Amalfi | Turin | 1864 |
| Giovanni II di Napoli | Naples | 1869 |
| I Promessi Sposi | Lecco | 1869 |

**Petrelli, Eleanora**                    *Soprano*
(*Née* Wigström)
b. Simtuna, Sweden, 1835: d. Chicago,
1904
A pupil of Viardot-Garcia.

**Petrov, Ossip Afanassievitch**          *Bass*
b. Elizavetgrad, Russia, 1807: d. St.
Petersburg, 1878
He was the first to sing Varlaam in a
concert performance of the Inn scene from
*Boris Godunov* before the opera had been
accepted by the officials. He was the first
Ivan Susanin, the first Russlan, and the
first Miller in Dargomyzhsky's *Russalka*.
He made his debut as Sarastro at St.
Petersburg in 1830.

**Pfitzner, Hans**                        *Composer*
b. Moscow, 1869: d. Salzburg, 1949

| Palestrina | Munich | 1917 |
| Der Arme Heinrich | Mainz | 1895 |

**Philidor, François André**             *Composer*
b. Dreux, France, 1726: d. London, 1795
The composer made his living as a
professional chess-player.

| Le Maréchal Ferrant | Comique | 1761 |
| Sancho Pança dans | | |
| son Isle | ,, | 1762 |
| Tom Jones | ,, | 1765 |
| Ernelinde (*Sandomir*) | ,, | 1767 |

**Phillipps, Adelaide**                  *Contralto*
b. Stratford on Avon, 1833: d. Karlsbad,
1882
She was a protegée of Jenny Lind. She
made her debut as Rosina (*Il Barbiere di
Siviglia*) at Milan in 1854 and as Azucena
in New York, 1856.

**Piccini, Niccolò**                      *Composer*
b. Bari, 1728: d. Passy, 1800

This unfortunate composer was made
the unwilling battle banner of the warriors
against the Gluckists. When they prevailed upon him to write an *Iphigénie en
Tauride* to contest Gluck's position (which
failed miserably), the war fizzled. Piccini
wrote one hundred thirty-nine operas,
ten of them during the single year 1761.

| La Cecchina | | 1760 |
| La Buona Figliuola | Rome | 1760 |
| Roland | Paris | 1778 |
| Iphigénie en Tauride | ,, | 1781 |
| Didon | ,, | 1783 |

**Pickhardt, Ione**                       *Composer*
b. New York, 1900:

| Moira | | 1931 |

**Pick-Mangiagalli, Riccardo**           *Composer*
b. Bohemia, 1882: d. Milan, 1949
The first opera to be broadcast by radio
anywhere was his *L'Ospite Inatteso*.

| Basi e Bote | Rome | 1927 |
| Casanova a Venezia | La Scala | 1929 |
| L'Ospite Inatteso | Milan Radio | 1931 |
| Il Notturno Romantico | Rome | 1936 |

**Pierné, Henri Constant Gabriel**
                                          *Composer*
b. Metz, 1863: d. Ploujean, 1937
A pupil of Massenet and Franck.

| La Coupe Enchantée | Royan | 1895 |
| Vendée | Lyons | 1897 |
| La Fille de Tabarin | Opéra- | |
| | Comique | 1901 |
| On ne Badine pas | | |
| avec l'Amour | ,, | 1910 |
| Sophie Arnould | ,, | 1927 |

**Pierson, Henry Hugo**                   *Composer*
(*Originally* Pearson)
b. Oxford. 1815: d. Leipzig, 1873

| Leila | Hamburg | 1848 |
| Contarini | ,, | 1872 |

**Pijper, Willem**                        *Composer*
b. Zeist, Holland, 1894: d. Leidschendam,
1947

| Halewijn | Amsterdam | 1933 |
| Merlijn (*unfinished*) | | 1946 |

**Pinza, Ezio** *Bass*
b. Rome, 1892: d. Stamford, Conn., 1957
Widely known not only for opera, but for his part in the Broadway show *South Pacific*. He made his operatic debut in Rome, 1920, as King Marke and his Metropolitan debut in 1926 as Pontifex Maximus (*La Vestale*). He sang the first Nerone (by Boito).

Archibaldo, Don Basilio (*Il Barbiere di Siviglia*), Boris Godunov, King Marke, Don Giovanni, Mefistofele (*Mefistofele*), Méphistophélès (*Faust*), Nerone (*Boite*), Nilakantha, Pontifex Maximus (*La Vestale*), Tcherevik (*The Fair at Sorotchinsk*).

**Pipkov, Lubomir** *Composer*
b. Lovetch, Bulgaria, 1904:
Nine Brothers of Yanina   Sofia   1937
Momtchil              ,,     1948

**Pizzeti, Ildebrando** *Composer*
b. Parma, 1880:

| | | |
|---|---|---|
| Fedra | Milan | 1915 |
| Débora e Jaéle | ,, | 1922 |
| Fra Gherardo | ,, | 1928 |
| Lo Straniero | Rome | 1930 |
| Orsèolo | Florence | 1935 |
| L'Oro | Milan | 1947 |
| Vanna Lupa | Florence | 1949 |
| Ifigenia | ,, | 1951 |
| Cagliostro | Milan | 1953 |
| La Figlia di Jorio | Naples | 1954 |
| L'Assassinio nel Cattedrale | Milan | 1958 |

**Plançon, Pol Henri** *Bass*
b. Ardennes, 1854: d. Paris, 1914
He made his debut at Lyons in 1877, at the Opéra, as Méphistophélès (*Faust*), in 1883, and at the Metropolitan in the same role ten years later.

Alvise, Balthasar (*La Favorita*), St. Bris, Capulet, Escamillo, Friar Laurence, Henry the Fowler, High Priest (*Aida*), Hermann (*Tannhäuser*), King (*Aida*), Méphistophélès (*La Damnation de Faust*), Méphistophélès (*Faust*), Oroveso, Phanuel (*Hérodiade*), Plunkett, Pogner.

**Planquette, Robert** *Composer*
b. Paris, 1848: d. there, 1903
Les Cloches de Corneville   Paris   1877
Rip van Winkle                 1882

**Polacco, Giorgio** *Conductor*
b. Venice, 1875:
Conductor at San Francisco, at the Metropolitan and at Chicago.

**Poleri, David** *Tenor*
b.
Alfredo, Mario Cavaradossi, Don José, Rodolfo, Turiddu.

**Polignac, Armande de** *Composer*
b. Paris, 1876:
A pupil of Fauré and D'Indy.
Morgane
L'Hypocrite Sanctifié

**Ponchielli, Amilcare** *Composer*
b. near Cremona, 1834: d. Milan, 1886

| | | |
|---|---|---|
| I Promessi Sposi | Cremona | 1856 |
| La Gioconda | Milan | 1876 |
| Il Figliuolo Prodigo | ,, | 1880 |
| Marion Delorme | ,, | 1885 |

**Poniatowski, Joseph** *Composer*
(*Fully* Prince Joseph Michael Xavier Francis John Poniatowski)
b. Rome, 1816: d. Chiselhurst, 1873
Ruy Blas            Lucca   1842
La Contessina     Paris   1868

**Pons, Lily** *Soprano*
b. Draguignon, France, 1904:
She made her debut in Mulhouse, singing Lakmé, and at the Metropolitan in 1931 as Lucia.

Gilda, Lakmé, Linda di Chamounix, Lucia, Marie (*La Figlia del Reggimento*), Rosina (*Il Barbiere di Siviglia*), Violetta.

**Ponselle, Carmela** *Soprano*
b. Schenectady, N.Y., 1892:
She made her debut at the Metropolitan as Amneris in 1925.

**Ponselle, Rosa** *Soprano*
(*Carmela Ponselle's sister*)
b. Meriden, Conn., 1897:

She made her debut at the Metropolitan as Leonora (*La Forza del Destino*) in 1918 opposite Caruso.

Aida, Carmen, Elisabetta (*Don Carlos*), Fiora, Gioconda, Leonora (*La Forza del Destino*), Margared (*Le Roi d'Ys*), Rachel, Rezia, Santuzza, Selika, Violetta.

**Ponte, Lorenzo da**  *Librettist*
b. Ceneda, near Venice 1749: d. New York, 1838
A very colorful poet, responsible for the librettos of some of the most famous operas. He was professor of rhetoric at Treviso until banished for speaking against the government there. He became laureate at Venice until banished in 1779. From 1782 to 1792 he worked in Vienna, where he created librettos for the Imperial Theater and for Mozart. After that he tried Paris and London. Arriving in New York in 1803 he dealt in tea, tobacco and drugs to make a living, but failing in this he took to teaching Italian. Again in Sunbury, Pennsylvania, he tried business as a manufacturer of liquors, but failed again. He taught Italian at Columbia College, now Columbia University. His famous libretti are: *Le Nozze di Figaro, Don Giovanni*, and *Così fan Tutte*.

**Poot, Marcel**  *Composer*
b. near Brussels, 1901:
A pupil of Dukas.
Moretus                           1943

**Porpora, Nicçolò Antonio**  *Composer*
b. Naples, 1686: d. there, 1768.
A famous singing teacher, and Handel's chief rival in London. He wrote 44 operas.
Siface                            1726

**Porrino, Ennio**  *Composer*
b. Sardinia, 1910:
Gli Orazi              Milan  1941

**Poulenc, Francis**  *Composer*
b. Paris, 1899:
One of "Les Six."

Les Gendarme Incompris           1920
Les Mamelles de    Opéra-
  Tirésias         Comique  1947
Les Dialogues des
  Carmélites       La Scala 1957

**Pratella, Francesco Balilla**  *Composer*
b. Romagna, 1880: d. Ravenna, 1955
Lilia                  Luga    1905
La Sina d'Uargoun
  (*his own libretto*)   Bologna  1909
L'Aviatore Dro
  (*his own libretto*)   Lugo    1920
Fabiano                Bologna  1939

**Pratt, Silas Gamaliel**  *Composer*
b. Addison, Vt., 1846: d. Pittsburgh, 1916
His niche in the hall of fame is due to what may be an apochryphal story: it is said that when he met Wagner in Germany the following conversation took place: Wagner: "I hear that you are the Richard Wagner of America." Pratt: "Then, Herr Wagner, you must be the Silas G. Pratt of Germany."
Zenobia           Chicago  1883
Triumph of Columbus         1892

**Price, Leontyne**  *Soprano*
b.
She made her name singing Bess in 1952. She first sang opera in 1955 as Tosca, on television. Her stage debut came in San Francisco as the Mother Superior in *Dialogues des Carmelites*.
Aida, Cio-Cio San, Donna Anna, Bess, Leonora (*Il Travatore*), Liù (Puccini's *Turandot*), Mother Superior, Pamina, Tosca.

**Prohaska, Felix**  *Conductor*
b. Vienna, 1912:
He conducted at Graz, Duisberg, and Strasbourg before going to Vienna in 1945.

**Prokofiev, Sergey**  *Composer*
b. near Ekaterinoslav, Russia, 1891: d. Moscow, 1953

He is famous for the musical fairy tale for narrator and orchestra, *Peter and the Wolf*. His best known opera, after a comedy by Carlo Gozzi, is *The Love for Three Oranges*.

| | | |
|---|---|---|
| Maddalena | | 1913 |
| The Flaming Angel | | 1919 |
| The Love for Three Oranges | Chicago | 1921 |
| The Gambler | Brussels | 1929 |
| War and Peace | Leningrad | 1946 |

**Provenzale, Francesco** *Composer*
b. Naples, 1627: d. there, 1704
A composer of operas, oratorios and other works. It is sometimes said that he "invented" the da capo aria.

**Puccini, Giacomo** *Composer*
(*Full Name* Giacomo Antonio Domenico Michele Secondo Maria Puccini)
b. Lucca, 1858: d. Brussels, 1924
One of the greatest opera composers after Verdi, and a very successful exponent of the style *verismo*. He was a pupil of Ponchielli.

| | | |
|---|---|---|
| Le Villi | Milan | 1884 |
| Edgar | La Scala | 1889 |
| Manon Lescaut | Turin | 1893 |
| La Bohème | ,, | 1896 |
| Tosca | Rome | 1900 |
| Madama Butterfly | La Scala | 1904 |
| La Fanciulla del West | Metropolitan | 1910 |
| La Rondine | Monte Carlo | 1917 |
| Il Trittico | Metropolitan | 1918 |
| Il Tabarro | | |
| Suor Angelica | | |
| Gianni Schicchi | | |
| Turandot | La Scala | 1928 |

(*Completed by Franco Alfano.*)

**Puente, Giuseppe del** *Baritone*
b. Naples, 1841: d. New York, 1900
He sang Valentin in the opening production of the Metropolitan.

Alfio, Barnaba, Escamillo, Figaro (*Il Barbiere di Siviglia*), Lescaut (*Manon*), De Nevers, Valentin (*Faust*).

**Purcell, Henry** *Composer*
b. London, 1658: d. Westminister, 1695
This greatest of English composers wrote several masques, but only one opera, and that was first produced not in a theater but in a boarding school for girls. He was a pupil of Pelham Humphries, who was, in turn, a pupil of Lully.

| | | |
|---|---|---|
| Dido and Aeneas | Chelsea | 1689 |

**Pylkkänen, Tauno** *Composer*
b. Helsinki, 1918:

| | |
|---|---|
| Jaakio Ilkka | 1937 |
| Bathsheba Saarenmaalla | 1940 |
| Mare ja hänen poikansa | 1945 |
| Simo Hurtta | 1948 |
| Suden Morsian | 1950 |
| Varjo | 1952 |

**Quagliati, Paolo** *Composer*
b. Chioggia, 1555: d. Rome, 1628

| | | |
|---|---|---|
| Carro di Fedeltà d'Amore | Rome | 1606 |

**Quinault, Phillipe** *Librettist*
b. Paris, 1635: d. there, 1688
Librettist for most of the operas of Lully.

**Raaff, Anton** *Tenor*
b. near Bonn, 1714: d. Munich, 1797
The first Idomeneo.

**Raalte, Albert van** *Conductor*
b. Amsterdam, 1890: d. there, 1952
Conductor at Leipzig and at the Hague until 1922, then an independent conductor.

**Rabaud, Henri** *Composer*
b. Paris, 1873: d. there, 1949

| | | |
|---|---|---|
| La Fille de Roland | Opéra-Comique | 1904 |
| Le premier glaive | Beziers | 1908 |
| Marouf | Opéra-Comique | 1914 |
| Antoine et Cléopâtre | | 1917 |
| L'Appel de la Mer | Leipzig | 1924 |
| Le Miracle des Loups | Comique | 1924 |
| Rolande et le Mauvais Garçon | Opéra | 1934 |

Le Jeu de l'amour
et du Hasard    Monte Carlo  1954

**Rachmaninov, Sergey**   *Composer*
b. near Novgorod, 1873: d. Beverly Hills,
Calif. 1943
Best known as a pianist, he was also
director of the Moscow Opera from 1904
to 1906.

Aleko    Moscow  1893
Francesca da Rimini   ,,  1906
The Miserly Knight   ,,  1906

**Radford, Robert**   *Bass*
b. Nottingham, England, 1874: d. London, 1933
A founder of the British National Opera
Company.
Boris Godunov, Commendatore (*Don Giovanni*), Fasolt, Louise's Father, Hunding, Méphistophélès (*Faust*), Osmin, Sarastro.

**Rains, Leon**   *Bass*
b. New York, 1870: d. Los Angeles, 1954
He made his debut at the Metropolitan
in 1908.

**Raisa, Rosa**   *Soprano*
b. Bialystok, Poland, 1893:
She made her debut at Parma in 1913,
and at Chicago the following year. She sang
the first Asteria (*Nerone*, Boito), and the
first Turandot.
Aida, Asteria (*Nerone*, Boito), Elena,
Francesca, Rachel, Turandot, Valentine
(*Les Huguenots*).

**Rameau, Jean Philippe**   *Composer*
b. Dijon, 1683: d. Paris, 1764
Rameau is frequently called the father
of harmony, for his treatise which was the
first on that subject.

Hippolyte et Aricie    Opéra  1733
Castor et Pollux    ,,  1737
Dardanus    ,,  1739

**Rangström, Ture**   *Composer*
b. Stockholm, 1884: d. there, 1947

Kronbruden    Stuttgart  1919
Middelalderlig    Stockholm  1921
Gilgamesh (*completed
by Fernström*)    ,,  1952

**Rankin, Nell**   *Mezzo-soprano*
b.
Amneris, Marina Mnishek, Carmen.

**Rankl, Karl**   *Conductor*
b. near Vienna, 1898:
Starting at Graz in 1932, he has conducted at Prague, Covent Garden, and in
Glasgow, among other places.

**Rappold, Marie**   *Soprano*
b. London, 1873: d. Hollywood, 1957
She sang Sulamith (*Die Königin von
Saba*) in her first appearance at the Metropolitan in 1905.
Aida, Desdemona, Elizabeth, Elsa, Euridice, Inez, Iphigénie (*Iphigénie en Tauride*),
Marguérite (*Faust*), Micaela, Princess
(*Lobetanz*), Sulamith, Venus.

**Rathaus, Karol**   *Composer*
b. Tarnopol, Poland, 1895: d. New York,
1954
Fremde Erde
(*Strange World*)    Berlin  1930

**Rauzzini, Venanzio**   *Composer*
b. Rome, 1747: d. Bath, England, 1810
Piramo e Tisbe    1775
Le Ali d'Amore    1776

**Ravel, Maurice**   *Composer*
b. Ciboure, France, 1875: d. Paris, 1937
Famous everywhere for his orchestral
*Bolero*.
L'Heure Espagnole   Opéra-
Comique  1911
L'Enfant et les
Sortilèges    Monte Carlo  1925

**Rebikov, Vladimir**   *Composer*
b. Siberia, 1866: d. Crimea, 1920
Rebikov is best known for his little
piano pieces for children.
In the Thunderstorm   Odessa  1894
The Christmas Tree   Moscow  1903

**Reed, Herbert Owen**  *Composer*
b. Odessa, Missouri, 1910:
Michigan Dream                    1955

**Reeves, Sims**  *Tenor*
(*Really* John Sims Reeves)
b. Woolwich, England, 1818: d. Worthing, 1900
A famous Captain MacHeath. He made his debut at Newcastle on Tyne as Rodolfo in *La Sonnambula* in 1839, and at La Scala as Edgardo in 1846.
Carlo (*Linda di Chamounix*), Dandini, Edgardo, Florestan, Sir Huon, MacHeath, Ottocar (*Der Freischütz*), Rodolfo (*La Sonnambula*).

**Refice, Licinio**  *Composer*
b. near Rome, 1883: d. Rio de Janeiro, 1954
Cecilia                    Rome   1934
Margherita da Cortona   Milan   1938

**Reichmann, Theodor**  *Bass*
b. Rostock, 1849: d. Marbach, 1903
The first Amfortas.
Amfortas, Creon (*Medea*), Dutchman, Hans Sachs, Pizzarro, Trompeter von Säkkingen, Wotan.

**Reinecke, Carl Heinrich Carsten**
*Composer*
b. Altona, Germany, 1824: d. Leipzig, 1910
An all-round musician, he was a pianist, a conductor and a famous teacher.
König Manfred      Weisbaden  1867
Auf hohen Befehl   Hamburg    1886

**Reiner, Fritz**  *Conductor*
b. Budapest, 1888:
Beginning at his birthplace in 1911, he subsequently conducted at Dresden, Cincinnati, San Francisco, Covent Garden, Pittsburgh, Chicago and the Metropolitan. In 1953 he became conductor of the Chicago Symphony Orchestra.

**Reiner, Karel**  *Composer*
b. Žatec, Czechoslovakia, 1910:

A pupil of Alois Hába.
Tale of an Enchanted Song         1949

**Reiss, Albert**  *Tenor*
b. Berlin, 1870: d. Nice, 1940
He made his debut at the Metropolitan in 1901 singing both the Sailor and the Shepherd in *Tristan und Isolde*. In the productions of *Der Schauspieldirektor* and *Bastien et Bastienne* in 1916, he both sang and directed.
Bastien (*Bastien et Bastienne*), Jacquino, Mozart (*Der Schauspieldirektor*), Sailor and Shepherd (*Tristen und Isolde*).

**Reizenstein, Franz**  *Composer*
b. Nuremberg, 1911:
A pupil of Paul Hindemith.
Men Against the Sea               1949
Anna Kraus                        1952

**Renan, Émile**  *Baritone*
b.
Alcindoro, Dr. Bartolo (*Le Nozze di Figaro*), Benoit, Court Attendant (*Der Prozess*), Dancairo, Doctor (*Wozzeck*), Masetto, Marquis d'Obigny, Oscar (*Regina*), Pantalone (*The Love for Three Oranges*), Remondado, Sacristan, Schaunard, Secret Police Agent (*The Consul*), Sharpless, Willem (*Der Prozess*), Yamadori.

**Renaud, Maurice Arnold**  *Baritone*
b. Bordeaux, 1861: d. Paris, 1933
He made his debut in Brussels in 1883.
Beckmesser, Escamillo, Germont (wearing eighteenth-century costume), Don Giovanni, Hamlet, Karnac (*Le Roi d'Ys*), Méphistophélès (*La Damnation de Faust*), Nelusko, de Nevers, Rigoletto, Valentin (*Faust*), Wolfram.

**Resnik, Regina**  *Soprano*
b. New York, 1922:
After a debut in Mexico City in 1943 she came out at the Metropolitan in *Il Trovatore* the following year. She sang the first Delilah (*The Warrior*), and the first Baroness in *Vanessa*.

Baroness (*Vanessa*), Delilah (*The Warrior*), Ellen (*Peter Grimes*), Donna Elvira, Leonore (*Fidelio*), Magdalene, Marcellina Marina Mnishek, Musetta, Rosalinda, Sieglinde, Venus.

**Resphighi, Ottorino**     *Composer*
b. Bologna, 1879: d. Rome, 1936
One of the principal Italian modernists; he made one of the standard arrangements of *La Favola d'Orfeo*. He is best known for his orchestral pieces *The Pines of Rome* and *The Fountains of Rome*.

| | | |
|---|---|---|
| Re Enzo | Bologna | 1905 |
| Belfagor | Milan | 1923 |
| La Campana | | |
| Sommersa | Hamburg | 1927 |
| Lucrezia | Milan | 1937 |

**Reszke, Edouard de**     *Bass*
b. Warsaw, 1853: d. Garnek, Poland,1917
Brother of Jean de Reszke. He made his debut singing Amonasro under Verdi's direction at Paris, 1876. He first appeared in the United States as Henry the Fowler in Chicago, 1891, and at the Metropolitan as Friar Laurence the same year.
Almaviva (*Le Nozze di Figaro*), Amonasro, Basilio, St. Bris, Count (*La Sonnambula*), Diego (*L'Africana*), Hagen, Hans Sachs, Henry the Fowler, Hunding, Indra (*Le Roi de Lahore*), King of Egypt, Kurnewal, Friar Laurence, Leporello, Marcel, King Marke, Mefistofele (*Mefistofele*), Méphistophélès (*Faust*), Nilakantha, Oberthal, Ramfis.

**Reszke, Jean de**     *Tenor*
b. Warsaw, 1850: d. Nice, 1925
Brother of Edouard de Reszke and a famous teacher. At first a baritone, he made his debut as Alfonso in *La Favorita* at Venice in 1874. As a tenor he first sang in Madrid, 1879, in the title role of Robert le Diable. With his brother he appeared in Chicago as Lohengrin in his first appearance in this country, 1891. He sang the first Cid, and the first stage performance of Faust (*La Damnation de Faust*).

Alfonso (*La Favorita*), Almaviva (*Il Barbiere di Siviglia*), Le Cid, Faust (*La Damnation de Faust*), Faust (*Faust*), Figaro (*Il Barbiere di Siviglia*), Don Giovanni, des Grieux (*Manon*), John of Leyden, St. John (*Hérodiade*), Don José, Lohengrin, Fra Melitone, de Nevers, Otello, Don Ottavio Radames, Raoul, Riccardo, Robert le Diable, Romeo, Tristan, Valentin (*Faust*), Walther, Werther.

**Reszke, Josephine de**     *Soprano*
b. Warsaw, 1855: d. there, 1891
Sister of the two brothers. She made her debut as Ophélie at the Opéra in 1875.
Aida, Marguérite, Ophélie.

**Rethberg, Elisabeth**     *Soprano*
(*Really* Sattler)
b. Saxony, 1894:
The first Helena (*Aegyptische Helene*). She made her debut at the Metropolitan in 1922, singing Aida.
Agathe, Aida, Cio-Cio San, Desdemona, Elisabeth, Fiora, Helene (*Die Aegyptische Helene*), Iris, Marenka, Sieglinde.

**Reusse-Belce, Luise**     *Soprano*
b. Vienna, 1860: d. Aibach, Germany, 1945
She was the first woman stage manager at Nuremberg in 1913. She made her debut as Elsa at Karlsruhe in 1881, and at the Metropolitan in 1902.

**Reutter, Hermann**     *Composer*
b. Stuttgart, 1900:

| | | |
|---|---|---|
| Saul | Baden-Baden | 1928 |
| Der Verlorene Sohn | Stuttgart | 1929 |
| Doktor Johannes | | |
| Faust | Frankfurt | 1936 |
| Odysseus | ,, | 1942 |
| Don Juan und Faust | Stuttgart | 1950 |
| Ballade der | | |
| Landstrasse | ,, | 1952 |
| The Bridge of | Frankfurt | |
| San Luis Rey | Radio | 1954 |
| Die Witwe von | | |
| Ephesus | Cologne | 1954 |

**Rey, Cemal Reschid** *Composer*
b. Istanbul, 1904:
Notable Turkish composer, who studied in Paris.

| | |
|---|---|
| Faire sans Dire | 1920 |
| Yann Marek | 1922 |
| Sultan Cem | 1923 |
| Zeybeck | 1926 |

**Reyer, Louis Étienne Ernest** *Composer*
(*Originally* Rey)
b. Marseilles, 1823: d. Hyères, 1909

| | | |
|---|---|---|
| Sigurd | Brussels | 1884 |
| La Statue | Paris | 1861 |
| Salammbô | Brussels | 1890 |

**Reznieck, Emil Nicolaus von** *Composer*
b. Vienna, 1860: d. Berlin, 1945

| | | |
|---|---|---|
| Donna Diana | Prague | 1894 |
| Till Eulenspiegel | Karlsruhe | 1902 |
| Ritter Blaubart | Darmstadt | 1920 |
| Holofernes | Berlin | 1923 |
| Spiel oder Ernst | Dresden | 1930 |
| Der Gondoliere des Dogen | Stuttgart | 1931 |

**Ricci, Luigi** *Composer*
b. Naples, 1805: d. Prague, 1859

| | | |
|---|---|---|
| Chiara di Rosemberg | Milan | 1831 |
| Crispino e la Comare | Venice | 1850 |

**Richter, Hans** *Conductor*
b. Raab, Hungary, 1843: d. Bayreuth, 1916
He conducted the first performance of *Siegfried*.

**Rieti, Vittorio** *Composer*
b. Alexandria, Egypt, 1898:

| | | |
|---|---|---|
| Orfeo | | 1928 |
| Teresa nel Bosco | Venice | 1934 |
| Don Perlimplin | Urbana, Ill. | 1952 |
| The Pet Shop | New York | 1958 |

**Righini, Vincenzo** *Composer*
b. Bologna, 1756: d. there, 1812
Like many of his contemporaries, he not only composed but also conducted and sang.

| | | |
|---|---|---|
| Selva Incantata | | 1802 |
| Gerusalemme Liberata | | 1802 |
| Il Convietato di Pietra (*Don Giovanni*) | Vienna | 1777 |

**Rimsky-Korsakov, Nicolai** *Composer*
b. near Novgorod, 1844; d. near St. Petersburg, 1908
Rimsky-Korsakov was one of the most prolific composers of his time in Russia. But he was also a tireless editor and advocate of the works of others. It was he who brought Moussorgsky's masterpiece, *Boris Godunov*, the fame which it now has by reorchestrating and editing it in detail. He performed the same service for *Prince Igor* by Borodin. He is well known for one of his orchestral pieces, the orchestral fairy tale *Scherherazade*.

| | | |
|---|---|---|
| Pskovityanka (*The Maid of Pskov*) | St. Petersburg | 1873 |
| Maiskaya Notch (*May Night*) | ,, | 1880 |
| Snyegurotchka (*Snow* Maiden) | ,, | 1882 |
| Mlada | ,, | 1892 |
| Notch pered Rozhdestrom (*The Night before Christmas*) | ,, | 1895 |
| Sadko | Moscow | 1898 |
| Mozart i Salieri | ,, | 1898 |
| Boyarynia Vera Sheloga | ,, | 1898 |
| Tsarskaya Neviesta (*The Tsar's Bride*) | ,, | 1899 |
| Tsar Sultan | ,, | 1900 |
| Servilia | St. Petersburg | 1902 |
| Kaschey Bezmertny (*Kaschey the Immortal*) | Moscow | 1902 |
| Pan Voyevoda (*The Commander*) | St. Petersburg | 1904 |
| Kitezh | ,, | 1907 |
| Le Coq d'Or | Moscow | 1909 |

**Rinuccini, Ottavio** *Librettist*
b. Florence, 1562: d. there, 1621
The author of the first operas, *Dafne*, *Euridice* and *Arianna*. He was, of course, a most influential member of the Florentine Camerata (*see* Bardi and Corsi).

**Rivier, Jean** *Composer*
b. Villemonble, France, 1896:
Vénitienne      Paris   1937

**Rocca, Lodovico** *Composer*
b. Turin, 1895:
| | | |
|---|---|---|
| In Terra di Leggenda | Milan | 1933 |
| Il Dibuk | ,, | 1934 |
| La Morte di Frine | ,, | 1937 |
| Monte Ivnor | Rome | 1939 |
| L'Uragano | Milan | 1952 |

**Rogatis, Pascual de** *Composer*
b. Teora, Italy, 1881:
| | | |
|---|---|---|
| Amfion y Zeto | Buenos Aires | 1915 |
| Huémac | ,, | 1916 |
| La Novia del Hereje | ,, | 1935 |

**Roger, Gustave Hippolyte** *Tenor*
b. near Paris, 1815: d. there, 1879
The first John of Leyden. He made his debut at the Opéra-Comique in 1838, but his operatic career was cut short when he lost his right arm in a hunting accident and was forced to retire from the stage.

**Roger-Ducasse, Jean Jules Aimable**
*Composer*
b. Bordeaux, 1873: d. near there, 1954
A pupil of Fauré.
Cantegril    Opéra-Comique   1931

**Rogers, Bernard** *Composer*
b. New York, 1893:
| | | |
|---|---|---|
| The Marriage of Aude | Rochester, N.Y. | 1931 |
| The Warrior | Metropolitan | 1947 |
| The Veil | Bloomington, Ind. | 1950 |

**Rogers, Clara Kathleen** *Soprano*
(*Née* Barnett)
b. Cheltenham, England, 1844: d. Boston, 1931

She made her debut as Isabella in *Robert le Diable*, Turin 1863. She came out in New York ten years later.

**Roland-Manuel, Alexis** *Composer*
(*Really* Lévy)
b. Paris, 1891:
| | | |
|---|---|---|
| Isabelle et Pantalon | Paris | 1922 |
| Le Diable Amoureux | | 1929 |

**Romani, Felice** *Librettist*
b. Genoa, 1788: d. Riviera, 1865
He is said to have written nearly one hundred libretti. Among the best known are: *La Sonnambula*, *Norma*, *L'Elisir d'Amore*, *Lucrezia Borgia*, *Il Turco in Italia*, and *Il Pirata*.

**Ronconi, Giorgio** *Baritone*
b. Milan, 1810: d. Madrid, 1890
Don Basilio (*Il Barbiere di Siviglia*), Belcore, Enrico, Figaro (*Il Barbiere di Siviglia*), Don Giovanni, Riccardo (*I Puritani*), Rigoletto, Tasso.

**Rooy, Anton van** *Bass*
b. Rotterdam, 1870: d. Munich, 1932
This famous basso made his debut in Bayreuth in 1897 and at the Metropolitan the following year as Wotan.
Dutchman, Escamillo, Hans Sachs, Jokanaan, Kurnewal, Valentin (*Faust*), Wolfram, Wotan.

**Ropartz, Guy** *Composer*
b. Guingamp, France, 1864: d. there, 1955
Le Pays      Nancy   1912

**Rorem, Ned** *Composer*
b. Richmond, Ind., 1923:
| | | |
|---|---|---|
| A Childhood Miracle | New York | 1952 |
| The Robbers | ,, | 1958 |

**Rosa, Carl August** *Conductor*
(*Originally* Rose)
b. Hamburg, 1842: d. Paris, 1889
Founder of the Carl Rosa Opera Company. In 1867 he married Euphrosyne Parepa.

**Roselius, Ludwig** *Composer*
b. Kassel, 1902:
Doge und
  Dogaressa    Dortmund  1928
Godiva         Nuremberg  1933
Gudrun         Graz  1939

**Rosenberg, Hilding** *Composer*
b. Bosjökloster, Sweden, 1892:
Resan till America
  (*Voyage to*
  *America*)    Stockholm  1932
Marionettes    ,,  1939

**Rosenstock, Joseph** *Conductor*
b. Cracow, 1895:
Beginning in Darmstadt in 1922, he has conducted in Wiesbaden, Mannheim, Tokyo, New York City and Cologne.

**Rossi, Giulio** *Bass*
b. Rome, 1865: d. Milan, 1931
He made his debut at Parma in 1887 and at the Metropolitan in 1908.

**Rossi, Luigi** *Composer*
b. Foggia, 1597: d. Rome, 1653
He produced the first Italian opera in Paris.
Le Mariage d'Orphée et Euridice

**Rossi-Lemeni, Nicola** *Bass*
b. Constantinople, 1922:
The first Tomasso Becket, he first appeared in the United States at San Francisco in 1951, as Boris Godunov.
Abbot (*La Forza del Destino*), Archibaldo, Don Basilio (*Il Barbiere di Siviglia*), Boris Godunov, Sir George (*I Puritani*), Don Giovanni, Guillaume Tell, Macbeth (by Bloch), Mefistofele, Oroveso, Selim, Tomasso Becket, Uberto (*La Serva Padrona*).

**Rossini, Gioacchino Antonio** *Composer*
b. Pesaro, Italy, 1792: d. Paris, 1868
The son of the town trumpeter. This genius of opera retired as a composer at the age of thirty-seven and did not write another note for the stage for the rest of his long life.

| | | |
|---|---|---|
| Tancredi | Venice | 1813 |
| L'Italiana in Algeri | ,, | 1813 |
| Aureliano in Palmira | Milan | 1813 |
| Il Turco in Italia | ,, | 1814 |
| Elisabetta, Regina d'Inghilterra | Naples | 1815 |
| Torvaldo e Dorliska | Rome | 1815 |
| Il Barbiere di Siviglia | ,, | 1816 |
| Otello | Naples | 1816 |
| La Cenerentola | Rome | 1817 |
| La Gazza Ladra | Milan | 1817 |
| Armida | Naples | 1817 |
| Mosè in Egitto | ,, | 1818 |
| Semiramide | Venice | 1823 |
| Le Siège de Corinthe | Paris | 1826 |
| Guillaume Tell | Opéra | 1829 |

**Roswaenge, Helge** *Tenor*
b. Copenhagen, 1897:
Ivan Susanin, Florestan, Oberon, Tamino.

**Rota, Nino** *Composer*
b. Milan, 1911:
Ariodante    Parma  1942
I Due Timidi    1950

**Rothier, Léon** *Baritone*
b. Reims, 1874: d. New York, 1951
He made his debut as Jupiter in *Philémon et Baucis* at the Opéra-Comique, then appeared at the Metropolitan for the first time in 1910 as Méphistophélès (*Faust*).
Barbe-Bleue, Comte des Grieux, Jupiter (*Philémon et Baucis*), Méphistophélès (*Faust*), Nilakantha.

**Rothmüller, Marko** *Baritone*
b. Yugoslavia, 1908:
Jokanaan, Macbeth, Scarpia, Wozzeck.

**Rousseau, Jean Jacques** *Composer*
b. Geneva, 1712: d. near Paris, 1778
Famous as a philosopher, Rousseau was also a music theorist and composer.
Les Muses Galantes    1745
Le Devin du
  Village    Fontainebleau  1752

**Rousseau, Marcel August**  *Composer*
(*Professional name* Samuel-Rousseau)
b. Paris, 1882: d. there, 1955

| | | |
|---|---|---|
| Tarass Boulba | Paris | 1919 |
| Le Hulla | „ | 1923 |
| Le Bon Roi Dagobert | „ | 1927 |
| Kerkeb | „ | 1951 |

**Roussel, Albert Charles**  *Composer*
b. Tourcoing, France, 1869: d. Royan 1937

| | | |
|---|---|---|
| Le Testament de la Tante Caroline | Olomouc, Czechoslovakia | 1936 |

**Roze, Marie Hippolyte**  *Soprano*
(*Née* Ponsin)
b. Paris, 1846: d. near there, 1926
She made her debut at the Opéra-Comique as Marie (by Hérold) in 1865.
Carmen, Elsa, Leonore (*Fidelio*), Manon, Marguérite (*Faust*), Marie (by Hérold).

**Rubini, Giovanni Battista**  *Tenor*
b. near Bergamo, 1794: d. there 1854
The first Arturo (*I Puritani*), he made his debut at Pavia in 1814.
Arturo (*I Puritani*), Otello (by Rossini), Don Ottavio.

**Rudolf, Max**  *Conductor*
b. Frankfurt, 1902:
He has conducted in Germany, Prague and at the Metropolitan. In 1958 he was appointed conductor of the Cincinnati Symphony Orchestra.

**Ruffo, Titta**  *Baritone*
(*Really* Ruffo Titta)
b. Pisa, 1877: d. Florence, 1953
One of the great baritones of all time, whom many consider to have possessed the largest voice ever heard on the operatic stage. He made his debut in Rome in 1898 as the Herald in *Lohengrin*, and his American debut in Philadelphia in 1912 as Rigoletto. He first appeared at the Metropolitan in 1922, singing Figaro in the *Il Barbiere di Siviglia*.

**Rysanek, Leonie**  *Soprano*
b. Vienna
She made her debut in Innsbrück, Austria.
Agathe, Aida, Ariadne (*Ariadne auf Naxos*), Brünnhilde, Danae, Elisabeth of Valois, Empress (*Die Frau ohne Schatten*), Gilda, Lady Macbeth.

**Sabata, Victor de**  *Composer*
b. Trieste, 1892:
He is best known as a conductor, at Monte Carlo and La Scala.

| | | |
|---|---|---|
| Il Macigno | La Scala | 1917 |

**Sack, Erna**  *Soprano*
b. Berlin, 1906:
Famous for her extraordinary range which included the C above high C. She appeared in concert in New York in 1937 and 1955.

**Saint-Saëns, Charles Camille**  *Composer*
b. Paris, 1835: d. Algiers, 1921
A composer in all forms, not excluding music for films (silent films with an orchestra in the pit). He is best known for his orchestral *Danse Macabre*, and the poetic cello piece, *Le Cygne*, from the orchestral suite *Le Carnaval des Animaux*.

| | | |
|---|---|---|
| La Princesse Jaune | Paris | 1872 |
| Le Timbre d'Argent | „ | 1877 |
| Samson et Dalila | Weimar | 1877 |
| Étienne Marcel | Lyons | 1879 |
| Henry VIII | Paris | 1883 |
| Proserpine | „ | 1887 |
| Ascanio | „ | 1890 |
| Phryné | „ | 1893 |
| Les Barbares | „ | 1901 |
| Hélène | Monte Carlo | 1904 |
| L'Ancêtre | „ | 1906 |
| Déjanire | „ | 1911 |

**Saléza, Albert**  *Tenor*
b. near Bayonne, 1867: d. Paris, 1916
He made his debut as Mylio (*Le Roi d'Ys*) at the Opéra-Comique, 1888.
Le Cid, Faust (*Faust*), Don José, Mylio (*Le Roi d'Ys*), Otello, Romeo, Siegmund.

**Salieri, Antonio** *Composer*
b. Legnano, 1750: d. Vienna, 1825
One of Beethoven's teachers, and a teacher of Schubert and Liszt. He wrote thirty-nine operas.

| | | |
|---|---|---|
| La Grotto di Trionfonio | Vienna | 1785 |
| Tarare | Opéra | 1787 |

**Salmhofer, Franz** *Composer*
b. Vienna, 1900:

| | | |
|---|---|---|
| Die Dame in Traum | Vienna | 1935 |
| Iwan Tarassenko | ,, | 1938 |
| Das Werbekleid | ,, | 1946 |

**Saltzmann-Stevens, Minnie** *Soprano*
b. Bloomington, Ill., 1878:
A famous Brünnhilde and Kundry.
Brünnhilde, Kundry, Sieglinde.

**Saminsky, Lazare** *Composer*
b. Odessa, 1882: d. Port Chester, N.Y., 1959
A pupil of Rimsky-Korsakov, and a specialist in Jewish liturgical music.

| | | |
|---|---|---|
| The Vision of Ariel | | 1916 |
| Gagliarda of a Merry Plague | New York | 1925 |
| The Daughter of Jephta | | 1929 |
| Julian the Apostate Caesar | | 1938 |

**Sammarco, Mario** *Baritone*
b. Palermo, 1873: d. Milan, 1930
The first Gérard (*Andrea Chénier*). He made his debut at Milan, 1894. In 1905 he came out as Scarpia at Covent Garden, and in 1908 as Tonio in his first New York appearance.
Alvise, Falstaff (*Falstaff*), Gérard (*Andrea Chénier*), Gil (*Il Segreto di Susanna*), Don Giovanni, Iago, Orfeo (*La Favola d'Orfeo*), Rafaele, Rigoletto, Scarpia, Tonio.

**Sanderson, Sybil** *Soprano*
b. Sacramento, Calif., 1865: d. Paris, 1903
The first Thaïs, and the first Phryné (by Saint-Saëns). She made her Metropolitan debut in 1895 as Manon.

**Sandi, Luis** *Composer*
b. Mexico City, 1905:

| | | |
|---|---|---|
| Carlota | Mexico City | 1948 |

**Santley, Charles** *Baritone*
b. Liverpool, 1834: d. near London, 1922
A pupil of Manuel García. Gounod wrote two of his most famous airs, *Avant de quitter ces lieux* and *Dio Possente*, for Santley.
Almaviva (*Le Nozze di Figaro*), Caspar, Fra Diavolo, Doctor Grenvil (*La Traviata*), Dutchman, Herr Fluth, Hoël, de Nevers, Peter the Great, Valentin (*Faust*).

**Sargent, Harold Malcolm Watts**
*Conductor*
b. London, 1895:
He conducted the first performance of *Hugh the Drover*.

**Sarti, Giuseppe** *Composer*
b. Faenza, 1729: d. Berlin, 1802
Sarti remains audible on the opera stage principally because of Mozart's quotation of an aria from his *I Due Litiganti* in *Don Giovanni*.

| | | |
|---|---|---|
| Il Re Pastore | Venice | 1753 |
| I Due Litiganti | Milan | 1782 |
| Armida e Rinaldo | St. Petersburg | 1786 |

**Sass, Marie** *Soprano*
(*Really* Marie Saxe)
b. Ghent, 1838: d. St. Perine, 1907
The first Elisabeth (*Don Carlos*), and the first Selika.
Elisabeth (*Don Carlos*), Elisabeth (*Tannhäuser*), Donna Anna, Selika.

**Sauguet, Henri** *Composer*
b. Bordeaux, 1901:

| | | |
|---|---|---|
| Le Plumet du Colonel | Paris | 1924 |
| La Contrebasse | ,, | 1932 |
| La Chartreuse de Parme | ,, | 1939 |
| La Gageuse Imprévue | ,, | 1944 |
| Les Caprices de Marianne | Aix-en-Provence | 1954 |

**Saville, Frances** *Soprano*
b. San Francisco, 1862: d. Burlingame, Calif., 1935
She made her debut at Brussels in 1892. Three years later she appeared at the Metropolitan for the first time, singing Juliette.

**Sayao, Bidu** *Soprano*
b. Rio de Janeiro, 1902:
A pupil of Jean de Reszke. She made her debut at the Metropolitan in 1937 as Manon.
Gilda, Juliette, Manon, Marguérite (*Faust*), Mélisande, Mimi, Nedda, Norina (*Don Pasquale*), Serpina, Susanna (*Le Nozze di Figaro*).

**Saygun, Ahmed Adnam** *Composer*
b. Izmir, Turkey, 1907:
A pupil of Vincent d'Indy; he composed operas on Turkish subjects.

| | | |
|---|---|---|
| Tas Babek | Ankara | 1934 |
| Keren | ,, | 1953 |

**Scalchi, Sofia** *Contralto*
b. Turin, 1850: d. Rome, 1922
One of the company in the Metropolitan's opening season, 1883. She made her debut at Mantua in 1866, singing Ulrica. In 1868 she came out at Covent Garden as Azucena.
Azucena, La Cieca, Frédéric (*Mignon*), Martha (*Faust*), Pierotte (*Linda di Chamounix*), Semiramide, Siebel, Ulrica, Vania (*Ivan Susanin*).

**Scaria, Emil** *Bass*
b. Graz, Austria, 1838: d. Blasewitz, 1886
The very first to sing Gurnemanz, there having been two singers for the role in opening performances of *Parsifal*.
Bertram, St. Bris, Escamillo, Gurnemanz, Hans Sachs, Marcel, Wotan.

**Scarlatti, Alessandro** *Composer*
b. Palermo, Sicily, 1660: d. Naples, 1725
The founder of the Neapolitan school of opera. He is said to have made the

first use of accompanied recitatives in 1693 in his opera *Teodora Augusta*. In all he turned out one hundred fifteen operas.

| | | |
|---|---|---|
| Olimpia Vendicata | Naples | 1685 |
| Teodora Augusta | Rome | 1693 |
| Il Tigrane | Naples | 1715 |
| Il Trionfo dell'Onore | ,, | 1718 |

**Schack, Benedict** *Tenor*
(*Original spelling Žak*)
b. Bohemia, 1758: d. Munich, 1826
The first Tamino. He not only sang but also composed some operas himself.
Count Almaviva (*Le Nozze di Figaro*), Don Ottavio, Tamino.

**Schalk, Franz** *Conductor*
b. Vienna, 1863: d. Edlach, 1931
He conducted at the Metropolitan from 1898 to 1899, then went to Berlin, and later to Vienna.

**Scharwenka, Xaver** *Composer*
b. Samter, Germany, 1850: d. Berlin, 1924
Famous as a composer for piano and for orchestra.

| | | |
|---|---|---|
| Mataswintha | Weimar | 1896 |

**Scheidemantel, Karl** *Baritone*
b. Weimar, 1859: d. there, 1923
He wrote a new text for *Così fan Tutte*, after Calderón, produced in Dresden in 1909 as *Die Dame Kobold*.
Amfortas, Dutchman, Don Fernando (*Fidelio*), Hans Heiling, Hans Sachs, Herald (*Lohengrin*), Klingsor, Kothner, Kurnewal, Wolfram.

**Scherman, Thomas** *Conductor*
b. New York, 1917:
In 1947 he organized the Little Orchestra Society of New York, and has performed many otherwise forgotten operatic works in concert form with that group.

**Schibler, Armin** *Composer*
b. Kreuzlingen, Switzerland, 1920:

| | | |
|---|---|---|
| Der Spanische | | |
| Rosenstock | Bern | 1950 |

Der Teufel im Winterpalais 1953
Das Bergwerk von Falun 1953
Die Füsse im Feuer Zürich 1955

**Schick, George** *Conductor*
b. Prague, 1908:
He made his debut at the Metropolitan conducting *Rigoletto*.

**Schick, Margarete Luise** *Soprano*
(*Née* Hanel)
b. Mainz, 1773: d. Berlin, 1809
Susanna (*Le Nozze di Figaro*), Zerlina (*Don Giovanni*).

**Schikaneder, Emanuel Johann**
*Librettist*
b. Straubing, Austria, 1751: d. Vienna, 1812
The subject of Mozart's *Der Schauspieldirektor*. With the help of Gieseke, he completed the libretto for *Die Zauberflöte*. He had been an actor, and had even played Hamlet. A lover of comic parts, he was the first Papageno. It was Schikaneder, as a manager, who commissioned Beethoven's *Fidelio*.

**Schillings, Max von** *Composer*
b. Düren, Germany, 1868: d. Berlin, 1933
Chiefly known for his opera *Mona Lisa*, he also was active as conductor and opera director.
Mona Lisa Stuttgart 1915

**Schipa, Tito** *Tenor*
b. Lecce, 1889:
The first Ruggero (*La Rondine*). He made his debut in Chicago in 1920. Twelve years later he first appeared at the Metropolitan as Nemerino, a part for which he was famous.
Fra Diavolo, Duke, Ernesto (*Don Pasquale*), Federico (*L'Arlesiana*), Fritz, des Grieux(*Manon*), Nemerino, Don Ottavio, Ruggero, Werther, Wilhelm.

**Schippers, Thomas** *Conductor*
b. Kalamazoo, Mich., 1930:
He has conducted opera at the New York City Center, beginning in 1951, and at the Metropolitan since 1955.

**Schiuma, Alfredo** *Composer*
b. Buenos Aires, 1885:

| | | |
|---|---|---|
| Amy Robsart | Buenos Aires | 1920 |
| La Sirocchia | „ | 1922 |
| Tabaré | „ | 1925 |
| Las Virgenes del Sol | „ | 1939 |
| La Infanta | „ | 1941 |

**Schlusnus, Heinrich** *Baritone*
b. Braubach, Germany, 1888: d. Frankfurt, 1952
Famous as Amfortas and as Montforte (*I Vespri Siciliani*).

**Schmedes, Erik** *Tenor*
b. near Copenhagen, 1868: d. Vienna, 1931
He made his debut at Wiesbaden in 1891 singing the Herald in *Lohengrin*. In 1908 he came out at the Metropolitan as Siegmund.
Herald (*Lohengrin*), Palestrina, Parsifal, Pedro (*Tiefland*), Siegmund, Tannhäuser, Tristan.

**Schmidt, Franz** *Composer*
b. Pressburg, 1874: d. near Vienna, 1939

| Notre Dame | Vienna | 1914 |
|---|---|---|
| Fredigundis | Berlin | 1922 |

**Schnorr von Carolsfeld, Ludwig** *Tenor*
b. Munich, 1836: d. Dresden, 1865
The first Tristan, playing opposite his wife. Forty-one days after the première he died. He was also a pianist, a poet and a painter.
Lohengrin, Naphtali, Robert le Diable, Tristan.

**Schnorr von Carolsfeld, Malwina**
*Soprano*
b. Copenhagen, 1832: d. Karlsruhe, 1904
In 1865 she sang the first Isolde, opposite her husband. Later she became a famous teacher of singers.

**Schoeck, Othmar** *Composer*
b. Brunnen, Switzerland, 1886: d. Zürich, 1957

Don Ranudo de
Colibrados Zürich 1919
Das Wandbild Halle 1921
Venus Zürich 1922
Penthesilea Dresden 1927
Massimilla Doni „ 1937
Das Schloss Dürande Berlin 1943

**Schoemaker, Maurice** *Composer*
b. near Brussels, 1890:
Swane 1933

**Schoenberg, Arnold** *Composer*
b. Vienna, 1874: d. Los Angeles, 1951
One of the most influential musical minds of the twentieth century, creator of the twelve-tone method of composition (known also as the dodecaphonic system), in which all principal themes are constructed on a basic series of twelve different notes. One of his best known works is *Verklärte Nacht* (*Transfigured Night*).
Von Heute auf
Morgen Frankfurt 1930

**Schöffler, Paul** *Baritone*
b. Dresden, 1897:
This famous Hans Sachs made his New York debut as Jokanaan at the Metropolitan in 1949.
Hans Sachs, High Priest (*Alceste*), Jokanaan, Jupiter (*Die Liebe der Danae*), Orest (*Elektra*).

**Schorr, Friedrich** *Bass*
b. Nagyvárad, Hungary, 1888: d. Farmington, Conn., 1953
He made his debut at Chicago in 1911, but it was thirteen years before he made his first appearance at the Metropolitan as Wolfram.
Altair, Amfortas, Dutchman, Hanns Sachs, Jokanaan, Orest (*Elektra*), Wolfram, Wotan.

**Schott, Anton** *Tenor*
b. Swabia, 1846: d. Stuttgart, 1913
He made his debut as Max in *Der Freischütz*. In 1884 he appeared for the first

time at the Metropolitan, singing Tannhäuser.
Benvenuto Cellini, Florestan, Max (*Der Freischütz*), Rienzi, Siegmund, Tannhäuser.

**Schreker, Franz** *Composer*
b. Monaco, 1878: d. Berlin, 1934
Der Ferne Klang (*The
Distant Sound*) Frankfurt 1912
Die Gezeichneten
(*The Stigmatized*) „ 1918
Der Schatzgräber (*The
Treasure Hunter*) „ 1920

**Schröder-Devrient, Wilhelmine**
*Soprano*
b. Hamburg, 1804: d. Coburg, 1860
The first Adriano (*Rienzi*), the first Senta, and the first Venus. She made her debut as Pamina in Vienna, 1822.
Adriano (*Rienzi*), Agathe, Amina, Desdemona, Iphigénie (*Iphigénie en Aulide*), Leonore (*Fidelio*), Marie (*Barbe-Bleue* by Grétry), Norma, Pamina, Senta, Venus.

**Schubert, Franz Peter** *Composer*
b. Vienna, 1797: d. there, 1828
The great composer of German *Lieder*.
Alfonso und Estrella Weimar 1854
Der Häusliche Krieg Frankfurt 1861
Fierrebras Karlsruhe 1897

**Schuch, Ernst von** *Conductor*
b. Graz, 1846: d. Dresden, 1914
The first to conduct *Feuersnot, Salome, Elektra* and *Der Rosenkavalier*.

**Schumann, Elisabeth** *Soprano*
b. Merseburg, Germany, 1885: d. New York, 1952
She made her debut at Hamburg in 1910, and at the Metropolitan, singing Sophie, in 1914. She was especially known for her singing of the works of Bach and Richard Strauss.
Donna Anna, Constance, Ilia (*Idomeneo*), Marzelline, Sophie (*Der Rosenkavalier*).

**Schumann, Robert Alexander**
*Composer*
b. Zwickau, Saxony, 1810: d. near Bonn, 1856
The celebrated composer, creator of the romantic style in piano compositions, songs and symphonies. He died insane.
Genoveva              Leipzig  1850

**Schumann-Heink, Ernestine**   *Contralto*
(*Née* Rössler)
b. Lieben, Czeckoslovakia, 1861: d. Hollywood, 1936
The first Klytemnestra (*Elektra*); and therein lies a story: she came away after that first night completely annoyed and disgusted with what she thought was a harsh, unmusical and unrewarding role.
She made her debut as Azucena at Dresden in 1878, as Erda at Covent Garden in 1892 and as Ortrud at Chicago in 1898 and at the Metropolitan the following year. For years after she had retired she made a ritual of singing the hymn *Silent Night* over the air on Christmas Eve.
Azucena, Brangäne, Carmen, The Countess (*Der Trompeter von Säkkingen*), Erda, Fides, Fricka, Klytemnestra, Ortrud, Waltraute.

**Schütz, Heinrich**           *Composer*
b. Köstritz, Germany, 1585: d. Dresden, 1672
The great predecessor of Bach, best known for his organ works and his numerous *Sacred Concerts*. His *Dafne* was the first German opera. It had a text by Opitz after Rinuccini, but the music is lost.
Dafne                 Torgau  1627

**Schützendorf, Gustav**        *Baritone*
b. Cologne, 1883: d. Berlin, 1937
He made his debut at the Metropolitan in 1922 singing von Faninal.

**Schwarzkopf, Elisabeth**      *Soprano*
b. near Poznan, 1915:

She made her debut in Berlin in 1938. She was the first Anne Trulove.
Anne Trulove, Blondchen, Cio-Cio San, Constanze, Countess (*Capriccio*), Elsa, Donna Elvira, Esmeralda (*Prodaná Nevesta*), Eva, Gilda, Lauretta (*Gianni Schicchi*), Liù, Manon, Margherita (*Mefistofele*), Marzellina, Mimi, Musetta, Pamina, Rosina (*Il Barbiere di Siviglia*), Sophie (*Der Rosenkavalier*), Violetta, Waldvogel (*Siegfried*), Zerbinetta.

**Scontrino, Antonio**          *Composer*
b. Trapani, Sicily, 1850: d. Florence, 1922
Matelda               Milan  1879
Sortilegio            Turin  1882

**Scott, Cyril**               *Composer*
b. Oxton, England, 1879:
The Alchemist         Essen  1925

**Scott, Tom**                 *Composer*
b. Campbellsburg, Ky., 1912:
American folk singer.
The Fisherman                 1956

**Scotti, Antonio**            *Baritone*
b. Naples, 1866: d. there, 1936
He made his debut at Malta in 1889 as Amonasro. In 1899, as Don Giovanni, he came out at the Metropolitan and at Covent Garden. He sang with the Metropolitan for thirty-four years.
Almaviva (*Le Nozze di Figaro*), Amonasro, Ashton, Belcore, Escamillo, Falstaff (*Falstaff*), Germont, Gil, Don Giovanni, Iago, Lescaut (*Manon Lescaut*), Marcel, de Nevers, Rigoletto, Scarpia, Sharpless, Tonio, Valentin (*Faust*).

**Scribe, Augustin Eugène**     *Librettist*
b. Paris, 1791: d. there, 1861
Scribe was one of the most prolific of successful librettists, numbering the following among his works:
Fra Diavolo, La Juive, Les Huguenots, Le Prophète, L'Africaine, L'Etoile du Nord, Gustave III, I Vespri Siciliani (with Duveyier), Masaniello and Robert le Diable (with Delavigne).

**Sebastian, George**     *Conductor*
b. Budapest, 1903:
He has conducted at Hamburg, Leipzig, and the Metropolitan.

**Seefried, Irmgard**     *Soprano*
b. Köngetried, Bavaria, 1919:
She made her debut at Vienna as Eva in 1943 and at the Metropolitan as Susanna (*Le Nozze di Figaro*) ten years later.
Agathe, Antonia, Cio-Cio San, Composer (*Ariadne auf Naxos*), Eva, Fiordiligi, Giulietta, Marenka, Marzelline, Nanetta (*Falstaff*), Nedda, Nuri (*Tiefland*), Olympia, Pamina, Stella, Susanna (*Le Nozze di Figaro*).

**Seidl, Anton**     *Conductor*
b. Budapest, 1850: d. New York, 1898
From 1873 to 1879 he conducted at Bayreuth. After a short time in Bremen, he conducted at the Metropolitan from 1885 until his death. He married Auguste Krauss in 1885.

**Seidl-Krauss, Auguste**     *Soprano*
b. Vienna, 1853: d. Kingston, N.Y., 1939
The wife of the conductor Anton Seidl.
Agathe, Annchen (*Der Freischütz*), Brünnhilde, Elisabeth, Elsa, Eva, Irene, Isolde, Leonore (*Fidelio*), Rezia, Senta, Sieglinde.

**Sekles, Bernhardt**     *Composer*
b. Frankfurt, 1872: d. there, 1934
| Scheherazade | Mannheim | 1917 |
| Die Zehn Küsse | Frankfurt | 1926 |

**Sembrich, Marcella**     *Soprano*
b. Galicia, 1858: d. New York, 1935
One of the most accomplished musicians who ever sang in opera. On 21 April 1884 she took part in a benefit at the Metropolitan, playing the *Violin Concerto* by Bériot, a Chopin *Mazurka* on the piano, and singing. She made her debut in Athens in 1877 as Elvira (*I Puritani*), and in London, 1880, as Lucia. In 1883 she appeared for the first time at the Metropolitan in the same role.

Amina, Elvira (*Ernani*), Elvira (*I Puritani*), Eva, Frau Fluth, Gilda, Harriett (*Martha*), Lucia, Marie (*La Figlia del Reggimento*), Norina, Rosina (*Il Barbiere di Siviglia*), Susanna (*Le Nozze di Figaro*), Valentine (*Les Huguenots*), Violetta, Zerlina (*Don Giovanni*).

**Serafin, Tullio**     *Conductor*
b. near Venice, 1878:
Conductor at the Metropolitan from 1924 to 1935.

**Serov, Alexander**     *Composer*
b. St. Petersburg, 1820: d. there, 1871
| Judith | St. Petersburg | 1863 |
| Rogneda | „ | 1865 |
| Vrazhya Sila (*The Power of Evil*) (*Finished by Soloviev*) | „ | 1871 |

**Sessions, Roger**     *Composer*
b. Brooklyn, N.Y., 1896:
One of the most important American composers of the modern school; also a distinguished teacher.
| The Trial of Lucullus | Berkeley, Calif. | 1947 |
| Montezuma | | 1947 |

**Seymour, John Laurence**     *Composer*
b. Los Angeles, 1893:
A pupil of Vincent d'Indy.
| In the Pasha's Garden | Metropolitan | 1935 |

**Shacklock, Constance**     *Soprano*
b.
Carmen, Octavian, Salome.

**Shaporin, Yuri**     *Composer*
b. Ukraine, 1889:
| The Decembrists | Moscow | 1953 |

**Sheridan, Margaret**     *Soprano*
b. County Mayo, Ireland, 1889: d. near Dublin, 1958
Cio-cio San, Desdemona, Iris, Maddalena (*Andrea Chénier*), Manon Lescaut, Wally.

**Shostakovitch, Dmitri**     *Composer*
b. St. Petersburg, 1906:
Celebrated Soviet symphonist, who ceased to write operas after the official condemnation he received for his *Lady Macbeth of Minsk*. In 1959 he produced a light opera.

| | | |
|---|---|---|
| The Nose | Leningrad | 1930 |
| Lady Macbeth of Minsk | ,, | 1934 |
| Moskva | | |
| Tchernomushki | Moscow | 1959 |

**Shuard, Amy**     *Soprano*
b. London, 1924:
Aida, Amelia (*Simon Boccanegra*), Carmen, Cio-Cio San, Princess Eboli, Freia, Gerhilde, Giorgetta (*Il Tabarro*), Giulietta (*Les Contes d'Hoffmann*), Káta Kabanová, Magda Sorel, Marguérite (*Faust*), Musetta, Nedda, Santuzza, Venus.

**Sibelius, Jean**     *Composer*
b. Tavastehus, Finland, 1865: d. Järvenpää, 1957
Finland's most illustrious composer

| | | |
|---|---|---|
| Jungfruburen | Helsinki | 1896 |

**Siems, Margarete**     *Soprano*
b.
The first Chrysothemis (*Elektra*), the first Marschallin, and the first Zerbinetta (*Ariadne auf Naxos*).

**Siepi, Cesare**     *Bass*
b. Milan, 1923:
He made his debut in Rigoletto in Venice, 1941.
Alvise, Don Basilio (*Il Barbiere di Siviglia*), Don Giovanni, Boris Godunov, Colline, Figaro (*Le Nozze di Figaro*), Mefistofele (*Mefistofele*), Oreveso, Padre Guardiano, Philip II, Sparafucile.

**Simionato, Giulietta**     *Mezzo-soprano*
b. Forli, Italy, 1916:
Azucena, Charlotte, Isabella (*L'Italiana in Algeri*), Marina Mnishek, Mignon, Preziosilla (*La Forza del Destino*), Rosina

(*Il Barbiere di Siviglia*), Sorceress (*Dido and Aeneas*).

**Singher, Martial**     *Baritone*
b. Oloron, Ste. Marie, France, 1904:
He made his debut at the Metropolitan in 1943.
Coppelius, Dapertutto, Golaud, High Priest (*Alceste*), Lindorf, Marouf, Dr. Miracle, Pelléas.

**Skilton, Charles Sanford**     *Composer*
b. Northampton, Mass., 1868: d. Lawrence, Kans., 1941

| | |
|---|---|
| The Sun Bride | 1930 |

**Slezak, Leo**     *Tenor*
b. Moravia, 1875: d. Bavaria, 1946
A pupil of Jean de Reszke. He made his London debut and his Metropolitan debut both in 1909, singing Otello. His first appearance in opera was in Brünn, 1896, singing Lohengrin. He is the father of the actor Walter Slezak.
Hermann (*Pique-Dame*), Julien, Lohengrin, Manrico, Otello, Radames, Tannhäuser, Walther.

**Smallens, Alexander**     *Conductor*
b. St. Petersburg, 1889:
He is usually the conductor of productions of *Porgy and Bess*, of which he conducted the première. He has conducted at Boston, Chicago and Philadelphia.

**Smetana, Bedřich**     *Composer*
b. Litomysl, Bohemia, 1824: d. Prague, 1884
National Bohemian composer, best known for his orchestral music, especially *The Moldau*.

| | | |
|---|---|---|
| Braniboři v Čechách (*The Brandenburgers in Bohemia*) | Prague | 1866 |
| Prodaná Nevěsta (*The Bartered Bride*) | ,, | 1866 |
| Dalibor | ,, | 1868 |
| Dvě vdovy (*The Two Widows*) | ,, | 1874 |

Hubička (*The Kiss*) Prague 1876
Tajemství (*The Secret*) „ 1878
Libuše „ 1881
Čertova stěna
(*The Devil's Wall*) „ 1882

**Smyth, Ethel Mary** *Composer*
b. Kent, England, 1858: d. Surrey, 1944
England's most famous woman composer and a fervid believer in the rights of women; fervid enough to have been arrested and jailed in 1911 for her agitations in favor of woman's suffrage.

Der Wald (*The Forest*) Dresden 1901
Fantasio Weimar 1902
The Wreckers Leipzig 1906
The Boatswain's Mate London 1916
Fête Galante Birmingham 1923
Entente Cordiale Bristol 1926

**Sodero, Cesare** *Conductor*
b. Naples, 1886: d. New York, 1947
Music Director of NBC and the Mutual Network Conductor of the San Carlo Opera and the Philadelphia Opera.

**Solti, Georg** *Conductor*
b. Budapest, 1912:
Conductor at Munich, Frankfurt and San Francisco.

**Sontag, Henriette** *Soprano*
(Countess Rossi)
b. Coblenz, 1806: d. Mexico City, 1854
The first Euryanthe.
Amina, Donna Anna, Desdemona, Elvira (*I Puritani*), Euryanthe, Isabella (*L'Italiana in Algeri*), Lucrezia Borgia, Marie (*La Figlia del Reggimento*), Norina, Rosina (*Il Barbiere di Siviglia*), Semiramide, Susanna (*Le Nozze di Figaro*), Zerlina (*Don Giovanni*).

**Spelman, Timothy** *Composer*
b. Brooklyn, N.Y., 1891:
La Magnifica 1920
The Sunken City 1930
The Courtship of Miles Standish 1943

**Spohr, Ludwig** *Composer*
b. Brunswick, 1784: d. Kassel, 1859
Famous as a violinist and composer of instrumental music. He wrote eleven operas. As a conductor he brought out *Der Fliegende Holländer* and *Tannhäuser*, but was officially restrained from bringing out *Lohengrin*.

Faust Prague 1816
Jessonda Kassel 1823
Zemire und Azor Frankfurt 1819

**Spontini, Gasparo** *Composer*
b. near Ancona, Italy, 1774: d. there, 1851
A prolific composer of operas and other works. He met his greatest successes in France where *La Vestale*, which took him fifteen years to compose, was finally performed. There he was director of the Italian Opera, and later became court composer. He also held the latter post in Berlin for a few years.

La Vestale Opéra 1807
Fernand Cortez „ 1809
Olympie „ 1819

**Stabile, Mariano** *Baritone*
b. Palermo, 1888:
Alfonso (*Così fan Tutte*), Falstaff (*Falstaff*), Giovanni (*Francesca da Rimini*), Don Giovanni, Iago, Lescaut (*Manon Lescaut*), Plunkett, Poet (*Il Turco in Italia*), Rigoletto, Scarpia.

**Stagno, Roberto** *Tenor*
b. Palermo, 1836: d. Genoa, 1897
The first Turiddu. He was among the company in the Metropolitan's opening season, 1883.
Grimaldo, Lionel, Manrico, Don Ottavio, Turiddu.

**Stanford, Charles Villiers** *Composer*
b. Dublin, 1852: d. London, 1924
Savonarola Hamburg 1884
The Canterbury
Pilgrims London 1884

**Starer, Robert** *Composer*
b. Vienna, 1924
The Intruder    New York    1956

**Staudigl, Josef** *Bass*
b. Wöllersdorf, Austria, 1807: d. near Vienna, 1861
King Marke, Pietro (*Masaniello*), Pizarro, Pogner, Sarastro, Wotan.

**Staudigl, Josef, Jr.** *Baritone*
b. Vienna, 1850: d. Karlsruhe, 1910
Pogner, Rocco, King Marke.

**Steber, Eleanor** *Soprano*
b. Wheeling, W.Va., 1916:
The first Vanessa. She made her debut at the Metropolitan in 1940 as Sophie.
Alice Ford, Countess Almaviva, Donna Anna, Antonia, Arabella, Constanze, Desdemona, Elizabeth de Valois, Elsa, Eva, Donna Elvira, Fiordiligi, Giulietta, Marguérite (*Faust*), Marie (*Wozzeck*), Marschallin, Micaela, Minnie, Sophie, Tosca, Vanessa, Violetta, Barak's Wife (*Die Frau ohne Schatten*).

**Stefano, Giuseppe di** *Tenor*
b. Catania, 1921:
Alfredo, Arthur (*I Puritani*), Canio, Duke, Edgar, Manrico, Mario Cavaradossi, Riccardo (*Un Ballo in Maschera*), Rodolfo, Turiddu, Wilhelm.

**Stehle, Sophie** *Soprano*
b. Hohenzollern-Sigmaringen, Germany, 1838: d. near Hanover, 1921
The first Fricka, Brünnhilde (*Walküre*), Alice Ford, Nedda, and Walter (*La Wally*).
Agathe, Alice Ford, Brünnhilde, Elisabeth, Elsa, Eva, Fricka, Nedda, Senta, Walter (*La Wally*).

**Steinberg, William** *Conductor*
b. Cologne, 1899:
Conductor at Cologne, Prague and elsewhere. In 1952 he was engaged as conductor of the Pittsburgh Symphony Orchestra.

**Stephens, Catherine** *Soprano*
b. London, 1794: d. there, 1882
Polly Peachum, Susanna (*Le Nozze di Figaro*), Rosetta (*Love in a Village*).

**Stevens, Risë** *Mezzo-soprano*
b. New York, 1913:
She made her debut in Prague in 1938 as Mignon, and at the Metropolitan the same year in the same role.
Carmen, Dalila, Mignon, Octavian.

**Stiedry, Fritz** *Conductor*
b. Vienna, 1883:
Has conducted at Berlin, Vienna, and the Metropolitan.

**Stignani, Ebe** *Mezzo-soprano*
b. Italy, 1905:
Adalgisa, Amneris, Dalila, Princess Eboli, Fidalma, Laura, Leonora (*La Favorita*), Martha (*Khovantchina*), Rosa (*L'Arlesiana*), Rubria (*Nerone* by Boito), Ulrica.

**Still, William Grant** *Composer*
b. Woodville, Miss., 1895:

| | |
|---|---|
| Blue Steel | 1935 |
| Troubled Island | 1938 |
| A Bayou Legend | 1940 |
| Miss Sally's Party | 1940 |
| A Southern Interlude | 1942 |
| Castasio | 1949 |

**Stokowski, Leopold** *Conductor*
b. London, 1882:
Celebrated conductor, especially noted for his zeal in bringing new works and new composers to public notice.

**Stoltz, Rosina** *Mezzo-soprano*
(*Really* Victoire Noël)
b. Paris, 1815: d. there, 1903
The first Leonora (*La Favorita*), the first Agathe, Desdemona (Rossini's *Otello*), and Zayda (*Dom Sébastien*).
Agathe, Desdemona (by Rossini), Fides, Leonora (*La Favorita*), Rachel, Zayda (*Dom Sébastien*).

**Stolz, Teresa** *Soprano*
b. Bohemia, 1834: d. Milan, 1902
Aida, Leonora (*La Forza del Destino*).

**Storace, Ann Selina** *Soprano*
b. London, 1766: d. Dulwich, 1817
A sister of Stephen Storace. The first
Susanna in *Le Nozze di Figaro*.

**Storace, Stephen** *Composer*
b. London, 1763: d. there, 1796
Brother of Ann Storace.

| | | |
|---|---|---|
| The Haunted Tower | London | 1789 |
| No Song, No Supper | „ | 1790 |
| Cherokee | „ | 1794 |
| Mahmoud (*completed by* | | |
| Kelly and Ann Storace) | „ | 1796 |

**Stradella, Alessandro** *Composer*
b. Montefestino, Italy, 1642: d. (*murdered*)
Genoa, 1682
A composer of opera, but most famous
because of the opera made about him by
Flotow in which speculations about his
murder are greatly romanticized.

**Strakosch, Maurice** *Manager*
b. Moravia, 1825: d. Paris, 1887
He presented Italian opera in New York
in 1857, and in Chicago in 1859.

**Strauss, Johann, Jr.** *Composer*
b. Vienna, 1825: d. there, 1899
The Waltz King.

| | | |
|---|---|---|
| Indigo | Vienna | 1871 |
| Der Karneval in Rome | „ | 1873 |
| Die Fledermaus (*The Bat*) | „ | 1874 |
| Cagliostro in Wien | „ | 1875 |
| Zigeunerbaron | | |
| (*The Gypsy Baron*) | „ | 1885 |

**Strauss, Richard Georg** *Composer*
b. Munich, 1864: d. Garmisch-Parten-
kirchen, 1949
The celebrated composer of operas and
symphonic poems, among which *Don
Juan, Till Eulenspiegel, Death and Trans-
figuration* are famous. He also arranged
*Iphigénie en Tauride* for the Metropolitan
in 1916, and *Idomeneo* for Vienna in 1931.

| | | |
|---|---|---|
| Guntram | Weimar | 1894 |
| Feuersnot | Dresden | 1901 |
| Salome | „ | 1905 |
| Elektra | „ | 1909 |
| Der Rosenkavalier | „ | 1911 |
| Ariadne auf Naxos | Stuttgart | 1912 |
| Die Frau ohne Schatten | Vienna | 1919 |
| Intermezzo | Dresden | 1924 |
| Die Aegyptische | | |
| Helene | „ | 1928 |
| Arabella | „ | 1933 |
| Die Schweigsame Frau | „ | 1935 |
| Friedenstag | Munich | 1938 |
| Daphne | Dresden | 1938 |
| Capriccio | Munich | 1942 |
| Die Liebe der Danae | Salzburg | 1952 |

**Stravinsky, Feodor** *Bass*
b. Tchernigov, Russia, 1843: d. Wildun-
gen, Germany, 1902
Father of Igor Stravinsky. His most
famous role was Méphistophélès in *Faust*.

**Stravinsky, Igor** *Composer*
b. Orianienbaum, Russia, 1882:
One of the great composers of the
twentieth century, and a tremendous
influence on the music of the generations
that followed him. Stravinsky began in a
style somewhat like that of Rimsky-
Korsakov, with whom he had taken a few
lessons. Some of his most popular ballets
date from that period. But he effectively
demolished that reputation with the
astonishingly primitive orchestral work
*Le Sacre du Printemps*, which became a
landmark in the change of direction of
musical composition. His later works
have shown no diminution of originality
but have tended to be more of a religious
and poetic nature than the ballets which
made him famous. Like the last quartets
of Beethoven, Stravinsky's latest works
are of a new style, somewhat neoclassic
but harmonically very complex. After
many years in Paris he settled in California. His *Oedipus Rex* was performed in
New York with magnificent, sticklike

marionettes by Bufano, twice the size of human beings. These acted out the story over the heads of the chorus, which was only dimly visible below.

| Rossignol | | |
| (*The Nightingale*) | Paris | 1914 |
| Mavra | „ | 1922 |
| Renard (*The Fox*) | „ | 1922 |
| Oedipus Rex | „ | 1927 |
| The Rake's Progress | Venice | 1951 |

**Strepponi, Giuseppina**                *Soprano*
b. Lodi, Italy, 1815: d. Busseto, 1897
The first Abigaille in *Nabucco*. In 1859 she married Verdi.

**Stückgold, Grete**                *Soprano*
b. London, 1895:
She made her Metropolitan debut as Eva in 1927.

**Sucher, Rosa**                *Soprano*
(*Née* Hasselbeck)
b. Velburg, Germany, 1849: d. Berlin, 1927
As Isolde she made her Covent Garden debut in 1892 and her Metropolitan three years later.
Brünnhilde, Elsa, Euryanthe, Eva, Isolde, Kundry, Senta.

**Sullivan, Arthur Seymour**                *Composer*
b. London, 1842: d. Westminster, 1900
In association with W. S. Gilbert, he wrote the music of some of the most famous English light operas, which have a style of their own. All those listed below were with Gilbert. His other works, of which there were many, do not survive on the stage. His "grand opera," *Ivanhoe*, produced in London in 1891, had only a transitory success.

| Trial by Jury | London | 1875 |
| The Sorcerer | „ | 1877 |
| HMS Pinafore | „ | 1878 |
| The Pirates of | | |
| Penzance | New York | 1878 |
| Patience | London | 1881 |
| Iolanthe | | 1882 |
| Princess Ida | | 1884 |
| The Mikado | | 1885 |
| Ruddigore | | 1887 |
| Yeomen of the Guard | | 1888 |
| The Gondoliers | | 1889 |

**Sullivan, Brian**                *Tenor*
b.
He made his Vienna debut as Erik (*Der Fliegende Holländer*) in 1959.
Alfred (*Die Fledermaus*), Avito, Erik (*Der Fliegende Holländer*), Ferrando, Grigori, Don José, Lohengrin, Pinkerton, Rodolfo, Walther.

**Sundelius, Marie**                *Soprano*
b. Karlsbad, Sweden, 1884: d. Boston, 1958
She made her debut at the Metropolitan in 1916. Subsequently, she became a singing teacher.

**Supervia, Conchita**                *Mezzo-soprano*
b. Barcelona, 1899: d. London, 1936
Her records reveal that this was a great voice.
Carmen, Concepcion (*L'Heure Espagnole*).

**Suppé, Franz von**                *Composer*
(*Really* Francesco Ezechiele Ermenegildo)
b. Dalmatia, 1819: d. Vienna, 1895
Only the overtures to his operas remain popular today.

| The Poet and Peasant | Vienna | 1846 |
| Boccaccio | „ | 1879 |
| Light Cavalry | „ | 1866 |

**Sutherland, Joan**                *Soprano*
b. Sydney, Australia, 1926:
Gifted with a remarkable capacity for study and control of a fine voice, she made her English opera debut at Covent Garden in 1952, and appeared at the Metropolitan in 1961. She ranks with Tebaldi and Callas as one of the most important singers of her time.
Amina, Desdemona, Dido, Elvira, Judith.

**Svanholm, Set**                    *Tenor*
b. Västeras, Sweden, 1904:
He made his debut at Stockholm as
Silvio in *Pagliacci*. In 1957 he became
General Manager of the Stockholm opera.
Aegisth, Figaro (*Il Barbiere di Siviglia*),
Parsifal, Siegfried, Siegmund, Silvio,
Tristan, Walther.

**Swarthout, Gladys**              *Contralto*
b. Deepwater, Missouri, 1904:
She made her debut at the Metropolitan
as La Cieca in 1929, five years after her
first appearance in opera in Chicago.
Carmen, La Cieca, Stéphano (*Roméo et
Juliette*).

**Szell, George**                  *Conductor*
b. Budapest, 1897:
He has conducted at Strasbourg, Prague,
Darmstadt, Düsseldorf, Berlin and at the
Metropolitan in New York (1942–1945).
In 1946 he became conductor of the
Cleveland Orchestra.

**Tagliavini, Ferruccio**              *Tenor*
b. Reggio, Italy, 1913:
In Florence, 1939, he made his debut
singing Rodolfo. He came out at the
Metropolitan in the same role in 1947.
Duke, Faust (*Mefistofele*), Fritz, des
Grieux (*Manon*), Mario Cavaradossi,
Rodolfo, Werther.

**Tajo, Italo**                         *Bass*
b. Pinerolo, 1915:
Don Basilio (*Il Barbiere di Siviglia*),
Colline, Gianni Schicchi, Leporello, Ramfis, Timur (*Turandot*).

**Talley, Marion**                   *Soprano*
b. Nevada, Missouri, 1907:
She made her debut as Gilda at the
Metropolitan in 1926. She was one of the
few American singers to be engaged there.
Her career was, however, soon ended.

**Tamagno, Francesco**                 *Tenor*
b. Turin, 1850: d. Varese, 1905

The first Otello (Verdi's opera), he made
his debut as Riccardo in *Un Ballo in
Maschera* at Palermo, 1874. His first
appearance at the Metropolitan took place
in 1894 when he sang Arnold in *Guillaume
Tell*.
Arnold (*Guillaume Tell*), Otello, Radames, Riccardo (*Un Ballo in Maschera*),
Samson.

**Tamberlik, Enrico**                  *Tenor*
b. Rome, 1820: d. Paris, 1889
The first Don Alvaro (*La Forza del
Destino*). He made his debut at Covent
Garden in 1850 singing Masaniello.

**Tamburini, Antonio**              *Baritone*
b. Faenza, Italy, 1800: d. Nice, 1876
The first Riccardo (*I Puritani*), and the
first Doctor Malatesta (*Don Pasquale*).

**Taneyev, Sergey Ivanovich**     *Composer*
b. Vladimir, Russia, 1856: d. Moscow,
1915
Orestes
    (*trilogy*)        St. Petersburg  1895

**Tansman, Alexander**             *Composer*
b. Lodz, 1897:
La Nuit Kurde                      1927
Le Serment           Brussels     1955

**Taskin, Émile Alexandre**            *Bass*
b. Paris, 1853: d. there, 1897
Taskin received a medal for his success
in calming the audience at the Opéra-
Comique when a fire broke out during a
performance of *Mignon* in 1887 and destroyed the theater. He was singing
Lotario at the time.

**Tauber, Richard**                    *Tenor*
(*Really* Ernest Seiffert)
b. Linz, Austria, 1892: d. London, 1948
He made his debut as Tamino at Frankfurt in 1913. He also, however, wrote and
produced his own opera:
Old Chelsea           London      1943

**Taylor, Deems**                  *Composer*
b. New York, 1885:

Well known as a critic and as a broadcast commentator on music. His suite *Through the Looking Glass* is still popular.

| The King's Henchman | Metropolitan | 1927 |
| Peter Ibbetson | ,, | 1931 |

**Tchaikovsky, Modest**     *Librettist*
b. St. Petersburg, 1850: d. Moscow, 1916
Brother of the symphonist Piotr Ilyich Tchaikovsky, and librettist for two operas by him: *Pique-Dame* and *Iolanthe*.

**Tchaikovsky, Piotr Ilyitch**     *Composer*
b. near Viatka, Russia, 1840: d. St. Petersburg, 1893
Famous everywhere for his romantic music, which is well exemplified in his last three symphonies, and his *Romeo and Juliet* Overture. Equally celebrated are his ballets (*The Swan Lake*, *The Sleeping Beauty*, *The Nutcracker*).

| Voyevode | Moscow | 1869 |
| Undine | | 1869 |
| Opritchnik | St. Petersburg | 1874 |
| Vakula the Smith | ,, | 1876 |
| Eugene Onegin | Moscow | 1879 |
| The Maid of Orleans | St. Petersburg | 1881 |
| Mazeppa | Moscow | 1884 |
| Tcherevichki (*a revision of* Vakula the Smith) | ,, | 1887 |
| The Sorceress | St. Petersburg | 1887 |
| Pique-Dame | ,, | 1890 |
| Iolanthe | ,, | 1892 |

**Tcherepnin, Alexandre**     *Composer*
b. St. Petersburg, 1899:
He completed Mussorgsky's *Zhenitba* for the performance in Essen, 1937. His father had done the same for the same composer's *Fair at Sorochintsky* in performance at Monte Carlo, 1923.

| Ol-ol | Weimar | 1928 |
| Die Hochzeit der Sobeide | Vienna | 1933 |
| The Farmer and the Fairy | Aspen, Colo., | 1952 |

**Tebaldi, Renata**     *Soprano*
b. Pesaro, Italy, 1922:
This great artist of the voice made her debut at Trieste in 1946 as Desdemona, then at Covent Garden in 1950 and the Metropolitan, 1955, in the same role. She is remarkable among prima donnas for her calm approach and her intense study of the emotional and musical fabric of each role.

Aida, Amelia (*Simon Boccanegra*), Cio-Cio San, Desdemona, Elsa, Helen of Troy (*Mefistofele*), Leonora (*La Forza del Destino*), Leonora (*Il Trovatore*), Maddalena (*Andrea Chénier*), Manon Lescaut, Margherite (*Mefistofele*), Mathilde (*Guillaume Tell*), Mimi, Olimpia (Spontini's opera), Tosca, Violetta, Wally.

**Telemann, Georg Philip**     *Composer*
b. Magdeburg, 1681: d. Hamburg, 1767
Best known for his chamber works, especially those including flute, strings, and harpsichord. He wrote forty operas.

| Der Gedultige Socrates | Hamburg | 1721 |
| Der Neu-Modische Liebhaber Damon | ,, | 1724 |

**Ternina, Milka**     *Soprano*
b. near Zagreb, 1863: d. there, 1941
She made her debut at her birthplace in 1882, and at the Metropolitan as Elsa in 1896.

Aida, Amelia (*Un Ballo in Maschera*), Brünnhilde, Elisabeth, Elsa, Gretchen (*Der Wildschütz*), Isolde, Kundry, Leonore (*Fidelio*), Selika, Tosca.

**Tetrazzini, Eva**     *Soprano*
b. Milan, 1862: d. Salsomaggiore, 1938
Sister of Luisa Tetrazzini. She made her debut as Marguérite (*Faust*) in Florence, 1882. Five years later she married Cleofonte Campanini.

**Tetrazzini, Luisa**     *Soprano*
b. Florence, 1871: d. Milan, 1940
Sister of Eva Tetrazzini, and a very

famous singer. As Melba toast was named for Nellie Melba, so Chicken Tetrazzini preserves this soprano's name for people who know nothing of opera. She made her debut as Inez in Florence, 1895. In London, 1907 and at the Manhattan opera 1908, she made debuts as Violetta.

Amina, Desdemona, Dinorah, Elvira (*I Puritani*), Gilda, Inez, Lakmé, Leila, Lucia, Marie (*La Figlia del Reggimento*), Rosina (*Il Barbiere di Siviglia*), Violetta.

**Teyte, Maggie** *Soprano*
(*Née* Tate)
b. Wolverhampton, England, 1888:
A pupil of Jean de Reske. She changed the spelling of her name in order to avoid popular mispronunciations in France. She is usually associated with the role of Mélisande. It was in Monte Carlo that she made her debut in 1907 as Zerlina (*Don Giovanni*).

Antonia, Cherubino, Cio-cio San, Giulietta, Mélisande, Mimi, Olympia (*Les Contes d'Hoffmann*), Stella, Zerlina (*Don Giovanni*).

**Thebom, Blanche** *Mezzo-soprano*
b. Monessen, Pa., 1918:
She made her debut as Fricka at the Metropolitan in 1944.

Adalgisa, Amneris, Azucena, Baba the Turk, Brangäne, Carmen, Dalila, Dorabella, Princess Eboli, Fricka, Laura Adorno, Marina Mnishek, Orlovsky, Ortrud, Venus.

**Thiriet, Maurice** *Composer*
b. Meulan, France, 1906:
Le Bourgeois de
Falaise     Paris   1937
La Véridique Histoire
du Docteur       1937

**Thoma, Therese** *Soprano*
b. Tutzing, Germany, 1845: d. Munich, 1921

The first Sieglinde. She married Heinrich Vogl in 1868.
Brünnhilde, Isolde, Sieglinde.

**Thomas, Charles Louis Ambroise**
*Composer*
b. Metz, 1811: d. Paris, 1896
A French composer of romantic operas. He taught at the Paris Conservatory for many years, and in 1871 became its director.

| | | |
|---|---|---|
| Le Caïd | Paris | 1849 |
| Le Songe d'une Nuit d'Été | ,, | 1850 |
| Raymond | ,, | 1851 |
| Mignon | ,, | 1866 |
| Hamlet | ,, | 1868 |

**Thomas, John Charles** *Baritone*
b. Meyersdale, Pa., 1891: d. Los Angeles, 1960
This famous singer of concert and radio made his operatic debut in Brussels in 1925. He came out as Valentin (*Faust*) in Covent Garden, 1928, and as Giorgio Germont at the Metropolitan in 1934.

Amonasro, Athanaël, Figaro (*Il Barbiere di Siviglia*), Giorgio Germont, Valentin (*Faust*).

**Thompson, Randall** *Composer*
b. New York, 1899:
Solomon and
Balkis    New York (radio)   1942

**Thomson, Virgil** *Composer*
b. Kansas City, Missouri, 1896:
His scores have a certain brash simplicity that wins them popularity. He has been an influential critic in New York.

| | | |
|---|---|---|
| Four Saints in Three Acts | Ann Arbor, Mich. | 1933 |

(*First stage performance, Hartford, Conn., 1934*)

| | | |
|---|---|---|
| The Mother of us All | New York | 1947 |

**Thorborg, Kerstin** *Contralto*
b. Venjan, Sweden, 1896:

296

Eleven years after her debut in Stockholm, 1925, she came out as Fricka at the Metropolitan.

Eglantine, Fricka, Herodias (*Salome*), Klytemnestra (*Elektra*), Kundry, Marina Mnishek, Doña Mercedes (*Der Corregidor*), Orfeo, Ulrica.

**Thuille, Ludwig Wilhelm Andreas Maria**          *Composer*
b. Bolzano, 1861: d. Munich, 1907
He is best known for his treatise on harmony.

| | | |
|---|---|---|
| Theuerdank | Munich | 1894 |
| Lobetanz | Karlsruhe | 1898 |
| Gugeline | Bremen | 1901 |

**Tibbett, Lawrence**          *Baritone*
b. Bakersfield, Calif., 1896: d. New York, 15 July 1960
A famous radio singer in the United States. He made his debut at the Metropolitan in 1923.

Don Carlo (*La Forza del Destino*), Ford (*Falstaff*), Iago, Michele (*Il Tabarro*), Rance, Scarpia, Simon Boccanegra, Valentin (*Faust*), Wolfram.

**Tichatschek, Joseph Aloys**          *Tenor*
b. Bohemia, 1807: d. Dresden, 1886
The first Cola Rienzi, the first Tannhäuser.

**Tietjens, Therese**          *Soprano*
b. Hamburg, 1831: d. London, 1877
She made her debut at Hamburg in 1849 and at London in 1858.

Alice Ford (*Falstaff*), Countess Almaviva, Amelia (*Un Ballo in Maschera*), Donna Anna, Elvira (*Ernani*), Fidès, Frau Fluth (*Die Lustigen Weiber von Windsor*), Iphigénie (*Iphigénie en Tauride*), Leonore (*Fidelio*), Leonora (*La Forza del Destino*), Leonora (*Il Trovatore*.) Lucrezia Borgia, Marguérite (*Faust*), Martha, Medea, Mireille, Norma, Ortrud, Pamina, Rezia, Semiramide, Valentine (*Les Huguenots*).

**Tippett, Michael**          *Composer*
b. London, 1905:

| | | |
|---|---|---|
| The Midsummer Marriage | London | 1955 |

**Toch, Ernst**          *Composer*
b. Vienna, 1887:

| | | |
|---|---|---|
| Wegwende | | 1925 |
| Die Prinzessin auf der Erbse (*The Princess on the Pea*) | Baden Baden | 1927 |
| Egon und Emilie | Mannheim | 1928 |
| Der Fächer (*The Fan*) | Königsberg | 1930 |

**Tokatyan, Armand**          *Tenor*
b. Bulgaria, 1899:
He made his operatic debut at Milan in 1921, and came out as Lucio (*Anima Allegra* by Vittadini) at the Metropolitan two years later.

Avito, Lucio (*Anima Allegra* by Vittadini), Paco (*La Vide Breve*).

**Tomasi, Henri**          *Composer*
b. Marseille, 1901:

| | | |
|---|---|---|
| Atlantide | Mulhouse | 1954 |
| Don Juan de Mañara | Munich | 1956 |
| Sampiero Corso | Bordeaux | 1956 |

**Tosatti, Vieri**          *Composer*
b. Rome, 1920:

| | | |
|---|---|---|
| Dionisio | | 1947 |
| Il Sistema della Dolcezza (*The System of Sweetness*) | | 1949 |
| La Partita a Pugni (*Prize Fight*) | Venice | 1953 |

**Toscanini, Arturo**          *Conductor*
b. Parma, 1867: d. New York, 1957
So famous a conductor as to be a legend in his own time even among people who never heard a concert. His career began in Rio de Janeiro where he stepped up from the orchestra to conduct Aida, taking the place of a conductor who had been hissed out of the house by the hostile audience. He conducted the first *Pagliacci*,

the first *La Bohème*, and the first United States performances of *Armide*, *Ariane et Barbe-Bleue*, *Boris Godunov*, *L'Amore dei Tre Re*, and many more. He became more widely known through his regular broadcasts with the NBC symphony orchestra which became the Symphony of the Air after his retirement. Because of his near blindness, he habitually committed each work to his fabulous memory and conducted without score.

**Tourel, Jennie**          *Mezzo-soprano*
b. Montreal, 1910:
   The first to sing Baba the Turk in *The Rake's Progress*. She made her debut at the Opéra-Comique in 1933 as Carmen.

**Tovey, Donald Francis**          *Composer*
b. Eton, 1875: d. Edinburgh, 1940
   Tovey is primarily known to students of music as the author of a series of critical analyses of music, with particular study of Beethoven.
   The Bride of
      Dionysius          Edinburgh 1932

**Tozzi, Giorgio**          *Bass*
b. Chicago:
   Tozzi began as a baritone but became a bass in 1950. He came to the Metropolitan in 1955 as Alvise (*La Gioconda*).
   Ashby, Amonasro, Commendatore (*Don Giovanni*), Count di Luna, Germont (*La Traviata*), Phillip the Second, Pimen, Pogner, Prince Gremin (*Eugene Onegin*), Count Rodolfo (*La Sonnambula*), Samuele (*Un Ballo in Maschera*), Sarastro, Tarquinius (*The Rape of Lucretia*), Tonio.

**Traetta, Tommaso**          *Composer*
b. Naples, 1727: d. Venice, 1779
   He wrote nearly forty operas.
   Ippolito ed Aricie          Parma     1759
   Ifigenia in Aulide          Vienna    1759
   Armida                         „          1761

**Tranchell, Peter**          *Composer*
b. Cuddalore, India, 1922:

   The Mayor of
      Casterbridge          Cambridge,
                                     England   1951

**Traubel, Helen**          *Soprano*
b. St. Louis, 1899:
   Famous as Isolde and as Brünnhilde, she made her debut at the Metropolitan as Sieglinde in 1939.

**Trebelli, Zelia**          *Mezzo-soprano*
(*Really* Gilbert)
b. Paris, 1838: d. Étretat, 1892
   She made her debut at Madrid, 1859, singing Rosina in *Il Barbiere di Siviglia*.
   Amneris, Arsace, Azucena, Carmen, Elena (*Mefistofele*), Fatima (*Oberon*), Frédéric (*Mignon*), Nancy (*Martha*), Maffeo Orsini, Rosina (*Il Barbiere di Siviglia*), Urbain.

**Tréville, Yvonne de**          *Soprano*
(*Really* Edyth la Gierse)
b. Galveston, Tex., 1881: d. New York, 1954
   She made her debut as Marguérite in New York, 1898.

**Tucker, Richard**          *Tenor*
b. New York, 1914:
   He made his debut at the Metropolitan in 1945, singing Enzo.
   Don Alvaro, Don Carlos, Enzo, Ferrando, Des Grieux (*Manon Lescaut*), Don José, Lensky, Mario Cavaradossi, Radames, Rodolfo, Turiddu.

**Turina, Joaquín**          *Composer*
b. Seville, 1882: d. Madrid, 1949
   Margot                      Madrid    1914
   Jardín de Oriente        „          1923

**Turner, Claramae**          *Mezzo-soprano*
b. Dinuba, Calif., 1920:
   The first Madame Flora (*The Medium*).
   Azucena, Carmen, Madame Flora, La Frugola (*Il Tabarro*), La Vecchia (*Gianni Schicchi*), Madame de Croissy (*Les Dialogues des Carmélites*), Marquise de

Berkenfield, Princess (*Suor Angelica*),
Witch (*Hänsel und Gretel*).

**Ugalde, Delphine**        *Soprano*
(*Née* Beaucé)
b. Paris, 1829: d. there, 1910
    This capable woman was manager of
the Bouffes-Parisiens from 1866 to 1871,
and the composer of an opera. She made
her debut as a soprano in Auber's *Domino
Noir* in 1848, singing Angèle.
    Angèle (*Domino Noir*), Blonde, Eurid-
ice (*Orphée aux Enfers*), Leonora (*Il
Trovatore*), Papagena, Rezia, Susanna (*Le
Nozze di Figaro*), Taven (*Mireille*),
    She composed:
La Halte au Moulin     Paris   1867

**Uhde, Hermann**        *Baritone*
    A member of the Metropolitan Opera
Company in 1960 noted for his interpretation of the role of Scarpia. He was also a
magnificent Wozzeck.

**Ullmann, Viktor**        *Composer*
b. Teschen, Austria, 1898:
    Peer Gynt
    Der Sturz des Anti-Christ

**Unger, Georg**        *Tenor*
b. Leipzig, 1837: d. there, 1887
    A famous Siegfried.

**Unger, Hermann**        *Composer*
b. Kamenz, Germany, 1886: d. Cologne,
    1958
    Der Zauberhandschuh
    (*The Magic Glove*)       1927
    Richmodis von Aducht     1928

**Uppman, Theodor**        *Baritone*
b.
    The first Billy Budd.
    Billy Budd, Masetto, Papageno, Paquil-
lo (*La Périchole*), Pelléas.

**Urlus, Jacques**        *Tenor*
b. near Aachen, 1867: d. Noordwijk,
    1935

In 1894 in Amsterdam he made his
debut as Beppo. As Tristan he came out
in Boston in 1912 and at the Metropolitan
the following year.
    Beppo, Florestan, Lohengrin, Parsifal,
Siegmund, Tristan.

**Ursuleac, Viorica**        *Soprano*
b. Cernauti, Romania, 1899:
    The first Arabella, Maria (*Friedenstag*),
Danae, and Countess (*Capriccio*). To her
and to Clemens Krauss, whom she
married, Strauss dedicated *Friedenstag*.
Her debut came at Berlin, in 1933.
    Arabella, Countess (*Capriccio*), Danae,
Helena (*Die Aegyptische Helena*), Maria
(*Friedenstag*).

**Usandizaga, José-María**        *Composer*
b. San Sebastien, Spain, 1887: d. Yanti,
    1915
    A pupil of d'Indy.
    Mendy-Mendiyan     Bilbao   1910
    Las Golondrinas
    (*The Swallows*)     Madrid   1914
    La Llama (*The Flame*)    ,,     1915

**Valleria, Alvina**        *Soprano*
(*Really* Schoening)
b. Baltimore, Md., 1848: d. Nice, 1925
    She made her debut in London in 1871,
then at the Metropolitan as Marguérite
(*Faust*), in 1879.
    Aida, Elisabeth, Leonore (*Fidelio*), Linda
di Chamounix, Marguérite (*Faust*), Margherite (*Mefistofele*), Martha, Micaela.

**Valleti, Cesare**        *Tenor*
b.
    Alfredo Germont, Almaviva (*Il Barbiere
di Siviglia*), Lindoro (*Il Turco in Italia*),
Don Ottavio, Werther.

**Vanesi, Felice**        *Baritone*
b. Calais
    The first Giorgio Germont, the first
Rigoletto, and the first Macbeth. His
place in history is not so much due to his
singing the first Giorgio Germont, but to

the fact that his annoyance at that part, for some reason or another, caused him to make a fool of himself and nearly of Verdi by sauntering throughout the evening, thus destroying any sense of stage timing.

**Vanni, Helen**　　　　　　*Soprano*
b.
Cherubino, Inez (*Il Travatore*).

**Varnay, Astrid**　　　　　　*Soprano*
b. Stockholm, 1918:
The first Telea (*The Island God*), she made her debut at the Metropolitan in 1941 by singing, without rehearsal, the part of Sieglinde.
Aida, Brünnhilde, Elektra, Elisabeth, Elsa, Isolde, Kundry, Lady Macbeth, Leonore (*Fidelio*), Leonora (*Il Trovatore*), Marschallin, Ortrud, Salome, Santuzza, Senta, Sieglinde, Telea (*The Island God*), Tosca, Venus.

**Vaughan Williams, Ralph**　　*Composer*
b. Gloucestershire, England, 1872: d. London, 1958
His characteristically English style is well illustrated in his remarkable work for string orchestra, the *Fantasy on a Theme by Thomas Tallis*, and in his choral and operatic music.

| | | |
|---|---|---|
| Hugh the Drover | London | 1924 |
| Sir John in Love | ,, | 1929 |
| The Poisoned Kiss | | |
| (*composed* 1928) | Cambridge | 1936 |
| Riders to the Sea | London | 1937 |
| The Pilgrim's Progress | | |
| (*Incorporating* | | |
| The Shepherds of the | | |
| Delectable Mountains) | | |
| | London | 1951 |

**Vecchi, Orazio**　　　　　　*Composer*
b. Modena, 1550: d. there, 1605
A canon of the Cathedral of Modena, he wrote a series of madrigals based upon Commedia dell'Arte technique, which was the immediate precursor of real opera.

| | | |
|---|---|---|
| L'Amfiparnaso | Modena | 1594 |

**Venth, Karl**　　　　　　*Composer*
b. Cologne, 1860: d. San Antonio, Tex., 1938

| | | |
|---|---|---|
| The Rebel | Fort Worth | 1926 |

**Verdi, Giuseppe Francesco**　*Composer*
b. Le Roncole, Italy, 1813: d. Milan, 1901
Verdi was one of the most famous and most prolific of opera composers of all time. One of his masterpieces, *Falstaff*, was completed in his eightieth year. During most of his life he was involved somewhat in the political turmoil of the unification of Italy. Many of his works bear evidence of this, for instance in the choice of subjects of a highly patriotic nature. He himself may not have taken an active role in that revolution, but his choruses were frequently used as signals for great demonstrations of patriotism among the people. He also found turmoil outside national politics, however. He tried twice to cope with the strict requirements of the formal French Opéra and was twice depressed by the results. But in other directions his fame helped him greatly by bringing in magnificent commissions such as that of the Khedive of Egypt who wished to have an opera to mark the opening of the Suez Canal. *Aida* was that work.

| | | |
|---|---|---|
| Oberto | La Scala | 1839 |
| Un Giorno di Regno | ,, | 1840 |
| Nabucco | ,, | 1842 |
| I Lombardi | ,, | 1843 |
| Ernani | Venice | 1844 |
| Macbeth | Florence | 1847 |
| Luisa Miller | Naples | 1849 |
| Rigoletto | Venice | 1851 |
| Il Trovatore | Rome | 1853 |
| La Traviata | Venice | 1853 |
| I Vespri Siciliani | Opéra | 1855 |
| Simon Boccanegra | Venice | 1857 |
| Un Ballo in Maschera | Rome | 1859 |
| La Forza del | | |
| Destino | St. Petersburg | 1862 |
| Don Carlos | Opéra | 1867 |

| Aida | Cairo | 1871 |
|---|---|---|
| Otello | La Scala | 1887 |
| Falstaff | „ | 1893 |

**Vere, Clementine de** *Soprano*
b. Paris, 1864: d. Mt. Vernon, N.Y., 1954
She made her debut as Marguerite de Valois in Florence, 1880. She came out at the Metropolitan in 1896 as Marguerite in *La Damnation de Faust*.

Aida, Dinorah, Gilda, Infanta (*Le Cid*), Lucia, Marguerite (*La Damnation de Faust*), Marguérite (*Faust*), Marguerite de Valois, Micaela, Ophélie, Rachel, Violetta.

**Verrall, John** *Composer*
b. Britt, Iowa, 1908:
A pupil of Zoltán Kodály, and Aaron Copland.

| The Cowherd and the Sky Maiden | Seattle | 1952 |
|---|---|---|
| The Wedding Knell | „ | 1952 |
| Three Blind Mice | „ | 1955 |

**Vestris, Lucia Elizabeth** *Mezzo-soprano*
b. London, 1797: d. Fulham, 1856
The first Fatima in Oberon.
Blonde, Fatima, Pippo (*La Gazza Ladra*), Susanna (*Le Nozze di Figaro*).

**Vianesi, Auguste** *Conductor*
b. Livorno, 1837: d. New York, 1908
He conducted the opening performance of the Metropolitan Opera, in 1883, the opera that night being *Faust*.

**Viardot-Garcia, Pauline** *Mezzo-soprano*
b. Paris, 1821: d. there, 1910
Famous daughter of the tenor Garcia, she studied piano with Liszt and composition with Reicha. She was an accomplished pianist, composer and singer. She sang the first Sapho and the first Fidès. Her debut was in London, 1839, as Desdemona in Rossini's *Otello*.

Alceste, Alice Ford, Amina, Donna Anna, Arsace, Desdemona (*Otello* by Rossini), Fidès, Iphigénie (*Iphigénie en Tauride*), Isabelle, Lady Macbeth, Leonora (*La Favorita*), Lucia, Norma, Orfeo, Rachel, Romeo (*I Capuletti ed I Montecchi*), Rosina, Sapho, Valentine (*Les Huguenots*), Zerlina (*Don Giovanni*).

**Vieuille, Félix** *Bass*
b. Saugeon, France, 1872: d. there, 1953
The first Father-in-law (*Le Pauvre Matelot*), the first Barbe-Bleue, and the first Arkel.

**Villa-Lobos, Heitor** *Composer*
b. Rio de Janeiro, 1887: d. there 1959
Villa-Lobos is very well known for his series called Chôros, especially the Chôros for an orchestra of cellos, of which instrument he is very fond, being a cellist himself.

| Izaht (*composed* 1914, revised 1932) | Rio de Janeiro (Concert) | 1940 |
|---|---|---|
| Zoé | | 1919 |
| Malazarte | | 1921 |
| Magdalena | Los Angeles | 1948 |

**Vinay, Ramon** *Tenor*
b. Chile
Canio, Don José, Otello, Parsifal, Radames, Samson, Tannhäuser, Tristan.

**Violette, Wesley La** *Composer*
b. St. James, Minn., 1894:

| Shylock | Chicago (in part) | 1930 |
|---|---|---|
| The Enlightened One | | 1955 |

**Vitalis, George** *Composer*
b. Athens, 1895:
Perseus and Andromeda
The Return of the Gods

| Golfo | New York (Concert) | 1949 |
|---|---|---|

**Vittadini, Franco** *Composer*
b. Pavia, 1884: d. there, 1948

| Anima Allegra | Rome | 1921 |
|---|---|---|
| Nazareth | Pavia | 1928 |
| La Sagredo | La Scala | 1930 |
| Caracciolo | Rome | 1938 |

**Vivaldi, Antonio** *Composer*
b. Venice, circa 1669: d. Vienna, 1741

301

Vivaldi, so famous for his pieces for string orchestra, such as *The Seasons*, may have written as many as forty operas.

| | | |
|---|---|---|
| Ipermestra | Florence | 1727 |
| L'Olimpiade | Venice | 1734 |

**Vix, Geneviève**  *Soprano*
b. Nantes, 1879: d. Paris, 1939
She made her debut at Chicago in 1917 as Manon.

**Vogl, Heinrich**  *Tenor*
b. near Munich, 1845: d. Munich, 1900
The first Loge, the first Siegmund. He made his debut as Max in *Der Freischütz* at Munich, 1865. In 1868 he married Therese Thoma. He also composed an opera:

| | | |
|---|---|---|
| Der Fremdling | Munich | 1899 |

**Völker, Franz**  *Tenor*
b. Neu-Isenburg, 1899:
A famous Lohengrin.
Dalibor, Fra Diavolo, Florestan, Lohengrin, Menelaus, Pedro (*Tiefland*), Siegmund.

**Votipka, Thelma**  *Soprano*
b.
La Ciesca (*Gianni Schicchi*), Curra (*La Forza del Destino*), Gerhilde, Inez (*Il Trovatore*), Giovanna (*Rigoletto*), Lucia (*Cavalleria Rusticana*), Marianne, Marta (*Mefistofele*), A Woman (*Boris Godunov*).

**Voyer, Giovanni**  *Tenor*
b. Benicarlo, Spain, 1901:
Faust (*La Damnation de Faust*), Hagenbach, Maurizio, Nerone (*Boito*).

**Vroons, Franz**  *Tenor*
b.
Don Basilio (*Il Barbiere di Siviglia*), Oberon, Oedipus, Paco (*La Vida Breve*), Riccardo (*Un Ballo in Maschera*).

**Wachtel, Theodor**  *Tenor*
b. Hamburg, 1823: d. there, 1893
He made his debut in Berlin in 1865.
Chappelou (*Le Postillion de Longjumeau*), Raoul, Stradella, Vasco da Gama.

**Wagenaar, Bernard**  *Composer*
b. Arnhem, Netherlands, 1894:

| | | |
|---|---|---|
| Pieces of Eight | New York | 1944 |

**Waghalter, Ignatz**  *Composer*
b. Warsaw, 1882: d. New York, 1949

| | | |
|---|---|---|
| Der Teufelsweg | Berlin | 1911 |
| Mandragola | „ | 1914 |
| Jugend | „ | 1917 |
| Der Späte Gast | „ | 1922 |
| Sataniel | „ | 1923 |

**Wagner, Cosima**  *Manager*
b. Bellaggio, near Lake Como, 1837: d. Bayreuth, 1930
Daughter of Liszt, she first married the conductor and pianist von Bülow, then left him for Richard Wagner in 1870. After Wagner's death she managed the Festspielhaus at Bayreuth and established many of the forms of education and production which it follows today.

**Wagner, Johanna**  *Soprano*
b. Hanover, 1826: d. Wurzberg, 1894
Richard Wagner's niece. She was a pupil of Viardot-García, and was the first to sing Elisabeth in *Tannhäuser*. Her debut was in *Der Freischütz* at Dresden in 1843, when she sang Agathe.
Adriano (*Rienzi*), Agathe, Donna Anna, Elisabeth, Euryanthe, Fidès, Leonore (*Fidelio*), Leonora (*La Favorita*), Lucrezia, Norma, Rezia, Romeo, Susanna (*Le Nozze di Figaro*), Tancredi, Valentine (*Les Huguenots*).

**Wagner, Richard**  *Composer*
b. Leipzig, 1813: d. Venice, 1883
Wagner attempted to create a German myth in opera, upon libretti of his own. He accomplished his aim, producing an incalculable effect on the writing of opera for the next generations. In the nineteenth century, any progress in the art was therefore usually hooted down as "Wagnerism," whether the composer, thus vilified, admired Wagner or not.

Die Feen
| | | |
|---|---|---|
| (composed 1833) | Munich | 1888 |
| Das Liebesverbot | Magdeburg | 1836 |
| Rienzi | Dresden | 1842 |
| Der Fliegende | | |
| Holländer | ,, | 1843 |
| Tannhäuser | ,, | 1845 |
| Lohengrin | Weimar | 1850 |
| Tristan und Isolde | Munich | 1865 |
| Die Meistersinger | ,, | 1868 |
| Das Ring des Nibelungen | | |
| (Prologue and Trilogy): | | |
| Das Rheingold | ,, | 1869 |
| Die Walküre | ,, | 1870 |
| Siegfried | Bayreuth | 1876 |
| Götterdammerung | ,, | 1876 |
| Parsifal | ,, | 1882 |

**Wagner, Siegfried**          *Composer*
b. Triebchen, 1869: d. Bayreuth, 1930
He was director of his father's operas at
Bayreuth from 1894 until his death.

| | | |
|---|---|---|
| Der Bärenhäuter | Munich | 1899 |
| Der Kobold | Hamburg | 1904 |

**Wagner, Wieland**          *Manager*
b. Bayreuth, 1917
Grandson of Richard Wagner. As stage
director in Bayreuth, he proved a most
radical innovator, particularly in his
simplified manner of staging Wagner's
operas.

**Walker, Edyth**          *Mezzo-soprano*
b. Hopewell, N.Y., 1867: d. New York,
1950
She made her debut at Berlin as Fidès
in 1894, and at the Metropolitan as
Amneris in 1903.
Amneris, Elektra, Fidès, Kundry, Leonora (La Favorita), Nancy (Martha).

**Wallace, William Vincent**          *Composer*
b. Waterford, Iowa, 1812: d. Pyrenees,
1865
| | | |
|---|---|---|
| Maritana | Drury Lane | 1845 |
| Lurline | Covent Garden | 1860 |

**Walter, Bruno**          *Conductor*
(Really B. W. Schlesinger)
b. Berlin, 1876:
Conductor at the Vienna Opera from
1901, at Munich from 1914, and at the
Metropolitan from 1941. He was renowned also for his conducting of symphonic works, especially those of Mahler.

**Walton, William**          *Composer*
b. Lancashire, England, 1902:
| | | |
|---|---|---|
| Troilus and Cressida | London | 1954 |

**Ward, Robert**          *Composer*
b. Cleveland, 1917:
A pupil of Bernard Rogers and Howard
Hanson.
He Who Gets
| | | |
|---|---|---|
| Slapped | New York | 1956 |

**Warren, Leonard**          *Baritone*
b. New York, 1911: d. there, 1960
He made his debut at the Metropolitan
as Paolo in 1939, and became one of the
leading singers of the company. He died
as he began his exit after his last aria in
the second act of La Forza del Destino.
Amonasro, Barnaba, Don Carlo (La
Forza del Destino), High Priest (Alceste),
Iago, Ilo (The Island God), Macbeth,
Paolo, Rigoletto, Scarpia, Tonio.

**Weber, Carl Maria von**          *Composer*
(Full name Carl Maria Friedrich Ernst von
Weber)
b. near Oldenberg, Germany, 1786: d.
London, 1826
His first successful opera, but not his
first work in the form, was Das Waldmäd-
chen, which he wrote at the age of fourteen. His innovations in harmony and in
the romantic continuity of his operas had
a very deep influence on other composers,
particularly Wagner.
| | | |
|---|---|---|
| Das Waldmädchen | Freiberg | 1800 |
| Der Freischütz | Berlin | 1821 |
| Euryanthe | Vienna | 1823 |
| Oberon | London | 1826 |

**Weede, Robert**      *Baritone*
b. Baltimore, 1903:
He made his debut at the Metropolitan in 1937.
Giorgio Germont, Manfredo (*L'Amore dei Tre Re*), Michele (*Il Tabarro*), Rance, Scarpia.

**Weigel, Eugene**      *Composer*
b. Cleveland, 1910:
A pupil of Hindemith.

| | | |
|---|---|---|
| The Lion Makers | | 1953 |
| The Mountain | | |
| Child | Missoula, Montana | 1958 |

**Weil, Hermann**      *Baritone*
b. Karlsruhe, 1877: d. Blue Mountain, N.Y., 1949
The first in the United States to sing Orfeo (*La Favola d'Orfeo*), in a concert at the Metropolitan in 1912. He made his debut at Freiberg in 1901 as Wolfram.
Amfortas, Hans Sachs, Kurnewal, Orfeo (*La Favola d'Orfeo*), Pylade (*Iphigénie en Tauride*), Wolfram.

**Weill, Kurt**      *Composer*
b. Dessau, 1900: d. New York, 1950
A composer in the more or less popular style of whatever country he happened to be working in, he is very well known in the United States for his high-school operetta *Down in the Valley*, and for his highly sophisticated *The Three-penny Opera*, *Street Scene*, and *Lost in the Stars*.

| | | |
|---|---|---|
| Der Protagonist | Dresden | 1926 |
| The Royal Palace | Berlin | 1927 |
| Mahagonny | Baden-Baden | 1927 |
| Die Dreigroschenoper | | |
| (*The Threepenny Opera*) | | |
| | Berlin | 1928 |
| Die Bürgschaft | ,, | 1932 |
| Der Silbersee | | 1933 |
| Marie Galante | | 1933 |
| Street Scene | New York | 1947 |
| Lost in the Stars | ,, | 1949 |

**Weinberg, Jacob**      *Composer*
b. Odessa, 1879: d. New York, 1956

| | | |
|---|---|---|
| Hechalutz (*The Pioneers* | | |
| of Israel*) | New York | 1934 |

**Weinberger, Jaromir**      *Composer*
b. Prague, 1896:
The Polka and Fugue from *Schwanda* are very popular in the United States.

| | | |
|---|---|---|
| Švanda Dudák (*Schwanda* | | |
| the Bagpiper*) | Prague | 1927 |
| Die Geliebte Stimme | Munich | 1930 |
| Lidé z Pokerflatu (*The* | | |
| Outcasts of Poker Flat*) | Brno | 1932 |
| A Bed of Roses | Prague | 1934 |
| Wallenstein | Vienna | 1937 |

**Weingartner, Felix**      *Composer*
b. Dalmatia, 1863: d. Winterthur, Switzerland, 1942
Not only a composer, he conducted opera at Berlin, Vienna, and Boston.

| | | |
|---|---|---|
| Sakuntala | Weimar | 1884 |
| Die Dame Kobold | | 1916 |
| Orestes (*trilogy*) | | 1925 |

**Weisgall, Hugo**      *Composer*
b. Czechoslovakia, 1912:
A pupil of Roger Sessions.

| | | |
|---|---|---|
| Night | | 1932 |
| Lilith | | 1934 |
| The Tenor | Baltimore | 1952 |
| The Stronger | Westport, Conn. | 1952 |
| Six Characters in Search | | |
| of an Author | | 1956 |

**Weldon, John**      *Composer*
b. Chichester, England, 1676: d. London, 1736

| | |
|---|---|
| She Would and She | |
| Would Not | 1703 |
| The Agreeable Disappointment | 1715 |

**Welitsch, Ljuba**      *Soprano*
b. near Varna, Bulgaria, 1913:
She made her debut as Nedda at Graz in 1936, as Donna Anna at London in 1947, and as Salome at the Metropolitan in 1949.

Aida, Amelia (*Un Ballo in Maschera*), Donna Anna, Barbarina, Cherubino, Cio-cio San, Composer (*Ariadne auf Naxos*), Fiordiligi, Hansel, Jenufa, Leonora (*Il Trovatore*), Lisa, Manon Lescaut, Mimi, Minnie, Musetta, Nedda, Rosalinda, Salome, Tatyana, Tosca.

**Wellesz, Egon**                          *Composer*
b. Vienna, 1885:
A scholar, theorist, and composer. He was an associate in Vienna of Schoenberg. He eventually settled in England.

| Die Prinzessin | | |
|---|---|---|
| Girnara | Hanover | 1921 |
| Alkestis | Mannheim · | 1924 |
| The Bacchae | Vienna | 1931 |
| Incognita | Oxford | 1951 |

**Werrenrath, Reinald**                  *Baritone*
b. Brooklyn, N.Y., 1883: d. Pittsburg, 1953
He made his debut at the Metropolitan in 1919, singing Silvio in *I Pagliacci*.

**Wettergren, Gertrud**                *Contralto*
(*Née* Palson)
b. Eslov, Sweden, 1897:
She made her debut in Stockholm in 1922 and at the Metropolitan, singing Amneris, in 1935.

**White, Carolina**                          *Soprano*
b. Dorchester, Mass., 1883:
Gutrune, Maliella, Susanna (*Il Segreto di Susanna*).

**White, Clarence Cameron**        *Composer*
b. Clarksville, Tenn., 1880: d. New York, 1960

| Ouanga | Chicago (*in part*) | 1932 |
|---|---|---|

**Whitehill, Clarence Eugene**          *Bass*
b. Mareno, Iowa, 1871: d. New York, 1932
The first American male singer to appear at the Opéra-Comique where he made his debut in 1900, the same year that he had come out at the Metropolitan.
Altair, Amfortas, Athanaël, Hans Sachs, Jokanaan, Friar Laurence.

**Wickham, Florence Pauline**      *Contralto*
b. Beaver, Pa., 1882:
She made her American debut as Kundry in 1904.
Adriano (*Rienzi*), Amneris, Brangäne, Emilia (*Otello*), Fricka, Kundry, Laura, Adorno, Maddalena, Orfeo, Ortrud, Waltraute.

**Wilder, Alec**                              *Composer*
b. Rochester, N.Y., 1907:

| The Lowland Sea | 1951 |
|---|---|
| Sunday Excursion | 1953 |
| Kittiwake Island | 1955 |

**Wildgans, Friedrich**                    *Composer*
b. Vienna, 1913:

| Der Baum der Erkenntniss | 1935 |
|---|---|

**Williams, Camilla**                        *Soprano*
b. Danville, Virginia:
Aida, Cio-cio San, Mimi.

**Williams, Ralph Vaughan**
*See* Vaughan Williams, Ralph

**Winkelmann, Hermann**                  *Tenor*
b. Brunswick, Germany, 1849: d. Vienna, 1912
The very first to sing Parsifal, being the first of the three who shared the opening performances.
Admetus, Lohengrin, Otello, Parsifal, Rinaldo (*Armida*), Tannhäuser, Tristan, Walther.

**Winter, Peter**                            *Composer*
b. Mannheim, 1754: d. Munich, 1825
Winter spent most of his creative life in Munich, although he had successes in other cities, especially Vienna.

| Der Bettelstudent | Munich | 1785 |
|---|---|---|
| Das Unterbrochene Opferfest | Vienna | 1796 |
| Marie von Montalban | Munich | 1800 |
| Colmal | ,, | 1809 |

**Wissmer, Pierre**                        *Composer*
b. Geneva, 1915:

| Marion | Geneva Radio | 1947 |
|---|---|---|
| Capitaine Bruno | Geneva | 1952 |
| Léonidas | Paris | 1958 |

**Witherspoon, Herbert** *Bass*
b. Buffalo, N.Y., 1873: d. New York, 1935
He made his debut at the Metropolitan in 1908 singing Titurel.

**Wittich, Marie** *Soprano*
b. Giessen, 1868: d. Dresden, 1931
The first Salome. She tried dancing the dance of the veils herself, but Strauss was appalled by the performance and stopped her. Since then a dancer generally has taken the place of the singer in that scene. Isolde, Kundry, Salome, Sieglinde.

**Wolf, Hugo** *Composer*
b. Windischgraz, 1860: d. Vienna, 1903
Famous as a composer of songs.
| Der Corregidor | Mannheim | 1896 |
| Manuel Venegas | „ (*in part*) | 1903 |

**Wolf-Ferrari, Ermanno** *Composer*
b. Venice, 1876: d. there, 1948
| Cenerentola | Venice | 1900 |
| Le Donne Curiose | Munich | 1903 |
| Il Segreto di Susanna | „ | 1909 |
| I Quattro Rusteghi | „ | 1906 |
| I Gioielli della Madonna | Berlin | 1911 |

**Wolff, Albert** *Composer*
b. Paris, 1884:
He was also conductor at the Opéra-Comique and at the Metropolitan.
| L'Oiseau Bleu | Metropolitan | 1919 |

**Wolpe, Stefan** *Composer*
b. Berlin, 1902:
| Schöne Geschichten | | 1927 |
| Zeus und Elida | | 1927 |

**Yamada, Kosçak** *Composer*
b. Tokyo, 1886:
| Alladine et Palomides | | 1913 |
| The Depraved Heavenly Maiden (*composed* 1908) | Tokyo | 1929 |
| Ayame | „ | 1935 |
| The Black Ships | „ | 1940 |
| Yoake | „ | 1940 |
| Hsiang Fei | | 1946 |

**Yeend, Frances** *Soprano*
b.
She made her Metropolitan debut in 1961 as Chrysothemis (*Elektra*)
Countess Almaviva, Marguérite (*Faust*), Micaela, Mimi, Turandot, Violetta.

**Young, Alexander** *Tenor*
b. London, 1920:

**Ysaÿe, Eugène** *Composer*
b. Liège, 1858: d. Brussels, 1931
A famous violinist. His only opera, which he wrote in the last years of his life, was to a libretto in the Walloon dialect.
| Piér li Hovieu (*Peter the Miner*) | Liège | 1931 |

**Zadek, Hilde** *Soprano*
b. Bromberg, 1917:
Aida, Donna Anna, Ariadnę (*Ariadne auf Naxos*), Elsa, Eva, Magda (*The Consul*), Vitellia (*La Clemenza di Tito*).

**Zádor, Eugene** *Composer*
b. Bátaszék, Hungary, 1894:
Zádor now lives in the United States.
| Diana | Budapest | 1923 |
| A Holtak Szigete (*The Island of the Dead*) | „ | 1928 |
| Columbus | New York | 1939 |

**Zandonai, Riccardo** *Composer*
b. Trentino, 1883: d. Pesaro, 1944
| Il Grillo del Focolare (*The Cricket on the Hearth*) | Turin | 1908 |
| Conchita | Milan | 1911 |
| Francesca da Rimini | Turin | 1914 |
| Giulietta e Romeo | Rome | 1922 |

**Zandt, Marie van** *Soprano*
b. New York, 1861: d. Cannes, 1919
The first Lakmé. She made her debut at Turin in 1879, and at the Metropolitan in 1891.
Amina, Cherubino, Dinorah, Lakmé, Manon, Mignon, Rosina (*Il Barbiere di Siviglia*), Zerlina (*Don Giovanni*).

**Zanten, Cornelia van** *Soprano*
b. Dordrecht, Netherlands, 1855: d. The Hague, 1946

**Zeisl, Eric** *Composer*
b. Vienna, 1905: d. Los Angeles, 1959
Leonce und Lena Prague 1937

**Zemlinsky, Alexander von** *Composer*
b. Vienna, 1872: d. Larchmont, N.Y., 1942
He was a conductor and a teacher. Arnold Schoenberg was among his pupils.
Es War Einmal Vienna 1900
Kleider Machen Leute „ 1910

**Zenatello, Giovanni** *Tenor*
b. Verona, 1876: d. New York, 1949
The first Pinkerton. He married Maria Gay in 1913.
Andrea Chenier, Canio, Enzo, Hermann (*Pique-Dame*), Loris, Manrico, Otello, Pinkerton, Radames, Silvio.

**Zeno, Apostolo** *Librettist*
b. Venice, 1668: d. there, 1750
He was court poet to the Emperor Charles VI. He wrote seventy-one libretti for the Italian opera at Vienna.

**Zerr, Anne** *Soprano*
b. Baden-Baden, 1822: d. Winterbach, 1881
The first Harriett (*Martha*).
Astrifiammante, Harriett (*Martha*), Lucia, Rosa (*Faust* by Spohr).

**Zingarelli, Niccolo Antonio** *Composer*
b. Naples, 1752: d. Torre del Greco, 1837
He wrote thirty-seven operas.
Giulietta e Romeo La Scala 1796
Clitemnestra „ 1800

**Zolotarev, Vassily** *Composer*
b. Taganrog, Russia, 1873:
A pupil of Rimsky-Korsakov.
The Decembrists Moscow 1925
Ak-gul 1942

# THE CHARACTERS IN THE OPERAS

After the name of each important character you will find a list of some of the important singers who have undertaken the role. In some cases the first to perform the role is indicated at the beginning of the list, as: 1st Grisi.

An index to this section, in which the characters are arranged according to voice, will be found at the end of the book.

| CHARACTER | | ROLE | SINGER | OPERA |
|---|---|---|---|---|
| **Abate di Chazeuil** | Tenor | | | *Adriana Lecouvreur* |
| **Abbate Cospicuo** | Baritone | | | *Arlecchino* |
| **Abbé** | Tenor | | | *Andrea Chénier* |
| **Abbess** | Silent | | | *Robert le Diable* |
| **Abbess** | Mezzo-soprano | | | *Suor Angelica* |
| **Abdallo** | Tenor | Nabucco's officer | | *Nabucco* |
| **Abdisa** | Tenor | Patriarch of Assyria | | *Palestrina* |
| **Abdullah** | Speaker | A pirate | | *Oberon* |
| **Abigaille** | Soprano | Slave, supposed daughter of Nabucco | 1st Giuseppina Strepponi | *Nabucco* |
| **Abimilech** | Bass | Philistine Satrap of Gaza | Burke | *Samson et Dalila* |
| **Abraham** | Speaker | Innkeeper | | *Háry János* |
| **Abul Hassan Ali Ebn Bekar** | Bass | A barber | Gura | *Barbier von Bagdad, Der* |
| **Achilles** | Tenor | Thessalian warrior | 1st Legros; Bentonelli | *Iphigénie en Aulide* |
| **Actors** | Chorus | | | *Gloriana, Mignon* |
| **Actresses** | Chorus | | | *Mignon* |

| CHARACTER | ROLE | SINGER | OPERA |
|---|---|---|---|
| **Adalgisa** Mezzo-soprano | Temple virgin | 1st Grisi; Barbieri, Stignani, Thebom | *Norma* |
| **Adelaide** Mezzo-soprano | Arabella's mother | Dunn | *Arabella* |
| **Adele** Soprano | Eisenstein's maid | Munsel, Peters | *Die Fledermaus* |
| **Adelma** Mezzo-soprano | Turandot's slave | | *Turandot* (Busoni) |
| **Adina** Soprano | Wealthy young farm owner | Lind | *L'Elisir d'Amore* |
| **Admetus** Baritone | Alceste's husband | 1st Giuseppe Tibaldi; Maison, Rakewski, Winkelmann | *Alceste* |
| **Admiral Lefort** *See* Lefort, Admiral | | | |
| **Adolar** Tenor | | Alvary, Nachbauer | *Euryanthe* |
| **Adonisedek** Baritone | | | *Debora* |
| **Adorno** *See* Gabriel Adorno | | | |
| **Adriana Lecouvreur** Soprano | Actress, in love with Maurizio | 1st Pandolfini; Brema, Caniglia, Cavalieri, Cobelli, Favero, Giachetti, Olivero, Oltra-Bella | *Adriana Lecouvreur* |
| **Adriano** Mezzo-soprano | Collonna's son | 1st Schröder-Devrient; Wagner, Wickham | *Rienzi* |
| **Aegisth** Tenor | Klytemnestra's lover | 1st Semback; Lorenz, Svanholm, Wölfl | *Elektra* |
| **Aeneas** Tenor | Trojan general | Pears | *Dido and Aeneas* |
| **Aeneas** *See also* Eneé | | | |
| **Aennchen** Soprano | Agathe's cousin | Seidl-Krauss | *Freischütz, Der* |
| **Afanasy Viazemsky, Prince** Tenor | | | *Pskovityanka* |

| CHARACTER | | ROLE | SINGER | OPERA |
|---|---|---|---|---|
| **Afra** | Tenor | Landlady, in love with Hagenbach | 1st Stehle; Bertana | *La Wally* |
| **Afron, Prince** Baritone | | | | *Coq d'Or, Le* |
| **Agamemnon** Baritone | | King of Mycenae | 1st Larrivée; Baklanov | *Iphigénie en Aulide* |
| **Agata** | Contralto | | Kobart | *Maria Golovin* |
| **Agathe** | Soprano | Cuno's daughter | 1st Stoltz; Borkh, Fisher, Gadski, Goltz, Kronold, Larsen-Todsen, Lind, Malten, Morena, Paton, Peschka-Leutner, Rethberg, Rysanek, Schröder-Devrient, Seefried, Seidl-Krauss, Stehle, Wagner | *Der Freischütz* |
| **Agnes** Mezzo-soprano | | Micha's wife | | *Prodana Nevešta* |
| **Agricultural laborers** Chorus | | | | *The Boatswain's Mate* |
| **Ahmed** | Bass | Pastry cook | | *Marouf* |
| **Aida** | Soprano | Ethiopian princess, slave to Amneris | 1st Pozzini; Alda, Arangi-Lombardi, Bampton, Boninsegna, Borkh, Brouwenstijn, Callas, Caniglia, Cigna, Cross, Destinn, Eames, Easton, Flagstad, Fursch-Madi, Gadski, Giannini, Goltz, Hauk, Juch, Kellogg, Krauss, Lilli Lehman, Litvinne, Mantelli, Matzenauer, Milanov, Muzio, | *Aida* |

# THE CHARACTERS IN THE OPERAS

| CHARACTER | ROLE | SINGER | OPERA |
|---|---|---|---|
| | | Nordica, Patti, Pauly, Ponselle, Price, Raisa, Rappold, Josephine de Reszke, Rethberg, Rysanek, Shuard, Teresa Stoltz, Tebaldi, Ternina, Torriani, Eva Turner, Valleria, Varnay, Vere, Welitsch, Williams, Zadek | |
| **Aithra**      Soprano | A sorceress | 1st Rajdl; Fleischer, Heidersbach | *Die Aegyptische Helene* |
| **Alberich**      Bass Baritone | Nibelung dwarf, Wotan's enemy | 1st Hill; Bispham | *Das Ring des Nibelungen* |
| **Albert**      Bass | Sergeant | | *La Juive* |
| **Albert**      Baritone | Charlotte's fiancé | | *Werther* |
| **Albert Herring**      Tenor | Greengrocer's assistant | | *Albert Herring* |
| **Albert K**      Bass | | | *Der Prozess* |
| **Albine**      Contralto | Abbess | | *Thaïs* |
| **Albrecht**  *See* Alberich | | | |
| **Albrecht von Brandenburg, Cardinal**      Tenor | Archbishop of Mainz | | *Mathis der Maler* |
| **Alcalde**      Bass | | | *Maritana* |
| **Alcalde, The**  *See* Juan Lopez | | | |
| **Alceste**      Soprano | Wife of Admetus | 1st Antonia Bernasconi; Cigna, Flagstad, Lawrence, Levasseur, Lubin, Milder, Viardot-Garcia | *Alceste* |
| **Alcindoro**      Bass | Musetta's latest escort | Baccaloni, Renan | *La Bohème* |

| CHARACTER | | ROLE | SINGER | OPERA |
|---|---|---|---|---|
| **Alcmene** Mezzo-soprano | | A queen, formerly beloved by Jupiter | | *Die Liebe der Danae* |
| **Alessio** | Bass | Villager | | *La Sonnambula* |
| **Alfio** | Baritone | Village teamster | 1st Salasso; Bispham, Franci, Panerai, del Puente | *Cavalleria Rusticana* |
| **Alfonso, Don** Baritone | | | 1st Benucci; Lorenzo Alvary, Brownlee, Stabile | *Così fan Tutte* |
| **Alfonso, XI** Baritone | | King of Castile | Ancona, Jean de Reszke | *La Favorita* |
| **Alfonso D'Arcos** Tenor | | Son of the Viceroy in Naples | Koegel | *Masaniello* |
| **Alfonso D'Este** Baritone | | Duke of Ferrara | Faure, Novara | *Lucrezia Borgia* |
| **Alfred** | Tenor | A singer | Sullivan | *Die Fledermaus* |
| **Alfredo Germont** Tenor | | Violetta's lover | 1st Graziani; Conley, Gigli, Hislop, Mario, McCormack, Peerce, Poleri, di Stefano, Valletti | *La Traviata* |
| **Ali** | Baritone | Marouf's friend | | *Marouf* |
| **Alice** Mezzo-soprano | | Lucia's companion | | *Lucia di Lammermoor* |
| **Alice** | Soprano | Robert's foster sister | 1st Derus-Gras; Caron, Falcon, Lind, Paton, Peschka-Leutner, Viardot-Garcia | *Robert le Diable* |
| **Alice Ford** | Soprano | Ford's wife | 1st Stehle; Curtin, Eames, Steber, Tietjens | *Falstaff* |
| **Alice Ford** *See also* Fluth, Frau | | | | |
| **Alidoro** | Bass | A philosopher and magician | | *La Cenerentola* |

| CHARACTER | ROLE | SINGER | OPERA |
|---|---|---|---|
| **Alisa** *See* Alice | | | |
| **Alladine** Pantomine | Former wife of Barbe-Bleue | | *Ariane et Barbe-Bleue* |
| **Almanzor** Speaker | Emir of Tunis | | *Oberon* |
| **Almaviva, Count** Tenor | | 1st Manuel Garcia, Sr; Hackett, Mario, Phillips, Jean de Reszke, Schack, Valleti | *Il Barbiere di Siviglia* |
| **Almaviva, Count** Baritone | | 1st Mandini; Bassi, Beck, Brownlee, Capoul, Cassell, Duprez, Landi, Maurel, T. Phillips, Poell, Edouard de Reszke, Santley, Scotti | *Le Nozze di Figaro* |
| **Almaviva, Countess** Soprano | | 1st Laschi; della Casa, Carvalhe, Cruvelli, Eames, Brouwenstijn, Faull, Hempel, Jurinac, Christine Nilsson, Steber, Tietjens, Yeend | *Le Nozze di Figare* |
| **Almira** Soprano | | Peschka-Leutner | *Almira* (Handel) |
| **Alms Collector** Soprano | | | *Suor Angelica* |
| **Alwa** Tenor | Schon's son, a writer | | *Lulu* |
| **Altair** Baritone | | 1st Burg; Hotter, Prohaska, Schorr, Whitehill | *Die Aegyptische Helena* |
| **Altichiara** Mezzo-soprano | Francesca's woman | | *Francesca da Rimini* |
| **Alto, The** Contralto | Klymene in Lully's Opera | | *Cardillac* |
| **Altoum, Emperor** Bass | Turandot's father | de Paolis, Fried | *Turandot* (Busoni) |

| CHARACTER | ROLE | SINGER | OPERA |
|---|---|---|---|
| **Alvar, Don** Tenor | Councillor | | *L'Africaine* |
| **Alvaro, Don** Tenor | Leonora's lover | 1st Tamberlik; Baum, Caruso, Gigli, del Monaco, Tucker | *La Forza del Destino* |
| **Alvise, Badoero** Bass | Inquisitor | Moscona, Novara, Pasero, Sammarco, Siepi | *La Gioconda* |
| **Amalia** Soprano | | 1st Lind | *I Masnadieri* (Verdi) |
| **Amantio di Nicolao, Ser** Baritone | Lawyer | | *Gianni Schicchi* |
| **Amaryllus** Tenor | Son of the empress | | *The Poisoned Kiss* |
| **Ambassadors** Chorus | | | *Rienzi* |
| **Ambrogio** Bass | Bartolo's servant | | *Il Barbiere di Siviglia* |
| **Ambroise, Maître** Bass | Vincent's father | Gassier | *Mireille* |
| **Amelfa** Contralto | Royal housekeeper | | *Le Coq d'Or* |
| **Amelia** Soprano | Renato's wife, beloved by Riccardo | Brouwenstijn, Callas, Caniglia, Cigna, Cross, Destinn, Goltz, Grob-Prandl, Hempel, Lilli Lehmann, Matzenauer, Milanov, Nordica, Ternina, Tietjens, Eva Turner, Welitsch | *Un Ballo in Maschera* |
| **Amelia Boccanegra** Soprano | Simon's daughter brought up as Maria Grimaldi | Milanov, Shuard, Tebaldi | *Simon Boccanegra* |
| **Amfortas** Baritone | Ruler of the Kingdom of the Grail | 1st Reichmann; Amato, Bender, Burke, Gura, Janssen, London, Perron, Plaschke, | *Parsifal* |

# THE CHARACTERS IN THE OPERAS

| CHARACTER | ROLE | SINGER | OPERA |
|---|---|---|---|
| | | Scheidl, Scheider-mantel, Schlusnus, Scherr, Weil, Whitehill | |
| **Amina** Soprano | The sleepwalker, engaged to Elvine | 1st Pasta; Albani, Callas, Charton-Demeur, Cole, Galli-Curci, Gerster, Hauk, Lind, Malibran, Murska, Nevada, Parepa-Rosa, Patti, Schröder-Devrient, Sembrich, Sontag, Luisa Tetrazzini, Viardot-Garcia, van Zandt | *La Sonnambula* |
| **Aminta** Soprano | Wife of Henry Morosus. An actress. | 1st Cebotari; Carosio, Carroll | *Die Schweigsame Frau* |
| **Amme, Die** *See* Nurse | | | |
| **Amneris** Contralto | Daughter of the King of Egypt | 1st Grossi; Barbieri, Bible, Brandt, Brema, Cary, Castagna, Fornia-Labey, Gulbranson, Harshaw, Homer, Kirkby-Lunn, Langendorf, Madeira, Mantelli, Matzenauer, Meisle, Mildenburg, Minghini-Cattaneo, Nikolaidi, Ober, Onegin, Carmela Ponselle, Rankin, Stignani, Thebom, Trebelli, Walker, Wettergren, Wickham | *Aida* |

| CHARACTER | ROLE | SINGER | OPERA |
|---|---|---|---|
| **Amonasro,** Baritone | King of Ethiopia. Aida's father | 1st Costa; Ancona, Beck, Formichi, Gobbi, Kaschmann, London, Maurel, Edouard de Reszke, Scolera, Scotti, Thomas, Tibbett, Warren | *Aida* |
| **Amor** Soprano | God of love | Gluck, Gueden | *Orfeo ed Euridice* |
| **Anabaptists** Chorus | | | *Le Prophète* |
| **Anaide** Contralto | Zaza's mother | | *Zaza* |
| **Anatol** Tenor | Son of Vanessa's only lover | 1st Gedda | *Vanessa* |
| **Anckarström** | | | *Gustave III* |
| **Anckarström** *See* Renato | | | |
| **Anckarström, Mrs.** Soprano | | 1st Falcon | *Gustave III* |
| **Andrea Chénier** Tenor | Revolutionary and poet | 1st Borgatti; Beval, Gigli, Lauri-Volpi, del Monaco, Zenatello | *Andrea Chénier* |
| **Andreloux** Mezzo-soprano | Shepherd | | *Mireille* |
| **Andrès** Tenor | Stella's servant | | *Les Conte d'Hoffmann* |
| **Andres** Tenor | | | *Wozzeck* |
| **Andrew J.** Tenor | | | *The Mother of Us All* |
| **Andrew Khovansky, Prince** Tenor | Ivan's son | | *Khovantschina* |
| **Andromaque** Pantomine | Hector's widow | | *Les Troyens* |
| **Anfinomo** Tenor | Penelope's suitor | | *Il Ritorno d'Ulisse in Patria* |
| **Angel More** Soprano | | | *The Mother of Us All* |

| CHARACTER | | ROLE | SINGER | OPERA |
|---|---|---|---|---|
| **Angèle** | Soprano | | Ugalde | *Domino Noir* (Auber) |
| **Angelic Voices** (Three) | Sopranos | | | *Palestrina* |
| **Angelica** | Soprano | Tormentilla's maid | | *The Poisoned Kiss* |
| **Angelica, Suor** | Soprano | A nun | 1st Farrar; dalla Rizza, Mazzolini, Carena, Oltra-Bella | *Suor Angelica* |
| **Angelina** | Contralto | Don Magnifico's step-daughter, Cinderella | 1st Giorgi-Righetti; Bible, Malibran | *La Cenerentola* |
| **Angelotti** *See* Cesare Angelotti | | | | |
| **Angels** | Chorus | | | *Faust, Palestrina, Pilgrim's Progress* |
| **Angels** (Two) | Soprano and Mezzo-soprano | | | *Le Jongleur de Nôtre Dame* |
| **Animal Tamer** | | (Later Redrig) | | *Lula* |
| **Animal Tamer** | Tenor | | | *Der Rosenkavalier* |
| **Animals** | Chorus | | | *L'Enfant et les Sortilèges* |
| **Anita** | Soprano | | 1st Calvé | *La Navarraise* |
| **Anna** | Contralto | Servant of Inez | | *L'Africaine* |
| **Anna** | Soprano | Gaveston's ward, the White Lady | 1st Rigaut; Gadski, Krauss | *La Dame Blanche* |
| **Anna** | Soprano | Chambermaid | | *Intermezzo* |
| **Anna** | Soprano | Zaccaria's sister | | *Nabucco* |
| **Anna** | Contralto | Didon's sister | | *Les Troyens* |
| **Anna Bolena** | Soprano | Mother of Elisabeth, and wife of Henry VIII | 1st Pasta; Grisi | *Anna Bolena* |
| **Anna, Donna** | Soprano | Don Ottavio's fiancée | 1st Teresa Saporiti; Camporese, Danco, Destinn, Dickons, | *Don Giovanni* |

317

| CHARACTER | ROLE | SINGER | OPERA |
|---|---|---|---|
| | | della Casa, Falcon, Faull, Fisher, Fursch-Madi, Harshaw, Krauss, Lilli Lehmann, Lind, Litvinne, Matzenauer, Milanov, Nordica, Parepa-Rosa, Price, Schumann, Sontag, Steber, Tietjens, Viardot-Garcia, Wagner, Welitsch, Zadek | |
| **Anna Gomez** Soprano | | | *The Consul* |
| **Anna Hope** Mezzo-soprano | | | *The Mother of Us All* |
| **Anna Reich** Soprano | Ann Page | Flagstad | *Die Lustigen Weiber von Windsor* |
| **Anne** Soprano | | | *The Mother of Us All* |
| **Anne** *See* Ninetta *See also* Aennchen | | | |
| **Anne Page** *See* Anna Reich | | | |
| **Anne Trulove** Soprano | | 1st Schwarzkopf; Gueden, Morison, Berger, Harvey | *The Rake's Progress* |
| **Annina** Contralto | Valzacchi's partner | Evans, Glaz, Lipton | *Der Rosenkavalier* |
| **Annina** Soprano | Violetta's confidante | | *La Traviata* |
| **Annius** Mezzo-soprano | Young patrician of Rome | | *La Clemenza di Tito* |
| **Annunziata** Silent | Matteo's wife | | *Arlecchino* |
| **Anthony, Susan B.** *See* Susan B. Anthony | | | |
| **Antigonae** Soprano | Daughter of Oedipus | Goltz | *Antigonae (Orff)* |

| CHARACTER | | ROLE | SINGER | OPERA |
|---|---|---|---|---|
| **Antinoo** | Bass | Penelope's suitor | | *Il Ritorno d'Ulisse in Patria* |
| **Anton Buis von Müglitz** | Bass | Archbishop of Prague | | *Palestrina* |
| **Antonia** | Soprano | Singer | 1st Isaac; Amara, della Casa, Fremstad, Hempel, Jurinach, Seefried, Steber, Teyte | *Les Contes d'Hoffmann* |
| **Antonia** | Soprano | | | *Tiefland* |
| **Antonia's Mother's Voice** Mezzo-soprano | | | | *Les Contes d'Hoffmann* |
| **Antonida** | Soprano | Ivan's daughter | Albani, Cebotari | *Ivan Susanin* |
| **Antonio** | Baritone | Linda's father | | *Linda di Chamounix* |
| **Antonio** | Bass | Servant | | *Mignon* |
| **Antonio** | Bass | Susanna's uncle, a gardener | 1st Bussani; Pröglhof | *Le Nozze di Figaro* |
| **Apollo** | Tenor | | | *Daphne* |
| **Apollo** See Bass, The | | | | |
| **Apollon** | Bass | A voice | 1st Laschi | *Alceste* |
| **Apollon** | Baritone | | | *Eumenides* |
| **Apollyon** | Bass | | | *Pilgrim's Progress* |
| **Apparition of a Youth** | Tenor | | | *Die Frau ohne Schatten* |
| **Apprentice** | Baritone | | | *Louise* |
| **Apprentices** | Chorus | | | *Die Meistersinger* |
| **Arabella** | Soprano | | 1st Ursuleac; della Casa, Steber | *Arabella* |
| **Arbace** | Tenor | Idomeneo's confidant | 1st Panzacchi | *Idomeneo* |
| **Arcas** | | Agamemnon's messenger | | *Iphigénie en Aulide* |

| CHARACTER | ROLE | SINGER | OPERA |
|---|---|---|---|
| **Archbishop** *See* Albrecht Von Brandenburg | | | |
| **Archdale, Mr.** Speaker | A white man | | *Porgy and Bess* |
| **Archer** Tenor | | | *Francesca da Rimini* |
| **Archer, First** Bass | | | *Khovantschina* |
| **Archer, Second** Bass | | | *Khovantschina* |
| **Archer, Third** Tenor | | | *Khovantschina* |
| **Archers** Chorus | | | *Francesca da Rimini, Khovantschina, Luisa Miller, Pskovityanka* |
| **Archibaldo** Bass | King of Altura | 1st de Angelis; Autori, Didur, Lazzari, Mardonis, Pasero, Pinza, Rossi-Lemeni | *L'Amore dei Tre Re* |
| **Ariadne** Soprano *Also called* Prima Donna | | 1st Jeritza; Goltz, Jurinac, Rysanek, Zadek | *Ariadne auf Naxos* |
| **Ariane** Mezzo-soprano | Bluebeard's sixth wife | 1st Leblanc; Farrar | *Ariane et Barbe-Bleue* |
| **Arianna** Soprano | | 1st Virginia Andreini | *Arianna* |
| **Aristée** *See* Pluton | | | |
| **Arithmetic** Tenor | A little old man | (*The same singer sings* La Rainette) | *L'Enfant et les Sortilèges* |
| **Arkel** Bass | King of Allemonde, Pelléas' grandfather | 1st Vieuille; Lorenzo Alvary, Hines, Morena | *Pelléas et Mélisande* |
| **Arlecchino** Speaker | Harlequin | | *Arlecchino* |
| **Arlecchino** *See also* Beppe | | | |
| **Arline** Soprano | The Count's daughter | Kemp, Lussan, Peters | *The Bohemian Girl* |

| CHARACTER | | ROLE | SINGER | OPERA |
|---|---|---|---|---|
| **Armida** | Soprano | | 1st Levasseur; Callas, Fremstad, Gluck, Malten | *Armida* (Gluck) |
| **Armored Men** See Men in Armor (Two) | | | | |
| **Arnheim, Count** | Bass | Governor | | *The Bohemian Girl* |
| **Arnold** | Tenor | Swiss patrol, Mathilde's suitor | 1st Nourrit; Tamagno | *Guillaume Tell* |
| **Arrigo** | Tenor | Young Sicilian in love with Elena | | *I Vespri Siciliani* |
| **Arsace** | Contralto | General of the Assyrians | Viardot-Garcia, Trebelli | *Semiramide* |
| **Arsena** | Soprano | Zsupan's daughter | | *Zigeunerbaron* |
| **Artaban** | Tenor | Financier | | *Esther de Carpentras* |
| **Artemis** (*This part was inserted by Richard Wagner in Act III in his revision of 1846.*) | | The goddess | | *Iphigénie en Aulide* |
| **Arthur Bucklaw, Lord** | Tenor | | | *Lucia di Lammermoor* |
| **Arthur Jones** | Baritone | Impressed seaman | | *Billy Budd* |
| **Arthur Talbot** | Tenor | Cavalier, Elvira's lover | 1st Rubini; Bonci, di Stefano | *I Puritani* |
| **Artilleryman, First and Second** | Speakers | | | *Háry János* |
| **Artists** | Chorus | | | *La Rondine* |
| **Arturo** See Arthur Bucklaw See also Arthur Talbot | | | | |
| **Arvidson** See Ulrica | | | | |

| CHARACTER | | ROLE | SINGER | OPERA |
|---|---|---|---|---|
| **Ascagne** | Soprano | Aeneas' son | | *Les Troyens* |
| **Ascanio** | | Cellini's apprentice | | *Benvenuto Cellini* |
| | Mezzo-soprano | | | |
| **Ashby** | Bass | Wells-Fargo man | Tozzi | *La Fanciulla del West* |
| **Ashton** | | | | |
| *See* Enrico | | | | |
| **Asmodus** | Baritone | Spirit voice | | *Doktor Faustus* |
| **Aspasia** | Soprano | | Bernasconi | *Mitridate* |
| **Aspirant Sisters** | | | | *Suor Angelica* |
| | Mezzo-sopranos | | | |
| **Assad** | Tenor | | | *Die Königin von Saba* |
| **Assan** | Baritone | Sorel's friend | | *The Consul* |
| **Assur** | Baritone | Prince, accomplice of Semiramide | Faure, Foli, Gassier, Lablache | *Semiramide* |
| **Astaroth** | Soprano | Slave of the Queen of Sheba | | *Die Königin von Saba* |
| **Asteria** | Soprano | | 1st Raisa; Cigna, Arangi-Lombardi, Laszlo, Scacciati | *Nerone* |
| **Astolfo** | Bass | Lucrezia's servant | | *Lucrezia Borgia* |
| **Astrologer** | Tenor | | | *Le Coq d'Or* |
| **Astynax** | Pantomime | Andromaque's son | | *Les Troyens* |
| **Athanaël** | Baritone | Young monk | 1st Delmas; Bechi, Thomas, Whitehill | *Thaïs* |
| **Athena's Statue** | | | | |
| *See* Statue d'Athéna, La | | | | |
| **Attendants** | Chorus | | | *L'Africaine, La Favorita, Lohengrin* |
| **Augusta Tabor** | | | Bible | *The Ballad of Baby Doe* |
| | Mezzo-soprano | | | |
| **Auguste** | Tenor | | | *Zaza* |
| **Augustin Moser** | | Mastersinger and tailor | | *Die Meistersinger* |
| | Tenor | | | |

| CHARACTER | ROLE | SINGER | OPERA |
|---|---|---|---|
| **Aunt** Contralto | | | *Její Pastorkyňa* (Jenufa) |
| **Auntie** Contralto | Landlady of The Boar | 1st Coates | *Peter Grimes* |
| **Avis** Soprano | Laurence's daughter, 17 | | *The Wreckers* |
| **Avito** Tenor | Former prince, in love with Fiora | 1st Ferrari-Fontana; F. Albanese, Crimi, Gigli, Le Giudice, Jagel, Kullman, Marcato, Martin, Merli, Piccaluga, Sullivan, Tokatyan | *L'Amore dei Tre Re* |
| **Avosmediano** Bass-baritone | Bishop of Cadiz | | *Palestrina* |
| **Azema** Soprano | Princess, beloved by Arsace | | *Semiramide* |
| **Azriel** Tenor | | | *Debora e Jaele* |
| **Azucena** Mezzo-soprano | Old gypsy woman of Biscay | 1st Goggi; Barbieri, Brandt, Cary, Dalis, Fremstad, Gay, Harshaw, Homer, Howard, Langendorf, Matzenauer, Ober, Phillips, Scalchi, Schumann-Heink, Simoniato, Thebom, Trebelli, Claramae Turner, Viardot-Garcia | *Il Trovatore* |
| **Ball Hanan** Baritone | Palace overseer | | *Die Königin von Saba* |
| **Baba** Contralto | Madame Flora, a medium | 1st C. Turner; Powers, Pederzini | *The Medium* |
| **Baba Mustapha** Tenor | A cadi | | *Der Barbier von Bagdad* |
| **Baba the Turk** Mezzo-soprano | A bearded lady | 1st Tourel; Madeira, Thebom | *The Rake's Progress* |
| **Babekan** Speaker | Saracen prince | | *Oberon* |

| CHARACTER | ROLE | SINGER | OPERA |
|---|---|---|---|
| **Babinsky**  Tenor | Romantic bandit | | *Švanda Dudák* |
| **Baby Doe**  Soprano | | | *The Ballad of Baby Doe* |
| **Bacchantes**  Chorus | | | *Fête Galante, Tannhäuser* |
| **Bacchus**  Tenor  *Also called* The Tenor | | McCracken | *Ariadne auf Naxos* |
| **Bacchus**  Speaker | A god | | *Orphée aux Enfers* |
| **Baculus**  Bass | Schoolmaster | | *Der Wildschütz* |
| **Baggott, Miss**  Contralto | Housekeeper, *called* Gladys Parworthy *in Acts I and II* | | *Let's Make an Opera* |
| **Bailli, Le**  Bass | Charlotte's father, 50 | Lorenzo Alvary | *Werther* |
| **Baldassare**  Baritone | Old shepherd | | *L'Arlesiana* |
| **Baldassare**  *See also* Balthazar | | | |
| **Balducci**  Bass | Papal Treasurer and Teresa's father | | *Benvenuto Cellini* |
| **Ballad Seller**  Tenor | | | *Hugh the Drover* |
| **Ballad Singer**  Bass | A blind man | | *Gloriana* |
| **Ballad Singer**  *See also* Gioconda | | | |
| **Balstrode, Captain**  Baritone | Retired merchant skipper | 1st Roderick Jones; Pease | *Peter Grimes* |
| **Balthasar Zorn**  Tenor | Mastersinger and pewterer | de Paolis | *Die Meistersinger* |
| **Balthazar**  Bass | Superior of the monastery | Plançon | *La Favorita* |
| **Bandit Chief** | | | *Don Quichotte* |
| **Bandits**  Chorus | | | *Don Quichotte, Ernani* |
| **Banquo**  Bass | A general, Macbeth's rival | Hines | *Macbeth* |
| **Barak**  Bass | Jewish commander | | *Debora e Jaele* |

| CHARACTER | ROLE | SINGER | OPERA |
|---|---|---|---|
| **Barak** Bass-baritone | A dyer | | *Die Frau ohne Schatten* |
| **Barak** Baritone | Calaf's servant | | *Turandot* (Busoni) |
| **Barak's Wife** Soprano | | Steber | *Die Frau ohne Schatten* |
| **Barbacan** Baritone | Concierge of the synagogue | | *Esther de Carpentras* |
| **Barbara** Mezzo-soprano | Foster child of the Kabanovs | | *Katya Kabanova* |
| **Barbarina** Soprano | Antonio's daughter | 1st Nanetta Gottlieb; Feldbermayer, Welitsch | *Le Nozze di Figaro* |
| **Barbe-Bleue** Bass | Bluebeard | 1st Vieuille; Rothier | *Ariane et Barbe-Bleue* |
| **Barber** See Abul Hassan See also Figaro See also Schneiderbart | | | |
| **Barce** Soprano | Servant | | *Hubička* |
| **Bard** Speaker | Narrator | | *Duke Bluebeard's Castle* |
| **Bardolph** Tenor | Falstaff's friend | | *Falstaff* |
| **Barena** Soprano | Servant at the mill | | *Její Pastorkyňa* (*Jenufa*) |
| **Barinkay** See Sandor Barinkay | | | |
| **Barnaba** Baritone | Inquisition spy | Bassi, Bonelli, Colzani, Franci, Giraldoni, Inghilleri, Morelli, del Puento, Warren | *La Gioconda* |
| **Baroncelli** Tenor | Roman citizen | | *Rienzi* |
| **Baroness, The Old** Soprano | | 1st Resnik | *Vanessa* |

| CHARACTER | ROLE | SINGER | OPERA |
|---|---|---|---|
| **Bartolo, Doctor** Bass | Rosina's guardian | d'Angelo, Baccaloni, Corsina | Il Barbiere di Siviglia |
| **Bartolo, Doctor** Bass | | 1st Bussani; Allin, Baccaloni, Corena, Mariz, Renan | Le Nozze di Figaro |
| **Basilio** Bass | A singing teacher | Chaliapin, Foli, Formes, Hines, Mirabella, Pinza, Edouard de Reszke, Ronconi, Rossi-Lemeni, Siepi, Tajo, Vroons | Il Barbiere di Siviglia |
| **Basilio, Don** Tenor | Organist and music-master | 1st Michael Kelly; Murray Dickie, de Paolis | Le Nozze di Figaro |
| **Bass, The** Bass | Apollo in Lully's opera | | Cardillac |
| **Bayan** Tenor | Bard | | Russlan and Ludmilla |
| **Bear** Silent | | | Siegfried |
| **Béatrice** Mezzo-soprano | Leonato's niece | 1st Charton-Demeur | Béatrice et Bénédict |
| **Beauty** From Chorus | | | Iris |
| **Beckmesser, Sixtus** Bass | Mastersinger and Town Clerk | 1st Hölzel; Bispham, Doench, Griswold, Kunz, Renaud | Die Meistersinger |
| **Beelzebub** Tenor | Spirit voice | | Doktor Faustus |
| **Beggar** Speaker | | | The Beggar's Opera |
| **Belcore** Baritone | Sergeant | Ronconi, Scotti | L'Elisir d'Amore |
| **Belinda** Soprano | Dido's lady in waiting | | Dido and Aeneas |
| **Bellangère** Soprano | Former wife of Barbe-Bleue | | Ariane et Barbe-Bleue |
| **Belmonte** Tenor | Spanish nobleman | 1st Ademberger; Kullmann, Rounseville | Die Entführung aus dem Serail |

| CHARACTER | ROLE | SINGER | OPERA |
|---|---|---|---|
| **Ben** Baritone | | 1st Kwarton | *The Telephone* |
| **Ben Budge** From Chorus | Gentleman of the road | Rogier | *The Beggar's Opera* |
| **Bench, The** Child | | | *L'Enfant et les Sortilèges* |
| **Bénédict** Tenor | An officer | | *Béatrice et Bénédict* |
| **Benes** Bass | Jailer | | *Dalibor* |
| **Benn, Harry** Tenor | Former boatswain | | *The Boatswain's Mate* |
| **Benno Robertson, Sir** Tenor | Puritan | | *I Puritani* |
| **Benoit** Bass | Landlord | Baccaloni, Renan | *La Bohème* |
| **Benton, Mistress** Mezzo-soprano | Governess and chaperone | | *Lakmé* |
| **Benvenuto Cellini** Tenor | Goldsmith and sculptor | 1st Duprez; Schott | *Benvenuto Cellini* |
| **Benvolio** Tenor | A Montague retainer | | *Roméo et Juliette* |
| **Beppe** Mezzo-soprano | A gypsy | | *L'Amico Fritz* |
| **Beppe** Tenor | Harlequin | Urlus | *I Pagliacci* |
| **Beppo** Tenor | Bandit | | *Fra Diavolo* |
| **Bergère, La** Soprano | The Louis XV Chair | | *L'Enfant et les Sortilèges* |
| **Bermate** Bass | | | *Snyegurotchka* |
| **Bernardino** Bass | Artisan for Cellini | | *Benvenuto Cellini* |
| **Bernardo Novagerio** Tenor | Papal legate | | *Palestrina* |
| **Bersi** Mezzo-soprano | Madeleine's maid | | *Andrea Chénier* |
| **Berta** Soprano | Marcellina, Rosina's governess | Madeira, Petina | *Il Barbiere di Siviglia* |
| **Bertha** Soprano | John's bride | Alvarez, Lilli Lehmann, Muzio | *Le Prophète* |
| **Bertram** Bass | The Devil disguised | Foli, Formes, Scaria | *Robert le Diable* |

| CHARACTER | | ROLE | SINGER | OPERA |
|---|---|---|---|---|
| **Bess** | Soprano | Crown's girl | 1st Anne Brown; Leontyne Price | Porgy and Bess |
| **Beth** | Soprano | A child | 1st Newton | The Tender Land |
| **Béthune, Di** | Bass | French officer | | I Vespri Siciliani |
| **Betto di Signa** | Bass | Dead Buoso's brother-in-law | Cehanovsky | Gianni Schicchi |
| **Betty Doxy** From Chorus | | Lady of the town | | The Beggar's Opera |
| **Bianca** | Contralto | Lucretia's nurse | | The Rape of Lucretia |
| **Bianca** | Soprano | Magda's friend | | La Rondine |
| **Biancofiore** | Soprano | Francesca's woman | | Francesca de Rimini |
| **Biaso** | Tenor | Scribe | | I Gioielli della Madonna |
| **Bijou** | Baritone | Chappelou's friend | | Le Postillion de Longjumeau |
| **Billows, Lady** Soprano | | Elderly autocrat | 1st Cross | Albert Herring |
| **Billy Budd** Baritone | | Seaman, stammerer | 1st Uppman | Billy Budd |
| **Billy Jackrabbit** Bass | | An (American) Indian | | La Fanciulla del West |
| **Bird** See Waldvogel | | | | |
| **Birdie** | Soprano | | Faull | Regina |
| **Bishop** | Baritone | | | Friedenstag |
| **Bishop** See Cardinal See also Ercole Severolus | | | | |
| **Bishop of Budoja** Tenor | | Italian bishop | | Palestrina |
| **Bishop of Thelesia** Silent | | | | Palestrina |
| **Biterolf** | Bass | Knight and minnesinger | | Tannhäuser |

THE CHARACTERS IN THE OPERAS

| CHARACTER | ROLE | SINGER | OPERA |
|---|---|---|---|
| **Black Bob** Bass | Sweepmaster, *called* Norman Chaffinch in *Acts I and II. Also plays* The Coachman. | | *Let's Make an Opera* |
| **Blanche** Soprano | | Duval, Kirsten | *Les Dialogues des Carmélites* |
| **Blanche** Soprano | | | *Louise* |
| **Blind, Doctor** Tenor | Eisenstein's attorney | Franke | *Die Fledermaus* |
| **Blondchen** *See* Blonde | | | |
| **Blonde** Soprano | Constanze's maid | 1st Therese Teyber; Haskins, Schwarzkopf, Ugalde, Vestris | *Die Entführung aus dem Serail* |
| **General Blood and Thunder** Speaker | | | *Háry János* |
| **Bluebeard, Duke** Bass | | | *Duke Bluebeard's Castle* |
| **Bluebeard** *See also* Barbe-bleue | | | |
| **Blunt** *See* Henry Morosus Blunt *See also* Morusus Blunt, Sir | | | |
| **Bob Boles** Tenor | Fisherman and Methodist | 1st M. Jones | *Peter Grimes* |
| **Bobil** Tenor | | | *Snyegurotchka* |
| **Bobilicka** Mezzo soprano | | | *Snyegurotchka* |
| **Bodyguards** Chorus | | | *Khovantschina, Pskovityanka* |
| **Bohemian, Old** Baritone | | | *Louise* |
| **Bois-Rosé** Tenor | Huguenot soldier | | *Huguenots, Les* |

| CHARACTER | | ROLE | SINGER | OPERA |
|---|---|---|---|---|
| **Boleslav Lazinski** Pantomime | | Pianist | | *Fedora* |
| **Bombasto, Doctor** | Bass | | | *Arlecchino* |
| **Bomely** | Bass | | | *Pskovityanka* |
| **Boniface** | Baritone | Monastery cook | | *Le Jongleur de Notre Dame* |
| **Bonze, The** | Bass | Cio-cio San's uncle, Priest | Lorenzo Alvary | *Madama Butterfly* |
| **Bonze** | Bass | | | *Le Rossignol* |
| **Barella** | Bass | Fisherman | | *Masaniello* |
| **Boris Godunov** | Baritone | Tsar of Russia | 1st Melnikov; Baklanov, Chaliapin, Christoff, Didur, Kipnis, London, Marcoux, Pinza, Radford, Rossi-Lemeni, Siepi, Silveri, Stear | *Boris Godunov* |
| **Boris Grigorievitch** | Tenor | In love with Katya | Jones | *Kata Kabanova* |
| **Borov** | Baritone | Doctor | | *Fedora* |
| **Borromeo** *See* Carlo Borromeo | | | | |
| **Borsa** *See* Matteo Borsa | | | | |
| **Bostana** | Mezzo soprano | Baba Mustapha's servant | | *Der Barbier von Bagdad* |
| **Bosun** | Baritone | Boatswain | | *Billy Budd* |
| **Bourdon** | Bass | | | *Le Postillon de Longjumeau* |
| **Boy** | Soprano | | | *The Warrior* |
| **Boy (John)** | Silent | Apprentice | | *Peter Grimes* |
| **Boyar Chruschtschov** *See* Khrushchev | | | | |

| CHARACTER | ROLE | SINGER | OPERA |
|---|---|---|---|
| **Boyar Guard** Tenor | | | *Boris Godunov* |
| **Boyars** Chorus | | | *Boris Godunov, Pskovityanka, Prince Igor* |
| **Boys** Chorus | | | *Carmen, Cavalleria Rusticana, Hugh the Drover, Pskovityanka* |
| **Boy's Voice** | | | *L'Amore dei Tre Re* |
| **Boys and Girls** Chorus | | | *La Bohème, Hänsel und Gretel* |
| **Branda** Bass | | | *Damnation de Faust* |
| **Brangäne** Mezzo soprano | Isolde's maid | 1st Anne Deinet; Brandt, Branzell, Brema, Cahier, Fremstad, Gay, Homer, Kirkby-Lunn, Klose, Lipton, Ober, Olczewska, Schumann-Heink, Thebom, Wickham | *Tristan und Isolde* |
| **Bretigny, De** Baritone | Nobleman | | *Manon* |
| **Bridal Couples** (Three) | | | *Guillaume Tell* |
| **Brighella** Tenor | | Curzi | *Ariadne auf Naxos* |
| **Bronislawa, Countess** Soprano | Laura's sister | | *Der Bettelstudent* |
| **Brünnhilde** Soprano | A Valkyr | 1st (In Walküre) Stehle; Brema, Easton, Fischer, Flagstad, Fremstad, Fuchs, Gadski, Grob-Prandl, Gulbranson, Harshaw, Kappel, Klafsky, Larsen-Todsen, Lawrence, Leffler-Burchhard, Lilli Lehmann, Leider, Litvinne, Malten, Marchesi, | *Das Ring des Nibelungen* |

331

| CHARACTER | ROLE | SINGER | OPERA |
|---|---|---|---|
| | | Materna, Matzenauer, Melba, Mildenburg, Mödl, Morena, Nordica, Ohms, Osborn, Rysanek, Saltzmann-Stevens, Seidl-Krauss, Sucher, Ternina, Thoma, Traubel, Varnay | |
| **Bubble, Madam** Mezzo-soprano | | | *Pilgrim's Progress* |
| **Buda** Soprano | Arline's attendant | | *The Bohemian Girl* |
| **Budd, Superintendant** Bass | | | *Albert Herring* |
| **Budivoj** Baritone | Captain of the guard | | *Dalibor* |
| **Buffoons, Four** Two Mezzo-sopranos, Tenor, Bass | | | *Sadko* |
| **Bugler** Bass | | | *Friedenstag* |
| **Burghers** Chorus | | | *Falstaff* |
| **Burghers** Chorus | Guildsmen | | *Die Meistersinger* |
| **Burghers' Sons** Chorus | | | *Pskovityanka* |
| **Burgomaster** Tenor | | Patzak | *Friedenstag* |
| **Bürstner, Fräulein** Soprano | | 1st della Casa; Curtin | *Der Prozess* |
| **Bussy** Baritone | Journalist | | *Zaza* |
| **Butterfly** *See* Cio-cio San | | | |
| **By-ends, Madame** Contralto | | | *Pilgrim's Progress* |
| **By-ends, Mister** Tenor | | | *Pilgrim's Progress* |
| **Cabin Boy** Speaker | | | *Billy Budd* |
| **Cacan** Baritone | Theater lover | | *Esther de Carpentras* |

| CHARACTER | | ROLE | SINGER | OPERA |
|---|---|---|---|---|
| **Cacique** | Baritone | | Faure, Maurel | *Il Guarany* |
| **Cadi** | Bass | | | *Marouf* |
| **Caesar de Bazan**<br>Tenor<br>*See also* César de<br>Bazan, Don | | | | *Maritana* |
| **Caius, Doctor** | Bass | Unsuccessful suitor<br>to Anne Page | | *Die Lustigen Weiber<br>von Windsor* |
| **Cajus, Peter** | Tenor | Unsuccessful suitor<br>to Nanetta | Bada | *Falstaff* |
| **Calaf** | Tenor | Unknown prince,<br>suitor to Turandot | | *Turandot* (Busoni) |
| **Calaf** | Tenor | Son of Timur,<br>suitor to Turandot | Gismondo, Lauri-<br>Volpi, Martinelli,<br>Merli, Tobin | *Turandot* (Puccini) |
| **Calchas** | | High priest | | *Iphigénie en Aulide* |
| **Caliph, The**<br>Baritone | | | | *Der Barbier von<br>Bagdad* |
| **Caliph's Entourage**<br>Chorus | | | | *Der Barbier von<br>Bagdad* |
| **Camilla** | Soprano | | Parepa-Rosa | *Zampa* |
| **Camille** | Soprano | | | *Louise* |
| **Camille<br>Desmoulins** | Tenor | | 1st Patzak | *Dantons Tod* |
| **Canciano** | Bass | Wealthy merchant | | *I Quattro Rusteghi* |
| **Canio** | Tenor | Pagliaccio, chief of<br>the players | 1st Giraud; Caruso,<br>Ferrari-Fontana,<br>Gigli, Lucia, Martin,<br>Martinelli, Melchior,<br>del Monaco,<br>di Stefano, Vinay,<br>Zenatello | *I Pagliacci* |
| **Capito, Wolfgang**<br>Tenor | | Cardinal's councillor,<br>Lutheran | | *Mathis der Maler* |
| **Cappadocian** | Bass | | | *Salome* |
| **Captain** | Bass | | | *Eugene Onegin* |

| CHARACTER | ROLE | SINGER | OPERA |
|---|---|---|---|
| **Captain**  Tenor | | | *Simon Boccanegra* |
| **Captain**  Tenor | | Franke | *Wozzeck* |
| **Captain of Hell's Guard**  Tenor | | | *Švanda Dudák* |
| **Captain of the Guard**  Bass | | | *The Bohemian Girl* |
| **Captain of the Guard**  Baritone | | | *Maritana* |
| **Captains, Three** Two Tenors, Baritone | | | *The Warrior* |
| **Captains**  Chorus | | | *Aida, Boris Godunov, L'Africaine* |
| **Capuchin Monks** Chorus | | | *Lucrezia Borgia* |
| **Capulet, Count** Bass | | Plançon | *Roméo et Juliette* |
| **Cardillac**  Baritone | A famous goldsmith | | *Cardillac* |
| **Cardinal** From Chorus | | | *Tosca* |
| **Cardinal** *See* Albrecht von Brandenburg *See also* Carlo Borromeo *See also* Christoph Madruscht | | | |
| **Cardinal, Le**  Tenor | Bishop of Carpentras | | *Esther de Carpentras* |
| **Cardinal de Brogni** Bass | | | *La Juive* |
| **Cardinal of Lorraine**  Bass | | | *Palestrina* |
| **Cardinal Salviati** *See* Salviati, Cardinal | | | |
| **Card Players, Three** From Chorus | | | *Arabella* |

| CHARACTER | ROLE | SINGER | OPERA |
|---|---|---|---|
| **Caribiniers** Chorus | | | *Fra Diavolo* |
| **Carlo Borromeo, Cardinal** Baritone | | | *Palestrina* |
| **Carlo di Vargas, Don** Baritone | Leonora's brother | de Luca, Tagliabue, Tibbett, Warren | *La Forza del Destino* |
| **Carlos, Don** Tenor | Heir to the Spanish throne | Martinelli, Tucker | *Don Carlos* |
| **Carlos, Don** Baritone | King of Castile | 1st Superchi; Betz, Graziani | *Ernani* |
| **Carlotta** Mezzo-soprano | Actress | R. Sarfaty | *Die Schweigsame Frau* |
| **Carmela** Mezzo-soprano | Gennaro's mother | Gay | *I Gioielli della Madonna* |
| **Carmele** Mezzo-soprano | Young girl who marries Paco | | *La Vide Breve* |
| **Carmen** (Mezzo) Soprano | Gypsy | 1st Galli-Marié; Ambré, Barbieri, Bellincioni, Besanzoni, Bourguignon, Brehms, Bressler-Giandi, Cahier, Calvé, Castagna, Coates, Djanel, Easton, Farrar, Fornia-Labey, Fremstad, Garden, Gay, Giannini, Gilly, Gutheil-Schoder, Hauk, Jeritza, Labia, Lilli Lehmann, Lucca, Lussan, Matzenauer, Miller, Mödl, Olczewska, Onegin, Patti, Pederzini, Ponselle, Rankin, Roze, Schumann-Heink, Shacklock, Shuard, Stevens, Supervia, Swarthout, Thebom, Tourel, Trebelli, Claramae Turner | *Carmen* |

| CHARACTER | | ROLE | SINGER | OPERA |
|---|---|---|---|---|
| **Carnero** | | | | |
| *See* Conte Carnero | | | | |
| **Carolina** | Soprano | Geronimo's younger daughter, secretly married to Paolino | | *Il Matrimonio Segreto* |
| **Carthaginians** | | | | *Les Troyens* |
| | Chorus | | | |
| **Cascart** | Baritone | Music hall performer | | *Zaza* |
| **Caspar** | Bass | Forester | Bohnen, Faure, Foli, Formes, Koegel, O. Krauss, Santley | *Der Freischütz* |
| **Cassandre** | Soprano | Trojan prophetess | | *Les Troyens* |
| **Cassandre, The Ghost of** | | | | *Les Troyens* |
| | Mezzo-soprano | | | |
| **Cassio** | Tenor | Otello's lieutenant | | *Otello* |
| **Cat** | Mezzo-soprano | | | *L'Enfant et les Sortilèges* |
| **Cats (Two)** | | Behind the scenes | | *The Boatswain's Mate* |
| **Catarina** | Soprano | | Farrar | *Madame Sans-Gêne* |
| **Caterina** | Soprano | Fritz's housekeeper | | *L'Amico Fritz* |
| **Catherine** | Soprano | | Curtin | *Wuthering Heights* |
| **Catholic Ladies and Gentlemen** | | | | *Les Huguenots* |
| | Chorus | | | |
| **Cavalier** | Tenor | | | *Cardillac* |
| **Cavaradossi, Mario** | | | | |
| *See* Mario Cavaradossi | | | | |
| **Cecco del Vecchio** | | Roman citizen | | *Rienzi* |
| | Bass | | | |
| **Cecil, Sir Robert** | | Secretary to the council | | *Gloriana* |
| | Baritone | | | |
| **Celestial Messenger** | | | | *Pilgrim's Progress* |
| | Tenor | | | |

| CHARACTER | ROLE | SINGER | OPERA |
|---|---|---|---|
| **Celestial Phalanxes** Chorus | | | *Mefistofele* |
| **Celio** Bass | Magician, the King's protector | | *The Love for Three Oranges* |
| **Cellini, Benvenuto** *See* Benvenuto Cellini | | | |
| **Cenerentola, La** *See* Angelina | | | |
| **Ceprano, Count** Bass | | | *Rigoletto* |
| **Ceprano, Countess** Mezzo Soprano | | Amara | *Rigoletto* |
| **Cerinto** Contralto | | | *Nerone* |
| **Certain Persons Cloth'd in Gold** Chorus | | | *Pilgrim's Progress* |
| **César de Bazan, Don** Baritone *See also* Caesar de Bazan | | 1st Bouhy; Maas | *Don César de Bazan* |
| **Cesare Angelotti** Bass | Escaped political prisoner | Lorenzo Alvary | *Tosca* |
| **Chamber Maid** | | | *Adriana Lecouvreur* |
| **Chamberlain** Bass | | | *Le Rossignol* |
| **Chappelou** Tenor | Postillion with a fine voice | 1st Chollet; Wachtel | *Le Postillion de Longjumeau* |
| **Charlemagne** Speaker | Emperor of the Franks | | *Oberon* |
| **Charles** Tenor | Vicomte, in love with Linda | | *Linda di Chamounix* |
| **Charles Gérard** Baritone | Revolutionary leader | 1st Sammarco; Danise, Formichi, Franci, Guelfi, Inghilleri, Silveri | *Andrea Chénier* |
| **Charlotte** Mezzo-soprano | Le Bailli's daughter, Albert's wife, in love with Werther | 1st Marie Renard; Delna, Eames, Farrar, Gay, Heidt, Lowe, Pederzini, Simoniato | *Werther* |

| CHARACTER | ROLE | SINGER | OPERA |
|---|---|---|---|
| **Chateauneuf**<br>*See* Marquis de<br>Chateauneuf | | | |
| **Chauve-Souris, Le**<br>Soprano | The Bat | | *L'Enfant et les*<br>*Sortilèges* |
| **Cheap Jack**<br>Baritone | | | *Hugh the Drover* |
| **Cheap Jewelry**<br>**Woman**<br>Mezzo-soprano | | | *A Village Romeo and*<br>*Juliette* |
| **Cherubino**  Soprano | Page to the Count-<br>ess Almaviva | 1st Bussani;  Adams,<br>Bible, Carvalho,<br>Cross, Danco,<br>Evans, Farrar,<br>Gueden, Lucca,<br>Miller, Christine<br>Nilsson, Novotna,<br>Teyte, Vanni,<br>Welitsch, van Zandt | *Le Nozze di Figaro* |
| **Cherubs**  Chorus | | | *Mefistofele* |
| **Chief Sailor**  Tenor | | | *Marouf* |
| **Chiffres, Les**<br>Children | Numbers | | *L'Enfant et les*<br>*Sortilèges* |
| **Child**<br>Mezzo-soprano | | | *L'Enfant et les*<br>*Sortilèges* |
| **Children**  Chorus | Children of the<br>Boyars | | *Boris Godunov* |
| **Children**  Chorus | | | *Esther de Carpentras,*<br>*Pique-Dame, Le*<br>*Prophète, Les*<br>*Troyens, Werther,*<br>*Wozzeck* |
| **Childrens' Voices,**<br>**Six**<br>Sopranos, Contraltos | | | *Die Frau Ohne*<br>*Schatten* |
| **Chinese Cup**<br>Mezzo-contralto | | | *L'Enfant et les*<br>*Sortilèges* |
| **Chloé**  Soprano | In a masque | | *Pique-Dame* |

| CHARACTER | | ROLE | SINGER | OPERA |
|---|---|---|---|---|
| **Chorèbe** | Baritone | Cassandra's lover | | *Les Troyens* |
| **Chorèbe's Ghost** Baritone | | | | *Les Troyens* |
| **Chorus** | Chorus | | | *Agamemnon, Choëphores, Gloriana* |
| **Chorus, Female** Soprano | | | | *The Rape of Lucretia* |
| **Chorus, Male** Tenor | | | 1st Peter Pears; | *The Rape of Lucretia* |
| **Choryphée** | | | | *Alceste* |
| **Chouette, La** Soprano | | The little owl | | *L'Enfant et les Sortilèges* |
| **Chris the Citizen** Baritone | | | | *The Mother of Us All* |
| **Christians** | Chorus | | | *La Juive, Nerone* |
| **Christine** | Soprano | Storch's wife who nags | 1st Lotte Lehmann | *Intermezzo* |
| **Christoph** | Tenor | Kepler's brother | | *Die Harmonie der Welt* |
| **Christoph Madruscht, Cardinal** | Bass | | | *Palestrina* |
| **Christopher Columbus (I)** Baritone | | As an old man | | *Christophe Colomb* |
| **Christopher Columbus (II)** Baritone | | As a young man | | *Christophe Colomb* |
| **Chronicler** *See* Pimen | | | | |
| **Cho-Cho San** *See* Cio-Cio San | | | | |
| **Chruschtschov** *See* Khrushchev | | | | |
| **Chrysothemis** Soprano | | Elektra's sister | 1st Siems; Hilde Konetzni, Faull, Yeend | *Elektra* |

| CHARACTER | | ROLE | SINGER | OPERA |
|---|---|---|---|---|
| **Church-Goers** Chorus | | | | *Doktor Faustus* |
| **Cicillo** | Tenor | Cammorist | | *I Gioielli della Madonna* |
| **Cieca, La** | Contralto | Gioconda's blind mother | Madeira, Schalchi, Swarthout | *La Gioconda* |
| **Cieco, Il** | Bass | Blind man, Iris's father | | *Iris* |
| **Ciesca, La** | Mezzo-soprano | Marco's wife, 38 | Votipka | *Gianni Schicchi* |
| **Cigarette Girls** Chorus | | | | *Carmen* |
| **Cinderella** *See* Angelina | | | | |
| **Cio-Cio San** | Soprano | Pinkerton's Japanese wife | 1st Storchio; Adami-Corradetti, Albanese, de los Angeles, Callas, della Casa, Cebotari, Cross, Destinn, Farrar, Faull, Favero, Giannini, Kirsten, Krusceniski, dal Monte, Price, Rethberg, Schwarzkopf, Seefried, Sheridan, Shuard, Tebaldi,Teyte, Welitsch, Williams | *Madama Butterfly* |
| **Cirillo** | Baritone | Coachman | | *Fedora* |
| **Cis** | Soprano | Child | | *Albert Herring* |
| **Citizens** | Chorus | | | *Andrea Chénier, La Bohème, Damnation de Faust, Les Huguenots, Iris, Mefistofele, Le Prophète, The Rake's Progress, Roméo et Juliette, La Rondine, Tosca, Les Troyens* |

# THE CHARACTERS IN THE OPERAS

| CHARACTER | ROLE | SINGER | OPERA |
|---|---|---|---|
| **City Crier**  Baritone | | | *Gloriana* |
| **Claggert**  Bass | Master at Arms | | *Billy Budd* |
| **Claison**  Contralto | Actress | Christa Ludwig | *Capriccio* |
| **Clara**  Soprano | Jake's wife | 1st Abbie Mitchell | *Porgy and Bess* |
| **Claretta**  Soprano | | | *Zaza* |
| **Clarissa, Princess**  Contralto | The King's niece | | *The Love for Three Oranges* |
| **Claudio**  Baritone | An officer in love with Hero | | *Béatrice et Bénédict* |
| **Clem**  Tenor | Black Bob. *Also plays* Max Westleton *in Acts I and II, and* Alfred the gardener | | *Let's Make an Opera* |
| **Clémence**  Soprano | | | *Mireille* |
| **Cleopatra**  Pantomime | | | *Faust* |
| **Clorinda**  Soprano | Don Magnifico's daughter | | *La Cenerentola* |
| **Clorinda**  Pantomime | Saracen maiden in man's armor | | *Il Combattimento di Tancredi e Clorinda* |
| **Clotilde**  Soprano | Norma's friend | | *Norma* |
| **Clytemnestra**  Soprano | Agamemnon's wife | | *Agamemnon* |
| **Clytemnestra**  Mezzo-soprano | Agamemnon's wife | 1st du Plant; Cyrena von Gordon | *Iphigénie en Aulide* |
| **Clytemnestra**  *See also* Klytemnestra | | | |
| **Clytemnestra's Ghost**  *See* Spectre de Clytemnestra, Le | | | |
| **Coal Gatherer**  Mezzo-soprano | | | *Louise* |
| **Coaxer, Mrs.**  From Chorus | Lady of the town | | *The Beggar's Opera* |

| CHARACTER | ROLE | SINGER | OPERA |
|---|---|---|---|
| **Chochenille** Tenor | Spalanzani's servant | | *Les Contes d'Hoffmann* |
| **Cockburn Lord** Tenor | Tourist | | *Fra Diavolo* |
| **Cockerel, The Golden** Soprano | | | *Le Coq d'Or* |
| **Coigny, Comtesse de** Mezzo-soprano | Madeleine's mother | | *Andrea Chénier* |
| **Cola Rienzi** Tenor | Roman tribune | 1st Tichatschek; Althouse, Max Alvary, Lorenz, Mass, Schott | *Rienzi* |
| **Colas** Baritone | | Bispham | *Bastien et Bastienne* |
| **Collatinus** Bass | Soldier, Lucretia's husband | | *The Rape of Lucretia* |
| **Colline** Bass | Young, starving philosopher | Moscona, Siepi, Tajo | *La Bohème* |
| **Colonna** *See* Steffano Colonna | | | |
| **Columbine** Mezzo-soprano | Arlecchino's wife | | *Arlecchino* |
| **Columbine** Soprano | | | *Fête Galante* |
| **Columbine** *See* Nedda | | | |
| **Comedians and Clowns** Chorus | | | *Prodana Neveta* |
| **Commandant** Bass | | | *Christophe Colomb* |
| **Commandant** Baritone | of the beseiged town | 1st Hotter; Prohaska | *Friedenstag* |
| **Commendatore** Bass | Donna Anna's father | 1st Giuseppe Lelli; Böhme, Foli, Radford, Tozzi, Wildermann | *Don Giovanni* |
| **Commercial Councillor** Baritone | Storch's friend | | *Intermezzo* |

| CHARACTER | ROLE | SINGER | OPERA |
|---|---|---|---|
| **Commère** <br> Mezzo-soprano | | 1st A. Hines | Four Saints in Three Acts |
| **Commissioner, Imperial** <br> *See* Imperial Commissioner | | | |
| **Companion** Tenor | of Cardillac's daughter | | Cardillac |
| **Compère** Bass | | 1st Abner Dorsey | Four Saints in Three Acts |
| **Composer** Soprano | | 1st Lotte Lehmann; Jurinac, Mödl, Seefried, Welitsch | Ariadne auf Naxos |
| **Concepcion** <br> Soprano | Torquemada's wife | 1st. Vix; Albanese, Bori, Franca Duval, Supervia | L'Heure Espagnole |
| **Concetta** Soprano | | | I Gioielli della Madonna |
| **Conductor** <br> *Also* Mr. Harper *in acts I and II* | | | Let's Make an Opera |
| **Confidante** <br> Soprano | to Klytemnestra | | Elektra |
| **Conrad Nachtigall** <br> Bass | Mastersinger and bucklemaker | | Die Meistersinger |
| **Constable** Bass | | | Hugh the Drover |
| **Constable** <br> From Chorus | | | Il Barbiere di Siviglia |
| **Constance Fletcher** <br> Soprano | | | The Mother of Us All |
| **Constanze** Soprano | A Spanish lady | | Die Entführung aus dem Serail |
| **Conte Carnero** <br> Baritone | Commissioner of morals | | Zigeunerbaron |
| **Conte di Luna** <br> Baritone | of Aragon | Maurel, Tozzi, Panerai | Il Trovatore |
| **Cook** Tenor | | | Christophe Colomb |

| CHARACTER | ROLE | SINGER | OPERA |
|---|---|---|---|
| **Cook**      Bass | An evil giant | | *The Love for Three Oranges* |
| **Cook**      Mezzo-soprano | to the Emperor | | *Le Rossignol* |
| **Coppelius**   Baritone | Scientist, Spalanzani's rival | London | *Les Contes d'Hoffmann* |
| **Coq d'Or, Le** *See* Cockerel, the Golden | | | |
| **Corcy, Marquis de**      Tenor | Head of the Paris Opèra | | *Le Postillon de Longjumeau* |
| **Corentini**   Tenor | Bagpiper | | *Dinorah* |
| **Corifeas (Two)** | | | *L'Assassinio nel' Cattedrale* |
| **Coroner**   Speaker | | | *Porgy and Bess* |
| **Corporal**      Bass | of the grenadiers | Cehanovsky | *La Figlia del Reggimento* |
| **Corporal**   Baritone | | | *Friedenstag* |
| **Corporal** *See also* José, Don | | | |
| **Corregidor, Der** *See* Eugenio di Zuniga, Don | | | |
| **Cossacks**   Chorus | | | *The Fair ot Sorochintsky* |
| **Cossé**   Tenor | | | *Les Huguenots* |
| **Councillors** | | | *L'Africaine* |
| **Counsel for the Prosecution**      Speaker | | | *Christophe Colomb* |
| **Count**   Baritone | Brother of the countess | Wächter | *Capriccio* |
| **Count** *See under proper name as:* Almaviva, Count *See also* Conte | | | |

| CHARACTER | ROLE | SINGER | OPERA |
|---|---|---|---|
| **Countess**  Soprano | The Count's sister | 1st Ursuleac; Cebotari, della Casa, Schwarzkopf | *Capriccio* |
| **Countess**  Mezzo-soprano | | | *Pique-Dame* |
| **Countess**  Contralto | | Schumann-Heink | *Der Trompeter von Säkkingen* |
| **Countess**  *See under proper name, as:* Almaviva, Countess | | | |
| **Country People**  Chorus | | | *Doktor Faustus* |
| **Counts**  Chorus | | | *Lohengrin* |
| **Coupava**  *See* Koupava | | | |
| **Carrier**  Tenor | | | *La Fanciulla del West* |
| **Court Attendant**  Bass | | Renan | *Der Prozess* |
| **Court Officials**  Chorus | | | *Nabucco* |
| **Court Servants**  Chorus | | | *Háry János* |
| **Courtiers**  Chorus | | | *Un Ballo in Maschera, Christophe Colomb, Le Coq d'Or, Dido and Aeneas, Doktor Faustus, La Favorita, Fête Galante, The Love for Three Oranges, Martha, Rigoletto, Le Rossignol, Les Troyens* |
| **Courtois**  Bass | | | *Zaza* |
| **Crab Man**  Tenor | | | *Porgy and Bess* |
| **Crébillon**  Bass-baritone | Perichaud's friend | | *La Rondine* |
| **Creditors**  Chorus | | | *Christophe Colomb* |

| CHARACTER | | ROLE | SINGER | OPERA |
|---|---|---|---|---|
| **Creditors** | Chorus | | | *Die Liebe der Danae* |
| **Creon** | Bass-baritone | Jocasta's brother | | *Oedipus Rex* |
| **Crespel** | Baritone | Antonia's father | | *Les Contes d'Hoffmann* |
| **Cretans** See People of Crete | | | | |
| **Cricket, A** | Soprano | | | *Das Heimchen am Herd* |
| **Cristian** See Silvano | | | | |
| **Crobyle** | Soprano | A slave | | *Thaïs* |
| **Croupiers** | Chorus | | | *Manon* |
| **Crowd** | Chorus | | | *Ariane et Barbe-Bleue* |
| **Crowds, Mute** Silent | | | | *Der Prozess* |
| **Crown** | Baritone | Stevedore | 1st Coleman | *Porgy and Bess* |
| **Crusty** See Lunardo | | | | |
| **Cuno** | Bass | Head forester | | *Der Freischütz* |
| **Cupidon** | Soprano | Cupid | | *Orphée aux Enfers* |
| **Curra** Mezzo-soprano | | Leonora's maid | Votipka | *La Forza del Destino* |
| **Don Curzio** | Tenor | A lawyer | 1st Michael Kelly; Meyer-Wolfing | *Le Nozze di Figaro* |
| **Customs Officer** Bass | | | | *La Bohème* |
| **Cutbeard** | | A barber | Ukena | *Die Schweigsame Frau* |
| **Cypriotes** | Chorus | | | *Otello* |
| **Czar** See Tsar | | | | |
| **Czipra** Mezzo-soprano | | Gypsy woman | | *Zigeunerbaron* |
| **Daland** | Bass | Norwegian sea-captain | Fischer, Foli, Griswold | *Der Fliegende Holländer* |

| CHARACTER | ROLE | SINGER | OPERA |
|---|---|---|---|
| **Dalibor** Tenor | Knight, imprisoned for murder | 1st Lukas; Völker | *Dalibor* |
| **Dalila** Mezzo-soprano | Philistine seductress | 1st Müller; Barbieri, Brema, Gay, Hastreiter, Homer Kirkby-Lunn, Langendorf, Matzenauer, Ober, Onegin, Stevens, Stignani, Thebom, Wettergren | *Samson et Dalila* |
| **Dalila** *See also* Delilah | | | |
| **Dalua** Baritone | Lord of shadow | 1st Boughton (*The composer*) | *The Immortal Hour* |
| **Danae** Soprano | Daughter of Pollux | 1st Ursuleac; Dow, Kupper, Rysanek | *Die Liebe der Danae* |
| **Dancairo, El** Baritone | A smuggler | Cehanovsky, Renan | *Carmen* |
| **Dancer** Dancer | | | *Capriccio, Louise* |
| **Dancers** Dancers | | | *Gloriana, Mefistofele, La Rondine, La Traviata, Turandot* (Busoni), *I Vespri Siciliani* |
| **Dancers (Six)** Dancers | | | *Four Saints in Three Acts* |
| **Dancing Girl** Dancer | | | *Hugh the Drover* |
| **Dancing Master** Tenor | | Fried | *Ariadne auf Naxos* |
| **Dandini** Bass | The prince's valet | Lablache, Reeves, Tamburini | *La Cenerentola* |
| **Dangeville, Mlle.** Mezzo-soprano | of the Comedie Française | | *Adriana Lecouvreur* |
| **Daniel** Tenor | | Capoul | *Le Chalet* |
| **Daniel Hizler** Bass | Vicar of Linz, *later* Vicar of Regensburg, *also* Mercury | | *Das Harmonie der Welt* |

| CHARACTER | ROLE | SINGER | OPERA |
|---|---|---|---|
| **Daniel Webster** Baritone | | | *The Mother of Us All* |
| **Danieli** Tenor | Young Sicilian | | *I Vespri Siciliani* |
| **Dansker** Bass | An old seaman | | *Billy Budd* |
| **Danton** *See* Georg Danton | | | |
| **Dapertutto** Baritone | A sorcerer | London | *Les Contes d'Hoffmann* |
| **Daphne** Soprano | | Bampton, Cebotari, Cigna | *Daphne* |
| **Daphnis** Contralto | Character in a masque, *played by* Pauline | | *Pique-Dame* |
| **Da-Ud** Tenor | Altair's son | | *Die Aegyptische Helene* |
| **Daughter of Cardillac** Soprano | | | *Cardillac* |
| **David** Baritone | A rabbi | Danise | *L'Amico Fritz* |
| **David** Tenor | Hans Sachs' apprentice | Franke | *Die Meistersinger* |
| **Dead Composers (Nine)** Three Tenors, Three Baritones, Three Basses | | | *Palestrina* |
| **Death** From Chorus | | | *Iris* |
| **Death** Contralto | | | *Le Rossignol* |
| **Death** Bass | | | *Savitri* |
| **Debora** Mezzo-soprano | Prophetess | 1st Tess; Spani, Carbone | *Debora* |
| **Delilah** (Mezzo) Soprano | | 1st Resnik | *The Warrior* |
| **Delilah** *See also* Dalila | | | |
| **Demas** Baritone | | | *Pilgrim's Progress* |
| **Demi-Mondaines** Chorus | | | *La Rondine* |

348

| CHARACTER | ROLE | SINGER | OPERA |
|---|---|---|---|
| **Demons** Chorus | | | *Faust* |
| **Desdemona** Mezzo-soprano | Otello's wife | 1st Stoltz; Viardot-Garcia | *Otello* (Rossini) |
| **Desdemona** Soprano | Otello's wife | 1st Pantaleone; Albani, Alda, Caniglia, Caron, Charton-Demeur, Ciani, Cross, Brouwenstijn, Eames, Farrar, Fodor-Mainvielle, Goltz, Ilitsch, Lilli Lehmann, Lussan, Malibran, Milanov, Christine Nilsson, Norena, Pampanini, Rappold, Rethberg, Scacciati, Schröder-Devrient, Sheridan, Sontag, Steber, Tebaldi, Eva Tetrazzini, Luisa Tetrazzini | *Otello* (Verdi) |
| **Desiré** Tenor | Valet | | *Fedora* |
| **Desmoulins** *See* Camille Desmoulins | | | |
| **Despina** Soprano | Fiordiligi's and Dorabella's maid | 1st Bussani; Gueden, Peters | *Così fan Tutte* |
| **Detective** Speaker | | | *Porgy and Bess* |
| **Devil, The** Bass | | | *Švanda Dudák* |
| **Devil's Familiar Spirit** Tenor | | | *Švanda Dudák* |
| **Devilshoof** Bass | Chief of the gypsies | | *The Bohemian Girl* |
| **Dew Fairy** Soprano | | | *Hänsel und Gretel* |
| **Dewman** Soprano | | Nicholls | *Hänsel und Gretel* |
| **Diana** Soprano | Goddess | | *Iphigénie en Tauride* |
| **Diane** Soprano | Goddess | | *Orphée aux Enfers* |

| CHARACTER | | ROLE | SINGER | OPERA |
|---|---|---|---|---|
| **Dickson** | Tenor | Tenant of the White Lady | | *La Dame Blanche* |
| **Dido** | Soprano | Queen of Carthage | Flagstad, Nicholls, Pederzini | *Dido and Aeneas* |
| **Didon** Mezzo-soprano | | Queen of Carthage | 1st Charton-Demeur; Delna, Mandikian | *Les Troyens* |
| **Diego, Don** | Bass | Councillor, Vasco's rival | Edouard de Reszke | *L'Africaine* |
| **Diemut** | Soprano | | Destinn | *Feuersnot* |
| **Dikoy** | Bass | Merchant, uncle of Boris | | *Katya Kabanova* |
| **Dimitri** | Contralto | Groom | | *Fedora* |
| **Dimitri** *See* Grigorij | | | | |
| **Dinorah** | Soprano | A peasant girl | 1st Cabel; Barrientos, Carvalho, Galli-Curci, Murska, Patti, Luisa Tetrazzini, Vere, van Zandt | *Dinorah* |
| **Dipsacus** | Bass | Magician, Tormentilla's father | | *The Poisoned Kiss* |
| **Director-Representative** Bass | | | | *Der Prozess* |
| **Disguised Jews** Chorus | | | | *Esther de Carpentras* |
| **Djamileh** Mezzo-soprano | | A slave | 1st Prelly | *Djamileh* |
| **Djura** | | Mandryka's servant | | *Arabella* |
| **Dmitri** *See* Grigorij | | | | |
| **Doctor** | | | | *Arabella* |
| **Doctor** | Speaker | | | *Lulu* |
| **Doctor** | Bass | | | *Macbeth* |

| CHARACTER | ROLE | SINGER | OPERA |
|---|---|---|---|
| **Doctor** Bass | | Doench, Renan | *Wozzeck* |
| **Doctor, The Old** Bass | | 1st Tozzi | *Vanessa* |
| **Doctor, Jewish** *See* Médicin Juif, Le | | | |
| **Doctor of Natural History** Baritone | | | *Doktor Faustus* |
| **Doctor Thorp** Silent | | | *Peter Grimes* |
| **Doctors (Eight)** Tenors, Basses | | | *Turandot* (Busoni) |
| **Doctors** Chorus | | | *The Love for Three Oranges* |
| **Dodon, King** Bass | | | *Le Coq d'Or* |
| **Dolcina, Suor** Mezzo-soprano | A nun | | *Suor Angelica* |
| **Doleful Creatures** Chorus | | | *Pilgrim's Progress* |
| **Dolly Trull** From Chorus | Lady of the town | | *The Beggar's Opera* |
| **Dominik, Graf** Baritone | Arabella's suitor | | *Arabella* |
| **Don** *See proper name, as:* Giovanni, Don | | | |
| **Doña Mercedes** *See* Mercedes, Doña | | | |
| **Donald** Baritone | A seaman | | *Billy Budd* |
| **Donald Gallop** Tenor | | | *The Mother of Us All* |
| **Donato** Bass-baritone | A young blind man | | *Maria Golovin* |
| **Donella** Mezzo-soprano | Francesca's woman | | *Francesca da Rimini* |
| **Donner** Bass Baritone | Norse god | Gura, Hargrave | *Das Ring des Nibelungen* |
| **Dorabella** Soprano | Fiordiligi's sister | 1st Villeneuve; Jurinac, Miller, Mödl, Thebom | *Così fan Tutte* |

| CHARACTER | | ROLE | SINGER | OPERA |
|---|---|---|---|---|
| **Dorotka** | Soprano | Schwanda's wife | | *Švanda Dudák* |
| **Dositheus** | Bass | Leader of the Old Believers, and enemy of the Tsar | Allin | *Khovantschina* |
| **Dositeo** | Baritone | A Roman | | *Nerone* |
| **Dot** | Soprano | John's wife | | *Das Heimchen am Herd* |
| **Douphol, Baron** | Baritone | Alfredo's rival for Violetta | Cehanovsky | *La Traviata* |
| **Dragoons** | Chorus | | | *Carmen* |
| **Dressmaker** | Soprano | | | *Der Rosenkavalier* |
| **Dressmakers** | Chorus | | | *The Poisoned Kiss* |
| **Druids** | Chorus | | | *The Immortal Hour* |
| **Drum-Major** | Tenor | | Baum | *Wozzeck* |
| **Drummers** | Chorus | | | *Billy Budd* |
| **Drunkards** | Chorus | | | *The Love for Three Oranges* |
| **Dryade** | Contralto | A nymph | | *Ariadne auf Naxos* |
| **Duchess of Parma** | Soprano | | | *Doktor Faustus* |
| **Duchesse de Krakenthorp** | Soprano | | | *La Figlia del Reggimento* |
| **Duclou** | Baritone | Stage manager | | *Zaza* |
| **Duenna** | | | | *Arabella* |
| **Duenna** | Mezzo-soprano | | | *Der Corregidor* |
| **Dufla, General** | Speaker | | | *Háry János* |
| **Dufresne, Mme** | Mezzo-soprano | Milio's wife | | *Zaza* |

# THE CHARACTERS IN THE OPERAS

| CHARACTER | ROLE | SINGER | OPERA |
|---|---|---|---|
| **Duke of Mantua** Tenor | | 1st Mirate; Bjoerling, Bonci, Borgioli, Caruso, Conley, Gigli, Hislop, Lauri-Volpi, Mario, Martini, McCormack, Peerce, Piccaver, Schipa, di Stefano, Tagliavini | *Rigoletto* |
| **Duke of Parma** Tenor | | | *Doktor Faustus* |
| **Duke of Verona** Bass | | | *Roméo et Juliette* |
| **Dulcamara** Bass | Quack, peddler of aphrodisiacs | Baccaloni | *L'Elisir d'Amore* |
| **Dulcinée, La Belle** Contralto | | 1st Lucy Arbell; Easton, Garden, Lyne | *Don Quichotte* |
| **Dumas** Baritone | President of the Tribunal | | *Andrea Chénier* |
| **Duncan** Silent | King of Scotland | | *Macbeth* |
| **Dutchman, The** Baritone | A damned soul | 1st Wächter; Berglund, Bertram, Bispham, Bockelmann, Hotter, Janssen, Maurel, Reichmann, Rooy, Santley, Scheidermantel, Schorr | *Der Fliegende Holländer* |
| **Dwarf** *See* Alberich *See also* Mime | | | |
| **Earth** *See* Johannes Kepler | | | |
| **Ebelasztin, Ritter Von** Tenor | Marie's chamberlain | | *Háry János* |
| **Eberbach, Count** Baritone | | | *Der Wildschütz* |

| CHARACTER | ROLE | SINGER | OPERA |
|---|---|---|---|
| **Eberbach, Countess** Contralto | | | *Der Wildschütz* |
| **Eboli, Principessa** Mezzo-soprano | Lady in waiting, in love with Don Carlos | Barbieri, Mödl, Shuard, Stignani, Thebom | *Don Carlos* |
| **Echo** Soprano | | | *Ariadne auf Naxos* |
| **Ecureuil, L'** Mezzo-soprano | The squirrel | | *L'Enfant et les Sortilèges* |
| **Edgar** *See* Edgardo | | | |
| **Edgardo** Tenor | Edgar of Ravens-wood | 1st Duprez; Campanini, Caruso, Nicolini, Peerce, Reeves, de Stefano | *Lucia di Lammermoor* |
| **Edmondo** Tenor | A student | | *Manon Lescaut* |
| **Edward Plummer** Tenor | | | *Das Heimchen am Herd* |
| **Eglantine** Soprano | | Brandt, Borkh, Ober, Peschka-Leutner, Thorborg | *Euryanthe* |
| **Egyptians** Chorus | | | *Aida* |
| **Eisenstein** *See* Gabriel von Eisenstein | | | |
| **Elder Gleaton** Tenor | | | *Susannah* |
| **Elder Hayes** Tenor | | | *Susannah* |
| **Elder McLean** Baritone | | | *Susannah* |
| **Elder Ott** Bass | | Hecht | *Susannah* |
| **Elders** Chorus | | | *Friedenstag* |
| **Elders (Two)** Tenor, Bass | of Novgorod | | *Sadko* |
| **Elders of Thebes** Chorus | | | *Antigonae* (Orff) |
| **Eléazar** Tenor | Jewish goldsmith | 1st Nourrit; Caruso, Duprez, Koegel, Martinelli | *La Juive* |

| CHARACTER | | ROLE | SINGER | OPERA |
|---|---|---|---|---|
| **Electors** | Chorus | | | *Ernani* |
| **Electra** | Soprano | Greek princess | 1st Elisabeth Wendling; Birgit Nilsson | *Idomeneo* |
| **Electre** | Soprano | | | *Les Choéphores* |
| **Elektra** | Soprano | Agamemnon's daughter | 1st Anny Krull; Borkh, Easton, Gutheil-Schoder, Kappel, Anni Konetzni, Kruscenski, Marcel, Pauly, Varnay, Walker | *Elektra* |
| **Elemer, Graf** | Tenor | Arabella's suitor | | *Arabella* |
| **Elena** | Soprano | Helen of Troy | Arangi-Lombardi, Cary, Easton, Fenn, Martinis, Christine Nilsson, Raisa, Rasa, Tebaldi, Trebelli | *Mefistofele* |
| **Elena, Duchess** | Soprano | | 1st Cruvelli; Callas, Anni Konetzni | *I Vespri Siciliani* |
| **Elisabeth** | Soprano | Niece of the Land-grave Hermann | 1st J. Wagner; Ackté, Albani, Eames, Cross, Brouwenstijn, Farrar, Fisher, Flagstad, Fornia-Labey, Fremstad, Gadski, Goltz, Harshaw, Jeritza, Juch, Kurt, Leffler-Burckhard, Malten, Marchesi, Materna, Moody, Morena, Birgit Nilsson Osborn, Rappold, Rethberg, Sass, Seidl-Krauss, Stehle, Ternina, Valleria, Varnay | *Tannhäuser* |

# THE CHARACTERS IN THE OPERAS

| CHARACTER | ROLE | SINGER | OPERA |
|---|---|---|---|
| **Elisabeth the First** Soprano | Queen of England | 1st Cross | *Gloriana* |
| **Elisabetta di Valois** Soprano | Queen of Spain, beloved by Don Carlos | 1st Sass; Brouwenstijn, Cigna, Caniglia, Grandi, Lucca, Ponselle, Rysanek, Steber | *Don Carlos* |
| **Elise** Soprano | | | *Louise* |
| **Elisetta** Soprano | Geronimo's older daughter | | *Il Matrimonio Segreto* |
| **Ellen** Soprano | An English lady | | *Lakmé* |
| **Ellen Orford** Soprano | Widow, schoolmistress | 1st Cross; Danco, Fisher, Manning, Resnik | *Peter Grimes* |
| **Elsa of Brabant** Soprano | | 1st Agthé; Ackté, Albani, Brandt, Destinn, Eames, Easton, Cross, Farrar, Fisher, Flagstad, Fremstad, Gadski, Jeritza, Juch, Krauss, Leffller-Burckhard, Mallinger, Marchesi, Melba, Moody, Morena, Christine Nilsson, Nordica, Osborn, Parepa-Rosa, Rappold, Reuss-Belce, Roze, Malvina Schnorr von Carolsfield, Schwarzkopf, Seidl-Krauss, Steber, Stehle, Sucher, Tebaldi, Ternina, Varnay, Vere, Zadek | *Lohengrin* |
| **Elvino** Tenor | Farmer, engaged to Amina | | *La Sonnambula* |
| **Elvira** Soprano | Spanish princess | | *Masaniello* |

| CHARACTER | | ROLE | SINGER | OPERA |
|---|---|---|---|---|
| **Elvira** | Soprano | Silvano's relative, beloved by Ernani | Lucca, Sembrich, Tietjens | *Ernani* |
| **Elvira** | Soprano | The Bey's wife | 1st Grisi; Barrientos, Callas, Gerster, Pinkert, Literazzini, | *L'Italiana in Algeri* |
| **Elvira** | Soprano | Lord Gaulthier Walton's daughter | | *I Puritani* |
| **Elvira, Donna** | Soprano | A lady from Burgos, deserted by Don Giovanni | 1st Catarina Micelli; Adams, Brandt, Carvalho, Casa, Cross, Farrar, Galli-Curci, Eugenie Garcia, Gerster, Jurinac, Lewis, Matzenauer, Milde, Christine Nilsson, Nordica, Resnik, Schwarz-kopf, Steber | *Don Giovanni* |
| **Elves (Three)** Sopranos, Contralto | | | | *Die Aegyptische Helene* |
| **Emilia** Mezzo-soprano | | Iago's wife, Desdemona's lady | Wickham | *Otello* (Verdi) |
| **Emma** | Soprano | Young girl | Ziliani | *Khovantschina* |
| **Emma** | Soprano | | Grisi | *Zelmira* (Handel) |
| **Emmie** | Soprano | A child | | *Albert Herring* |
| **Emperor** | Tenor | | | *Die Frau ohne Schatten* |
| **Emperor Altoum** Tenor | | Turandot's father | | *Turandot* (Puccini) |
| **Emperor of China** Baritone | | | | *Le Rossignol* |
| **Empress** | Soprano | The woman who had no shadow | 1st Lotte Lehmann; Kemp, Hilde Konetzni, Pauly, Rysanek | *Die Frau ohne Schatten* |
| **Empress of Austria** Soprano | | | | *Háry János* |

# THE CHARACTERS IN THE OPERAS

| CHARACTER | ROLE | SINGER | OPERA |
|---|---|---|---|
| **Empress Persicaria** Contralto | Mother of Amaryllus | | *The Poisoned Kiss* |
| **Enan, The Blind** Bass | | | *Debora e Jaele* |
| **Enée** Tenor | Aeneas, Trojan hero | 1st Monjauze; Kentish | *Les Troyens* |
| **Enrichetta** *See* Henrietta | | | |
| **Enrico** Baritone | Lord Henry Ashton of Lammermoor | Galassi, Lassalle, Ronconi, Scotti | *Lucia di Lammermoor* |
| **Enterich** Baritone | Prison governor | | *Der Bettelstudent* |
| **Entourage, The Caliph's** Chorus | | | *Der Barbier von Bagdad* |
| **Envoy of Japan** *See* Japanese Envoy | | | |
| **Envy** Bass | | | *Pilgrim's Progress* |
| **Enzo Grimaldo** Tenor | Genoese nobleman in love with Laura | Baum, Caruso, Gigli, Marconi, Martin, Martinelli, Merli, del Monaco, Tucker, Zenatello | *La Gioconda* |
| **Eochaidh** Baritone | King in love with Etain | | *The Immortal Hour* |
| **Ercole Severolus, Bishop** Bass Baritone | | | *Palestrina* |
| **Erda** Mezzo-soprano | Goddess of Earth | Homer, Matzenauer, Meisle, Ober, Schumann-Heink | *Das Ring des Nibelungen* |
| **Eric** Tenor | A huntsman | Althouse, Berger, Sullivan | *Der Fliegende Holländer* |
| **Ericlea** Mezzo-soprano | Penelope's nurse | | *Il Ritorno d'Ulisse in Patria* |
| **Erika** Mezzo-soprano | Vanessa's niece | 1st Elias | *Vanessa* |

| CHARACTER | ROLE | SINGER | OPERA |
|---|---|---|---|
| **Ernani** Tenor | Really John of Aragon, as a bandit chieftain in love with Elvira | 1st Guasio | *Ernani* |
| **Ernesto** Tenor | Don Pasquale's nephew | 1st Mario; Schipa | *Don Pasquale* |
| **Eroshka** Tenor | Gudok player | | *Prince Igor* |
| **Errand Girl** Soprano | | | *Louise* |
| **Erinnyes** Chorus | | | *Eumenides* |
| **Erster Bürger** Tenor | First citizen | | *Die Lustigen Weiber von Windsor* |
| **Escamillo** Baritone | Famous toreador | 1st Bouhy; Amato, Bispham, Campanari, Cassel, Galassi, Guarrera, Journet, Lassalle, London, Merrill, Plançon, del Puente, Renaud, van Rooy, Scaria, Scotti, Tibbett | *Carmen* |
| **Esmeralda** Soprano | A dancer | Schwarzkopf | *Prodana Nevešta* |
| **Esquires** Chorus | | | *Tristan und Isolde* |
| **Esquires (Four)** Sopranos, Tenors | | | *Parsifal* |
| **Essex, Robert Devereux Earl of** Tenor | Favorite of Queen Elisabeth | 1st Pears | *Gloriana* |
| **Estrella** Speaker | Lady in waiting | | *Háry János* |
| **Etain** Soprano | Manru's daughter | | *The Immortal Hour* |
| **Ethiopian Slaves** Chorus | | | *Aida* |
| **Eudoxia, Princess** Soprano | The emperor's niece | | *La Juive* |
| **Eugene Onegin** Baritone | | London, de Luca, Sved | *Eugene Onegin* |
| **Eugenio de Zuniga, Don** Tenor | The magistrate | 1st Breuer; Kelley | *Der Corregidor* |

| CHARACTER | | ROLE | SINGER | OPERA |
|---|---|---|---|---|
| **Eumete** | Tenor | Swineherd | | *Il Ritorno d'Ulisse in Patria* |
| **Eunuchs** | Chorus | | | *Turandot* (Busoni) |
| **Eunuchs of the Harem** | Chorus | | | *L'Italiana in Algeri* |
| **Euridice** | Soprano | Orfeo's wife | Gatti | *La Favola d'Orfeo* |
| **Euridice** | Soprano | Orphée's wife | | *Les Malheurs d'Orphée* |
| **Euridice** | Soprano | Orfeo's wife | Adams, Arnould, Billington, Gadski, Hasteriter, Novotna, Rappold | *Orfeo ed Euridice* |
| **Euridice** | Soprano | Orphée's wife | Ugalde | *Orphée aux Enfers* |
| **Eurimacho** | Tenor | Melanto's lover | | *Il Ritorno d'Ulisse in Patria* |
| **Europa** | Soprano | A Queen, formerly loved by Jupiter | | *Die Liebe der Danae* |
| **Euryanthe of Savoy** | Soprano | | 1st Sontag; Flagstad, Hempel, Lilli Lehmann, Lind, Sucher, Wagner | *Euryanthe* |
| **Eurydice** *See* Euridice | | | | |
| **Eva** | Soprano | Pogner's daughter | 1st Mathilde Mallinger; Albani, de los Angeles, Brandt, Dux, Eames, Farrar, Gadski, Goltz, Hempel, Jurinac, Leffler-Burckhard, Lemnitz, Marchesi, Moody, Morena, Osborn, Schwarzkopf, Seidle-Krauss, Sembrich, Steber, Stehle, Stückgold, Sucher, Zadek | *Die Meistersinger* |
| **Evander** | Tenor | | | *Alceste* |

| CHARACTER | ROLE | SINGER | OPERA |
|---|---|---|---|
| **Evangelist**  Bass | | | *Pilgrim's Progress* |
| **Evil, Choir of**  Chorus | | | *The Poisoned Kiss* |
| **Evil Spirits**  Chorus | | | *Robert le Diable* |
| **Executioner**  Tenor | | | *Švanda Dudak* |
| **Executioners**  Chorus | | | *La Juive* |
| **Fafner**  Bass | Giant, builder of Valhalla | List | *Das Ring des Nibelungen* |
| **Fairies**  Chorus | | | *La Damnation de Faust* |
| **Fairy**  *See* Dew Fairy | | | |
| **Falcon's Voice, The**  Soprano | | | *Die Frau ohne Schatten* |
| **Falke, Doctor**  Baritone | Eisenstein's friend | Brownlee | *Die Fledermaus* |
| **Falstaff, Sir John**  Baritone | | 1st Maurel; Tibbett, Gobbi, Stabile | *Falstaff* |
| **Falstaff, Sir John**  Bass | | 1st Zschiesche; Allin, Betz, Bispham, Sammarco, Scotti | *Die Lustigen Wieber von Windsor* |
| **Faninal, Herr von**  Baritone | Sophie's father | Brownlee, Schützendorf | *Der Rosenkavalier* |
| **Fanuèl**  Baritone | A Christian | 1st Galeffi;  Franci | *Nerone* |
| **Farfallo**  Bass | An actor | Hecht | *Die Schweigsame Frau* |
| **Farfarello**  Bass | A devil | | *The Love for Three Oranges* |
| **Farlaf**  Bass | Suitor of Ludmilla, a warrior | | *Russlan and Ludmilla* |
| **Farmer**  Bass | | | *Die Kluge* |
| **Farmers**  Chorus | | | *Martha* |
| **Farmer's Daughter**  Soprano | The wise maiden | | *Die Kluge* |

| CHARACTER | ROLE | SINGER | OPERA |
|---|---|---|---|
| **Fasolt**  Bass Baritone | Giant, builder of Valhalla | Radford | *Das Rheingold* |
| **Fata Morgana** Soprano | A witch, Leandro's protectress | Faull | *The Love for Three Oranges* |
| **Father-in-Law**  Bass | | 1st Vieuille; Nissen, Inghilleri | *Le Pauvre Matelot* |
| **Father of Louise** Bass | | Radford | *Louise* |
| **Fatima** Mezzo-soprano | Reiza's companion | 1st Vestris; Matzenauer, Trebelli | *Oberon* |
| **Fatimah**  Soprano | Marouf's shrewish wife | | *Marouf* |
| **Fauns**  Chorus | | | *Les Troyens* |
| **Faust**  Tenor | A learned man | 1st Jean de Reszke; Alvarez, Binci, Campanini, Dalmorès, Merli, Rousseliere, Voyer | *La Damnation de Faust* |
| **Faust**  Tenor | A learned doctor | 1st Barbot; Alvarez, Ansseau, Bonci, Campanini, Capoul, Caruso, Dalmorès, Hislop, Jadlowker, Kullmann, Maas, MacLennan, R. Martin, McCormack, Muratore, Nicolini, Jean de Reszke, Saléza, Tagliavini | *Faust* |
| **Faust**  Tenor | A learned doctor | Campanini, Caruso, Gigli, Masini, McCormack, Merli, del Monaco, Peerce, Pertile, Tagliavini | *Mefistofele* |
| **Faust, Doktor** Baritone | A learned man | | *Doktor Faust* |

| CHARACTER | | ROLE | SINGER | OPERA |
|---|---|---|---|---|
| **Fauteuil, Le** | Bass | The armchair | | L'Enfant et les Sortilèges |
| **Federica** | Contralto | Duchess, Walter's niece | | Luisa Miller |
| **Federico** | Tenor | Fritz's friend | | L'Amico Fritz |
| **Federico** | Tenor | Rosa's son, in love with the girl from Arles | 1st Caruso; Schipa | L'Arlesiana |
| **Fedora Romanov, Princess** | Soprano | | 1st Bellincioni; Caniglia, Cavalieri, Giachetti, Jeritza, Pederzini | Fedora |
| **Feklusha** | Mezzo-soprano | Servant | | Katya Kabanova |
| **Felice** | Soprano | Canciano's wife | | I Quattro Rusteghi |
| **Felicia** | Contralto | | 1st Malibran | Crociato (Meyerbeer) |
| **Felicia** See Felice | | | | |
| **Fellah** | Tenor | | | Marouf |
| **Femme du Peuple** See Woman | | | | |
| **Fenella** | Pantomime | Masaniello's sister, in love with Alfonso | | Masaniello |
| **Fenena** | Soprano | Nabucco's daughter | | Nabucco |
| **Fenton** | Tenor | Young gentleman in love with Nanetta | Bonci | Falstaff |
| **Fenton** | Tenor | Anne Page's lover | Dippel | Die Lustigen Weiber von Windsor |
| **Feodor** | Mezzo-soprano | Son of Boris Godunov | Miller | Boris Godunov |
| **Ferdinand** | Tenor | Young novice, in love with Leonora | Campanini, Caruso | La Favorita |
| **Ferdinand** See King of Spain | | | | |
| **Ferdinand II, Kaiser** Also Rudolf, also The Sun | Bass | | | Die Harmonie der Welt |

| CHARACTER | ROLE | SINGER | OPERA |
|---|---|---|---|
| **Fernando** Tenor | Rosario's lover | 1st Martinelli; Civil | *Goyescas* |
| **Fernando** Baritone | | 1st Galli; Faure | *La Gazza Ladra* |
| **Fernando, Don** Bass | The King's minister | Gura, Middleton, Scheidermantl | *Fidelio* |
| **Fernando** *See also* Ferdinand | | | |
| **Ferrando** Bass | Captain of the guard of di Luna | Gassier, Moscona | *Il Trovatore* |
| **Ferrando** Tenor | Dorabella's fiancé | 1st Calvesi; F. Austin, Lewis, Nash, Pears, Sullivan, Tucker | *Così fan Tutte* |
| **Fiakermilli** Soprano | Singer at the Fiaker Ball | | *Arabella* |
| **Fidalma** Mezzo-soprano | Geronimo's sister | Stignani | *Il Matrimonio Segreto* |
| **Fiddler, The Dark** Baritone | Real owner of the disputed land | | *A Village Romeo and Juliet* |
| **Fidelio** *See* Leonora | Really Leonora, disguised as a man | | |
| **Fidès** Mezzo-soprano | Mother of John of Leyden | 1st Viardot-Garcia; Alboni, Brandt, Brema, Homer, Ober, Schumann-Heink, Stoltz, Tietjens, Wagner, Walker | *Le Prophète* |
| **Fieramosca** Baritone | Cellini's rival, a papal sculptor | | *Benvenuto Cellini* |
| **Fiesco** *See* Jacopo Fiesco | | | |
| **Figaro** Baritone | A barber | 1st Zamboni; Ancona, Balfe, Forti, Manuel Garcia II, Gassier, Gobbi, Guarrera, Ludikar, Merrill, del Puente, Jean de Reszke, Ronconi, Ruffo, Svanholm, Thomas | *Il Barbiere di Siviglia* |

| CHARACTER | | ROLE | SINGER | OPERA |
|---|---|---|---|---|
| **Figaro** | Bass | Servant to Count Almaviva | 1st Benucci; Carey, Faure, Forti, Gassier, Kinder-mann, Kunz, Siepi | *Le Nozze di Figaro* |
| **Filch** | Tenor | Pickpocket, employed by Mr. Peachum | | *The Beggar's Opera* |
| **Filina** *See* Philine | | | | |
| **Filipeto** | Tenor | Maurizio's son | | *I Quattro Rusteghi* |
| **Filipievna** Mezzo-soprano | | Tatiana's nurse | | *Eugene Onegin* |
| **Filippo II** | Bass | King of Spain | Christoff, Hines, Siepi, Tozzi | *Don Carlos* |
| **Finn** | Tenor | Good wizard | | *Russlan and Ludmilla* |
| **Fiora** | Soprano | Manfredo's wife | 1st Villani; Bori, Cobelli, Edvina, Jepson, Kirsten, Moore, Muzio, Petrella, Rethberg, Ponselle, dalla Rizza, Scuderi | *L'Amore dei Tre Re* |
| **Fiordiligi** | Soprano | Dorabella's sister | 1st Farrarese del Bene; Danco, Goltz, Gueden, Hempel, Jurinac, Seefried, Steber, Welitsch | *Così fan Tutte* |
| **Fiorello** | Bass | Almaviva's servant | Cehanovsky, de Paolis | *Il Barbiere di Siviglia* |
| **Fiorilla** | Soprano | | Callas | *Il Turco in Italia* |
| **Fire** Soprano *Also* Princess, *also* Le Rossignol | | | | *L'Enfant et les Sortilèges* |
| **First Citizen** *See* Erster Bürger | | | | |
| **Fisherfolk** | Chorus | | | *Peter Grimes* |
| **Fisherman** | Tenor | | | *Le Rossignol* |

| CHARACTER | ROLE | SINGER | OPERA |
|---|---|---|---|
| **Fishermen** Chorus | | | *Les Pêcheurs de Perles, The Wreckers* |
| **Flamand** Tenor | A musician | Gedda | *Capriccio* |
| **Flaminio** Tenor | Castle guard | | *L'Amore dei Tre Re* |
| **Flavio** Tenor | A centurion | Franke | *Norma* |
| **Fleance** Silent | Banquo's son, Macbeth's nemesis | | *Macbeth* |
| **Fléville** Baritone | Cavalier | | *Andrea Chénier* |
| **Flint, Mr.** Baritone | Sailing master | | *Billy Budd* |
| **Flora** Soprano | | 1st Olive Dyer | *The Turn of the Screw* |
| **Flora Bervoix** Mezzo-soprano | Violetta's friend | 1st Speranza; Evans | *La Traviata* |
| **Flora, Madame** *See* Baba | | | |
| **Florence Pike** Contralto | Lady Billow's housekeeper | | *Albert Herring* |
| **Florestan** Tenor | A Spanish nobleman | 1st Demmer; Davies, Niemann, Patzak, Reeves, Schott, Urlus, Völker | *Fidelio* |
| **Florestein** Tenor | Count Arnheim's nephew | | *The Bohemian Girl* |
| **Floria Tosca** *See* Tosca | | | |
| **Floriana** Soprano | Music hall singer | | *Zaza* |
| **Flosshilde** Mezzo-soprano | A Rhinemaiden | | *Das Ring des Nibelungen* |
| **Flower Maidens, Choirs of** Sopranos, Contraltos | | | *Parsifal* |
| **Flower Maidens (Six)** Sopranos | | | *Parsifal* |
| **Flute Player** Silent | | | *Der Rosenkavalier* |

| CHARACTER | ROLE | SINGER | OPERA |
|---|---|---|---|
| **Fluth, Frau** Soprano | Mrs. Ford | Sembrich, Tietjens | *Die Lustigen Weiber von Windsor* |
| **Fluth, Herr** Baritone | Mr. Ford | Santley | *Die Lustigen Weiber von Windsor* |
| **Followers of Count di Luna** Chorus | | | *Il Trovatore* |
| **Followers of Danae** Chorus | | | *Die Liebe der Danae* |
| **Followers of Don Carlos** Chorus | | | *Ernani* |
| **Followers of Manrico** Chorus | | | *Il Trovatore* |
| **Followers of Pollux** Chorus | | | *Die Liebe der Danae* |
| **Followers of Silva** Chorus | | | *Ernani* |
| **Foltz** *See* Hans Folz | | | |
| **Fool** Bass | | | *Hugh the Drover* |
| **Fool** Tenor | | de Paolis | *Wozzeck* |
| **Fool** *See also* Simpleton | | | |
| **Footman** | | 1st Nagy | *Vanessa* |
| **Ford** Baritone | A wealthy burgher | Cassell, Tibbett | *Falstaff* |
| **Ford** *See also* Fluth, Herr | | | |
| **Ford, Mrs.** *See* Fluth, Frau *See also* Alice Ford | | | |
| **Foreign Woman** Soprano | | | *The Consul* |
| **Foreman** Baritone | At the mill | | *Její Pastorkyňa* (Jenufa) |
| **Forest Bird** *See* Waldvogel | | | |
| **Forest Rangers (Two)** Tenor, Bass | | | *Švanda Dudák* |

| CHARACTER | ROLE | SINGER | OPERA |
|---|---|---|---|
| **Forewoman** Mezzo-soprano | | | *Louise* |
| **Former Wives (Three)** | | | *Duke Bluebeard's Castle* |
| **Fortune Teller** Soprano | | | *Arabella* |
| **Fouquier-Tinville** Baritone | Attorney General | | *Andrea Chénier* |
| **Fra Diavolo** Tenor | Bandit chieftain | 1st Chollet; Bonci, Cox, Pertile, Santley, Schipa, Völker | *Fra Diavolo* |
| **Frances, Countess of Essex** Mezzo-soprano | | | *Gloriana* |
| **Francesca da Rimini** Soprano | Beloved by Paolo | 1st Edvina; Alda, Caniglia, Carbone, Cigna, Raisa, dalla Rizza, Somigli | *Francesca da Rimini* |
| **Francesco** Tenor | Artisan for Cellini | | *Benvenuto Cellini* |
| **Francesco** Bass | | Bohnen | *Mona Lisa* |
| **Françoise** Contralto | | Delna | *L'Attaque du Moulin* |
| **Frank** Baritone | Prison governor | | *Die Fledermaus* |
| **Frantz** Tenor | Crespel's servant | | *Les Contes d'Hoffmann* |
| **Franz** Bass | | | *Der Prozess* |
| **Frasquita** Soprano | A gypsy, friend of Carmen | | *Carmen* |
| **Frasquita** Mezzo-soprano | Tio Lucas' wife | Cross, Forster-Lauterer, Lipton, Novotna | *Der Corregidor* |
| **Frazier** Tenor | Self-styled lawyer for Catfish Row | | *Porgy and Bess* |
| **Frédéric** Baritone | An English officer | | *Lakmé* |
| **Frédéric** Tenor/Contralto | Young nobleman | Scalchi, Trebelli (The role has been sung by contraltos since Trebelli first undertook it) | *Mignon* |

| CHARACTER | ROLE | SINGER | OPERA |
|---|---|---|---|
| **Frederick of Telramund** Baritone | Count of Brabant | 1st Milde; Ancona, Bispham, Lassalle, Ludwig, Maurel | *Lohengrin* |
| **Freia** Soprano | Goddess of youth and beauty | 1st Haupt; Borkh, Jurinac, Novotna, Shuard | *Das Ring des Nibelungen* |
| **Freimann, Baroness** Soprano | Count Eberbach's sister | | *Der Wildschütz* |
| **Fricka** Mezzo-soprano | Goddess, Wotan's wife | 1st Stehle; Branzell, Brema, Cahier, Fremstad, Homer, Klose, Langendorf, Larsen-Todsen, Ober, Schumann-Heink, Thebom, Thorborg, Wickham | *Das Rheingold* |
| **Friend** Baritone | | 1st Musy; Beuf | *Le Pauvre Matelot* |
| **Friends** Chorus | | | *Der Barbier von Bagdad, Don Quichotte, Lucia di Lammermoor, Madama Butterfly, Le Postillion de Longjumeau* |
| **Friends of Esther** Chorus | | | *Esther de Carpentras* |
| **Friends of the Marquise** Chorus | | | *La Figlia del Reggimento* |
| **Fritz Kobus** Tenor | A wealthy bachelor | D. Borgioli, Schipa, Tagliavini | *L'Amico Fritz* |
| **Fritz Kothner** Bass | Mastersinger and baker | Brownlee, Harrell, Scheidermantel | *Die Meistersinger* |
| **Frogs** Chorus | | | *L'Enfant et les Sortilèges* |
| **Froh** Tenor | Norse god | Darcy | *Das Ring des Nibelungen* |
| **Front Line Officer** Baritone | | | *Friedenstag* |

| CHARACTER | | ROLE | SINGER | OPERA |
|---|---|---|---|---|
| **Frosch** | Speaker | Jailer | | *Die Fledermaus* |
| **Frost, King** | Bass | The winter | | *Snyegurotchka* |
| **Frugola, La** Mezzo-soprano | | Talpa's wife, 50 | Claramae Turner | *Il Tabarro* |
| **Furies** | Chorus | | | *Alceste* |
| **Fyodor** *See* Feodor | | | | |
| **Gabriel** | Bass | Employed by Dickson | | *La Dame Blanche* |
| **Gabriele Adorno** Tenor | | A patrician | | *Simon Boccanegra* |
| **Gabriel von Eisenstein** Tenor | | | Kullmann | *Die Fledermaus* |
| **Gaea** | Contralto | Daphne's mother | | *Daphne* |
| **Galitzky** *See* Vladimir Jaroslavitch | | | | |
| **Gallanthus** Baritone | | Amaryllus's sister | | *The Poisoned Kiss* |
| **Gamblers** | Chorus | | | *Manon, Pique-Dame* |
| **Gaoler** *See* Jailer | | | | |
| **Garcias** | Soprano | Admirer of Dulcinée | | *Don Quichotte* |
| **Garsenda** | Soprano | Francesca's woman | | *Francesca da Rimini* |
| **Gaspar, Don** | Tenor | The King's minister | | *La Favorita* |
| **Gastone de Letorières** Tenor | | | de Paolis | *La Traviata* |
| **Gauls** | Chorus | | | *Norma* |
| **Gaulthiers Walton, Lord** Bass | | A Puritan | | *I Puritani* |
| **Gaveston** | Bass | | | *La Dame Blanche* |
| **Gay Brook** | Treble | Age 13; Bruce *in* Acts I and II | | *Let's Make an Opera* |

# THE CHARACTERS IN THE OPERAS

| CHARACTER | ROLE | SINGER | OPERA |
|---|---|---|---|
| **Gazello** Bass | | | *Lucrezia Borgia* |
| **Gedge, Mr.** Baritone | Vicar | | *Albert Herring* |
| **Geishas** Chorus | | | *Iris* |
| **Gellner** Baritone | In love with Wally | | *La Wally* |
| **Generals** Chorus | | | *Háry János* |
| **Geneviève** Contralto | Mother of Pelléas | 1st Gerville-Reache; Gay | *Pelléas et Mélisande* |
| **Genii, Three** Sopranos, Mezzo-soprano | | | *Die Zauberflöte* |
| **Gennaro** Tenor | Blacksmith | Bassi, Jagel, Mario, Martinelli, Merli | *I Gioielli della Madonna* |
| **Gennaro** Tenor | Nobleman of the Venetian Republic | Campanini | *Lucrezia Borgia* |
| **Genoveva** Soprano | | Malten | *Genoveva* |
| **Genoveva, Suor** Soprano | A nun | | *Suor Angelica* |
| **Gentlemen** Chorus | | | *Manon* |
| **Gentlewoman** *See* Lady in waiting | | | |
| **Georg Danton** Baritone | French revolutionary | 1st Schöffler | *Dantons Tod* |
| **George Walton, Sir** Bass | Puritan, brother of Gaulthier | 1st Lablache; Rossi-Lemeni | *I Puritani* |
| **Georges Brown** Tenor | English officer | 1st Ponchard; Naval | *La Dame Blanche* |
| **Gérald** Tenor | English officer | 1st Talazac; Jagel, Martinelli, McCormack, Thill | *Lakmé* |
| **Gerard** *See* Charles Gerard | | | |
| **Gerhilde** Soprano | A valkyr | 1st Haupt; Brandt, Shuard, Votipka | *Die Walküre* |

371

| CHARACTER | ROLE | SINGER | OPERA |
|---|---|---|---|
| **Germont** *See* Giorgio Germont *See also* Alfredo Germont (Generally the sur-name serves to designate Giorgio Germont) | | | |
| **Geronimo** Bass | Carolina's father | Lablache | *Il Matrimonio Segreto* |
| **Geronte di Ravoir** Bass | Treasurer General | Didur | *Manon Lescaut* |
| **Gertrude** Soprano | Mother of Hansel and Gretel | | *Hänsel und Gretel* |
| **Gertrude** Contralto | | | *Louise* |
| **Gertrude** Mezzo-soprano | Juliette's nurse | | *Roméo et Juliette* |
| **Gertrude S.** Mezzo-soprano | | | *The Mother of Us All* |
| **Geschwitz, Gräfin** Mezzo-soprano | One of Lulu's later lovers | | *Lulu* |
| **Gessler** Bass | Tyrannical governor over Switzerland | | *Guillaume Tell* |
| **Gherardino** Contralto | Gherardo's son, 7 | | *Gianni Schicchi* |
| **Gherardo** Tenor | Dead Buoso's nephew, 40 | de Paolis | *Gianni Schicchi* |
| **Ghost of Max's Mother, The** | | | *Der Freischütz* |
| **Ghost of Nino** Bass | Semiramide's husband | | *Semiramide* |
| **Ghost** *See also* Cassandre's Ghost *See also* Chorèbe's Ghost *See also* Commendatore *See also* Quint's Ghost | | | |

| CHARACTER | | ROLE | SINGER | OPERA |
|---|---|---|---|---|
| **Ghosts** | Chorus | | | *Le Rossignol* |
| **Ghosts, Invisible** | | | | *Les Troyens* |
| | Chorus | | | |
| **Giacomo** | Bass | Bandit | | *Fra Diavolo* |
| **Gianetta** | Soprano | Peasant girl | | *L'Elisir d'Amore* |
| **Gianni Schicchi** | | A sly trickster, | 1st de Luca; S. | *Gianni Schicchi* |
| | Baritone | age 50 | Austin, Baccaloni, Badini, Corena, Galeffi, Stabile, Tajo | |
| **Giarno** | Bass | A gypsy | | *Mignon* |
| **Gil, Count** | | Susanna's husband, | Biasini, Noble, | *Il Segreto di Susanna* |
| | Baritone | 30 | Parvis, Sammarco, Scotti | |
| **Gilda** | Soprano | Rigoletto's daughter | 1st Brambilla; Ackté, Adams, Albani, Alda, Callas, Dobbs, Farrar, Galli-Curci, Gerster, Gueden, Hempel, Ivogün, Kellogg, Krauss, Kurz, Lipovska, Lyne, Melba, dal Monte, Munsel, Nordica, Norena, Paghliughi, Patti, Peters, Pons, Rysanek, Sayao, Schwarzkopf, Sembrich, Talley, Luisa Tetrazzini, Vere | *Rigoletto* |
| **Gingerbread Woman** | Soprano | | | *A Village Romeo and Juliet* |
| **Gioconda, La** | Soprano | The ballad singer | 1st Mariani; Arangi-Lombardi, Bampton, Callas, Cerquetti, Cigna, Destinn, Dow, Durand, Litvinne, Matzenauer, Milanov, Christine Nilsson, Nordica, Ponselle, Roman | *La Gioconda* |

| CHARACTER | ROLE | SINGER | OPERA |
|---|---|---|---|
| **Giorgetta**　Soprano | Michele's wife, 25, in love with Luigi | 1st Muzio; Albanese, Carbone, Kennard, Labia, Lewis, Shuard | *Il Tabarro* |
| **Giorgio** *See* George Walton, Sir | | | |
| **Giorgio Germont** Baritone | Alfredo's father | 1st Vanesi; Amato, Bonelli, Cassell, Gobbi, Renaud, Scotti, Thomas, Tibbett, Weede | *Il Traviata* |
| **Giovanna**　Soprano | Elvira's servant | | *Ernani* |
| **Giovanna** Mezzo-soprano | Gilda's duenna | Votipka | *Rigoletto* |
| **Giovanni, Don** Baritone | A licentious nobleman | 1st Bassi; Beck, Braham, Carey, Cassell, Faure, Forsell, Forti, G. Garcia M., Garcia I, Lablache, Lassalle, London, Maurel, Pinza, Renaud, Jean de Reszke, Ronconi, Rossi-Lemeni, Sammarco, Scotti, Siepi, Stabile | *Don Giovanni* |
| **Giovanni da Prodica**　Bass | Sicilian revolutionary | Christoff | *I Vespri Siciliani* |
| **Giovanni lo Sciancato**　Baritone | Lame son of Malatesta | 1st Cigada; Amato, Biasini, Danise, Maugeri, Ronconi, Stabile | *Francesca da Rimini* |
| **Giovanni Morone** Baritone | Papal legate | | *Palestrina* |
| **Giove**　Tenor | Jove, chief of the gods | | *Il Ritorno d'Ulisse in Patria* |
| **Girl with the Hunch-Back** Soprano | | | *Der Prozess* |

| CHARACTER | ROLE | SINGER | OPERA |
|---|---|---|---|
| **Girls** Chorus | | | L'Arlesiana, Die Meistersinger |
| **Girls from Sandomir** Chorus | | | Boris Godunov |
| **Giulia** Soprano | | Lind | La Vestale |
| **Giulietta** Soprano | A Capulet in love with Romeo | 1st Grisi | I Capuletti ed I Montecchi |
| **Giulietta** Soprano | Courtesan | 1st Isaac; Elias, Fremstad, Hempel, Jurinac, Seefried, Shuard, Steber, Teyte | Les Contes d'Hoffmann |
| **Giuseppe** Silent | | | Palestrina |
| **Giuseppe** Tenor | Violetta's servant | | La Traviata |
| **Giuseppe Hagenbach** See Hagenbach | | | |
| **Glasha** Mezzo-soprano | Servant | | Katya Kabanova |
| **Gleaton, Mrs.** Soprano | | | Susanna |
| **Gloster Heming** Mezzo-soprano | | | The Mother of Us All |
| **Gluttons** Chorus | | | The Love for Three Oranges |
| **Goatherds (Two)** Soprano, Contralto | | | Dinorah |
| **Gob** | Evil assistant of Dipsacus | | The Poisoned Kiss |
| **Gobin** Tenor | Perichaud's friend | | La Rondine |
| **Gobineau, Mr.** Baritone | Baba's client | | The Medium |
| **Gobineau, Mrs.** Soprano | Baba's client | | The Medium |
| **Gobrias** Tenor | Follower of Simon Mago | | Nerone |
| **Godfrey, Duke** Silent | Elsa's brother | | Lohengrin |

| CHARACTER | ROLE | SINGER | OPERA |
|---|---|---|---|
| **Godunov**<br>*See* Boris Godunov | | | |
| **Golaud** Baritone | Arkel's grandson, half-brother to Pelléas | 1st Dufranne; Amato, Singher, London | *Pelléas et Mélisande* |
| **Gonsalve** Tenor | Poet and Concepcion's lover | Kelley, Lloyd | *L'Heure Espagnole* |
| **Good, Choir of** Chorus | | | *The Poisoned Kiss* |
| **Gorislava** Soprano | Ratmir's slave | | *Russlan and Ludmilla* |
| **Goro** Tenor | Marriage broker | Franke, de Paolis | *Madama Butterfly* |
| **Governess** Mezzo-soprano | | | *Pique-Dame* |
| **Government Director** Bass | | | *Der Prozess* |
| **Graf von Helfenstein** Silent | | | *Mathis der Maler* |
| **Gräfin von Helfenstein** Contralto | | | *Mathis der Maler* |
| **Grand Inquisitor** Bass | | Hines | *L'Africaine* |
| **Grand Inquisitor** Bass | | | *Don Carlos* |
| **Grandmother** Mezzo-soprano | Salud's grandmother | | *La Vida Breve* |
| **Grandmother Buryja** Contralto | Mill owner | | *Její Pastorkyňa* (Jenufa) |
| **Gravis** Bass | Spirit voice | | *Doktor Faustus* |
| **Grazia** Dancer | | | *I Gioielli della Madonna* |
| **Grech** Bass | Policeman | | *Fedora* |
| **Greek Captain** Bass | | | *Les Troyens* |
| **Greek Chorus** Chorus | | | *Mefistofele* |

| CHARACTER | ROLE | SINGER | OPERA |
|---|---|---|---|
| **Greek Soldiers** Chorus | | | *Les Troyens* |
| **Greeks** Chorus | | | *Iphigénie en Aulide, Iphigénie en Tauride* |
| **Gregory** Baritone | Retainer to Capulet | | *Roméo et Juliette* |
| **Gregory** *See also* Grigorij | | | |
| **Gremin, Prince** Bass | An old general | Didur, Tozzi | *Eugene Onegin* |
| **Grenadiers** Chorus | | | *La Figlia del Reggimento* |
| **Grenvil, Doctor** Bass | | Santley | *La Traviata* |
| **Gretchen** Soprano | Baculus' fiancée | Ternina | *Der Wildschütz* |
| **Gretel** Soprano | Hänsel's sister | Gruhn, Mario | *Hänsel und Gretel* |
| **Grieux, Chevalier des** Tenor | In love with Manon | 1st Talazac; Ansseau, Bentonelli, Bjoerling, Caruso, Clément, Crooks, van Dyke, Gigli, Maas, Jean de Reszke, Schipa, Tagliavini | *Manon* |
| **Grieux, Count des** Bass | Father of the Chevalier | Rothier | *Manon* |
| **Grieux, Chevalier des** Tenor | In love with Manon Lescaut | Bevel, Bjoerling, Caruso, Gigli, del Monaco, Pertile, Tucker | *Manon Lescaut* |
| **Grigorij** Tenor | The false Dimitri, pretender to the throne of Russia | 1st Komissarzhevsky; Althouse, Baum, Sullivan | *Boris Godunov* |
| **Grimes** *See* Peter Grimes | | | |
| **Grimgerde** Soprano | A valkyr | Elias | *Die Walküre* |
| **Gritzko** Tenor | In love with Parassia | McCormack | *The Fair at Sorochintsky* |

| CHARACTER | ROLE | SINGER | OPERA |
|---|---|---|---|
| **Groom**<br>From Chorus | | | *Arabella* |
| **Grose, Mrs.**<br>Soprano | | 1st Cross | *The Turn of the Screw* |
| **Grubach, Frau**<br>Mezzo-soprano | | Evans | *Der Prozess* |
| **Gruff**<br>*English version of the name* Simon *in I Quattro Rusteghi* | | | |
| **Grüsser, Ulrich**<br>*See* Ulrich Grüsser | | | |
| **Guard**    Tenor | of the frontier | | *Hubička* |
| **Guard**<br>*See* Boyar Guard | | | |
| **Guardiano, Padre**<br>Bass | Franciscan superior | Hines, Rossi-Lemeni, Siepi | *La Forza del Destino* |
| **Guards**    Chorus | | | *Un Ballo in Maschera, Boris Godunov, Die Entführung aus dem Serail, Esther de Carpentras, La Favorita, Fête Galante, La Gioconda, Guillaume Tell, The Love for Three Oranges, Manon, Oberon, Semiramide* |
| **Gubetta**    Bass | Serving Lucrezia | | *Lucrezia Borgia* |
| **Guccio**    Bass | Painter, witness for the will | | *Gianni Schicchi* |
| **Guests**    Chorus | | | *Arabella, Ariadne auf Naxos, Fête Galante, Eugene Onegin, Pique-Dame, La Traviata* |
| **Guglielmo**    Bass | Fiordiligi's fiancé | 1st Bussani; Austin, Didur, Guarrera | *Così fan Tutte* |

| CHARACTER | ROLE | SINGER | OPERA |
|---|---|---|---|
| **Guide** Silent | | | *Carmen* |
| **Guido di Monforte** Baritone | Governor of occupied Sicily | Schlusnus | *I Vespri Siciliani* |
| **Guidon, Prince** Tenor | | | *Le Coq d'Or* |
| **Guildsmen** Chorus | | | *Die Meistersinger* |
| **Guillaume Tell** Baritone | Swiss patriot and hero | Beck, Braham, Faure, Lassalle, Maurel, Rossi-Lemeni | *Guillaume Tell* |
| **Guillot de Morfontaine** Tenor | An old roué | | *Manon* |
| **Gunther** Baritone | Hagen's half-brother | Austin, Gura | *Götterdämmerung* |
| **Gurnemanz** Bass | Knight of the Grail | 1st Scaria and Siehr; Allin, Andresen, Bohnen, Braun, Delmas, Grengg, Griswold, Hines, Kipnis, F. Kraus, Manowarda, Mayr, Weber | *Parsifal* |
| **Gustave III** *See* Riccardo | | | |
| **Gutrune** Soprano | Gunther's sister | Flagstad, Fornia-Labey, White | *Götterdämmerung* |
| **Gypsies** Chorus | | | *Carmen, The Fair at Sorochintsky, Maritana, Mignon, Il Trovatore* |
| **Gypsy** Bass | | | *The Fair at Sorochintsky* |
| **Gypsy** *See also* Azucena *See also* Carmen *See also* Giarno *See also* Preziosilla | | | |
| **Gzak** Bass | Polovtsian Khan (A Tartar) | | *Prince Igor* |

| CHARACTER | | ROLE | SINGER | OPERA |
|---|---|---|---|---|
| **Hadassa** Mezzo-soprano | | Esther | | *Esther de Carpentras* |
| **Hadji** | Tenor | Nilakantha's servant | | *Lakmé* |
| **Hagen** | Bass | Alberich's descendant, Siegfried's enemy | 1st Siehr; Griswold, Hofmann, F. Kraus, Mayr, Edouard de Reszke | *Götterdämmerung* |
| **Hagenbach** | Tenor | Of Sölden | Renato Gigli, R. Martin, Merli, Voyer | *La Wally* |
| **Hairdresser** | Silent | | | *Der Rosenkavalier* |
| **Haly** | Bass | The Bey's captain of corsairs | | *L'Italiana in Algeri* |
| **Hamlet** | Baritone | Danish prince | 1st Faure; Beck, Maurel, Renaud | *Hamlet* |
| **Hämon** | Tenor | | | *Antigonae* (Orff) |
| **Handmaiden** | | | | *L'Amore dei Tre Re* |
| **Handsome** | Baritone | A miner | | *La Fanciulla del West* |
| **Hanezò** | Bass | Fritz's friend | | *L'Amico Fritz* |
| **Hangmen (Two)** Tenors | | | | *Dantons Tod* |
| **Hans Foltz** | Bass | Coppersmith and Mastersinger | Lorenzo Alvary | *Die Meistersinger* |
| **Hans Heiling** Baritone | | | Beck, Scheidermantel | *Hans Heiling* |
| **Hans Sachs** | Bass | Mastersinger and cobbler | 1st Betz; Ancona, Bender, Berglund, Bockelmann, Delmas, Edelman, Fischer, Griswold, Gura, Hotter, Lassalle, Ludwig, Nissen, Prohaska, Reichmann, Edouard de Reszke, van Rooy, Rode, Scaria, Scheidermantel, Schöffler, Schorr, Soomer, Weil, Whitehill | *Die Meistersinger* |

| CHARACTER | ROLE | SINGER | OPERA |
|---|---|---|---|
| **Hans Schwarz** Bass | Mastersinger and stocking weaver | | *Die Meistersinger* |
| **Hänsel** Mezzo-soprano | Gretel's brother | Bible, Welitsch | *Hänsel und Gretel* |
| **Happy** Baritone | A miner | | *La Fanciulla del West* |
| **Hardstone** | | | *English version for the name* Maurizio *in I Quattro Rusteghi* |
| **Harlequin** Baritone | | | *Ariadne auf Naxos* |
| **Harlequin** Tenor | | | *Fête Galante* |
| **Harlequin** *See also* Arlecchino *See also* Beppe | | | |
| **Haroun** Tenor | A prince | 1st Duchesne | *Djamileh* |
| **Haroun al Rashid** Speaker | Calif of Bagdad | | *Oberon* |
| **Harriet Durham, Lady** Soprano | Maid of honour to the Queen, disguised as "Martha" | 1st Zerr; Alda, Favero, Mason, Sembrich | *Martha* |
| **Harry** Treble | A child | | *Albert Herring* |
| **Harry** Tenor | A miner | | *La Fanciulla del West* |
| **Harry Paddington** From Chorus | Gentleman of the road | | *The Beggar's Opera* |
| **Harvester** Tenor | | | *Dinorah* |
| **Harvey** Bass | Lawrence's brother-in-law | | *The Wreckers* |
| **Háry János** Baritone | A great liar | | *Háry János* |
| **Hate-Good, Lord** Bass | | | *Pilgrim's Progress* |
| **Hayes, Mrs.** Soprano | | | *Susannah* |
| **Heavenly Beings (Two)** Soprano, Contralto | | | *Pilgrim's Progress* |

| CHARACTER | ROLE | SINGER | OPERA |
|---|---|---|---|
| **Hebrew**<br>*See* Old Hebrew | | | |
| **Hebrews**   Chorus | | | *Nabucco, Samson et Dalila* |
| **Hector's Ghost**<br>Bass | | | *Les Troyens* |
| **Hécube**   Mezzo-soprano | Priam's wife | | *Les Troyens* |
| **Hedwige**   Soprano | Tell's wife | Brandt | *Guillaume Tell* |
| **Heinrich der Schreiber**   Tenor | Knight and Minnesinger | | *Tannhäuser* |
| **Helen of Troy**<br>Pantomime | | | *Faust* |
| **Helen of Troy**<br>*See* Elena | | | |
| **Helena**   Soprano | Wife of Menelaus | 1st Rethberg; Jeritza, Müller, Ursuleac | *Die Aegyptische Helena* |
| **Hélène**   Soprano | | 1st Melba | *Hélène* (Saint Saëns) |
| **Helenus**   Tenor | Priam's son | | *Les Troyens* |
| **Helmsman**<br>Baritone | | | *Tristan und Isolde* |
| **Helmsman**<br>*See also* Steersman | | | |
| **Helmwige**   Soprano | A valkyr | Amara, Faull | *Die Walküre* |
| **Henrici** | Saxon officer | | *Der Bettelstudent* |
| **Henrietta**   Soprano | Widow of Charles the First of France | | *I Puritani* |
| **Henry Ashton**<br>*See* Enrico | | | |
| **Henrietta M**<br>Soprano | | | *The Mother of Us All* |
| **Henry B**   Tenor | | | *The Mother of Us All* |
| **Henry Cuffe**<br>Baritone | Follower of Essex | | *Gloriana* |

| CHARACTER | | ROLE | SINGER | OPERA |
|---|---|---|---|---|
| **Henry Morosus Blunt** | Tenor | Actor, nephew to Sir Morosus | | *Die Schweigsame Frau* |
| **Henry the Fowler** | Bass | King of Germany | Delmas, Fischer, Griswold, Hinckley, Hotter, Plançon, Edouard de Reszke | *Lohengrin* |
| **Herald** | Baritone | | | *Alceste* |
| **Herald** | Tenor | | | *Don Carlos* |
| **Herald** | Bass | | | *The Love for Three Oranges* |
| **Herald** | Bass | | | *Otello* |
| **Herald** | Baritone | | | *Pilgrim's Progress* |
| **Herald** *See* King's Herald | | | | |
| **Herault de Sechelles** | Tenor | | 1st P. Klein | *Dantons Tod* |
| **Hercules** | Baritone | | | *Alceste* |
| **Herman Altan** | Baritone | | | *The Mother of Us All* |
| **Hermann** | Baritone | Student | | *Les Contes d'Hoffman* |
| **Herrmann** | Baritone | | 1st Alsen | *Dantons Tod* |
| **Hermann** | Tenor | Gambler, in love with Lisa | 1st Figner; Slezak, Zenatello | *Pique-Dame* |
| **Hermann** | Bass | Landgrave of Thuringia | 1st Dettmer; Griswold, Hines, Journet, List, Plançon | *Tannhäuser* |
| **Hermann Ortel** | Bass | Mastersinger and soap boiler | | *Die Meistersinger* |
| **Hermione** | Soprano | Child of Helena and Melenaus | | *Die Aegyptische Helena* |
| **Hermit** | Bass | | Foli | *Der Freischütz* |
| **Hermit** *See* Pimen | | | | |
| **Hero** | Baritone | Leonato's daughter in love with Claudio | | *Béatrice et Bénédict* |

| CHARACTER | ROLE | SINGER | OPERA |
|---|---|---|---|
| **Herod Antipas** Tenor | Governor of Judea | 1st Burrian; Borgatti, Dalmorès, Kirchoff, Krauss, Lorenz, Maison, Patzak, Pölzer | *Salome* |
| **Herodias** Mezzo-soprano | Herod's wife | 1st Chavanne; Olszewska, Shacklock, Thorborg | *Salome* |
| **Herring, Mrs.** Mezzo-soprano | Albert's mother | | *Albert Herring* |
| **Hester Prynne** Soprano | | 1st Gadski | *The Scarlet Letter* (Damrosch) |
| **Hester Prynne** Soprano | | 1st Giannini | *The Scarlet Letter* (Giannini) |
| **Hever**   Baritone | A spy | | *Debora e Jaele* |
| **High Priest** Baritone | | 1st Laschi; Franci, Schöffler, Singher, Warren | *Alceste* |
| **High Priest**   Bass | | | *Die Königin von Saba* |
| **High Priest** *See also* Ramfis | | | |
| **High Priest of Babylon**   Bass | | | *Nabucco* |
| **High Priest of Brahma**   Baritone | | | *L'Africaine* |
| **High Priest of Dagon**   Baritone | | Bouhy, Lassalle, Milde | *Samson et Dalila* |
| **High Priest of Neptune**   Tenor | | | *Idomeneo* |
| **Highbrows**   Chorus | | | *The Love for Three Oranges* |
| **Hindu Merchant** Tenor | | | *Sadko* |
| **Hob** | Evil servant of Dipsacus | | *The Poisoned Kiss* |
| **Hobson**   Bass | A carrier | 1st Vaughan | *Peter Grimes* |

| CHARACTER | ROLE | SINGER | OPERA |
|---|---|---|---|
| **Hoël** Baritone | Goatherd | Faure, de Luca, Maurel, Santley | *Dinorah* |
| **Hoffmann** Tenor | Poet, lover of Antonia, Giulietta, Olympia and Stella | Gedda | *Les Contes d'Hoffmann* |
| **Holsteiner** Bass | Commander of the besiegers | | *Friedenstag* |
| **Homonay** *See* Peter Homonay | | | |
| **Horace Adams, Reverend** Tenor | | 1st Culbert | *Peter Grimes* |
| **Horace Tabor** Baritone | | Cassell | *The Ballad of Baby Doe* |
| **Horloge Comptoise, L'** Baritone | The grandfather clock | | *L'Enfant et les Sortilèges* |
| **Horn, Count** *See* Tomaso | | | |
| **Horn-Player, The Poor** Tenor | | | *A Village Romeo and Juliet* |
| **Hortensio** Bass | Steward of the Marquise | Lorenzo Alvary | *La Figlia del Reggimento* |
| **Hostess** *See* Innkeeper | | | |
| **Housekeeper** Contralto | | Kobart | *Die Schweigsame Frau* |
| **Housewife** Mezzo-soprano | | | *Gloriana* |
| **Hugh Crome** Treble | Age 8, Ralph *in Acts I and II* | | *Let's Make an Opera* |
| **Hugh the Drover** Tenor | | 1st Davies | *Hugh the Drover* |
| **Huguenot Ladies and Gentlemen** Chorus | | | *Les Huguenots* |
| **Hunchback** Tenor | Barak's brother | | *Die Frau ohne Schattan* |
| **Hunchbacked Bass Fiddler** Bass | | | *A Village Romeo and Juliet* |

| CHARACTER | | ROLE | SINGER | OPERA |
|---|---|---|---|---|
| **Hunding** | Bass | Siegmund's enemy | 1st Niering; Griswold, Hinckley, Hotter, Koegel, Radford, Edouard de Reszke | *Die Walküre* |
| **Hungarian Sentry** Speaker | | | | *Háry János* |
| **Hunters** | Chorus | | | *Doktor Faustus, Der Fliegende Holländer, Guillaume Tell, Lucia di Lammermoor Martha, Les Troyens* |
| **Huntresses** | Chorus | | | *Martha* |
| **Huntsmen** | Bass | | | *Dinorah, Mefistofele, Pskovityanka, Der Wildschütz* |
| **Huon de Bordeaux, Sir** | Tenor | | 1st Braham; Althouse, Kullmann, Reeves | *Oberon* |
| **Hussars (Two)** Speakers | | | | *Háry János* |
| **Hylas** | Tenor | Trojan sailor | | *Les Troyens* |
| **Iago** | Baritone | Otello's underling | Faure | *Otello* (Rossini) |
| **Iago** | Baritone | Otello's ensign | 1st Maurel; Bechi, Biasini, Bispham, Formichi, Galassi, Inghilleri, Rimini, Sammarco, Scotti, Stabile, Tibbett | *Otello* |
| **Idamante** | Soprano | Idomeneo's son | 1st del Prato; Simoneau | *Idomeneo* |
| **Idiot** *See* Simpleton *See also* Fool | | | | |
| **Idomeneo** | Tenor | King of Crete | 1st Anton Raaf; Lewis | *Idomeneo* |
| **Idreno** | Tenor | Indian prince | | *Semiramide* |
| **Ighino** | Soprano | Palestrina's son | 1st Ivogün; Jurinac | *Palestrina* |

| CHARACTER | | ROLE | SINGER | OPERA |
|---|---|---|---|---|
| **Igor Sviatoslavitch** Baritone | | Prince Igor | Burke | *Prince Igor* |
| **Ilia** | Soprano | Trojan princess | 1st Dorothea Wendling; Gueden, Jurinac, Schumann | *Idomeneo* |
| **Ilka** | Soprano | Háry's fiancée | | *Háry János* |
| **Imperial Commissioner** Bass | | | | *Madama Butterfly* |
| **Incredibile** | Tenor | A Spy | | *Andrea Chénier* |
| **Indiana Elliott** Mezzo-soprano | | | | *The Mother of Us All* |
| **Indians** | Chorus | East Indians | | *Lakmé* |
| **Indians** | Chorus | | | *L'Africaine* |
| **Inez** | Soprano | Don Diego's daughter | Hauk, Murska, Luisa Tetrazzini | *L'Africaine* |
| **Inez** | Soprano | Leonora's confidante | Albanese | *La Favorita* |
| **Inez** | Soprano | Leonora's confidante | 1st Quadri; Rappold, Vanni, Votipka | *Il Trovatore* |
| **Infanta** | Soprano | | Vere | *Le Cid* |
| **Innkeeper** Mezzo-soprano | | | Lipton | *Boris Godunov* |
| **Innkeeper** | Bass | | | *Hugh the Drover* |
| **Innkeeper** From Chorus | | | | *Manon* |
| **Innkeeper** | Bass | | | *Manon Lescaut* |
| **Innkeeper** | Tenor | | | *Der Rosenkavalier* |
| **Innkeeper** *See also* Lillas Pastia | | | | |
| **Innocente, L'** Mezzo-soprano | | Rosa's retarded youngest son | | *L'Arlesiana* |
| **Inquisitor** *See* Grand Inquisitor | | | | |

| CHARACTER | ROLE | SINGER | OPERA |
|---|---|---|---|
| **Inquisitors** Chorus | | | *L'Africaine* |
| **Inigo Gomez, Don** Bass | Banker | | *L'Heure Espagnole* |
| **Intendant** Tenor | | | *Linda di Chamounix* |
| **Interpreter** Tenor | | | *Pilgrim's Progress* |
| **Iolanthe** Soprano | | 1st Fremstad | *Der Wald* |
| **Iopas** Tenor | Poet of Carthage | | *Les Troyens* |
| **Iphigénie** Soprano | Daughter of Agamemnon | 1st Sophie Arnould; Brouwenstijn, Levasseur, Schröder-Devrient, Tentoni | *Iphigénie en Aulide* |
| **Iphigénie** Soprano | Priestess of Diana | 1st Levasseur; Bernasconi, Caniglia, Kurt, Malten, Milder, Müller, Neway, Rappold, Tietjens, Viardot-Garcia | *Iphigénie en Tauride* |
| **Irene** Soprano | Rienzi's sister | 1st Schröder-Devrient; Brandt, Lilli Lehmann, Moody, Osborn, Seidl-Krauss | *Rienzi* |
| **Iris** Soprano | | 1st Darclée; Bori, Eames, Pampanini, Rethberg, Sheridan | *Iris* |
| **Irma** Soprano | Louise's fellow worker | Cavan | *Louise* |
| **Iro** Tenor | Jester for the suitors | | *Il Ritorno d'Ulisse in Patria* |
| **Isabel Wentworth** Mezzo-soprano | | | *The Mother of Us All* |
| **Isabella** Soprano | Queen of Spain | | *Christophe Colomb* |
| **Isabella** Soprano | Princess of Sicily | Juch, Peschka-Leutner, Rogers, Viardot-Garcia | *Robert le Diable* |
| **Isabelle** Contralto | Lindoro's beloved | Simionato, Sontag | *L'Italiana in Algeri* |

| CHARACTER | | ROLE | SINGER | OPERA |
|---|---|---|---|---|
| **Isabelle** | Soprano | | Carvalho | *Le Pré aux Clercs* |
| **Isèpo** | Tenor | Public scribe | de Paolis | *La Gioconda* |
| **Ismaele** | Tenor | Nephew of the king of Jerusalem | | *Nabucco* |
| **Ismene** Mezzo-soprano | | Antigone's sister | | *Antigonae* (Orff) |
| **Isolde** | Soprano | Irish princess, engaged to King Marke | 1st Malvina Schnorr von Carolsfield; Albani, Cobelli, Fisher, Flagstad, Fremstad, Fuchs, Gadski, Grob-Prandl, Harshaw, Kappel, Kurt, Larsen-Todsen, Leffler-Burckhard, Lilli Lehman, Leider, Litvinne, Lubin, Malten, Marchesi, Milden-burg, Mödl, Moody, Morena, Nordica, Osborn, Seidl-Krauss, Sucher, Ternina, Thoma, Traubel, Varnay, Wittich | *Tristan und Isolde* |
| **Isotta** | Soprano | An actress | Moody | *Die Schweigsame Frau* |
| **Italian Singer (Soprano)** Soprano | | | | *Capriccio* |
| **Italian Singer (Tenor)** | Tenor | | | *Capriccio* |
| **Ivan Khovansky, Prince** | Bass | Leader of the Archers, enemy of the Tsar | | *Khovantschina* |
| **Ivan Susanin** | Bass | Peasant | 1st Petrov; Prohaska, Ros-waenge | *Ivan Susanin* |
| **Ivan Vassilievitch, Tsar** | Bass | Ivan the Terrible | Chaliapin | *Pskovityanka* |

| CHARACTER | ROLE | SINGER | OPERA |
|---|---|---|---|
| **Ivanov**<br>*See* Peter Ivanov | | | |
| **Jack**  Mezzo-soprano | Tallan's son, 15 | | *The Wreckers* |
| **Jacquino**  Tenor | Rocco's assistant | | *Fidelio* |
| **Jacopo Fiesco**  Bass | Patrician | | *Simon Boccanegra* |
| **Jaele**  Soprano | Hever's wife,<br>Sisera's lover | 1st Tess;  Spani | *Debora e Jaele* |
| **Jafia**  Tenor | | | *Debora e Jaele* |
| **Jago**  Bass | Silva's squire | | *Ernani* |
| **Jahel**  Baritone | | | *Le Roi d'Ys* |
| **Jailer**  Bass | | | *Die Kluge* |
| **Jailer**  Bass | | | *Tosca* |
| **Jailer**  From Chorus | | | *Il Trovatore* |
| **Jake**  Baritone | Fisherman | 1st Matthews | *Porgy and Bess* |
| **Jake Wallace**<br>Baritone | Minstrel | | *La Fanciulla del West* |
| **Jan Janitzky**  Tenor | Simon's fellow<br>prisoner | | *Der Bettelstudent* |
| **Jane, Aunt**<br>Contralto | Sister of the<br>constable | | *Hugh the Drover* |
| **Janissaries**  Chorus | | | *Die Entführung aus dem Serail* |
| **Jankel** | Mandryka's servant | | *Arabella* |
| **Jano**  Soprano | Shepherd boy | | *Jeji Pastorkyňa* (Jenufa) |
| **Japanese Envoy I**<br>Tenor | | | *Le Rossignol* |
| **Japanese Envoy II**<br>Baritone | | | *Le Rossignol* |
| **Japanese Envoy III**<br>Tenor | | | *Le Rossignol* |
| **Jaroslavna**  Soprano | Prince Igor's wife | Brouwenstijn | *Prince Igor* |
| **Javotte**  Soprano | An Actress | | *Manon* |
| **Jean**  Tenor or<br>Soprano | A tumbler | 1st Maréchal;<br>Garden | *Le Jongleur de Notre Dame* |

| CHARACTER | ROLE | SINGER | OPERA |
|---|---|---|---|
| **Jean, Friar** Bass | | | *Roméo et Juliette* |
| **Jemmy** Soprano | Tell's son | | *Guillaume Tell* |
| **Jemmy Twitcher** From Chorus | Gentleman of the road | | *The Beggar's Opera* |
| **Jenik** Tenor | Micha's son by his first wife | Davies, Kullmann, Pears | *Prodana Nevešta* |
| **Jenny** Soprano | Dickson's wife | | *La Dame Blanche* |
| **Jenny Diver** From Chorus | A lady of the town | | *The Beggar's Opera* |
| **Jenny Reefer** Soprano | | | *The Mother of Us All* |
| **Jenufa** Soprano | Kostelnika's foster daughter | 1st Kabelacova; Brouwenstijn, Caleva, Goltz, Jeritza, Lemnitz, Müller, Welitsch | *Její Pastorkyňa* (Jenufa) |
| **Jessel, Miss** Mezzo-soprano | | | *The Turn of the Screw* |
| **Jesser** Baritone | | | *Debora e Jaele* |
| **Jester** Bass | | | *Francesca da Rimini* |
| **Jester** Dancer | | | *Pilgrim's Progress* |
| **Jesuit** See Lowitski See also Rangoni See also Tschernjakovsky | | | |
| **Jesuits** Silent | | | *Palestrina* |
| **Jewish Doctor** See Médicin juif, Un | | | |
| **Jews (Five)** Four Tenors, Bass | | | *Salome* |
| **Jews** Chorus | | | *Debora e Jaele, The Fair at Sorochintsky, La Juive* |
| **Jews** See also Disguised Jews | | | |

| CHARACTER | | ROLE | SINGER | OPERA |
|---|---|---|---|---|
| **Jim** | Baritone | Cotton picker | | *Porgy and Bess* |
| **Jitka** | Soprano | | | *Dalibor* |
| **Jo the Loiterer** Tenor | | | | *The Mother of Us All* |
| **Jocasta** Mezzo-soprano | | Wife of Oedipus, widow of Laius | Bouvier, Danco, Mödl, Zareska | *Oedipus Rex* |
| **Joe** | Tenor | A miner | | *La Fanciulla del West* |
| **Johann** | Bass | Le Bailli's friend | | *Werther* |
| **Johannes Kepler** Baritone | | Astronomer, also The Earth | | *Die Harmonie der Welt* |
| **John** | Baritone | | | *Das Heimchen am Herd* |
| **John** | Silent | Peter's apprentice | | *Peter Grimes* |
| **John Adams** Tenor | | | | *The Mother of Us All* |
| **John Bunyan** Bass Baritone | | Poet | | *Pilgrim's Progress* |
| **John Crome** Treble | | Age 15. *Also called* Peter *in Acts I and II* | | *Let's Make an Opera* |
| **John of Aragon** *See* Ernani | | | | |
| **John of Leyden** Tenor | | The Prophet | 1st Roger; Alvarez, Caruso, Martinelli, Niemann, Jean de Reszke | *Le Prophète* |
| **John Sorel** Baritone | | Member of the underground | | *The Consul* |
| **John the Baptist** *See* Jokanaan | | | | |
| **John the Butcher** Bass Baritone | | Mary's fiancé | | *Hugh the Drover* |
| **Johnson, Dick** Tenor | | Ramerrez, the bandit | 1st Caruso; Lauri-Volpi, Martinelli, Merli, del Monaco | *La Fanciulla del Wes* |
| **Jokanaan** Baritone | | John the Baptist, captive | 1st Perron; Berger, Berglund, Cassell, Dalmorès, Hotter, Prohaska, van Rooy, Schöffler, Schorr, Whitehill | *Salome* |

| CHARACTER | ROLE | SINGER | OPERA |
|---|---|---|---|
| **Jokers** Chorus | | | *The Love for Three Oranges* |
| **Jonas** Tenor | Anabaptist | | *Le Prophète* |
| **José Castro** Bass | Bandit | | *La Fanciulla del West* |
| **José de Santarem, Don** Baritone | Courtier | | *Maritana* |
| **José, Don** Tenor | Corporal in the guard | 1st Lherie; Alvarez, Max Alvary, Ansseau, Baum, Campanini, Caruso, Clément, Dalmorès, Ferrari-Fontana, Giraldoni, Hamlin, Lestellier, Maison, Martinelli, del Monaco, Muratore, Poleri, Jean de Reszke, Saléza, Sullivan, Thill, Tucker, Vinay | *Carmen* |
| **Josef K** Tenor | The defendant | | *Der Prozess* |
| **Monsieur Jourdain** | Owner of the house | | *Ariadne auf Naxos* |
| **Journeymen** Chorus | | | *Die Meistersinger* |
| **Jouvenot, Mlle.** Soprano | of the Comédie Française | | *Adriana Lecouvreur* |
| **Jove** *See* Giove | | | |
| **Juan** Tenor | Admirer of Dulcinée | | *Don Quichotte* |
| **Juan Lopez** Bass | The Mayor | | *Der Corregidor* |
| **Judas Iscariot** Baritone | | | *Pilgrim's Progress* |
| **Judge** From Chorus | | | *Un Ballo in Maschera* |
| **Judge** Tenor | | | *Švanda Dudak* |
| **Judge** | | | *Tosca* |
| **Judge, Examiner** Baritone | | | *Der Prozess* |

| CHARACTER | ROLE | SINGER | OPERA |
|---|---|---|---|
| **Judges** Chorus | | | *Pskovityanka* |
| **Judith** Mezzo-soprano | Bluebeard's last wife | | *Duke Bluebeard's Castle* |
| **Juggler** Silent | | | *Hugh the Drover* |
| **Juggler** *See* Jean | | | |
| **Julie** Mezzo-soprano | Danton's wife | 1st G. Thury | *Dantons Tod* |
| **Julie** Soprano | | Falcon | *La Vestale* |
| **Julien** Tenor | Artist in love with Louise | 1st Maréchal; Ansseau, Dalmorès, Maison, Pertile, Slezak, Trantoul, Ziliani | *Louise* |
| **Juliet** *See* Juliette *See also* Giulietta | | | |
| **Juliet** Soprano | Age 14. *Called* Anne Dougall *in Acts I and II* | | *Let's Make an Opera* |
| **Juliette** Soprano | Capulet's daughter | 1st Carvalho; Ackté, Adams, Alda, Bori, Eames, Farrar, Galli-Curci, Hauk, Lipovska, Lussan, Malibran, Mason, Melba, Munsel, Patti, Perli, Saville, Sayao, Schröder-Devrient | *Roméo et Juliette* |
| **Junius** Baritone | Roman General | | *The Rape of Lucretia* |
| **Junkman** Bass | | | *Louise* |
| **Junon** Mezzo-soprano | Juno, wife of Jupiter | | *Orphée aux Enfers* |
| **Jupiter** Baritone | Chief of the gods | 1st Hotter; Poell, Schöffler | *Die Liebe der Danae* |
| **Jupiter** Baritone | King of gods | | *Orphée aux Enfers* |
| **Jupiter** Tenor | Also Wallenstein | | *Die Harmonie der Welt* |

| CHARACTER | ROLE | SINGER | OPERA |
|---|---|---|---|
| **Jupiter**<br>*See also* Giove | | | |
| **Jurist** Bass | | | *Doktor Faustus* |
| **Justizrat** Baritone | Storch's friend | | *Intermezzo* |
| **Kabanicha**<br>*See* Marfa<br>Kabanova | | | |
| **Kaiser Franz of**<br>**Austria** Speaker | | | *Háry János* |
| **Kaiser**<br>*See* Rudolf Kaiser<br>*See also* Ferdinand<br>Kaiser | | | |
| **Kalman Zsupan**<br>Baritone | Pig farmer | | *Zigeunerbaron* |
| **Kammersänger**<br>Bass | Storch's friend | | *Intermezzo* |
| **Karnac** Baritone | Enemy general | Renaud | *Le Roi d'Ys* |
| **Karolka**<br>Mezzo-soprano | The mayor's<br>daughter | | *Její Pastorkyňa*<br>(Jenufa) |
| **Kate Pinkerton**<br>Mezzo-soprano | Pinkerton's<br>American wife | | *Madama Butterfly* |
| **Katharina**<br>Contralto | Kepler's mother,<br>also the Moon | | *Die Harmonie der*<br>*Welt* |
| **Katherine**<br>Contralto | | 1st Gerville-Réache | *Le Juif Polonais* |
| **Kathinka** Soprano | Marenka's mother | | *Prodana Nevešta* |
| **Katya (Katerina)**<br>**Kabanova**<br>Soprano | Tichon's wife | 1st Vesela; Pauly,<br>Shuard | *Katya Kabanova* |
| **Kecal** Bass | Marriage broker | | *Prodana Nevešta* |
| **Keeper of the Mad-**<br>**house** Bass | | 1st Emanuel Menkes | *The Rake's Progress* |
| **Kepler, Johannes**<br>*See* Johannes Kepler | | | |
| **Khivria**<br>Mezzo-soprano | Tcherevik's wife | | *The Fair at*<br>*Sorochintsky* |

| CHARACTER | ROLE | SINGER | OPERA |
|---|---|---|---|
| **Khrushchev**   Tenor | Boyard | | *Boris Godunov* |
| **Kilian**   Tenor | Rich peasant | | *Der Freischütz* |
| **King**   Bass Baritone | | | *Fête Galante* |
| **King**   Baritone | | | *Die Kluge* |
| **King**   Bass | | | *Maritana* |
| **King**<br>See also Roi | | | |
| **King Marke**   Bass | King of Cornwall, | 1st Zottmayer;<br>Bohnen, Fischer,<br>Griswold, Gura,<br>Hotter, Kipnis,<br>Mayr, Pinza,<br>Edouard de Reszke,<br>Staudigl I,<br>Staudigl II, Weber | *Tristan und Isolde* |
| **King of Clubs**   Bass | Ruler of the<br>Kingdom | | *The Love for Three Oranges* |
| **King of Egypt**<br>   Bass | | Scolara, Plançon,<br>Edouard de Reszke | *Aida* |
| **King of Fools**<br>   Tenor | | | *Louise* |
| **King of Spain**   Bass | | | *Christophe Colomb* |
| **King of the Ocean**<br>   Bass | | | *Sadko* |
| **King Solomon**<br>   Baritone | | | *Die Königin von Saba* |
| **Kings (Four)**<br>   Tenors, Basses | Nephews of Pollux | | *Die Liebe der Danae* |
| **King's Herald, The**<br>   Bass | | Huehn, Ruffo,<br>Scheidermantel,<br>Schmedes | *Lohengrin* |
| **Klingsor**   Bass | A magician | 1st Hill and Fuchs;<br>Goritz, Scheider-<br>mantel | *Parsifal* |
| **Kluge, Die**<br>See Farmer's<br>daughter | | | |

# THE CHARACTERS IN THE OPERAS

| CHARACTER | ROLE | SINGER | OPERA |
|---|---|---|---|
| **Klymene**<br>*See* Alto, the | | | |
| **Klytemnestra**<br>Mezzo-soprano | Agamemnon's widow | 1st Schumann-Heink; Klose, Mildenburg, Mödl, Thorborg | *Elektra* |
| **Klytemnestra**<br>Soprano | Agamemnon's wife | Ober | *Iphigénie en Aulide* |
| **Knight, First**<br>Tenor | | | *Parsifal* |
| **Knight, Second**<br>Bass | | | *Parsifal* |
| **Knights**     Chorus | | | *Guillaume Tell, Tannhäuser, Tristan und Isolde* |
| **Knights (Four)** | | | *L'Assassinio nel Cattedrale* |
| **Knights of the Grail**     Chorus | | | *Parsifal* |
| **Kofner**<br>Bass Baritone | | | *The Consul* |
| **Kontchak**     Bass | Polovtsian (Tartar) Khan | | *Prince Igor* |
| **Kontchakovna**<br>Mezzo-soprano | Kontchak's daughter | | *Prince Igor* |
| **Kostelnika, Buryjovka**<br>Soprano | Widow, Jenufa's foster mother | Braun, Fisher, Fuchs, Matzenauer, Pederzini | *Její Pastorkyňa* (Jenufa) |
| **Kothner**<br>*See* Fritz Kothner | | | |
| **Koupava**<br>Soprano | In love with Misgir | | *Snyegurotchka* |
| **Kouzka**     Baritone | Archer | | *Khovantschina* |
| **Kreon**     Baritone | King, Antigonae's uncle | | *Antigonae* (Orff) |
| **Kronthal, Baron**<br>Tenor | Brother of the Countess of Eberbach | | *Der Wildschütz* |
| **Kruschina**     Baritone | Peasant, Marenka's father | | *Prodana Nevešta* |

| CHARACTER | | ROLE | SINGER | OPERA |
|---|---|---|---|---|
| **Kuligen** | Baritone | Vanja's friend | | *Katya Kabanova* |
| **Kundry** | Soprano | A bewitched, cursed woman | 1st Brandt; Brema, Flagstad, Fuchs, Gulbranson, Harshaw, Kemp, Kirkby-Lunn, Kurt, Leider, Lubin, Malten, Marchesi, Materna, Matzenauer, Mildenburg, Mödl, Moody, Saltzmann-Stevens, Sucher, Ternina, Thorborg, Varnay, Walker, Wickham, Wittich | *Parsifal* |
| **Kunz Vogelgesang** | Tenor | Mastersinger and furrier | | *Die Meistersinger* |
| **Kurvenal** | Baritone | Tristan's retainer | 1st Mitterwurzer; Bispham, Hotter, Edouard de Reszke, van Rooy, Scheidermantel, Weil | *Tristan und Isolde* |
| **Kyoto** | Baritone | Japanese pimp | | *Iris* |
| **Laborers** | Chorus | | | *Les Troyens* |
| **Laca Klemen** | Tenor | Stepbrother of Stewa, in love with Jenufa | | *Její Pastorkyňa (Jenufa)* |
| **Lackey** | Bass | | | *Ariadne auf Naxos* |
| **Ladies** | Chorus | | | *L'Africaine, Ernani, La Favorita, Guillaume Tell, Luisa Miller, Manon, Martha, Roméo et Juliette, Tannhäuser, Tosca* |
| **Ladies (Three)** | Sopranos, Mezzo-soprano | Attendants to the Queen of the Night | | *Die Zauberflöte* |

| CHARACTER | ROLE | SINGER | OPERA |
|---|---|---|---|
| **Ladies and Gentlemen** Chorus | | | *Adriana Lecouvreur, Andrea Chénier, La Gioconda, Otello, La Rondine, La Traviata* |
| **Ladies in Waiting** Chorus | | | *Lucrezia Borgia* |
| **Ladies of Honor** Chorus | | | *Lohengrin* |
| **Lady** Soprano | | | *Dantons Tod* |
| **Lady Essex** *See* Frances, Countess | | | |
| **Lady in Waiting** Soprano | | | *Gloriana* |
| **Lady in Waiting** Soprano | to Lady Macbeth | | *Macbeth* (Verdi) |
| **Lady Macbeth** Soprano | | Pederzini | *Macbeth* (Bloch) |
| **Lady Macbeth** Soprano | | Borkh, Callas, Dow, Grandi, Mödl, Onegin, Rysanek, Viardot-Garcia, Varnay | *Macbeth* (Verdi) |
| **Laertes** Tenor | Actor | Gassier | *Mignon* |
| **Laetitia** Soprano | | Hurley | *The Old Maid and the Thief* |
| **Laïs** Pantomime | | | *Faust* |
| **Lakmé** Soprano | Nilakantha's daughter | 1st Van Zandt; Barrientos, Galli-Curci, Lipovska, Munsel, Patti, Pons, Luisa Tetrazzini, Tréville | *Lakmé* |
| **Lamoral, Graf** Bass | Arabella's suitor | | *Arabella* |
| **Lamplighter** Tenor | | | *Manon Lescaut* |
| **Landgrave** *See* Hermann | | | |
| **Larina** Mezzo-soprano | Tatyana's mother | | *Eugene Onegin* |

| CHARACTER | ROLE | SINGER | OPERA |
|---|---|---|---|
| **Larkens** Bass | A miner | | *La Fanciulla del West* |
| **Lartigen** Bass | Monologuist | | *Zaza* |
| **Laundry Girls** Chorus | | | *Iris* |
| **Laura** Mezzo-soprano | Alvise's wife, in love with Enzo | 1st Biancolini-Rodriguez; Barbieri, Castagna, Fursch-Madi, Homer, Kirkby-Lunn, Minghini-Cattaneo, Ober, Stignani, Thebom, Wickham | *La Gioconda* |
| **Laura** Contralto | Peasant girl | | *Luisa Miller* |
| **Laura** Soprano | | 1st Ivogün | *Das Ring des Polycrates* |
| **Laura, Countess** Soprano | Palmatica's daughter | | *Der Bettelstudent* |
| **Laurence, Friar** Bass | | Marcoux, Plançon, Edouard de Reszke, Whitehill | *Roméo and Juliette* |
| **Lauretta** Soprano | Gianni's daughter, 21 | 1st Easton; Albanese, Naylor, dalla Rizza, Schwarzkopf | *Gianni Schicchi* |
| **Laurie** Soprano | | 1st Carlos | *The Tender Land* |
| **Lawrence** Baritone | Lighthousekeeper | | *The Wreckers* |
| **Lawyer** | | | *Die Harmonie der Welt* |
| **Lawyer** Baritone | | | *Der Prozess* |
| **Lawyer** *See also* Frazier | | | |
| **Lazarillo** Mezzo-soprano | A poor boy | | *Maritana* |
| **Leaders of the People** Soprano, Mezzo-soprano, and Baritone | | | *Alceste* |

| CHARACTER | | ROLE | SINGER | OPERA |
|---|---|---|---|---|
| **Leandro** | Tenor | Columbine's lover | | *Arlecchino* |
| **Leandro** | Barítone | Prime minister, King of Spades | | *The Love for Three Oranges* |
| **Lechery, Lord** | Tenor | | | *Pilgrim's Progress* |
| **Leda** | Contralto | A queen, formerly loved by Jupiter | | *Die Liebe der Danae* |
| **Lefort, Admiral** | Bass | Russian ambassador | | *Zar und Zimmerman* |
| **Lehl** | Contralto | Shepherd | | *Snyegurotchka* |
| **Leïla** | Soprano | Priestess of Brahma | 1st de Maesen; Berger, Calvé, Carosio, Fohström, Galli-Curci, Hempel, Pareto, Luisa Tetrazzini | *Les Pêcheurs de Perles* |
| **Leni** | Soprano | | 1st della Casa; Curtin | *Der Prozess* |
| **Lensky** | Tenor | Olga's fiancé | Figner, Jones, Martinelli, Tucker | *Eugene Onegin* |
| **Leonato** | Bass | Governor of Messina | | *Béatrice et Bénédict* |
| **Leonora** | Soprano | | 1st Falcon | *Alessandro Stradella* (Niedemayer) |
| **Leonora** | Soprano | Florestan's wife. When disguised as a man she is called Fidelio | 1st Milder; Borkh, Brandt, Brouwen-stijn, Caron, Cruvelli, Fisher, Flagstad, de Gunst, Fornia-Labey, Goltz, Krauss, Larsen-Todsen, Leffller-Burckhard, Lilli Lehman, Lotte Lehmann, Malibran, Malten, Matzenauer, Mödl, Pauly, Resnik, Roze, Schröder-Devrient, Seidl-Krauss, Ternina, Tietjens, Valleria, Varnay, Wagner, Wildbrunn | *Fidelio* |

| CHARACTER | | ROLE | SINGER | OPERA |
|---|---|---|---|---|
| **Leonora** | Soprano | A duchess, beloved of Manrico | 1st Penio; Bampton, Brouwenstijn, Callas, Goldini, Krauss, Litvinne, Milanov, Price, Tebaldi, Tietjens, Ugalde, Varnay, Welitsch | *Il Trovatore* |
| **Leonora di Gusman** | | The King's mistress | 1st Stoltz; Borghi-Mamo, Cary, Homer, Lucca, Mantelli, Viardot-Garcia, Wagner, Walker | *La Favorita* |
| **Leonora di Vargas, Donna** | Soprano | | Callas, Cigna, Milanov, Muzio, Ponselle, Stignani, Teresa Stoltz, Tebaldi, Tietjens | *La Forza del Destino* |
| **Léopold** | Tenor | Prince. Working for Eléazar as an apprentice under the name of Samuel | Koegel | *La Juive* |
| **Leporello** | Bass | Don Giovanni's servant | 1st Felice Ponziani; Baccaloni, Benucci, Chaliapin, Corena, Formes, Manuel García, I, Kunz, Lablache, Mirabella, Edouard de Reszke, Tajo | *Don Giovanni* |
| **Lerma, Count** | Tenor | | Franke | *Don Carlos* |
| **Lescaut** | Baritone | Manon's cousin | del Puente | *Manon* |
| **Lescaut** | Baritone | Manon's brother | Guarrera, Scotti, Stabile | *Manon Lescaut* |
| **Leukippos** | Tenor | Shepherd in love with Daphne | | *Daphne* |
| **Leuthold** | Bass | Swiss patriot, shepherd | | *Guillaume Tell* |

| CHARACTER | | ROLE | SINGER | OPERA |
|---|---|---|---|---|
| **Levis** | Bass | Spirit voice | | *Doktor Faustus* |
| **Libellule, La** Mezzo-soprano | | Dragonfly | | *L'Enfant et les Sortilèges* |
| **Lieutenant** | Tenor | | | *Doktor Faustus* |
| **Lillas Pastia** From Chorus | | Innkeeper | | *Carmen* |
| **Lillian Russell** Soprano | | | | *The Mother of Us All* |
| **Lily** Mezzo-soprano | | Strawberry woman, Peter's wife | | *Porgy and Bess* |
| **Linda** | Soprano | Beloved of Charles | Barili, Barrientos, Kellogg, Murska, Pons, Valleria | *Linda di Chamounix* |
| **Lindorf** | Bass | Councillor of Nuremburg | London | *Les Contes d'Hoffmann* |
| **Lindoro** | Tenor | Italian lover of Isabella | Valletti | *L'Italiana in Algeri* |
| **Linette** | Contralto | Princess hidden in an orange | | *The Love for Three Oranges* |
| **Lion Tamer** Soprano | | | Lewis | *He Who Gets Slapped* |
| **Lionel** | Tenor | Plunkett's foster brother | Caruso, Gigli, Mario, Pertile, Stagno, Tucker | *Martha* |
| **Lisa** | Soprano | In love with Hermann | Corsi, Destinn, Jurinac, Hilde Konetzni, Welitsch | *Pique-Dame* |
| **Lisa** | Soprano | Innkeeper, rival for Elvino's love | | *La Sonnambula* |
| **Lisette** | Soprano | Magda's maid, in love with Prunier | 1st Ferraris; Fleisher | *La Rondine* |
| **Little Bat McLean** Tenor | | | | *Susannah* |
| **Little Devils** Chorus | | | | *The Love for Three Oranges* |
| **Little Franz** | | Storch's 8 year old son | | *Intermezzo* |

403

| CHARACTER | | ROLE | SINGER | OPERA |
|---|---|---|---|---|
| **Little Suzanne** Soprano | | Kepler's daughter by his first wife | | *Die Harmonie der Welt* |
| **Liù** | Soprano | Faithful slave girl of Timur | 1st Zamboni; Albanese, Favero, Norena, Pampanini, Price, Schwarzkopf, Tebaldi | *Turandot* |
| **Livoretto** | Tenor | Nobleman of the Venetian Republic | | *Lucrezia Borgia* |
| **Lob** | | Evil assistant of Dipsacus | | *The Poisoned Kiss* |
| **Lockit** | Baritone | Jailer, Lucy's father | | *The Beggar's Opera* |
| **Lodovico** | Bass | Venetian ambassador | | *Otello* |
| **Loge** | Tenor | Norse god | 1st Vogl; Garris | *Das Ring des Nibelungen* |
| **Lohengrin** | Tenor | Knight of the Grail, son of Parsifal | 1st Beck, Althouse, Max Alvary, Berger, Campanini, Caruso, Dalmorès, van Dyke, Gigli, Hensel, Hopf, Maas, Nachbauer, Nicolini, Niemann, Jean de Reszke, Ludwig Schnorr von Carolsfield, Slezak, Sullivan, Urlus, Völker, Winkelmann | *Lohengrin* |
| **Lola** Mezzo-soprano | | Alfio's wife, having an affair with Turiddu | Bible, Brema, Evans, Homer | *Cavalleria Rusticana* |
| **Lorance** | Soprano | | 1st Caron | *Jocelyn* |
| **Lords (Four)** Tenor, Baritone and Bass | | | | *The Warrior* |
| **Lorek** | Baritone | A surgeon | | *Fedora* |
| **Lorenz von Pommersfelden** Bass | | Dean of Mainz | | *Mathis der Maler* |

| CHARACTER | | ROLE | SINGER | OPERA |
|---|---|---|---|---|
| **Lorenzo** | Tenor | Officer of the carabiniers | Matters | *Fra Diavolo* |
| **Lorenzo** | Tenor | Alfonso's confidant | | *Masaniello* |
| **Loris Ipanov, Count** | Tenor | Accused of murder | 1st Caruso; Gigli, Martinelli, Pertile, Zenatello | *Fedora* |
| **Lotario** | Bass | Deranged minstrel, old man | Faure, Taskin | *Mignon* |
| **Louis the Sixth** | Bass | | Fischer | *Euryanthe* |
| **Louise** | Soprano | In love with Julien | 1st Martha Rioton; Alda, Bori, Destinn, Edvina, Farrar, Favero, Garden, Gutheil-Schoder, Kirsten, dalla Rizza | *Louise* |
| **Lover** | Tenor | | | *Fête Galante* |
| **Lowbrows** | Chorus | | | *The Love for Three Oranges* |
| **Lowitsky** | Bass | Jesuit | | *Boris Godunov* |
| **Lubava** | Mezzo-soprano | Sadko's wife | | *Sadko* |
| **Lucia** | Soprano | Lucy of Lammermoor | 1st Tacchinardi-Persiani; Albani, Barrientos, Callas, Carvalho, Charton-Demeur, Galli-Curci, Gerster, Hauk, Hempel, Kellogg, Krauss, Liebling, Lind, Lucca, Melba, Moffo, Munsel, Murska, Nevada, Christine Nilsson, Nordica, Pacini, Pareto, Patti, Pons, Sembrich, Luisa Tetrazzini, Vere, Viardot-Garcia, Zerr | *Lucia di Lammermoor* |

| CHARACTER | | ROLE | SINGER | OPERA |
|---|---|---|---|---|
| Lucia | Soprano | Lucretia's attendant | Gueden | The Rape of Lucretia |
| Lucia *See also* Mamma Lucia | | | | |
| Lucieta | Soprano | Lunardo's daughter by his first wife | | I Quattro Rusteghi |
| Lucile | Soprano | Desmoulins' wife | 1st Cebotari | Dantons Tod |
| Lucinda | | | | English version for the name Lucieta in I Quattro Rusteghi |
| Lucretia | Contralto | Palestrina's dead wife | | Palestrina |
| Lucretia | Contralto | Wife of Collatinus | 1st Ferrier | The Rape of Lucretia |
| Lucrezia Borgia | Soprano | | Fursch-Madi, Grisi, Krauss, Sontag, Tietjens, Wagner | Lucrezia Borgia |
| Lucy *See* Lucia | | | | |
| Lucy Lockit | Soprano | The Jailer's daughter | | The Beggar's Opera |
| Ludmilla | Soprano | In love with Russlan | | Russlan and Ludmilla |
| Luigi | Tenor | Stevedore, 20 | 1st Montesanti; Jagel, Johnson, Merli, del Monaco | Il Tabarro |
| Luisa | Soprano | Rodolfo's beloved | 1st Gavazzaniga; Ponselle | Luisa Miller |
| Lukas | Tenor | Young widower in love with Vendulka | | Hubička |
| Lulu | Soprano | | 1st Hadzic; Styx, Spletter | Lulu |
| Lummer, Baron | Tenor | | | Intermezzo |
| Luna, Count | Baritone | Envoy from Spain | | Palestrina |
| Luna *See also* Conte di Luna | | | | |

| CHARACTER | | ROLE | SINGER | OPERA |
|---|---|---|---|---|
| **Lunardo** | Bass | Merchant, Lucieta's father | | *I Quattro Rusteghi* |
| **Luther** | Bass | Innkeeper | | *Les Contes d'Hoffmann* |
| **Lysiart** | Baritone | | Gura | *Euryanthe* |
| **Macbeth** | Baritone | A general, ambitious for the Scottish throne | 1st Vanesi; Chapman, Rothmuller, Taddei, Warren | *Macbeth* |
| **Macduff** | Tenor | Scots nobleman, Macbeth's enemy | Bergonzi | *Macbeth* |
| **Macheath, Captain** | Tenor | A notorious highwayman | 1st John Beard; Incledon, Pears, Reeves, Ranalow | *The Beggar's Opera* |
| **MacIrton** | Bass | Justice of the Peace | | *La Dame Blanche* |
| **Madame de Croissy** | Mezzo-soprano | | Claramae Turner | *Les Dialogues des Carmélites* |
| **Maddalena** | Soprano | Linda's mother | | *Linda di Chamounix* |
| **Maddalena** | Contralto | Sparafucile's sister | Gay, Glaz, Lipton, Madeira | *Rigoletto* |
| **Maddalena** *See also* Madeleine *See also* Magdalena | | | | |
| **Madeleine** | Contralto | | | *Louise* |
| **Madeleine** | Soprano | Chappelou's wife | 1st Roy; de Garmo, Charton-Demeur | *Le Postillion de Longjumeau* |
| **Madeleine de Coigny** | Soprano | In love with Andrea Chénier | 1st Carrera; Caniglia, Milanov, Muzio, Sheridan, Strakosch, Tebaldi | *Andrea Chénier* |
| **Madelon** | Mezzo-soprano | Old woman | | *Andrea Chénier* |
| **Madmen** | Chorus | | | *The Rake's Progress* |
| **Maffio Orsini** | Contralto | Lucrezia's enemy | Alboni, Trebelli | *Lucrezia Borgia* |
| **Magda** | Soprano | Rambaldo's mistress | 1st dalla Rizza; Bori, Favero | *La Rondine* |

| CHARACTER | ROLE | SINGER | OPERA |
|---|---|---|---|
| **Magda Sorel**<br>Soprano | John's wife | 1st Neway; Borkh,<br>Mödl, Petrella,<br>Shuard, Zadek | *The Consul* |
| **Magdalena**<br>Mezzo-soprano | Eva's nurse | 1st Sophie Dietz;<br>Glaz, Homer,<br>Resnik, Wickham | *Die Meistersinger* |
| **Magi**　　Chorus | | | *Semiramide* |
| **Magician**　　Bass | | | *Švanda Dudak* |
| **Magician**<br>*See* Nika<br>Magadoff | | | |
| **Magistrate** | | | *Die Harmonie der<br>Welt* |
| **Magistrate**<br>*See also* Eugenio de<br>Zuniga, Don | | | |
| **Magnates**　　Chorus | | | *Boris Godunov* |
| **Magnifico, Don**<br>Bass | Baron of<br>Montflagon | | *La Cenerentola* |
| **Mago**<br>*See* Simon Mago | | | |
| **Mahomet**<br>Pantomime | Negro page | | *Der Rosenkavalier* |
| **Maid**<br>Mezzo-soprano | | | *Její Pastorkyňa<br>(Jenufa)* |
| **Maid of Honor**<br>Mezzo-soprano | to the princess | | *Masaniello* |
| **Maid Servants<br>(Three)**<br>Sopranos,<br>Mezzo-soprano | | | *Martha* |
| **Maid Servants**<br>Contralto,<br>2 Mezzo-sopranos,<br>2 Sopranos | | | *Elektra* |
| **Maiden**　　Soprano | A Polovtsian<br>(Tartar) | | *Prince Igor* |
| **Maiden**<br>*See* Farmer's<br>daughter | | | |

| CHARACTER | | ROLE | SINGER | OPERA |
|---|---|---|---|---|
| **Maidens** | Chorus | | | *Der Fliegende Holländer, Der Prozess* |
| **Maids** | Chorus | | | *Pskovityanka, Wozzeck* |
| **Maids (Two)** Sopranos | | | | *Daphne* |
| **Maids in Waiting** Chorus | | | | *Khovantschina* |
| **Maintop** | Tenor | | | *Billy Budd* |
| **Maive** | Contralto | Etain's mother | | *The Immortal Hour* |
| **Majas and Majos** | Chorus | Ladies and gentlemen | | *Goyescas* |
| **Major-Domo** Tenor | | | | *Adriana Lecouvreur* |
| **Major-Domo** Baritone | | | | *Andrea Chénier* |
| **Major-Domo** Speaker | | | Louw | *Ariadne auf Naxos* |
| **Major-Domo** | Bass | | | *Capriccio* |
| **Major-Domo** Tenor | | | | *Christophe Colomb* |
| **Major-Domo** Tenor | | to von Faninal | Franke | *Der Rosenkavalier* |
| **Major-Domo** Tenor | | to the Marschallin | | *Der Rosenkavalier* |
| **Major-Domo** Baritone | | | 1st Cehanovsky | *Vanessa* |
| **Malatesta, Doctor** Baritone | | Don Pasquale's friend | 1st Tamburini; de Luca, Gassier | *Don Pasquale* |
| **Malatestino dall' Occhio** | Tenor | One-eyed son of Malatesta | | *Francesca da Rimini* |
| **Malcolm** | Tenor | Duncan's son | | *Macbeth* |
| **Malice** | Soprano | | | *Pilgrim's Progress* |
| **Maliella** | Soprano | Carmela's adopted daughter | Edvina, Giannini, Jeritza, White | *I Gioielli della Madonna* |
| **Mallika** Mezzo-soprano | | Lakmé's slave | | *Lakmé* |

# THE CHARACTERS IN THE OPERAS

| CHARACTER | ROLE | SINGER | OPERA |
|---|---|---|---|
| **Mama** | | | *The Ballad of Baby Doe* |
| **Mama Lucia** Contralto | Turiddu's mother | Votipka | *Cavalleria Rusticana* |
| **Mamalik (Two)** Bass | | | *Marouf* |
| **Man** Speaker | | | *Der Prozess* |
| **Man Servants (Three)** Tenor, Basses | | | *Martha* |
| **Man with the Donkey** Tenor | | | *Die Kluge* |
| **Man with the Mule** Baritone | | | *Die Kluge* |
| **Mancini, Count** Tenor | | Norman Kelley | *He Who Gets Slapped* |
| **Mandarin** Baritone | | | *Turandot* |
| **Mandryka** Baritone | Arabella's suitor | London | *Arabella* |
| **Manfredo** Baritone | Archibaldo's son | 1st Galeffi; Amato, Bonelli, Cigada, Danise, Guarrera, Inghilleri, Morelli, Tagliabue, Weede | *L'Amore dei Tre Re* |
| **Manfredo** Tenor | A Sicilian | | *I Vespri Siciliani* |
| **Manon** Soprano | | 1st Marie Heilbronn; Alda, de los Angeles, Bori, Edvina, Farrar, Favero, Garden, Hauk, Jurinac, McWatters, Moore, Muzio, Roze, Schwarzkopf, Sanderson, Vix, van Zandt | *Manon* |
| **Manon Lescaut** Soprano | | 1st Cesira-Ferrani; Alda, Barbato, Bori, Caniglia, Cavalieri, Favero, Kirsten, Lipovska, Oltrabella, Pampanini, Sheridan, Tebaldi, Welitsch | *Manon Lescaut* |

| CHARACTER | | ROLE | SINGER | OPERA |
|---|---|---|---|---|
| **Manrico** | Tenor | Troubadour, Leonora's lover. The supposed son of Azucena | 1st Boucardé; Bjoerling, Campanini, Caruso, Martin, Martinelli, del Monaco, Slezak, Stagno, di Stefano, Zenatello | *Il Trovatore* |
| **Manuel** | Baritone | Carmela's brother | | *La Vida Breve* |
| **Manuela** Mezzo-soprano | | A maid | | *Der Corregidor* |
| **Manufacturer** Baritone | | | | *Der Prozess* |
| **Manus** | Bass | Etain's father | | *The Immortal Hour* |
| **Manz** | Baritone | Rich farmer, Sali's father | | *A Village Romeo and Juliet* |
| **Maometto** | Bass | | 1st Galli | *Maometto* (Rossini) |
| **Mara** Mezzo-soprano | | | | *Debora e Jaele* |
| **Marcel** | Bass | Huguenot soldier | Foli, Formes, Edouard de Reszke, Scaria, Scotti | *Les Huguenots* |
| **Marcellina** | Soprano | Rocco's daughter | 1st Müller; della Casa, Schumann, Schwarzkopf, Seefried | *Fidelio* |
| **Marcellina** | Soprano | Dr. Bartolo's housekeeper | 1st Mandini; Rossel-Majdan | *Le Nozze di Figaro* |
| **Marcellina** *See also* Berta | | | | |
| **Marcelline** Mezzo-soprano | | | | *L'Attaque du Moulin* |
| **Marcello** | Baritone | Young starving painter | Franci, Guarrera, Panerai, Pinza, Tagliabue | *La Bohème* |
| **Marchand de Masques, La** Soprano | | Mask seller | | *Esther de Carpentras* |
| **Marchese di Calatrava** | Bass | Leonora's father | | *La Forza del Destino* |

| CHARACTER | ROLE | SINGER | OPERA |
|---|---|---|---|
| **Marchese d'Obigny** Baritone | | Renan | *La Traviata* |
| **Marchioness of Montefiore** Mezzo-soprano | | | *Maritana* |
| **Marco** Bass | Rosa's brother | | *L'Arlesiana* |
| **Marco** Baritone | Simone's son, 45 | | *Gianni Schicchi* |
| **Marco** Tenor | Dufresne's butler | | *Zaza* |
| **Marenka** Soprano | In love with Jenik | Cross, Destinn, Jurinac, Hilde Konetzni, Müller, Novotna, Oltrabella, Rethberg, Seefried | *Prodana Nevešta* |
| **Marfa Kabanova** Contralto | Widow (Kabanicha), Katya's mother in law | | *Katya Kabanova* |
| **Margared** Soprano | The king's daughter | 1st Deschamps; Ponselle | *Le Roi d'Ys* |
| **Margarethe** Soprano | | Brandt | *Genoveva* |
| **Margarita** Mezzo-soprano | Lunardo's second wife | | *I Quattro Rusteghi* |
| **Margery** | | | English version for the name Margarita *in* *I Quattro Rusteghi* |
| **Margherita** Soprano | Beloved of Faust | Alda, Albanese, Borgi-Mamo, Calvé, Canetti, Caniglia, Eames, Farrar, Lilli Lehmann, Muzio, Christine Nilsson, Scacciati, Schwarz-kopf, Spani, Tebaldi, Valleria | *Mefistofele* |
| **Margiana** Soprano | Baba Mustapha's daughter | | *Der Barbier von Bagdad* |
| **Margret** Contralto | | Evans | *Wozzeck* |
| **Marguerite** Soprano | | Calvé, Cigna, Farrar, Gatti, Melba, Vere | *La Damnation de Faust* |

| CHARACTER | ROLE | SINGER | OPERA |
|---|---|---|---|
| **Marguerite** Soprano | Old servant | | *La Dame Blanche* |
| **Marguérite** Soprano | Beloved of Faust | 1st Miolan-Carvalho; Ackté, Adams, Albani, Alda, de los Angeles, Borghi-Mamo, Calvé, Carvalho, Eames, Edvina, Farrar, Fursch-Madi, Garden, Hauk, Jeritza, Juch, Jurinac, Kellogg, Lucca, Malten, Melba, Christine Nilsson, Nordica, Patti, Rappold, Josephine de Reszke, Roze, Sayao, Shuard, Steber, Eva Tetrazzini, Tietjens, Treville, Valleria, Vere, Yeend | *Faust* |
| **Marguerite** Soprano | | | *Louise* |
| **Marguerite de Valois** Soprano | Betrothed to Henri IV | 1st Dorus-Gras; Hempel, Juch, Melba, Peschka-Leutner, Luisa Tetrazzini, Vere | *Les Huguenots* |
| **Maria** Soprano | The commandant's wife | 1st Ursuleac; Grandi, Weber | *Friedenstag* |
| **Maria** Contralto | Cookshop keeper | | *Porgy and Bess* |
| **Maria** *Another name for* Amelia Boccanegra | | | |
| **Maria** *English version of* Marina, *in I Quattro Rusteghi* | | | |
| **Maria Golovin** Soprano | | Franca Duval | *Maria Golovin* |

413

| CHARACTER | | ROLE | SINGER | OPERA |
|---|---|---|---|---|
| **Marianne** | Soprano | Sophie's duenna | Votipka | *Der Rosenkavalier* |
| **Marie** | Soprano | | Schröder-Devrient | *Barbe-Bleue* (Grétry) |
| **Marie** | Soprano | Foster daughter of a regiment | Lind, Lucca, Patti, Pons, Sembrich, Sontag, Luisa Tetrazzini | *La Figlia del Reggimento* |
| **Marie** | Soprano | | Roze | *Marie* (Hérold) |
| **Marie** | Soprano | Prostitute | 1st Sigrid Johanson; Borkh, Danco, Dow, Gatti, Goltz, Mödl, Neway, Pauly, Steber | *Wozzeck* |
| **Marie** | Soprano | Van Bett's niece | | *Zar und Zimmerman* |
| **Marie-Louise** | Mezzo-soprano | Napoleon's second wife | | *Háry János* |
| **Marie's Child** | Treble | | | *Wozzeck* |
| **Mariette** | Soprano | | Jeritza | *Die Tote Stadt* |
| **Marina** | Soprano | Filipeto's aunt | | *I Quattro Rusteghi* |
| **Marina Mnishek** | Mezzo-soprano | Daughter of the Voyevode of Sandomir | 1st Platonova; Castagna, Elias, Ober, Rankin, Resnik, Simionato, Thebom, Thorborg | *Boris Godunov* |
| **Marines** | Chorus | | | *Billy Budd* |
| **Mario Cavaradossi** | Tenor | Painter in love with Tosca | 1st de Marchi; Baum, Borgatti, Borgioli, Caruso, Conley, Cremonini, Crooks, Fernandi, Hamlin, Lucia, Martin, McCormack, del Monaco, Peerce, Pertile, Poleri, di Stefano, Tagliavini, Tucker | *Tosca* |
| **Maritana** | Soprano | A gypsy | | *Maritana* |

## THE CHARACTERS IN THE OPERAS

| CHARACTER | ROLE | SINGER | OPERA |
|---|---|---|---|
| **Mark** Tenor | A fisherman, Thirza's lover | | *The Wreckers* |
| **Mark** *See also* King Marke | | | |
| **Marlardot** Tenor | Music Hall proprietor | | *Zaza* |
| **Marouf** Baritone | Henpecked cobbler | Singher | *Marouf* |
| **Marquis** Silent | | | *Cardillac* |
| **Marquis de Boisfleury** Baritone | | | *Linda di Chamounix* |
| **Marquis de Chateauneuf** Tenor | French ambassador | | *Zar und Zimmermann* |
| **Marquis of Montefiore** Bass | | | *Maritana* |
| **Marquise de Birkenfeld** Soprano | | Claramae Turner | *La Figlia del Reggimento* |
| **Mars** Tenor | The planet, also Ulrich Grüsser | | *Die Harmonie der Welt* |
| **Mars** Bass | A god | | *Orphée aux Enfers* |
| **Marschallin, The** Soprano | Princess von Werdenberg | 1st Siems; Cross, Easton, della Casa, Fisher, Hempel, Anni Konetzni, Lotte Lehmann, Leider, Lemnitz, Lewis, Steber, Varnay | *Der Rosenkavalier* |
| **Marta** Soprano | | Barrientos, Hempel, Juch, Kellogg, Murska, Patti, Tietjens, Valleria | *Marta* |
| **Marta** Soprano | Sebastiano's mistress | Destinn | *Tiefland* |
| **Martha** Contralto | | 1st Duclos; Scalchi | *Faust* |

415

| CHARACTER | ROLE | SINGER | OPERA |
|---|---|---|---|
| **Martha** Mezzo-soprano | One of the Old Believers | Stignani | *Khovantschina* |
| **Martha** Contralto | | | *Mefistofele* |
| **Martha** *See also* Harriett | | | |
| **Martha Schwerlein** Mezzo-soprano | Marguerite's neighbor | | *Faust* |
| **Marti** Baritone | Rich farmer, Vreli's father | | *A Village Romeo and Juliet* |
| **Martinka** Contralto | Vendulka's aunt | | *Hubička* |
| **Marullo, Cavaliere** Baritone | A courtier | | *Rigoletto* |
| **Mary** Contralto | Senta's nurse | | *Der Fliegende Holländer* |
| **Mary** Soprano | Constable's daughter | 1st Lewis; Cross | *Hugh the Drover* |
| **Mary** Soprano | | Bori | *Peter Ibbetson* |
| **Mary Ann** Speaker | Servant | | *The Boatswain's Mate* |
| **Marzci, Old** Baritone | Marie's coachman | | *Háry János* |
| **Marzelline** *See* Marcellina | | | |
| **Masaniello** Tenor | Fisherman, Fenella's brother | 1st Nourrit; Braham, Tamberlik | *Masaniello* |
| **Masha** Soprano | Lisa's maid | | *Pique-Dame* |
| **Masetto** Bass | Peasant | 1st Giuseppe Lolli; Walter Berry, Lorenzo Alvary, Bispham, Renan, Uppmann | *Don Giovanni* |
| **Mask Seller** *See* Marchand de Masques, La | | | |
| **Masks** Chorus | | | *La Traviata* |
| **Masquers** Chorus | | | *La Gioconda* |
| **Massarelli** Silent | | | *Palestrina* |

| CHARACTER | | ROLE | SINGER | OPERA |
|---|---|---|---|---|
| **Master of Ceremonies** | Tenor | | | *Christophe Colomb* |
| **Master of Ceremonies** | Bass | | | *Doktor Faustus* |
| **Master of Ceremonies** | Tenor | | | *Gloriana* |
| **Master of Ceremonies** | Tenor | | | *The Love for Three Oranges* |
| **Master of Ceremonies** | Tenor | | | *Pique-Dame* |
| **Mat of the Mint** | From Chorus | Gentleman of the Road | | *The Beggar's Opera* |
| **Mates, First and Second** | Baritones | | | *Billy Budd* |
| **Mathieu** | Baritone | Waiter | | *Andrea Chénier* |
| **Mathilde** | Soprano | Gessler's sister | Carvalho, Krauss, Tebaldi | *Guillaume Tell* |
| **Mathis** | Baritone | The painter Grünewald | | *Mathis der Maler* |
| **Matous** | Bass | A smuggler | | *Hubička* |
| **Matuta, Boyard Nikita** | Tenor | | | *Pskovityanka* |
| **Matteo** | Tenor | | Morell | *Arabella* |
| **Matteo** | Bass | Innkeeper | Autori, Goritz | *Fra Diavolo* |
| **Matteo Borsa** | Tenor | A courtier | Franke, de Paolis | *Rigoletto* |
| **Matteo del Sarto** | Baritone | Tailor and cuckold | Morell | *Arlecchino* |
| **Matthisen** | Bass | Anabaptist | | *Le Prophète* |
| **Maurevert** | Bass | Catholic noble | | *Les Huguenots* |
| **Maruizio** | Tenor | Count of Saxony | 1st Caruso; Campora, Pertile, Voyer | *Adriana Lecouvreur* |

| CHARACTER | ROLE | SINGER | OPERA |
|---|---|---|---|
| **Maurizio** Bass Baritone | Merchant, Filipeto's father | | *I Quattro Rusteghi* |
| **Max** Tenor | Forester | Althouse, Braham, Schott, Udvardy, Vogl | *Der Freischütz* |
| **May** Soprano | A pretty young toy-maker | | *Das Heimchen am Herd* |
| **Mayor** Bass | of the village | | *Jéjí Pastorkyňa (Jenufa)* |
| **Mayor of Hornachuelos** Bass | | | *La Forza del Destino* |
| **Mayor's Wife** Mezzo-soprano | | | *Jéjí Pastorkyňa (Jenufa)* |
| **McLean, Mrs.** Mezzo-soprano | | | *Susannah* |
| **Medea** Soprano | | Callas, Tietjens | *Medea* (Cherubini) |
| **Médecin Juif, Un** Baritone | A Jewish doctor | | *Esther de Carpentras* |
| **Medium, I** | Servant of the empress | | *The Poisoned Kiss* |
| **Medium, II** | Servant of the empress | | *The Poisoned Kiss* |
| **Medium, III** | Servant of the empress | | *The Poisoned Kiss* |
| **Medium, The** *See* Baba | | | |
| **Mefistofele** Bass | | de Angelis, Burke, Chaliapin, Didur, Nanetti, Pasera, Pinza, Edouard de Reszke, Rossi-Lemeni, Siepi | *Mefistofele* |
| **Megärus** Tenor | A spirit voice | | *Doktor Faust* |
| **Melanto** Mezzo-soprano | Penelope's servant | | *Il Ritorno d'Ulisse in Patria* |
| **Melcthal** Bass | Arnold's father, Swiss patriot | | *Guillaume Tell* |

| CHARACTER | | ROLE | SINGER | OPERA |
|---|---|---|---|---|
| **Mélisande** | Soprano | Former wife of Barbe-Bleu | | *Ariane et Barbe-Bleue* |
| **Mélisande** | Soprano | Golaud's wife, beloved of Pelléas | 1st Garden; de los Angeles, Bori, Connor, Edvina, Jepson, Perli, Sayao, Teyte | *Pelléas et Mélisande* |
| **Melitone, Fra** | Baritone | Franciscan | Corena, Gassier, Jean de Reszke | *La Forza del Destino* |
| **Melnik** | Bass | | Chaliapin | *Roussalka* |
| **Melot** | Baritone | A courtier | Cehanovsky | *Tristan und Isolde* |
| **Melusine, Countess** | Speaker | Lady in waiting | | *Háry János* |
| **Members of the Revolutionary Tribunal** | Chorus | | | *Andrea Chénier* |
| **Memucan** | Tenor | (Aman) | | *Esther de Carpentras* |
| **Men (Three)** | Tenor, | Baritone, Bass | | *Der Prozess* |
| **Men** | Chorus | | | *Pilgrim's Progress, Tiefland* |
| **Men and Women** | Chorus | | | *Dalibor, La Damnation de Faust* |
| **Men at Arms** | Chorus | | | *Lucrezia Borgia, Mefistofele, I Puritani, Tristan und Isolde* |
| **Men in Armor (Two)** | Tenor, Bass | | | *Zauberflöte* |
| **Menelaus** | Tenor | Helena's husband | 1st Tauche; Laubenthal, Völker | *Die Aegyptische Helena* |
| **Méphistophélès** | Bass | | Formichi, Galeffi, Gobbi, Plançon, Renaud | *La Damnation de Faust* |
| **Mephistopheles** | Tenor | | | *Doktor Faustus* |

| CHARACTER | ROLE | SINGER | OPERA |
|---|---|---|---|
| **Méphistophélès** Bass | | 1st Balanqué; Bouhy, Chaliapin, Christoff, Delmas, Faure, Foli, Gassier, Giraudet, Hinshaw, Journet, Lablache, List, London, Marcoux, Novara, Pinza, Plançon, Radford, Edouard de Reszke, Rothier, F. Stravinski | *Faust* |
| **Mephistopheles** *See also* Mefistofele | | | |
| **Mercedes** Mezzo-soprano | A gypsy | Cross, Evans, Glaz | *Carmen* |
| **Mercedes, Doña** Contralto | | Thorborg | *Der Corregidor* |
| **Merchants** Chorus | | | *The Fair at Sorochintsky* |
| **Merchants (Two)** Tenor, Bass | | | *Marouf* |
| **Merchants and Wives** Chorus | | | *Manon* |
| **Mercure** Tenor | The god Mercury | | *Orphée aux Enfers* |
| **Mercury** Bass | The planet, also Daniel Hizler | | *Die Harmonie der Welt* |
| **Mercury** Tenor | | | *Die Liebe der Danae* |
| **Mercury** Bass | The god | | *Les Troyens* |
| **Mercutio** Baritone | Romeo's friend | | *Roméo et Juliette* |
| **Merry-go-round Man** Baritone | | | *A Village Romeo and Juliet* |
| **Méru** Baritone | Catholic gentleman | | *Les Huguenots* |
| **Messagera; La** Soprano | The messenger | | *La Favola d'Orfeo* |
| **Messenger** Tenor | | Franke | *Aida* |
| **Messenger** Baritone | | | *Antigonae* (Orff) |

| CHARACTER | ROLE | SINGER | OPERA |
|---|---|---|---|
| **Messenger** Baritone | | | *Christophe Colomb* |
| **Messenger** Bass-baritone | | | *Oedipus Rex* |
| **Messenger** From Chorus | | | *Il Trovatore* |
| **Messenger** Tenor | | | *La Wally* |
| **Messenger of Peace** Soprano | | | *Rienzi* |
| **Messengers** Chorus | | | *Rienzi* |
| **Metifio** Baritone | Horse tender | | *L'Arlesiana* |
| **Micaela** Soprano | Village girl from Navarra | 1st Chapuy; Adams, Alda, Amara, de los Angeles, Bori, Conner, Eames, Farrar, Gueden, Hurley, Mario, Melba, Rappold, Steber, Valleria, Vere, Yeend | *Carmen* |
| **Micha** Bass | Landlord, Jenik's father | | *Prodaná Nevĕsta* |
| **Michael Andreievitch Toucha** Tenor | In love with Olga | | *Pskovityanka* |
| **Michele** Baritone | Barge man, 50 | 1st Didur; Franci, Galeffi, Tibbett, Weede | *Il Tabarro* |
| **Michelin** Baritone | A journalist | | *Zaza* |
| **Michonnet** Baritone | Stage director | | *Adriana Lecouvreur* |
| **Midas** Tenor | King of Lydia whose touch turns things to gold | 1st Taubmann; Patzak | *Die Liebe der Danae* |
| **Midir** Tenor | | | *The Immortal Hour* |
| **Midshipmen (Four)** Chorus | | | *Billy Budd* |

| CHARACTER | ROLE | SINGER | OPERA |
|---|---|---|---|
| **Mignon** Mezzo-soprano | Foundling brought up as a gypsy | 1st Galli-Marie; Albani, Barrientos, Bori, Destinn, Farrar, Juch, Lussan, Matzenauer, Morris, Christine Nilsson, Pederzini, Simionato, Stevens, van Zandt | *Mignon* |
| **Milada** Soprano | Dalibor's accuser | Hilde Konetzni, Lemnitz | *Dalibor* |
| **Milio Dufresne** Tenor | Zaza's lover | Gigli | *Zaza* |
| **Milkwoman** Soprano | | | *Louise* |
| **Miller** Baritone | An old soldier, Luisa's father | | *Luisa Miller* |
| **Milliners** Chorus | | | *The Poisoned Kiss* |
| **Mime** Tenor | A Nibelung | Nachbauer | *Das Ring des Nibelungen* |
| **Mimi** Soprano | Embroiderer, consumptive | 1st Cesari-Ferrani; Albanese, Alda, Amara, de los Angeles, Bori, Callas, Cavan, Cebotari, Connor, Cross, della Casa, Esty, Farrar, Favero, Flagstad, Gluck, Gueden, Hempel, Jurinac, Kirsten, Labia, Lipovska, Melba, Moffo, Moore, Norena, Perli, Sayao, Schwarzkopf, Tebaldi, Teyte, Welitsch, Williams, Yeend | *La Bohème* |
| **Miners** Chorus | | | *The Wreckers* |

| CHARACTER | | ROLE | SINGER | OPERA |
|---|---|---|---|---|
| **Minerve** | Soprano | Goddess | | Orphée aux Enfers |
| **Minerva** | Soprano | | | Il Ritorno d'Ulisse in Patria |
| **Mingo** | Tenor | | | Porgy and Bess |
| **Minister, The King's** See Fernando, Don | | | | |
| **Ministers** | Chorus | | | Aida |
| **Minnesingers** See the opera Tannhäuser | | | | |
| **Minnie** | Soprano | Saloon keeper | 1st Destinn; Barbato, Caniglia, Cobelli, Flagstad, Jeritza, Kirk, dalla Rizza, Steber, Tebaldi, Welitsch | La Fanciulla del West |
| **Mirabella** | Contralto | Carnero's long lost wife | | Zigeunerbaron |
| **Miracle, Doctor** | Baritone | | London | Les Contes d'Hoffmann |
| **Mireille** | Soprano | In love with Vincent | 1st Carvalho; Barrientos, Blauvelt, Eames, Nevada, Patti, Tietjens | Mireille |
| **Mizgir** | Baritone | In love with the Snow Maiden | | Snyegurotchka |
| **Missail** | Tenor | A vagrant | | Boris Godunov |
| **Mistress of the Novices** | Mezzo-soprano | | | Suor Angelica |
| **Mistrust** | Baritone | A neighbor | | Pilgrim's Progress |
| **Mitrane** | Tenor | Captain of the guard | | Semiramide |
| **Mityukh** | Bass | One of the people | | Boris Godunov |

| CHARACTER | ROLE | SINGER | OPERA |
|---|---|---|---|
| **Mityusha**<br>*See* Mityukh | | | |
| **Mnishek, Marina**<br>*See* Marina<br>Mnischek | | | |
| **Molly Brazen**<br>From Chorus | A lady of the town | | *The Beggar's Opera* |
| **Mona**   Soprano | | Kemp | *Mona Lisa*<br>(Schillings) |
| **Mona Lisa**  Soprano | | Borkh | *Mona Lisa* |
| **Monforte**<br>*See* Guido di<br>Monforte | | | |
| **Monastery**<br>**Attendant**<br>From Chorus | | | *Manon* |
| **Monica**   Soprano | Baba's daughter | 1st Keller | *The Medium* |
| **Monk**       Bass | | | *Don Carlos* |
| **Monks**    Chorus | | | *La Favorita, La Gioconda, I Gioielli della Madonna, Les Huguenots, Rienzi, Roméo et Juliette, Thaïs* |
| **Monks, Franciscan**<br>Chorus | | | *La Forza del Destino* |
| **Monostatos**  Tenor | Sarastro's Moorish servant | Perier | *Zauberflöte* |
| **Monsters**  Chorus | | | *The Love for Three Oranges* |
| **Montano**    Bass | Otello's predecessor in Cyprus | | *Otello* |
| **Monterone, Count**<br>Baritone | | | *Rigoletto* |
| **Moon, The**<br>Contralto | Also Katherina | | *Die Harmonie der Welt* |
| **Morales**    Bass | Officer of the guard | | *Carmen* |
| **Morbio**  Baritone | An actor | Newman | *Die Schweigsame Frau* |

# THE CHARACTERS IN THE OPERAS

| CHARACTER | ROLE | SINGER | OPERA |
|---|---|---|---|
| **Morena** Bass | A fisherman | | *Masaniello* |
| **Morgiana** Soprano | | 1st Falcon | *Ali Baba* (Cherubini) |
| **Morosus Blunt** Bass | An old bachelor | 1st Plaschke; Beattie | *Die Schweigsame Frau* |
| **Morphée** Tenor | A god | | *Orphée aux Enfers* |
| **Moruccio** Baritone | Miller | | *Tiefland* |
| **Mosè** Bass | Moses | Christoff | *Mosè* (Rossini) |
| **Moser, Augustin** Tenor | Mastersinger and tailor | | *Die Meistersinger* |
| **Mother** Soprano | Amahl's mother | Neway | *Amahl and the Night Visitors* |
| **Mother** Contralto | | | *The Consul* |
| **Mother** Contralto | | | *L'Enfant et les Sortilèges* |
| **Mother** | | Neway | *Maria Golovin* |
| **Mother Goose** Mezzo-soprano | | 1st Nell Tangeman; Lipton, Madeira | *The Rake's Progress* |
| **Mother of Louise** Contralto | | Gay | *Louise* |
| **Mountaineers** Chorus | | | *Ernani* |
| **Mountjoy, Charles Blount, Lord** Baritone | | | *Gloriana* |
| **Mister, or Mrs.** *See proper name, as:* Day, Mr. *or* Ford, Mrs. | | | |
| **Muezzin (Two)** Tenors | | | *Marouf* |
| **Muff** Tenor | A comedian | | *Prodaná Nevěsta* |
| **Muleteers** Chorus | | | *La Forza del Destino* |
| **Muse of Poetry** Soprano | | | *Les Contes d'Hoffmann* |

| CHARACTER | | ROLE | SINGER | OPERA |
|---|---|---|---|---|
| **Musetta** | Soprano | In love with Marcello | 1st Pacini; Fenn, Goltz, Gueden, Lewis, Lussan, Munsel, Resnik, Schwarzkopf, Shuard, Welitsch | *La Bohème* |
| **Music Master** | Baritone | | Herbert | *Ariadne auf Naxos* |
| **Music Master** | Tenor | | | *Manon Lescaut* |
| **Music Master** See Basilio, Don | | | | |
| **Musician** | Mezzo-soprano | | Vanni | *Manon Lescaut* |
| **Musician Monk** | Baritone | | | *Le Jongleur de Notre Dame* |
| **Musicians** | | | Players of the Violin, Cello and Cembalo | *Capriccio* |
| **Musicians** | Chorus | | | *Il Barbiere di Siviglia, Francesca da Rimini, Gloriana, Její Pastorkyňa (Jenufa)* |
| **Musketeer** | Bass | | | *Friedenstag* |
| **Mustafa** | Bass | The Bey of Algiers | | *L'Italiana in Algeri* |
| **Mustapha** See Baba Mustapha | | | | |
| **Mute** | Silent | | | *Die Entführung aus dem Serail* |
| **Mylio** | Tenor | Victorious general | Gigli, Saléza | *Le Roi d'Ys* |
| **Myrrha** | Soprano | | 1st Christine Nilsson | *Sardanapale* |
| **Myrtale** | Mezzo-soprano | A slave | | *Thaïs* |
| **Mystic Choir** | Chorus | | | *Mefistofele* |

| CHARACTER | | ROLE | SINGER | OPERA |
|---|---|---|---|---|
| **Nabi** | Baritone | Prince of Nephthali | | *Debora e Jaele* |
| **Nabucco** | Baritone | Nebuchadnezzar, King of Babylon | | *Nabucco* |
| **Nabucodonosor** *See* Nabucco | | | | |
| **Nadina** | Speaker | Member of Almanzor's harem | | *Oberon* |
| **Nadir** | Tenor | Fisherman | 1st Morini; T. Burke, Caruso, Cremonini, Delmas, Garulli, Lugo | *Les Pêcheurs de Perles* |
| **Naiade** | Soprano | A nymph | | *Ariadne auf Naxos* |
| **Naiads** | Chorus | | | *Mefistofele, Tannhäuser, Les Troyens* |
| **Naina** | Mezzo-soprano | An evil witch | | *Russlan and Ludmilla* |
| **Namouna** | Speaker | Fatima's grand-mother | | *Oberon* |
| **Nancy** | Mezzo-soprano | The baker's assistant | | *Albert Herring* |
| **Nancy** | Contralto | | | *Hugh the Drover* |
| **Nancy** | Contralto | Harriett's waiting maid | Elmo, Howard, Pederzini, Trebelli, Walker | *Martha* |
| **Nandro** | Tenor | Shepherd | | *Tiefland* |
| **Nanetta** | Soprano | Ford's daughter, in love with Fenton | Lussan, Seefried | *Falstaff* |
| **Nanette** | Soprano | Maid to the Baroness Freimann | | *Der Wildschütz* |
| **Napoleon, Emperor** | Baritone | | | *Háry János* |
| **Napoleone** | Baritone | | Amato | *Madame Sans-Gêne* |
| **Narbal** | Bass | Dido's minister | | *Les Troyens* |
| **Narciso, Don** | Tenor | | Gedda | *Il Turco in Italia* |

| CHARACTER | | ROLE | SINGER | OPERA |
|---|---|---|---|---|
| **Narraboth** | Tenor | Captain of the guard | | *Salome* |
| **Narrator** | Speaker | | | *Christophe Colomb* |
| **Narumoff** | Baritone | A gambler | | *Pique-Dame* |
| **Natalia** | Mezzo-soprano | Zaza's maid | | *Zaza* |
| **Nathanael** | Tenor | A student | | *Les Contes d'Hoffmann* |
| **Naval Captain** | Bass | | | *Manon Lescaut* |
| **Nazarenes (Two)** | Tenor, Bass | | | *Salome* |
| **Nebuchadnezzar** *See* Nabucco | | | | |
| **Ned Keene** | Baritone | Apothecary and quack | 1st Donlevy | *Peter Grimes* |
| **Nedda** | Soprano | "Columbine," Canio's wife in love with Silvio | 1st Stehle; Ackté, Amara, Callas, Destinn, della Casa, Fenn, Fornia-Labey, Ilitsch, Kronold, Labia, Lussan, Melba, Sayao, Seefried, Shuard, Welitsch | *I Pagliacci* |
| **Neighbor, A** | Tenor | | | *Der Corregidor* |
| **Neighbors** | Chorus | | | *Arlecchino, Benvenuto Cellini, Werther* |
| **Nejata** | Mezzo-soprano | Musician from Kiev | | *Sadko* |
| **Nella** | Soprano | Gherardo's wife, 34 | | *Gianni Schicchi* |
| **Nelly** | Soprano | | Neway | *Wuthering Heights* |
| **Nelson** | Tenor | | | *Porgy and Bess* |
| **Nelusko** | Baritone | Slave, captured by Vasco da Gama | Ancona, Basiola, Beck, Borgioli, Faure, Lassalle, Renaud, Edouard de Reszke | *L'Africaine* |

| CHARACTER | ROLE | SINGER | OPERA |
|---|---|---|---|
| **Nemorino** Tenor | Young peasant | 1st Genero; Caruso, Gigli, Schipa | *L'Elisir d'Amore* |
| **Neptune** *See* Nettuno *See also* Voice of Neptune | | | |
| **Nereo** Tenor | | | *Mefistofele* |
| **Nerone** Bass | The emperor Nero | Pinza | *Nerone* (Boito) |
| **Nerone** Tenor | The emperor Nero | 1st Pertile; Lauri-Volpi, Voyer | *Nerone* (Mascagni) |
| **Nettuno** Bass | Neptune | | *Il Ritorno d'Ulisse in Patria* |
| **Nevers, Count de** Baritone | Catholic nobleman | 1st Derivis; Ancona, Faure, Lassalle, Maurel, del Puente, Renaud, Jean de Reszke, Santley, Scotti | *Les Huguenots* |
| **Newspaper Girl** Soprano | | | *Louise* |
| **Nibelungs** Chorus | | | *Das Ring des Nibelungen* |
| **Nicias** Tenor | An Alexandrian | 1st Alvarez | *Thaïs* |
| **Nick** Tenor | Bartender | | *La Fanciulla del West* |
| **Nick Shadow** Baritone | | 1st Otakar Kraus; Harrell, Hines | *The Rake's Progress* |
| **Nicklausse** Mezzo-soprano | Hoffman's friend | Varno | *Les Contes d'Hoffmann* |
| **Nicola** Tenor | Footman | | *Fedora* |
| **Nicoletta** Mezzo-soprano | Princess hidden in an orange | | *The Love for Three Oranges* |
| **Nieces (Two)** Sopranos | Main attractions of "The Boar" | 1st Iacopi, Blanche Turner | *Peter Grimes* |
| **Night Watch** Chorus | | | *Les Huguenots* |
| **Night Watchman** Bass | | | *Die Meistersinger* |
| **Nightingale** *See* Rossignol, Le | | | |

| CHARACTER | ROLE | SINGER | OPERA |
|---|---|---|---|
| **Nightwatchmen's Voices (Three)** <br> Basses | | | *Die Frau ohne Schatten* |
| **Nika Magadoff** <br> Tenor | The magician | Kelley | *The Consul* |
| **Nikititsch** Bass | | | *Boris Godunov* |
| **Nilakantha** <br> Bass Baritone | Brahmin priest | E. Burke, Pinza, Edouard de Reszke, Rothier | *Lakmé* |
| **Nimming Ned** <br> From Chorus | Gentleman of the road | | *The Beggar's Opera* |
| **Ninetta** Soprano | | Grisi | *La Gazza Ladra* |
| **Ninetta** Soprano | Princess hidden in an orange | Hurley | *The Love for Three Oranges* |
| **Ninetta** Soprano | Elena's attendant | | *I Vespri Siciliani* |
| **Nino** <br> *See* Ghost of Nino | | | |
| **Noble Pages (Four)** <br> Sopranos, Contraltos | | | *Tannhäuser* |
| **Nobles** Chorus | | | *Dalibor, Lohengrin, Le Prophète, Rienzi, Rigoletto, Le Roi d'Ys Roméo et Juliette, Tannhäuser, Tosca* |
| **Nobles of the Venetian Republic** Chorus | | | *Lucrezia Borgia* |
| **Noctambulist** <br> Tenor | | | *Louise* |
| **Noctambulist** <br> *See also* Amina | | | |
| **Nolan, Mrs.** <br> Mezzo-soprano | Baba's client | Bible, Evans | *The Medium* |
| **Norina** Soprano | Young widow | 1st Grisi; Bori, Gueden, Mildmay, Noni, Pareto, Sayao, Sembrich, Sontag | *Don Pasquale* |

| CHARACTER | | ROLE | SINGER | OPERA |
|---|---|---|---|---|
| **Norma** | Soprano | Druid High Priestess | 1st Pasta; Bampton, Callas, Hauk, Krauss, Lilli Lehmann, Lucca, Mallinger, Matzenauer, Milanov, Muzio, Parepa-Rosa, Ponselle, Schröder-Devrient, Tietjens, Viardot-Garcia, Wagner | *Norma* |
| **Norman** | Tenor | Follower of Ashton | | *Lucia di Lammermoor* |
| **Normando** *See* Norman | | | | |
| **Norma's Children** | | | | *Norma* |
| **Norn, First** | Contralto | One of the Fates | | *Götterdämmerung* |
| **Norn, Second** | Mezzo-soprano | One of the Fates | | *Götterdämmerung* |
| **Norn, Third** | Soprano | One of the Fates | | *Götterdämmerung* |
| **Notary** | | | | *Il Barbiere di Siviglia* |
| **Notary** | Baritone | | | *Intermezzo* |
| **Notary** | Baritone | | | *Don Pasquale* |
| **Notary** | Bass | | | *Der Rosenkavalier* |
| **Notary** | Silent | | | *La Sonnambula* |
| **Notary's Wife** | Soprano | | | *Intermezzo* |
| **Nourabad** | Bass | High Priest of Brahma | 1st Guyot; Baronti, E. Burke, Miranda | *Les Pêcheurs de Perles* |
| **Nourrice** | Contralto | Nurse | | *Ariane et Barbe-Bleue* |
| **Novice** | Tenor | | | *Billy Budd* |
| **Novice's Friend** | Baritone | | | *Billy Budd* |
| **Novices** | Chorus | | | *Suor Angelica* |

# THE CHARACTERS IN THE OPERAS

| CHARACTER | ROLE | SINGER | OPERA |
|---|---|---|---|
| **Nowalska, Countess** See Palmatica | | | |
| **Nuns** Chorus | | | Robert le Diable, Il Trovatore |
| **Nuns** See also the opera Suor Angelica | | | |
| **Nureddin** Tenor | | | Il Barbier von Bagdad |
| **Nuri** Soprano | | Flagstad, Seefried | Tiefland |
| **Nurse** Mezzo-soprano | Xenia's nurse | Madeira | Boris Godunov |
| **Nurse** Mezzo-soprano | | 1st Jeritza | Die Frau ohne Schatten |
| **Nurse** Soprano | to Jaroslavna | | Prince Igor |
| **Nursing Sister** Soprano | | | Suor Angelica |
| **Nymphs** Chorus | | | Russlan and Ludmilla, Tannhäuser, Les Troyens |
| **Nymphs and Shepherds** Chorus | | | La Favola d'Orfeo |
| **Oberon** Tenor | King of the fairies | 1st Bland; Martinelli, Vrooms | Oberon |
| **Oberthal, Count** Baritone | | Didur, Edouard de Reszke | Le Prophète |
| **Obigny, Marchese d'** See Marchese d'Obigny | | | |
| **Obstinate** Bass | A neighbor | | Pilgrim's Progress |
| **Ochs von Lerchenau, Baron** Bass | Sophie's would-be suitor | 1st Perron; Lorenzo Alvary, Bender, Kipnis, List, Mayr, Stear | Der Rosenkavalier |

432

| CHARACTER | ROLE | SINGER | OPERA |
|---|---|---|---|
| **Octavian** Mezzo-soprano | Bearer of the Rose | Bible, della Casa, Evans, Goltz, Gutheil-Schoder, Hadrabova, Jurinac, Lotte Lehmann, Miller, Mödl, Novotna, Ober, Olczewska, Shacklock, Stevens, Thebom | *Der Rosenkavalier* |
| **Oedipus** Tenor | King of Thebes | Malipiero, Pears, Simoneau, Vrooms | *Oedipus* |
| **Officer** Tenor | | | *Ariadne auf Naxos* |
| **Officer** Tenor | | | *The Bohemian Girl* |
| **Officer** Bass | | | *Cardillac* |
| **Officer** From Chorus | | | *Christophe Colomb* |
| **Officer** Baritone | | | *Friedenstag* |
| **Officer** From Chorus | | | *Tosca* |
| **Officer** Baritone | | | *The Warrior* |
| **Officers** Chorus | | | *Billy Budd, Carmen, Lucrezia Borgia, Pskovityanka* |
| **Official Registrar** Baritone | | | *Madama Butterfly* |
| **Officials** Chorus | | | *Aida* |
| **Old Bard** Bass | | | *The Immortal Hour* |
| **Old Believers** Chorus | | | *Khovantschina* |
| **Old-Clothes Man** Tenor | | | *Louise* |
| **Old Gypsy** Baritone | | | *Il Trovatore* |
| **Old Hebrew** Bass | | Allin, Moscona | *Samson et Dalila* |
| **Old Men** Chorus | | | *Prince Igor* |
| **Old Men of Thebes** Chorus | | | *Oedipus Rex* |

| CHARACTER | ROLE | SINGER | OPERA |
|---|---|---|---|
| **Old Servant** Bass | | | *Elektra* |
| **Old Woman** From Chorus | | | *L'Amore dei Tre Re* |
| **Olga** Contralto | Tatiana's sister | Elias | *Eugene Onegin* |
| **Olga Sukarev, Countess** Soprano | | | *Fedora* |
| **Olga Yourievna Tokmakov, Princess** Soprano | In love with Michael | | *Pskovityanka* |
| **Olimpia** Soprano | | Tebaldi | *Olympia* (Spontini) |
| **Olin Blitch** Bass-baritone | Evangelist | | *Susannah* |
| **Olivier** Baritone | Poet | Fischer-Dieskau | *Capriccio* |
| **Ollendorf, Colonel** Bass | Governor of Cracow | | *Der Bettelstudent* |
| **Olympia** Soprano | A mechanical doll | 1st Isaac; Dobbs, Fremstad, Hempel, Seefried, Teyte | *Les Contes d'Hoffmann* |
| **Omniscient Mussel, The** Contralto | | | *Die Aegyptische Helena* |
| **One-Arm** Bass | Barak's brother | | *Die Frau ohne Schatten* |
| **One-Eye** Bass | Barak's brother | | *Die Frau ohne Schatten* |
| **Opera Singers** Chorus | | | *Le Postillion de Longjumeau* |
| **Ophélie** Soprano | Hamlet's beloved | 1st Christine Nilsson; Ackté, Albani, Barrientos, Calvé, Gerster, Melba, Mignon Nevada, Nordica, Patti, Josephine de Reszke, Vere | *Hamlet* |
| **Opinion Publique, L'** Mezzo-soprano | Public Opinion | | *Orphée aux Enfers* |
| **Oracle** | | | *Alceste* |
| **Orator** Bass | | | *Die Zauberflöte* |

| CHARACTER | | ROLE | SINGER | OPERA |
|---|---|---|---|---|
| **Orest** | Baritone | Agamemnon's son, Elektra's brother | 1st Perron; Janssen, Nissen, Schorr, Schöffler | *Elektra* |
| **Oreste** | Baritone | | | *Les Choëphores* |
| **Oreste** | Baritone | | | *Eumenides* |
| **Oreste** | Baritone | Iphigénie's brother | 1st Larrivée; Beck | *Iphigénie en Tauride* |
| **Orfeo** | Baritone | | 1st Giovanni Gualberto; Franci, Galeffi, Kullmann, Sammarco, Weil | *La Favola d'Orfeo* |
| **Orfeo** | Contralto | | 1st Guadagni; Ansseau (*Tenor*), Barbieri, Brema, Butt, Delna, Ferrier, Gay, Gerville-Réache, Hastreiter, Homer, Legros (*Tenor*), Thorborg, Viardot-Garcia, Wickham | *Orfeo ed Euridice* |
| **Orford, Ellen** *See* Ellen Orford | | | | |
| **Orlovsky** Mezzo-soprano | | Rich Russian | Miller, Novotna, Thebom | *Die Fledermaus* |
| **Oroe** | Bass | High Priest of the Magi | Foli | *Semiramide* |
| **Oroveso** | Bass | Norma's father, Archdruid | Lablache, Moscona, Plançon, Rossi-Lemeni, Siepi, Weiss | *Norma* |
| **Orphans (Three)** Soprano, Mezzo-soprano, Contralto | | | | *Der Rosenkavalier* |
| **Orphée** | Baritone | | | *Les Malheurs d'Orphée* |
| **Orphée** | Tenor | A superb violinist | | *Orphée aux Enfers* |
| **Orsini** *See* Paolo Orsini *See also* Maffio Orsini | | | | |

| CHARACTER | | ROLE | SINGER | OPERA |
|---|---|---|---|---|
| **Ortlinde** | Soprano or Mezzo-soprano | A Valkyr | Flagstad | *Die Walküre* |
| **Ortrud** | Mezzo-soprano | Wife of Frederick of Telramund | 1st Fasztlinger; Brema, Cahier, Carey, Fisher, Fornia-Labey, Fursch-Madi, Harshaw, Hastreiter, Homer, Kirkby-Lunn, Langendorf, Lilli Lehmann, Matzenauer, Mödl, Ober, Schumann-Heink, Thebom, Tietjens, Varnay, Wickham | *Lohengrin* |
| **Osaka** | Tenor | Rich young man in love with Iris | Caruso, Gigli, Pertile | *Iris* |
| **Oscar** | Soprano | A page | Carvalho, Grandi, Kurz, Thorborg, Schwarzkopf | *Un Ballo in Maschera* |
| **Osmin** | Bass | Overseer of the harem | 1st Ludwig Fischer; Ernster, Radford | *Die Entführung aus dem Serail* |
| **Osmina, Suor** | Soprano | A nun | | *Suor Angelica* |
| **Ostasio** | Baritone | Francesca's brother | | *Francesca da Rimini* |
| **Otello** | Tenor | A moor, Venetian governor of Cyprus | 1st Tamagno; Alvarez, Campanini, Lauri-Volpi, Marconi, Martinelli, McCracken, Melchior, Merli, del Monaco, Mullings, Pertile, Jean de Reszke, Rubini, Saléza, Slezak, Trantoul, Vinay, Winkelmann, Zanello, Zenatello | *Otello* (Verdi) |

| CHARACTER | ROLE | SINGER | OPERA |
|---|---|---|---|
| **Ott, Mrs.**  Contralto | | | *Susannah* |
| **Ottakar, Prince** | | Reeves, Robinson | *Der Freischütz* |
| **Ottavio, Don**      Tenor | Betrothed to Donna Anna | 1st Antonio Baglioni; Bjoerling, Conley, Dermota, Lucia, Mario, McCormack, Peerce, Jean de Reszke, Rubini, Schack, Schipa, Stagno, Valletti | *Don Giovanni* |
| **Ottokar**      Tenor | Arsena's lover | | *Zigeunerbaron* |
| **Ottoman**      Child | Le Pouf | | *L'Enfant et les Sortilèges* |
| **Ourrias**      Baritone | Bulltender, rival for Mireille's love | | *Mireille* |
| **Overseer**      Soprano | | | *Elektra* |
| **Overseer**      Baritone | | | *Der Prozess* |
| **Ovlour**      Tenor | Polovtsian traitor | | *Prince Igor* |
| **Paco**      Tenor | | 1st Devries; Masini, Tokatyan, Vroons | *La Vida Breve* |
| **Page**      Contralto | Of Hérodias | Bible | *Salome* |
| **Page**      Mezzo-soprano | | | *Snyegurotchka* |
| **Page, Mr.**      *See* Reich, Herr | | | |
| **Page, Mistress**      Mezzo-soprano | | | *Falstaff* |
| **Page, Mrs.**      *See* Reich, Frau | | | |
| **Pages**      Chorus | | | *Ernani, Guillaume Tell, Les Huguenots, Lohengrin, Luisa Miller, Martha, Pskovityanka, I Puritani, Rigoletto, Roméo et Juliette* |

| CHARACTER | | ROLE | SINGER | OPERA |
|---|---|---|---|---|
| **Pages** | | | | |
| *See* Noble Pages (Four) | | | | |
| **Painter** | Bass | | | *Louise* |
| **Painter** | Tenor | | • | *Lulu* |
| **Painter-Monk** | Baritone | | | *Le Jongleur de Notre Dame* |
| **Pagliaccio** | | | | |
| *See* Canio | | | | |
| **Palémon** | Bass | An old Cenobite monk | | *Thaïs* |
| **Palestrina, Giovanni Pierluigi** | Tenor | The composer | 1st Karl Erb; Patzak, Schmedes | *Palestrina* |
| **Pali** | Bass | A gypsy | | *Zigeunerbaron* |
| **Palmatica** | Mezzo-soprano | The Countess Nowalska | | *Der Bettelstudent* |
| **Paloucky** | Bass Baritone | Peasant | | *Hubička* |
| **Pamela** | Mezzo-soprano | Cockburn's wife, a tourist | 1st Boulanger; Matters | *Fra Diavolo* |
| **Pamina** | Soprano | Daughter of the queen of the night | 1st Nanetta Gottlieb; Carvalho, Davy, Dux, Eames, Cross, della Casa, Hempel, Jurinac, Lemnitz, Malten, Novotna, Schröder-Devrient, Schwarzkpof, Seefried, Siems, Tietjens | *Die Zauberflöte* |
| **Pancratius** | Speaker | The Count's major-domo | | *Der Wildschütz* |
| **Pang** | Tenor | Supreme lord of provisions | | *Turandot* |
| **Pantalis** | Contralto | | | *Mefistofele* |
| **Pantalone** | Bass | Minister | | *Turandot* (Busoni) |
| **Pantaloon** | | | | *Fête Galante* |

| CHARACTER | | ROLE | SINGER | OPERA |
|---|---|---|---|---|
| **Pantaloon** | Baritone | The king's friend | Renan | *The Love for Three Oranges* |
| **Panthée** | Bass | Priest of Troy | | *Les Troyens* |
| **Paolino** | Tenor | Carolina's secret husband | | *Il Matrimonio Segreto* |
| **Paolo Albiani** Baritone | | A plebian | | *Simon Boccanegra* |
| **Paolo il Bello** | Tenor | Handsome son of Malatesta | 1st Martinelli; Crimi, Parmeggiani, Pertile, Prandelli, Ziliani | *Francesca da Rimini* |
| **Paolo Orsini** | Bass | Roman patrician | Griswold | *Rienzi* |
| **Papagena** | Soprano | Destined to be Papageno's wife | 1st Gerl; Ugalde | *Die Zauberflöte* |
| **Papageno** | Baritone | A bird catcher | 1st Schikaneder; Balfe, Carey, Kunz, Uppmann | *Die Zauberflöte* |
| **Papal Nuncios (Two)** | Silent | | | *Palestrina* |
| **Paquiro** | Baritone | Toreador | 1st de Luca; Poli | *Goyescas* |
| **Parassia** | Soprano | In love with Gritzko | | *The Fair at Sorochintsky* |
| **Paris, Count** Baritone | | | | *Roméo et Juliette* |
| **Parpignol** | Tenor | Toy peddler | Franke | *La Bohème* |
| **Parsifal** | Tenor | An innocent and pure youth | 1st Winkelmann, Gudehus and Jäger; Althouse, Max Alvary, Berger, Burgstaller, Burrian, Dalmorès, Dippel, van Dyke, Hensel, Hutt, Hyde, Laubenthal, MacLennan, Melchior, Mullings, Niemann, Schmedes, Svanholm, Urlus, Vinay, Winkelmann, Wölfl, Sembach | *Parsifal* |

| CHARACTER | ROLE | SINGER | OPERA |
|---|---|---|---|
| **Pascoe**　Baritone | Headman and preacher | | *The Wreckers* |
| **Pasha**<br>*See* Selim Pasha | | | |
| **Pasquale, Don**　Bass | An old bachelor | 1st Leblache;<br>Baccaloni, Corena,<br>de Luca | *Don Pasquale* |
| **Passer-By**　Baritone | | | *Der Prozess* |
| **Pastourelle, Une**<br>　　　Soprano | Shepherd girl | | *L'Enfant et les<br>Sortilèges* |
| **Pâtre, Un**<br>　　　Contralto | Shepherd | | *L'Enfant et les<br>Sortilèges* |
| **Patricians**　Chorus | | | *Simon Boccanegra* |
| **Patroclus** | Friend of Achilles | | *Iphigénie en Aulide* |
| **Pauline**　Contralto | Lisa's friend | | *Pique-Dame* |
| **Peachum, Mr.**　Bass | A fence, an organizer of thieves | Austin | *The Beggar's Opera* |
| **Peachum, Mrs.**<br>　　　Mezzo-soprano | Peachum's wife,<br>Polly's mother | | *The Beggar's Opera* |
| **Peasant**　Tenor | | | *La Figlia del<br>Reggimento* |
| **Peasant, First**　Bass | | | *Ariane et Barbe-Bleue* |
| **Peasant, Second**<br>　　　Tenor | | | *Ariane et Barbe-Bleue* |
| **Peasant, Third**<br>　　　Bass | | | *Ariane et Barbe-Bleue* |
| **Peasants**　Chorus | | | *Andrea Chénier,<br>Ariane et Barbe-Bleue,<br>Cavalleria Rusticana,<br>L'Elisir d'Amore,<br>La Figlia del<br>Reggimento,<br>Guillaume Tell,<br>Háry János, Ivan<br>Susanin, Linda di<br>Chamounix, Mathis<br>der Maler, Le<br>Prophète, Der<br>Wildschütz* |

# THE CHARACTERS IN THE OPERAS

| CHARACTER | ROLE | SINGER | OPERA |
|---|---|---|---|
| **Peasants (Two)** Speakers | | | *Háry János* |
| **Peasants (Two)** Baritones | | | *A Village Romeo and Juliet* |
| **Pedlars** Chorus | | | *La Bohème, Louise* |
| **Pedrillo** Tenor | Belmonte's servant | | *Die Entführung aus dem Serail* |
| **Pedro, Don** Bass | A general | | *Béatrice et Bénédict* |
| **Pedro** Tenor | The mayor's secretary | | *Der Corregidor* |
| **Pedro** Tenor | | Dalmorès | *La Habanera* |
| **Pedro** Soprano | Dulcinée's admirer | | *Don Quichotte* |
| **Pedro** Tenor | Shepherd | Schmedes, Völker | *Tiefland* |
| **Pedro, Don** Bass | The king's councillor | | *L'Africaine* |
| **Pelléas** Tenor | Arkel's grandson, Golaud's half brother | 1st Perier; Singher, Uppmann | *Pelléas et Mélisande* |
| **Peneios** Bass | Fisherman, Daphne's father | | *Daphne* |
| **Penelope** Soprano | | 1st Goltz | *Penelope (Liebermann)* |
| **Penelope** Contralto | Wife of Ulisse | | *Il Ritorno d'Ulisse in Patria* |
| **Penitents** Chorus | | | *Mefistofele* |
| **People** Chorus | | | *L'Amore dei Tre Re, Cardillac, Le Coq d'Or, Dido and Aeneas, Eumenides, Fidelio, I Gioielli della Madonna, Die Harmonie der Welt, Háry János, Le Jongleur de Notre Dame, Khovantschina, Manon, Prince Igor, Pskovityanka, Le Roi d'Ys, Die Zauberflöte* |

| CHARACTER | ROLE | SINGER | OPERA |
|---|---|---|---|
| **People of Bagdad** Chorus | | | *Der Barbier von Bagdad* |
| **People of Crete** Chorus | | | *Idomeneo* |
| **People of Naples** Chorus | | | *Masaniello* |
| **People of New Hope Valley** Chorus | | | *Susannah* |
| **Pepa** Mezzo-soprano | Paquiro's sweetheart | 1st Perini; Elmo | *Goyescas* |
| **Pepa** Soprano | | | *Tiefland* |
| **Perfilievna** Mezzo-soprano | Nurse | | *Pskovityanka* |
| **Perichaud** Bass-baritone | | | *La Rondine* |
| **Perside** Soprano | A Christian | | *Nerone* |
| **Peter** Baritone | Father of Hansel and Gretel | | *Hänsel und Gretel* |
| **Peter** Tenor | The honey-man | | *Porgy and Bess* |
| **Peter** *English version of the name* Filipeto *in* I Quattro Rusteghi | | | |
| **Peter I** Baritone | Young Tsar of Russia | Santley, Faure, Maurel | *Zar und Zimmermann* |
| **Peter Grimes** Tenor | A fisherman | 1st Pears; Horne | *Peter Grimes* |
| **Peter Homonay, Graf** Baritone | Recruiting officer | | *Zigeunerbaron* |
| **Peter Ibbetson** Tenor | | Johnson | *Peter Ibbetson* |
| **Peter Ivanov** Tenor | Russian deserter | | *Zar und Zimmermann* |
| **Peter the Great** *See* Peter I | | | |

| CHARACTER | ROLE | SINGER | OPERA |
|---|---|---|---|
| **Phaecian Sailors** Chorus | | | *Il Ritorno d'Ulisse in Patria* |
| **Phaeton** *See* Tenor, The | | | |
| **Philine** Soprano | An actress, in love with Wilhelm | Garrison, Kellogg, Lilli Lehmann, Nordica, Talley | *Mignon* |
| **Philip the Second** *See* Filipso II | | | |
| **Philistine Messenger** Tenor | | 1st de Paolis | *Samson et Dalila* |
| **Philistines** Chorus | | | *Samson et Dalila* |
| **Philosophers (Two)** Tenor, Bass | | | *Louise* |
| **Phryné** Pantomime | | | *Faust* |
| **Phryné** Soprano | | 1st Sanderson | *Phryné (by* Saint-Saëns) |
| **Physician** Bass | | | *Pelléas et Mélisande* |
| **Pianist** *See* Boleslav Lazuiski | | | |
| **Pickthank** Contralto | | | *Pilgrim's Progress* |
| **Piedmontese, A** Tenor | | | *Friedenstag* |
| **Pierrot** Baritone | | | *Fête Galante* |
| **Pierrotto** Contralto | | Scalchi | *Linda di Chamounix* |
| **Pietists** Chorus | | | *The Wreckers* |
| **Pietro** Baritone | Masaniello's friend | Faure, Staudigl | *Masaniello* |
| **Pietro** Bass | Plebeian | | *Simon Boccanegra* |
| **Pilgrim** Tenor | A traveller through life | 1st Matters | *Pilgrim's Progress* |
| **Pilgrims** Chorus | | | *Boris Godunov, Faust, La Forza del Destino, Mireille, Tannhäuser* |

| CHARACTER | | ROLE | SINGER | OPERA |
|---|---|---|---|---|
| **Pilot** | Bass | | | *La Gioconda* |
| **Pimen** | Bass | Hermit and chronicler | Lorenzo Alvary, Gobbi, Hines, Tozzi | *Boris Godunov* |
| **Pinchbeck, Sir James** *English version of the name* Canciano *in I Quattro Rusteghi* | | | | |
| **Pinellino** | Bass | Cobbler, witness for the will | | *Gianni Schicchi* |
| **Ping** | Baritone | Grand Chancellor of China | | *Turandot* |
| **Pinkerton, Lieutenant B.F.** | Tenor | Of the United States Navy | 1st Zenatello; Caruso, Conley, Gedda, Hyde, Kullmann, Lloyd, Lugo, R. Martin, McCormack, del Monaco, Pertile, Sullivan | *Madama Butterfly* |
| **Pinkerton, Miss (Two)** | Soprano | | Faull | *The Old Maid and the Thief* |
| **Pinkerton, Kate** *See* Kate Pinkerton | | | | |
| **Pippo** | Mezzo-soprano | | Vestris | *La Gazza Ladra* |
| **Piram** | Baritone | | | *Debora e Jaele* |
| **Pirates** | Chorus | | | *Oberon* |
| **Pirro** | Baritone | | Gassier | *I Lombardi* |
| **Pisandro** | Tenor | One of Penelope's suitors | | *Il Ritorno d'Ulisse in Patria* |
| **Pistol** | Bass | Falstaff's friend | | *Falstaff* |
| **Pittichinaccio** | Tenor | Giulietta's admirer | | *Les Contes d'Hoffmann* |
| **Pizarro, Don** | Bass | Prison governor | 1st Meier; Bender, Bispham, Forti, Goritz, Reichmann, Staudigl | *Fidelio* |

# THE CHARACTERS IN THE OPERAS

| CHARACTER | ROLE | SINGER | OPERA |
|---|---|---|---|
| **Plainclothes Men** (Two)  Silent | Detectives | | *The Consul* |
| **Players**  Chorus | | | *Iris* |
| **Plebeians**  Chorus | | | *Simon Boccanegra* |
| **Pliable**  Tenor | A neighbor | | *Pilgrim's Progress* |
| **Plunkett**  Bass | Young farmer | de Luca, Maugeri, Stabile | *Martha* |
| **Pluto** | God of the underworld | | *La Favola d'Orfeo* |
| **Pluton**  Tenor | God of the underworld, on earth called Aristée | | *Orphée aux Enfers* |
| **Plutus**  Baritone | A role in a masque played by Tomsky | | *Pique-Dame* |
| **Poet**  Baritone | | | *Louise* |
| **Poet Monk**  Tenor | | | *Le Jongleur de Notre Dame* |
| **Pogner, Veit**  Bass | Mastersinger, goldsmith, Eva's father. | 1st Bausewein; Burke, Griswold, Hotter, Kipnis, Mayr, Plançon, Staudigl I, Staudigl II, Tozzi | *Die Meistersinger* |
| **Poisson**  Tenor | of the Comedie Française | | *Adriana Lecouvreur* |
| **Police**  Chorus | | | *Le Postillion de Longjumeau, Tosca* |
| **Police Commissioner**  Bass | | | *Der Rosenkavalier* |
| **Policeman**  Bass | | | *The Boatswain's Mate* |
| **Policeman**  Speaker | | | *Porgy and Bess* |
| **Policemen (Two)**  Baritones | | | *Louise* |
| **Polish Commander**  Baritone | | | *Ivan Susanin* |

| CHARACTER | ROLE | SINGER | OPERA |
|---|---|---|---|
| **Polish Ladies** Chorus | | | *Boris Godunov* |
| **Polkan, General** Bass | | | *Le Coq d'Or* |
| **Pollione** Tenor | Proconsul of Rome in Gaul | | *Norma* |
| **Pollux** Tenor | King of Eos, Danea's father | | *Die Liebe der Danae* |
| **Polly Peachum** Soprano | | 1st Lavinia Fenton; Cibber, Dickons, Stephens | *The Beggar's Opera* |
| **Polovtsian Chiefs** Chorus | | | *Prince Igor* |
| **Polyxène** Soprano | Priam's daughter | | *Les Troyens* |
| **Pompeo** Baritone | | | *Benvenuto Cellini* |
| **Pong** Tenor | Supreme lord of the imperial kitchen | Curzi | *Turandot* (Puccini) |
| **Pontius Pilate** Bass | | | *Pilgrim's Progress* |
| **Pope Pius IV** Bass | | | *Palestrina* |
| **Populace** Chorus | | | *Un Ballo in Maschera, La Gioconda, Les Huguenots, Maritana* |
| **Porgy** Bass Baritone | A crippled poor man | 1st Todd Duncan; Warfield | *Porgy and Bess* |
| **Porter** From Chorus | | | *Manon* |
| **Pousette** Soprano | An actress | | *Manon* |
| **Powder Monkeys** Chorus | | | *Billy Budd* |
| **Preacher** | | | *The Wreckers* |
| **Prefect** Bass | | | *Linda di Chamounix* |
| **Prelates** Chorus | | | *Esther de Carpentras* |
| **Preziosilla** Mezzo-soprano | A gypsy | Miller, Simionato | *La Forza del Destino* |

| CHARACTER | ROLE | SINGER | OPERA |
|---|---|---|---|
| **Priam** Bass | King of Troy | | *Les Troyens* |
| **Priam's Ghost** Bass | | | *Les Troyens* |
| **Priest** | | | *Turandot* (Busoni) |
| **Priest** *See also* High Priest | | | |
| **Priestesses of Diana** Chorus | | | *Iphigénie en Tauride* |
| **Priests** Chorus | | | *L'Africaine, Rienzi, Tiefland, Die Zauberflöte* |
| **Priests (Two)** Tenor, Bass | | | *Die Zauberflöte* |
| **Priests (Three)** | | | *L'Assassinio nel Cattedrale* |
| **Priests and Priestesses** Chorus | | | *Aida, Norma* |
| **Priests of Neptune** Chorus | | | *Idomeneo* |
| **Priest's Son, The** Tenor | Khivria's lover | | *The Fair at Sorochintsky* |
| **Prima Donna** Soprano | Who plays Ariadne | | *Ariadne auf Naxos* |
| **Primrose Seller** Contralto | | | *Hugh the Drover* |
| **Prince** Tenor | Hypochondriac | Lloyd | *The Love for Three Oranges* |
| **Prince** Tenor | A traveller in Africa | | *Lulu* |
| **Prince de Bouillon** Bass | | 1st de Luca; Sammarco | *Adriana Lecouvreur* |
| **Prince Ottakar** *See* Ottakar, Prince | | | |
| **Princes and Princesses** Chorus | | | *Prince Igor* |

447

| CHARACTER | | ROLE | SINGER | OPERA |
|---|---|---|---|---|
| **Princess** | Soprano | Also Fire, also Le Rossignol | | *L'Enfant et Les Sortilèges* |
| **Princess** | Soprano | | Rappold | *Lobetanz* |
| **Princess** | Soprano | | Alda, Favero | *Marouf* |
| **Princess** | Contralto | Angelica's aunt | 1st Perini; Palombini, Claramae Turner | *Suor Angelica* |
| **Princess von Werdenberg** *See* Marschallin, The | | | | |
| **Princess de Bouillon** Mezzo-soprano | | In love with Maurizio | Elmo, Pederzini | *Adriana Lecouvreur* |
| **Prior, The** | Bass | | | *Le Jongleur de Notre Dame* |
| **Prisoner** | | | | *Maria Golovin* |
| **Prisoners** | Chorus | | | *Andrea Chénier, Fidelio, Prince Igor, Le Prophète* |
| **Private Soldier** Tenor | | | | *Friedenstag* |
| **Prodica** *See* Giovanni da Prodica | | | | |
| **Prophète, Le** *See* John of Leyden | | | | |
| **Proserpina** | | | | *La Favola d'Orfeo* |
| **Prunier** | Tenor | A poet | 1st Dominici | *La Rondine* |
| **Public Opinion** *See* Opinion Publique | | | | |
| **Publius** | Bass | Captain of the Praetorian guard | Edelmann | *La Clemenza di Tito* |
| **Puck** | Soprano | Oberon's runner | | *Oberon* |
| **Puppets (Four)** Soprano, Contralto, Tenor, Bass | | | | *Fête Galante* |

# THE CHARACTERS IN THE OPERAS

| CHARACTER | ROLE | SINGER | OPERA |
|---|---|---|---|
| **Puritans** Chorus | | | *I Puritani* |
| **Pylade** Tenor | Oreste's friend | 1st Legros; Nourrit, Weil | *Iphigénie en Tauride* |
| **Pythie, La** Soprano | | | *Eumenides* |
| **Queen** Mezzo-soprano | | | *Fête Galante* |
| **Queen Iceheart** Mezzo-soprano | | | *Švanda Dudák* |
| **Queen Mother of Samarkand** Soprano | A negress | | *Turandot* (Busoni) |
| **Queen of Sheba, The** Mezzo-soprano | | Lilli Lehmann, Malten | *Die Königin von Saba* |
| **Queen of Shemakha** Soprano | | Dobbs | *Le Coq d'Or* |
| **Queen of the Gypsies** Contralto | | | *The Bohemian Girl* |
| **Queen of the Night** Soprano | | 1st Josefa Hofer; Juch, Peters | *Die Zauberflöte* |
| **Quichotte, Don** Bass | Don Quixote | 1st Chaliapin; Vanni-Marcoux | *Don Quichotte* |
| **Quickly, Dame (or Mistress)** Contralto | | Homer | *Falstaff* |
| **Quinault** Bass | Of the Comédie Française | | *Adriana Lecouvreur* |
| **Quint's Ghost** Tenor | | 1st Pears | *The Turn of the Screw* |
| **Quixote** *See* Quichotte | | | |
| **Rachel** Soprano | Eleazar's daughter | 1st Falcon; Brandt, Easton, Krauss, Lilli Lehmann, Materna, Ponselle, Raisa, Stoltz, Viardot-Garcia, Vere | *La Juive* |

| CHARACTER | | ROLE | SINGER | OPERA |
|---|---|---|---|---|
| **Radames** | Tenor | Captain of the guard | 1st Mongini; Baum, Campanini, Caruso, Graziani, Jagel, Lauri-Volpi, Maas, Martinelli, Merli, del Monaco, Mullings, Pertile, Jean de Reszke, Slezak, Tamagno, Tucker, Vinay, Zenatello | *Aida* |
| **Rafaele** | Baritone | Camorrist leader | Danise, Sammarco, Czaplicki | *I Gioielli della Madonna* |
| **Ragman** | Bass | | Allin | *Louise* |
| **Ragpicker** Mezzo-soprano | | | | *Louise* |
| **Ragpickers** | Chorus | | | *Iris* |
| **Raimbaut** | Tenor | Minstrel | | *Robert le Diable* |
| **Raimondo** | Bass | Papal legate | | *Rienzi* |
| **Raimondo** *See* Raymond | | | | |
| **Rainette, La** | Tenor | The frog | | *L'Enfant et les Sortilèges* |
| **Rakewell** *See* Tom Rakewell | | | | |
| **Raleigh, Sir Walter** | Bass | Captain of the guard | | *Gloriana* |
| **Rambaldo** Baritone | | Wealthy Parisian | | *La Rondine* |
| **Ramfis** | Bass | High priest | 1st Medini; Didur, Moscona, Nanetti, Plançon, Edouard de Reszke, Tajo | *Aida* |
| **Ramiro** | Baritone | Muleteer | Cassell, Vieuille | *L'Heure Espagnole* |
| **Ramiro, Don** Tenor | | Prince of Salerno | Lloyd | *La Cenerentola* |
| **Ramon, Maître** Bass | | Mireille's father | | *Mireille* |

| CHARACTER | ROLE | SINGER | OPERA |
|---|---|---|---|
| **Ramphis**<br>*See* Ramfis | | | |
| **Rance, Jack**<br>Baritone | Sheriff | 1st Amato;<br>Borgioli, Franci,<br>Galeffi, Tibbett,<br>Weede | *La Fanciulla del<br>West* |
| **Rangoni** Bass | A Jesuit | | *Boris Godunov* |
| **Raoul de Nangis**<br>Tenor | Huguenot nobleman | 1st Nourrit;<br>Campanini, Caruso,<br>Dippel, Lauri-<br>Volpi, Maas, Mario,<br>Martinelli, Nicolini,<br>Niemann, Jean de<br>Reszke, Wachtel | *Les Huguenots* |
| **Ratcliffe, Lt.** Bass | | | *Billy Budd* |
| **Ratmir** Contralto | Oriental prince,<br>suitor to Ludmilla | | *Russlan and Ludmilla* |
| **Raymond** Baritone | Chaplain of<br>Lammermoor | | *Lucia di Lammermoor* |
| **Reapers** Chorus | | | *Eugene Onegin* |
| **Recorder of<br>Norwich** Bass | | | *Gloriana* |
| **Recruits** Chorus | | | *Její Pastorkyňa*<br>(*Jenufa*) |
| **Rector**<br>*See* Horace Adams | | | |
| **Red Whiskers**<br>Tenor | An impressed sea-<br>man | | *Billy Budd* |
| **Redburn, Mr.**<br>Baritone | First lieutenant | | *Billy Budd* |
| **Registrar**<br>*See* Official<br>Registrar | | | |
| **Regnard, Baron**<br>Baritone | | Renan | *He Who Gets<br>Slapped* |
| **Regina** Soprano | Schwalb's daughter | | *Mathis der Maler* |
| **Regina Giddens**<br>Soprano | | Lewis | *Regina* |
| **Reich, Frau**<br>Mezzo-soprano | Mrs. Page | | *Die Lustigen Weiber<br>von Windsor* |

| CHARACTER | | ROLE | SINGER | OPERA |
|---|---|---|---|---|
| **Reich, Herr** | Bass | Mr. Page | Gassier | *Die Lustigen Weiber von Windsor* |
| **Reinmar von Zweter** | Bass | Knight and Minnesinger | | *Tannhäuser* |
| **Reiza** *See* Rezia | | | | |
| **Relatives** | Chorus | | | *Madama Butterfly, Lucia di Lammermoor* |
| **Remondado, El** | Tenor | A smuggler | de Paolis, Renan | *Carmen* |
| **Renato** | Baritone | The governor's secretary, Amelia's husband (Anckarström) | Bechi, Gobbi, Sved | *Un Ballo in Maschera* |
| **Repela** | Bass | Valet to the Magistrate | Hesch | *Der Corregidor* |
| **Representative of the Sailors** | Speaker | | | *Christophe Colomb* |
| **Retainers** | Chorus | | | *Lucia di Lammermoor* |
| **Retz, De** | Baritone | | | *Les Huguenots* |
| **Rezia** | Soprano | Daughter of Haroun el Rashid | 1st Paton; Brouwenstijn, Flagstad, Goltz, Anni Konetzni, Milanov, Müller, Pederzini, Ponselle, Seidl-Krauss, Tietjens, Ugalde, Wagner | *Oberon* |
| **Rhadames** *See* Radames | | | | |
| **Ribbing, Count** *See* Samuele | | | | |
| **Riccardo** | Tenor | Count of Warwick (Gustavus III) | Bjoerling, Bonci, Borgioli, Caruso, Gigli, Martinelli, Peerce, Jean de Reszke, di Stefano, Tamagno, Vroons | *Un Ballo in Maschera* |

| CHARACTER | ROLE | SINGER | OPERA |
|---|---|---|---|
| **Riccardo, Don** Tenor | The King's squire | | *Ernani* |
| **Riccardo** *See* Richard Forth, Sir | | | |
| **Riccardo Accolai, Count** Tenor | Visitor | | *I Quattro Rusteghi* |
| **Rich, Lady Penelope** Soprano | Sister of Essex | | *Gloriana* |
| **Richard Forth, Sir** Baritone | Puritan | 1st Tamburini; Beck, Galassi, Gerster, Ronconi, Panerai | *I Puritani* |
| **Richtofen** | Saxon officer | | *Der Bettelstudent* |
| **Riedinger** Bass | Rich Lutheran | | *Mathis der Maler* |
| **Rienzi** *See* Cola Rienzi | | | |
| **Rigoletto** Baritone | The Duke's jester, Gilda's father | 1st Vanesi; Baklanov, Basiola, Brownlee, Formichi, Franci, Galassi, Gobbi, Lassalle, de Luca, Merrill, Renaud, Ronconi, Ruffo, Sammarco, Scotti, Schwarz, Stabile, Warren, Weede | *Rigoletto* |
| **Rinuccio** Tenor | Zita's nephew, 24, in love with Lauretta | Conley, Crimi, Davies, Johnson, T. Burke | *Gianni Schicchi* |
| **Roaring Boys and Whores** Chorus | | | *The Rake's Progress* |
| **Robbins** Tenor | | | *Porgy and Bess* |
| **Robert** Bass | | | *Hugh the Drover* |
| **Robert** Tenor | Son of the Devil, Duke of Normandy | 1st Nourrit; Mario, Jean de Reszke, Schnorr von Carolsfield | *Robert le Diable* |

| CHARACTER | | ROLE | SINGER | OPERA |
|---|---|---|---|---|
| **Roberti** From Chorus | | Executioner | | *Tosca* |
| **Roberto** | Bass | French Soldier | | *I Vespri Siciliani* |
| **Robespierre** | Tenor | | 1st Witt | *Dantons Tod* |
| **Robinson, Count** | Bass | An English lord | | *Il Matrimonio Segreto* |
| **Rocco** | Bass | Chief jailer | 1st Rothe; Braun, Formes, Kipnis, Staudigl II | *Fidelio* |
| **Rocco** | Bass | Camorrist | | *I Gioielli della Madonna* |
| **Roche, La** | Bass | Theater director | Hotter | *Capriccio* |
| **Roderigo** | Tenor | Venetian gentleman | | *Otello* |
| **Rodolfo** | Tenor | Starving young poet | Bonci, Borgioli, Caruso, Conley, Cunningham, Gigli, Hislop, Jagel, Kiepura, Lauri-Volpi, Martin, Martinelli, McCormack, Peerce, Pertile, Poleri, di Stefano, Sullivan, Tagliavini, Tucker | *La Bohème* |
| **Rodolfo** | Tenor | In love with Luisa, son of Count Walter | | *Luisa Miller* |
| **Rodolpho, Count** | Bass | Lord of the castle | Faure, Foli, Gassier, Reeves, Edouard de Reszke | *La Sonnambula* |
| **Rodrig** | Bass | Athlete (also plays Animal Tamer) | | *Lulu* |
| **Rodrigo** | Baritone | Marquis of Posa | 1st Faure; de Luca, Merrill | *Don Carlos* |
| **Rodriguez** | Tenor | Admirer of Dulcinée | | *Don Quichotte* |
| **Roi d'Ys, Le** | Bass | King of Ys | | *Le Roi d'Ys* |
| **Romans** | Chorus | | | *Nerone, Rienzi* |
| **Romantics** | Chorus | | | *The Love for Three Oranges* |
| **Romeo** | Contralto | A Montague in love with Giulietta | 1st Giuditta Grisi; Viardot-Garcia, Wagner | *I Capuletti ed I Montecchi* |

| CHARACTER | | ROLE | SINGER | OPERA |
|---|---|---|---|---|
| **Roméo** | Tenor | A Montague, enemy to the Capulets | 1st Michot; Alvarez, Ansseau, Capoul, Crooks, Gigli, Hislop, Mario Muratore, Jean de Reszke, Saléza | *Roméo et Juliette* |
| **Rosa** | Soprano | | Zerr | *Faust* (Spohr) |
| **Rosa Mamai** | Mezzo-soprano | Federico's mother | 1st Fraces; Stignani, Pederzini | *L'Arlesiana* |
| **Rosalia** | Contralto | | | *Tiefland* |
| **Rosalinda** | Soprano | Eisenstein's wife | Gueden, Hurley, Resnik, Welitsch | *Die Fledermaus* |
| **Rosario** | Soprano | A lady in love with Fernando | 1st Fitziu; Carbone | *Goyescas* |
| **Roschana** | Speaker | Almanzor's wife | | *Oberon* |
| **Rose** | Soprano | An English lady | | *Lakmé* |
| **Rose** | Soprano | | | *Le Postillion de Longjumeau* |
| **Rossetta** | Soprano | | Billington, Stephens | *Love in a Village* |
| **Rosette** | Soprano | An actress | | *Manon* |
| **Rosina** | Mezzo-soprano | Dr. Bartolo's ward | 1st Giorgi-Righetti; Alboni, de los Angeles, Callas, Carvalho, Dickons, Fodor-Mainvielle, Fornia-Labey, Galli-Curci, Hempel, Holman, Lessugg, Macbeth, Malibran, Melba, Munsel, Mignon, Nevada, Patti, Peters, Phillips, Pons, Schwarzkopf, Sembrich, Simionato, Sontag, Luisa Tetrazzini, Trebelli, Tuminia, Viardot-Garcia, van Zandt | *Il Barbiere di Siviglia* |
| **Rossignol, Le** | Soprano | *Also plays* Fire *and* The Princess | | *L'Enfant et les Sortilèges* |

| CHARACTER | ROLE | SINGER | OPERA |
|---|---|---|---|
| **Rossignol, Le** Soprano | The Nightingale | | *Le Rossignol* |
| **Rossweisse** Soprano *or* Mezzo-soprano | A Valkyr | | *Die Walküre* |
| **Roucher** Bass | Andrea's friend | | *Andrea Chénier* |
| **Rouvel, Baron** Tenor | | | *Fedora* |
| **Rowan** Soprano | Nurse (*Called Pamela Wilton in Acts I and II*) | | *Let's Make an Opera* |
| **Rozenn** Soprano | The king's daughter | Alda | *Le Roi d'Ys* |
| **Rubria** Mezzo-soprano | Vestal virgin, secretly a Christian | 1st Bertana; Stignani | *Nerone* |
| **Rudolf II, Kaiser** Bass *Also* Ferdinand, *also* The Sun | | | *Die Harmonie der Welt* |
| **Rudolph** Tenor | Captain of the guard | | *Guillaume Tell* |
| **Rudolph** *See also* Rodolfo | | | |
| **Ruedi** Tenor | Fisherman | | *Guillaume Tell* |
| **Ruggero** Tenor | Young man | 1st Schipa; Gigli | *La Rondine* |
| **Ruggiero** Baritone | Provost | | *La Juive* |
| **Ruiz** Tenor | Manrico's soldier | Grazzi | *Il Trovatore* |
| **Rusalka** Soprano | | Brouwenstijn | *Rusalka* |
| **Russian Sentry** Speaker | | | *Háry János* |
| **Russlan** Bass | | 1st Petrov | *Russlan and Ludmilla* |
| **Rustighello** Tenor | Serving Alfonso d'Este | | *Lucrezia Borgia* |
| **Ruy Gomez di Silva, Don** Bass | Spanish grandee | Mayr | *Ernani* |
| **Saamcheddine, Princess** Soprano | | 1st Davelli; Favero, Alda | *Marouf* |
| **Sachs** *See* Hans Sachs | | | |

| CHARACTER | ROLE | SINGER | OPERA |
|---|---|---|---|
| **Sacristan** Baritone | | Baccaloni, Corena, Renan | *Tosca* |
| **Sadko** Tenor | Singer | | *Sadko* |
| **Saffi** Soprano | Czipra's foster daughter | | *Zigeunerbaron* |
| **Sailor** Tenor | | | *Dido and Aeneas* |
| **Sailor** Tenor | Returned after fifteen years | 1st Legrand; Kreuger, Malipiero, Ostertag, Schiffler | *Le Pauvre Matelot* |
| **Sailor** Tenor | | Reiss | *Tristan und Isolde* |
| **Sailors** Chorus | | | *L'Africaine, Billy Budd, Dido and Aeneas, Der Fliegende Holländer, La Gioconda, Idomeneo, Lakmé, Marouf, Otello, Tristan und Isolde, Les Troyens* |
| **Saints** Double Chorus | | | *Four Saints in Three Acts* |
| **St. Bris** Baritone | Catholic nobleman | 1st Serda; Delmas, Faure, Foli, Kaschmann, Lassalle, Plançon, Edouard de Reszke, Scaria | *Les Huguenots* |
| **St. Chavez** Tenor | | 1st Embry Bonner | *Four Saints in Three Acts* |
| **St. Corentin** Bass | Patron of Ys | | *Le Roi d'Ys* |
| **St. Ignatius Loyola** Baritone | | 1st Edward Matthews | *Four Saints in Three Acts* |
| **St. Just** Bass | | 1st L. Weber | *Dantons Tod* |
| **St. Settlement** Soprano | | 1st Bertha Baker | *Four Saints in Three Acts* |
| **St. Therese I** Soprano | | 1st Beatrice Wayne | *Four Saints in Three Acts* |
| **St. Therese II** Contralto | | 1st B. Howard | *Four Saints in Three Acts* |
| **Sali** Soprano | Manz's son, as a child | | *A Village Romeo and Juliet* |

| CHARACTER | | ROLE | SINGER | OPERA |
|---|---|---|---|---|
| **Sali** | Tenor | Manz's son, in love with Vreli | | *A Village Romeo and Juliet* |
| **Salome** (The part requires both a Soprano and a Dancer) | Soprano | Herod's step-daughter | 1st Wittich; Ackté, Borkh, Cebotari, Curtin, Destinn, Djanel, Easton, Fremstad, Garden, Goltz, Gutheil-Schoder, Jeritza, Krusceniski, Lawrence, Birgit Nilsson, Shacklock, Varnay, Welitsch | *Salome* |
| **Salud** | Soprano | Gypsy in love with Paco | 1st Lillian Grenville; de los Angeles, Bori, Carré, dalla Rizza | *La Vida Breve* |
| **Salviati, Cardinal** | Bass | | | *Benvenuto Cellini* |
| **Sam** | Treble | Sweepboy, 8 (*called John in Acts I and II*) | | *Let's Make an Opera* |
| **Sam Polk** | Tenor | Susannah's brother | | *Susannah* |
| **Samaritana** | Soprano | Francesca's sister | | *Francesca da Rimini* |
| **Samiel** | Speaker | The wild huntsman (the Devil) | | *Der Freischütz* |
| **Samson** | Tenor | Hebrew hero | Caruso, Merli, del Monaco, Tamagno, Vinay | *Samson and Dalila* |
| **Samson** | Baritone | | 1st Harrell | *The Warrior* |
| **Samuel** *See* Léopold | | | | |
| **Samuele** | Bass | The governor's enemy (Count Ribbing) | Lorenzo Alvary | *Un Ballo un Maschera* |
| **Samurai** | Chorus | | | *Iris* |
| **Sancho** | Baritone | Don Quixote's squire | 1st Gresse; de Luca | *Don Quichotte* |
| **Sandman** | Soprano | Bringer of sleep to little children | | *Hänsel und Gretel* |

# THE CHARACTERS IN THE OPERAS

| CHARACTER | | ROLE | SINGER | OPERA |
|---|---|---|---|---|
| **Sandor Barinkay** | Tenor | | | *Zigeunerbaron* |
| **Sante** | Silent | Count Gil's servant | | *Il Segreto di Susanna* |
| **Santuzza** | Soprano | Village girl in love with Turiddu | 1st Bellincioni; Barbieri, Brouwenstijn, Callas, Calvé, Destinn, Eames, Easton, Fremstad, Gay, Goltz, Jeritza, Kronold, Labia, Masiani, Matzenauer, Milanov, Neway, Ponselle, Shuard, Varnay | *Cavalleria Rusticana* |
| **Sapho** | Soprano | | 1st Viardot-Garcia; Krauss | *Sapho* (Gounod) |
| **Sapho** | Soprano | | Bellincioni, Calvé, Garden | *Sapho* (Massenet) |
| **Sarastro** | Bass | High priest of Isis and Osiris | 1st Gerl; Bender, Foli, Formes, Kipnis, Petrov, Radford, Staudigl, Tozzi | *Die Zauberflöte* |
| **Sarvaor, Uncle** | Bass | | 1st Cotreuil; d'Angelo | *La Vida Breve* |
| **Satraps** | Chorus | | | *Semiramide* |
| **Saturn** *Also plays* Tansur | Bass | | | *Die Harmonie der Welt* |
| **Satyavan** | Tenor | Woodman | | *Savitri* |
| **Satyrs** | Chorus | | | *Fête Galante, Les Troyens* |
| **Savitri** | Soprano | Satyavan's wife | | *Savitri* |
| **Savoyard** | Mezzo-soprano | | | *Fedora* |
| **Savoyards** | Chorus | | | *Linda di Chamounix* |
| **Scaramuccio** | Tenor | | Manton | *Ariadne auf Naxos* |

| CHARACTER | ROLE | SINGER | OPERA |
|---|---|---|---|
| **Scarpia, Baron** Baritone | Chief of police | 1st Giraldoni; Baklanov, Cassell, Formichi, Franci, Galeffi, Gobbi, London, Rothmuller, Sammarco, Scotti, Stabile, Taddei, Tibbett, Uhde, Warren, Weede | *Tosca* |
| **Schaunard** Baritone | Starving young musician | Cehanovsky, Renan | *La Bohème* |
| **Schigolch** Bass | Old man | | *Lulu* |
| **Schikaneder** Baritone | Opera manager | Bispham | *Der Schauspieldirektor* |
| **Schlemil** Bass | Giulietta's lover | | *Les Contes d'Hoffmann* |
| **Schmidt** Baritone | Jailer | | *Andrea Chénier* |
| **Schmidt** Tenor | Le Bailli's friend | | *Werther* |
| **Schneidebart** Baritone | Barber | | *Die Schweigsame Frau* |
| **Scholar** Silent | | | *Der Rosenkavalier* |
| **Schön, Doctor** Baritone | An editor | Stig | *Lulu* |
| **Schoolboy** Contralto | Gymnasiast, *also plays* Wardrobe Mistress | | *Lulu* |
| **Schoolboys** Chorus | | | *Der Wildschütz* |
| **Schouisky** *See* Schuisky | | | |
| **Schtschelkalov** *See* Shchelkalov | | | |
| **Schuisky, Wassili Ivanovitsh** Tenor | Boyard, ambitious to become Tsar | Bada, Franke, Kullmann, de Paolis | *Boris Godunov* |
| **Schwalb, Hans** Tenor | Peasant leader | | *Mathis der Maler* |
| **Schwanda the Bagpiper** Baritone | Švanda Dudák | | *Švanda Dudák* |

| CHARACTER | ROLE | SINGER | OPERA |
|---|---|---|---|
| **Schwertleite** Soprano or Mezzo-soprano | A Valkyr | Madeira | *Die Walküre* |
| **Sciarrone** Bass | Gendarme | Cehanovsky | *Tosca* |
| **Scindia** Baritone | | 1st Lassalle; Ancona | *Le Roi de Lahore* |
| **Scipio** Speaker | A small boy | | *Porgy and Bess* |
| **Scribe** From Chorus | | | *Tosca* |
| **Scrivener** Tenor | | | *Khovantschina* |
| **Sculptor** Baritone | | | *Louise* |
| **Sculptor Monk** Bass | | | *Le Jongleur de Notre Dame* |
| **Scythians** Chorus | | | *Iphigénie en Tauride* |
| **Sea Nymph** Soprano | | | *Oberon* |
| **Sebastiano** Baritone | Rich land owner | | *Tiefland* |
| **Secret Police Agent** Bass | | Renan | *The Consul* |
| **Secretary** *See* Shchelkalov | | | |
| **Secretary** Mezzo-soprano | | 1st Powers | *The Consul* |
| **Secretary** Silent | | | *Palestrina* |
| **Sedley, Mrs.** Mezzo-soprano | Rentier, widow of an East India Company's factor | 1st Valetta Jacopi | *Peter Grimes* |
| **Selika** Soprano | Captured African queen | 1st Sass; Barrientos, Brandt, Caniglia, Fremstad, Anni Konetzni, Lucca, Materna, Matzenauer, Nordica, Ponselle, Rasa, Ternina | *L'Africaine* |
| **Selim** Speaker | The pasha | | *Die Entführung aus dem Serail* |
| **Sellem** Tenor | Auctioneer | 1st Hugues Cuenod; Franke | *The Rake's Progress* |

| CHARACTER | | ROLE | SINGER | OPERA |
|---|---|---|---|---|
| **Selva** | Bass | Officer of the guard | | *Masaniello* |
| **Sélysette** Mezzo-soprano | | Former wife of Barbe-bleu | | *Ariane et Barbe-Bleue* |
| **Semele** | Soprano | A queen, formerly loved by Jupiter | | *Die Liebe der Danae* |
| **Semiramide** Soprano | | Queen of Babylon | Alboni, Fodor-Mainvielle, Grisi, Krauss, Scalchi, Sontag, Tietjens | *Semiramide* |
| **Senators** | Chorus | | | *La Gioconda* |
| **Senta** | Soprano | Daland's daughter | 1st Schröder-Devrient; Borkh, Corsi, Destinn, Flagstad, Hastreiter, Juch, Leider, Marchesi, Moody, Murska, Osborn, Seidl-Krauss, Stehle, Sucher, Varnay | *Der Fliegende Holländer* |
| **Sentry** | Tenor | | | *Pskovityanka* |
| **Serena** | Contralto | | | *I Gioielli della Madonna* |
| **Serena** | Soprano | Robbins' wife | | *Porgy and Bess* |
| **Sergeant** | Bass | | | *Friedenstag* |
| **Sergeant** | Baritone | | | *Hugh the Drover* |
| **Sergeant** From Chorus | | | | *Manon* |
| **Sergeant** From Chorus | | | | *Tosca* |
| **Sergeant of Archers** | Bass | | | *Manon Lescaut* |
| **Sergio** | Baritone | Footman | | *Fedora* |
| **Serpina** | Soprano | Uberto's servant | 1st Laura-Monti; Easton, Fleisher, Galli-Marie, Sayao | *La Serva Padrona* |
| **Servant** From Chorus | | | | *Arabella* |
| **Servant** From Chorus | | | | *Un Ballo in Maschera* |

| CHARACTER | ROLE | SINGER | OPERA |
|---|---|---|---|
| **Servant**<br>From Chorus | | | *Christophe Colomb* |
| **Servant** | | | *Maria Golovin* |
| **Servant** | Silent | | *Palestrina* |
| **Servant** | Baritone | of Nicias | *Thaïs* |
| **Servants** | Chorus | | *Adriana Lecouvreur, Andrea Chénier, Der Barbier von Bagdad, Le Coq d'Or, Falstaff, La Forza del Destino, Die Frau ohne Schatten, Die Liebe der Danae, The Love for Three Oranges, Luisa Miller, Martha, Mignon, Madama Butterfly, Pique-Dame, The Rake's Progress, Rigoletto, La Traviata, Der Wildschütz, Wozzeck* |
| **Servants (Two)**<br>Baritones | | | *Don Quichotte* |
| **Servants (Four)**<br>Tenors, Basses | of the Marschallin | | *Der Rosenkavalier* |
| **Servants (Eight)**<br>Four Tenors,<br>Four Basses | | | *Capriccio* |
| **Servants of Aithra (Two)**<br>Soprano,<br>Mezzo-soprano | | | *Die Aegyptische Helena* |
| **Servilia** | Soprano | Wife of Sextus | *La Clemenza di Tito* |
| **Sesto**<br>*See* Sextus | | | |
| **Sextus** | Contralto | Young patrician of Rome | *La Clemenza di Tito* |
| **Shades of Trojans**<br>Chorus | | | *Die Aegyptische Helena* |

| CHARACTER | | ROLE | SINGER | OPERA |
|---|---|---|---|---|
| **Shadow, Nick** *See* Nick Shadow | | | | |
| **Shaklovity, Boyard** | Baritone | | | *Khovantschina* |
| **Sharpers** | Chorus | | | *Manon* |
| **Sharpless** | Baritone | United States Consul at Nagasaki | 1st de Luca; Brownlee, Paci, Renan, Scotti | *Madama Butterfly* |
| **Shchelkalov** | Baritone | Clerk of the Douma (the parliament) | Cehanovsky | *Boris Godunov* |
| **Shellfish Seller** | Bass | | | *Hugh the Drover* |
| **Shepherd** | Tenor | | | *Oedipus Rex* |
| **Shepherd** | Tenor | | Franke, Reiss | *Tristan und Isolde* |
| **Shepherd** *See also* Young Shepherd | | | | |
| **Shepherd Boy** | Contralto | | Evans, Glaz | *Tosca* |
| **Shepherds (Three)** | Tenor, Baritone and Bass | | | *Pilgrim's Progress* |
| **Shepherds (Four)** | Tenor, Baritone, Two Basses | | | *Daphne* |
| **Shepherds** | Chorus | | | *L'Enfant et les Sortilèges, Les Troyens, The Wreckers* |
| **Sherasmin** | Baritone | Sir Huon's squire | | *Oberon* |
| **Sheriff** | Bass | | | *Martha* |
| **Shillem** | Tenor | | | *Debora e Jaele* |
| **Shining Ones (Three)** | Soprano, Mezzo-soprano, Contralto | | | *Pilgrim's Progress* |
| **Shopkeepers** | Chorus | | | *La Bohème, Iris* |

| CHARACTER | ROLE | SINGER | OPERA |
|---|---|---|---|
| **Showman** Baritone | | | *Hugh the Drover* |
| **Showman** Tenor | | | *The Village Romeo and Juliet* |
| **Shuisky** *See* Schuisky | | | |
| **Sicilians** Chorus | | | *I Vespri Siciliani* |
| **Sid** Baritone | Butcher's assistant | | *Albert Herring* |
| **Sid** Baritone | | | *La Fanciulla del West* |
| **Siebel** Mezzo-soprano | Youth in love with Marguerite | 1st Faivre; Bible, Scalchi | *Faust* |
| **Siegfried** Tenor | Posthumous son of Siegmund and Sieglinde | 1st Betz; Althouse, Max Alvary, Berger, Burgstaller, Hartmann, Lorenz, Melchior, Mullings, Niemann, Svanholm, Unger | *Das Ring des Nibelungen* |
| **Sieglinde** Soprano | Hunding's wife, Siegfried's sister | 1st Thoma; Ackté, Bampton, Borkh, Caron, Eames, Easton, Fisher, Flagstad, Fornia-Labey, Fremstad, Gadski, Jeritza, Juch, Klafsky, Lilli Lehmann, Lotte Lehmann, Lemnitz, Marchesi, Moody, Morena, Müller, Resnik, Rethberg, Saltzmann-Stevens, Seidl-Krauss, Traubel, Varnay, Wittich | *Die Walküre* |
| **Siegmund** Tenor | Mortal son of the god Wotan | 1st Vogl; Althouse, Max Alvary, Berger, van Dyke, Hyde, Lorenz, Melchior, Niemann, Saléza, Schmedes, Schott, Svanholm, Urlus, Völker | *Die Walküre* |

| CHARACTER | ROLE | SINGER | OPERA |
|---|---|---|---|
| **Siegrune** Soprano or Mezzo-soprano | A Valkyr | Glaz | *Die Walküre* |
| **Silberklang, Madame** Soprano | | Cavalieri | *Der Schauspieldirektor* |
| **Silla** Mezzo-soprano | Palestrina's pupil | | *Palestrina* |
| **Silva** *See* Ruy Gomez di Silva, Don | | | |
| **Silvano** Baritone | A sailor (Cristian) | Cehanovsky | *Un Ballo in Maschera* |
| **Silvio** Baritone | A villager in love with Nedda | Ancona, Cehanovsky, Svanholm, Panerai, Werrenrath, Zenatello | *I Pagliacci* |
| **Simon** Tenor | Polish beggar student | | *Der Bettelstudent* |
| **Simon** Bass | | 1st G. Hamm | *Dantons Tod* |
| **Simon** Bass-baritone | Marina's husband | | *I Quattro Rusteghi* |
| **Simon Boccanegra** Baritone | Plebeian, elected Doge | Colzani, Gobbi, Tibbett, Warren | *Simon Boccanegra* |
| **Simon Mago** Baritone | Sorcerer | 1st Journet; Maugeri | *Nerone* |
| **Simon Magus** Baritone | | | *Pilgrim's Progress* |
| **Simona** Soprano | | | *Zaza* |
| **Simone** Bass | Dead Buoso's cousin, 70 | Lorenzo Alvary | *Gianni Schicchi* |
| **Simpleton, The** Tenor | | Franke | *Boris Godunov* |
| **Singer** Soprano | The first singer of the opera | | *Cardillac* |
| **Singer** Tenor | | Baum | *Der Rosenkavalier* |
| **Singer** Mezzo-soprano | | | *Turandot* (Busoni) |
| **Singer** Baritone | | | *La Vida Breve* |
| **Singers** Chorus | of the Papal Chapel | | *Palestrina* |

| CHARACTER | ROLE | SINGER | OPERA |
|---|---|---|---|
| **Singers (Five)** Two Tenors, Three Basses | from the Chapel of St. Maria Maggiore | | *Palestrina* |
| **Sirens** Chorus | | | *Mefistofele, Russlan and Ludmilla, Tannhäuser* |
| **Sirieux, De** Baritone | French diplomat | | *Fedora* |
| **Sisera** Tenor | Enemy of the Jews | 1st Sample; Folco, Parmeggiani | *Debora e Jaele* |
| **Sister** *See the opera* Suor Angelica | | | |
| **Sisters** Chorus | | | *Suor Angelica* |
| **Sixtus Beckmesser** *See* Beckmesser, Sixtus | | | |
| **Skula** Bass | Gudok player | | *Prince Igor* |
| **Slammekin, Mrs.** From Chorus | A lady of the town | | *The Beggar's Opera* |
| **Slave** Contralto | of Francesca | | *Francesca da Rimini* |
| **Slave Merchant** Pantomime | | | *Djamileh* |
| **Slaves** Chorus | | | *Die Aegyptische Helena, Le Coq d'Or, Die Entführung aus dem Serail, Khovantschina, Oberon, Prince Igor Semiramide, Turandot* (Busoni), *Die Zauberflöte* |
| **Slender** *See* Spärlich | | | |
| **Slim Girl** Soprano | | | *A Village Romeo and Juliet* |
| **Smeraldina** Mezzo-soprano | Fata Morgana's servant | Bible, Evans | *The Love for Three Oranges* |
| **Smugglers** Chorus | | | *Carmen, Hubička* |
| **Snyegurotchka** Soprano | The Snow-Maiden, daughter of Winter and Spring | Bori | *Snyegurotchka* |

467

| CHARACTER | | ROLE | SINGER | OPERA |
|---|---|---|---|---|
| **Sobinjin** | Tenor | Soldier, Antonida's bridegroom | | *Ivan Susanin* |
| **Sofa** | Child | Le Canapé | | *L'Enfant et Les Sortilèges* |
| **Soldier** | Baritone | Brother of the girl Faust betrayed | | *Doktor Faustus* |
| **Soldier, First** Baritone | | | | *Les Troyens* |
| **Soldier, Second** Bass | | | | *Les Troyens* |
| **Soldiers** | Chorus | | | *L'Africaine Aida, Andrea Chénier, Il Barbiere di Siviglia, La Bohème, Carmen, Dalibor, La Damnation de Faust, Debora, Doktor Faustus, L'Elisir d'Amore, Faust, Fidelio, La Figlia del Reggimento, La Forza de Destino, Friedenstag, Guillaume Tell, Die Harmonie der Welt, Háry János, Hugh the Drover, Les Huguenots, Idomeneo, Ivan Susanin, La Juive, Lakmé, The Love for Three Oranges, Manon, Maritana, Marouf, Masaniello, Mathis der Maler, Otello (Verdi), Prince Igor, Le Prophète, Der Prozess, Rienzi, Le Roi d'Ys, Roméo et Juliette, Tosca, Turandot (Busoni), Il Trovatore, I Vespri Siciliani, Wozzeck* |

| CHARACTER | ROLE | SINGER | OPERA |
|---|---|---|---|
| **Soldiers (Two)** Basses | | | *Salomé* |
| **Soldiers of Babylon** Chorus | | | *Nabucco* |
| **Soldiers of the Commonwealth** Chorus | | | *I Puritani* |
| **Solo Contralto** From Chorus | | | *Les Choëphores* |
| **Solo Soprano** From Chorus | | | *Les Choëphores* |
| **Solomon** *See* King Solomon | | | |
| **Somarona** Bass | Orchestra conductor | | *Béatrice et Bénédict* |
| **Song Writer** Baritone | | | *Louise* |
| **Sonora** Baritone | A miner | | *La Fanciulla del West* |
| **Sophie** Soprano | Daughter of von Faninal | 1st Minnie Nast; Berger, Conner, Dux, della Casa, Gueden, Peters, Schumann, Schwarzkopf, Steber | *Der Rosenkavalier* |
| **Sophie** Soprano | Charlotte's sister | 1st Forster; Gluck | *Werther* |
| **Sophie Brook** Soprano | Age 10, *called* Monica *in Acts I and II* | | *Let's Make an Opera* |
| **Sorceress** Mezzo-soprano | | Simionato | *Dido and Aeneas* |
| **Sourin** Bass | Officer | | *Pique-Dame* |
| **Spalanzani** Tenor | Inventor of a mechanical doll | | *Les Contes d'Hoffmann* |
| **Sparafucile** Bass | A professional assassin | Foli, Hines, Moscona, Siepi | *Rigoletto* |
| **Spärlich, Junker** Tenor | Slender, unsuccessful suitor to Ann Page | | *Die Lustigen Weiber von Windsor* |

| CHARACTER | ROLE | SINGER | OPERA |
|---|---|---|---|
| **Spectators, Ten Reasonable**<br>Five Tenors, Five Basses | | | *The Love for Three Oranges* |
| **Spectre de Clytemnestra, Le**<br>Mezzo-soprano | | | *Eumenides* |
| **Spinellocchio, Maestro**   Bass | Doctor | | *Gianni Schicchi* |
| **Spirit**   Soprano | | | *Dido and Aeneas* |
| **Spirit Messenger**<br>Baritone | | | *Die Frau ohne Schatten* |
| **Spirit of the Forest**<br>Tenor | | | *Snyegurotchka* |
| **Spirit of the Masque**   Tenor | | | *Gloriana* |
| **Spirits of Trees**<br>Chorus | | | *The Immortal Hour* |
| **Spirit Voice**<br>Mezzo-soprano | | | *The Immortal Hour* |
| **Spirits**   Chorus | | | *Die Frau ohne Schatten* |
| **Splendiano**   Tenor | Secretary to the prince | Potel | *Djamileh* |
| **Spoletta**   Tenor | Police agent | de Paolis | *Tosca* |
| **Sportin' Life**<br>Tenor | Dope peddler | 1st Bubbles; Long, Calloway (*written for* Calloway) | *Porgy and Bess* |
| **Spring**<br>Mezzo-soprano | | | *Snyegorochka* |
| **Springer**   Tenor | Manager of a theatrical troupe | | *Prodaná Nevěsta* |
| **Squeak**   Tenor | Ship's corporal | | *Billy Budd* |
| **Stallkeeper**<br>From Chorus | | | *Hugh the Drover* |
| **Starbemberg, Baron**   Baritone | | | *Die Harmonie der Welt* |

| CHARACTER | ROLE | SINGER | OPERA |
|---|---|---|---|
| **Stars, The**   Chorus | | | *Die Harmonie der Welt* |
| **Statue d'Athena, La**   Soprano, Mezzo-soprano and Contralto | A triple-voice role | | *Eumenides* |
| **Steersman**   Tenor | | Dippel | *Der Fliegende Holländer* |
| **Steffano Colonna**   Bass | Roman Patrician | Fischer | *Rienzi* |
| **Stella**   Soprano | Opera singer | 1st Isaac;  Fremstad, Hempel, Seefried, Teyte | *Les Contes d'Hoffman* |
| **Stella**   Soprano | | | *I Gioielli della Madonna* |
| **Stefanida Matuta, Boyardin**   Soprano | Olga's friend | | *Pskovityanka* |
| **Stephano**   Soprano | Romeo's page | Swarthout | *Roméo et Juliette* |
| **Steurman**   *See* Steersman | | | |
| **Stewa Buryja**   Tenor | Step brother of Laca | | *Její Pastorkyňa* (Jenufa) |
| **Steward**   Bass | | | *La Rondine* |
| **Storch, Hofkapell-meister Robert**   Baritone | Christine's husband | | *Intermezzo* |
| **Strange Children**   Chorus | | | *Die Frau ohne Schatten* |
| **Street Arab**   Soprano | | | *Louise* |
| **Street Folk**   Chorus | | | *Falstaff* |
| **Street Sweeper**   Mezzo-soprano | | | *Louise* |
| **Streltzy**   Chorus | Archers | | *Boris Godunov, Khovantschina* |
| **Streshniev**   Tenor | | | *Khovantschina* |

| CHARACTER | ROLE | SINGER | OPERA |
|---|---|---|---|
| **Stroh, Kapell-meister** Tenor | Storch's friend | | *Intermezzo* |
| **Stromminger** Bass | Wally's father | | *La Wally* |
| **Student** Speaker | | | *Háry János* |
| **Student** Tenor | | | *Louise* |
| **Student** Tenor | | | *Der Prozess* |
| **Students** Chorus | | | *La Bohème, La Damnation de Faust, Doktor Faustus, Faust, Les Huguenots, Manon, Mefistofele, La Rondine* |
| **Students (Three) from Krakov** Tenor, Two Basses | | | *Doktor Faustus* |
| **Students (Four) from Wittemberg** Tenors | | | *Doktor Faustus* |
| **Styx, John** Baritone | A fool | | *Orphée aux Enfers* |
| **Suky Tawdry** From Chorus | A lady of the town | | *The Beggar's Opera* |
| **Sulamith** Soprano | High priests' daughter | Lilli Lehmann, Rappold | *Die Königin von Saba* |
| **Sulpice** Bass | Sergeant of grenadiers | Baccaloni | *La Figlia del Reggimento* |
| **Sultan Miramoulin** Tenor | | | *Christophe Colomb* |
| **Sultan of Khaitan** Bass | | | *Marouf* |
| **Sun, The** Bass Also Rudolf II, and Ferdinand II | | | *Die Harmonie der Welt* |
| **Suor** *See proper name, as* Angelica, Suor | | | |
| **Superstition** Tenor | | | *Pilgrim's Progress* |
| **Surgeon** Tenor | | Cehanovsky | *La Forza del Destino* |
| **Susan** Soprano | | | *Hugh the Drover* |

| CHARACTER | | ROLE | SINGER | OPERA |
|---|---|---|---|---|
| **Susan B. Anthony** Soprano | | Leader in the cause for woman's suffrage | | *The Mother of Us All* |
| **Susanna** | Soprano | Later Kepler's wife, also Venus | | *Die Harmonie der Welt* |
| **Susanna** | Soprano | An old believer | | *Khovantschina* |
| **Susanna** | Soprano | Maid to Countess Almaviva, Figaro's bride | 1st Storace; Camporese, Catalani, Farrar, Gueden, Hurley, Lind, Milder, Moffo, Nordica, Paton, Peters, Sayao, Schick, Seefried, Sembrich, Sontag, Ugalde, Vestris, Wagner, Welitsch White | *Le Nozze di Figaro* |
| **Susanna, Countess** Soprano | | Gil's wife, 20 | Erminia Borghi, Bori, Olive Dyer, Farrar, Lipovska, Oltrabella, Vallin, White | *Il Segreto di Susanna* |
| **Susannah Polk** Soprano | | | Curtin | *Susanna* |
| **Suzanne** | Contralto | | | *Louise* |
| **Suzel** | Soprano | Farmer's daughter | 1st Calvé; Bori, Favero, Marengo, Magnoni | *L'Amico Fritz* |
| **Suzuki** Mezzo-soprano | | Cio-cio San's servant | 1st Giaconia; Bible, Evans, Gay, Homer, Lejeune, Miller, Novotna | *Madama Butterfly* |
| **Suzy** Mezzo-soprano | | Magda's friend | | *La Rondine* |
| **Svietozar** | Bass | Prince of Kiev, Ludmilla's father | | *Russlan and Ludmilla* |
| **Swallow** | Bass | A lawyer | 1st Brannigan | *Peter Grimes* |
| **Sylvester von Schaumberg** Tenor | | Army officer | | *Mathis der Maler* |

| CHARACTER | | ROLE | SINGER | OPERA |
|---|---|---|---|---|
| **Syndham, Lord** | Bass | British ambassador | | *Zar und Zimmermann* |
| **Tackleton** | Bass | Dot's employer, a toymaker | | *Das Heimchen am Herd* |
| **Taddeo** | Baritone | An old Italian | | *L'Italiana in Algeri* |
| **Taddeo** *See also* Tonio | | | | |
| **Tallan** | Tenor | | | *The Wreckers* |
| **Talpa** | Bass | Stevedore, 55 | Moscona | *Il Tabarro* |
| **Tamino** | Tenor | An Egyptian prince | 1st Schack; Gedda, Gudehus, Kraus, Tauber | *Die Zauberflöte* |
| **Tanato** | Baritone | Thanatos, God of death | | *Alceste* |
| **Tancredi** | Pantomine | A Christian knight | | *Il Combattimento di Tancredi e Clorinda* |
| **Tannhäuser** | Tenor | Knight and minne-singer, enthralled by Venus | 1st Tichatschek; Althouse, Alvarez, Max Alvary, Berger, Burrian, Dippel, van Dyke, Hartmann, Hoose, Kullmann, Melchior, Mullings, Niemann, Schmedes, Slezak, Vinay, Winkelmann | *Tannhäuser* |
| **Tansur** Also Saturn | Bass | | | *Die Harmonie der Welt* |
| **Tarquinius** | Baritone | Tyrant of Rome | | *The Rape of Lucretia* |
| **Tartaglia** | Bass | Minister | | *Turandot* (Busoni) |
| **Tartars** | Chorus | | | *Prince Igor* |
| **Tatyana** | Soprano | In love with Eugene | Amara, Brouwenstijn, Cross, Destinn, Lotte Lehmann, Lipovska, Lemnitz, Miller, Muzio, Welitsch | *Eugene Onegin* |

| CHARACTER | ROLE | SINGER | OPERA |
|---|---|---|---|
| **Taupe, Monsieur** Tenor | | | *Capriccio* |
| **Tavannes** Tenor | Catholic gentleman | | *Les Huguenots* |
| **Taven** Mezzo-soprano | Old woman | Ugalde | *Mireille* |
| **Tchaplitsky** Tenor | Gambler | | *Pique-Dame* |
| **Tchekalinsky** Tenor | Officer | | *Pique-Dame* |
| **Tchelkalov** *See* Shchelkalov | | | |
| **Tcherevik** Bass | Parassia's father | Pinza | *The Fair at Sorochintsky* |
| **Tcherevik's Friend** Bass | | | *The Fair at Sorochintsky* |
| **Tchernikovsky** Bass | Jesuit | | *Boris Godunov* |
| **Tchernomor** | Evil dwarf | | *Russlan and Ludmilla* |
| **Tebaldo** Soprano | Elisabeth's page | | *Don Carlos* |
| **Tebaldo** Tenor | French soldier | | *I Vespri Siciliani* |
| **Telea** Soprano | | 1st Varnay | *The Island God* |
| **Telemaco** Mezzo-soprano | Son of Ulisse | | *Il Ritorno d'Ulisse in Patria* |
| **Telramund** *See* Frederick of Telramund | | | |
| **Temple Gate- Keeper** Soprano or Tenor | | | *Die Frau ohne Schatten* |
| **Temple Virgins** Chorus | | | *Norma* |
| **Tempters (Four)** | | | *L'Assassinio nel Cattedrale* |
| **Tenebrun** From Chorus | | | *Don Quichotte* |
| **Tenor** Tenor Also Bacchus | | | *Ariadne auf Naxos* |

| CHARACTER | ROLE | SINGER | OPERA |
|---|---|---|---|
| **Tenor, The**   Tenor | Phaeton in Lully's opera | | *Cardillac* |
| **Teresa**   Soprano | Cellini's love, Balducci's daughter | 1st Dorus-Gras | *Benvenuto Cellini* |
| **Teresa**   Soprano | Miller, Amina's foster mother | | *La Sonnambula* |
| **Testo**   Narrator | | | *Il Combattimento di Tancredi e Clorinda* |
| **Thaddeus**   Tenor | | Maas | *The Bohemian Girl* |
| **Thaddeus Stevens** Tenor | | | *The Mother of Us All* |
| **Thaïs**   Soprano | A courtesan | 1st Sanderson; Edvina, Farrar, Favero, Garden, Jepson, Jeritza | *Thaïs* |
| **Thanatos** See Tanato | | | |
| **Theater Director** Bass | | | *Lulu* |
| **Theater Personnel** Chorus | | | *Cardillac* |
| **Theière, La**   Tenor | The tea pot | | *L'Enfant et les Sortilèges* |
| **Theologian**   Bass | | | *Doktor Faustus* |
| **Theophilus of Imola** Tenor | Italian bishop | | *Palestrina* |
| **Thessalians**   Chorus | | | *Iphigénie en Aulide* |
| **Thirza** Mezzo-soprano | Pascoe's wife, 22, in love with Mark | | *The Wreckers* |
| **Thisbe** Mezzo-soprano | Don Magnifico's daughter | | *La Cenerentola* |
| **Thoas**   Bass | The king of Scythia | Braun, Gassier | *Iphigénie en Tauride* |
| **Thomas à Becket** See Tommaso Becket | | | |
| **Thoré**   Baritone | Catholic gentleman | | *Les Huguenots* |
| **Thrasher, The**   Bass | | | *Der Prozess* |

| CHARACTER | | ROLE | SINGER | OPERA |
|---|---|---|---|---|
| **Tikhon Ivanovitch Kabanov** | Tenor | Katya's husband | | *Kata Kabanova* |
| **Tigellino** | Bass | | | *Nerone* |
| **Timorous** | Tenor | A neighbor | | *Pilgrim's Progress* |
| **Timur** | Bass | Blind, exiled Tartar king | Tajo | *Turandot* (Puccini) |
| **Tina Crome** | Soprano | Age 8, *called* Mavis *in Acts I and II* | | *Let's Make an Opera* |
| **Tinca** | Tenor | Stevedore, 35 | 1st Crimi | *Il Tabarro* |
| **Tio Lucas** | Baritone | A miller | 1st Demuth | *Der Corregidor* |
| **Tiresias** | Tenor | Blind seer | | *Antigonae* (Orff) |
| **Tiresias** | Bass | Blind soothsayer | | *Oedipus Rex* |
| **Tisbe** | Mezzo-soprano | | Evans | *La Cenerentola* |
| **Titania** | Speaker | Oberon's wife | | *Oberon* |
| **Titurel** | Bass | Father of Amfortas, former king | Kindermann, Witherspoon | *Parsifal* |
| **Titurelli** | Tenor | | | *Der Prozess* |
| **Titus** | Tenor | Emperor of Rome, 79–81 A.D. | Patzak | *La Clemenza di Tito* |
| **Toby** | Dancer | A mute | | *The Medium* |
| **Tokmakov, Prince Youry Ivanovitch** | Bass | Mayor of Pskov | | *Pskovityanka* |
| **Toldo Berardengo, Ser** | Tenor | Lawyer | | *Francesca da Rimini* |
| **Tom Cat** | Baritone | | | *L'Enfant et les Sortilèges* |
| **Tom Rakewell** | Tenor | The rake | 1st Rounseville; Conley, Lewis, Young | *The Rake's Progress* |
| **Tomaso** | Bass | The governor's enemy (Count Horn) | | *Un Ballo in Maschera* |
| **Tommaso** | Bass | Village elder | | *Tiefland* |
| **Tomasso Becket** | Bass | Archbishop of Canterbury | 1st Rossi-Lemeni | *L'Assassinio nel Cattedrale* |

| CHARACTER | | ROLE | SINGER | OPERA |
|---|---|---|---|---|
| **Tomes** | Baritone | Lucas' brother in law | | *Hubička* |
| **Tomsky, Count** | Baritone | | | *Pique-Dame* |
| **Tonio** | Tenor | Tyrolean peasant, Marie's lover | | *La Figlia del Reggimento* |
| **Tonio** | Baritone | A clown called Taddeo | 1st Maurel; Ancona, Bonelli, Campanari, Delmas, Formichi, Gobbi, Guarrera, McCormack, Merrill, Sammarco, Scotti, Warren | *I Pagliacci* |
| **Tonuelo** | Bass | Court messenger | | *Der Corregidor* |
| **Torchbearer** | Baritone | | | *Francesca da Rimini* |
| **Torchbearers** | Chorus | | | *Francesca da Rimini* |
| **Tormentilla** | Soprano | Daughter of Dipsacus, brought up on a diet of poisons | | *The Poisoned Kiss* |
| **Torquemada** | Tenor | Clock maker, husband of Concepcion | | *L'Heure Espagnole* |
| **Tosca, Floria** | Soprano | Celebrated singer in love with Mario | 1st Darclée; Albanese, Brouwenstijn, Borkh, Callas, Caniglia, Cavalieri, Cigna, Cobelli, Destinn, Eames, Edvina, Farrar, Fremstad, Goltz, Grandi, Jeritza, Kirsten, Labia, Lotte Lehmann, Marcel, Melis, Milanov, Muzio, Pacetti, Price, Scacciati, Steber, Tebaldi, Ternina, Varnay, Welitsch | *Tosca* |

| CHARACTER | | ROLE | SINGER | OPERA |
|---|---|---|---|---|
| **Toto** | Soprano | Dufresne's child | | *Zaza* |
| **Tourists** | Chorus | | | *Lakmé* |
| **Townspeople** | Chorus | | | *Carmen, Friedenstag, Hugh the Drover, Mignon, Peter Grimes* |
| **Toysellers** | Chorus | | | *Hugh the Drover* |
| **Trabucco** | Tenor | Muleteer | | *La Forza del Destino* |
| **Traders** | Chorus | | | *Pilgrim's Progress* |
| **Trainbearer** | Soprano | to Clytemnestra | | *Elektra* |
| **Tramps (Three)** | Tenor, Baritone and Bass | | | *Die Kluge* |
| **Trapes, Mrs.** | Mezzo-soprano | The tally woman | | *The Beggar's Opera* |
| **Travellers** | Chorus | | | *Manon* |
| **Travers, Ned** | Baritone | Former soldier | | *The Boatswain's Mate* |
| **Tree** | Bass | | | *L'Enfant et les Sortilèges* |
| **Trees** | Chorus | | | *L'Enfant et les Sortilèges* |
| **Trim** | Tenor | A miner | | *La Fanciulla del West* |
| **Triquet, Monsieur** | Tenor | | | *Eugene Onegin* |
| **Tristan** | Tenor | Cornish knight in love with Isolde | 1st Ludwig Schnorr von Carolsfield; Althouse, Max Alvary, Berger, Borgatti, Dalmorès, Gudehus, Hartmann, Kalisch, Lorenz, MacLennan, Melchior, Mullings, Niemann, Jean de Reszke, Schmedes, Svanholm, Urlus, Vinay, Vogl, Winkelmann | *Tristan und Isolde* |

| CHARACTER | ROLE | SINGER | OPERA |
|---|---|---|---|
| **Tristan de Mickleford, Lord** Bass | Harriett's cousin | | *Martha* |
| **Trojan Captains** Chorus | | | *Les Troyens* |
| **Trojan Captains (Two)** Baritone, Bass | | | *Les Troyens* |
| **Trojan Prisoners** Chorus | | | *Idomeneo* |
| **Trojan Soldier** Baritone | | | *Les Troyens* |
| **Trojan Soldiers** Chorus | | | *Les Troyens* |
| **Trottolo** Boy soprano | | | *Maria Golovin* |
| **Trouble** Silent | Cio-cio San's child | | *Madama Butterfly* |
| **Truchsess von Waldburg** Bass | Leader of the army | | *Mathis der Maler* |
| **Truffaldino** Bass | | Lorenzo Alvary | *Ariadne auf Naxos* |
| **Truffaldino** Tenor | Jester | | *The Love for Three Oranges* |
| **Truffaldino** Tenor | Chief eunuch | | *Turandot* (Busoni) |
| **Trulove** Bass | Anne's father | 1st Raffaele Arié | *The Rake's Progress* |
| **Trumpeter** From Chorus | | | *Hugh the Drover* |
| **Trumpeter** Bass Trombone | | | *The Love for Three Oranges* |
| **Tsar Berendey** Tenor | | | *Snyegurotchka* |
| **Turandot** Soprano | Daughter of Altoum | | *Turandot* (Busoni) |
| **Turandot, Princess** Soprano | Daughter of Altoum | 1st Raisa; Borkh, Callas, Cigna, Easton, Grob-Prandl, Jeritza, Muzio, Nemeth, Rysanek, Salvatini, Scacciati, Yeend | *Turandot* (Puccini) |

| CHARACTER | | ROLE | SINGER | OPERA |
|---|---|---|---|---|
| **Turiddu** | Tenor | Young soldier | 1st Stagno; Baum, Bjoerling, Conley, Lucia, McCormack, Masini, Peerce, Poleri, di Stefano, Tucker | Cavalleria Rusticana |
| **Turk, Baba The** See Baba the Turk | | | | |
| **Turkish Soldiers** | Chorus | | | Die Entführung aus dem Serail |
| **Turkish Women** | Chorus | | | Die Entführung aus dem Serail |
| **Turnkey** | Tenor | | | Hugh the Drover |
| **Tutor** | Bass | To Orest | | Elektra |
| **Tybalt** | Tenor | Capulet's nephew | | Roméo et Juliette |
| **Tyroleans** | Chorus | | | La Wally |
| **Uberto** | Bass | | 1st Gioacchino Corrado; d'Angelo, Baccaloni, Rossi-Lemeni | La Serva Padrona |
| **Ulisse** | Tenor | Ulysses, Greek hero | | Il Ritorno d'Ulisse in Patria |
| **Ulysses S. Grant** | Baritone | | | The Mother of Us All |
| **Ulrica** | Contralto | Fortune teller (Arvidson) | Anderson, Klose, Madeira, Matzenauer, Schalchi, Stignani, Thorborg | Un Ballo in Maschera |
| **Ulrich Grüsser** | Tenor | Kepler's assistant, later a soldier, also Mars | | Die Harmonie der Welt |
| **Ulrich Eisslinger** | Tenor | Mastersinger and grocer | | Die Meistersinger |
| **Undertaker** | Baritone | | | Porgy and Bess |
| **Undine** | Soprano | | Gadski | Undine (Lortzing) |
| **Upfold, Mr.** | Tenor | The mayor | | Albert Herring |

| CHARACTER | | ROLE | SINGER | OPERA |
|---|---|---|---|---|
| **Urbain** Mezzo-soprano | | Marguerite's page | | *Les Huguenots* |
| **Ursula** | Contralto | Hero's friend | | *Béatrice et Bénédict* |
| **Ursula** | Soprano | Riedinger's daughter, loved by Mathis | | *Mathis der Maler* |
| **Usher** | Tenor | | | *Pilgrim's Progress* |
| **Valentin** | Baritone | Marguerite's brother | 1st Reynald; Bonelli, Dufranne, de Luca, Maurel, del Puente, Renaud, Jean de Reszke, van Rooy, Santley, Thomas, Tibbett | *Faust* |
| **Valentine** | Soprano | In love with Raoul, betrothed to de Nevers | 1st Falcon; Borini, Cruvelli, Destinn, Juch, Krauss, Lind, Lucca, Materna, Christine Nilsson, Nordica, Raisa, Scacciati, Sembrich, Tietjens, Viardot-Garcia, Wagner | *Les Huguenots* |
| **Valkyr** *See the opera* Die Walküre | | | | |
| **Valzacchi** | Tenor | Scandalmonger | de Paolis | *Der Rosenkavalier* |
| **Vampire** From Chorus | | | | *Iris* |
| **Van Bett** | Bass | Burgomaster of Sardam | | *Zar und Zimmermann* |
| **Vanessa** | Soprano | Spinster | 1st Steber | *Vanessa* |
| **Vanja** | Contralto | Orphan adopted by Ivan | Leonova, Scalchi | *Ivan Susanin* |
| **Vanya Kudras** | Tenor | Dikoy's clerk, in love with Barbara | | *Katá Kabanová* |
| **Vanuzzi** | Bass | An actor | Voketaitis | *Die Schweigsame Frau* |
| **Varlaam** | Bass | Vagrant | 1st Petrov; Baccaloni, Flagello | *Boris Godunov* |

# THE CHARACTERS IN THE OPERAS

| CHARACTER | ROLE | SINGER | OPERA |
|---|---|---|---|
| **Varsonofiev** Baritone | Vassily's attendant | | *Khovantschina* |
| **Vasco da Gama** Tenor | Portuguese explorer | 1st Naudin; Gigli, Martinelli, Piccaver, Jean de Reszke, Wachtel | *L'Africaine* |
| **Vasek** Tenor | Micha's second son, quite timid | | *Prodaná Nevěsta* |
| **Vassals** Chorus | | | *Die Götterdämmerung* |
| **Vassily Galitsin, Prince** Tenor | | | *Khovantschina* |
| **Vaucluse** Tenor | The bishop's valet | | *Esther de Carpentras* |
| **Vaudemont, Count** Bass | French officer | | *I Vespri Siciliani* |
| **Vecchia, La** *See Zita* | | | |
| **Veit Pogner** *See Pogner, Veit* | | | |
| **Vendors** Chorus | | | *I Gioielli della Madonna* |
| **Vendulka** Soprano | Paloucky's daughter | | *Hubička* |
| **Venetian Merchant** Baritone | | | *Sadko* |
| **Venus** Contralto | Goddess | | *Orphée aux Enfers* |
| **Venus** Soprano | Supernatural seductress | 1st Schröder-Devrient; Fornia-Labey, Fremstad, Lawrence, Matzenauer, Rappold, Resnik, Shuard, Thebom, | *Tannhäuser* |
| **Venus** *See also Susanna* | | | |
| **Vera Boronel** Contralto | | Evans | *The Consul* |
| **Vere, Captain** Tenor | In command of the ship | 1st Pears | *Billy Budd* |
| **Vespone** Silent | A servant | | *La Serva Padrona* |

| CHARACTER | ROLE | SINGER | OPERA |
|---|---|---|---|
| **Viking Merchant** Baritone | | | Sadko |
| **Village Elder** Speaker | | | Háry János |
| **Villagers** Chorus | | | L'Arlesiana, Cavalleria Rusticana, La Dame Blanche, Faust, La Forza del Destino, Hubička, Její Pastorkyňa (Jenufa), Luisa Miller, Le Nozze di Figaro, I Pagliacci, Prodaná Nevěsta, La Sonnambula |
| **Vincent** Tenor | In love with Mireille | 1st Michot | Mireille |
| **Vincenzo Gellner** See Gellner | | | |
| **Violetta Valery** Soprano | A courtesan | 1st Salvini-Donatelli; Albanese, Alda, Bellincioni, Bevy, Callas, Cross, Farrar, Fenn, Galli-Curci, Hempel, Jeritza, Juch, Kellogg, Kirsten, Kurz, Labia, Lilli Lehmann, Lipovska, Melba, Munsel, Muzio, Christine Nilsson, Nordica, Novotna, Patti, Pons, Ponselle, Schwarzkopf, Sembrich, Steber, Tebaldi, Luisa Tetrazzini, Vere, Yeend | La Traviata |
| **Virgil T.** Baritone | | | The Mother of Us All |
| **Vitek** Tenor | Dalibor's squire | | Dalibor |

484

# THE CHARACTERS IN THE OPERAS

| CHARACTER | | ROLE | SINGER | OPERA |
|---|---|---|---|---|
| **Vitellia** | Soprano | Daughter of the deposed emperor of Rome | Zadek | *La Clemenza di Tito* |
| **Vitellozzo** | Bass | Nobleman of the Venetian Republic | | *Lucrezia Borgia* |
| **Vivetta** | Soprano | Rosa's god-daughter, in love with Federico | | *L'Arlesiana* |
| **Vixen, Miss** From Chorus | | A lady of the town | | *The Beggar's Opera* |
| **Vizier** | Baritone | The Sultan's adviser | | *Marouf* |
| **Vladimir Igorevitch** Tenor | | Igor's son | | *Prince Igor* |
| **Vladimir Yaroslavovitch** Bass | | Yaroslavna's brother | | *Prince Igor* |
| **Vladislav** | Baritone | King of Bohemia | | *Dalibor* |
| **Vlassievna** Contralto | | Nurse | | *Pskovityanka* |
| **Vogelgesang** *See* Kunz Vogelgesang | | | | |
| **Voice** From Chorus | | | | *L'Amore dei tre Re* |
| **Voice** | Tenor | In the forge, later of a street seller, later from a distance | | *La Vida Breve* |
| **Voice from Above** Contralto | | | | *Die Frau ohne Schatten* |
| **Voice from Heaven** Soprano | | | Amara | *Don Carlos* |
| **Voice of a Bird** Soprano | | | | *Pilgrim's Progress* |
| **Voice of Neptune** Bass | | | | *Idomeneo* |
| **Voice of the Temple Watchman** Bass | | | | *Die Königin von Saba* |
| **Voice on a Record** Soprano | | | | *The Consul* |
| **Volkhova** | Soprano | Princess of the ocean | | *Sadko* |

| CHARACTER | | ROLE | SINGER | OPERA |
|---|---|---|---|---|
| **Vreli** | Soprano | Marti's daughter, in love with Sali | | *A Village Romeo and Juliet* |
| **Wagner** | Baritone | Faust's attendant | | *Doktor Faustus* |
| **Wagner** | Baritone | A student | | *Faust* |
| **Wagner** | Tenor | | Ferrari-Fontana | *Mefistofele* |
| **Wailing Women** | Chorus | | | *Der Barbier von Bagdad* |
| **Waiters** | Chorus | | | *La Bohème* |
| **Waiters (Four)** | Tenor, Three Basses | | | *Der Rosenkavalier* |
| **Waldner, Graf** | Bass | Arabella's father, a gambler | London | *Arabella* |
| **Waldvogel** | Soprano | A forest bird | Schwarzkopf | *Siegfried* |
| **Wallenstein** | Tenor | Commander-in-chief, also Jupiter | | *Die Harmonie der Welt* |
| **Wally** | Soprano | In love with Hagenbach | 1st Darclée; Caniglia, Cigna, Destinn, Guerrini I, Guerrini II, Sheridan, Tebaldi | *La Wally* |
| **Walter** | Soprano | Strolling minstrel | 1st Stehle | *La Wally* |
| **Walter, Count** | Bass | Rodolfo's father | | *Luisa Miller* |
| **Walter Furst** | Bass | Swiss patriot | | *Guillaume Tell* |
| **Walther von der Vogelweide** | Tenor | Knight and minnesinger | | *Tannhäuser* |
| **Walther von Stolzing** | Tenor | Franconian knight | 1st Betz; Althouse, Alvarez, Max Alvary, Berger, Dippel, Gudehus, Hopf, Hyde, Lorenz, Maison, Nachbauer, Niemann, Jean de Reszke, Slezak, Sullivan, Svanholm, Winkelmann | *Die Meistersinger* |

| CHARACTER | ROLE | SINGER | OPERA |
|---|---|---|---|
| **Waltraute** Soprano or Mezzo-soprano | A valkyr | Homer, Ober, Schumann-Heink, Wickham | Das Ring des Nibelungen |
| **Wangenheim** | Saxon officer | | Der Bettelstudent |
| **Wanton, Madam** Soprano | | | Pilgrim's Progress |
| **Wardrobe Mistress** Contralto | Also plays the schoolboy | | Lulu |
| **Warlaam** See Varlaam | | | |
| **Warrior** See Samson | | | |
| **Warriors** Chorus | | | The Immortal Hour, Prince Igor, Le Roi d'Ys |
| **Wat Dreary** From Chorus | A gentleman of the road | | The Beggar's Opera |
| **Watch, The** Chorus | | | Cardillac |
| **Watchful** Baritone | Porter | | Pilgrim's Progress |
| **Watchman** Tenor | | | Antigonae (Orff) |
| **Watchmen (Four)** Basses | | | Die Liebe der Danae |
| **Waters, Mrs.** Soprano | Landlady | | The Boatswain's Mate |
| **Wayfarers** Chorus | | | Mefistofele |
| **Weeping Women** Chorus | | | Turandot (Busoni) |
| **Welko** From Chorus | Mandryka's servant | | Arabella |
| **Wellgunde** Soprano | A Rhine maiden | | Das Ring des Nibelungen |
| **Werther** Tenor | Poet, 23 | 1st van Dyke; Clément, Conley, Jones, Jean de Reszke, Schipa, Tagliavini, Valletti | Werther |

| CHARACTER | ROLE | SINGER | OPERA |
|---|---|---|---|
| **Wheel of Fortune Woman**  Soprano | | | *A Village Romeo and Juliet* |
| **Whores and Roaring Boys**  Chorus | | | *The Rake's Progress* |
| **Wicker Chair, The**  Child | | | *L'Enfant et les Sortilèges* |
| **Widow**  Silent | | | *Der Rosenkavalier* |
| **Widow Browe** *See* Witwe Browe | | | |
| **Wife**  Contralto | | | *Dantons Tod* |
| **Wife**  Soprano | Faithful to her sailor husband | 1st Madeleine Sibille; Enk, Favero, Leskaya, Novotna, Teschemacher | *Le Pauvre Matelot* |
| **Wife of the Court Attendant**  Soprano | | | *Der Prozess* |
| **Wigmaker**  Baritone | | | *Ariadne auf Naxos* |
| **Wigmaker**  Silent | | | *Manon Lescaut* |
| **Wild Girl**  Mezzo-soprano | | | *A Village Romeo and Juliet* |
| **Wilhelm Meister**  Tenor | Student on his travels | 1st Achard; Capoul, Davies, Gigli, Maas, Schipa, de Stefano | *Mignon* |
| **Willem**  Baritone | | Renan | *Der Prozess* |
| **William**  Tenor | | | *Hugh the Drover* |
| **William Jennings Bryan**  Bass | | Hecht | *The Ballad of Baby Doe* |
| **William Tell** *See* Guillaume Tell | | | |
| **Witch**  Mezzo-soprano | | Homer, Ober, Claramae Turner | *Hänsel und Gretel* |
| **Witches**  Chorus | | | *Dido and Aeneas, Macbeth, Mefistofele* |

| CHARACTER | ROLE | SINGER | OPERA |
|---|---|---|---|
| **Witches (Two)** Sopranos | | | *Dido and Aeneas* |
| **Wits** Chorus | | | *The Love for Three Oranges* |
| **Witwe Browe** Contralto | | | *Zar und Zimmermann* |
| **Wizards** Chorus | | | *Mefistofele* |
| **Woglinde** Soprano | A Rhine maiden | Fornia-Labey, Lilli Lehmann | *Das Ring des Nibelungen* |
| **Wolfram von Eschenbach** Baritone | Knight and minnesinger | 1st Mitterwurzer; Ancona, Bispham, Gura, London, Ludwig, Maurel, Morelli, Renaud, van Rooy, Scheidermantel, Schorr, Tibbett, Weil | *Tannhäuser* |
| **Woman, A** Soprano | | | *Alceste* |
| **Woman, A** Soprano | | | *Friedenstag* |
| **Women** Chorus | | | *Friedenstag, Götter-dämmerung, Pilgrim's Progress, Prince Igor, I Puritani, Tiefland, Les Troyens, A Village Romeo and Juliet, The Wreckers* |
| **Women (Two)** Soprano and Mezzo-soprano | | | *Dido and Aeneas* |
| **Women Wailing** *See* Wailing Women | | | |
| **Woodcutter's Boy** Soprano | | | *Pilgrim's Progress* |
| **Wordsworth, Miss** Soprano | Church school teacher | | *Albert Herring* |
| **Workmen** Chorus | | | *Louise, Les Troyens* |

489

| CHARACTER | ROLE | SINGER | OPERA |
|---|---|---|---|
| **Workmen (Two)** Baritone, Bass | | | *Wozzeck* |
| **Worldly Glory** Baritone | | | *Pilgrim's Progress* |
| **Wotan** Bass Baritone | Norse god | 1st Kindermann; Bender, Berglund, Betz, Bispham, Bockelmann, Delmas, Griswold, Hotter, Janssen, Ludwig, Mayr, Nissen, Reichmann, van Rooy, Rode, Scaria, Schorr, Staudigl II | *Das Ring des Nibelungen* |
| **Wowkle** Mezzo-soprano | Billy's squaw | | *La Fanciulla del West* |
| **Wozzeck**  Baritone | A soldier | 1st Scheele-Müller; Fehr, Gobbi, Hermann, Manowarda, Nillius, Rothmuller, Uhde | *Wozzeck* |
| **Wreckers**  Chorus | | | *The Wreckers* |
| **Wurm**  Bass | | | *Luisa Miller* |
| **Xanthe**  Soprano | Danae's servant | | *Die Liebe der Danae* |
| **Xenia**  Soprano | Daughter of Boris Godunov | | *Boris Godunov* |
| **Xenia's Nurse** *See* Nurse | | | |
| **Yamadori**  Baritone | Rich Japanese | Cehanovsky, Renan | *Madama Butterfly* |
| **Yeletsky, Prince**  Baritone | Lisa's fiancé | | *Pique-Dame* |
| **Ygraine**  Soprano | Former wife of Barbe-Bleue | | *Ariane et Barbe-Bleue* |
| **Yniold**  Soprano | Golaud's son | 1st Blondin | *Pélleas et Mélisande* |
| **Young Girl** From Chorus | | | *L'Amore dei Tre Re* |
| **Young Girl** From Chorus | | | *Iris* |

| CHARACTER | ROLE | SINGER | OPERA |
|---|---|---|---|
| **Young Maid**<br>From Chorus | | | *I Quattro Rusteghi* |
| **Young Men (Two)**<br>Tenors | | | *Dantons Tod* |
| **Young Men and**<br>**Women**   Chorus | | | *The Fair at*<br>*Sorochintsky* |
| **Young People**<br>**(Three)**<br>Tenor, Baritone,<br>and Bass | | | *Der Prozess* |
| **Young Servant**<br>Tenor | | | *Elektra* |
| **Young Shepherd**<br>Soprano | | Peters | *Tannhäuser* |
| **Youshko Velebin**<br>Bass | Messenger | | *Pskovityanka* |
| **Youth**<br>From Chorus | | | *L'Amore dei Tre Re* |
| **Youth**   Tenor | | | *Der Prozess* |
| **Youths and Boys**<br>Chorus | | | *Parsifal* |
| **Yvette**   Soprano | Magda's friend | | *La Rondine* |
| **Zaccaria**   Bass | High priest of<br>Jerusalem | | *Nabucco* |
| **Zacharias**   Bass | An Anabaptist | | *Le Prophète* |
| **Zaretsky**   Bass | | | *Eugene Onegin* |
| **Zayda**<br>Mezzo-soprano | | 1st Stoltz | *Dom Sebastiano* |
| **Zaza**   Soprano | Music-hall singer | 1st Storchio;<br>Farrar, Favero | *Zaza* |
| **Zdenek's Ghost** | | | *Dalibor* |
| **Zdenka**   Soprano | Arabella's sister,<br>brought up as a boy | della Casa<br>Rothenberger | *Arabella* |
| **Zerbinetta**   Soprano | | 1st Siems;  Gueden,<br>Ivogün, Kurz,<br>Schwarzkopf,<br>Streich | *Ariadne auf Naxos* |

| CHARACTER | | ROLE | SINGER | OPERA |
|---|---|---|---|---|
| **Zerlina** | Soprano | Matteo's daughter | 1st Alboni; Berger, Carosio, Carvalho, Naylor, Parepa-Rosa, Patti | *Fra Diavolo* |
| **Zerlina** | Soprano | Peasant girl engaged to Matteo | 1st Teresa Bondini; Adams, Carosio, Carvalho, Connor, della Casa, Farrar, Fleisher, Fodor-Mainvielle, Gueden, Hauk, Hurley, Kellogg, Lucca, Lussan, Malibran, Munsel, Naylor, Parepa-Rosa, Patti, Peters, Schick, Sembrich, Sontag, Teyte, Viardot-Garcia, van Zandt | *Don Giovanni* |
| **Zinida** Mezzo-soprano | | | Sarfaty | *He Who Gets Slapped* |
| **Zita** | Contralto | Dead Buoso's cousin, 60 | Claramae Turner | *Gianni Schicchi* |
| **Zora** | Soprano | | Nevada | *La Perle du Brésil* |
| **Zsupan** *See* Kalman Zsupan | | | | |
| **Zuane** | Bass | A boatman | Cehanovsky | *La Gioconda* |
| **Zuckertanz, Doctor** Tenor | | | | *Maria Golovin* |
| **Zulma** | Contralto | Elvira's companion | | *L'Italiana in Algeri* |
| **Zuniga** | Bass | Captain of the guard | Lorenzo Alvary | *Carmen* |
| **Zurga** | Baritone | King of the fishermen | 1st Ismael; Ancona, Badini, Biasini, Lherie, de Luca, Soulacroix | *Les Pêcheurs de Perles* |

# FIRST LINES AND TITLES OF FAMOUS MUSICAL NUMBERS

NOTE: In this section the English that appears below first lines in other languages is not necessarily a literal translation since it is an adaptation suited to the music.

| FIRST LINE | ROLE | OPERA |
|---|---|---|
| **A lonely Arab maid** | Fatima<br>(Mezzo-soprano) | *Oberon*<br>(Act II) |
| **A red-headed woman** | Crown<br>(Baritone) | *Porgy and Bess*<br>(Act II) |
| **A Serpina penserate**<br>(Think about me when you're away) | Serpina<br>(Soprano) | *La Serva Padrona*<br>(Part II) |
| **A tanto amor**<br>(Thou beautiful flower) | Alfonso<br>(Baritone) | *La Favorita*<br>(Act III) |
| **A te o cara**<br>(To thee, my dearest) | Arturo Talbot<br>(Tenor) | *I Puritani*<br>(Act I) |
| **A un dottor della mia sorte***<br>(To a doctor of my luck) | Doctor Bartolo<br>(Bass) | *Il Barbiere di Siviglia*<br>(Act I) |
| **A una fonte aflito e solo**<br>(Just by a fountain alone and in sorrow) | Elvira<br>(Soprano) | *I Puritani*<br>(Act III) |
| **A woman is a sometime thing** | Jake<br>(Baritone) | *Porgy and Bess*<br>(Act I) |
| **Abends will ich schlafen gehen**<br>(When at night I go to sleep)<br>"The Children's Prayer" | Hänsel, Gretel<br>(Soprano,<br>Mezzo-soprano) | *Hänsel und Gretel*<br>(Act II) |
| **Abscheulicher! wo eilst du hin?**<br>(Accursed one! where go you now?) | Leonora<br>(Soprano) | *Fidelio*<br>(Act I) |

* Note: This aria is sometimes replaced with *Manca un foglio*.

493

| FIRST LINE | ROLE | OPERA |
|---|---|---|
| **Ach, das Leid hab' ich getragen** (Ah, what grief must I now bear) | Nureddin (Tenor) | *Der Barbier von Bagdad* (Act I) |
| **Ach, ich fühl's, es ist verschwunden** (Ah, 'tis gone, 'tis gone forever) | Pamina (Soprano) | *Die Zauberflöte* (Act II) |
| **Ach, ich hab' sie ja nur auf die Schulter gekusst** (Ah! upon her shoulder have I kissed her) | Colonel Ollendorf (Bass) | *Der Bettelstudent* (Act I) |
| **Ach, ich liebte, war so glücklich** (Ah, my love, 'twas so pleasant) | Constanze (Soprano) | *Die Entführung aus dem Serail* (Act I) |
| **Adamastor, re dell' onde profonde** (Adamastor, ruler of ocean) | Nelusko (Baritone) | *L'Africaine* (Act III) |
| **Addio alla madre** "Turiddu's Farewell" | Turiddu (Tenor) | *Cavalleria Rusticana* |
| **Addio del passato** (Farewell to bright visions) | Violetta (Soprano) | *La Traviata* (Act III) |
| **Addio di Mimi** *See* Donde lieta usci | | |
| **Addio dolce svegliare** (Farewell sweet love) | Mimi, Musetta, Rodolfo, Marcello (Two Sopranos, Tenor, Baritone) | *La Bohème* (Act III) |
| **Adieu, Mignon** (Goodbye, Mignon) | Wilhelm (Tenor) | *Mignon* (Act II) |
| **Adieu, notre petite table** (Goodbye, our little table) | Manon (Soprano) | *Manon* (Act II) |
| **Agathe's Prayer** *See* Leise, leise, fromme Weise | | |
| **Ah, Belinda, I am prest with torment** | Dido (Soprano) | *Dido and Aeneas* (Act I) |
| **Ah! che la morte ognora** (Ah! pray that peace may attend us) "The Miserere" | Leonora, Manrico (Soprano, Tenor) | *Il Trovatore* (Act III) |
| **Ah! I am suffocating** (The Clock Scene) | Boris (Bass) | *Boris Godunov* (Act III) |

| FIRST LINE | ROLE | OPERA |
|---|---|---|
| **Ah! j'ai baisée ta bouche** (Ah! I have kissed your mouth) | Salome (Soprano) | *Salome* |
| **Ah, je ris de me voir si belle** (Ah! I laugh to see me so beautiful) "The Jewel Song" | Marguérite (Soprano) | *Faust* (Act III) |
| **Ah! lève-toi, soleil** (Ah! rise up fair sun!) | Romeo (Tenor) | *Roméo et Juliette* (Act II) |
| **Ah, lo veggio, quell' anima bella** (Well I know that a maid so enchanting) | Ferrando (Tenor) | *Così fan Tutte* (Act II) |
| **Ah, malgré moi** (Against my will) | Alceste (Soprano) | *Alceste* (Act II) |
| **Ah! mon fils** (Ah! my son) | Fidès (Contralto) | *Le Prophète* (Act II) |
| **Ah, non credea mirarti** (Ah, I could not believe) | Amina (Soprano) | *La Sonnambula* (Act II) |
| **Ah, non giunge uman pensiero** (Ah, the depths of human thought) | Amina (Soprano) | *La Sonnambula* (Act II) |
| **Ah! per sempre io ti perdei** (Ah! forever have I lost thee) | Riccardo (Baritone) | *I Puritani* (Act I) |
| **Ah! perchè non posso odiarti?** (Ah! why is it I don't hate thee?) | Amina (Soprano) | *La Sonnambula* (Act II) |
| **Ah, chi mi dice mai quel barbaro dov'è** (Where shall I find the traitor who stole my heart?) | Donna Elvira (Soprano) | *Don Giovanni* (Act I) |
| **Ah, del Tebro** (Ah, thou Roman!) | Oroveso (Bass) | *Norma* (Act III) |
| **Ah! dite alla giovine** (Ah! tell it to your daughter) | Violetta (Soprano) | *La Traviata* (Act II) |
| **Ah! fors'è lui** (Ah! but for him) | Violetta (Soprano) | *La Traviata* (Act I) |
| **Ah, fuggi il traditore** (Ah, the traitor escapes me!) | Donna Elvira (Soprano) | *Don Giovanni* (Act I) |
| **Ah! fuyez, douce image!** (Ah! leave me, fairest sight!) | des Grieux (Tenor) | *Manon* (Act III) |

| FIRST LINE | ROLE | OPERA |
|---|---|---|
| **Ah, pescator, affonda l'esca** (Fisherman, now throw in your bait) | Barnaba (Baritone) | *La Gioconda* (Act II) |
| **Ah, pietà! Signori miei** (Spare me, spare my life I pray) | Leporello (Bass) | *Don Giovanni* (Act II) |
| **Ah, se l'error t'ingombra** (Ah, mid the shadows of error) "The Nun's Chorus" | Count di Luna, Nuns (Baritone, Chorus) | *Il Trovatore* (Act II) |
| **Ah sì ben mio coll'essere** (The vows we fondly plighted) | Manrico (Tenor) | *Il Trovatore* (Act III) |
| **Ah sì! che feci** (What was I doing?) "The Quintet" | Violetta, Flora Bervoix, Alfredo, Giorgio Germont, Baron Douphol (Two Sopranos, Tenor, two Baritones) | *La Traviata* (Act II) |
| **Ahi! casa acerba** (Ah! house of sadness!) | La Messagera (Soprano) | *La Favola d'Orfeo* (Act II) |
| **Ai nostri monti** (Back home the mountains) | Azucena, Manrico (Contralto, Tenor) | *Il Trovatore* (Act III) |
| **Alerte! Alerte!** (Leave her! Leave her!) | Marguérite, Faust, Méphistophélès, Chorus (Soprano, Tenor, Bass, Chorus) | *Faust* (Act V) |
| **Alles fühlt der Liebe Freuden** (All with passion's fever tingle) | Monostatos (Tenor) | *Zauberflöte* (Act II) |
| **Almighty Virgin** "Elisabeth's Prayer" | Elisabeth (Soprano) | *Tannhäuser* (Act III) |
| **Als Büblein klein** (As little knaves) "The Drinking Song" | Sir John Falstaff (Bass) | *Die Lustigen Weiber von Windsor* (Act II) |
| **Als flotter Geist** (As merry a spirit) | Barinkay (Tenor) | *Zigeunerbaron* (Act I) |
| **Am stillen Herd** (By silent hearth) | Walther (Tenor) | *Die Meistersinger* (Act I) |
| **Amfortas, die Wunde!** (Amfortas, the wound!) | Parsifal (Tenor) | *Parsifal* (Act II) |
| **Amor ti vieta** (My love forbids thee) | Count Loris (Tenor) | *Fedora* (Act II) |

| FIRST LINE | ROLE | OPERA |
|---|---|---|
| **Amour, viens aider ma faiblesse** (Ah love, come aid my weakness) | Dalila (Mezzo-soprano) | *Samson et Dalila* (Act II) |
| **Andrò ramingo e solo** (I go, wandering and alone) | Elektra, Ilia, Idamante, Idomeneo (Three Sopranos, Tenor) | *Idomeneo* (Act III) |
| **Angel's Pantomime** | Orchestra | *Hänsel und Gretel* (Act II) |
| **Anvil Chorus** | Gypsies (Chorus) | *Il Trovatore* (Act II) |
| **Aprite un po' quegli occhi** (Just open your eyes and you'll see them) | Figaro (Baritone) | *Le Nozze di Figaro* (Act IV) |
| **Au fond du temple saint** (In the depths of the temple) | Nadir, Zurga (Tenor, Bass) | *Les Pêcheurs de Perles* (Act I) |
| **Avant de quitter ces lieux** (Now before I leave my home) | Valentin (Baritone) | *Faust* (Act II) |
| **Ave Maria** (Hail Mary) | Desdemona (Soprano) | *Otello* (Act IV) |
| **Avec de la tendresse** *See* Durch Zärtlichkeit | | |
| **Bacchanale** | Ballet | *Samson et Dalila* (Act III) |
| **Bald prangt den Morgen zu verkünden** (The rosy dawn that greets us early) | Three Genii (Two sopranos, Mezzo-soprano) | *Die Zauberflöte* (Act II) |
| **Ballabile** | Ballet | *Aida* (Act II) |
| **Ballad of the King of Thule** *See* Il était un roi de Thulé | | |
| **Ballatella** *See* Che volo d'augelli | | |
| **Bannis la crainte et les alarmes** (Banish your fears and your alarms) | Admetus (Baritone) | *Alcestis* (Act II) |
| **Barcarolle** *See* Belle nuit ô nuit d'amour | | |

| FIRST LINE | ROLE | OPERA |
|---|---|---|
| **Batti, batti, o bel Masetto** (Chide me, chide me, oh fine Masetto) | Zerlina (Soprano) | *Don Giovanni* (Act I) |
| **Bei Männern, welche Liebe fühlen** (The kindly voice of Mother Nature) | Pamina (Soprano) | *Zauberflöte* (Act I) |
| **Bel raggio lusinghier** (Bright ray of hopefulness) | Semiramide (Soprano) | *Semiramide* (Act I) |
| **Bell Song, The** *See* Où va la jeune hindoue? | | |
| **Bella figlia dell' amore** (Fairest daughter of the graces) | Gilda, Maddalena, The Duke, Rigoletto (Soprano, Contralto, Tenor, Baritone) | *Rigoletto* (Act IV) |
| **Belle nuit ô nuit d'amour** (Fairest night, oh night of love) "The Barcarolle" | Nicklausse, Giulietta (Two Mezzo-sopranos) | *Les Contes d'Hoffmann* (Act II) |
| **Berceuse** (Lullaby) | Louise's father (Bass) | *Louise* (Act IV) |
| **Berceuse** *See* Cachés dans cet asile | | |
| **Bess, you is my woman now** | Bess, Porgy (Soprano, Baritone) | *Porgy and Bess* (Act II) |
| **Bevi, bevi** | Chorus | *Otello* |
| **Bildnis Aria** *See* Dies Bildnis ist bezaubernd schön | | |
| **Blick ich umher** (Gazing upon you) | Hermann (Baritone) | *Tannhäuser* (Act II) |
| **Brahma! grand dieu!** (Brahma, great god!) | Leïla (Soprano) | *Les Pêcheurs de Perles* (Act II) |
| **Brangäne's Warning** | Brangäne (Mezzo-soprano) | *Tristan und Isolde* (Act II) |
| **Bridal Chamber Scene** *See* Das süsse Lied verhallt | | |
| **Bridal Chorus** | Chorus, Orchestra | *Lohengrin* (Act III) |

| FIRST LINE | ROLE | OPERA |
|---|---|---|
| **Bridal Procession** | Orchestra | *Le Coq d'Or*<br>(Act III) |
| **Brindisi** (Drinking Songs)<br>*See* Viva il vino spumeggiante<br>*See* Il segreto per esser felice<br>*See* Libiamo, libiamo<br>*See* O vin, dissipe la tristesse<br>*See* Bevi, bevi | | |
| **Brunnhilde's Battle Cry**<br>*See* Ho yo to ho | | |
| **Buona sera, mio Signore**<br>(Then good evening, dear milord) | Rosina, Almaviva,<br>Figaro, Doctor Bartolo,<br>Don Basilio<br>(Mezzo-soprano,<br>Tenor, Baritone, two<br>Basses) | *Il Barbiere di Siviglia*<br>(Act II) |
| **By Wisla's blue waters** | Chorus | *Boris Godunov*<br>(Act III) |
| **Cachés dans cet asile**<br>(Hidden in this place) | (Tenor) | *Jocelyn* |
| **Calezeva, La***  | Soprano | |
| **Calf of Gold**<br>*See* Le Veau d'Or | | |
| **Canon**<br>*See* Mir ist so wunderbar | | |
| **Cantiamo, facciam brindisi**<br>(Let us sing, let us drink together) | Chorus | *L'Elisir d'Amore*<br>(Act II) |
| **Caro nome**<br>(Dearest name) | Gilda<br>(Soprano) | *Rigoletto*<br>(Act II) |
| **Casta diva**<br>(Queen of heaven) | Norma<br>(Soprano) | *Norma*<br>(Act I) |
| **Catalog Aria**<br>*See* Madamina | | |
| **Celeste Aida**<br>(Heavenly Aida) | Radames<br>(Tenor) | *Aida*<br>(Act I) |
| **Chanson du Toréador**<br>*See* Vôtre toast | | |

* A Spanish song sometimes used by Adelina Patti in the Music Lesson scene of *Il Barbiere di Siviglia*.

| FIRST LINE | ROLE | OPERA |
|---|---|---|
| **Chaste fille de Latone** (Chaste daughter of Latona) "The Hymn to Diana" | Iphigénie (Soprano) | *Iphigénie en Tauride* |
| **Che farò senza Euridice** (I have lost my Euridice) | Orfeo (Contralto) | *Orfeo ed Euridice* (Act III) |
| **Che fiero momento** (What a proud moment) | Orfeo, Euridice (Soprano, Contralto) | *Orfeo ed Euridice* (Act III) |
| **Che gelida manina** (Your tiny hand is frozen) "Rodolfo's Narrative" | Rodolfo (Tenor) | *La Bohème* (Act I) |
| **Che puro ciel** (What heavenly light) | Orfeo (Contralto) | *Orfeo ed Euridice* (Act II) |
| **Che soave zeffiretto** (How soft the breezes) | Susanna, the Countess (Two Sopranos) | *Le Nozze di Figaro* (Act III) |
| **Che volo d'augelli** (Ye birds without number) | Nedda (Soprano) | *I Pagliacci* (Act I) |
| **Ch'ella mi creda libero** (Let her believe they let me go) | Dick Johnson (Tenor) | *La Fanciulla del West* (Act III) |
| **Chi mai dell' Erebo** (Who can return from Hell?) | Furies and Demons (Chorus) | *Orfeo ed Euridice* (Act II) |
| **Chi mi frena** (What restrains me?) "The Sextet" | Lucia, Alisa, Edgardo, Arturo, Enrico, Raimondo (Soprano, Contralto, two Tenors, two Baritones) | *Lucia di Lammermoor* (Act II) |
| **Chiamo il mio ben così** (I call to my happiness) | Orfeo (Contralto) | *Orfeo ed Euridice* (Act I) |
| **Children's Prayer** *See* Abends will ich schlafen gehen | | |
| **Chimes in the valley** | Euryanthe (Soprano) | *Euryanthe* (Act I) |
| **Chorus of the Girls of Sandomir** *See* By Wisla's blue waters | | |
| **Cielo e mar** (Heaven and sea) | Enzo Grimaldo (Tenor) | *La Gioconda* (Act II) |
| **Cinta di fiori** (Circled by flowers) | George Walton (Bass) | *I Puritani* (Act II) |

| FIRST LINE | ROLE | OPERA |
|---|---|---|
| **Clapping Game Song** | Nurse, Feodor (Soprano, Mezzo-soprano) | *Boris Godunov* (Act II) |
| **Clock Scene** *See* Ah! I am suffocating | | |
| **Cobbler's Song** *See* Schusterlied | | |
| **Come un bel dì di Maggio** (As one fine day in May) | Andrea (Tenor) | *Andrea Chénier* (Act IV) |
| **Connais-tu le pays?** (Knowest thou the land?) | Mignon (Mezzo-soprano) | *Mignon* (Act I) |
| **Conoscete, signor Figaro, questo foglio chi vergò?** (Do you recognize, my Figaro, this most shameful little note?) | Almaviva (Baritone) | *Le Nozze di Figaro* (Act II) |
| **Coronation March** | Orchestra | *Le Prophète* (Act IV) |
| **Coronation Scene** | Boris, the People (Bass, Chorus) | *Boris Godunov* (Prologue) |
| **Cortigiani, vil razza dannata!** (Vile race of courtiers!) | Rigoletto (Baritone) | *Rigoletto* (Act III) |
| **Couplets** *See* Sittencommissions couplets | | |
| **Credeasi misera** (Believe me, this miserable one) | Arturo, Elvira (Soprano, Tenor) | *I Puritani* (Act III) |
| **Credo in un Dio crudel** (I believe in a cruel god) | Iago (Baritone) | *Otello* (Act II) |
| **Crudel, perchè finora?** (O why are you so cruel?) | Susanna, Almaviva (Soprano, Baritone) | *Le Nozze di Figaro* (Act III) |
| **Csardas** *See* Klänge der Heimat | | |
| **D'amour l'ardente flamme** (The ardent flame of love) | Marguerite (Soprano) | *La Damnation de Faust* (Act IV) |
| **Dance in Six** | Orchestra | *Guillaume Tell* (Act I) |
| **Dance of the Apprentices** | Chorus | *Die Meistersinger* (Acts I and III) |

| FIRST LINE | ROLE | OPERA |
|---|---|---|
| **Dance of the Camorrists** | Orchestra | *I Gioielli della Madonna* (Act III) |
| **Dance of the Hours** | Ballet | *La Gioconda* (Act III) |
| **Dance of the Seven Veils\*** | Salome | *Salome* |
| **Das süsse Lied verhallt** (That sweetest song is dead) "The Love Duet" | Elsa, Lohengrin (Soprano, Tenor) | *Lohengrin* (Act III) |
| **De' miei bollenti spiriti** (Wild was my ardent spirit) | Alfredo (Tenor) | *La Traviata* (Act II) |
| **De noirs pressentiments** (The dark presentiments) | Thoas (Bass) | *Iphigénie en Tauride* (Act IV) |
| **Death Scene** *See* Hark! the tolling bell *See* Io muojo *See* Sono andate | | *Boris Godunov* *La Forza del Destino* *La Bohème* |
| **Death of Don Quixote** | Dulcinée, Don Quixote, Sancho Panza (Soprano, two Basses) | *Don Quichotte* (Act V) |
| **Deh non volerli vittimi** (They shall not be the victims) | Norma, Pollione, Oroveso (Soprano, Tenor, Bass) | *Norma* (Act II) |
| **Deh per questo istante solo** (O this once they grace accord me) | Sextus (Tenor) | *La Clemenza di Tito* (Act II) |
| **Deh vieni alla finestra** (Look down now from your window) "Don Giovanni's Serenade" | Don Giovanni (Baritone) | *Don Giovanni* (Act II) |
| **Deh vieni non tardar** (Then come to me my love) | Susanna (Soprano) | *Le Nozze di Figaro* (Act IV) |
| **Dell' elisir mirabile** (Miraculous, this mixture) | Nemerino (Tenor) | *L'Elisir d'Amore* (Act II) |
| **Depuis le jour** (E'er since the day) | Louise (Soprano) | *Louise* (Act III) |
| **Der Arme kann von Strafe sagen** ('Tis hard such punishment to suffer) | Three Ladies, Tamino, Papageno (Two Sopranos, Mezzo-soprano, Tenor, Baritone) | *Die Zauberflöte* (Act I) |

\* Usually performed by a dancer in place of the prima donna.

| FIRST LINE | ROLE | OPERA |
|---|---|---|
| **Der Freund ist dein** (The friend is yours) | Sulamith (Soprano) | *Die Königen von Saba* (Act III) |
| **Der Gnade Heil** *See* Pilgrim's Chorus | | |
| **Der Hölle Rache kocht in meinem Herzen** (I'll have revenge, no longer can I bear it) | Queen of the Night (Soprano) | *Die Zauberflöte* (Act II) |
| **Der kleine Sandmann bin ich** (The little Sandman am I) | Sandman (Soprano) | *Hänsel und Gretel* (Act II) |
| **Der Männer Sippe sass hier im Saal** (The host of kinsmen sat in this hall) | Sieglinde (Soprano) | *Die Walküre* (Act I) |
| **Der Vogelfänger bin ich ja** (I am the jolly bird catcher) | Papageno (Baritone) | *Die Zauberflöte* (Act I) |
| **Dew Fairy's Song, The** | Dew fairy (Soprano) | *Hänsel und Gretel* (Act III) |
| **Di provenza il mar** (In the country by the sea) | Giorgio Germont (Baritone) | *La Traviata* (Act II) |
| **Di quella pira** (On such a pyre) | Manrico (Tenor) | *Il Trovatore* (Act III) |
| **Di tanti palpiti*** (Such palpitations) | Soprano | *Tancredi* |
| **Dich selig Frau** (Thou blessed one) | Siegmund (Tenor) | *Die Walküre* (Act I) |
| **Dich, teure Halle** (Hail, hall of song) | Elisabeth (Soprano) | *Tannhäuser* (Act II) |
| **Dido's Lament** *See* When I am laid in earth | | |
| **Die Frist ist um** (The time has passed) | Dutchman (Baritone) | *Der Fliegende Holländer* (Act I) |
| **Dies Bildnis ist bezaubernd schön** (O loveliness beyond compare) "The Portrait Aria" | Tamino (Tenor) | *Die Zauberflöte* (Act I) |

* This is the so-called *Aria dei Rizzi*, having been composed while Rossini was cooking rice. It is sometimes used in the Music Lesson scene of *Il Barbiere di Siviglia*.

| FIRST LINE | ROLE | OPERA |
|---|---|---|
| **Dieu, que me voix tremblante** (O God, with my trembling voice) | Eléazar (Tenor) | *La Juive* (Act II) |
| **Dir, Göttin der Liebe soll mein Lied ertönen** (Thou, goddess of love shall be my muse of singing) "The Hymn to Venus" | Tannhäuser (Tenor) | *Tannhäuser* (Act II) |
| **Divinités du Styx** (Divinities of death) | Alceste (Soprano) | *Alceste* (Act I) |
| **Doch dich rührt kein Flehen** (Firm is thy decision) | Constanze (Soprano) | *Die Entführung aus dem Serail* (Act II) |
| **Doll's Song** *See* Les oiseaux dans la charmille | | |
| **Donde lieta usci** (Whence did our happiness come?) "Mimi's farewell" | Mimi (Soprano) | *La Bohème* (Act III) |
| **Donne mie la fate a tanti** (Ladies have such variation) | Guglielmo (Bass) | *Così fan Tutte* (Act II) |
| **Donna non vidi mai** (Maiden so very fair) | des Grieux (Tenor) | *Manon Lescaut* (Act I) |
| **Dormirò sol nel manto** (I shall sleep soundly) | Philip the Second (Bass) | *Don Carlos* (Act IV) |
| **Dove sono** (I remember) | Countess Almaviva (Soprano) | *Le Nozze di Figaro* (Act III) |
| **Dream** *See* En fermant les yeux | | |
| **Dream Pantomime** | Orchestra | *Hänsel und Gretel* (Act II) |
| **Drinking Song** *See* Als Büblein klein *See* Trinke, Liebchen, trinke schnell *See* Brindisi | | |
| **Du bist der Lenz** (You are my spring) | Sieglinde (Soprano) | *Die Walküre* (Act I) |
| **Duetto d'Amore** *See* Vieni la sera *See* Love Duet | | |

| FIRST LINE | ROLE | OPERA |
|---|---|---|
| **Duidu** | Chorus | *Die Fledermaus* (Act II) |
| **D'un pensiero e d'un accento** (But one thought and one accent) | Amina, Elvino (Soprano, Tenor) | *La Sonnambula* (Act I) |
| **Dunque io son, tu non m'inganni** (Tell me he loves, say you speak truly) | Rosina, Figaro (Mezzo-soprano, Baritone) | *Il Barbiere di Siviglia* (Act I) |
| **Durch die Wälder, durch die Auen** (Through the forest, over meadows) | Max (Tenor) | *Der Freischütz* (Act I) |
| **Durch Zärtlichkeit und Schmeicheln** (With tenderness and coaxing) | Constanze (Soprano) | *Die Entführung aus dem Serail* (Act II) |
| **È il sol dell' anima** (Love's the sun within my heart) | Gilda, the Duke (Soprano, Tenor) | *Rigoletto* (Act II) |
| **E la fede delle femine** (And the faithlessness of women) | Guglielmo, Ferrando, Alfonso (Tenor, Baritone, Bass) | *Così fan Tutte* (Act I) |
| **E lucevan le stelle** (The stars were brightly shining) | Mario (Tenor) | *Tosca* (Act III) |
| **E quest' asilo ameno e grato** (In this tranquil and lovely abode) | A Happy Spirit (Soprano) | *Orfeo ed Euridice* (Act II) |
| **E scherzo ed è follia** ('Tis funny and 'tis madness) "The Quintet" | Amelia, Oscar, Riccardo, Samuele, Tommaso (Two Sopranos, Tenor, two Basses) | *Un Ballo in Maschera* (Act I) |
| **È sogno, o realtà?** (A dream or reality?) | Ford (Baritone) | *Falstaff* (Act II) |
| **Ecco ridente in cielo\*** (O see it smile in the eastern sky) | Count Almaviva (Tenor) | *Il Barbiere di Siviglia* (Act I) |
| **Eccomi a vostri piedi** (Behold me at your feet) | Figaro (Baritone) | *Le Nozze di Figaro* (Act IV) |
| **E'er since the day** *See* Depuis le jour | | |
| **Ein Kobold** (A goblin) | Hans Sachs (Bass) | *Die Meistersinger* (Act III) |

\* This aria was added for the second performance of the opera, after a fiasco in which García sang a Spanish song of his own. This one was originally written for the opera *Aureliano in Palmira*.

| FIRST LINE | ROLE | OPERA |
|---|---|---|
| **Ein Mädchen oder Weibchen** (A maiden or a housewife) | Papageno (Baritone) | *Die Zauberflöte* (Act II) |
| **Elisabeth's Prayer** *See* Almighty Virgin | | |
| **Elle a fui, la tourterelle** (The dove has flown) | Antonia (Soprano) | *Les Contes d'Hoffmann* (Act IV) |
| **Elle ne croyait pas** (Ah! hardly thinking) | Wilhelm (Tenor) | *Mignon* (Act III) |
| **Elsa's Dream** | Elsa (Soprano) | *Lohengrin* (Act I) |
| **Elvira's Mad Scene** *See* Qui la voce sua soave | | |
| **En fermant les yeux** (Now closing my eyes) "The Dream" | des Grieux (Tenor) | *Manon* (Act II) |
| **Entrance of the gods into Valhalla** | Orchestra | *Das Rheingold* (Finale) |
| **Enzo Grimaldo, Principe di Santafiore** (Enzo Grimaldo, Prince of Santa Fiore) | Enzo, Barnaba (Tenor, Baritone) | *La Gioconda* (Act I) |
| **Er kommt, er kommt, o Wonne meiner Brust** (He comes, he comes, o joy within my breast) | Margiana, Bostana, Baba Mustapha (Soprano, Mezzo-soprano, Tenor) | *Der Barbier von Bagdad* (Act II) |
| **Er sterbe** (He dies) | Leonora, Florestan, Rocco, Pizzaro (Soprano, Tenor, Baritone, Bass) | *Fidelio* (Act II) |
| **Erda's Warning** *See* Weiche, Wotan, Weiche! | | |
| **Eri tu che macchiavi** (Was it you who stained my name?) | Renato (Baritone) | *Un Ballo in Maschera* (Act V) |
| **Ernani, involami** (Ernani, escape with me) | Elvira (Soprano) | *Ernani* (Act I) |
| **Erzählung der Waltraute** (Waltraute's Narrative) | Waltraute (Mezzo-soprano) | *Siegfried* (Act I) |

| FIRST LINE | ROLE | OPERA |
|---|---|---|
| **Et ta langue elle ne remue plus** (And your tongue, it speaks no more) | Salome (Soprano) | *Salome* |
| **Euch lüften, die mein Klagen** (You breezes, take my wailings) | Elsa (Soprano) | *Lohengrin* (Act II) |
| **Evening Prayer** *See* Abends will ich schlafen gehen | | |
| **Evening Star** *See* O du mein holder Abendstern | | |
| **Fairy's Song, The** *See* Dew Fairy's Song, The | | |
| **Faites-lui mes aveux** (Give her my avowals) | Siebel (Mezzo-soprano) | *Faust* (Act III) |
| **Farewell, O earth** *See* O terra addio | | |
| **Farewell** *See* Addio *See* Adieu | | |
| **Femme sensible** (O lady bright) | A Bard (Baritone) | *Ariodant* (Act II) |
| **Figlia dei re** (Daughter of kings) | Nelusko (Baritone) | *L'Africaine* (Act II) |
| **Figlia, tal nome palpita** (Daughter, your name strikes memories) | Simon Boccanegra (Baritone) | *Simon Boccanegra* (Act II) |
| **Finch' han dal vino** (While we have wine) | Don Giovanni (Bass) | *Don Giovanni* (Act I) |
| **Fledermaus Waltz, The** *See* Duidu | | |
| **Flower Song** *See* Faites-lui mes aveux *See* Le fleur que tu m'avais jetée | | |
| **Forest Murmurs** *See* Waldweben | | |
| **Forging Scene** *See* Nothung! Nothung! *See* Anvil Chorus | | |

| FIRST LINE | ROLE | OPERA |
|---|---|---|
| **Fredda ed immobile** <br> (Coldly and immovable) <br> "The Sextet" | Berta, Rosina, Almaviva, <br> Figaro, Bartolo, Don <br> Basilio <br> (Soprano, Mezzo- <br> soprano, Tenor, <br> Baritone, Two Basses) | *Il Barbiere di Siviglia* <br> (Act I) |
| **Frisch weht der Wind der Heimath zu** <br> (Fresh blows the wind unto my home) | Sailor <br> (Tenor) | *Tristan und Isolde* <br> (Act I) |
| **Fuggiam gli ardori inospiti** <br> (Let's fly from these hostile skies) | Aida, Radames <br> (Soprano, Tenor) | *Aida* <br> (Act III) |
| **Fünftausend Thaler** <br> (Five thousand dollars) | Baculus <br> (Bass) | *Der Wildschütz* <br> (Act II) |
| **Fuor del mar ho un mar in seno*** <br> (Away from the sea I have a sea in my heart) | Idomeneo <br> (Tenor) | *Idomeneo* <br> (Act II) |
| **Garden Scene** <br> *See* Figlia, tal nome palpita | | |
| **Gavotte** <br> *See* Me voici dans son boudoir <br> *See* Obeissons quand leur voix <br> appelle | | *Mignon* <br> *Manon* |
| **Già i sacerdoti adunanzi** <br> (Now have the priests come together) | Amneris <br> (Contralto) | *Aida* <br> (Act IV) |
| **Già mi dicon venal** <br> (Enemies call me venal) <br> "Scarpia's Cantabile" | Scarpia <br> (Baritone) | *Tosca* <br> (Act II) |
| **Già nella notta densa** <br> (Dark is the night around us) <br> "The Love Duet" | Desdemona, Otello <br> (Soprano, Tenor) | *Otello* <br> (Act I) |
| **Giorno d'orrore** <br> (Day of horror) | Semiramide, Arsace <br> (Soprano, Contralto) | *Semiramide* |
| **Giusto cielo rispondete** <br> (God of justice hear my prayer) | Edgardo, Enrico <br> (Tenor, Bass) | *Lucia di Lammermoor* <br> (Act III) |

* Written as a show piece for Raaff.

| FIRST LINE | ROLE | OPERA |
|---|---|---|
| **Gloire immortelle de nos aïeux** (Immortal glory of our forefathers) "The Soldier's Chorus" | Soldiers (Chorus) | *Faust* (Act IV) |
| **Gloria all' Egitto ed ad Iside** (Glory unto Egypt and to Isis) "The Grand March" | Chorus | *Aida* (Act II) |
| **Golden Calf, The** *See* Le veau d'Or | | |
| **Good Friday Spell** | Orchestra | *Parsifal* (Act III) |
| **Grand March, The** *See* Gloria all' Egitto ed ad Iside | | |
| **Grand March** | Orchestra | *Tannhäuser* (Act II) |
| **Gypsy Chorus** *See* Anvil Chorus | | |
| **Ha, seht es winkt?** (Ha, see it wink?) "The Treasure Waltz" | Saffi, Czipra, Barinkay (Soprano, Mezzo-soprano, Tenor) | *Zigeunerbaron* (Act II) |
| **Ha! welch' ein Augenblick** (Ha! now's the proper time) | Don Pizzaro (Bass) | *Fidelio* (Act I) |
| **Ha, wie will ich triumphieren** (Ha, how I shall triumph here) | Osmin (Bass) | *Die Entführung aus dem Serail* (Act III) |
| **Habanera** *See* L'amour est un oiseau rebelle | | |
| **Hammer Song** *See* Ho Ho | | |
| **Hark! the tolling bell** | Boris (Bass) | *Boris Godunov* (Act III) |
| **Hat man nicht auch Gold bei neben** (Life is nothing without money) | Rocce (Bass) | *Fidelio* (Act I) |
| **Hat denn Himmel mich verlassen?** (Am I then to be forsaken?) | Max (Tenor) | *Der Freischütz* (Act II) |
| **Heavenly Aida** *See* Celeste Aida | | |

| FIRST LINE | ROLE | OPERA |
|---|---|---|
| **Heil diesem Hause**<br>(Hail to this house!) | Chorus | *Der Barbier von Bagdad*<br>(Act III) |
| **Herz, versage nicht geschwind***<br>(Heart, fail me not too quickly) | The Magistrate<br>(Bass) | *Der Corregidor*<br>(Act II) |
| **Hier soll' ich dich denn sehen, Constanze**<br>(Here shall I see you quite soon, Constanze) | Belmonte<br>(Tenor) | *Die Entführung aus dem Serail*<br>(Act I) |
| **Ho capito, signor si**<br>(I do understand it, sir) | Masetto<br>(Baritone) | *Don Giovanni*<br>(Act I) |
| **Ho Ho! Schmiede, mein Hammer**<br>(Ho Ho! Smith, my hammer!)<br>"The Hammer Song" | Siegfried<br>(Tenor) | *Siegfried*<br>(Act I) |
| **Horch die Lerche singt im Hain**<br>(Hark, the skylark sings in the woods) | Fenton<br>(Tenor) | *Die Lustigen Weiber von Windsor*<br>(Act II) |
| **Ho yo to ho**<br>(Brunnhilde's Battle Cry) | Brünnhilde<br>(Soprano) | *Die Walküre*<br>(Act II) |
| **Hungarian March**<br>*See* Marche Hongroise | | |
| **Huntsman's Song**<br>*See* Le jour est levé | | |
| **Hymn to the Evening Star**<br>*See* O du mein holder Abendstern | | |
| **Hymn to the Sun**<br>*See* Salut a toi soleil de flamme | | |
| **Hymn to Venus**<br>*See* Dir Göttin der Liebe soll mein Lied ertönen | | |
| **I got plenty o' nuttin'** | Porgy<br>(Baritone) | *Porgy and Bess*<br>(Act I) |
| **I have attained the highest power** | Boris<br>(Bass) | *Boris Godunov*<br>(Act II) |
| **I revel in hope and joy again** | Sir Huon<br>(Tenor) | *Oberon*<br>(Act III) |

* The words of this song are by Heinrich Heine.

| FIRST LINE | ROLE | OPERA |
|---|---|---|
| **Ich baue ganz auf deine Stärke** (I dedicate my all to your power) | Belmonte (Tenor) | *Die Entführung aus dem Serail* (Act III) |
| **Ich hab' kein Geld, bin vogelfrei** (I have no gold, I'm free as a bird) | Simon (Tenor) | *Der Bettelstudent* (Act III) |
| **Ich knüpfte manche zarte Bänder** (I have tied many delicate bands) | Simon (Tenor) | *Der Bettelstudent* (Act I) |
| **Ich lade gern mir Gäste ein** (I like my guest to be most glad) | Prince Orlovsky (Mezzo-soprano) | *Die Fledermaus* (Act II) |
| **Ich sah das Kind** (I saw the child) | Kundry (Soprano) | *Parsifal* (Act II) |
| **Ich setz den Fall** (I set the trap) | Laura, Simon (Soprano, Tenor) | *Der Bettelstudent* (Act II) |
| **Il cavallo scalpita** (Proudly prancing sturdy steed) | Alfio (Baritone) | *Cavalleria Rusticana* |
| **Il core vi dono** (This heart that I give you) | Dorabella, Guglielmo (Soprano, Bass) | *Così fan Tutte* (Act II) |
| **Il est doux, il est bon** (He is kind, he is good) | Salome (Soprano) | *Hérodiade* (Act I) |
| **Il était un roi de Thulé** (It was the king of Thule) "The Ballad of the King of Thule" | Marguérite (Soprano) | *Faust* (Act III) |
| **Il lacerato spirito** (A wounded spirit) | Jacopo Fiesco (Bass) | *Simon Boccanegra* (Act I) |
| **Il mio tesoro intanto** (Speak, my heart, to my lady) | Don Ottavio (Tenor) | *Don Giovanni* (Act II) |
| **Il nome vostro ditemi** (But tell me just your name) | Gilda, the Duke (Soprano, Tenor) | *Rigoletto* (Act II) |
| **Il Padre adorato ritrovo e lo perdo** (I've found my beloved father and lost him again) | Idamante (Soprano) | *Idomeneo* (Act I) |
| **Il segreto per esser felice** (The secret of living in pleasure) | Maffio Orsini (Contralto) | *Lucrezia Borgia* (Act II) |
| **Im Mohrenland gefangen wir** (We found ourselves in Moorish lands) | Pedrillo (Tenor) | *Die Entführung aus dem Serail* (Act III) |

| FIRST LINE | ROLE | OPERA |
|---|---|---|
| **Imponete** (Now command me) | Violetta, Giorgio Germont (Soprano, Baritone) | *La Traviata* (Act II) |
| **In dem Schatten meiner Locken***  (In the shadow of my curls) | Frasquita (Mezzo-soprano) | *Der Corregidor* |
| **In des Lebens Frühlingstagen** (In the springtime of my life) | Florestan (Tenor) | *Fidelio* (Act II) |
| **In diesen heil'gen Hallen** (In this most holy hall) | Sarastro (Bass) | *Zauberflöte* (Act II) |
| **In fernem Land** (In distant lands) | Lohengrin (Tenor) | *Lohengrin* (Act III) |
| **In mia man alfin tu sei** (At last you are now in my hands) | Norma, Pollione (Soprano, Tenor) | *Norma* (Act II) |
| **In quelle trine morbide** (Between these silken curtains) | Manon Lescaut (Soprano) | *Manon Lescaut* (Act II) |
| **In uomini, in soldati** (In men as in soldiers) | Despina (Soprano) | *Così fan Tutte* (Act I) |
| **Infelice, e tu credevi** (Thou unfaithful! yet I believed thee) | Don Silva (Bass) | *Ernani* (Act I) |
| **Innkeeper's Song** *See* Song of the Drake | | |
| **Invano, Alvaro!** (In vain, Alvaro!) | Carlo, Alvaro (Tenor, Baritone) | *La Forza del Destino* (Act IV) |
| **Invocation** *See* Avant de quitter ces lieux *See* O Isis und Osiris *See* In diesen heil'gen Hallen | | |
| **Io muojo** (I am dying) | Leonora (Soprano) | *La Forza del Destino* (Act IV) |
| **Io sono ricco e tu sei bella** (I'm a rich one, and you are pretty) | Adina, Dulcamara (Soprano, Bass) | *L'Elisir d'Amore* (Act II) |
| **Io sono docile** (But I am most docile) | Rosina (Mezzo-soprano) | *Il Barbiere di Siviglia* (Act I) |

* A concert song by Hugo Wolf.

| FIRST LINE | ROLE | OPERA |
|---|---|---|
| **Isolde! Tristan! Geliebter!** (Isolde! Tristan! Beloved!) "The Love Duet" | Tristan, Isolde (Soprano, Tenor) | *Tristan und Isolde* (Act II) |
| **Isolde's Narrative** | Isolde (Soprano) | *Tristan und Isolde* (Act I) |
| **It ain't necessarily so** | Sportin' Life (Tenor) | *Porgy and Bess* (Act II) |
| **It takes a long pull to get there** | Jake, Chorus (Baritone, Chorus) | *Porgy and Bess* (Act II) |
| **Ja, das Schreiben und das Lesen** (Yes, the writing and the reading) | Zsupan (Baritone) | *Zigeunerbaron* (Act I) |
| **Je dis que rien ne m'épouvante** (I tell you I'm not weak at heart) | Micaela (Soprano) | *Carmen* (Act III) |
| **Je suis Titania** (I am Titania) "The Polonaise" | Philine (Soprano) | *Mignon* (Act II) |
| **Je t'implore et je tremble** (I implore you, I tremble) | Iphigénie (Soprano) | *Iphigénie en Tauride* (Act IV) |
| **Je veux vivre dans ce rêve** (In this dream I would stay) "Juliette's waltz" | Juliette (Soprano) | *Roméo et Juliette* (Act I) |
| **Je viens célébrer la victoire** (I will celebrate the triumph) | Samson (Tenor) | *Samson et Dalila* (Act I) |
| **Jerum! Jerum!** *See* Schusterlied | | |
| **Jewel Song** *See* Ah, je ris de me voir si belle | | |
| **Juliette's Waltz** *See* Je veux vivre dans ce rêve | | |
| **King Marke's Soliloquy** | King Marke (Bass) | *Tristan und Isolde* (Act II) |
| **King of Thule, The** *See* Il était un roi de Thulé | | |
| **Klänge der Heimat** (Sounds of Home) | Rosalinda (Soprano) | *Die Fledermaus* (Act II) |
| **Kommt ein schlanker Bursch gegangen** (Comes a handsome boy a-wooing) | Aennchen (Soprano) | *Der Freischütz* (Act II) |

| FIRST LINE | ROLE | OPERA |
|---|---|---|
| **La biondina in gondolete\*** | Soprano | |
| **La calunnia** (See what calumny) | Don Basilio (Bass) | *Il Barbiere di Siviglia* (Act II) |
| **Là ci darem la mano** (Let me adore your hand, love) | Zerlina, Don Giovanni (Soprano, Baritone) | *Don Giovanni* (Act I) |
| **La donna è mobile** (Woman is fickle) | The Duke of Mantua (Tenor) | *Rigoletto* (Act IV) |
| **La fatal pietra** (The fatal stone) | Aïda, Radames (Soprano, Tenor) | *Aïda* (Act IV) |
| **La fleur que tu m'avais jetée** (The flower that you threw to me) | Don José (Tenor) | *Carmen* (Act II) |
| **Le Rêve** *See* En fermant les yeux | | |
| **La vendetta** (Now the vengeance) | Doctor Bartolo (Bass) | *Le Nozze di Figaro* (Act I) |
| **La vergine degli angeli** (The Virgin of the angels) | Leonora, Padre Guardiano (Soprano, Bass) | *La Forza del Destino* (Act II) |
| **L'Amour est un oiseau rebelle** (Love is a wild bird) "The Habanera" | Carmen (Soprano) | *Carmen* (Act I) |
| **Largo** *See* Ombra mai fu | | |
| **Largo al factotum della città** (Way for the city's factotum) | Figaro (Baritone) | *Il Barbiere di Siviglia* (Act I) |
| **Lasciatemi morire†** (O let me die) "The Lament of Arianna" | Arianna (Soprano) | *Arianna* |
| **Last rose of summer, The** *See* Qui sola vergin rosa | | |
| **Laughing Song** *See* Mein Herr Marquis *See* Ah! je ris de me voir si belle *See* L'Ora o Tirsi | | |

\* A barcarolle used by Giorghi-Righetti in the Music Lesson scene of *Il Barbiere di Siviglia*.
† This is all that remains of the opera.

# FIRST LINES AND TITLES OF FAMOUS NUMBERS

| FIRST LINE | ROLE | OPERA |
|---|---|---|
| **Lay of Sorrow** | Shepherd <br>(Tenor) | *Tristan und Isolde* <br>(Act III) |
| **Le jour est levé** <br>(The day is breaking) | Huntsman <br>(Bass) | *Dinorah* <br>(Act III) |
| **Le minaccie** <br>(All your threatening) | Carlo, Alvaro <br>(Tenor, Baritone) | *La Forza del Destino* <br>(Act IV) |
| **Le veau d'Or** <br>(The Golden Calf) | Faust, Méphistophélès <br>(Tenor, Bass) | *Faust* <br>(Act II) |
| **Lebewohl mein flandrisch Mädchen** <br>(Now farewell my Flemish maiden) | Marquis de Chateauneuf <br>(Tenor) | *Zar und Zimmermann* <br>(Act II) |
| **L'Éclat de rire** <br>*See* L'Ora o Tirsi | | |
| **Leise, leise fromme Weise** <br>(Softly, softly, day is ending) | Agathe <br>(Soprano) | *Der Freischütz* <br>(Act II) |
| **Leonora Overture No. III*** | Orchestra | |
| **Leporello's Catalog** <br>*See* Madamina | | |
| **Les Oiseaux dans la charmille** <br>(The birds in the bushes) "The Mechanical Doll's Song" | Olympia <br>(Soprano) | *Les Contes d'Hoffmann* <br>(Act I) |
| **Letter Duet** <br>*See* Che soave zeffiretto | | |
| **Libiamo, libiamo ne' lieti calici** <br>(Let's drink, then let's drink from happy glasses) "The Brindisi" | Violetta, Alfredo, Chorus <br>(Soprano, Tenor, Chorus) | *La Traviata* <br>(Act I) |
| **Liebesnacht** <br>*See* Isolde! Tristan! Geliebte! | | |
| **Liebestod** <br>*See* Mild und leise | | |
| **Lohengrin's Farewell** | Lohengrin <br>(Tenor) | *Lohengrin* <br>(Act III) |
| **L'Ora o Tirsi†** <br>(L'Eclat de rire) | Manon Lescaut <br>(Soprano) | *Manon Lescaut* <br>(Act II) |

* The most famous of the four overtures to *Fidelio*, now used most often between the scenes of Act II.
† Sometimes used in the Music Lesson scene of *Il Barbiere di Siviglia*.

| FIRST LINE | ROLE | OPERA |
|---|---|---|
| **Love Death** | | |
| *See* Mild und leise | | |
| **Love Duet** | | |
| *See* Das süsse Lied verhallt | | Lohengrin |
| *See* Già nella notte densa | | Otello |
| *See* Isolde! Tristan! Geliebte! | | Tristan und Isolde |
| *See* Non la sospiri la nostra casetta | | Tosca |
| *See* Vieni la sera | | Madama Butterfly |
| **Lullaby** | | |
| *See* Berceuse | | |
| *See* Summertime | | |
| **Ma dall' avido stelo divulsa** | Amelia | Un Ballo in Maschera |
| (Beneath yonder magic flower) | (Soprano) | (Act II) |
| **Ma se m'è forza perderti** | Riccardo | Un Ballo in Maschera |
| (But if I am forced to lose you) | (Tenor) | (Act III) |
| **Mad Scene** | | |
| *See* Ophélie's Mad Scene | | Hamlet |
| *See* Qui la voce sua soave | | I Puritani |
| **Mad Scene from Lucia** | Lucia | Lucia di Lammermoor |
| | (Soprano) | (Act II) |
| **Mad Scene of Oreste** | Oreste | Iphigénie en Tauride |
| | (Baritone) | (Act II) |
| **Madamina** | Leporello | Don Giovanni |
| (Sweet my lady) "The Catalog" | (Bass) | (Act I) |
| **Magic Fire Music** | Orchestra | Die Walküre |
| | | (Act III) |
| **Magische Töne** | Assad | Die Königen von Saba |
| (Magical music) | (Tenor) | (Act II) |
| **Mal reggendo all' aspro assalto** | Azucena, Manrico | Il Trovatore |
| (Ill sustaining the vicious assault) | (Contralto, Tenor) | (Act II) |
| **Maledizione (The Malediction)** | | |
| *See* Cortigiani, vil razza dannata | | Rigoletto |
| *See* Vous qui de Dieu vivant | | La Juive |
| **Manca un foglio** | Doctor Bartolo | Il Barbiere di Siviglia |
| (A letter's missing) | (Bass) | (Act I) |
| **March of the Mastersingers** | Orchestra | Die Meistersinger |
| | | (Act III) |

| FIRST LINE | ROLE | OPERA |
|---|---|---|
| **Marche Hongroise** (Hungarian March) "The Rákóczy March" | Orchestra | *La Damnation de Faust* (Act I) |
| **Marsch, Marsch, Marsch** (March, March, March) | Pedrillo, Osmin, Belmonte (Two Tenors, Bass) | *Die Entführung aus dem Serail* (Act I) |
| **Martern aller Arten** (Tortures unabating) | Constanze (Soprano) | *Die Entführung aus dem Serail* (Act II) |
| **Me voici dans son boudoir** (Here am I in her boudoir) | Frédéric (Tenor) | *Mignon* (Act II) |
| **Meco all' altar di Venere** (With me at the altar of Venus) | Pollione (Tenor) | *Norma* (Act I) |
| **Meditation** | Orchestra | *Thaïs* (Act II) |
| **Mein Aug' bewacht** (My eyes on guard) | Saffi, Czipra, Barinkay (Soprano, Mezzo-soprano, Tenor) | *Zigeunerbaron* (Act II) |
| **Mein Freund, in holder Jungendzeit** (My friend, in my younger days) | David, Hans Sachs (Tenor, Baritone) | *Die Meistersinger* (Act III) |
| **Mein Herr Marquis** (My dear Marquis) | Adele (Soprano) | *Die Fledermaus* (Act II) |
| **Menuet des feux-follets** (Minuet of the will-o-the-wisps) | Orchestra | *La Damnation de Faust* (Act III) |
| **Metà di voi quà vadano** (Let half of you go down the road) | Don Giovanni (Baritone) | *Don Giovanni* (Act II) |
| **Mi chiamano Mimi** (My name is Mimi) | Mimi (Soprano) | *La Bohème* (Act I) |
| **Mi par d'udir ancora** (To me as in a dream) | Nadir (Tenor) | *Les Pêcheurs de Perles* (Act I) |
| **Mi tradì quel alma ingrate** (All my love was given to him) (This aria was inserted by Mozart for Katharina Cavalieri) | Donna Elvira (Soprano) | *Don Giovanni* (Act II) |
| **Mild und leise** (Mild and softly) "The Liebestod" | Isolde (Soprano) | *Tristan und Isolde* (Act III) |

| FIRST LINE | ROLE | OPERA |
|---|---|---|
| **Mimi's Farewell**<br>*See* Donde lieta usci | | |
| **Minuet from Don Giovanni** | Orchestra | *Don Giovanni*<br>(Act I) |
| **Minuet**<br>*See also* Menuet | | |
| **Mir ist so wunderbar***<br>(How wondrous the emotion) | Leonora, Marcellina,<br>Jacquino, Rocco<br>(Two Sopranos, Tenor,<br>Bass) | *Fidelio*<br>(Act I) |
| **Mira, O Norma**<br>(Hear me, O Norma) | Norma, Adalgisa<br>(Two sopranos) | *Norma*<br>(Act II) |
| **Miserere**<br>*See* Ah! che la morta ognora | | |
| **Mit Gewitter und Sturm**<br>(With thunder and storm) | Steersman<br>(Tenor) | *Der Fliegende Holländer*<br>(Act I) |
| **Mon coeur s'ouvre à ta voix**<br>(My heart at thy sweet voice) | Dalila<br>(Mezzo-soprano) | *Samson et Dalila*<br>(Act II) |
| **Monologue**<br>*See* È sogno o realtà<br>*See* I have attained the highest<br>    power<br>*See* Nemico della patria<br>*See* O monumento<br>*See* Pari siamo<br>*See* Wie duftet doch der Flieder | | *Falstaff*<br>*Boris Godunov*<br><br>*Andrea Chénier*<br>*La Gioconda*<br>*Rigoletto*<br>*Die Meistersinger* |
| **Monstre affreux!**<br>(Fearsome fiend!) | (Bass) | *Dardanus* |
| **Morgenlich leuchtend in rosigem Schein**<br>(Morning was gleaming with<br>roseate light) "The Prize Song" | Walther<br>(Tenor) | *Die Meistersinger*<br>(Act III) |
| **Morir! si pura e bella**<br>(To die! so pure and lovely) | Radames<br>(Tenor) | *Aida*<br>(Act IV) |
| **Musetta's Waltz**<br>*See* Quando me'n vo'soletta | | |
| **Music Lesson†** | Rosina<br>(Soprano or<br>Mezzo-soprano) | *Il Barbiere di Siviglia*<br>(Act II) |

\* This is a canon for four voices.

† By tradition, this scene consists of practically any arias and show-pieces the prima donna wishes to display.

# FIRST LINES AND TITLES OF FAMOUS NUMBERS

| FIRST LINE | ROLE | OPERA |
|---|---|---|
| **My man's gone now** | Serena (Soprano) | *Porgy and Bess* (Act I) |
| **My name is Mimi** See Mi chiamano Mimi | | |
| **My native land** See O patria mia | | |
| **Nacqui all' affanno, al pianto** (In anxiety and in tears) | Angelina (Contralto) | *La Cenerentola* (Act II) |
| **'Neath almond trees in bloom** | Count Adolar (Tenor) | *Euryanthe* (Act I) |
| **Nemico della patria** (Enemy of the Fatherland) "The Monologue" | Charles Gérard (Baritone) | *Andrea Chénier* (Act III) |
| **Nessun dorma** (None shall sleep) | Calaf (Tenor) | *Turandot* (Act III) |
| **No! Pagliaccio non son!** (No! I'm an actor no more!) | Canio (Tenor) | *Pagliacci* (Act II) |
| **Nobles seigneurs, salut** (Noble lords, my greeting) | The Page (Contralto) | *Les Huguenots* (Act I) |
| **Nocturne** See Tornami | | |
| **Non, ce n'est point un sacrifice** (No, it is hardly a sacrifice) | Alceste (Soprano) | *Alceste* (Act I) |
| **Non imprecare** (Cast no more blame) | Leonora, Alvaro, Padre Guardiano (Soprano, Tenor, Bass) | *La Forza del Destino* (Act IV) |
| **Non la sospiri la nostra casetta** (Do you not long for our secluded cottage) "The Love Duet" | Tosca, Mario (Soprano, Tenor) | *Tosca* (Act I) |
| **Non mi dir, bell' idol mio** (Say no more, my beloved) | Donna Anna (Soprano) | *Don Giovanni* (Act II) |
| **Non più andrai*** (No more so slyly) | Figaro (Baritone) | *Le Nozze di Figaro* (Act I) |
| **Non più di fiori vaghe catene** (O ne'er shall Hymen spread out his roses) | Vitellia (Soprano) | *La Clemenza di Tito* (Act II) |

* Sometimes this aria is played during the second act of *Don Giovanni*.

| FIRST LINE | ROLE | OPERA |
|---|---|---|
| **Non siate ritrosi** <br> (O vision so charming) | Guglielmo <br> (Bass) | *Così fan Tutte* <br> (Act I) |
| **Non so più cosa son, cosa faccio** <br> (I don't know what it can be <br> that ails me) | Cherubino <br> (Soprano) | *Le Nozze di Figaro* <br> (Act I) |
| **Nothung! Nothung!** <br> (*Nothung* is the name of <br> Siegfried's sword) "The <br> Forging Scene" | Siegfried <br> (Tenor) | *Siegfried* <br> (Act I) |
| **Notte e giorno faticar** <br> (Night and day am I weary) | Leporello <br> (Bass) | *Don Giovanni* <br> (Act I) |
| **Nume, custode e vindici** <br> (God, guardian and avenger) | Radames, Ramfis, Chorus <br> (Tenor, Bass, Chorus) | *Aida* <br> (Act I) |
| **Nun's Chorus** <br> *See* Ah! se l'error t'ingombra | | |
| **Nur eine Waffe taugt** <br> (Only one weapon serves) | Parsifal <br> (Tenor) | *Parsifal* <br> (Act III) |
| **Nurse's Song** <br> (Once a girl was languishing <br> alone) | Nurse <br> (Contralto) | *Boris Godunov* <br> (Act II) |
| **Nurse's Song** <br> *See also* Song of the Gnat | | |
| **O Araby, dear Araby** | Fatima <br> (Mezzo-soprano) | *Oberon* <br> (Act III) |
| **O Carlo, ascolta!** <br> (O Carlos, hear me!) | Rodrigo <br> (Baritone) | *Don Carlos* <br> (Act IV) |
| **O cieli azzuri** <br> *See* O patria mia | | |
| **O diese Sonne** <br> (How bright the sunlight) | Max, Cuno, Caspar <br> (Tenor, Two Basses) | *Der Freischütz* <br> (Act I) |
| **O Dieu, Dieu de nos pères** <br> (O God, God of our fathers) <br> "The Passover Scene" | Rachel, Eléazar <br> (Soprano, Tenor) | *La Juive* <br> (Act II) |
| **O don fatale** <br> (O fatal gift) | Princess Eboli <br> (Contralto) | *Don Carlos* <br> (Act IV) |
| **O du mein holder Abendstern** <br> (Thou brightly shining evening <br> star) | Wolfram <br> (Baritone) | *Tannhäuser* <br> (Act III) |

| FIRST LINE | ROLE | OPERA |
|---|---|---|
| **O holdes Bild** (O lovely picture) | Nureddin, Margiana (Soprano, Tenor) | *Der Barbier von Bagdad* (Act II) |
| **O Isis und Osiris** (O Isis and Osiris) | Sarastro (Bass) | *Zauberflöte* (Act II) |
| **O Lola** "The Siciliana" | Turiddu (Tenor) | *Cavalleria Rusticana* |
| **O malheureuse Iphigénie** (O unhappy Iphigénie) | Iphigénie (Soprano) | *Iphigénie en Tauride* |
| **O Mimi, tu più** (O Mimi, false one) | Rodolfo, Marcello (Tenor, Baritone) | *La Bohème* (Act IV) |
| **O mio babbino caro** (O my beloved daddy) | Lauretta (Soprano) | *Gianni Schicchi* |
| **O mio Fernando** (O my Ferdinand) | Leonora (Mezzo-soprano) | *La Favorita* (Act III) |
| **O monumento** "Barnaba's Monologue" | Barnaba (Baritone) | *La Gioconda* (Act I) |
| **O namenlose Freude** (O joy inexpressible) | Leonora, Florestan (Soprano, Tenor) | *Fidelio* (Act II) |
| **O paradiso** (O paradise) | Vasco da Gama (Tenor) | *L'Africaine* (Act III) |
| **O patria mia** (O my native land) | Aida (Soprano) | *Aida* (Act III) |
| **O prêtres de Baal** (O priests of Baal) "The Prison Scene" | Fidès (Contralto) | *Le Prophète* (Act V) |
| **O soave fanciulla** (O lovely maiden) | Rodolfo (Tenor) | *La Bohème* (Act I) |
| **O sommo Carlo** (O noble Carlos) | Elvira, Ernani, Don Silva, Chorus (Soprano, Tenor, Baritone, Chorus) | *Ernani* (Act III) |
| **O statua gentilissima** (O statue, most respectfully) | Leporello, Don Giovanni (Baritone, Bass) | *Don Giovanni* (Act II) |
| **O terra addio** (Farewell, Oh earth) | Aida, Radames (Soprano, Tenor) | *Aida* (Act IV) |
| **O toi qui prolongeas** (O thou who prolongest) | Iphigénie (Soprano) | *Iphigénie en Tauride* |

| FIRST LINE | ROLE | OPERA |
|---|---|---|
| **O tu che in seno agli angeli** (O thou who in the breast of the angels) | Alvaro (Tenor) | *La Forza del Destino* (Act III) |
| **O vin, dissipe la tristesse** (O wine, dismiss our heavy thoughts) | Hamlet (Baritone) | *Hamlet* (Act II) |
| **O wär ich schon mit dir vereint** (O were I but with you united) | Leonora (Soprano) | *Fidelio* (Act I) |
| **O welche Lust** (O what joy) "The Prisoners' Chorus" | Prisoners (Chorus) | *Fidelio* (Act I) |
| **O wie ängstlich, o wie feurig** (O how anxious, o how fiery) | Belmonte (Tenor) | *Die Entführung aus dem Serail* (Act I) |
| **O zittre nicht, mein lieber Sohn** (Be not afraid, o noble youth) | Queen of the Night (Soprano) | *Die Zauberflöte* (Act I) |
| **Obbligato, obbligato** (Thank you kindly, thank you kindly) | Nemerino, Dulcamara (Tenor, Bass) | *L'Elisir d'amore* (Act I) |
| **Obeissons, quand leur voix appelle** (We must obey them when they call) "The Gavotte" | Manon (Soprano) | *Manon* (Act III) |
| **Oh, pourquoi ne m'as-tu regardé?** (Oh why did you not look at me?) | Salome (Soprano) | *Salome* |
| **Ombra mai fu** (Deeply the shadow) "The Largo" | Xerxes (Contralto) | *Serse* |
| **Ombre légère** (Shadows so light) "The Shadow Song" | Dinorah (Soprano) | *Dinorah* (Act II) |
| **Ophélie's Mad Scene** | Ophélie (Soprano) | *Hamlet* (Act IV) |
| **Or sai chi l'onore** (Now you know for certain) | Donna Anna (Soprano) | *Don Giovanni* (Act I) |
| **Ora e per sempre addio** (Now and forever farewell) | Otello (Tenor) | *Otello* (Act II) |

| FIRST LINE | ROLE | OPERA |
|---|---|---|
| **Où va la jeune Hindoue?** (Where goes the Hindu maiden?) "The Bell Song" | Lakmé (Soprano) | *Lakmé* (Act II) |
| **Ozean, du Ungeheuer** (Ocean, thou mighty monster) | Reiza (Soprano) | *Oberon* (Act II) |
| **Pace, pace mio Dio** (Peace, peace, o Lord) | Leonora (Soprano) | *La Forza del Destino* (Act IV) |
| **Padre, germani, addio** (Father, my cousins, goodbye) | Ilia (Soprano) | *Idomeneo* (Act I) |
| **Paradiso** *See* O Paradiso | | |
| **Pari siamo** (How like we are) "Rigoletto's monologue" | Rigoletto (Baritone) | *Rigoletto* (Act II) |
| **Parigi, o cara, noi lasceremo** (Forever, my dear, must I leave thee) | Violetta, Alfredo (Soprano, Tenor) | *La Traviata* (Act III) |
| **Parmi veder le lagrime** (Among the tears that fall) | The Duke of Mantua (Tenor) | *Rigoletto* (Act III) |
| **Passover Scene** *See* O Dieu, Dieu de nos pères | | |
| **Patria mia** *See* O patria mia | | |
| **Patter song** (Farlaf's Rondo) | Farlaf (Bass) | *Russlan and Ludmilla* (Act II) |
| **Per me ora fatale** (Now is the fatal time) | Count di Luna (Baritone) | *Il Trovatore* (Act II) |
| **Per pietà, ben mio, perdona** (Ah my love, forgive my madness) | Fiordiligi (Soprano) | *Così fan Tutte* (Act II) |
| **Piangea cantando** (With weeping I sing) "The Willow Song" | Desdemona (Soprano) | *Otello* (Act IV) |
| **Piango si voi** (I weep for you) | Maria, Gabriele, Simon Boccanegra, Jacopo Fiesco (Soprano, Tenor, Baritone, Bass) | *Simon Boccanegra* (Act III) |
| **Piff! Paff!** | Marcel (Baritone) | *Les Huguenots* (Act I) |

| FIRST LINE | ROLE | OPERA |
|---|---|---|
| **Pilgrim's Chorus** | Chorus | *Tannhäuser*<br>(Acts I, III) |
| **Placido è il mar, andiamo**<br>(The sea is quiet now, let's leave here) | Chorus | *Idomeneo*<br>(Act II) |
| **Pogner's Address** | Veit Pogner<br>(Bass) | *Die Meistersinger*<br>(Act I) |
| **Polonaise**<br>*See* Je suis Titania | | |
| **Polonaise from "Boris Godunov"** | Orchestra | *Boris Godunov*<br>(Act III) |
| **Polovtsian Dances** | Ballet | *Prince Igor*<br>(Act II) |
| **Porgi amor**<br>(God of love) | Countess Almaviva<br>(Soprano) | *Le Nozze di Figaro*<br>(Act II) |
| **Portrait Aria**<br>*See* Dies Bildnis ist bezaubernd schön | | |
| **Pourquoi me reveiller?**<br>(O why did you wake me?) | Werther<br>(Tenor) | *Werther*<br>(Act III) |
| **Preislied "Prize song"**<br>*See* Morgenlich leuchtend in rosigem Schein | | |
| **Près des ramparts de Séville**<br>(Under the walls of Seville)<br>"The Seguidilla" | Carmen<br>(Soprano) | *Carmen*<br>(Act II) |
| **Pria di partir**<br>(Before we do leave) | Idamante, Elektra,<br>Idomeneo<br>(Two sopranos, Tenor) | *Idomeneo*<br>(Act II) |
| **Printemps qui commence**<br>(Spring is beginning) | Dalila<br>(Soprano) | *Samson et Dalila*<br>(Act I) |
| **Prisoner's Chorus**<br>*See* O welche Lust | | |
| **Prison Scene**<br>*See* Alerte! Alerte!<br>*See* O prêtres de Baal | | |
| **Prize Song**<br>*See* Morgenlich leuchtend in rosigem Schein | | |

| FIRST LINE | ROLE | OPERA |
|---|---|---|
| **Procession of the Mastersingers** | Orchestra | *Die Meistersinger* (Act III) |
| **Protegga il giusto cielo** (May heaven protect us) "The Trio of the Masks" | Donna Anna, Donna Elvira, Don Ottavio (Two Sopranos, Tenor) | *Don Giovanni* (Act I) |
| **Pur ti riveggo mia dolce Aida** (I see you again, my sweet Aida) | Radames (Tenor) | *Aida* (Act III) |
| **Qual cor tradisti** (The treacherous heart) | Norma, Pollione (Soprano, Tenor) | *Norma* (Act II) |
| **Quado me'n vo'soletta** (When I am alone) "Musetta's Waltz" | Musetta (Soprano) | *La Bohème* (Act II) |
| **Quanto amore** (What a false love!) | Adina, Dulcamara (Soprano, Baritone) | *L'Elisir d'amore* (Act II) |
| **Quanto e bella** (How beautiful) | Nemerino (Tenor) | *L'Elisir d'amore* (Act I) |
| **Quartet from La Bohème** *See* Addio dolce svegliare | | |
| **Quartet from Rigoletto** *See* Bella figlia dell' amore | | |
| **Queen of the Night's Aria** *See* Der Hölle Rache kocht in meinem Herzen *See also* O zittre nicht mein lieber Sohn | | |
| **Questa o quella** (This or that one?) | The Duke of Mantua (Tenor) | *Rigoletto* (Act I) |
| **Qui la voce sua soave** (How smooth his voice) "Elvira's Mad Scene" | Elvira (Soprano) | *I Puritani* (Act II) |
| **Qui sola vergine rosa** ('Tis the last rose of Summer) | Martha (Soprano) | *Martha* (Act II) |
| **Quintet from Un Ballo in Maschera** *See* É scherzo ed è follia | | |
| **Quintet from Die Meistersinger** *See* Selig wie die Sonne | | |
| **Quintet from La Traviata** *See* Ah si! che feci | | |

| FIRST LINE | ROLE | OPERA |
|---|---|---|
| **Rachel! quand du seigneur*** (Rachel, when from the Lord) | Eléazar (Tenor) | *La Juive* (Act IV) |
| **Rákóczy march** See Marche Hongroise | | |
| **Recondita armonia** (Strange harmony) | Mario (Tenor) | *Tosca* (Act I) |
| **Return victorious!** See Ritorna Vincitor! | | |
| **Ride of the Valkyries** | Orchestra | *Die Walküre* (Act III) |
| **Rienzi's Prayer** | Rienzi (Tenor) | *Rienzi* (Act V) |
| **Ritorna vincitor** (Return in victory) | Aida (Soprano) | *Aida* (Act I) |
| **Rivolgete a lui lo sguardo†** | Bass | |
| **Rodolfo's Narrative** See Che gelida manina | | |
| **Roi de Thulé, Le** See Il était un roi de Thulé | | |
| **Rom Erzählung** (Rome Narrative) | Tannhäuser (Tenor) | *Tannhäuser* (Act III) |
| **Room for the factotum** See Largo al factotum | | |
| **Rosa del ciel** (Rose of heaven) | Orfeo (Tenor) | *La Favola d'Orfeo* (Act I) |
| **Rudolph's Narrative** See Che gelida manina | | |
| **Sach's Monologue** See Wie duftet doch der Flieder | | |
| **Salomé, Salomé, demande** (Salome, Salome, but ask) | Herod (Baritone) | *Hérodiade* (Act III) |
| **Salut a toi soleil de flamme** (I hail the day's bright light, the sun) "Hymn to the Sun" | Queen (Soprano) | *Le Coq d'Or* (Act II) |

* According to Kobbé, Nourrit may have had a hand in the composition of this aria.
† This aria, K.584, was originally planned for Guglielmo in Act I of *Così fan Tutte*, but was not so used.

| FIRST LINE | ROLE | OPERA |
|---|---|---|
| **Salut, demeure chaste et pure**<br>(Hail, thou dwelling chaste and pure) | Faust<br>(Tenor) | *Faust*<br>(Act III) |
| **Sandman's Lullaby**<br>*See* Der kleine Sandmann bin ich | | |
| **Scarpia's Aria**<br>*See* Giá mi dicon venal | | |
| **Schattentanz**<br>*See* Ombre légère | | |
| **Schusterlied**<br>(*Cobbler's Song*) | Hans Sachs<br>(Baritone) | *Die Meistersinger*<br>(Act II) |
| **Scintille, diamant**<br>(Sparkle, diamond) | Dapertutto<br>(Baritone) | *Les Contes d'Hoffmann*<br>(Act III) |
| **Se a caso Madama**<br>(If milady should call you) | Figaro<br>(Baritone) | *Le Nozze di Figaro*<br>(Act I) |
| **Se il mio nome saper**<br>(Shall I then tell you his name?) | Figaro<br>(Tenor) | *Il Barbiere di Siviglia*<br>(Act I) |
| **Se il padre perdei**<br>(If I should lose my father) | Ilia<br>(Soprano) | *Idomeneo*<br>(Act II) |
| **Se vuol ballare**<br>(Would you like dancing?) | Figaro<br>(Baritone) | *Le Nozze di Figaro*<br>(Act I) |
| **Secondate aurette amiche**<br>(Gentle breezes softly sighing) | Ferrando, Guglielmo<br>(Tenor, Baritone) | *Così fan Tutte*<br>(Act II) |
| **Selig wie die Sonne**<br>(Brightly as the sun) | Eva, Magdalena, David,<br>Walther, Hans Sachs<br>(Soprano, Mezzo-<br>soprano, Two Tenors,<br>Bass) | *Die Meistersinger*<br>(Act III) |
| **Sempre libera**<br>(Now so freely) | Violetta<br>(Soprano) | *La Traviata*<br>(Act I) |
| **Seguidilla**<br>*See* Près des ramparts de Séville | | |
| **Sempre in contrasti**<br>(Always in contrasts) | Uberto<br>(Bass) | *La Serva Padrona*<br>(Part I) |
| **Sento, O Dio!**<br>(Courage fails me) "The<br>Quintet" | Fiordiligi, Dorabella,<br>Ferrando, Guglielmo,<br>Alfonso<br>(Two Sopranos, Tenor,<br>Baritone, Bass) | *Così fan Tutte*<br>(Act I) |

| FIRST LINE | ROLE | OPERA |
|---|---|---|
| **Serenade** | | |
| *See* Deh vieni alla finestra | | *Don Giovanni* |
| *See* Se il mio nome | | *Il Barbiere di Siviglia* |
| *See* Vous qui faites l'endormie | | *Faust* |
| **Sextet from "Lucia"** | | |
| *See* Chi mi frena? | | |
| **Shadow Song** | | |
| *See* Ombre légère | | |
| **Si la rigueur et la vengeance** | Cardinal de Brogni | *La Juive* |
| (If the rigor and the vengeance) | (Bass) | (Act I) |
| **Si, pel ciel marmoreo giuro** | Otello, Iago | *Otello* |
| (Now, we swear by heaven and earth) | (Tenor, Baritone) | (Act II) |
| **Si può? Signore, Signori** | Tonio | *I Pagliacci* |
| (May I, Ladies, Gentlemen?) | (Tenor) | (Prologue) |
| **Siciliana** | | |
| *See* O Lola | | |
| **Siccome un dì caduto** | Leïla | *Les Pêcheurs de Perles* |
| (As fugitive one day) | (Soprano) | (Act II) |
| **Siege of Kazan** | | |
| *See* Varlaam's Song | | |
| **Siegfrieds Erzählung** | Siegfried | *Siegfried* |
| (Siegfried's Narrative) | (Tenor) | (Act III) |
| **Siegfried's Rhine Journey** | Orchestra | *Siegfried* |
| | | (Prelude) |
| **Siegmund heiss ich** | Siegmund | *Die Walküre* |
| (Siegmund am I) | (Tenor) | (Act I) |
| **Siegmund's Spring Song** | | |
| *See* Winterstürme wichen | | |
| **Simpleton's Lament** | Simpleton | *Boris Godunov* |
| (Flow, ah! flow my bitter tears) | (Tenor) | (Finale) |
| **Sittencommissions couplets** | Mirabella, Zsupan, Carnero (Contralto, Two Baritones) | *Zigeunerbaron* (Act II) |
| **Sleepwalking Scene** | Lady Macbeth | *Macbeth* |
| | (Soprano) | (Act IV) |

| FIRST LINE | ROLE | OPERA |
|---|---|---|
| **Sleepwalking Scene** | Amina<br>(Soprano) | *La Sonnambula*<br>(Act III) |
| **Smanie implacabile**<br>(Frenzied and implacable) | Dorabella<br>(Soprano) | *Così fan Tutte*<br>(Act I) |
| **So elend und so treu**<br>(So miserable and true) | Saffi<br>(Soprano) | *Zigeunerbaron*<br>(Act I) |
| **Soave sia il vento**<br>(O may the sea flow calmly) | Fiordiligi, Dorabella,<br>Alfonso<br>(Two Sopranos,<br>Baritone) | *Così fan Tutte*<br>(Act I) |
| **Sogno soave e casto**<br>(Dream so fair and chaste) | Ernesto<br>(Tenor) | *Don Pasquale*<br>(Act III) |
| **Soldiers' Chorus**<br>*See* Gloire immortelle | | |
| **Solenne in quest' ora**<br>(Solemnly this hour) | Carlo, Alvaro<br>(Tenor, Baritone) | *La Forza del Destino*<br>(Act III) |
| **Son imbrogliato io già**<br>(I'm embroiled in it already) | Uberto<br>(Bass) | *La Serva Padrona*<br>(Part II) |
| **Son vergin vezzosa**<br>(I am a blithesome maiden) | Elvira<br>(Soprano) | *I Puritani*<br>(Act I) |
| **Song of Battles**<br>*See* Varlaam's Song | | |
| **Song of India** | The Indian Merchant<br>(Tenor) | *Sadko*<br>(Act II) |
| **Song of the Drake**<br>(Once I caught a drake with<br>feathers) | Innkeeper<br>(Mezzo-soprano) | *Boris Godunov*<br>(Act I) |
| **Song of the Gnat** | Nurse<br>(Mezzo-soprano) | *Boris Godunov*<br>(Act II) |
| **Song of the Valkyr**<br>*See* Ho yo to ho | | |
| **Song of the Viking** | The Viking Merchant<br>(Bass) | *Sadko*<br>(Act II) |
| **Song to the evening star**<br>*See* O du mein holder Abendstern | | |
| **Sono andati**<br>(Have they all gone now?) | Mimi, Rodolfo<br>(Soprano, Tenor) | *La Bohème*<br>(Act IV) |

| FIRST LINE | ROLE | OPERA |
|---|---|---|
| **Sonst spielt ich mit Szepter und Kron**<br>(I played with the scepter and crown) | Peter I<br>(Tenor) | *Zar und Zimmermann*<br>(Act III) |
| **Splendon più belle in ciel**<br>(The splendor of the sky) | Baldassare<br>(Bass) | *La Favorita*<br>(Act IV) |
| **Standin' in need of prayer** | Emperor Jones<br>(Baritone) | *The Emperor Jones*<br>(Act II) |
| **Steuermannslied**<br>*See* Mit Gewitter und Sturm | | |
| **Stizzoso, mio stizzoso**<br>(You vex me, how you vex me!) | Serpina<br>(Soprano) | *La Serva Padrona*<br>(Part I) |
| **Stride la vampa**<br>(Let the flames roar) | Azucena<br>(Mezzo-soprano) | *Il Trovatore*<br>(Act II) |
| **Su, e con me vieni, o cara**<br>(Come, then, come with me, my dearest) | Euridice, Orfeo<br>(Soprano, Contralto) | *Orfeo ed Euridice*<br>(Act III) |
| **Suicidio!**<br>(Suicide!) | La Gioconda<br>(Soprano) | *La Gioconda*<br>(Act IV) |
| **Summertime and the livin' is easy**<br>"The Lullaby" | Bess<br>(Soprano) | *Porgy and Bess*<br>(Act I) |
| **Suoni la tromba**<br>(O sound the trumpet) | Richard Forth, George Walton<br>(Baritone, Bass) | *I Puritani*<br>(Act II) |
| **Swan Song**<br>*See* Lohengrin's Farewell | | |
| **Tacea la notte placida**<br>(Calmly and gracefully night time) | Leonora<br>(Soprano) | *Il Trovatore*<br>(Act I) |
| **Tannhäuser's Song**<br>*See* Göttin der Liebe soll mein Lied ertönen | | |
| **Te Deum**<br>(Thou, o Lord) | Scarpia, Chorus<br>(Baritone, Chorus) | *Tosca*<br>(Act I) |
| **Te souvient-il du lumineux voyage**<br>(Do you remember the luminous voyage) | Athanael, Thaïs<br>(Soprano, Baritone) | *Thaïs*<br>(Act III) |

| FIRST LINE | ROLE | OPERA |
|---|---|---|
| **Temple Scene** *See* Nume custode | | |
| **Terra addio, O** *See* O terra addio | | |
| **The last rose of summer** *See* Qui sola vergine rose | | |
| **There's a boat that's leavin' soon for New York** | Sportin' Life (Tenor) | *Porgy and Bess* (Act III) |
| **Threatful gather clouds about me** | Euryanthe, Eglantine (Soprano, Mezzo-soprano) | *Euryanthe* (Act I) |
| **To you my soul I give** | Euryanthe, Count Adolar) (Soprano, Tenor) | *Euryanthe* (Act II) |
| **Toreador's Song** *See* Votre toast | | |
| **Torna la pace al core\*** (Now take peace into your heart) | Idomeneo (Tenor) | *Idomeneo* (Act III) |
| **Torna, torna, deh torna, Ulisse** (Back, come back, o return, Ulysses) | Penelope (Contralto) | *Il Ritorno d'Ulisse in Patria* (Act I) |
| **Tornami a dir che m'ami** (Turn to me and say you love me) | Norina, Ernesto (Soprano, Tenor) | *Don Pasquale* (Act III) |
| **Tortures unabating** *See* Martern aller Arten | | |
| **Traurigkeit ward mir zum Lose** (Sadness was all my destiny) | Constanze (Soprano) | *Die Entführung aus dem Serail* (Act II) |
| **Treasure Waltz** *See* Ha, seht es winkt | | |
| **Trinke, Liebchen, trinke schnell** (Drink, my darling, drink it up) | Rosalinda, Alfred (Soprano, Tenor) | *Die Fledermaus* (Act I) |
| **Trio of the Masks** *See* Protegga il giusto cielo | | |
| **Tu che a Dio spiegasti l'ali** (Thou who to God has spread thy wings) | Edgardo, Raimondo (Tenor, Bass) | *Lucia di Lammermoor* (Act III) |

\* This aria was not sung in the first performance of the opera.

| FIRST LINE | ROLE | OPERA |
|---|---|---|
| **Ah! du wolltest mich nicht deinen Mund küssen lassen** (You would not kiss me) | Salome (Soprano) | *Salome* |
| **Tu sè morta, sè morta mia vita** (Thou art dead, my life dies with you) | Orfeo (Tenor) | *La Favola d'Orfeo* (Act II) |
| **Tutte le feste al tempio** (On every festal morning) | Gilda (Soprano) | *Rigoletto* (Act III) |
| **Udite, udite, o rustici** (O hear me, o hear me, dear villagers) | Dulcamara (Bass) | *L'Elisir d'amore* (Act I) |
| **Un' aura amorosa** (Her eyes so alluring) | Ferrando (Tenor) | *Così fan Tutte* (Act II) |
| **Un bel dì vedremo** (One fine day I'll see him) | Cio-cio San (Soprano) | *Madama Butterfly* (Act II) |
| **Un dì felice eterea** (One day of rapture) | Violetta, Alfredo (Soprano, Tenor) | *La Traviata* (Act I) |
| **Una donna a quindici anni** (Once a lady fifteen years old) | Despina (Soprano) | *Così fan Tutte* (Act II) |
| **Una furtiva lagrima** (A furtive tear) | Nemerino (Tenor) | *L'Elisir d'amore* (Act II) |
| **Una voce poco fa** (Just a while ago I heard) | Rosina (Mezzo-soprano) | *Il Barbiere di Siviglia* (Act I) |
| **Und ob die Wolke** (Although a cloud comes) | Agathe (Soprano) | *Der Freischütz* (Act III) |
| **Unis dès la plus tendre enfance** (Together since earliest childhood) | Pylade (Tenor) | *Iphigénie en Tauride* (Act III) |
| **Va crudele, al dio spietato** (Go, O cruel one, to God the implacable) | Adalgisa, Pollione (Soprano, Tenor) | *Norma* (Act I) |
| **Va, pensiero** (Go, my thoughts) | Hebrew captives (Chorus) | *Nabucco* (Act III) |
| **Vallons de l'Helvétie** (O valleys of Helvetia) | (Bass) | *Le Chalet* |
| **Varlaam's Song** (Long ago at Kazan) | Varlaam (Bass) | *Boris Godunov* (Act I) |

| FIRST LINE | ROLE | OPERA |
|---|---|---|
| **Vedrai carino, se sei buonino**<br>(O shall I tell you, my dearest) | Zerlina<br>(Soprano) | *Don Giovanni*<br>(Act II) |
| **Vedrò mentr'io sospiro**<br>(I'll go while still I have breath) | Almaviva<br>(Baritone) | *Le Nozze di Figaro*<br>(Act III) |
| **Vengeance Aria**<br>*See* Or sai che l'onore | | |
| **Venite inginocchiatevi**<br>(Come here and kneel before me) | Countess Almaviva<br>(Soprano) | *Le Nozze di Figaro*<br>(Act II) |
| **Venusberg Music** | Orchestra | *Tannhäuser*<br>(Prelude) |
| **Vesti la giubba**<br>(On with the play) | Canio<br>(Tenor) | *Pagliacci*<br>(Act I) |
| **Vi ravviso o luoghi ameni**<br>(As I gaze on the scenes of my<br>childhood) | Count Rodolpho<br>(Bass) | *La Sonnambula*<br>(Act I) |
| **Vi ricordo o boschi ombrosi**<br>(I recall now the shadowy forest) | Orfeo<br>(Tenor) | *La Favola d'Orfeo*<br>(Act II) |
| **Vien, diletto**<br>(Come, beloved) | Elvira<br>(Soprano) | *I Puritani*<br>(Act I) |
| **Vieni fra queste braccia**<br>(Come into my arms) | Elvira, Arturo<br>(Soprano, Tenor) | *I Puritani*<br>(Act III) |
| **Vieni la sera**<br>(Evening's coming) | Cio-cio San, Pinkerton<br>(Soprano, Tenor) | *Madama Butterfly*<br>(Act I) |
| **Vision fugitive**<br>(Fleeting vision) | Herod<br>(Baritone) | *Hérodiade*<br>(Act II) |
| **Vissi d'arte**<br>(Thus love and music) | Tosca<br>(Soprano) | *Tosca*<br>(Act II) |
| **Viva il vino spumeggiante**<br>(Long live the wine effervescent)<br>"The Brindisi" | Turiddu, Chorus<br>(Tenor, Chorus) | *Cavalleria Rusticana* |
| **Vivat Bacchus**<br>(Long live Bacchus) | Pedrillo, Osmin<br>(Tenor, Bass) | *Die Entführung aus dem<br>Serail*<br>(Act II) |
| **Voce di donna o d'angelo**<br>(Voice of the lady, or of angels) | La Cieca<br>(Mezzo-soprano) | *La Gioconda*<br>(Act I) |
| **Voi che sapete**<br>(Tell me fair ladies) | Cherubino<br>(Soprano) | *Le Nozze di Figaro*<br>(Act II) |

| FIRST LINE | ROLE | OPERA |
|---|---|---|
| **Voi lo sapete**<br>(Well do you know it) | Santuzza<br>(Soprano) | *Cavalleria Rusticana* |
| **Votre toast je peux vous le rendre**<br>(To your toast I'll give another)<br>"The Toreador's Song" | Escamillo<br>(Baritone) | *Carmen*<br>(Act II) |
| **Vous qui du Dieu vivant**<br>(You who of the living God)<br>"Malediction" | Cardinal de Brogni<br>(Bass) | *La Juive*<br>(Act III) |
| **Vous qui faites l'endormie**<br>(You pretend to be sleeping) | Méphistophélès<br>(Bass) | *Faust*<br>(Act IV) |
| **Wach! auf! es nahet gen den Tag***<br>(Awake, draws near the break of day) | Chorus | *Die Meistersinger*<br>(Act III) |
| **Wahn! Wahn! Überall Wahn!**<br>(Mad, mad, all the world's mad!) | Hans Sachs<br>(Baritone) | *Die Meistersinger*<br>(Act III) |
| **Waldweben**<br>(Forest weaving) | Orchestra | *Siegfried*<br>(Act II) |
| **Walpurgis night** | Ballet | *Faust*<br>(Act V) |
| **Walther's Prize Song**<br>*See* Morgenlich leuchtend in rosigem Schein | | |
| **Waltraute's Narrative**<br>*See* Erzählung der Waltraute | | |
| **Waltz from Eugene Onegin** | Orchestra | *Eugene Onegin*<br>(Act I) |
| **Waltz from Faust** | Orchestra | *Faust*<br>(Act II) |
| **Waltz from Roméo et Juliette**<br>*See* Je veux vivre dans ce rêve | | |
| **Waltz from La Bohème**<br>*See* Quando me'n vo'soletta | | |
| **Waltz from Die Fledermaus** | Orchestra | *Die Fledermaus*<br>(Act II) |
| **Waltz from Der Rosenkavalier** | Orchestra | *Der Rosenkavalier*<br>(Act II) |

* The words to this chorale are by the real Hans Sachs.

| FIRST LINE | ROLE | OPERA |
|---|---|---|
| **Wedding March**<br>*See* Bridal Chorus | | |
| **Weiche, Wotan, weiche!**<br>(Waver, Wotan, waver!) | Erda<br>(Contralto) | *Das Rheingold* |
| **Welch ein Geschick**<br>(What dexterity!) | Constanze, Belmonte<br>(Soprano, Tenor) | *Die Entführung aus dem Serail*<br>(Act III) |
| **Welche Wonne, welche Lust**<br>(What delight, what freedom) | Blonde<br>(Soprano) | *Die Entführung aus dem Serail*<br>(Act II) |
| **Welcher Kummer herrscht in meiner Seele**<br>(What conflicting feelings rule my soul) | Constanze<br>(Soprano) | *Die Entführung aus dem Serail*<br>(Act II) |
| **Wenn der Freuden Thränen fliessen**<br>(When the tears of joy are flowing) | Belmonte<br>(Tenor) | *Die Entführung aus dem Serail*<br>(Act II) |
| **Wer ein Liebchen hat gefunden**<br>(When a maiden takes your fancy) | Osmin<br>(Bass) | *Die Entführung aus dem Serail*<br>(Act I) |
| **Wer uns getraut?**<br>(Who married us?) | Saffi, Barinkay<br>(Soprano, Tenor) | *Zigeunerbaron*<br>(Act II) |
| **When a maiden takes your fancy**<br>*See* Wer ein Liebchen hat gefunden | | |
| **When I am laid in earth** | Dido<br>(Soprano) | *Dido and Aeneas*<br>(Act III) |
| **When zephyrs waft me peace** | Count Adolar<br>(Tenor) | *Euryanthe*<br>(Act II) |
| **Where seek to hide** | Count Lysiart<br>(Baritone) | *Euryanthe*<br>(Act II) |
| **Wie duftet doch der Flieder**<br>(How sweetly smells the elder)<br>"Hans Sach's Narrative" | Hans Sachs<br>(Bass) | *Die Meistersinger*<br>(Act II) |
| **Wie oft in Meers tiefsten Schlund**<br>(How often in the ocean's caves) | Dutchman<br>(Baritone) | *Der Fliegende Holländer*<br>(Act I) |
| **Wie stark ist nicht dein Zauberton**<br>(O voice of magic melody) | Pamino<br>(Tenor) | *Die Zauberflöte*<br>(Act I) |

| FIRST LINE | ROLE | OPERA |
|---|---|---|
| **Willow Song**<br>*See* Piangea cantando | | |
| **Winterstürme weichen**<br>(Winter's storms are lightening)<br>"Siegmund's spring song" | Siegmund<br>(Tenor) | *Die Walküre*<br>(Act I) |
| **Witch's Song** | The Witch<br>(Mezzo-soprano) | *Hänsel und Gretel*<br>(Act III) |
| **Zefiretti lusinghieri**<br>(Little breezes, little flatteries) | Ilia<br>(Soprano) | *Idomeneo*<br>(Act III) |
| **Zitti, zitti, piano**<br>(Quickly, quickly, softly) | Rosina, Almaviva,<br>Figaro<br>(Mezzo-soprano,<br>Tenor, Baritone) | *Il Barbiere di Siviglia*<br>(Act II) |

# CHRONOLOGY OF OPERA

| YEAR | GENERAL HISTORY | OPERA HISTORY | FIRST PERFORMANCES |
|------|-----------------|---------------|--------------------|
| 1285 | | | Le Jeu de Robin et Marion |
| 1472 | | | Orfeo (Poliziano) |
| 1492 | Columbus discovered the West Indies. | | |
| 1513 | Balboa discovered the Pacific Ocean. | | |
| 1540 | DIED: Dr. Johann Faust. | | |
| 1542 | De Soto died on the Mississippi River. | | |
| 1546 | DIED: Martin Luther. | BORN: Caccini. | |
| 1548 | BORN: El Greco (?). | | |
| 1550 | | BORN: Vecchi, Cavalieri. | |
| 1553 | DIED: Rabelais. | | |
| 1554 | England became reconciled to the Papal Court. | | |
| 1556 | DIED: Charles V of Spain. | | |
| 1558 | Elizabeth I became Queen of England. | | |
| 1560 | | BORN: Corsi. | |
| 1561 | The Huguenots got their name. | BORN: Peri. | |
| 1564 | BORN: Shakespeare, Galileo Galilei, DIED: John Calvin. | | |
| 1567 | | BORN: Monteverdi. | |
| 1568 | Mary, Queen of Scots defeated at Langside. | | |

537

| YEAR | GENERAL HISTORY | OPERA HISTORY | FIRST PERFORMANCES |
|------|-----------------|---------------|--------------------|
| 1572 | Massacre of St. Bartholomew. | | |
| 1576 | First theater built in England. | | |
| 1581 | | | Circe, a ballad opera at the Louvre |
| 1584 | DIED: Ivan the Terrible. | | |
| 1585 | | BORN: Schütz. | |
| 1587 | Published: *Historia von D. Johann Fausten.* | | |
| 1588 | Spanish Armada destroyed. First newspaper in England. | | |
| 1590 | Written: Marlowe's *Doctor Faustus.* | | |
| 1597 | Shakespeare's *Romeo and Juliet.* | Published: *L'Amfiparnaso.* | |
| 1598 | Boris Godunov became Tsar of Russia. | | |
| 1600 | | | Euridice (Peri): La Rappresentazione dell' Anima e del Corpo |
| 1602 | First Englishman lands in New England. | DIED: Cavalieri. | |
| 1603 | DIED: Elizabeth I. Shakespeare's *Hamlet.* | | |
| 1604 | French establish colony in Maine. | DIED: Corsi. | |
| 1605 | DIED: Boris Godunov. Published: *Don Quixote.* | DIED: Vecchi. | |
| 1607 | Jamestown colony founded. | | La Favola d'Orfeo |
| 1608 | BORN: John Milton. | | Dafne (Gagliano); Arianna |
| 1610 | Coffee first used in Europe. | | |

| YEAR | GENERAL HISTORY | OPERA HISTORY | FIRST PERFORMANCES |
|------|-----------------|---------------|--------------------|
| 1613 | Pocahontas converted to Christianity. | Monteverdi moved to Venice. | |
| 1614 | A colony founded at the mouth of the Hudson. | | |
| 1616 | DIED: Shakespeare. | BORN: Perrin. | |
| 1617 | DIED: Pocahontas. | | |
| 1618 | Beginning of the Thirty Years' War. | DIED: Caccini. | |
| 1619 | Discovery of the circulation of the blood. BORN: Cyrano de Bergerac. | | |
| 1620 | Colony founded at Plymouth. Invention of the thermometer. | | |
| 1622 | BORN: Molière. | | |
| 1624 | | | Il Combattimento di Tancredi e Clorinda |
| 1625 | Nieuw Amsterdam founded. DIED: El Greco. | | |
| 1627 | | | Dafne, the first German opera |
| 1628 | Bernini began the tomb of Urban. | BORN: Cambert. | |
| 1632 | Maryland chartered. | BORN: Lully. | |
| 1633 | First schoolmaster arrived in America. | DIED: Peri. | |
| 1634 | First hackney coaches in London | BORN: M. A. Charpentier. | |
| 1635 | The French Academy founded. | BORN: Quinault. | |
| 1636 | Harvard College founded. | | |
| 1637 | War between settlers and Pequot Indians in Massachusetts. | First public opera house opened at Venice. | |

| YEAR | GENERAL HISTORY | OPERA HISTORY | FIRST PERFORMANCES |
|---|---|---|---|
| 1638 | First log cabin in America. | Published: *Il Combattimento di Tancredi e Clorinda.* | |
| 1639 | First American post office. | | L'Adone |
| 1641 | First colonial American patent. | | Il Ritorno d'Ulisse in Patria |
| 1642 | DIED: Galileo Galilei. | | L'Incoronazione di Poppea |
| 1643 | Invention of the barometer. | DIED: Monteverdi. | |
| 1644 | Cromwell defeated Prince Rupert. | | |
| 1645 | | First Italian opera troupe visits Paris. | |
| 1648 | End of the Thirty Years' War. | | |
| 1649 | Charles I beheaded. | | |
| 1653 | Cromwell made Lord Protector of England. | | |
| 1655 | DIED: Cyrano de Bergerac. | | Triomphe de l'Amour sur Bergers et Bergères, the first French opera |
| 1656 | First Quakers arrive in America. | | The Siege of Rhodes, the first English opera |
| 1658 | First hospital established at Nieuw Amsterdam. | BORN: Purcell. | |
| 1660 | English monarchy restored. Tea introduced to England. | BORN: Campra and A. Scarlatti. | Serse (Cavalli) |
| 1661 | Louis XIV established the court of Versailles. | | |
| 1662 | Connecticut colony chartered. | Covent Garden theatre opened. | |
| 1664 | The English establish New York. | | |
| 1665 | Molière wrote *Le Festin de Pierre* (*Don Juan*). The Great Plague. | | |

| YEAR | GENERAL HISTORY | OPERA HISTORY | FIRST PERFORMANCES |
|---|---|---|---|
| 1666 | The Great Fire of London. | | |
| 1669 | BORN: Antonio Vivaldi. | | |
| 1670 | Charleston, S.C. founded. | BORN: Caldara | |
| 1671 | | Louis XIV permits the establishment of the Académie Royale de Musique (L'Opéra). | Pomona |
| 1672 | First book copyrighted in America. | Lully took over the Opéra. DIED: Schütz. | Les Fêtes de l'Amour et de Bacchus. |
| 1673 | DIED: Molière. The first mail carried from New York to Boston. | | |
| 1674 | DIED: John Milton. | | Alceste (Lully) |
| 1675 | Indian raid upon Deerfield, Massachusetts. | DIED: Perrin. | |
| 1677 | Racine wrote *Phèdre*. | DIED: Cambert. | Isis |
| 1678 | First book of poems by Anne Bradstreet, first American poetess. | First opera house built in Germany at Hamburg. | |
| 1679 | Great fire at Boston. | | Gli Equivoci nel Sembiante (Scarlatti) |
| 1682 | First marriage in Pennsylvania. | Stradella murdered. | |
| 1683 | The Poles break the Turkish siege of Vienna. | BORN: Rameau. | |
| 1685 | BORN: J. S. Bach, Handel and John Gay. | | |
| 1686 | Charter of Connecticut hidden in an oak tree from Governor Andros. | | Acis et Galathée (Lully); Armide (Lully) |
| 1687 | | DIED: Lully. | |
| 1688 | Bacon's *Essays* printed in America. | DIED: Quinault. | |
| 1689 | Peter the Great made Tsar of Russia. | | Dido and Aeneas |

| YEAR | GENERAL HISTORY | OPERA HISTORY | FIRST PERFORMANCES |
|---|---|---|---|
| 1690 | Battle of the Boyne, Ireland | | |
| 1691 | First ducking stool in New York. | | King Arthur |
| 1692 | Salem witch hunt began. | | The Fairy Queen |
| 1693 | | | Medea (Charpentier) |
| 1694 | BORN: Voltaire. | | |
| 1695 | First streetcleaners in New York. | DIED: Purcell. | |
| 1698 | | BORN: Metastasio. | |
| 1704 | Louis XIV defeated at Blenheim. Massacre at Deerfield, Massachusetts. | DIED: M. A. Charpentier. | Iphigénie en Tauride (Campra) |
| 1705 | Newcomen's steam engine. | | Almira (Handel) |
| 1706 | BORN: Benjamin Franklin. | BORN: Galuppi. | |
| 1707 | England and Scotland united. | | |
| 1709 | First copyright by statute granted in England. | | Agrippina |
| 1710 | Three thousand refugees from Germany arrive in America. | BORN: Arne, Favart and Pergolesi. | |
| 1712 | Carolina divided into North and South parts. | BORN: Rousseau. | Il Pastor Fido—first version |
| 1714 | Tea imported to America. | BORN: Gluck. | |
| 1720 | New York City had 7000 residents. | Royal Academy of Music established in London. | |
| 1721 | First inoculation against smallpox. | | |
| 1722 | | Bach's *Wohltemperiertes Klavier*, celebrating the equal-tempered system of tuning. | |
| 1725 | First newspaper in New York. | DIED: A. Scarlatti. | |

| YEAR | GENERAL HISTORY | OPERA HISTORY | FIRST PERFORMANCES |
|---|---|---|---|
| 1726 | | | Alessandro |
| 1728 | First organ in Philadelphia. | BORN: Piccini. | The Beggar's Opera |
| 1730 | Baltimore settled. | | Partenope |
| 1731 | First circulating library in America. | | Il Maestro di Musica |
| 1732 | BORN: G. Washington. | BORN: Beaumarchais, J. Haydn. DIED: John Gay. | Acis and Galatea (Handel) |
| 1733 | Savannah, Ga., settled. | | La Serva Padrona; Rosamund; Hippolyte et Aricie |
| 1734 | The "Great Awakening" religious revival in New England. | | Il Pastor Fido—second version |
| 1735 | First settlers in Indiana. | BORN: J. C. Bach. | Flora, at Charleston, S.C., the first opera in America |
| 1736 | First diagnosis of scarlet fever. | DIED: Pergolesi. | Atalanta |
| 1737 | | | Castor et Pollux |
| 1738 | First umbrella in America. | DIED: Caldara. | Serse (Handel) |
| 1739 | | | Dardanus |
| 1740 | France and Prussia attack Southern Germany. | BORN: Paisiello, Sophie Arnould. | |
| 1741 | First symphony orchestra in America, at Bethlehem, Pa. | BORN: Grétry. DIED: Vivaldi. | |
| 1743 | BORN: Thomas Jefferson. | BORN: Adamberger. | |
| 1744 | First brewery in Baltimore. | DIED: Campra. | |
| 1746 | Defeat of the Scots at Culloden. | | |
| 1748 | | | Semiramide Riconosciuta |
| 1749 | | BORN: Cimarosa, da Ponte and Goethe. | |

| YEAR | GENERAL HISTORY | OPERA HISTORY | FIRST PERFORMANCES |
|---|---|---|---|
| 1750 | First human dissection in America. DIED: J. S. Bach. | BORN: Salieri. | The Beggar's Opera, in New York |
| 1752 | England adopted the Gregorian Calendar. | | Le Devin du Village |
| 1756 | Beginning of the Seven Years' War. | BORN: Mozart. | |
| 1757 | Clive opened India for England. | | |
| 1759 | Wolfe defeated Montcalm at Quebec. BORN: Robert Burns. | DIED: Handel. | |
| 1762 | Catherine the Great became ruler of Russia. | BORN: Michael Kelly. | Orfeo ed Euridice Love in a Village |
| 1763 | Otis outlined reasons for the American Revolution. | BORN: Incledon, Méhul. | |
| 1764 | First spinning mill in Philadelphia. | DIED: Rameau. | Rose et Colas |
| 1767 | (Probably) first libretto published in America. | Gluck published his famous preface. | Alceste (Gluck); La Cantarina; The Disappointment |
| 1768 | New York Chamber of Commerce founded. | | Bastien et Bastienne; Iphigénie en Tauride (Galuppi) |
| 1769 | Watt patented his steam engine. | | La Finta Semplice; Le Déserteur; Le Tableau Parlant |
| 1770 | The Boston Massacre. | BORN: Beethoven. | Mitridate |
| 1771 | Benjamin Franklin began his autobiography. | | Ascanio in Alba; Zémire et Azor |
| 1772 | First type foundry in America. | Gluck went to Paris. | Lucio Silla |
| 1773 | The Boston Tea Party. | | Hippolyte et Aricie; Céphale et Procris |
| 1774 | Discovery of oxygen. | BORN: Braham, Spontini. | Iphigénie en Aulide |
| 1775 | Battle of Lexington. Beaumarchais' Il Barbiere di Siviglia | BORN: M. García, Sr., Boieldieu. | La Finta Giardiniera |

| YEAR | GENERAL HISTORY | OPERA HISTORY | FIRST PERFORMANCES |
|---|---|---|---|
| 1776 | Washington crossed the Delaware. The Declaration of Independence. | | |
| 1777 | Battle of Saratoga. | | Armide (Gluck); Polly |
| 1778 | DIED: Voltaire. | DIED: Arne, Rousseau. | |
| 1779 | John Paul Jones captured the *Serapis* | | Iphigénie en Tauride (Gluck) |
| 1780 | Battle of King's Mountain, S.C./N.C. | | |
| 1781 | English surrender at Yorktown. Spanish capture St. Joseph, Ind. Kant's *Critique of Pure Reason*. | | Iphigénie en Tauride (Piccini); Idomeneo; Belmont et Constanze |
| 1782 | The American Revolution ends at Charleston. | BORN: Auber. DIED: Metastasio, J. C. Bach. | Die Entführung aus dem Serail; Fra i Due Litiganti; Il Barbiere di Siviglia (Paisiello) |
| 1783 | First balloon ascent. | | |
| 1784 | Slavery abolished in Connecticut and Rhode Island. | BORN: Spohr. | Richard Coeur de Lion |
| 1785 | First American turnpike. | BORN: Milder. DIED: Galuppi. | |
| 1786 | First *Hamlet* in America. | BORN: Weber. | Der Schauspieldirektor; Le Nozze di Figaro; Doktor und Apotheker; Una Cosa Rara |
| 1787 | Slavery prohibited in Northwest territories. | DIED: Gluck. | Don Giovanni |
| 1788 | The Constitution of the United States adopted. | | |
| 1789 | G. Washington made President. The Bastille riot. | | |
| 1790 | The Constitution ratified. | | Così fan Tutte |

| YEAR | GENERAL HISTORY | OPERA HISTORY | FIRST PERFORMANCES |
|---|---|---|---|
| 1791 | Congress passed first internal revenue act. | First company of French opera arrived at New Orleans. BORN: Hérold, Scribe, Meyerbeer. DIED: Mozart. | Lodoiska; La Clemenza di Tito; Die Zauberflöte |
| 1792 | French Republic victory at Valmy. | BORN: Rossini. DIED: Favart. | Il Matrimonio Segreto |
| 1793 | Louis XVI beheaded. | | |
| 1794 | | BORN: Lablache. | Tammany |
| 1795 | The French Directoire established. | BORN: Marschner. | |
| 1796 | Napoleon defeated the Austrians at Arcola. DIED: Robert Burns. | BORN: Pacini. | The Archers, the first American opera to be performed. |
| 1797 | | BORN: Donizetti, Schubert. | Anacreon chez Polycrate; Medea (Cherubini); Doktor Faust (Walter) |
| 1798 | Napoleon conquers Egypt. First income tax in England. | | Falstaff (Salieri) |
| 1799 | End of the Directoire. Napoleon made First Consul. | DIED: Beaumarchais. | The Vintage; Ariodant |
| 1800 | Spain ceded Louisiana to France. | DIED: Piccini. | Les Deux Journées |
| 1801 | Thomas Jefferson inaugurated as President of the United States. | BORN: Bellini, Lortzing. DIED: Cavalieri, Cimarosa. First signs of Beethoven's deafness. | |
| 1802 | The first lifeboats. | BORN: Nourrit. DIED: Sophie Arnould. | |
| 1803 | The Louisiana Purchase. | BORN: Adam, Berlioz. | La Selva Incantada |
| 1804 | Napoleon made Emperor. | BORN: Glinka, Schröder-Devrient. DIED: Adamberger. | |

| YEAR | GENERAL HISTORY | OPERA HISTORY | FIRST PERFORMANCES |
|---|---|---|---|
| 1805 | Nelson defeated the Spanish at Trafalgar. Fulton operated the first steamboat. | | Fidelio |
| 1806 | Webster's Dictionary published. | BORN: Sontag. | |
| 1807 | Napoleon defeated the Prussians. | BORN: Staudigl. | Joseph; La Vestale |
| 1808 | | BORN: Balfe, Malibran. | |
| 1809 | BORN: Lincoln. | BORN: Mendelssohn. DIED: J. Haydn. | Fernando Cortez |
| 1810 | BORN: Chopin. | BORN: David, Mario, Nicolai, R. Schumann. | Barber of Seville (Paisiello), at New Orleans |
| 1811 | First colony in Pacific Northwest. | BORN: Grisi, Liszt, Thomas. | |
| 1812 | Napoleon occupied Moscow. United States at war with England. | BORN: Von Flotow. | La Scala di Seta |
| 1813 | | BORN: Dargomizhsky, Verdi, Wagner, Fry. DIED: Grétry. | L'Italiana in Algeri; Tancredi |
| 1814 | Treaty of Ghent. The first gas lights in London. | | Il Turco in Italia |
| 1815 | Napoleon defeated at Waterloo. The Battle of New Orleans. | | |
| 1816 | The year in which the northern United States had no summer. | DIED: Paisiello. | Il Barbiere di Siviglia (Rossini); Undine; Faust (Spohr); Otello (Rossini) |
| 1817 | "Thanatopsis" by Bryant. | DIED: Méhul. | La Cenerentola; La Gazza Ladra |
| 1818 | Executive mansion in Washington painted white to cover scorch marks left by British invaders. | BORN: Gounod. | |
| 1819 | | BORN: Offenbach. | Olympia |
| 1820 | DIED: Daniel Boone. | BORN: Jenny Lind. | |

| YEAR | GENERAL HISTORY | OPERA HISTORY | FIRST PERFORMANCES |
|---|---|---|---|
| 1821 | Cherokees adopt the alphabet of Sequoia. BORN: Dostoevsky. DIED: Napoleon. | | Der Freischütz |
| 1822 | | BORN: Arditi, Franck. | |
| 1823 | The Monroe Doctrine. | BORN: Lalo. | Semiramide (Rossini); Euryanthe |
| 1824 | | BORN: Cornelius, Smetana. | |
| 1825 | First railroad in England. | BORN: J. Strauss, Jr. DIED: Salieri. | La Dame Blanche; Don Giovanni, in New York |
| 1826 | First locomotive in America. DIED: Thomas Jefferson. | DIED: Weber, Kelly, Incledon. García presented opera in New York. | Oberon |
| 1827 | | BORN: Marie Carvalho. DIED: Beethoven. | Die Hochzeit des Camacho; Il Pirata |
| 1828 | BORN: Tolstoi. | DIED: Schubert. | Masaniello; Der Vampyr |
| 1829 | First school for the blind in the U.S. | First Italian opera at New York. Rossini retired from opera. | Agnes von Hohenstaufen; Guillaume Tell; Der Templar und die Judin |
| 1830 | In a test race, a horse beat a locomotive. | BORN: von Bülow, J. B. Faure, Goldmark. | Fra Diavolo; I Capuletti ed I Montecchi; Anna Bolena. |
| 1831 | McCormick invented the reaping machine. | BORN: Tietjens. | La Sonnambula; Zampa; Robert le Diable; Norma |
| 1832 | DIED: Goethe. | BORN: L. Damrosch. DIED: M. García, Sr. | L'Elisir d'Amore; Le Pré aux Clercs |
| 1833 | BORN: Brahms. | BORN: Borodin. DIED: Hérold. | Hans Heiling; Lucrezie Borgia |
| 1834 | Electric motor invented in Vermont. | BORN: Ponchielli, Santley. DIED: Boieldieu. | Le Chalet |
| 1835 | Morse invented the telegraph. | BORN: Saint Saëns, Cui. DIED: Bellini. | I Puritani; La Juive; Le Cheval de Bronze; Lucia di Lammermoor |
| 1836 | Republic of Texas established. | BORN: Delibes. DIED: Malibran. | Les Huguenots; Le Postillion de Longjumeau; Ivan Susanin |

| YEAR | GENERAL HISTORY | OPERA HISTORY | FIRST PERFORMANCES |
|------|-----------------|---------------|--------------------|
| 1837 | Victoria became Queen of England. | | Alessandro Stradella; Zar und Zimmermann |
| 1838 | Boston added music to public school curriculum. | BORN: Bizet, Stehle. DIED: da Ponte, Milder. | Maria di Rudenz; Falstaff (Balfe); Benvenuto Cellini |
| 1839 | First photographs. BORN: Cézanne. | BORN: Mussorgsky. DIED: Nourrit. | Esmeralda; Oberto— Verdi's first |
| 1840 | First U.S. expedition to Antarctica. | BORN: Galli-Marié, Tchaikovsky. | La Figlia del Reggimento; Un Giorno di Regno; La Favorita |
| 1841 | First covered wagons arrive in California. | BORN: Chabrier, Dvořák. | |
| 1842 | N.Y. Philharmonic Society formed. | BORN: Boito, Brandt, Massenet. DIED: Cherubini. | Nabucco; Linda de Chamounix; Le Roi d'Yvetot (Auber); Rienzi; Russlan and Ludmilla; Der Wildschütz |
| 1843 | First soap powder in U.S. | BORN: Patti, Christine Nilsson. | Der Fliegende Holländer; Don Pasquale; I Lombardi; Medea (Pacini); Don Sebastian; The Bohemian Girl |
| 1844 | Stephen Foster's first published song. | BORN: Rimsky-Korsakov. | Ernani |
| 1845 | Texas annexed to U.S.A. | BORN: G. Fauré, I. Campanini. | Leonora; Tannhäuser; Maritana |
| 1846 | United States at war with Mexico. | | Attila; The Night Dancers; La Damnation de Faust |
| 1847 | DIED: Johnny Appleseed. | BORN: Albani. DIED: Mendelssohn. | Macbeth; Martha |
| 1848 | Revolution in Europe. BORN: Gauguin. | BORN: Maurel, Lilli Lehmann. DIED: Donizetti. | Die Lustigen Weiber von Windsor |
| 1849 | The California Gold Rush. DIED: Chopin. | BORN: Godard. | Le Caïd: Le Prophète; Luisa Miller |
| 1850 | Mormons reached Salt Lake, Utah. First international copyright. | BORN: J. de Reszke, Scalchi. | Le Songe d'Une Nuit d'Été; Lohengrin; Genoveva |

| YEAR | GENERAL HISTORY | OPERA HISTORY | FIRST PERFORMANCES |
|---|---|---|---|
| 1851 | *New York Times* founded. *Moby Dick* published. | BORN: d'Indy. DIED: Lortzing, Spontini. | Rigoletto; Sapho (Gounod); Raymond; La Perle du Brésil |
| 1852 | *Uncle Tom's Cabin* published. | BORN: Hauk. | |
| 1853 | BORN: Van Gogh. | BORN: E. de Reszke. | Il Trovatore; La Traviata |
| 1854 | The British light brigade died at Balaklava. | BORN: Chadwick, Janáček, Humperdinck, Plançon. DIED: Sontag. | Halka; L'Étoile du Nord; Alfonso und Estrella |
| 1855 | Crimean War ended. | | I Vespri Siciliani; L'Ebreo |
| 1856 | BORN: Sigmund Freud. | DIED: Adam, Braham, R. Schumann. | Manon Lescaut (Auber); Rusalka; Falstaff (Adam); Les Dragons de Villars |
| 1857 | Central Park, N.Y., laid out. | BORN: Nordica. DIED: Glinka. | Simon Boccanegra |
| 1858 | First cable across the Atlantic. | Covent Garden rebuilt. BORN: Calvé, Leoncavallo, Puccini, Sembrich. DIED: Lablache. | Orphée aux Enfers; Der Barbier von Bagdad |
| 1859 | Italy united. John Brown captured Harpers Ferry, W.Va. | BORN: V. Herbert. DIED: Spohr. | Un Ballo in Maschera; Faust; Dinorah |
| 1860 | Lincoln elected to presidency. | BORN: Wolf, Albéniz, Mahler, Alvarez, C. Campanini, G. Charpentier, Paderewski. DIED: Schröder-Devrient. | Philémon et Baucis; Lurline |
| 1861 | First great battle of the Civil War at Manassas. | BORN: Melba, Schumann-Heink. DIED: Marschner, Scribe, Staudigl. | La Statue; Der Häusliche Krieg |
| 1862 | Battles of Shiloh, Antietam, Vicksburg. | BORN: Debussy, Delius, W. Damrosch. | La Reine de Saba; Lalla Rookh; Béatrice et Bénédict; La Forza del Destino |

# CHRONOLOGY OF OPERA

| YEAR | GENERAL HISTORY | OPERA HISTORY | FIRST PERFORMANCES |
|---|---|---|---|
| 1863 | Battles of Chancellorsville and Gettysburg. | BORN: Juch, Ternina, Mascagni. | Judith (Serov); Notre Dame de Paris; Les Pêcheurs de Perles; Les Troyens—Part II |
| 1864 | Battles of the Wilderness and Atlanta. | BORN: d'Albert, R. Strauss. DIED: Fry, Meyerbeer. | Mireille; La Belle Hélène |
| 1865 | Booth shot Lincoln. | BORN: Dukas. | L'Africaine; Tristan und Isolde; Die Schöne Galathea; Rognyeda |
| 1866 | | BORN: Busoni, Cilèa, Scotti, Dippel. | Zaïda (Mozart); Prodana Nevěsta; Mignon |
| 1867 | Cigarettes appear in America. | BORN: Eames, Granados, Giordano, Toscanini. DIED: Pacini. | Don Carlos; La Grande Duchesse de Gérolstein; Roméo et Juliette; L'Oca del Cairo (Mozart); König Manfred; La Jolie Fille de Perth |
| 1868 | Little Women published. | BORN: Schmedes. DIED: Rossini. | Mefistofele (Boito); Hamlet; Dalibor; Die Meistersinger; La Périchole |
| 1869 | First transcontinental railroad completed. | DIED: Berlioz, Grisi, Dargomizhsky. | Das Rheingold |
| 1870 | War between France and Germany. | BORN: van Rooy. DIED: Balfe. MARRIED: Wagner to Cosima Liszt von Bülow | Il Guarany; Die Walküre; Der Fliegende Holländer; at Drury Lane, the first Wagner in England |
| 1871 | Gilbert and Sullivan commenced their collaboration. | BORN: Converse, Hadley, Dalmorès, Fremstad, Homer, Tetrazzini. DIED: Auber. | Aida |
| 1872 | | BORN: Vaughan Williams. | Kamenny Gost; Djamileh; Don César de Bazan; La Fille de Mme. Angot |
| 1873 | Financial panic in New York. | BORN: Caruso, Chaliapin, Rachmaninov. | Pskovityanka; Le Roi l'à Dit |
| 1874 | First public zoo in U.S. | BORN: Didur, Schönberg, DIED: Cornelius. | Boris Godunov; Die Fledermaus; Der Widerspänstigen Zähmung |

| YEAR | GENERAL HISTORY | OPERA HISTORY | FIRST PERFORMANCES |
|---|---|---|---|
| 1875 | First American university course in music. | BORN: Hahn, Ravel. DIED: Bizet. | Carmen; Die Königin von Saba; Das Goldene Kreuz |
| 1876 | Battle of the Little Big Horn. Custer's last stand. | BORN: Wolf-Ferrari, da Falla. | La Gioconda; Das Ring des Nibelungen (complete); Hubička; Paul et Virginie |
| 1877 | Selden invented a horseless carriage. | BORN: Mary Garden. DIED: Tietjens. | Le Roi de Lahore; Samson et Dalila |
| 1878 | Edison patented the phonograph. | BORN: Destinn. | |
| 1879 | BORN: Einstein, Stalin. | BORN: Beecham. | Eugene Onegin |
| 1880 | Sarah Bernhardt appeared in N.Y. | BORN: Bloch. DIED: Offenbach. | |
| 1881 | DIED: Dostoevski. | BORN: Bartók, Cadman, Enesco. DIED: Mussorgsky. | Les Contes d'Hoffmann; Libuše; Hérodiade |
| 1882 | First streetcars in U.S. (at Appleton, Wisc.) | BORN: Kodály, Farrar, Galli-Curci, Malipiero, Stravinsky. | Snyegurotchka; Françoise de Rimini; Zenobia; Parsifal; Dmitrij; Der Bettelstudent |
| 1883 | First vaudeville in U.S. Brooklyn Bridge opened. | BORN: Alda, Zandonai. DIED: Mario, Wagner, von Flotow. Opened: The Metropolitan Opera House. | Henry VIII; Lakmé |
| 1884 | | BORN: Easton, McCormack. DIED: Smetana. | Sigurd; Manon; Der Trompeter von Säkkingen |
| 1885 | Mark Twain published The Adventures of Huckleberry Finn | BORN: A. Berg, Hempel, E. Schumann, Martinelli. DIED: L. Damrosch. | Nadeshda; Der Zigeunerbaron |
| 1886 | Statue of Liberty unveiled. | DIED: Ponchielli, Liszt. | Khovantschina; Gwendoline |
| 1887 | | BORN: Villa-Lobos, Jeritza. DIED: Borodin, Jenny Lind. | Le Roi malgré Lui; Otello (Verdi) |
| 1888 | The Great Blizzard in New York | BORN: Lotte Lehmann, Teyte, Schorr. | Asrael; Jocelyn; Le Roi d'Ys |

| YEAR | GENERAL HISTORY | OPERA HISTORY | FIRST PERFORMANCES |
|------|-----------------|---------------|--------------------|
| 1889 | The Johnstown flood. | BORN: Muzio. | Edgar (Puccini) |
| 1890 | DIED: Van Gogh. | BORN: Gigli, Melchior, Ibert. DIED: Franck. | Salammbô; Cavalleria Rusticana; La Basoche; Robin Hood; Prince Igor; Pique-Dame; Les Troyens, complete |
| 1891 | Zipper patented. Carnegie Hall opened. | BORN: Kipnis, Prokofiev. DIED: Delibes. | Gunlöd; Le Rêve; L'Amico Fritz |
| 1892 | Dvořák visited U.S. | BORN: Honegger, Milhaud, Pinza, Rodjinski. DIED: Lalo. | La Wally; Werther; Mala Vita; I Pagliacci; Yolande; Cristoforo Colombo |
| 1893 | Financial panic in U.S. | BORN: Hába. DIED: Gounod, Tchaikovsky. | Mme. Chrysanthème; Manon Lescaut (Puccini); Falstaff (Verdi); Aleko; L'Attaque du Moulin; Hänsel und Gretel |
| 1894 | | BORN: Rethberg. DIED: Chabrier, Von Bülow. | Thaïs; Le Portrait die Manon; La Navarrase; Jeanie Deans |
| 1895 | Stephen Crane published *The Red Badge of Courage* | BORN: Hindemith, Orff, Flagstad. DIED: M. Carvalho, Godard. | Kenilworth; Enrico Clifford |
| 1896 | Langley's model airplane flew successfully. | BORN: Weinberger, Thorborg, Tibbett, Hanson. DIED: Thomas, I. Campanini | Pepita Jiménez; Sadko; La Bohème (Puccini); The Scarlet Letter (Damrosch); Shamus O'Brien; Andrea Chénier; Der Corregidor; Das Heimchen am Herd |
| 1897 | DIED: Brahms. | BORN: Ponselle. | Fierrebras (Schubert); La Bohème (Leoncavallo); L'Arlesiana; Sapho (Massenet); Šarka (Fibich) |
| 1898 | War between the United States and Spain. | BORN: Patzak, Gershwin. | Lobetanz; Fedora; Iris; Véronique |
| 1899 | | BORN: Traubel. DIED: J. Strauss. | Tsarskaya Nyevesta |

| YEAR | GENERAL HISTORY | OPERA HISTORY | FIRST PERFORMANCES |
|------|-----------------|---------------|---------------------|
| 1900 | Casey Jones died in a train wreck. | BORN: Weill, Krenek, Antheil, Copland. DIED: J. Strauss. | Tosca; Louise; Le Juif Polonais; Promethée; Zaza |
| 1901 | DIED: Queen Victoria. | BORN: Egk. DIED: Verdi. | Rusalka (Dvořák); Feuersnot |
| 1902 | | BORN: Walton, Sayao. | Orestes (Weingartner); Le Jongleur de Notre Dame; Merrie England; Der Wald; Pelléas et Mélisande; Adriana Lecouvreur |
| 1903 | DIED: Gauguin. First successful airplane. | BORN: Novotna. DIED: Arditi, Wolf. | Ilsebill; The Zaporogues; Tiefland; Siberia |
| 1904 | First subway in the world begun in New York. | BORN: Dallapiccola, Peerce, Pons. DIED: Dvorak. | Její Pastorkyňa ("Jenufa"); Madama Butterfly; Koanga; Sakuntala (Coerne); Risurrezione |
| 1905 | Japanese defeated the Russians in Manchuria. | DIED: Galli-Marié. | L'Oracolo; Salomé |
| 1906 | San Francisco earthquake. DIED: Cézanne. | BORN: Milanov. | The Pipe of Desire; Greysteel; Don Procopio; I Quattro Rusteghi; Aphrodite; The Wreckers |
| 1907 | | First American performance of Salome. Closed immediately. | Kitezh; A Village Romeo and Juliet; Ariane et Barbe-Bleue; Le Coq d'Or; Zenobia. |
| 1908 | Isadora Duncan at height of her dance career. | DIED: Rimsky-Korsakov. | La Habanera |
| 1909 | | DIED: Albéniz. | Monna Vanna; Elektra; Zhenitba; Safie; Pierrot et Pierrette; Il Segreto di Susanna |
| 1910 | DIED: Tolstoi, Mark Twain. | BORN: Pears, Tourel. DIED: Viardot-García. First production of an American opera at the Metropolitan, *The Pipe of Desire*. | Don Quichotte; Poia; Macbeth (Bloch); La Fanciulla del West; Königskinder; Noël |

| YEAR | GENERAL HISTORY | OPERA HISTORY | FIRST PERFORMANCES |
|------|-----------------|---------------|--------------------|
| 1911 | Charlie Chaplin appeared at New York City. | DIED: Mahler. | Der Rosenkavalier; Natoma; The Sacrifice; The Fair at Sorochintsky; La Jota; L'Heure Espagnole; I Gioielli della Madonna |
| 1912 | The steamship *Titanic* sank. | BORN: Ferrier, Mödl. DIED: Massenet. | Mona; Ariadne auf Naxos |
| 1913 | Panama Canal completed. | BORN: Britten, Stevens, Tagliavini. | La Forêt Bleue; Cyrano de Bergerac; Madeleine; Penelope; La Vide Breve; L'Amore dei Tre Re; Julien |
| 1914 | The First World War began at the Marne. | BORN: Tucker. DIED: J. B. Faure, Nordica, Plançon. | Francesca da Rimini; L'Ombra di Don Giovanni; Marouf; Le Rossignol; The Immortal Hour |
| 1915 | Allies defeated at Gallipoli. Poison gas used in war. | BORN: Del Monaco. DIED: Goldmark. | Mme. Sans-Gêne; Fedra |
| 1916 | Allies win Verdun and Jutland. | BORN: Steber. DIED: Granados. | Goyescas; The Boatswain's Mate; Savitri |
| 1917 | United States entered war. Russian Revolution. | BORN: Kirsten. DIED: E. de Reszke. | The Canterbury Pilgrims; La Rondine; Lodoletta; Arlecchino; Turandot (Busoni); Palestrina; Azora, the Daughter of Montezuma |
| 1918 | Second battle of the Marne. Paris bombed. Armistice. | BORN: Thebom. DIED: Debussy, Boito, Cui. | Shanewis; Duke Bluebeard's Castle; Il Trittico |
| 1919 | The liquor prohibition amendment (the eighteenth). | DIED: Patti, Leoncavallo, C. Campanini. | Monsieur Beaucaire; Les Choëphores; Die Frau ohne Schatten; Fennimore und Gerda |
| 1920 | Air mail service commenced in U.S. First regular radio broadcasting. | At Hammersmith the Beggar's Opera ran 1463 nights. | Rip van Winkle; Ritter Blaubart; Cleopatra's Night; The Tempest; Die Tote Stadt |
| 1921 | U.S. initiated quota limitations on immigration. | DIED: Caruso, Brandt, Humperdinck, Christine Nilsson, Saint-Saëns, Stehle. | Antar; Prince Ferelon; Mörder Hoffnung des Fraun; Nusch-Nuschi; Káta Kabanová; The Love for Three Oranges |

| YEAR | GENERAL HISTORY | OPERA HISTORY | FIRST PERFORMANCES |
|------|-----------------|---------------|--------------------|
| 1922 | Mussolini became dictator of Italy. | BORN: Tebaldi. DIED: Santley, Scalchi. | Sancta Susanna; Venus; Sakuntala (Alfano); Mavra; Alkestis |
| 1923 | | DIED: Maurel. | El Retablo de Maese Pedro; The Perfect Fool; Fête Galante; Debora e Jaele |
| 1924 | | DIED: G. Fauré, Puccini, Busoni, V. Herbert. | Nerone (Boito); Der Sprung über das Schatten; Hugh the Drover; The Queen of Cornwall; Intermezzo |
| 1925 | The Scopes trial, in which Darwin's theory of evolution was at issue. | DIED: J. de Reszke. | L'Enfant et les Sortilèges; Socrate; Doktor Faust; At the Boar's Head; Sarka (Janáček); Wozzeck |
| 1926 | The first radio network broadcast. | | Judith (Honegger); Der Protagonist; Turandot (Puccini); Les Malheurs d'Orphée; Háry János; Cardillac; Orpheus und Eurydike; A Witch of Salem |
| 1927 | Lindberg flew across the ocean alone, non-stop. Sacco and Vanzetti were executed. | | Jonny Spielt Auf; La Rosiera; The King's Henchman; Le Poirier de Misère; The Royal Palace; Naïla; Agamemnon; Švanda Dudák; Madonna Imperia; Oedipus Rex (Stravinsky); Hin und Züruck; L'Enlèvement d'Europe; La Campana Sommersa; Eumenides; Le Pauvre Matelot; Antigone (Honegger) |
| 1928 | First scheduled television broadcast. | DIED: Janáček. | Die Aegyptische Helena; Fredericka; Die Dreigroschenoper |
| 1929 | Collapse in Wall Street brought on the "Great Depression" | DIED: Hauk, Lilli Lehmann. | Sir John in Love; La Femme Nue; Jürg Jenatsch; Neues vom Tage; Judith (Goossens); Engelbrekt; Samuel Pepys |

| YEAR | GENERAL HISTORY | OPERA HISTORY | FIRST PERFORMANCES |
|------|-----------------|---------------|--------------------|
| 1930 | Four and a half million unemployed in the U.S.A. | DIED: Albani, Destinn. | Le Roi d'Yvetot (Ibert); Z mrtvého Domu; Christophe Colomb; Transatlantic; Wir bauen eine Stadt; Fremde Erde |
| 1931 | Many banks closed. | DIED: Melba, d'Indy, Chadwick, Schmedes. | Die Mutter; Peter Ibbetson |
| 1932 | Thirteen million unemployed. F. D. Roosevelt elected president. | DIED: d'Albert, Dippel, Van Rooy. | Maximilien |
| 1933 | Hitler assumed power in Germany. | DIED: Alvarez. | The Jolly Roger; The Emperor Jones; Arabella |
| 1934 | | DIED: Delius. | Madrisa; Lady Macbeth of Minsk; Four Saints in Three Acts; Merry Mount; Helen Retires; Lulu |
| 1935 | U.S. established its Social Security Administration. | DIED: A. Berg, Dukas, Sembrich. | Nerone (Mascagni); In the Pasha's Garden; Medea (Engel); Die Schweigsame Frau; Porgy and Bess |
| 1936 | Edward VIII abdicated. | DIED: Muzio, Scotti, Schumann-Heink. | Oedipus Tyrannus (Enesco); The Poisoned Kiss; Le Testament de la Tante Caroline; Pickwick |
| 1937 | Arturo Toscanini became conductor of the N.B.C. Symphony. | DIED: Gershwin, Ravel, Hadley. | Don Juan de Mañera; L'Aiglon; Massimilla Doni; The Man Without a Country; Wallenstein; Riders to the Sea |
| 1938 | | DIED: Chaliapin. | Esther de Carpentras; Peer Gynt; The Scarlet Letter (Giannini); Mathis der Maler; Karl V; Friedenstag; Daphne (Strauss) |
| 1939 | Hitler attacked Poland. DIED: Sigmund Freud. | DIED: Dalmorès, Juch. | The Old Maid and the Thief; Der Mond; Medée (Milhaud) |
| 1940 | The British evacuated Europe at Dunkirk. | DIED: Converse, Tetrazzini. | Volo di Notte |

| YEAR | GENERAL HISTORY | OPERA HISTORY | FIRST PERFORMANCES |
|---|---|---|---|
| 1941 | Japanese bombed Pearl Harbor. | DIED: Paderewski, Ternina. | Paul Bunyan |
| 1942 | Battles of Bataan, The Coral Sea, El Alamein, Guadalcanal, Midway Island. | DIED: Calvé. | Capriccio; Ginevra |
| 1943 | Battle of the Gilbert Islands. | DIED: Rachmaninov. | Barbe-Bleue; Die Kluge |
| 1944 | The Allied invasion of Europe. | DIED: Zandonai. | |
| 1945 | Atomic bomb dropped on Hiroshima, Japan. End of the Second World War. | DIED: Bartók, Mascagni, McCormack. | Peter Grimes; The Scarecrow |
| 1946 | U.S. joined UNESCO. | DIED: Didur, Cadman, Falla. | The Medium; The Rape of Lucretia |
| 1947 | First scheduled round-the-world commercial flight. | DIED: Hahn, Homer. | Street Scene; The Warrior; The Trial of Lucullus; Albert Herring; Dantons Tod |
| 1948 | | DIED: Wolf-Ferrari, Giordano. | |
| 1949 | Permanent United Nations Headquarters dedicated. | DIED: R. Strauss. | Let's Make an Opera; Till Eulenspiegel(Jeremias); Billy Budd (Ghedini); Regina |
| 1950 | The Korean War. | DIED: Weill, Cilèa, de Luca, W. Damrosch. | The Consul; Il Prigioniero; The Triumph of St. Joan; Bolivar |
| 1951 | First color-television broadcast. | DIED: Fremstad, Schönberg. | Pilgrim's Progress; The Rake's Progress; Billy Budd (Britten) |
| 1952 | | DIED: Alda, Eames, E. Schumann. | Leonore 40/45; Die Liebe der Danae |
| 1953 | DIED: Stalin. | DIED: Ferrier, Prokofiev, Schorr. | Gloriana; Der Prozess; The Taming of the Shrew |
| 1954 | First thermo-nuclear bomb exploded. | | The Tender Land; David; The Turn of the Screw; The Mother; Troilus and Cressida; Double Trouble; The Saint of Bleecker Street |

| YEAR | GENERAL HISTORY | OPERA HISTORY | FIRST PERFORMANCES |
|---|---|---|---|
| 1955 | DIED: Einstein. Salk vaccine against poliomyelitis developed. | DIED: Hempel, Honegger, Enesco. | Susannah |
| 1956 | Segregation in public schools outlawed by Supreme Court. | DIED: G. Charpentier. | He Who Gets Slapped; The Wife of Martin Guerre; The Ballad of Baby Doe |
| 1957 | Opening of International Geophysical Year, a cooperative scientific experiment. | DIED: Pinza, Toscanini, Gigli. | Les Dialogues des Carmelites; The Prodigal Son (Malipiero); Die Harmonie der Welt |
| 1958 | First U.S. artificial satellite put in orbit. | DIED: Vaughan Williams. | Vanessa; Wuthering Heights; Maria Golovin; L'Assassinio nell' Cattedrale |
| 1959 | Rocket to moon fired by Soviet scientists. | DIED: Bloch. | |
| 1960 | Unprecedented number of heads of state attend U.N. session. | DIED: Bjoerling, Warren. | |

# GLOSSARY

**a cappella** (It.) ah cahPELlah

Without accompaniment, particularly solo or choral music without instrumental accompaniment. The expression in Italian means "in the chapel style."

**a demi voix** (Fr.) ah d'MEE vwah

At half voice, in a singing whisper, sotto voce.

**accompanist**

One who accompanies, usually a pianist who substitutes for the orchestra in rehearsals of operatic scenes or in concerts of soloists. Sometimes a regular performance of opera contains passages in which a singer is accompanied by a keyboard instrument, the conductor relinquishing his direction until the passage is done. This is usual in the various kinds of dry recitative.

**act**

The largest formal unit of opera. Most operas have two, three or four acts which are themselves divided into scenes. The acts are usually separated by intermissions whereas the scenes are not. The separation into acts usually indicates the passage of time in the action, while the changes of scene usually involve less a change of time than one of locale.

**adagio** (It.) ahDAHzheeo

An indication of tempo; slowly, at a pace slower than a normal walk.

**adaptation**

An arrangement of the instrumentation, and/or a translation or alteration of the libretto of an opera. An adaptation is usually a fairly free alteration of the sequence and detail of the various scenes and musical pieces, made for the purpose of shortening an opera, or to render it more palatable for a particular audience. It is not to be confused with simple reorchestration, or with transposition of the music. But many so-called translations of libretti are adaptations.

**AGMA**

The American Guild of Musical Artists; one of the dominant unions for singers in opera in the United States.

**allegretto** (It.) ahlegGRETTo

Not as fast as allegro.

**allegro** (It.) ahLEGgro

A tempo indication; quickly, at a pace faster than a normal walk. The word has a connotation of lightness also, or of happiness, but in music the mood is not always involved.

**alto** (It.) AHLtoh

High. Formerly used to describe the highest male voice, otherwise sometimes known as the countertenor. Now used for the lowest female voice which sings in that same range, the contralto. For some reason the word *contralto* occurs more often in connection with solo voices, but *alto* with choral.

**alzamento** (It.) ahltzaMENtoh

Raising the voice, lightening the voice, bringing the tone, as it were, up from the depths of the chest.

**anacrusis**

From the Greek word which means "a striking-back." Hence an upward movement of the body which by the laws of Newtonian physics must be followed by a downward movement (what goes up must come down). The anacrusis is therefore the feeling of lifting up which prepares a heavy accent. It occurs once in each measure as the upbeat immediately preceding the bar line.

**andante** (It.) ahnDAHNtay

An indication of tempo; moving, going, at a normal walking pace.

**apron**

That part of the stage floor which projects toward the audience and beyond the curtain line. The term is usually restricted to the proscenium stage.

**arabesque** (Fr.) ahrahBESK

Ornament in Arabian style, hence usually a kind of ornamental turning figure on the upbeat, or the unaccented beat.

**arena stage**

A stage completely surrounded by its audience. This is a very ancient shape for the stage, having its origin perhaps in the threshing-circle at harvest time. It allows a much larger audience to view the action than does a proscenium, but it demands an entirely different concept of staging and acting.

**aria** (It.) AHree-ah

An air, a song. Usually a formal song within an opera or an oratorio. By nature it is separated in action from the general flow of the story and the scene around it.

**aria concertata** (It.) AHree-ah conchayrTAHtah

A concerted air. An aria with an accompaniment closely woven around the voice, as for instance those arias in which the flute accompanies the soprano very closely in duet while both are accompanied by the orchestra.

**aria da capo** (It.) AHree-ah dah CAHpo

An aria which ends with the same music as that with which it began.

**aria parlante** (It.) AHree-ah pahrLAHNtay

An aria which is sung in loose rhythm, closely parallel to the rhythm of speech. Not to be confused with *sprechstimme* which is a musical imitation of the tones and rhythms of speech.

**arioso** (It.) ahreeOHzo

In the manner of an aria. An air. Usually in a freer form than aria, or in closer musical relationship with its context. The arioso is sometimes no more than a melodious moment in music, sometimes an air of larger form and more fullness than an aria.

**arrangement**

A revision of the music of an opera or of a piece of music. Usually the arrangement involves mainly a change of instrumentation as in the modern arrangements of *La Favola d'Orfeo* which permit performance with modern instruments replacing those which Monteverdi called for but which are no longer available outside museums.

**artistic director**

The artistic director of an opera company is usually the one person responsible for the overall artistic conception of a particular production. He is therefore frequently the one who assigns the cast, appoints the conductor, the scene designer and stage director. He does not conduct rehearsals, but tells the others how he wants the rehearsals to be directed.

**atonality**

Literally without tonality, but usually used to describe a harmonic quality or a system with complex relationships of tonalities between different parts of the piece or different voices. Atonal music has tone, but is intended to sound free of any tonal center. It is not the same as dissonance. *See* dodecaphonism.

**avant garde** (Fr.) AHvah(n) gard

Those who search ahead. The innovators who attempt new styles and explore their techniques.

**backdrop**

The curtain, stretched on frames and painted or simply hanging behind the actors, which forms the rear wall of the visible part of the stage. It is to be distinguished from cyclorama in that it is usually painted to represent a definite plane of background, whereas the cyclorama generally represents the sky, or empty space.

**backstage**

The area behind the visible part of the stage; that which is behind the backdrop and outside the wings, wherever the audience is not permitted to see.

**baffleboard**

A sound-reflecting construction so placed behind and/or around the orchestra and the singers that their sound may be heard in the outer reaches of the audience. Generally necessary in outdoor productions.

**ballabile** (It.) bahLAHbeelay

In the style of dancing, a scene in popular dance style, not ballet.

**ballad opera**

An opera or operetta made for the most part of a series of well known popular songs, with new words arranged and edited to carry along a plot. A fine example of ballad opera is the perennial triumph, *The Beggar's Opera*.

**ballata** (It.) bahLAHta

A ballad. Also a dance.

**ballet** (Fr.) bahLAY

A theatrical dance, usually representative of a story or a plot and performed by dancers trained in its special technique. Not to be confused with pantomime, which lacks the fairly abstract form imposed upon ballet, nor with ordinary dancing, which lacks the purpose of story.

Also the group of dancers who perform such works.

Also that part of an opera which is to be performed in dance.

**barcarolle** (Fr.) bahrcahROHL

A song to be sung in a boat. Frequently associated with Venice, and sung by the gondoliers as they ply their trade along the canals in the quiet of evening.

**baritone**

The male voice whose range lies below that of the tenor and above that of the bass. Also the singer who has such a voice. Also the name of a deep-voiced brass instrument, not frequently employed in opera.

**barocco** (It.) bahROHKkoh

Baroque.

**baroque** (Fr.) bahROHK

The word comes from an obscure root meaning "irregular, bizarre." In music it describes a period and a style which is highly ornamented and in which the ornaments are frequently integrated with the

# GLOSSARY

actual structure of the piece. The baroque style crept into opera in the late seventeenth and early eighteenth centuries. Gluck fought against the kind of superficiality it produced.

**bass**
The lowest male voice, with a range extending below that of the baritone. Also a term designating the lowest of any combination of melodic lines.

**basso** (It.) BAHso
One who sings in the bass register.

**basso cantante** (It.) BAHso cahnTAHNtay
A lyric bass voice, a voice of exceptional smoothness in the very low range. The opposite of basso buffo. *See* buffo.

**basso continuo** (It.) BAHso conTEEnuo
A continuous accompaniment of instruments in which, generally, the harmonization is written not in notes but as a series of numbers indicating notes above the notes of the lowest instrument, to be improvised upon by the player of the keyboard. Frequently employed by the composers of the seventeenth and eighteenth centuries not only to save time in the writing but also to provide the performer a chance to show his abilities.

**basso profondo** (It.) BAHso proFONdo
A bass voice whose range extends far below the normal bass.

**baton** (Fr.) bahTO(N)
Literally, *stick*. The little wooden stick used by the conductor to make his hand movements more visible to the players in the pit and on the stage.

**beat**
The pulse of music. That which the conductor indicates by the regular motion of his baton. Not to be confused with

tempo, which is the frequency of the beats, nor with measure which is their grouping. Nor is beat always audible. When one refers to *the* beat, he frequently means the downbeat. If he means the rhythm, he's wrong.

**bel canto** (It.) bell CAHNto
"Beautiful song," the lyric style as distinguished from the dramatic or the buffo.

**benefit**
A performance the proceeds of which are to be donated to a specific charity. It used to be the practice for a composer to organize a benefit to keep himself from starvation. But nowadays the recipient is usually a charitable organization.

**berceuse** (Fr.) bayrSE(R)Z
A lullaby, a cradle song.

**bit**
Broadway slang for a very small role. The bit player is usually required to appear on stage and say a line or two, and is thus above the walk-on and the extra.

**bocca chiusa** (It.) BOCKka keeYUza
With mouth closed while singing; humming. It is worth noting that there are two methods of humming, one of which is employed by choruses who wish to be heard distinctly, and who hum without closed mouths. The directive *bocca chiusa* would prevent that variation.

**bouche fermée** (Fr.) BOOSH fayrMAY
*See* bocca chiusa.

**brasses**
The brass instruments of the orchestra. The trumpets, cornets, trombones, horns and tubas. Such metal instruments as the metal flute, the metal clarinet, and their like are called woodwinds.

**braut lied** (Ger.) BROWT leet
A wedding song.

**bravura** (It.) brahVOORa
Skill. Usually, in music, great brilliance of execution. The term *bravura* describes brilliance of tone and accuracy of execution at a high level of clarity and is sometimes called heroic.

**break**
The point at which the tone quality, or timbre of the low register of a voice changes to that of the high register.
Also used to indicate a free moment in an improvisatory piece, especially in jazz.

**brindisi** (It.) brinnDEEzee
A drinking song.

**buffo** (f. buffa) (It.) BOOfo (BOOfa)
Comic, in the style of comedy. This refers to the style of delivery of the lines, not to their content. An example of a buffo part would be Dr. Bartolo, in *Il Barbiere di Siviglia*.

**cabaletta** (It.) cahbahLETtah
A pleasing little song. In Spanish the root is associated with the horse, *caballo*; hence a cabaletta is sometimes a little song one would sing while riding. The cabaletta is the second or third (and usually the more difficult) part of a soprano aria, as in "*Casta diva*," "*Ernani, involami*," and "*Tacea la notte*."

**cadence**
Literally fall. The final moment of any melody or a phrase of music; usually the motion implied by the last two or three harmonic movements. It is a harmonic event, which can happen as a temporary stop or a permanent end to a phrase.

**cadenza** (It.) cahDENza
An ornamented passage in which the flow of the piece has been temporarily halted while the voice, perhaps accompanied by a solo instrument, indulges in a free improvisation. Sometimes the composer actually writes it out, maintaining the improvisatory quality. Strictly speaking, the cadenza was a florid ornament during the final cadence of a piece.

**Camerata, la** (It.) cahmayRAHtah, lah
The name applied to a group of Florentine noblemen who met together to discuss the possibility of a revival of the style of the classic drama of Greece. They produced, instead, the first operas. Chief among them were Bardi, Corsi, Peri, Rinuccini, Vincenzo Galilei, Strozzi, Mei, Caccini and Cavalieri.

**canon**
Literally, "rule". A piece of melodic music, usually sung and usually short, in which the first voice is precisely imitated by the second, then by the third and so forth as each enters the scheme. The simplest canons are rounds such as *Three Blind Mice*. In opera one of the most famous canons is *Mir ist so Wunderbar*. *See also* fugue.

**cantabile** (It.) cahnTAHbeelay
Singingly, in an easy flowing style. A direction to the singer to sing most smoothly. Also used to designate an air written to be sung or played in smooth style.

**cantando** (It.) cahnTAHNdoh
Singing. A directive to the orchestra to play as smoothly as singers should sing.

**cantata** (It.) cahnTAHta
A piece of vocal music, usually on a religious text but not always. The cantata is a large form, frequently containing arias, interludes and other smaller forms. It is best known as a form for chorus and soloists, differing from opera in that it is not acted and is usually fairly short.

**cantilena** (It.) cahnteeLAYna

A little song. Sometimes the highest of several singing parts.

**canzona** (It.) cahnZOHna

A song, but frequently an elaborate song distinguished from an aria by its informality.

**capacity house**

A full house, an auditorium filled to its capacity.

**capo, da**

See da capo. See also aria da capo.

**cast**

Those who appear upon the stage as actors, singers and dancers in a performance. But specifically those who have identity, as distinguished from the chorus and the ballet ensemble.

To cast means to assign people to play the roles required by the opera.

**castrato** (It.) cahSTRAHto

A male singer who has achieved an abnormally high voice by means of a surgical alteration of his gonadal system during his youth. A eunuch.

**cavatina** (It.) cahvahTEEna

A little song having only a single strain, and usually simple, expressive and gentle.

**chamber opera**

Opera intended to be played to a small audience and/or in a small place. Hence frequently an opera without chorus, with a small cast and a piano for accompaniment.

**chant**

A ritualistic song, a piece for solo or for chorus in ritualistic style. The *Miserere* in *Il Trovatore* is a good example. Another is the choral background for Pimen's monologue in *Boris Godunov*.

**chantant** (Fr.) shahnTAH(N)

Singing, in a singing style.

**chef d'orchestre** (Fr.) shay dorKEST

Chief of the orchestra, the conductor.

**chest tones**

See voce di petto.

**chiuso** (It.) keeYUzo

Closed. See bocca chiusa.

**choral conductor**

One who conducts a chorus, the chorus master. In opera the chorus is frequently so placed behind the scenes that the members cannot see the regular conductor. The choral conductor then places himself somewhere where he *can* see the conductor, and the chorus can see him. He then transmits the beat and the cues so that they may be on time. The choral conductor also conducts rehearsals especially for the chorus.

**choral opera**

An opera in which the chorus is predominant, as in *Boris Godunov*, most of the works of Gluck, *Oedipus Rex* and others. Many composers have sought, in choral opera, an approach to the classic style of Greek drama.

**choreography**

Dance writing. But in practice it has been such a complex problem to write dance down that the term has come to mean the composition of dance, whether or not any part of it is recorded in writing.

**chorus**

The group of singers who sing and act always en masse, never as soloists. In some operas, the chorus is not a group but is one singer who comments upon the action. See the opera *The Rape of Lucretia*.

**chorus master**

The leader of the chorus. Specifically the rehearsal director for the chorus, only infrequently the conductor during performance. *See* choral conductor.

**chromatic tones**

Tones which have been altered in pitch from the normal tones of any scale. The alteration is a raising by means of sharps, or a lowering by flats. *See* scale.

**claque** (Fr.) clak

A noisy little knot of people in the audience, or surreptitiously spread among the audience, whose main purpose is to stimulate and to simulate great applause for a certain performer so that that worthy may seem to be more popular than is really the case, and thus more to be respected and salaried for his fame. Most singers, whether they want one or not, have their claques.

**classic**

Of classic time, standard. In music, generally, the classic period came after the baroque and before the romantic. Some composers, notably Gluck, wrote in a simple but large style, and their works are models of the genuine form of opera; hence they are classics. But any work which is of long-lasting worth becomes a model in the same way.

**clavier**

(Fr.) clahveeAY
(Ger.) clahVEER (spelled Klavier)
The keyboard. An instrument which is played by means of a keyboard; hence the harpsichord, the piano, etc.

**clef**

The symbol which designates the pitch range of the lines and spaces of the staff. The treble clef used to be the letter G, placed upon the line G above middle C.

The bass clef was an F, and points out the F below middle C. Between these is the C clef itself. Soprano and alto voices appear with the treble clef, tenors with the C, and baritones and basses with the F. Nowadays it is quite usual to use the treble clef for tenor, since the C clef is less familiar.

**coach**

An assistant to the director who helps a singer learn and establish his role during rehearsals. Also an advisor on technical matters to any performer.

**coda**

The tail end (from the Latin *cauda*, meaning "tail"). An extended embellishment of the ending of a piece of music. Distinguished from cadenza in that the coda involves a written recapitulation of the events of the piece, using the whole orchestra, while the cadenza is a free improvisation for the soloists alone. Frequently the coda is a recapitulation characterized by tremendous acceleration toward the ending—as in the *Viennese Waltz*. In opera many a coda remains buried under the unmusical applause of the audience after the singer has had her high note.

**coloratura** (*from* It.) coloraTOORah

Colored, that is; colorful. Florid music for the voice; a highly decorated style with many flourishes, trills and complex figures woven about it. Although it can occur in any voice, it appears most often in showpieces for the soprano. The most famous examples are the *Bell Song* from *Lakmé*, Juliette's *Jewel Song*, and the Queen of the Night's aria.

**comique** (Fr.) coMEEK

Not necessarily comic, but sometimes so. The word describes a style associated with the Opéra-Comique, in Paris. *See* opéra comique. The correct designation for a comic opera in Italian is *opera buffa*, and in French *opéra bouffe*.

**company**

The entire personnel of singers, actors, dancers and instrumentalists who perform opera. In practice the term is most usually applied to a more or less stable group such as the company that performs in repertory, or the touring company.

**concertmaster**

The leading violinist of the orchestra. He sits at the conductor's left and performs certain special duties such as to play the little solos that occur from time to time in the score, or to signal the orchestra to tune up before the conductor himself appears. He also establishes the bowing patterns for the first violins and, in general, acts as the playing leader of the orchestra.

**concert performance**

A performance of an opera without much staging and action, and usually without costumes. Very frequently a new work, or a work too expensive or experimental to warrant full performance receives a concert performance.

**concert pitch**

Standard pitch. Defined by the United States Bureau of Standards to be the pitch of 440 vibrations per second for the A above middle C. Many conductors surreptitiously tune their orchestras to a slightly higher pitch in the fond belief that the audience will think the total sound thus produced to be more brilliant than that of other conductors and orchestras.

**conductor**

He, or she, who leads the orchestra, the singers, the dancers and the chorus in the performance of opera. Not a director in the sense of the stage director.

**conservatory**

Specifically, a formal school of music.

**contralto**

The lowest female voice. Sometimes, as in the role of Orfeo, in *Orfeo ed Euridice*, a voice in that range which may be sung by a high male tenor or a female contralto.

**contratenor**

*See* countertenor.

**counterpoint**

Note-against-note. A style of music in which more than one melody may be heard at one time. A canon is a contrapuntal composition. A voice in counterpoint to another is one which serves as a rhythmic and melodic contrast to another, having its own melody.

**countertenor**

A tenor of exceptionally high range.

**crescendo** (It.) kraySHENdo

Increasing in volume, growing louder.

**czardas** (Hungarian) CHARdahsh

A hungarian dance in two movements, slow then fast.

**cue**

An indication to begin. The conductor gives a cue by signaling with his hand and eye. The score provides a cue by showing the notes or words which immediately preceded an entrance. On a player's part cues are written in very tiny notes.

**curtain raiser**

A short piece before the curtain rises. In opera generally a comic scene or play preceding the main work of the evening. Not an overture.

**cut**

A passage which has been deleted. Also that point in the score at which one skips several measures or several pages. Cuts serve to shorten an overlong piece, sometimes to clarify a murky passage, sometimes to relieve an overworked singer.

**cyclorama**

A backdrop, usually curved, which extends around the sides and rear of a set and which is usually lighted to represent sky or some other indefinite space. It is distinguished from a simple backdrop, which is usually flat and painted to represent a definite scene.

**da capo** (It.) dah CAHpo

From the top. A directive to the performer to return to the beginning of the piece. *See also* aria da capo.

**debut** (Fr.) dehBÜ

A coming out. A singer's first appearance on the stage.

**décor** (Fr.) dehKOR

The set considered as a work of color and design. The design of a setting. The word implies a quality of decoration.

**dialogue**

The conversation of characters upon the stage. Not their expressive solos, monologues and arias, nor their concerted pieces such as trios and septets, but their responsive talk (whether spoken or sung).

**diatonic**

Within the natural scale, without altered notes, nonchromatic. Whether or not a piece is based upon the classic major or minor modes, if it is diatonic it makes use of whatever modal system it has without temporary chromatism. In slang terms, diatonic music is "white note" music, as the diatonic function is represented by the white notes of the piano.

**diction**

Clarity of speech, the quality which makes spoken or sung words understandable. But it is important to keep in mind that for practical purposes diction means clarity of the consonants, since many a singer becomes so involved with the smoothness of his tone that he unconsciously tries to glide over consonants without sounding them. Diction is not to be confused with prosody. Prosody exists in the composition of words and music, while diction can be only in the actual sounding.

**diminuendo**

Diminishing, growing less in volume, becoming quieter.

**director**

He who directs. Usually, in opera, the director is primarily the instructor and constructor of stage movement and acting. Sometimes he is also the conductor of the performance. *See also* artistic director.

**diva** (It.) DEEva

A great lady in opera, a goddess among singers. A prima donna, but in a more complimentary sense.

**divisi**

Divided. A divisi passage is one in which two performers who have been singing the same line divide to sing different notes, as when the sopranos of the chorus divide to become first and second sopranos.

**dodecaphonism**

The theory of music based upon the consideration of the twelve equally spaced tones of the tempered system as of equal harmonic value. The composer establishes his thematic thesis as a series of twelve tones, using each of the available tones once. Upon this he builds his piece. This technique was promulgated by Arnold Schoenberg and used by many of his followers. It is the harmonic system of the opera *Lulu*.

**donna**

Lady, hence a female singer. *See* prima donna.

**double bill**

A performance consisting of two operas, as the double header in baseball consists of two games. A common double bill contains *Cavalleria Rusticana*, and *I Pagliacci*.

**downbeat**

The beat indicated by the conductor in moving his baton downward, hence in practice the first beat after the bar line in any measure, the heaviest beat of that measure (though not always).

**drama**

That which is acted. An acting-out. It is important to remember that drama is not the same as story, tableau, pageant or poem. Drama must be acted to exist, and within it there must be an irreversible transportation of the emotional being of the audience. Drama may not merely portend, it must actually allow that which is portentous to move into its action.

**dramma per musica** (It.) drahma payr MOOzicka

A play in music. One way to avoid the ambiguity of the word *opera*, which to many composers signifies a series of songs rather than a serious drama in music.

**drops**

Pieces of scenery which are hung from the flies of the stage, and which therefore can be dropped into place. In practice, drops are cloth hangings rather than constructions. *See also* flats.

**dry recitative**

*See* recitativo secco.

**duet**

A musical piece for two, or for two soloists plus their accompaniment.

**duo** (It.) DOO-oh

Two. Either a piece for two, or the two who perform it.

**durchcomponiert**

Through-composed; music written in a continuous, noncyclic form; music that has no "repeats" or simple recapitulations. The composer, having stated his theme once, never states it quite the same way again, but always with new material. The term has come into use to describe a tendency among many modern dramatic composers.

**dutchman**

A little strip of cloth glued over the joint between two adjacent flats, and painted so that the joint becomes invisible.

**dynamics**

The world of louds and softs, the crescendos and diminuendos of music. But in opera there is another meaning—the modulations of the tensions and relaxations of emotion that give evidence of the progress of the drama.

**eclogue**

A song of shepherds, a pastoral.

**encore** (Fr.) ah(n)KOR

Again. An added song, or other musical piece, to reward an audience for stopping the action of an opera with its tremendous applause. This is entirely pleasing to the performer, sometimes also to the composer and librettist, but hardly ever to the dramatist whose work has been brought to a grinding halt for it.

**ensemble** (Fr.) ah(n)SOMb

Together. The delicate quality of singing together in tonality and in emotional contact during a performance. It is easier to achieve ensemble in concerted pieces, such as the finale of an opera, but a performance becomes memorable when it has this quality throughout.

**entr'acte** (Fr.) AH(N)tract

Between the acts. A little piece of music, a ballet or even a little play between the acts of the opera. It may or may not have anything to do with the plot of the opera itself.

**entrance**

Not only a door or a place to enter upon the stage, but also the point at which a singer or an instrument begins to sing or to play. There is an entrance each time the singer begins, whether for the first time in the piece, or only after a short rest.

**epilogue**

In Greek, the root means "upon the word," hence it is a final action which comments upon the opera or which informs the audience what happened after the opera ended. In *Boris Godunov*, for instance, the Simpleton's song becomes an epilogue, as he voices the grief for Russia, torn by its czars. An epilogue is not merely a postlude, which can consist only of music.

**episode**

An event in a drama, not necessarily set apart from other events in form, but a complete event.

**extra**

Broadway slang for a person who appears as one of a crowd on the stage, a supernumerary, not a member of the company.

**fanfare**

A musical ovation, an elaborate musical announcement. Fanfares quite generally consist of a flourish or two from the brasses and drums before the entrance of some character of importance, or before the statement of some important idea.

**figured bass**

A line of music written in the bass clef with numbers inscribed over or under the notes, giving enough information so that a keyboard performer may improvise harmonies upon the bass line; a thorough bass, or basso continuo. The numbers tell the player the intervals of the chord to be built upon the bass note; 6/4 tells him to construct a chord whose tones, if reduced to the least space of one octave, would appear as the sixth and fourth notes above the bass, inclusively.

**filar la voce** (It.) feelahr la VOchay

To spin out the tone by alternating crescendos and diminuendos.

**finale** (It.) feeNAHlay

An ending. Usually a grand scene involving some recapitulation of the musical and dramatic events which preceded it, and using as many of the principals of the cast as possible. See the finale in *Don Giovanni*.

**Five, The**

Nickname for five Russians who collectively revolutionized Russian music. They were: Cui, Rimsky-Korsakov, Borodin, Balakirev and Mussorgsky.

**flat**

A symbol which lowers a tone the distance of one semitone. A singer who "sings flat" is one who is consistently out of tune downwards, not up to pitch.

**flats**

Pieces of scenery which are flat. They

usually are made of light canvas, stretched over wooden frames and painted.

**flies**

The rafters above a stage, the open space above the stage where drops may be hung.

**folk opera**

An opera made of folk songs and folk material—or what appear to be folk songs and folk material. *Porgy and Bess* has sometimes been called folk opera. The zarzuelas of Spain are more nearly the type.

**form**

The abstracted structure of a piece of music. The general skeleton into which the composer, ostensibly, fits his ideas. In the classics and romantics, forms seem easier to identify since they have recurring events which help us to reconstruct their skeletons in our minds. But one should not mistake nonrepetitive music for formless music.

Opera is a form of music, distinguished from symphony, cantata, etc. Within opera, aria is a form distinguishable from scena, recitative, and so forth. Music has been defined as organized sound, hence its form is its being.

**forte**

Strongly—therefore loudly. The opposite of piano. Marked *f* in music.

**fortissimo**

Most strongly, as loudly as possible. Marked *ff* on the music.

**fugue**

A form in music in which a theme, generally first stated in one voice, is successively taken up by another and another voice in imitation and in counterpoint to each other. It is a larger form than canon. Whereas canon is the strictest imitation, fugue is fairly free and may be developed considerably. In opera fugue hardly ever occurs except as a device to imitate increasing excitement, as in the overture to *Il Segreto di Susanna*, and that to *Die Zauberflöte*.

**gavotte** (Fr.) gahVOTT

A fairly slow dance in duple rhythm characterized by an even balance between its anacrusis and its metacrusis, or its upbeat and its downbeat.

**gigue** (Fr.) ZHEEG

Derived from the old German word for fiddle; a fast dance in triple time, a jig.

**glissando** (It.) gliSAHNdo

Sliding. Passing up or down the scale without stopping on the notes.

**grace note**

A little ornament of one note which introduces another. In vocal technique the grace note has a necessary function as a means of helping the vocal apparatus to commence a trill.

**grand opera**

Huge opera. That is to say, opera in the grand manner. In France the distinction used to be drawn between opéra comique, which could have spoken dialogue, and the opera, which could not and which had to have a ballet. But nowadays the term is highly emotional, signifying opera which moves by its grandeur, its size in cast, orchestra and sets.

**grease paint**

Make-up for the stage. Since stage lighting flattens details instead of flattering them, thick make-up is frequently the resort of the actor. It *is* greasy, after exposure to the heat of the lights and of the action.

**habanera** (Sp.) hahbahnAYRa

A slow Spanish dance in triple time, the most famous operatic example of which is the Habanera in *Carmen*.

**harmonics**

The overtones, the audible tones which can be distinguished within any tone as it is played or sung. Harmonics exist in an exact relationship to each other, the first harmonic being the basic tone produced, the second being its octave, the third a fifth above that octave, and so on. They are each a multiple of the basic pitch, so that if the basic pitch is 200 vibrations per second, the second harmonic is 400, the third 600, the fourth 800 and so forth. It has been determined that the differences between vowel sounds are caused by different balances of harmonics, and that the different timbres of instruments are similarly created. This is evident on an organ console, where one can mix various harmonic tones to produce imitations of various instruments. Upon the effect of the clash of the harmonics of one note with those of another note sounded simultaneously has been built the science of harmony in music.

**harmony**

The science of the relationship of tones sounded simultaneously. Harmony considers the tones in their static relationship, while counterpoint deals with the relationship of melodies to each other.

**harpsichord**

A keyboard instrument played like a piano, which produces its sound by plucking its strings. The keyboard appears as a piano keyboard, but in some instruments the color scheme of the black and white keys is reversed. The plucking is accomplished with little quills actuated by jacks attached to the keys. Frequently there is more than one keyboard, plus a set of stops which connect the keys together to produce different combinations of harmonics. The harpsichord was the standard instrument in the accompaniment of dry recitative. It is presently undergoing a resurgence as a solo instrument.

**head voice**

*See* voce di testa.

**heldentenor** (Ger.)

Heroic tenor. A tenor with a brilliant voice, suited to heroic parts and frequently unsuited for more subtle ones.

**heroic**

Brilliant, sometimes also dramatic or theatrical. Said of male voices. The opposite of bel canto.

**histrionic**

Theatrical, dramatic.

**house**

Where the audience sits. In a figurative sense, the audience itself, as in the expression "a good house," which is an audience that pleases the manager by filling the house, or the actor by being sympathetic to the opera.

**hymn**

A sacred song, usually in invocation to a deity, as the *Hymn to Venus*.

**impresario**

One who gathers up performers, finds a place for them to perform and entices the audience to come to see the performance. The impresario is the manager of the opera company rather than one of its directors. His job is the business of contracts and contacts.

**imbroglio** (It.) imBROlyo

A device which creates a confusion of rhythms, as for instance when a figure strongly suggestive of waltz measure is written out in a measure of four beats. This device occurs throughout opera as an evidence of excitement in any part, and is especially noticeable in the end of the *Leonora Overture No. 3* (*Fidelio*).

**incidental music**

Music which fills in the empty places in a play. In a good play the incidental music consists of the dances, the songs and perhaps the fanfares called for by the script. But in a bad play it also provides background noise where none should be. Some operas were originally conceived as incidental music to plays, for instance Busoni's *Turandot*.

**instrumentation**

The assignment of instruments to the orchestra; the use made of them in the score.

**interlude**

Literally, "between the games." A piece of music or a theatrical episode which comes between important episodes and which generally provides the audience some feeling of rest between activities.

**intermezzo** (It.) intayrMETzo

An interlude, but of larger proportions. The opera *La Serva Padrona* was conceived and first performed as an intermezzo for another opera. But on the other end of the scale, the little instrumental piece between the parts of *Cavalleria Rusticana* is also an intermezzo.

**intonation**

Putting into tone. Good intonation is accurately pitched, bad intonation is not. The term has less to do with the quality of tone than its precision.

**jeu** (Fr.) ZHE(R)

Play. The act of playing, or the play itself, as in *Le Jeu de Robin et Marion*.

**jig**

See gigue, for which it is the English equivalent.

**key**

That which one's fingers press to make instruments change their pitch.

Also the tonal system of a musical phrase, demarked by its central or basic note—its tonic, as in "the key of G." Distinguished from mode in that key is restricted to the system of European music, which has only the major and minor modes.

**Klavier**

See clavier.

**largo** (It.) LAHRgo

Slowly, slower than adagio.

**larynx**

The vocal organ, the upper part of the trachea. The seat of the vocal cords.

**léger** (f. légère) (Fr.) layZHAY (layZHAYR)

Light, lightly. A soprano légère is a soprano with a very light voice.

**leitmotiv** (Ger.) LIGHTmoteef

A significant phrase or fragment of music used to represent a person or an idea. Wagner made use of the term to describe his concept of the denotative possibilities in music. He gave every important character or object or idea in his operas a leitmotiv, and was thereby able, he claimed, to bring the item to mind via music whenever he wished to refer to it in the drama.

**libretto**

Literally, "little book." Particularly the book of the words of an opera. The libretto is usually an adaptation of a play or story, made by a librettist particularly for operatic performance; hence it is not a large book, since music manages to take the place of many descriptive words. The libretto of *Otello*, for an instance, contains slightly more than one fourth the lines of Shakespeare's play.

### light opera

Unserious opera, sometimes comic opera. The term describes the lightness with which the subject is treated, not the form of the piece.

### line

The line of musical notes on the page which the singer sings or the instrumentalist plays. Therefore, within instrumental music, a line is frequently called a voice. Hence a fugue is spoken of as having three or four voices. But in opera the real vocal line must be distinguished from the instrumental line, and so forth.

### lirico basso

*See* lyric bass.

### lullaby

A cradle song; a song, therefore, sung for the purpose of lulling someone to sleep in a pleasant manner. A berceuse.

### lute

A stringed instrument slightly similar to the guitar, but with more strings, some of which vibrate in sympathy with others, as resonators. The word is frequently used in a figurative sense; to "take up one's lute" means to sing one's song.

### lyre

The harp of the ancient Greeks, usually depicted as a small inverted omega, or the letter U with a bar across the top and six or seven vertical strings which the singer may pluck as a sort of limited

support to his song. It gave its name as an adjective—lyrical.

### lyric

From *lyre*, hence singable. Lyrics are words for song. Other words may be intended for scenas and other musical forms, but lyrics are essentially simple and gentle.

### lyric bass

A bass voice more suited to smooth singing than to dramatic exclamation.

### lyric tenor

As in lyric bass, a tenor voice more suited to smooth song than to heroic declamation.

### madrigal

A choral song for the pleasure of singing together. The madrigal was most popular around the sixteenth century, and its subject was usually love. Whereas a motet has a sacred text, a madrigal is always secular. One of the immediate predecessors of opera was *L'Amfiparnaso*, which was a little play made of madrigals. But the polyphonic style did not lend itself to clarity in presentation of a story. It took the re-application of monody, therefore, to make opera possible.

### maestro (It.) mahESSstro

The master, the orchestral conductor. One frequently uses the term as a complimentary title. Also, a singing teacher.

### major mode

One of the two prevalent modes in modern European music, the other being the minor mode. The major has been roughly characterized as the mode of happiness or brilliance, which is hardly an adequate description of something so applicable to any emotional event. The major mode actually is an entire group of modes in use since centuries before their notation was developed; they all can be reduced to scales in which the first two steps up from the tonic tone are whole tones. This provides a general difference from the minors, which have a half-tone for their second step. The major scale was one of the great joys of Beethoven, but one has only to hear *Orfeo ed Euridice* to realize that the happiness factor is not always there; Orfeo's lament at losing his wife the second time, *Che farò senz' Euridice*, is in a major mode.

### make-up

What every actor must paint upon his face and hands to (1) make them visible on the stage, and (2) make them appear to be someone else's face and hands. The term therefore covers more than the cosmetics of day wear; it includes false hair, false eyeglasses, false noses and so forth. But it does not include ornaments for the hair, for instance, which are part of the costume.

### mandolin

A stringed instrument with a body shaped like an idealized pear and a neck somewhat like that of a guitar. The mandolin has eight strings, tuned in four pairs with the same notes as the violin. One plays it with a plectrum and sustains a note by continuous plucking.

### mask

A false face, or something with which to cover the face or a part of it.

### masque (Fr.) mask

A show in which the actors are masked to represent personifications of abstract qualities such as temperance, the devil and what not. Usually performed by amateurs for their own entertainment. *See* the opera *Gloriana*.

### masqué (Fr.) masKAY

Masked. Said of a masked ball, which is one at which the participants hide their faces with masks, the better to effect liaisons without being caught at it. *See* the opera *Un Ballo in Maschera*.

### measure

A gross unit by which recurrent patterns of rhythm are delineated. A measure is one complete unit in a rhythmic pattern. It contains three motions: the anacrusis which is the lifting up, the crusis which is the main accent or downbeat, and the metacrusis which is the recovery. In the waltz *The Blue Danube*, the first four notes of the theme make the anacrusis, the heavy beat the crusis, and the repeated offbeat figure after it the metacrusis. The measure, therefore, is *not* contained always between the bar lines. Rather, the bar line is a symbol which indicates that the next beat is the crusis. A measure may be very long or very short, it may not have one or the other of the two offbeats, but it always has only one crusis, and that indicated by the bar. Many composers, of course, write with ambiguities for artistic reasons, so that the rule is violated on paper. But the ambiguity they create proves the rule in practice.

### melodrama

A drama in song, hence any drama in music. But the word has deteriorated somewhat in the last few decades so that it now represents a kind of play which satirizes the sentimentality of the late nineteenth century. Such plays have a hero, a heroine and a villain and revolve around some impending tragedy such as the foreclosure of the family mortgage. In opera, which should itself be called melodrama, the term serves only to denote passages of extreme sentimentality.

**melody**

The metaphysical motion of the attention from tone to tone. In practice *melody* is the technical word for any fairly coherent line of music, usually the line that is most prominent in any passage. It is frequently, therefore, the vocal line itself. But in a philosophical sense we should permit ourselves to describe the melody of composite lines. *See* melos.

**melos**

Greek for "song," hence used to designate the total emotional line of a musical piece, the musical-emotional line of opera.

**messa di voce** (It.) MESSa dee VOchay

A gradual swelling and diminishing of the volume of the tone of the voice on a single note, indicated in music by a small crescendo mark followed by an equivalent diminuendo under the same note.

**meter**

The unheard unit of time measurement in music. Upon the meter the composer builds rhythms. Meter is not to be confused with beat, which is the pulse of time in music. Meter in music is not the same as meter in poetry; in fact what the poet calls the beat is the composer's meter.

**metronome**

A mechanical device which beats time with an inverted pendulum and a clicking sound. It was invented by Beethoven's contemporary, Maelzel. The pace or tempo of music is usually indicated on the score by a figure which represents the number of beats per minute "m.m.", or on Maelzel's Metronome. Modern metronomes have dispensed with the mechanical pendulum and substituted an electronically actuated blinking light, which since it provides no visible movement does not give the performer quite the same information.

**mezza voce** (It.) METza VOchay

Half the power of the voice, softly. But not quite as secretly as sotto voce.

**mezzo-soprano** (It.) METzo soPRAHno

A soprano voice of slightly lower range than the full soprano, but not as low as contralto.

**microtone**

A very small division of the octave. The normal tuning of the tempered scale of the piano divides the octave into twelve equally spaced tones. This amounts to a practical compromise between the infinite division of the octave in pure intonation and the number of keys that a human hand can reach in playing. In order to notate the pure intonation more closely, many composers have devised systems of smaller intervals. Carrillo in Mexico uses numerals to indicate as many as ninety-six tones to the octave. Others have made more readable systems. Several operas have been written in microtone notation, notably by Alois Hába. Microtones do not constitute a system of harmonic structure as does dodecaphonism, but rather are a means of indicating more accurate variations of pitch on paper.

**mime** (Fr.) meem

One who pantomimes. An actor who uses no speech but only gesture and movement. Also the act of pantomiming.

**minnesinger**

A lover of singing and a singer himself. The minnesingers flourished in Germany from the twelfth to the fourteenth centuries. *See* the opera *Tannhäuser*. *See also* troubadour.

**minstrel**

An itinerant singer who accompanies himself on some instrument such as the guitar as he sings little songs. He is distinguished from the bard, who sings of epic events and so forth. In the United States the word became attached to a kind of actor who appeared in blackface. The minstrels toured the early Midwest and presented shows which consisted mostly of jokes and funny songs, sung by a dozen or so minstrels, playing banjos.

### minor mode

One of the two modes of modern tonal music, the other being the major mode. Like the major, the minor is really a class of modes, all of which have in common the fact that their second scalewise step upward is a semitone. *See* major mode.

### minuet

A formal dance in triple time, usually somewhat stately and slow.

### mise-en-scène (Fr.) MEEZ ah(n) SEN

The putting on the stage, the manner in which a scene is placed upon the stage. By extension, the set and costumes themselves.

### modality

The quality of being in a mode. The organization of sound which makes music forces, by definition, some formality onto the structure of a melody. This amounts to the fact that a melody uses a certain group of tones with which it completes its entire design, leaving out other tones which were not useful to it. The effect of whatever relationship the selected tones may produce is the modality of the melody. In practice one may reduce any melody to its notes and put those notes into a single scale (ignoring for the moment the fact that altered notes present some problems of classification). We speak of the tonal effect of that scale as its mode, and hence the mode of the melody. Modes lend themselves to description as

dark, light, sad, happy and so forth. But the adjectives have practically no real meaning.

### mode

The tonal structure of the system of any melody. The total tonal framework in which a melody is constructed. Not the same as scale. The mode is the total relationship of its tones. The American blues, for instance, is a mode. *See* modality.

### modulation

Change of key. The word would seem to indicate change of mode, but in practice the transition from A major to B-flat major, though the mode is the same, is a modulation. In early times, however, when scale was an unused concept, the harmonic differences between one major key and another had no meaning; hence the only effective change was one which changed the mode itself. Since the modes were identified with different levels on what we know as the chromatic scale the result *included* a change of key.

Modulation is the great dramatic device of harmony in opera. That sudden change of atmosphere when Florestan is about to be saved was accomplished by a modulation.

### monody

Single-voiced song. Theoretically monody should be the unaccompanied song of a single melodic line. But in practice, and in its most important sense, it is melody for solo voice with accompaniment. Monody is the opposite of polyphony. It was necessary for the Camerata (*q.v.*) to put monody to use before opera could be invented. Monody allowed a single person to sing a dramatic song, or to take part verbally in a dramatic event as a personality, whereas with polyphony, which was at that time the general tool of vocal music, no such personalization could occur. Any aria is monody; so is any recitative.

**motet**

A sacred choral song. The motet was the contemporary of the madrigal, but whereas the madrigal was sung by four or five people for their own pleasure, the motet is frequently sung by a chorus. The motet survives in opera as a choral hymn, but the madrigal which preceded opera does not so remain.

**motif**

*See* leitmotiv.

**musical**

A musical show, particularly the big and brassy kind played on Broadway and as a spectacle on TV. Musicals are a commercial approach to opera. Sometimes there has been a noteworthy bridging of the gap. *Carmen* was adapted as the musical *Carmen Jones*, which was a great hit and a compliment to the original. Bertolt Brecht and Kurt Weill have made several attempts to do likewise on a more bitter level.

**musical director**

Usually the chief conductor of the company, sometimes the conductor who actually directs the production itself; that is to say, the one who instructs the singers in rehearsal and conducts the performance.

**mute**

Among the cast of characters, the mute is the silent role.

In the orchestra the mute is the device which a performer attaches to his instrument to alter (i.e., cause mutation in) its tone. It also reduces the volume of its tone, but its primary purpose is the change, not the quietness.

**narrator**

One who tells the story to the audience. Sometimes, as in *Il Combattimento di Tancredi e Clorinda*, the narrator is a singer. At others it may be a speaker or even a chorus. Narrators are frequently employed in concert performances of operas, to fill in the gaps.

**neoclassic**

A style in music, not thoroughly associated with any particular era but distinguished by its use of classic forms with modern orchestration. Paul Hindemith, who writes in the most original style, still may be considered to be neoclassic at times in his use of old forms. Likewise Stravinsky evidences a considerable interest in the period of Bellini in his *Rake's Progress*.

**nocturne**

A night piece, a relatively quiet piece of music meant to be played in the evening or to evoke the atmosphere of night.

**notation**

The art and science of writing musical ideas on paper. There are many kinds of notation, such as the melodic symbols of the Byzantine church, the horseshoe-and-nail notation of medieval Europe, and the harmonic system of lines, spaces and circular notes which we use today. Several opera composers, realizing the value of accuracy in writing the highly complex intervals of the ordinary vocal melody, have attempted to invent systems which will allow exact reproduction. This has resulted in systems of writing microtones. But in actual practice, when vocal music is written without relationship to tempered instruments (instruments whose tuning is fixed to the twelve equally spaced tones of the tempered octave), the singer sings with microtonic accuracy of pitch and the audience hears it with great clarity.

**note**

The symbol on the page which indicates which pitch to sound and how long to sound it. Loosely speaking, the tone itself.

**notturno** (It.) notTOORno

A nocturne

**obbligato** (It.) obbleeGAHto

Obliged. An indispensable accompaniment, especially a contrapuntal accompaniment to a solo voice as in the case of the flute which plays a duet with the soprano during a coloratura aria, while the orchestra accompanies both of them.

**octave**

The harmonic distance from one tone to its double; the distance, therefore, of eight scale-notes up or down, counted inclusively. The octave of any tone is its second harmonic. It has the same name as the tone itself. In many harmonic systems it does not occur as the eighth note of a scale; in the pentatonic system of the music of the Scottish Highlands it is the sixth tone. But it is always of twice the frequency of the parent tone, and always has the same name.

**octet**

A group of eight performers or a piece of music written for such a group. In opera, commonly, an octet consists of eight principals, whether or not their number is augmented by a vast accompaniment. The octet is of infrequent occurrence in modern music. Usually, when eight voices are involved, the grouping is that of two quartets rather than as a single octet. This happens most frequently as four principals join with the chorus, which is also divided into four voices.

**open stage**

A stage made visible from more than one side. Since the proscenium stage is essentially a three-walled box, it permits a limited variation in style of performance. Forms of open staging are: the arena, visible from all sides; the strip stage, visible from opposite sides; the platform before a backdrop; and (it actually exists) the stage which completely surrounds the audience. Of these the term *open stage* most commonly refers to the platform and backdrop type.

**opera**

A kind of musical drama, mostly sung, consisting of arias, ensembles, choral scenes and dialogue. Opera is not the only kind of musical drama; the Greeks, for instance, probably presented their classic dramas as musical productions. The term *opera* has become so closely associated with its Italian interpretation that some composers have objected to it as a designation for what they produce. Among these was Wagner, who called his work music-drama or festival-play in order to escape the implication of a string of arias roughly tied together into a story. Even the Italians have objected, Verdi calling many of his works *dramma per musica*, and Monteverdi one of his "a fable." But in any case a good opera is a dramatic event in singing.

**opera buffa** (It.) opera BOOfa

Comic opera. This term is most useful in order to distinguish comic opera from opéra comique.

**opéra comique** (Fr.) ohpayrah coMEEK

Not necessarily comic opera, but by tradition an opera with spoken dialogue. Its opposite is grand opera. *Carmen*, as written by Bizet, was opéra comique. Giraud added music to support the dialogue (deleting much of the important dialogue in the process) to make it "grand." The style gets its name from the Opéra-Comique in Paris, which allowed its presentation, while the Académie Royale (the Opéra) did not.

**opera seria** (It.) opera SAYreeah
Serious opera.

**operetta**
Light opera.

**orchestration**
The science of writing music for instruments, or of assigning instruments to music. The orchestration is the arrangement thus made. It is written in the score.

**organ point**
An instrumental drone bass frequently employed as a dramatic and musical device to represent solidity, gravity. It gets its name from the fact that the pipe organ has a pedal keyboard which is frequently employed to hold a low note for a long time while the hands play fantasias.

**ouverture** (Fr.) oovayrTÜR
Overture.

**ovation**
Thunderous applause, great acclaim.

**overtones**
Those tones which can be heard within any musical tone and which are its harmonics. It is these, the balance of overtones, which create the differences of timbre of instruments.

**overture**
An opening piece. A rather extensive piece of music for the orchestra to play before the curtain opens. Gluck, in his preface to *Alceste*, says that an overture should prepare the audience for what is about to happen.

**pantomime**
An act or show without words in which the dramatic event is conveyed to the audience by means of gestures and bodily motion. Not to be confused with ballet and dance, which are formal and fairly abstract movements. Pantomime imitates natural motion in a somewhat conventionalized manner. Pantomime performers are called mimes. Their performances are frequently accompanied by music. In opera there is sometimes a pantomimed moment as when Hamlet presents the dumb show before Claudius in which the mimes mimic the murder Claudius committed.

**parlante** (It.) pahrLAHNtay
In a manner resembling speech, but particularly in a declamatory manner. Said of musical lines, and not to be confused with *Sprechstimme*, which is the formal imitation of the tones and rhythms of speech.

**part**
A role, one's part to be played. In the orchestra the part is the instrumental line each player reads. On the stage, the part is the characterization and vocal line each singer (or actor) follows.

**pasticcio** (It.) pahSTEEcheeo
A little play or story woven together as a sort of pasted-up opera, with music by more than one composer. Frequently the words are written to the music, instead of the reverse.

**pastiche** (Fr.) pahSTEESH
Pasticcio.

**pastoral** (*or* pastourelle)
A musical piece or a scene representative of meadows where shepherds and shepherdesses are supposed to frolic. The operas about Orpheus commonly begin with a pastoral. Sometimes complete operas can be called pastoral.

# GLOSSARY

**percussion**

The group of instruments in the orchestra which produce sound when struck. These include the drums, cymbals, marimbas, timpani, blocks and so forth. The piano is sometimes included, if the composer wishes to use it in that manner.

**phonetic**

Having to do with sound. The science of phonetics deals with the differences of sounds in various languages and dialects. Not to be confused with that other science of sound, harmonics.

**piano**

Softly, the opposite of forte. Its symbol on the page is *p*. Because it could be played both softly and loudly without the trouble of pulling out stops as in the harpsichord, allowing the player infinite subtlety of dynamic shading, the pianoforte got its name.

**piano score**

A score which has been reduced so that a pianist may reproduce its music on his instrument, substituting for the orchestra. Commonly synonymous with *vocal score*.

**pianissimo**

Most softly.

**pit**

The place, generally sunken below the line of sight of the audience, where the orchestra sits during a performance of opera.

**pitch**

Location in the spectrum of tone. Pitch is described in vibrations per second, high pitch being the pitch of higher frequency, and so forth. *See* concert pitch.

**pizzicato** (It.) pitzzeCAHto

Plucking, especially of the strings of the violin, viola, and other bowed instruments.

**plot**

The general skeleton of the story of an opera, reduced to simple terms. Not the same as a scenario.

**polonaise** (Fr.) pollohNEZ

A Polish dance in 3/4 time, containing all kinds of skips and turns, and with much syncopation. One of the most famous in opera runs throughout the Polish scenes of *Boris Godunov*.

**polyphony** (Greek) pollIFfonee

Music of many lines woven together, in other words, music of many voices, in the sense of melodic lines. The opposite of monody. Until the prevalence of polyphony was broken by the introduction of monody, it was impossible for opera to be invented. But polyphony as a technique abounds in opera now, as in the quintets, the septets and the great ensembles of such masters and Mozart and Gluck. Polyphony is the simultaneous singing of separate voices, not to be confused with chordal music, which is harmonically based.

**postlude**

An afterpiece. A postlude is short, usually without voices, not to be confused with an epilogue. The postlude is sometimes nothing more than the unheard music after the final curtain which accompanies the audience in its stumblings to the exits.

**prelude**

An opening piece, an introduction. A short piece of music intended to establish little more than the harmonic context of what is to follow, or briefly to set a mood. Not as big as an overture, and not to be confused with a prologue.

**première**

A first performance of an opera. A world premiere is the very first performance anywhere, but companies frequently use the word to indicate a first in their repertory, or in the city.

**presence**

*See* stage presence.

**prima donna** (It.) PREEma DONna

The first woman. Logically there can be but one prima donna in a company, and socially there should be but one in order to maintain peace. But the term is used to compliment any of the three or four highest-paid women on the roster. Because of the emotional history of such people, the term *prima donna* is also used to describe a singer who is belligerently defensive about her abilities and her fame.

**principal**

A leading singer, one of the important singers in the company, or one who sings an important role in the opera.

**production**

The total putting together and presentation of an opera. The physical equipment, the people in costume and the art of the presentation all make the production. A new production is one which has been newly designed and newly conceived, whether it has new singers and new sets or not. The person who makes the production is not called, as in the film world, a producer, but rather the artistic director.

**projection**

To a singer, projection is the process by which he makes his voice reach the farthest corner of the hall with clarity. As an actor he must add a psychological integration to his vocal technique so that the character is projected as clearly as the sound.

To the set designer, projection is the process by which he may flash an image on the backdrop to set the scene, thus allowing great speed of changes and less drain on the budget.

**prologue**

A foreword. A solo which announces the facts they need to know to the audience, as in *I Pagliacci*. But also the prologue may be an extensive scene or two, providing background information for the opera, as in the Coronation Scene and Pimen's monologue, which combine to become the prologue to *Boris Godunov*. The prologue has words, and is thereby distinguished from the prelude and the overture.

**prompter**

One who whispers or shouts a word or two to remind an actor of his next line. In opera the prompter has a little cabin in the footlights, visible to but hardly noticed by the audience. There he sits with the score before him and barks orders to the singers all the way through the performance. Thus a company may maintain a large repertory, or a singer keep many parts at the tip of his tongue.

**props**

Objects which help the audience identify the scene on the stage, or which are picked up and used by the actors. Books on the table, pistols, candles and so forth are props. But beds are scenery and hats and coats are costume.

**proscenium**

The arch or frame through which the audience can see the stage. It occurs, of course, only in those theaters which have the boxlike stage. *See* open stage.

**prosody**

The fitting of words into rhythm.

Good prosody allows words to retain their natural accent and weight in rhythm. Bad prosody does not. Opera abounds in bad prosody, which causes audiences to miss the meanings of the words that are being sung, thereby saving the day for many an impossible libretto.

**protagonist**
The first to act, therefore the character whose action starts the main dramatic movement of the play. Technically he is opposed to the antagonist, but that term is not so frequently used in opera. Carmen is the protagonist of her opera, the people of Russia sometimes receive that title in *Boris Godunov*.

**quartet**
A group of four performers or a piece written for four. In opera a quartet usually consists of four principals who are accompanied by the orchestra.

**quaver**
British term for the eighth-note.

**quintet**
A group of five performers, or music written for five. As in quartet, the quintet of an opera may consist of five principals plus the orchestra or chorus.

**reading**
The act of playing through a piece of music or a scene without rehearsal. Also a term used to describe the manner in which a performance was conducted, as "a brilliant reading" or "a sensuous reading."

**recapitulation**
Restatement in music. A re-use of previous thematic material with or without some variation or development of its harmonic structure.

**recitativo** (It.) raycheetahTEEvo
A passage of dialogue which, though in the tones of music, is recited more or less like prose speech, and which may be accompanied by anything from a chord or two to a complex web of counterpoint, depending upon the composer's style or intention. Same as *recitative*. See below.

**recitativo misurato** (It.)
rayseetahTEEvo meezooRAHto
Measured recitative. A recitative supported by measured music instead of the isolated, rhythmless chords of dry recitative. But not yet as musical as a real melody, or an arioso.

**recitativo secco** (It.)
rayseetahTEEvo SECKo
Dry recitative. One step removed from natural prose speech. The singer intones the words with harmonically determined notes, but not yet with anything that could be called melody. The accompaniment consists of isolated chords and cadences used mostly as punctuation and a means to keep on pitch. This accompaniment, in classic opera, was commonly played on the harpsichord.

**recitativo stromentato** (It.)
rayseetahTEEvo stromenTAHto
Instrumented recitative. A more musical line than in dry recitative, accompanied by more than a keyboard, and therefore usually the same as recitativo misurato.

**reduction**
The arrangement of a score for fewer instruments. Operas frequently suffer reduction to fit touring companies or for small theaters where a large orchestra could not be accommodated.

**refrain**
A stanza which occurs periodically

throughout a ballad or a song. Also, loosely, a memorable tune and thus the ballad or song itself. The word was frequently used as a title for melodies.

**régisseur** (Fr.) rayzheeSE(R)
The stage director.

**repertory**
The selection of operas which a company maintains in a state of readiness for production. Also the roles a singer keeps ready to sing with little or no rehearsal. Repertory is much more usual among opera companies than in the speaking theater.

**rest**
A symbol on the musical page which replaces a note with silence. Also the moment of silence itself.

**revival**
A new production of an old work, or of a work which has been out of repertory for some time. A revival need not be a really new production, but merely a re-establishment of an old production without significant change.

**rhapsody**
Literally a sewing together of songs. Hence rhapsody is one of the more remote ancestors of opera. According to some anthropological archaeologists, the ancient Greek rhapsodist was essentially an actor acting a play in music. The fact that he did it all solo only proved his versatility. He narrated his story in song, and embellished it with odes. Unfortunately the Florentines who searched for a way to invent opera did not know about this; they had to go through the process of discovering it as monody all over again.

**rhythm**
The changes and variations, arranged in patterns in time, which the composer builds upon the pulse of music. Although he uses percussion instruments to emphasize it, rhythm is not effected by drumbeats but by harmonic changes or changes of direction in melody. It is not to be confused with beat or with pulse, both of which are its tools; nor with tempo, which is its pace.

**ritornello** (It.) reetorNELlo
A little refrain which occurs again and again between stanzas of a ballad or rondo and which serves as a kind of little coda for each section of the piece. There is a ritornello which appears in many places during La Favola d'Orfeo.

**rococo** (It.) roKOko
A variant of baroque, usually associated with lighter and more florid music.

**role**
The part one plays, one's total action on the stage, all the words and singing the performer uses to create a character and to complete that character's life within an opera. A role is not just the image of the character sketched in gesture, but is the entire play of that character against and with the others in an opera.

**romance**
A song of amorous feeling, or a piece of music intended to stimulate amorous or pleasant imagination.

**romantic**
Having the quality of wishfulness. But also descriptive of a period in musical history, roughly the nineteenth century, during which many composers became interested in the narrative and descriptive possibilities in music. In concert music they developed the tone poem and its relatives. In opera there came a double result which had the look of extreme realism (verismo) on the one hand and sentimentality on the other. Such works

as *Louise*, *La Bohème*, and *Manon* are prime examples.

**rondeau** (Fr.) ronDOH

One of the simpler forms of French song.

**rondo** (It.) RONdoh

A musical piece which has a continually recurring stanza or theme which alternates with other themes or stanzas. The rondo is more usual as a dance piece, hence its recurrent theme is not quite the same thing as a refrain in a ballad.

**round**

The simplest canon. A canon may be a rather extended piece, even though it is required to be strictly imitative. But a round is a simple song which is sung in canon; i.e., after the first voice has begun, each of the other voices enters in succession until all are singing. Then it comes to an end in reverse fashion or in a tutti, without development.

**rubato** (It.) rooBAHto

Stolen, robbed. A term to describe the hesitation which is possible within rhythms. In rubato, a little extra time devoted to one beat is made up by hurrying through others within the measure, so that the following measure may occur on time.

**run**

A melodic passage which travels up or down the scale, either diatonically or chromatically, hitting every note but not dwelling on one more than another. Not to be confused with glissando, which does not sound each note separately, nor with arpeggio, which sounds only the notes of a chord without intermediates. The run is generally an ornamental device.

**scale**

The systematized reduction of the tones of any mode, gathered up and put into order. Since we have major, minor and other modes we have also major, minor and other scales which are their schematic pictures. The chromatic scale is a scale in the tempered system of tuning, as represented by the twelve tones of the piano's octave. It is common to use the word *scale* when we really mean mode, but it leads to a misunderstanding. Scales are not a natural phenomenon in music, they are orderly arrangements of notes made to help us identify and discuss modes.

**scena** (It.) SHAYna

A great scene in opera, but more particularly a musical episode wherein the action and dialogue are composed into the musical form as integrally as is an aria. In fact a scena is sometimes an extended aria with dramatic dialogue woven in. Thus the scena is the ultimate accomplishment of dramatic composition in music, being as thoroughly a dramatic event as a musical one. It is identified, when one refers to it, usually by the name of the chief character taking part, as "Lucia's Scena."

**scenario**

An outline of the sequence of scenes of an opera. The scenario is a working basis for the librettist, the composer and the scene designer. Ideally it is organized in terms of physical action on the stage.

**scene**

A section of an act of an opera. Nowadays a scene commonly consists of all the music and action which occurs between changes of setting, or important changes of cast. In the old days one scene would end and another begin if and when any member of the cast had an entrance or an exit. But now, since it is recognized that dramatic motion has a rhythm of its own the scene has become defined and bounded by episodes and thus most commonly by changes in setting or time.

Scene is also the setting itself, that which meets the eyes of the audience. This may even include the tableau of actors themselves, and in a psychological sense the emotional background.

**scherzo** (It.) SKAYRTzo

Literally, "joke." A humorous episode in music, generally one in which the music itself creates the mood, not the words or events.

**score**

The pages upon which all the vocal and instrumental music of the opera is written out. That which the conductor reads as he conducts. The score does not normally contain all the nonmusical passages of an opera, such as long periods of dialogue, but it does include every detail necessary for the conductor to carry out his job, even notes about the motion of actors on the stage wherever that may be important to the timing. One generally distinguishes the score of an opera from its reductions by calling it the full score. *See also* vocal score *and* piano score.

**secco** (It.) SECKo

Dry. *See* recitativo secco.

**segue** (It.) SAYgway

Continue as before, or continue into the next section. Not only a directive, but also the name of the bridge-passage by which different parts of the scene may be strung together.

**seguidilla** (Sp.) saygeeDEElya

A Spanish dance in 3/4 time. See the excellent example in the opera *Carmen* (*Près des ramparts de Séville*).

**semitone**

A half step in the diatonic scale, a chromatic step. It is the placement of the semitones in the various scales which identifies them. The major scale has half steps from its third to its fourth tones and from its seventh to its eighth. The natural minor has them both one step lower in the scale. The symbol for raising a tone one half step is the sharp, to lower it the same amount the flat.

**septet**

A group of seven performers or the music written for such a group. In opera it does not change their classification if the seven performers are accompanied by the orchestra or the chorus.

**serenade**

An evening song, therefore commonly associated with a lover's invocation to his beloved.

**seria**

*See* opera seria.

**set**

The entire combination of physical equipment which makes up the visible scene within which the actors play. On a proscenium stage the set consists usually of drops, flats and furniture.

**set piece**

A musical episode whose form and rhythmic organization within the context of the opera set it apart from the general flow of action, thus bringing that action to a halt. The sextet from *Lucia di Lammermoor* is such a set piece, as is the Toreador's song in *Carmen*.

Also a unit of the set, such as a tree or a papier-maché boulder.

**sextet**

A group of six performers or the music written for such a group. As in all other ensembles of opera, the fact that they are accompanied by numerous instruments does not affect their classification as a sextet.

# GLOSSARY

**signature**

The cluster of sharps or flats (or lack of them) which with the clef sign indicate the key of a line of music. Also, loosely, that key itself, expressed in terms of sharps and flats.

Sometimes a signature is a significant passage of music used to remind the audience of the identity of some character on the stage. *See* leitmotiv.

**simultaneous set**

A stage setting which contains all the elements for all the scenes of the opera, so arranged that changes of scene may be accomplished by no more than the movement of the actors into a new location. In medieval morality plays, the setting was commonly of this type, with the pearly gates of heaven at the one end and the mouth of hell at the other, leaving the characters free to march whichever way their parts led them.

**singspiel** (Ger.) ZINGshpeel

A play to be sung, a play in which dialogue is spoken between musical numbers. Akin to the ballad opera and the Broadway musical.

**solfeggio** (It.) solFEDGgio

Training of the ear and the voice so that the one may understand the pitch relationships of the notes it hears, and the other produce notes accurately as they are read from the page. A basic training for any composer or performer.

**solo** (It.) SOlo

Alone. A singer who sings a part more prominent than other parts which accompany it, or who sings alone. Also, music for one performer with or without accompaniment.

**song**

A piece to be sung. The song is the most ancient form of free expression in vocal music, and remains the simplest form, complete in itself. The word is inapplicable to extended arias with musical development. The song is essentially emotional and reflective, not dramatic or narrative.

**soprano**

The highest of the voices, the female voice of highest range. Hence also the highest in any group of melodic lines as the soprano part in a fugue, or the soprano saxophone among other saxophones.

**sotto voce** (It.) SOTto VOchay

Under the breath, without force in the voice (although still with dramatic intensity), quietly. Not the same, however, as piano or pianissimo. *Sotto voce* implies a quality of secrecy.

**soubrette** (Fr.) sooBRETT

A theatrical type; the coquettish lady's maid, or the girl of slightly scandalous reputation.

**spinto** (It.)

A term descriptive of the type of operatic voice that can be stretched to include roles of entirely different character. Most particularly used to describe a soprano voice capable of the whole range of roles from the dramatic, through the lyric to the coloratura. A singer possessing this triple ability would be an asset to any company, but few have it.

**Sprechstimme** (Ger.) SHPREKstimma

The speaking voice, hence music which is written to be sung in the manner of the speaking voice. *Sprechstimme* designates particularly a technique of imitating the tones and rhythms of speech with music, which permits the composer to direct the dialogue with absolute accuracy and to accompany it with music. It is not to be confused with recitative, which is a sort of chantlike melody with speech rhythm. Sprechstimme, as written on the page, imitates the rise and fall of natural speech as nearly as the composer can.

**staccato** (It.) staCAHto
Detached, hence notes sung with separation between them; the opposite of legato.

**staff**
The five-line system upon which one writes musical notes. Actually there have been staves of more or less than five lines.

**stage director**
The technical supervisor of a production, responsible for the operation of the stage and the set upon it, and the attendance of the actors at rehearsal.

**stage presence**
An intangible ability by which a performer projects the fact of his existence into the awareness of the audience. It takes a great actor to do this without distracting the audience from the opera itself.

**standard opera**
Opera which remains constantly in repertory and which rightly or wrongly becomes the measure of other operas.

**star system**
A system of casting by which the company selects operas to fit the abilities and desires of the famous singers it has available, counting on their names as stars to draw the audience. This can lead to the revival of forgotten works or the premières of new ones, but it also tends to subordinate the drama to the superficiality of the performance. The star system is really the negative of the repertory system, but many companies manage to make use of the advantages of both by having a very large, and very expensive roster of stars.

**strings**
The instruments of the orchestra which are bowed. Although the piano has strings it is not considered one of them because it is played by keys. Nor is the guitar included, but left in a class of its own.

**studio performance**
A performance presented in a small place (hardly ever actually in a studio), usually before a select audience of friends and possible patrons of the company. Sometimes equivalent to a reading, but usually put on with more formality and rehearsal in order to make a better impression.

**styling**
The overall color and effect of a production, its manner as indicated by the kind of detail in its sets, its costumes and so forth, and its musical reading.

**succès d'estime** (Fr.) sucsay desTEEM
A tremendous success, one which makes the reputation of its composer or performers.

**succès de scandale** (Fr.) sucsay duh scahnDAHL
A scandalous success, one attributable as much to scandal about its production as to its worth.

**sung recitative**
Dialogue in music. *See* recitativo secco, recitativo misurato *and* recitativo stromentato.

**super**
Slang for an extra; a person not a member of the company but hired at the moment to be a member of a crowd upon the stage, or to hold a spear or whatever. A supernumerary.

# GLOSSARY

**supporting cast**

Those in the cast who are not the principals. The captains of the guard, the notaries, the fathers-in-law and the duennas.

**syncopation**

The existence of syncopes.

**syncope**

A rhythmic break, a hesitation where there should have been a beat, or a beat where none should have existed. One can feel the effect of syncope by walking at a normal pace, but thinking of the "beat" as the upward movement of each step.

**tableau**

A static scene, a scene staged as if it were a picture. Also that quality of any scene which one can retain in the memory as a picture.

**tacet**

Be silent. A direction to the performer which indicates that he has nothing further to sing or play until the piece has ended, or until the end of the scene.

**tempo**

Literally, "time." The pace of music, the speed of the meter or the pulse.

**tenor**

The male voice of highest normal range, higher than the baritone, not as high as the contralto. Also, the person gifted with such a voice.

**terzetto** (It.) tayrtZETTo

A little piece for three. Terzetto implies a short piece, whereas *trio* does not. Unlike *trio*, *terzetto* may not be used to designate the performers themselves.

**tessitura**

The average working range of a musical line. The range which is most used throughout the piece, but not including the isolated and infrequent high and low extremes. Tessitura is a measurement of the effective labor the vocal chords must go through to produce the sound of a particular line. Thus an aria may have a high tessitura because most of its notes are in the high range, even though some may be low.

**tetralogy**

A group of four operas whose stories form a sequence, as does *The Ring of the Nibelungs* — although Wagner himself called the first of them, *Das Rheingold*, a prologue to the others.

**theatrical**

Quality of fitness for the theater. The word is frequently derisive, being used to describe flamboyant technique.

**theme**

A significant melody or a significant phrase upon which the composer builds his musical ideas. Also, in opera, the basic idea of the plot.

**time**

In music, its pace. *See* tempo. Also, the kind of measure, as in 3/4 time.

**timbre** (Fr.) TAMber

The quality of tone of any instrument or voice. The timbre of the oboe is remarkably different from that of the clarinet. Timbre is the result of the balance of the overtones of any note sounded by the instrument or voice. It has nothing to do with pitch. The vowels sounded by the human voice are strictly differences of timbre, whatever tone they may have.

**timpani**

Kettledrums, drums of definite pitch which can be altered by mechanical or pneumatic means.

**title role**

That role which represents the character named in the title, as does the role of Carmen, or Otello, or in *Il Barbiere di Siviglia*, Figaro.

**tone**

A musical sound of a single, steady pitch. Also the quality of sound, as in pure tone, or high tone, or reedy tone. Also short for whole tone, or scale tone. A tone is symbolized by a note on the staff, which gives rise to the use of the word *note* to designate tone.

**tonality**

Quality of having tone. In music, tonality is the specific quality of harmonic systems which have a fairly stable structure and which can be reduced to scales. Its opposite is atonality. Tonal relationships may be dissonant or consonant. The word is restricted to the harmonic organization of tones, while *modality* refers to their melodic relationship.

**tour**

A route of travel, a periplus, through which a company or a performer visits many cities away from its (or his) home base of operation, putting on performances.

**transpose**

To change the level of pitches of a piece of music. This occurs when an aria lies in a difficult range for a particular singer, or when the performer wishes to establish a different relationship with the context.

**trapdoor**

A portion of the stage floor which can be opened to permit exits and entrances, or which will permit parts of the set to be raised or lowered through it.

**traps**

Portions of the stage floor which can be opened. *See* trapdoor. Also, the collection of percussion instruments normally played by one person in a jazz band: the snare drum, cymbals, pedal bass drum, temple blocks, and so forth.

**treble**

A child's voice, a voice which sings in the range indicated by the treble clef.

Also the name of the clef which indicates the pitch for G above middle C, otherwise known as the G clef.

**tremolo**

Trembling sound, sound which wavers in volume upon its pitch. The tremolo does not involve a wavering in pitch. For that, *see* vibrato.

**trill**

A rapid alternation of two notes adjacent to each other. The trill often ends with a little turn, or flourish.

**trilogy**

A group of three full-length operas with a common thread of story or plot. There are several trilogies based upon the three stories of the life of Orestes.

**trio**

A group of three performers, or the music written for them. In opera the three may be and usually are accompanied by the orchestra.

**troubadour** (Fr.)

A wandering singer, a bard. He flourished in the twelfth century in southern France, composing his own words, his own music, and his own peculiar stanza forms. Some of them were the great poets of their age, such as was Bertrand de Born. The opera *Il Trovatore* deals with such a singer. Tannhäuser, the minnesinger, represents the German variation of the type.

**troupe**

The company or part of one considered as a touring unit. Usually it consists of a nucleus of singers and players which is augmented by local talent wherever it may perform. Many troupes have been organized by singers as vehicles for themselves.

**tune**

A simple melody. Also, accuracy of pitch. To be in tune signifies the quality of being in unison or harmony with others.

**tutti**

Everybody. A passage of music in which everybody joins in after a solo or a small ensemble.

**twelve-tone system**

A melodic and harmonic system of the composition of music based upon the equal temperament of the accurately tuned pianoforte. *See* dodecaphonism.

**unison**

As one, therefore singing or playing the same notes. The opposite of *divisi*. A canon at the unison is one in which all the entrances occur at the same pitch, although at different times.

**unit set**

A set which contains all the parts required for all the scenes of the opera. It may be necessary to shift the position of a part here or there to effect changes of scene, hence not necessarily the same as a simultaneous set.

**upbeat**

The beat which the conductor indicates by a rising motion of his baton, usually an unaccented beat. When one speaks of *the* upbeat, one generally means the anacrusis.

**valse** (Fr.) vAHLS

Waltz.

**vamp**

An improvised accompaniment, usually a simple figure more or less filled out for effect, but which can be played over and over until the singer is ready to begin singing.

**vaudeville** (Fr.) VOHdveel

A short theatrical caprice, usually of comic character, with dialogue and songs.

**vehicle**

An opera intended as a show piece for a certain singer or perhaps for a new production technique. Hence *Semiramide*, out of the repertory for years, was revived as a vehicle for Tebaldi.

**verismo** (It.) vayrIZmo

Realism. A style of opera highly developed in the nineteenth century in Italy, and made as imitative of the superficial aspects of real life as possible. Essentially the negative of drama, which is ritualistic. A good example of verismo is the opera *Tosca*; another is *La Fanciulla del West*.

**vibrato**

Vibrated. Since all musical sound is the result of vibrations, the word really means "wavering in pitch and volume," which produces the feeling of warmth in the human voice. As a matter of fact, it is a natural product of the act of remaining on pitch, the voice constantly moving around the desired pitch, allowing the mind to make constant corrections to keep it in the right place. It is otherwise psychologically impossible for the voice to maintain a pitch the way an instrument can.

**vocal score**

A score reduced to the vocal parts, and therefore of a size convenient for the singer to hold in his hand during rehearsal. Commonly, the vocal score has a reduction of the orchestral music for the piano written beneath the vocal parts, and is thus essentially a piano score.

**vocalise** (Fr.) vocahLEEZ

An exercise for voice, especially a repeating melodic exercise which gradually transposes itself to higher and higher ranges.

**voce** (It.) VOchay

The human voice.

**voce di petto** (It.) VOchay dee PETto

The chest tones of the voice.

**voce di testa** (It.) VOchay dee TESTa

The head tones of the voice.

**voice**

The sound produced by the larynx. Also any line of melody for any instrument, or a line of coherent melody within a context of other such lines, as one voice of a fugue.

**volume**

Relative loudness of sound. Not to be confused with intensity or projection, which are essentially complexities of voice, diction, rhythm and intonation.

**Vorspiel** (Ger.) FORshpeel

A prelude, a musical introduction leading directly into a scene.

**walk-on**

Broadway slang for a bit part without spoken lines, or an extra who appears apart from the crowd.

**waltz**

A revolving dance in alternating patterns of three steps each. It is therefore really a dance of two triple beats, but is generally written as two equivalent measures in 3/4 time. One of the most famous operatic waltzes runs through *Der Rosenkavalier*.

**winds**

Those instruments of the orchestra which are blown, both woodwinds and brasses. They do not include the pipe organ.

**wings**

The flats or drops which conceal the sides of the stage but between which entrances may be effected. Also, therefore, the concealed space to each side of the stage where performers wait before their entrances.

**woodwinds**

Those instruments which are, or used to be, made of wood and which are blown. Nowadays many of them are made of metal. They include flute, piccolo, clarinet, oboe, bassoon, saxophone and their families. Most of them might better be characterized as reed instruments, since it is the reed in the mouthpiece that vibrates to produce the tone.

**workshop**

A practical school of opera, or particularly that class in a school which actually mounts performances in order to learn the technique of operatic theater by experience. Most opera in the United States is produced by collegiate opera workshops.

**zarzuela** (Sp.) zahrzooWAYla

A kind of popular opera in Spain and Spanish-speaking countries. A cousin of the singspiel, the vaudeville and the ballad opera.

# THEMES OF THE MOST FAMOUS
# MUSICAL NUMBERS

While most of the translations which appear after these musical examples are traditional, some have been altered to match the original meanings and music more accurately.

**Aida** ACT I *Radames*

Ce- le- ste A- i- da for- ma di- vi- na,— mi- sti- co ser- to di lu- cee fior.

Celeste Aida, forma divina, mistico serto di luce e fior.

Heavenly Aida, divine form, beauteous mystery of flowers and light.

ACT II *Chorus*

Glo- riaall'E- git- to ed I- si- de cheil sac-ro suol pro- teg- ge! Al re cheil del- ta reg- ge Al re cheil del- ta reg- - - ge in- ni fe-sto-si al- ziam! S'intrec- ci ll lo- to al lau - ro sul

crin__ dei__ vin - ci - to- ri.

Gloria all' Egitto ed Iside che il sacro suol protegge! Al re che il delta
regge inni festosi alziam!

Glory to Egypt and to Isis who wards away disaster! To Egypt's royal master we raise our
festal song!

S'intrecci il loto al lauro sul crin dei vincitori.

Bind the lotus with the laurel to crown the victors.

MARCH

ACT IV *Amneris*

Già i sac-er- do- ti a du- nan-si

Ar - bi - tri del tuo fa- to

per dell' ac- cu- sa or- ri- bi- le sco-
par - ti an- cor t'e da- to.

Già i sacerdoti a dunansi Arbitri del tuo fato per dell' accusa orribile
scoparti ancor t'e dato.

Already the priests are meeting to decide your fate after this horribly sweeping
accusation which has been made against you.

ACT IV *Radames*

O ter- ra ad- di- o, ad-di- o, val- le di
pian- ti, sog- no di gau-dio che in do- lor___ svani. A noi si schiu- de si schiu- de il
ciel. ___

O terra addio, valle di pianti, sogno di gaudio che' in dolor svani. A
noi si schiude il ciel.

Farewell O earth, farewell thou vale of sorrow. Brief dream of joy condemned to end
in woe. To us now opens the sky.

**Alceste** ACT I *Alceste*

Di- vin- i- tés du Styx, Di- vin- i- tés du Styx, mi- ni- stres de la mort.

Divinités du Styx, ministres de la mort.

O gods of the Styx, ministers of death.

ACT II *Admetus*

O mes en- fants! O mes a- mis!

vous pé- né- trez mon coeur de la plus

douce —— iv- res- se.

O mes enfants! O mes amis! vous pénétrez mon coeur de la plus
douce ivresse.

O my children, O my friends! You wring my heart with the sweetest feelings.

### Arianna. LAMENTO D'ARIANNA. *Arianna*

Lasciatemi morire! lasciatemi morire e chi

volete che mi conforte in così dura sorte in così gran martire.

O, let me die, and let me have comfort in this hard fate, this great sacrifice.

### Il Barbiere di Siviglia. ACT I. *Almaviva*

Ecco ridente in cielo spunta la bella aurora, e tu non sorgi ancora e
puoi dormir così?
Day comes with all her roses, blushing they redden the distance. Flow'rs wake to new
existence and dost thou slumber yet?

Largo al factotum della città largo! la la la la
la la la! la! Presto a bottega che l'alba è già presto! la la la la la la! la!
Way for the city's factotum here! Make way! Quick to my business, daylight is near,
make way!

ACT I *Rosina*

U– na vo– ce po– co fa qui nel
cor mi ri– suo– no il mio
cor fe – ri– te e già è Lin–
do – ro fu che il pa go.

Una voce poco fa qui nel cor mi risuonò il mio cor ferite è gia e

Lindoro fu che il pagò.

Just a little while ago a voice within my heart, which already feels a wound, spoke of

Lindoro in words of hope.

The Beggar's Opera. ACT I. *Polly.* (Purcell)

Vir– gins are like the fair flower in its
lu – ster which in the gar– den e–
na – mels the ground.

Virgins are like the fair flower in its

luster which in the garden enamels the ground.

Were I laid on Greenland's
coast and in my arms embraced my lass, warm amidst eternal frosts, too soon the half
year's night would pass.

Let us take the road. Hark! I hear the sound of coaches—the
hour of attack approaches—t'your arms brave boys and load!

ACT II. *MacHeath*

Man may escape from rope and gun, nay, some have outliv'd the

doctor's pill. Who takes a woman must be undone,

**La Boheme** ACT I *Rodolfo*

Che ge-li-da ma - ni - na, se la las-ci ris-cal-dar. Cer - car che gio - va? Al bu - io non si tro - va.

Che gelida manina, se la lasci riscaldar. Cercar che giova? Al buio non si trova.

Your tiny hand is frozen, let me warm it up in mine. Why search for help there? In darkness you won't find it.

ACT I *Mimi*

Mi chia - ma - no Mi - mi ma'il mio no - me è Lu - ci - a.

Mi chiamano Mimi ma'il mio nome è Lucia.

They call me Mimi, but my real name is Lucia.

ACT II MUSETTA'S WALTZ. *Musetta*

Quan - do m'en vo?

Quando me'n vo', quando me'n vo' soletta per la

via la gente sosta e mira.

When I'm alone, whenever I'm alone on the street the gentlemen admire me.

### Boris Godunov PROLOGUE *Chorus*

Why do you abandon us, O father?

### PROLOGUE, CORONATION SCENE *Chorus*

To the sun in all splendor risen be glory.

ACT I *Boris*

My soul is sad. Against my will strange tremors and evil presentiments
oppress my mind.

ACT I *Innkeeper*

Once I caught a drake with feathers green and blue. O, thou my
darling drake, come again, my mate so true.

ACT I *Varlaam*                    THE SIEGE OF KAZAN

Long a - go at Ka - zan where I was figh - ting, Tsar I - van sat a - feas-ting with his lea - ders. There the Tar- tar horde he har - ried, spared not man, nor maid, nor mar - ried, then Rus - sia had___ fine times!

Long ago at Kazan where I was fighting, Tsar
Ivan sat afeasting with his leaders. There the Tartar horde he harried, spared not man
nor maid nor married, then Russia had fine times!

ACT II *Nurse*

Once a girl was lan - guish- ing a- lone.

Once a girl was languishing alone. To her came a boy, so handsome grown.

## ACT II SONG OF THE GNAT *Nurse*

Once a gnat was cutting wood, a flea was kneading dough. Soon a loaf crisp and good on the gnat she did bestow.

## ACT II CLAPPING GAME SONG *Feodor*

pig once laid a large white egg.

I'll tell you a tale and you'll laugh! How once

a hen did hatch a fine calf, how a pig once laid a large white egg.

ACT II *Boris*

I have at- tained to pow-er. Six years have

passed since first I ruled o'er Rus- sia. But

still no peace re- turns to my___ re-morse-ful soul.

The hea- vy hand of one a-bove doth press u-

pon my guil- ty soul re- quir- ing jus- tice!

I have attained to power. Six years have passed since first I ruled o'er

Russia. But still no peace returns to my remorseful soul. The heavy hand of one above

doth press upon my guilty soul requiring justice!

## ACT III *The Girls from Sandomir*

By Wisla's blue waters beneath an old willow one

flower is blooming with petals all like snowflakes.

## FINALE *Simpleton*

Flow, Ah! flow my bitter tears. Weep, lament all ye true believers.

Soon the foe will come, all the world grow dark, dark as blackest night, not a star

shines through.

## Carmen ACT I *Boys*

A- vec la gar- de mon-tante, nous ar-ri-vons nous voi- là! Son- ne trom-pette é-cla-tan-te! Ta ra ta ta ta ta ta ta ta l

Avec la garde montante nous arrivons nous voilà!  Sonne

trompette éclatante! Ta ra ta ta ta ra ta ta!

Marching with the changing guard, marching with them here we are.  Hear how the

bugles shall sound! Ta ra ta ta.

## ACT I HABANERA *Carmen*

L'a-mour est un oi- seau re- bel- le que nul ne peut____ ap- pri-voi- ser. Et c'est bien en vain qu'on l'ap- pei- le si lui con - vient____ de re- fu- ser. L'a-mour est en- fant de Bo- hème, il n'à ja- mais ja- mais con- nu de loi.

L'Amour est un oiseau rebelle que nul ne peut apprivoiser. Et
c'est bien en vain qu'on l'appelle si lui convient de refuser.

Love's a wild and rebellious bird that flies so free it cannot be tamed. Call in vain, it
will be not heard, for love's reluctant to come by name.

L'Amour est enfant de Bohème, il n'à jamais jamais connu la loi.

For love's a child of gypsy life and love will never never go by law.

ACT I SÉGUIDILLA *Carmen*

Près des ramparts de Séville chez
mon ami Lillas Pastia j'irai danser la Séguidilla et boire du Manzanilla, j'irai chez mon
ami Lillas Pastia.

Under the walls of Sevilla there lives my friend Lillas Pastia. I'll be there to dance
Seguidillas and I'll drink Manzanilla. I'll be waiting there at Lillas Pastia's.

Votre toast je peux vous le rendre, señors, señors,

car avec les soldats, Oui, les toréros peuvent s'entendre pour plaisirs, pour plaisirs, ils ont les combats!

To your toast I'll give another, señors, señors, to all the soldiers. And to toreros, brave men among us. For our pleasure, for our fun they fight. How they fight!

Toréador en garde! Toréador, Toréador, Et songe bien, oui, songe en combatant qu'un œil noir te regarde.

Toreador, be ready, Toreador, and remember as you prepare, dark eyes are upon you.

ACT II *Carmen, Mercédès, Frasquita*

Les trin- gles des sis- tres tin- taient_____ a-
vec un é- clat mé- tal- li- - que. Et
sur cette é- tran- ge mu- si- - que les
zin- ga- rel- las se le- vaient._____

Les tringles des sistres tintaient avec un éclat
métallique. Et sur cette étrange musique les zingarellas se levaient.

The tingling of the little bells surprises with metallic ringing. Upon the sound of such strange singing the gypsy girls dance for the day.

ACT II. *Don José*

Hal- te là, qui va là? Dra- gon d'Al- ca- la!

Où t'en vas- tu par là, Dra- gon d'Al- ca- la?

Halte là, qui va là? Dragon d'Alcala! Où t'en vas-tu par là, Dragon d'Alcala?

Who goes there? Who goes there? Man of Alcala. Where are you going there, man of Alcala?

**ACT III** *Micaela*

Je dis — que rien ne m'é-pou-van- te, je dis, Hé-las! que je ré- ponds de moi Mais j'ai beau fai - re la vail- lant- te, au fond du coeur __ je meurs d'ef- froi! __

Je dis que rien ne m'épouvante, je dis, Hélas! que je réponds de moi.

Mais j'ai beau faire la vaillante au fond du coeur je meurs d'effroi!

I say I will not be dismayed. I say, alas! but I'm trembling with fear! But my dear, as I answer your heart, at the bottom of mine I'm dying of fright.

**Les Contes d'Hoffmann** ACT I *Olympia*

Les oi- seaux dans la char -mil - - - - - - le.

Les oiseaux dans la charmille.

The birds in the grove.

Belle nuit, O nuit d'amour, souris à nos ivresses.

Beauteous night, O night of love, please smile at our excesses.

Ah, Ah! Ah, Belinda, I am prest with torment.

When I am laid in earth, may my wrongs create no trouble, no trouble

in thy breast.

### Don Giovanni ACT I *Donna Anna*

Fuggi, crudele, o fuggi, lascia che mora anch'io.

Leave me, my friend, O leave me, please let me bear my sorrow.

### ACT I *Donna Elvira*

ma - i, che mi man- cò di fè.

Ah chi mi dice mai quel barbaro dov'è. Che per mio scorno

amai, che mi mancò di fè.

Where shall I find the traitor who stole my heart away? I gave him all in earnest, he

took it all in play.

ACT I *Leporello*

Ma- da- mi- na, il ca- to- lo- go e

ques- to del- le bel- le che a-moil pa-dron mi- o.

In I- tal- ia sei cen- to e quar- an- ta,

In Al- ma- gna due cen- to e trent' u- na.

Cen- to in Fran- cia, Tur- chia no -vant'

u - na, ma, ma in Is- pa- gna, ma in Is-

pa- gna son già mil- le e tre!

Madamina, il catalogo è questo delle belle che ama il padron mio.

Dear my lady, let me draw your attention to this long list of names and addresses.

In Italia sei cento e quaranta, in Almagna due cento e trent' una. Cento in Francia, in Turchia novant' una, ma in Ispagna, ma in Ispagna son già mille e tre!

Of Italians six hundred and forty, and in Germany two hundred thirty. Hundred in France and in Turkey 'twas ninety, Ah! but in Spain, ah! but in Spain were a thousand and three!

ACT I *Don Giovanni*

Là ci darem la mano, là mi dirai di sì; vedi non è lontano
partiam ben mio da qui.

Let me adore your hand, love, then make your answer yes. See, it is not so far, love, to let your heart confess.

ACT I *Donna Elvira*

tor fal- la _____ ce ci- gli - o.

Ah, fuggi, il traditor! Non lo lasciar più dir. Il labbro è mentidor

fallace ciglio.

Be warned of him, my child, and hear his words no more. Do not become beguiled for

they'll deceive you.

ACT I QUARTET *D. Elvira, D. Anna, D. Ottavio, D. Giovanni*

Non _____ ti fi- dar, O mi- se- ra, di

quel ri- bal- do cor! Me già tra- di quel

bar- ba- ro te vuol tra- dir an- cor.

Non ti fidar,

O misera, di quel ribaldo cor! Me già tradi quel barbaro te vuol tradir ancor.

Do not confide, unhappy one, in such a trustless heart! Already has he betrayed me.

He'll be betraying you!

ACT I *Donna Anna*

Or sai che l'on- o - re ra- pi- re a me

vol - se chi fu il tra- di- to - re che il

pa- dre, cheil pa- dre ___ mi tol- se.

Or sai che l'onore rapire a me volse chi fu il traditore che il padre
mi tolse.

You know now for certain the name of the traitor who bartered my honor, who
murdered my father.

ACT I *Don Giovanni*

Fin ch'an del vi - no cal- da la tes- ta

u - na gran fes - ta va pre-pa- rar.

Fin ch' an del vino calda la testa una gran festa va preparar.

Song, wine and women, who'd be without them? I'll have my pleasure both morning
and night.

ACT I *Zerlina*

Bat- ti, bat- ti, O bel Ma - set- to, la tua

po- ve- ra Zer- li- na. Sta- rò qui comea-gnel-

li - na le tue bat- te as- pet- tar.

Batti, batti, O bel Masetto, la tua povera Zerlina.  Starò quì come
agnellina le tue batte aspettar.

Chide me, chide me, dear Masetto.  Chide your little poor Zerlina.  I can stand it like a
little lamb, your anger I will bear.

### ACT II *Don Giovanni*

Deh vieni alla finestra, O mio tesoro.  Deh vieni a consolar il
pianto mio.

Come near, lean out your window, my prize and my treasure.  Come here, console my
sorrow, come console my grief.

### ACT II *Zerlina*

Vedrai carino se sei buonino che bel rimedio ti voglio dar.

If you will promise me not to betray me I have a remedy to bring you health.

Il mio tesoro intanto, andate, andate a consolar.

Speak for me to the lady and tell her, and tell her all I know.

Avant de quitter ces lieux, sol natal de mes aïeux, à toi, Seigneur, et roi des cieux ma soeur je confie.

Now before I leave this place, the sun of my past, to you Lord, King of Heaven, I entrust my sister.

Salut, demeure chaste et pure!

O hail, thou dwelling chaste and pure!

Il était un roi de Thulé qui, jusqu'à la tombe fidèle.

Once there was a great king of Thule who to the last was faithful.

Ah, je ris de me voir si belle en ce miroir.

**Ah,** I laugh to see myself so pretty in the glass.

Vous qui faites l'endormie n'entendez-vous pas? O Catharine
ma mie, n'entendez vous pas ma voix et mes pas?

**While** you pretend you are sleeping, don't you hear my steps? O Catherine, my lovely,
don't you hear my song and my steps?

ACT IV SOLDIER'S CHORUS *SOLDIERS*

Gloire immortelle de nos aieux, sois nous fidèle,

mourons comme eux! Et sous ton aile, soldats vainqueurs, dirige nos pas, dirige nos

pas, enflamme nos coeurs.

Immortal glory of our ancestors, let us be faithful and die as they did. And under your

wing, soldiers and conquerors, direct our steps and enflame our hearts.

Fidelio ACT I QUARTET-Canon *Marcelline, Leonora, Jacquino, Rocco*

wer- de glück- lich, glück- lich sein.

Mir ist so wunderbar, es engt das Herz mir ein, er liebt mich, es ist klar,
ich werde glücklich sein.

To me he is so dear, it fills my heart with joy. He loves me, that is clear. How happy,
happy I shall be!

## Hänsel und Gretel ACT II *Hänsel, Gretel*

A- bends will ich schla- fen gehn, vier-zehn Eng-lein

um mich stehn; zwei zu mei-nen Häup- ten,

zwei zu mei- nen Füs - sen.

Abends will ich schlafen gehn, vierzehn
Englein um mich stehn; zwei zu meinen Häupten, zwei zu meinen Füssen.
When at night I go to sleep, fourteen angels round me keep. Two beside my head stay,
two down at my feet stay.

## Iphigénie en Tauride ACT I *Thoas*

De noirs pré-sen- ti- ments mon âme in-ti- mi-

dé - e. De si- nis- tres terreurs    est    sans    cesse    ob-  sé-  dé-         e.

De noirs présentiments mon âme intimidée. De

sinistres terreurs est sans cesse obsédée.

O dark, foreboding fears, my soul is quelled in terror. With most ominous fears and

unceasing obsessions.

## Lohengrin ACT III *Lohengrin*

In    fer- nem Land    un – nah-bar    eu – ren Schrit-ten

liegt ei-ne Burg    die    Mon-sal- vat    ge- nannt.

Ein lich-ter Tem-pel ste-het dort in  mit-ten        so

kost- bar  als auf Er – den nichts be-        kannt.

In fernem Land unnahbar euren Schritten liegt eine

Burg die Montsalvat genannt. Ein lichter Tempel stehet dort inmitten so kostbar als

auf Erden nichts bekannt.

In distant lands by ways remote and hidden there stands a tower we call Montsalvat. It

holds a shrine to the profane forbidden, more precious there is naught on earth than that.

## Lucia di Lammermoor ACT II SEXTET

Chi mi frena in tal momento? Chi troncò dell' ire il corso? Il suo duolo il suo spavento son la prova d'un rimorso!

What from vengeance yet restrains me, words suffice not to upbraid thee. Even terror that thus enchains thee proves that falsely thou betrayed me!

Chi raffrena il mio furore e la man che al brando corse? Della misera in favore nel mio netto un grido sorse!

What from vengeance now restrains me, will he madly dare upbraid her? Ah, she dreads me and disdains me. Nevermore will I thus persuade her.

## Macbeth ACT I *Banquo*

Co - me dal ciel pre - ci - pi - ta

l'om-bra più sem- pre os-cu- ra! In not- te u- gual tra-

fis - se- ro Dun- ca- no il mio si - gnor.

Come del ciel precipita l'ombra più sempre
oscura! In notte ugual trafissero Duncano il mio signor.
How dark the sky with heavy clouds, darker than any shadow! Such was the night they killed my lord, when Duncan met his death.

## Madama Butterfly ACT I *Cio-cio San*

Un bel di ve- dre- mo le var- si un fil di

fu- mo sull'es- tre- mo con- fin del ma-re e

poi la na- ve ap- pa- re.

Un bel dì vedremo le varsi un fil di fumo sull'

estremo confin del mare e poi la nave appare.

He'll return one fine day, I'll see the telltale smoke rise far above the far horizon before

his ship appears.

**Manon** ACT II *Manon*

A- dieu,    no- tre pe -    ti- te ta-    ble

qui nous ré - u - nit    si sou - vent!    A - dieu,

a - dieu,    no- tre pe -    ti- te ta -    ble    si

gran- de pour nous    ce- pen-    dant!

Adieu, notre petite table qui nous reunit si souvent! Adieu,

**si grande pour nous cependant!**

Goodbye, our little table, which brought us together so often, so large for us all the same.

ACT III *Des Grieux*

Ah,    fu - yez    douce    i- mage,

a    mon â-    me trop chè- re.    Res- pec-tez

un    re- pos    cru- el- le ment ga- gné.

Ah, fuyez douce image, a mon âme trop chère.  Respectez un

repos cruéllement gagné.

Leave me now, image fair, thou to me art too dear.  Pay respect to my peace, won by

the cruelest deed.

### Martha ACT II *Martha*

'Tis the last rose of sum-mer left bloo - ming a - lone.

'Tis the last rose of summer left blooming alone.

### ACT III *Lionello*

M'ap - pa - ri tutt' a - mor il mio sguar - do l'in - con - trò.

M'appari tutt' amor il mio sguardo l'incontrò.

Everywhere I see love, face to face in every look.

### Die Meistersinger – PROCESSION OF THE MASTERSINGERS

ACT I *Walther*

Am stil- len Herd___ in Win- ter-zeit___ wann

Burg und Hof mir ein- ge- scheidt, ___

wie einst der Lenz so lieb - lich lacht!

Am stillen Herd in Winterzeit wann Burg und Hof mir eingescheidt, wie
einst der Lenz so lieblich lacht!

By silent hearth in wintertime when town and farm are all cut off, oh how the lovely
springtime laughs!

ACT III THE PRIZE SONG *Walther*

Mor - gen- lich   leuch - tend__   im   ro -   si - gen

Schein von Blüth und  Duft   ge-schwellt die Luft, voll al - ler

Won - - - nen   nie er - son - nen.

Morgenlich leuchtend im rosigen Schein von Blüth und

Duft geschwellt die Luft, voll aller Wonnen nie ersonnen.

Morning now brightens with roseate light, and sweetest fragrance in the air fills me

with ecstasy in the sunlight.

Mignon ACT I *Mignon*

Con -   nais= tu   le   pays____

ou  fleu - rit  l'o - ran -  ger?____

le   pays  des  fruits   d'or____

____  et  des  ro - ses  ver -  meilles.____

Connais-tu le pays où fleurit l'oranger? Le pays des fruits d'or et des

roses vermeilles.

Do you know the countryside where the orange tree blooms? The country of golden

fruits and of roses.

ACT II *Philine*

Je suis Ti-ta-ni- a la blon- de, je suis Ti-ta-ni- a la fille de l'air.

Je suis Titania la blonde, je suis Titania fille de l'air.

I am Titania the blond one, I am Titania the daughter of air.

## Le Nozze di Figaro ACT I *Figaro*

Se vuol bal - la - re si - gnor con - ti - no,

se vuol bal - la - re si - gnor con - ti - no,

il chi - tar - ri - no le suo - ne - rò,

il chi – tar – ri – no  le  suo – ne – rò, si,

le  suo – ne – rò,  si,  le  suo – ne – rò.

Se vuol ballare signor contino, il chitarrino le suonerò, si.

If you would dance, then dance at your pleasure. Let the guitar beat the measure for you. Yes, beat you a measure with the guitar.

ACT I *Cherubino*

Non so  più  co - sa son, co - sa  fac – cio  or di

fo – co,o - ra  so – no  di  ghiac - cio.  O – gni

don –  na  can-giar  di  co –  lo – re,  o – gni

d on–  na  mi  far  pal – pi –  tar,  o – gni

don –  na  mi  far  pal –  pi – tar.

Non so più cosa son cosa faccio or di foco ora sono di ghiaccio. Ogni
donna cangiar di colore, ogni donna mi far palpitar.

I don't know what it can be that ails me, either fever or chills; sickness flails me. Any
lady can change all my color, any lady can make my heart beat.

Non più andrai farfallone amoroso notte e giorno d'intorno girando
della belle turbando il riposo Narcisetto, Adoncino d'amor.

Now no more escapades as a lover, day and night whispering lies under cover. Never
more shall you play as a Paris, as Adonis you'll sigh nevermore.

miei ___ sos- pir. ___

Porgi Amor, qualche ristoro me al mio duolo a' miei sospir.

God of Love, O do restore me. Hear my sadness and my supplication.

ACT II *Cherubino*

Voi che sa- pe- te che co- sa è a-

mor, don- ne ve- de- te

s'io l'ho nel cor.

Voi che sapete che cosa è amor, donne vedete s'io l'ho nel cor.

You who have seen him tell me about this Love; lady, you know him, say, do I love?

ACT III *Countess Almaviva*

Do - ve so - no i bei mo-

men - ti di dol - cez - za e

di pia - cer? ___

Dove sono i bei momenti di dolcezza e di piacer?

Now where are they, all those fine moments full of pleasure and sweetness and joy?

ACT IV *Susanna*

Deh vie - ni non tar- dar, O gio - ia

bel - la. Vie-'ni ove a - mo - re

per go - der t'ap- pel - la.

Deh vieni non tardar, O gioia bella. Vieni ove amore per goder t'appella.

O come and don't be slow, no more delaying. Come where my love is calling you to playing.

## Orfeo ed Euridice ACT III *Orfeo*

Che fa - rò sen-za Eu-ri - di - ce, dove an-

drò sen- za il mio ben? Che fa -

Che farò senza Euridice, dove andrò senza il mio

ben? Che farò? Dove andrò? Che farò senza il mio ben?

All my joy has now departed, nought but grief and woe I see. Would I ne'er had

known existence! Life alas is dark for me.

## Otello ACT I *Otello, Desdemona*

Già nella notte densa s'estingue ogni clamor, già il mio cor

fremebondo s'ammansa in quest' ampleso e si rinsensa.

Dark is the night around us. All clamors now have ceased. All the storm of my

passion I quell in your embrace in perfect peace.

Ora e per sempre addio, santo memorie, addio sublimi incanti del pensier!

Now and forever farewell, sacred remembrance, farewell, sublime music of my thought.

Piangea cantando nell' erma landa, piangea la mesta, O salce, salce!

With weeping I sing alone and lonely upon this lonely strand. O willow, willow!

## Pagliacci ACT I *Canio*

Vesti la giubba e la faccia infarina. Le gente paga e rider vuole qua.

Ridi, Pagliaccio, sul tuo amore in franto!

Put on your make-up and then smear on the powder! The people pay you and they
must have their laugh. Laugh now, Pagliaccio, for the love that is gone now.

## Rigoletto ACT I *Gilda*

Caro nome che il mio cor festi primo palpitar. Le delizie
dell' amor mi dei sempre rammentar!

Dearest name within my heart, name that makes my heartbeat start, O delight of love,
stay with me forever, love.

Questa o quella per me pari sono al quant' altre d'intorno mi vedo.

This or that one, O what does it matter to a man of my kind? One is like another.

La donna è mobile, qual piuma al vento, muta d'accento e di pensiero!

Woman is changeable, not to be trusted, just like the little breeze that rustles autumn
leaves.

Bella figlia dell' amore,

schiavo son de'vezzi tuoi. Con un detto sol tu puoi le mie pene a consolar.

I'm your slave, dear girl, believe me. Chains like yours cannot be broken. But a word in kindness spoken will my peace of mind restore.

long - temps en cor.

Je veux vivre dans ce rêve qui m'en ivre longtemps en cor.

I would go in this dream life that has kept my heart filled with joy.

## Der Rosenkavalier  THE WALTZ

## Samson et Dalila ACT II *Dalila*

Mon coeur s'ouvre à ta voix    com-me s'ou-vrient les

fleurs    aux bai- sers___ de l'au-ro- re!

Ah!___ ré -    ponds ___ à

ma___ ten-    dres- se.

Mon cœur s'ouvre à ta voix comme s'ouvrient les

fleurs aux baisers de l'aurore! Ah! réponds à ma tendresse!

My heart at thy sweet voice doth open like flowers at the dawn. Ah! respond to my

entreaty!

Dir Göttin der Liebe soll mein Lied ertönen.

Thou, Goddess of Love, art all the burden of my song.

O, du mein holder Abendstern, wohl grüsst' ich immer dich so gern.

O thou most holy evening star, how sweet your gaze from heaven far.

**ACT III** *Pilgrims*

Der Gna- de Heil ward dem Büs- ser be-

schie- den, nun geht er ein in__ der

Se - li- gen Frie - - - den.

Der Gnade Heil ward dem Büsser beschieden, nun geht er ein in der Seligen Frieden!

The grace of God to the sinner is given. His soul shall dwell with the blessed in heaven.

**La Tosca** **ACT II** *Tosca*

Vis - si d'ar - te, vis - si d'a-mo- re

non fe-ci mai male ad a - ni- ma vi - va!

Vissi d'arte, vissi d'amore, non feci mai male ad anima viva!

Thus did love and thus did my beauty both give to my art its greatest expression.

## La Traviata ACT I *Alfredo*

Libiamo, libiamo ne' lieti calici, che la bellezza in fiora.

Let's drink, let's drink and be merry. Now is the time for the beauties of living.

## ACT I *Violetta*

Ah, fors' è lui che l'anima solinga ne tumulti,

Ah, was it him my heart foretold, when in the rush of pleasure,

## ACT I *Violetta*

scor— ra il vi — ver mi — o pei sen —

tie — ri del pia — cer.

Sempre libera degg' io follegiare di gioia in gioia, vo' che scorra il

viver mio pei sentieri del piacer.

I'll fulfill the round of pleasure, joying, toying from flow'r to flow'r.  I will drain a

brimming measure from the cup of rosy joy.

ACT I *Alfredo*

A — mor, a — mor è

pal — pi — to del l'u— ni — ver — so del

u — ni— ver—so— in — te — ro.

Amor, amor è palpito del l'universo intero.

Love is the soul of the universe entire.

Di provenza il mar il suol chi dal cor ti cancellò?

Have the countryside and sea passed away from memory?

Addio del passato bei sogni ridenti.

Forever must I leave thee, thou fair world of sorrows.

re - mo, la vi- ta y- ni- ti tras- co-re-re-mo.

Parigi o cara noi lasceremo, la vita uniti trascoreremo.

Far from the noisy city I shall take thee, nothing from this hour shall keep you from me.

## Il Trovatore ACT II ANVIL CHORUS *Gypsies*

Chi del gi- ta - no i gior - ni ab-

bel - la? bel- la chi? Chi i

gior - ni ab- bel- la, chi?

Chi del gitano i giorni abbella? Chi? Chi i giorni abbella?

Cheer for the happy days when gypsies go a-roving.

### ACT III *Manrico*

Ah_____ che la mor- te o- gno - ra

e —— tar-da nel ve-nir a chi de-si-a, a chi de-si-a mo-rir. Ad-di-o ad-dio Leo-no-ra ad-di-o.

Ah che la morte ognora e tarda nel venir chi desia morir! Addio.

Ah, send thy light, Aurora, carry me soon to death. Tell her I love her, tell her of my desire, addio!

## Die Zauberflöte ACT I *Papageno*

Der Vog-el-fän-ger bin ich, ja, stets lus-tig heis-sa hop-sa-sa! Ich Vo-gel-fän-ger bin be-kannt bei alt und jung im gan-zen Land.

Der Vogelfänger bin ich, ja, stets lustig heissa

hopsasa! Ich Vogelfänger bin bekannt bei alt und jung im ganzen Land.

O where or when didst ever see as jolly fine a man as me? I am the best bird-catching man, say old and young in every land.

ACT I *Tamino*

Dies Bild- nis ist be-zau-bernd schön— wie noch kein Au- ge je ge- sehn.— Ich fühl' es, ich fühl es, wie dies Göt- ter-bild mein Herz _____ mit neu- er Re- gung füllt.

Dies Bildnis ist bezaubernd schön wie noch kein Auge gesehn. Ich fühl' es wie dies Göttebild mein Herz mit neuer Regung fühllt.

This portrait is beyond compare, as lovely as I've seen. I wonder, I wonder if it's joy that fills my heart with such a gripping pain?

ACT II *Sarastro*

O I- sis und O- si- ris schen-ket der Weis- heit Geist dem neu- en Paar. Die ihr der Wan- drer Schrit- te len- ket.

O Isis und Osiris schenket der Weisheit Geist dem neuen Paar. Die ihr der Wandrer Schritte lenket.

O Isis and Osiris, hear me pray for these that seek your light. Grant them patience for their wand'ring.

**ACT II** *Queen of the Night*

Der Hölle Rache kocht in meinem Herzen; Tod und

Verzweiflung flammen um mich her!

The fires of hell are blazing in my own heart! Death and vengeance fill my heart with joy!

**ACT III** *Sarastro*

In diesen heil'gen Hallen kennt man die Rache nicht.

In these most holy halls no wrath or sorrow stays.

# RECORDINGS OF
# COMPLETE OPERAS

**Aida**
Callas, Tucker, Barbieri, Gobbi, conducted by Serafin
ANGEL 3525–C/L
Tebaldi, del Monaco, Stignani, conducted by Erede
LONDON A–4308
Milanov, Bjoerling, Barbieri, Warren, conducted by Perlea
VICTOR LM–6122
Nelli, Tucker, Gustavson, Valdengo, conducted by Toscanini
VICTOR LM–6132

**Alceste**
Flagstad, Jobin, Hemsley, conducted by Jones
LONDON A–4411
The same cast, Stereo version
LONDON OSA–1403

**Amahl and the Night Visitors**
VICTOR LM–1701

**Amelia Goes to the Ball**
ANGEL D–35140

**Andrea Chénier**
Tebaldi, del Monaco, Corena, conducted by Gavazzeni
LONDON A–4332
The same cast, stereo version
LONDON OSA–1303

**Arabella**
Della Casa, Gueden, London, conducted by Solti
LONDON A–4412

The same cast, stereo version
LONDON OSA–1404

**Ariadne auf Naxos**
Schwarzkopf, Streich, Seefried, conducted by von Karajan
ANGEL 3532–C/L

**Arianna**
(Since all but the *Lament of Arianna* has been lost, this recording must be considered complete.)
WESTMINSTER XWN–18765

**Arlecchino** (Busoni)
VICTOR LM–1944

**Un Ballo in Maschera**
Callas, di Stefano, Barbieri, Gobbi, conducted by Votto
ANGEL 3557–C/L
Nelli, Peerce, Turner, Merrill, conducted by Toscanini
VICTOR LM–6112

**Il Barbiere di Siviglia** (Rossini)
Callas, Gobbi, Alva, conducted by Galliera
ANGEL 3559–C/L
The same cast, Stereo version
ANGEL S–3559 C/L
de los Angeles, Bechi, Rossi-Lemeni, conducted by Serafin
CAPITOL GCR–7138
VICTOR LM 6104
Simionato, Bastianini, Corena, Siepi, conducted by Erede
LONDON A–4327

654

# RECORDINGS OF COMPLETE OPERAS

**Der Barbier von Bagdad**
ANGEL 3553

**Bastien et Bastienne**
PERIOD 542

**The Beggar's Opera**
The Old Vic company, conducted by
Sargent
VICTOR LM–6048
Prietto, Lipton, Noble, conducted by
Austin
WESTMINSTER OPW–1201

**Der Bettelstudent**
VANGUARD 474–75

**La Bohème**
Callas, di Stefano, conducted by Votto
ANGEL 3560
Sayao, Tucker, Baccaloni
COLUMBIA 3SL–101
Stella, Poggi, conducted by Molinari
COLUMBIA M2L–401
Tebaldi, Gueden, Inghilleri, conducted by
Erede
LONDON A–4209
Albanese, Peerce, conducted by Toscanini
VICTOR LM–6006
de los Angeles, Bjoerling, Amara, Merrill,
conducted by Beecham
VICTOR LM–6042

**Boris Godunov**
Belgrade National Opera
LONDON A–4317
Bolshoi Theater
PERIOD 554
Christoff, Borg, Gedda, conducted by
Dobrowen
VICTOR LM–6403

**Carmen**
Opéra-Comique, conducted by Wolff
LONDON, A–4304
Stevens, Peerce, Albanese, Merrill
VICTOR LM–6102

**Cavalleria Rusticana**
Callas, Di Stefano, Panerai, conducted by
Serafin

ANGEL 3509–3S/L
ANGEL 3528–C/L*
Harshaw, Tucker, Guarrera, conducted by
Cleva
COLUMBIA SL–123
COLUMBIA SL–124*
del Monaco, Nicolai, conducted by
Ghione
LONDON A–4323*
LONDON A–4216
Zanelli, Visetti, Ferrari, conducted by
Falco
PERIOD 317
Milanov, Bjoerling, Merrill, conducted by
Cellini
VICTOR LM–6046
VICTOR LM–6106*
Tebaldi, Bjoerling, Bastianini, conducted
by Erede
VICTOR LM–6059
The same cast, Stereo version
VICTOR LSC–6059

**Les Choëphores**
DECCA 9956

**Il Combattimento di Tancredi e
Clorinda**
Conducted by Ephrikian
PERIOD 551
Milan Monteverdiana Ensemble
VOX 8560

**The Consul**
DECCA DXB–101

**Les Contes d'Hoffmann**
Dobbs, Simoneau, conducted by Le
Conte
EPIC SC–6028
The same cast, stereo version
EPIC BSC–101
Conducted by Beecham
LONDON A–4302

**Der Corregidor**
URANIA 208

* Recording of both *Cavalleria Rusticana* and *I Pagliacci*.

**La Damnation de Faust**
Conducted by Fournet
COLUMBIA 3SL–110
Danco, Poleri, Singher, conducted by
Munch
VICTOR LM–6114

**Le Devin du Village**
ANGEL D 35421
ANGEL T 35421

**Don Carlos**
VICTOR LM–6124

**Don Giovanni**
Simoneau, Jurinac, Zadek, London, con-
ducted by Moralt
EPIC 4SC–6010
Danco, Della Casa, Gueden, Siepi,
Corena, conducted by Krips
LONDON A–4406
The same cast, stereo version
LONDON OSA–1401

**Don Pasquale**
Capecchi, Rizzoli, Valdengo, conducted
by Molinari-Pradelli
EPIC 4SC–6016
Corena, La Gatta, Poli, Lazzari, conducted
by Parodi
URANIA 228

**Die Dreigroschenoper**
German cast
COLUMBIA O2L–257
The same cast, stereo version
COLUMBIA O2S–201
Lenya, Roswaenge, conducted by Adler
VANGUARD 9002
Original cast
TELEFUNKEN 66053

**L'Elisir d'Amore**
Gueden, Capecchi, di Stefano, Corena,
conducted by Molinari-Pradelli
LONDON A–4321
Carosio, Gobbi, Monti, Luise, conducted
by Santini
VICTOR LM–6024

**L'Enfant et les Sortilèges**
LONDON A–4105

**Eugene Onegin**
Belgrade National Opera
LONDON A–4324
Russian State Opera
PERIOD 507
Bolshoi Theater
WESTMINSTER OPW–1303

**The Fair at Sorochintsky**
EPIC 4SC–6017

**Falstaff**
Gobbi, Schwarzkopf, Barbieri, Panerai,
conducted by von Karajan
ANGEL 3552–C/L
The same cast, stereo version
ANGEL S–3552–C/L
Nelli, Merriman, Elmo, Guarrera, con-
ducted by Toscanini
VICTOR LM–6111

**La Fanciulla del West**
LONDON A–4338

**Faust**
Steber, Conley, Siepi
COLUMBIA 3SL–112
de los Angeles, Gedda, Christoff, con-
ducted by Cluytens
VICTOR LM–6400

**La Favola d'Orfeo**
DECCA ARC–3035/36

**La Favorita**
LONDON A–4322

**Fidelio**
Rysanek, Seefried, Häflinger, conducted
by Fricsay
DECCA DXH–147
Peerce, Bampton, Steber, conducted by
Toscanini
VICTOR LM–6025

**La Finta Semplice**
EPIC 4SC–6021

**Die Fledermaus**
Schwarzkopf, Streich, Gedda, Krebs, conducted by von Karajan
ANGEL 3539–B/L
Pons, Welitsch, Tucker, Kullmann, conducted by Ormandy
COLUMBIA 3SL–108
Gueden, Lipp, Parzak, Dermota, conducted by Krauss
LONDON A–4207

**Die Fliegende Holländer**
Radio Berlin production, conducted by Fricsay
DECCA–DXC–124
Uhde, Varnay, Weber, conducted by Keilberth
LONDON A–4325

**La Forza del Destino**
Callas, Tucker, Nicolai, conducted by Serafin
ANGEL 3531–C/L
Tebaldi, del Monaco, Simionato, Siepi, conducted by Molinari-Pradelli
LONDON A–4408
The same cast, stereo version
LONDON OSA–1405
Guerrini, Campora, Corena, conducted by Parodi
URANIA 226

**Fra Diavolo**
URANIA 204

**Die Frau ohne Schatten**
LONDON A–4505

**Der Freischütz**
Cunitz, Loose, Hopf, Poell, conducted by Ackermann
LONDON A–4303
Bohme, Trotschel, Aldenhoff, conducted by Kempe
URANIA 403

**La Grande Duchesse de Gérolstein**
URANIA UX–115–2
Stereo version
URANIA USD–1015–2

**La Gioconda**
Cerquetti, del Monaco, Simionato, Siepi, conducted by Gavazzeni
LONDON A–4331
The same cast, stereo version
LONDON OSA–1302
Corridori, Campora, Corena, conducted by Parodi
URANIA 241
Milanov, di Stefano, Elias, Warren, conducted by Previtali
VICTOR LM–2249
The same cast, stereo version
VICTOR LSC–6139

**Götterdämmerung**
LONDON A–4603

**Goyescas**
LONDON A–4121
Stereo version
LONDON OSA–1101

**Hänsel und Gretel**
Schwarzkopf, Grümmer, conducted by von Karajan
ANGEL 3506–B/L
Stevens, Conner, Brownlee, conducted by Rudolf
COLUMBIA SL–102
Berger, Radio Berlin production, conducted by Rothier
URANIA 212

**Die Harmonie der Welt**
DECCA 9765

**L'Heure Espagnole**
Duval, Giraudeau, conducted by Cluytens
ANGEL D (or T) 35018
Danco, Hamel, Durenne, conducted by Ansermet
LONDON A–4102

**Idomeneo**
ANGEL 3574
ANGEL T–35595/97

**L'Italiana in Algeri**
ANGEL 3529–B/L

**Ivan Susanin**
Belgrade National Opera
LONDON A–4409
Bolshoi Theater
VANGUARD 6010/12

**Khovantschina**
LONDON A–4405

**Kitezh**
URANIA 7115

**Die Kluge**
ANGEL 3551 or
ANGEL T–35389/90
Stereo version
ANGEL S–3551 B/L

**Lakmé**
LONDON A–4307

**Let's Make an Opera**
LONDON A–4107

**Lohengrin**
Bavarian Radio production, conducted by
Jochum
DECCA DXB–131
Steber, Varnay, conducted by Kleiber
LONDON A–4502
Schech, Klose, Bohme, conducted by
Kempe
URANIA 225

**Louise**
EPIC 4SC–6018

**The Love for Three Oranges**
EPIC 4SC–6013

**Lucia di Lammermoor**
Callas, di Stefano, Gobbi, conducted by
Serafin
ANGEL 3503 or T–35038/39
Pons, Tucker, Guarrera, conducted by
Cleva
COLUMBIA 3SL–127
Wilson, Poggi, Colzani, conducted by
Capuana
URANIA 232

Peters, Peerce, Tozzi, conducted by
Leinsdorf
VICTOR LM–6055

**Lulu**
COLUMBIA 5SL–121

**Die Lustigen Weiber von Windsor**
URANIA 214

**Madama Butterfly**
Callas, Gedda, Borriello, conducted by
von Karajan
ANGEL 3523 or T–35255/27
de los Angeles, di Stefano, Gobbi, con-
ducted by Gavazzeni
EMI-CAPITOL GCR–7137
VICTOR LM–6121
Steber, Tucker, Valdengo, conducted by
Rudolf
COLUMBIA 3SL–104
Tebaldi, Bergonzi, Sordello, conducted by
Serafin
LONDON A–4337
The same cast, stereo version
LONDON OSA–1406
Moffo, Valleti, conducted by Leinsdorf
VICTOR LM–6135
The same cast, stereo version
VICTOR LSC–6135

**Il Maestro di Musica**
WESTMINSTER XWN–18262

**Mahagonny**
COLUMBIA K3L–243

**Les Malheurs d'Orphée**
WESTMINSTER OPW–11031

**Manon**
Micheau, de Luca, conducted by Wolff
LONDON A–4305
de los Angeles, Legay, conducted by
Monteux
VICTOR LM–6402

**Manon Lescaut**
Tebaldi, del Monaco, Corena, conducted
by Molinari-Pradelli
LONDON A–4316

Albanese, Bjoerling, Merrill, conducted by Perlea
VICTOR LM–6116

**Maria Golovin**
VICTOR LM–6142
Stereo version
VICTOR LSC–6142

**Matrimonio Segreto, Il**
ANGEL 3549 or
ANGEL T–35375/77

**Medea** (Cherubini)
MERCURY OL–3–104
Stereo version
MERCURY SR–3–9000

**The Medium**
COLUMBIA OSL–154

**Mefistofele**
Dall' Argine, Noli, conducted by Capuana
URANIA 230
Christoff, Prandelli, conducted by Gui
VICTOR LM–6049

**Die Meistersinger**
Franz, Grümmer, Schock, conducted by Kempe
ANGEL 3572 E/L
Gueden, Treptow, Schöffler, conducted by Knappertsbusch
LONDON A–4601
Frantz, Lemnitz, Aldenhoff, conducted by Kempe
URANIA 206

**Mireille**
ANGEL 3533 or
ANGEL T–35210/12

**Der Mond**
ANGEL 3567 or
ANGEL T–35389/90

**Norma**
ANGEL 3517

**Le Nozze di Figaro**
Jurinac, Streich, Schöffler, conducted by Böhm
EPIC SC–6022

della Casa, Gueden, Danco, Siepi, conducted by Kleiber
LONDON A–4407
The same cast, stereo version
LONDON OSA–1402
Jurinac, Sciutti, Stevens, conducted by Gui
VICTOR LM–6401

**Oberon**
PERIOD 575

**Oedipus Rex**
Cocteau (narrating), conducted by Stravinsky
COLUMBIA ML–4644
Pasquier (narrating), conducted by Ansermet
LONDON A–4106

**Orfeo ed Euridice**
Gedda, Micheau, conducted by Froment
ANGEL 3569 or
ANGEL T–35554/55
Fischer-Dieskau, Streich, conducted by Fricsay
DECCA DXH–143
Simoneau, Danco, conducted by Rosbaud
EPIC 4SC–6019
Klose, Berger, Streich, conducted by Rothier
URANIA 223
Stevens, della Casa, Peters, conducted by Monteux
VICTOR LM–2253

**Otello** (Verdi)
del Monaco, Tebaldi, conducted by Erede
LONDON A–4312
Sarri, la Pollo, conducted by Peoletti
URANIA 216
Vinay, Nelli, Valdengo, conducted by Toscanini
VICTOR LM–6107

**Pagliacci, I**
Callas, di Stefano, Gobbi, conducted by Serafin
ANGEL 3527–3S/L
The same cast, together with *Cavalleria Rusticana*
ANGEL 3528 C/L

Amara, Valdengo, Tucker, conducted by Cleva
COLUMBIA SL–113
The same cast, together with *Cavalleria Rusticana*
COLUMBIA SL–124
del Monaco, Petrella, Poli, conducted by Erede
LONDON A–4214
The same cast, together with *Cavalleria Rusticana*
LONDON A–4323
de los Angeles, Bjoerling, Merrill, Warren, conducted by Cellini
VICTOR LM–6405
The same cast, together with *Cavalleria Rusticana*
VICTOR LM–6106

**Parsifal**
LONDON A–4602

**Le Pauvre Matelot**
WESTMINSTER OPW–11030

**Les Pêcheurs de Perles**
Opéra-Comique, conducted by Cluytens
ANGEL 3524 or
ANGEL T–35174/75
Lamoureux concerts, conducted by Fournet
EPIC 4SC–6002

**Pelléas et Mélisande**
de los Angeles, Janssen, Souzay, conducted by Cluytens
ANGEL 3561 or
ANGEL T–35478/80
Micheau, Maurane, Roux, conducted by Fournet
EPIC 4SC–6003
Danco, Mollet, Rehfuss, conducted by Ansermet
LONDON A–4401

**Pique-Dame**
LONDON A–4410

**Porgy and Bess**
Torme, Faye, Duke Ellington Orchestra,

Australian Jazz Quartet,
BETHLEHEM EXLP–1
Conducted by Engel
COLUMBIA OSL–162

**Prince Igor**
Belgrade National Opera
LONDON A–4503
USSR National Orchestra
PERIOD 552

**Prodaná Nevěsta**
Slovenian Opera
EPIC 4SC–6020
Richter, Hauser, Peters, Bohme, conducted by Lenzer
URANIA 210
Prague National Theater
URANIA 231

**I Puritani**
ANGEL 3502

**The Rake's Progress**
COLUMBIA 5SL–125

**El Retablo de Maese Pedro**
French Radio production
ANGEL D (or T)–35134
Spanish National Orchestra
LONDON LL–1739
Vienna Philharmonia conducted by Adler
SPA 43

**Rigoletto**
Callas, di Stefano, Gobbi, conducted by Serafin
ANGEL 3537–5S/L
del Monaco, Gueden, conducted by Erede
LONDON A–4313
Peerce, Warren, Berger, conducted by Cellini
VICTOR LM–6021
Merrill, Peters, Bjoerling, Tozzi, conducted by Perlea
VICTOR LM–6051

**Roméo et Juliette**
LONDON A–4310

## Der Rosenkavalier

Schwarzkopf, Edelmann, Ludwig, conducted by von Karajan
ANGEL 3563–D/L
The same cast, stereo version
ANGEL S 3563–D/L
Reining, Weber, Jurinac, conducted by Kleiber
LONDON A–4404
Baumer, Lemnitz, Bohme, conducted by Kempe
URANIA 201
Munich State Opera, conducted by Krauss
VOX 7774

## Le Rossignol
ANGEL D (or T)–35204

## Rusalka (Dvořák)
URANIA 219

## Russlan und Ludmilla
WESTMINSTER OPW–1401

## The Saint of Bleecker Street
VICTOR LM–6032

## Salome
LONDON A–4217

## Der Schauspieldirektor
PERIOD 532

## Die Schöne Galathee
URANIA 7167

## Il Segreto di Susanna
DECCA 9770

## La Serva Padrona
Carteri, Rossi-Lemeni, conducted by Giulini
ANGEL D (or T)–35279
Mazzoleni, Cortis, conducted by Leitner
DECCA ARC–3039

## Simon Boccanegra
EMI–CAPITOL GCR–7126

## Snyegurotchka
LONDON A–4504

## Socrate
ESOTERIC 510

## La Sonnambula
ANGEL 3568

## Street Scene
COLUMBIA OL–4139

## Suor Angelica
EMI–CAPITOL G–7115

## Il Tabarro
VICTOR LM–2057

## Tannhäuser
URANIA 211

## Thaïs
URANIA 227

## Tiefland
EPIC SC–6025

## Tosca
Callas, di Stefano, Gobbi, conducted by de Sabata
ANGEL 3508 or
ANGEL T–35060/61
Stella, Poggi, Taddei, conducted by Serafin
COLUMBIA M2L–402
Tebaldi, Campora, Mascherini, conducted by Erede
LONDON A–4213
Milanov, Bjoerling, Warren, conducted by Leinsdorf
VICTOR LM–6052
dall'Argine, Scattolini, Colombo, conducted by Quadri
WESTMINSTER OPW–1288

## La Traviata
Stella, di Stefano, Gobbi, conducted by Serafin
ANGEL 3545–B/L
Guerrini, Huder, Silveri
COLUMBIA, 3SL–103
Tebaldi, Poggi, Prottl, conducted by Molinari-Pradelli
LONDON A–4314

Albanese, Peerce, Merrill, conducted by
Toscanini
VICTOR LM–6003
Carteri, Valleti, Warren, conducted by
Monteux
VICTOR LM–6040

**Tristan und Isolde**
Flagstad, Suthaus, Thebom, Fischer-
Dieskau, conducted by Furtwängler
VICTOR LM–6700
Gewandhaus production, conducted by
Konwitschny
URANIA 202

**Il Trovatore**
Callas, di Stefano, Barbieri, Panerai, con-
ducted by von Karajan
ANGEL 3554–5S/L
Tebaldi, del Monaco, Simionato, Savarese,
conducted by Erede
LONDON A–4326
The same cast, stereo version
LONDON OSA–1304
Bjoerling, Milanov, Warren, conducted
by Cellini
VICTOR LM–6008

**Tsarskaya Nevyesta**
WESTMINSTER OPW–1301

**Turandot** (Puccini)
Callas, Schwarzkopf, Fernandi, conducted
by Serafin
ANGEL 3571–C/L
Borkh, Tebaldi, del Monaco, conducted
by Erede
LONDON A–4320

**Il Turco in Italia**
ANGEL 3535–C/L

**The Turn of the Screw**
LONDON A–4219

**Vanessa**
VICTOR LM–6138
Stereo version
VICTOR LSC–6138

**La Vida Breve**
VICTOR LM–6017

**Werther**
URANIA 233

**Wozzeck**
COLUMBIA 5SL–118

**Z Mrtvého Domu**
EPIC–4SC–6005

**Zar Und Zimmermann**
DECCA DXD–129

**Die Zauberflöte**
Streich, Stader, Häflinger, Fischer-
Dieskau, conducted by Fricsay
DECCA DXJ–134
Gueden, Lipp, Simoneau, Bohme, con-
ducted by Böhm
LONDON A–4319

**Zhenitba**
WESTMINSTER OPW–1202

**Zigeunerbaron**
Schwarzkopf, Gedda, Kunz, conducted by
Ackermann
ANGEL 3566–B/L
Zadek, Loose, Patzak, Poell, conducted by
Krauss
LONDON A–4208
Kunz, Loose, conducted by Paulk
VANGUARD 486/7

# SPECIAL INDEXES

## Sopranos

Aïno Ackté, Suzanne Adams, Rosa Agthé, Licia Albanese, Emma Albani, Frances Alda, Lucine Amara, Victoria de los Angeles, Sophie Arnould, Rose Bampton, Maria Barrientos, Gemma Bellincioni, Erna Berger, Elizabeth Billington, Lillian Evans Blauvelt, Lucrezia Bori, Inge Borkh, Hélène, Bouvier, Minnie Bower, Marianne Brandt, Gré Brouwenstijn, Maria Callas, Emma Calvé, Violante Camporese, Maria Caniglia, Rose Caron, Joan Carroll, Marie Carvalho, Lisa della Casa, Katharina Cavalieri, Marie Cavan, Maria Cebotari, Susanna Maria Cibber, Gina Cigna, Giuseppina Cobelli, Blanche Cole, Nadine Conner, Joan Cross, Jeanne Cruvelli, Phyllis Curtin, Suzanne Danco, Gloria Davy, Emmy Destinn, Mattiwilda Dobbs, Julie Dorus-Gras, Dorothy Dow, Denise Duval, Franca Duval, Claire Dux, Emma Eames, Florence Easton, Marie Louise Edvina, Eileen Farrell, Geraldine Farrar, Ellen Faull, Mafalda Favero, Jean Fenn, Lavinia Fenton, Sylvia Fisher, Kirsten Flagstad, Editha Fleischer, Josephine Fodor-Mainvielle, Olive Fremstad, Marta Fuchs, Emma Fursch-Madi, Johanna Gadski, Amelita Galli-Curci, Eugenie Garcia, Mary Garden, Mabel Garrison, Gabriele Gatti, Etelka Gerster, Dusolina Giannini, Alma Gluck, Christel Goltz, Margherita Grandi, Giulia Grisi, Gertrude Grob-Prandl, Nora Gruhn, Hilde Gueden, Ellen Gulbranson, Margaret Harshaw, Frieda Hempel, Emilie Herzog, Laurel Hurley, Daniza Ilitsch, Maria Ivogün, Helen Jepson, Maria Jeritza, Emma Juch, Sena Jurinac, Gertrude Kappel, Clara Louise Kellogg, Barbara Kemp, Dorothy Kirsten, Katharina Klafsky, Anny Konetzni, Hilde Konetzni, Marie Krauss, Selma Kronold, Melanie Kurt, Selma Kurz, Maria Labia, Nanny Larsen-Todsen, Marjorie Lawrence, Georgette Leblanc, Martha Leffler-Burckard, Lilli Lehmann, Lotte Lehmann, Frida Leider, Tiana Lemnitz, Rosalie Levasseur, Brenda Lewis, Estelle Liebling, Jenny Lind, Lydia Lipovska, Félia Litvinne, Göta Ljungberg, Aase Løveberg, Germaine Lubin, Pauline Lucca, Zélie de Lussan, Felice Lyne, Florence Macbeth, Mathilde Mallinger, Thérèse Malten, Dorothée Manski, Lucille Marcel, Blanche Marchesi, Queena Mario, Amalie Materna, Margarete Matzenauer, Nellie Melba, Carmen Melis, Zinka Milanov, Anna von Mildenburg, Anna Milder, Mildred Miller, Martha Mödl, Toti dal Monte, Fanny Moody, Grace Moore, Berta Morena, Maria Müller, Patrice Munsel, Ilma di Murska, Claudia Muzio, Emma Nevada, Mignon Nevada, Patricia Neway, Agnes Nicholls, Birgit Nilsson, Christine Nilsson, Lillian Nordica, Eide Norena, Jarmila Novotna, Margarete Ober, Jane Osborn, Euphrosyne Parepa-Rosa, Giuditta Pasta, Mary Anne Paton, Adelina Patti, Rose Pauly, Gianna Pederzini, Minna Peschka-Leutner, Roberta Peters, Eleonora Petrelli, Lily Pons, Carmela Ponselle, Rosa Ponselle, Leontyne

Price, Marie Rappold, Regina Resnik, Josephine de Reszke, Elizabeth Rethberg, Luise Reuss-Belce, Clara Kathleen Rogers, Marie Roze, Leonie Rysanek, Erna Sack, Minnie Saltzmann-Stevens, Sybil Sanderson, Marie Constance Sass, Frances Saville, Bidu Sayao, Margarete Luise Schick, Malvina Schnorr von Carolsfield, Wilhelmine Schröder-Devrient, Elizabeth Schumann, Elizabeth Schwarzkopf, Irmgard Seefried, Auguste Seidl-Kraus, Marcella Sembrich, Constance Shacklock, Margaret Sheridan, Amy Shuard, Margarete Siems, Henriette Sontag, Eleanor Steber, Sophie Stehle, Catherine Stephens, Teresa Stolz, Ann Storace, Giuseppina Strepponi, Joan Sutherland, Rosa Sucher, Marion Talley, Renata Tebaldi, Milka Ternina, Eva Tetrazzini, Luisa Tetrazzini, Maggie Teyte, Therese Thoma, Teresa Tietjens, Helen Traubel, Yvonne de Tréville, Delphine Ugalde, Viorica Ursuleac, Alvina Valleria, Astrid Varnay, Clementine de Vere, Geneviève Vix, Thelma Votipka, Johanna Wagner, Ljuba Welitsch, Carolina White, Camilla Williams, Marie Wittich, Frances Yeend, Hilda Zadek, Marie van Zandt, Cornelia van Zanten, Anna Zerr

**Mezzo-sopranos**

Frances Bible, Adelaide Borghi-Mamo, Marie Boulanger, Marianne Brandt, Marie Brema, Bruna Castagna, Anne Charton-Demeur, Rosalind Elias, Edith Evans, Rita Fornia-Labey, Olive Fremstad, Marie Galli-Curci, Giuditta Grisi, Marie Gutheil-Schoder, Margaret Harshaw, Minnie Hauk, Louise Homer, Louise Kirkby-Lunn, Margarete Klose, Lorri Lail, Martha Lipton, Margarete Matzenauer, Anna von Mildenberg, Nell Rankin, Giulietta Simionato, Risë Stevens, Eve Stignani, Rosina Stoltz, Marie Sundelius, Conchita Supervia, Blanche Thebom, Jennie Tourel, Zelia Trebelli, Claramae Turner, Lucia Elizabeth Vestris,

Pauline Viardot-Garcia, Edyth Walker

**Contraltos**

Marietta Alboni, Marian Anderson, Fedora Barbieri, Marianne Brandt, Clara Butt, Sara Jane Cahier, Anna Louise Cary, Edith Coates, Marie Delna, Cloe Elmo, Kathleen Ferrier, Olive Fremstad, Maria Gay, Jeanne Gerville-Réache, Herta Glaz, Margaret Harshaw, Helene Hastreiter, Kathleen Howard, Ruth Kobart, Frieda Langendorf, Darya Leonova, Jean Madeira, Maria Garcia Malibran, Kathryn Meisle, Elena Nikolaidi, Maria Olczewska, Sigrid Onegin, Flora Perini, Adelaide Phillips, Sofia Scalchi, Ernestine Schumann-Heink, Gladys Swarthout, Kerstin Thorborg, Gertrud Wettergren, Florence Pauline Wickham

**Male Contralto**

Gaetano Guadagni

**Tenors**

Valentin Adamberger, Paul Althouse, Albert Raymond Alvarez, Max Alvary, Fernand Ansseau, Joseph Barbot, Kurt Baum, John Beard, Joseph Bentonelli, Rudolf Berger, Jussi Bjoerling, Alesandro Bonci, Giuseppe Borgatti, Dino Borgioli, John Braham, Alois Burgstaller, Karel Burian, Italo Campanini, Joseph Capoul, Enrico Caruso, Jean Baptiste Chollet, Eugene Conley, Gaetano Crivelli, Richard Crooks, Hugues Cuenod, Charles Dalmorès, Tudor Davies, Andreas Dippel, Gilbert Duprez, Ernest van Dyke, Nicolay Figner, Paul Franke, Manuel del Popolo Vicente Garcia, Nicolai Gedda, Beniamino Gigli, Lodovico Graziani, Heinrich Gudehus, Charles Hackett, George Hamlin, Carl Hartmann, Heinrich Hensel, Joseph Hislop, Ellison van Hoose, Hans Hopf, Walter Hyde, Charles Benjamin Incledon, Herrmann Jadlowker, Frederick Jagel, Edward Johnson, Rowland Jones, Paul Kalisch, Norman Kelley, Michael Kelly,

Jan Kiepura, Heinrich Knote, Ernst Kraus, Charles Kullman, Giacomo Lauri-Volpi, Joseph Legros, Richard Lewis, David Lloyd, Max Lorenz, Fernando de Lucia, Joseph Maas, Francis MacLennan, René Maison, Giovanni Matteo Mario, Riccardo Martin, Giovanni Martinelli, Nino Martini, John McCormack, Lauritz Melchior, James Melton, Mario del Monaco, Frank Mullings, Lucien Muratore, Franz Nachbauer, Emilio Naudin, Nicolini, Albert Niemann, Adolphe Nourrit, Louis Nourrit, Alessio de Paolis, Julius Patzak, Peter Pears, Jan Peerce, Jean Perier, Aureliano Pertile, David Poleri, Anton Raaff, Sims Reeves, Albert Reiss, Jean de Reszke, Gustave Roger, Helge Roswaenge, Giovanni Battista Rubini, Albert Saléza, Benedict Schack, Tito Schipa, Erik Schmedes, Ludwig Schnorr von Carolsfield, Anton Schott, Leo Slezak, Roberto Stagno, Giuseppe di Stefano, Brian Sullivan, Set Svanholm, Ferrucio Tagliavini, Francesco Tamagno, Enrico Tamberlik, Richard Tauber, Joseph Aloys Tichatschek, Armand Tokatyan, Richard Tucker, Georg Unger, Jacques Urlus, Cesare Valleti, Ramon Vinay, Heinrich Vogl, Franz Völker, Giovanni Voyer, Franz Vroons, Theodor Wachtel, Hermann Winkelmann, Alexander Young, Giovanni Zenatello

## Baritones

Pasquale Amato, Mario Ancona, Sumner Austin, George Baklanov, Luigi Bassi, Johann Beck, Rudolf Berger, Franz Betz, David Bispham, Rudolf Bockelmann, Richard Bonelli, Jacques André Bouhy, John Brownlee, Giuseppe Campanari, Francis Carey, Walter Cassell, George Cehanovsky, Karl Doench, Hector Dufranne, Todd Duncan, Jean Baptiste Faure, Edoardo Ferrari-Fontana, Dietrich Fischer-Dieskau, Cesare Formichi, Anton Forti, Benvenuto Franci,

Antonio Galassi, Carlo Galeffi, Gustave García, Édouard Gassier, Eugenio Giraldoni, Tito Gobbi, Igor Gorin, Otto Goritz, Frank Guarrera, Eugen Gura, Mack Harrell, Max Heinrich, Josef Herrmann, William Hinshaw, Ludwig Hofmann, Hans Hotter, Julius Huehn, Giovanni Inghilleri, Herbert Janssen, August Kinderman, Otakar Kraus, Jean Louis Lassalle, Giuseppe de Luca, William Ludwig, Vanni Marcoux, Vasco Mariz, Victor Maurel, Robert Merrill, Hans von Milde, Anton Mitterwurzer, Carlo Morelli, Hans Hermann Nissen, Karl Perron, Giuseppe del Puente, Émile Renan, Maurice Arnold Renaud, Giorgio Ronconi, Leon Rothier, Marko Rothmüller, Titta Ruffo, Mario Sammarco, Charles Santley, Karl Scheidermantel, Heinrich Schlusnus, Paul Schöffler, Gustav Schützendorf, Antonio Scotti, Martial Singher, Mariano Stabile, Josef Staudigl Jr., Antonio Tamburini, John Charles Thomas, Lawrence Tibbett, Herman Uhde, Theodor Uppman, Felice Vanesi, Leonard Warren, Robert Weede, Hermann Weil, Reinald Werrenrath

## Basses

Norman Allin, Lorenzo Alvary, Louis d'Angelo, Frederick Austin, Federico Autori, Salvatore Baccaloni, Paul Bender, Michael Bohnen, Karl Braun, Edmund Burke, Feodor Chaliapin, Boris Christoff, Anselmo Colzani, Fernando Corena, Jean François Delmas, Adamo Didur, Emil Fischer, Ludwig Fischer, Allen James Foley, Karl Johann Formes, Filippo Galli, Manuel Patricio García, Alfred Auguste Giraudet, Putnam Griswold, Joshua Hecht, Allen Carter Hinckley, Jerome Hines, Marcel Journet, Alexander Kipnis, Felix von Kraus, Eric Kunz, Luigi Lablache, Nicholas Levasseur, Emanuel List, Pavel Ludikar, Charles Manners, Richard Mayr, Ivan Melnikov, Nicola Moscona, Ossip Petrov, Ezio Pinza, Pol

Henri Plançon, Robert Radford, Leon Rains, Theodor Reichmann, Edouard de Reszke, Anton van Rooy, Giulio Rossi, Nicola Rossi-Lemeni, Emil Scaria, Friedrich Schorr, Cesare Siepi, Josef Staudigl Sr., Feodor Stravinsky, Italo Tajo, Emile Taskin, Giorgio Tozzi, Félix Vieuille, Clarence Whitehill, Herbert Witherspoon

**Composers**

Adolphe Adam, Adam de la Halle, Isaac Albéniz, Eugene d'Albert, Franco Alfano, George Antheil, Luigi Arditi, Anton Arensky, Attilio Ariosti, Thomas Arne, Daniel François Auber, Louis François Aubert, Edmond Audran, Johann Christian Bach, Michael William Balfe, Granville Bantock, Samuel Barber, Giovanni Bardi, Béla Bartók, Giovanni Battista Bassani, Ludwig van Beethoven, Vincenzo Bellini, Herman Bemberg, Robert Russell Bennett, François Benoist, Peter Benoit, Alban Berg, Natanael Berg, William Bergsma, Lennox Berkeley, Hector Berlioz, Franz Berwald, Henry Bishop, Julius Bittner, Georges Bizet, Boris Blacher, Leo Blech, Marc Blitzstein, Ernest Bloch, Jan Blockx, François Boïeldieu, Arrigo Boïto, Giovanni Bononcini, Alexander Borodin, Giovanni Bottesini, Rutland Boughton, Walter Braunfels, Benjamin Britten, Ignaz Brüll, Bruneau, Ferrucio Busoni, Giulio Caccini, Charles Wakefield Cadman, Antonio Caldara, Robert Cambert, François van Campenhout, André Campra, Henry Carey, Benjamin Carr, Eleazar de Carvalho, Mario Castelnuovo-Tedesco, Alfredo Catalani, Emilio del Cavalieri, Pier Francesco Cavalli, Marcantonio Cesti, Emmanuel Chabrier, George Whitefield Chadwick, Gustave Charpentier, Marc Antoine Charpentier, Ernest Chausson, Luigi Cherubini, Francesco Cilea, Domenico Cimarosa, Albert Coates, Louis Adolphe Coerne, Lawrance Collingwood, Frederick Converse, Aaron Copland, Peter Cornelius, Henry Cowell, César Cui, Luigi Dallapiccola, Leopold Damrosch, Walter Damrosch, Alexander Dargomijsky, Félicien Cesar David, John Davis, Achille Claude Debussy, Marcel Delannoy, Leo Délibes, Frederick Delius, Karl Ditters von Dittersdorf, Gaetano Donizetti, Antonio Draghi, Paul Dukas, Gabriel Dupont, Antonin Dvořák, Werner Egk, Gottfried von Einem, Georges Enesco, Lehman Engel, Camille Erlanger, Frederic d'Erlanger, Oscar Esplà, Manuel de Falla, Gabriel Fauré, Benedetto Ferrari, Henri Fevrier, Zdenek Fibich, Paul le Flem, Friedrich von Flotow, Carlisle Floyd, Josef Foerster, Cecil Forsyth, Lucas Foss, Alberto Franchetti, César Franck, William Henry Fry, Marco da Gagliano, Hans Gal, Vincenzo Galilei, Amintore Galli, Baldassare Galuppi, Nicholas Gatty, Giuseppe Gazzaniga, Franz Richard Genée Edward German, George Gershwin, Ottmar Gerster, François Gevaert, Giorgio Ghedini, Vittorio Giannini, Cecil Armstrong Gibbs, Gilardo Gilardi, Umberto Giordano, Peggy Glanville-Hicks, Alexander Glazounov, Reinhold Glière, Michael Glinka, Christoph Willibald Ritter von Gluck, Vittorio Gnecchi, Benjamin Godard, Alexander Goedicke, Hermann Goetz, Theo Goldberg, Karl Goldmark, Carlos Gomez, Eugene Goossens III, Jakov Gotovac, Charles Gounod, Gabriel Grad, Paul Graener, Enrique Granados, André Grétry, Louis Gruenberg, Michel la Guerre, Guido Guerrini, Ernst Guiraud, Inglis Gundry, Jésus Guridi, Manfred Gurlitt, Adalbert Gyrowetz, Joseph Hass, Alois Hába, Karel Hába, Henry Hadley, Richard Hageman, Reynaldo Hahn, Jacques Halévy, Asger Hamerik, Ebbe Hamerik, Georg Frideric Handel, Howard Hanson, William Harling, Carter Harman, Lou Harrison, Tibor Harsanyi, Frederic Hart,

John Hartmann, Karl Hartmann, Josef Matthias, Hans Haug, Franz Josef Haydn, Robert Heger, Everett Helm, Albert Henneberg, Valdemar Henriques, Hans Henze, Victor Herbert, Louis Joseph Hérold, Bernard Herrmann, Hugo Herrmann, Ludwig Hess, James Hewitt, Juan Hidalgo, Paul Hindemith, Finn Höffding, Paul Höffer, Joseph Holbrooke, Stanley Hollingsworth, Ladislav Holoubek, Gustav Holst, Arthur Honegger, Jenö Hubay, Hans Huber, John Adam Hugo, Engelbert Humperdinck, Jacques Ibert, Vincent d'Indy, Emile Inghelbrecht, Michael Ippolitov-Ivanov, Carlo Jachino, William Jackson, Frederick Jacobi, Leos Janaček, Emile Jacques-Dalcroze, Georg Jarno, David Jenkins, Ludwig Jensen, Jaroslav Jeremias, Otakar Jeremiaš, Karel Jirák, Norman dello Joio, André Jolivet, Victorin de Joncières, Sidney Jones, John Joubert, Dmitri Kabalevsky, Paul Kadosa, Alfred Kalnins, Janis Kalnins, Manolis Kalomiris, Lucian Kamienski, Heinrich Kaminski, Eugen Kapp, Rudolf Karel, Theodore Karyotakis, Tadeusz Kassern, Alexander Kastalsky, Leonard Kastle, Leo Kauffmann, Walter Kaufmann, Hugo Kaun, Robert Keldorfer, Jenö Kenessy, Johann Caspar Kerll, Wilhelm Kienzl, Giselher Klebe, Bruno Oscar Klein, Paul von Klenau, Friedrich Klose, Erland von Kock, Zoltán Kodály, Michael Kondracki, Petar Konjovic, Gyorgy Kósa, Reginald de Koven, Hans Krasa, Alexander Krein, Iša Krejčí, Miroslav Krejčí, Ernst Křenek, Rodolphe Kreutzer, Jaroslav Křička, Robert Kurka, Mario Labroca, Franz Lachner, Ignaz Lachner, Louis Lacombe, László Lajtha, Edouard Lalo, Raoul Laparra, Lars Erik Larsson, Eduard Lassen, Felice Lattuade, Armas Launis, André Lavagne, Daniel Lazarus, Sylvio Lazzari, Alexandre Lecocq, Dai-Kong Lee, Charles Lefebvre, Ethel Leginska, Franz Léhar, Walter Leigh, Leonardo Leo Ruggiero Leoncavallo, Jean François Lesueur, Fran

Lhotka, Ivo Lhotka-Kalinski, Boris Liatoshinsky, Rolf Liebermann, Ingemar Lijefors, Oskar Lindberg, George Linley, George Frederick Linstead, George Lloyd, Matthew Locke, Normand Lockwood, George London, Clarence Loomis, Harvey Worthington Loomis, Nikolai Lopatnikov, Gustav Albert Lortzing, Antonio Lotti, Adriano Lualdi, Otto Luening, Jean Baptiste Lully, Ralph Lyford, Hamish Maccunn, Alexander MacKenzie, Alexander MacLean, Leevi Madetoja, Quinto Manganini, Albéric Magnard, Louis Maillart, Nina Makarova, Edmond Henri Malherbe, Gian Francesco Malipiero, Riccardo Malipiero, Witold Maliszewski, Luigi Mancinelli, Joan Manén, Kathleen Lockhart Manning, Gino Marinuzzi, Heinrich Marschner, Armand Marsick, Henri Marteau, Henri Martelli, Frank Martin, Vincente Martin, Jean Martinon, Bohuslav Martinu, Eugène Georges Marty, Pietro Mascagni, Juan Bautista Massa, Victor Massé, Jules Massenet, William McCoy, Janis Mediņš, Étienne Méhul, Wilfrid Mellers, Felix Mendelssohn-Bartholdy, Gian Carlo Menotti, Giuseppe Mercadante, Oskar Merikanto, André Messager, Joseph Messner, Giacomo Meyerbeer, Solon Michaelides, Francisco Mignone, Marcel Mihailovici, Philip Miles, Darius Milhaud. Karl Millöcker, Richard Mohaupt, Jean Joseph Mondonville, Stanisaus Moniuszko, Pierre Monsigny, Michel de Montéclair, Italo Montemezzi, Claudio Monteverdi, Emanuel Moor, Douglas Moore, Frank Ledlie Moore, Virgilio Mortari, Moritz Moszkowski, Jean Joseph Mouret, Wolfgang Amadeus Mozart, Herbert Murrill, Modeste Mussorgsky, Nicolas Nabokov, Jacopo Napoli, Edward Napravnik, Johann Gottlieb Naumann, Victor Nessler, Arthur Finley Nevin, Karl Otto Nicolai, Carl Nielsen Rudolf Nielsen, Vitezslav Novák, Robert Oboussier, Jacques Offenback, Max d'Ollone, Ole Olsen, Giacomo Orefice, Carl Orff, Ottokar Ostrčil, Giovanni Pacini, Leonardo Pacini, Fredrik Pacius, Ignacy Jan Paderewski, Ferdinando Paër, Jaime Pahissa, Giovanni Paisiello, Roman Palester, Athos Palma, Selin Palmgren, Boris Papandopulo, Horatio Parker, Joseph Parry, Bernardo Pasquini, Carlos Pedrell, Felipe Pedrell, Arrigo Pedrollo, Willem Pelemans, Victor Pelissier, John Pepusch, Mario Peragallo, Giovanni Battista Pergolesi, Jacopo Peri, Wilhelm Petersen, Goffredo Petrassi, Enrico Petrella, Hans Pfitzner, François André Philidor, Niccola Piccinni, Ione Pickhardt, Riccardo Pick-Mangiagalli, Gabriel Pierné, Henry Pierson, Willem Pijper, Lubomir Pipkov, Ildebrando Pizzetti, Robert Planquette, Armande de Polignac, Amilcare Ponchielli, Francis Poniatowski, Marcel Poot, Niccolo Porpora, Ennio Porrino, Francis Poulenc, Francesco Pratella, Silas Pratt, Sergei Prokofiev, Francesco Provenzale, Giacomo Puccini, Henry Purcell, Tauno Pylkkänen, Paolo Quagliati, Henri Rabaud, Sergei Rachmaninov, Jean Philippe Rameau, Ture Rangström, Karol Rathaus, Venanzio Rauzzini, Maurice Ravel, Vladimir Rebikov, Herbert Owen Reed, Licinio Refice, Carl Reinecke, Karol Reiner, Franz Reizenstein, Ottorino Respighi, Hermann Reutter, Cemal Rey, Louis Etienne Reyer, Emil von Rezniček, Luigi Ricci, Vittorio Rieti, Vincenzo Righini, Nicholas Rimsky-Korsakov, Jean Rivier, Lodovico Rocca, Pascual de Rogatis, Jean Roger-Ducasse, Bernard Rogers, Alexis Roland-Manuel, Guy Ropartz, Ned Rorem, Ludwig Roselius, Hilding Rosenberg, Luigi Rossi, Gioacchino Antonio Rossini, Nino Rota, Jean Jaques Rousseau, Marcel Rousseau, Albert Roussel, Camille Saint Saëns, Antonio Salieri, Franz Salmhofer, Lazare Saminsky, Luis Sandi, Giuseppe Sarti, Henri Sauguet, Ahmed Adam Saygun, Alessandro Scarlatti, Xaver Scharwenka,

Armin Schibler, Max von Schillings, Alfredo Schiuma, Franz Schmidt, Othmar Schoeck, Maurice Schoemaker, Arnold Schönberg, Franz Schreker, Franz Peter Schubert, Robert Schumann, Heinrich Schütz, Antonio Scontrino, Cyril Scott Tom Scott, Berhardt Sekles, Alexander Serov, Roger Sessions, John Seymour, Yuri Shaporin, Dmitri Shostakovich, Jan Sibelius, Charles Skilton, Bedřich Smetana, Ethel Smyth, Timothy Spelman, Ludwig Spohr, Gasparo Spontini, Charles Stanford, Robert Starer, William Grant Still, Stephen Storace, Alessandro Stradella, Johann Strauss Jr., Richard Strauss, Igor Stravinsky, Arthur Sullivan, Franz von Suppé, Heinrich Sutermeister, Sergius Taneiev, Alexander Tansman, Deems Taylor, Piotr Ilyich Tchaikovsky, Alexander Tcherepnin, Georg Philip Telemann, Maurice Thiriet, Ambroise Thomas, Randall Thompson, Virgil Thomson, Ludwig Thuille, Michael Tippett, Ernst Toch, Henri Tomasi, Vieri Tosatti, Donald Francis Tovey, Tommaso Traetta, Peter Tranchell, Joaquín Turina, Viktor Ullmann, Hermann Unger, José Usandizaga, Ralph Vaughn Williams, Orazio Vecchi, Karl Venth, Giuseppe Verdi, Renaat Veremans, John Verrall, Heitor Villa-Lobos, Wesley la Violette, George Vitalis, Franco Vittadini, Antonio Vivaldi, Bernard Wagenaar, Ignatz Waghalter, Richard Wagner, Vincent Wallace, William Walton, Robert Ward, Carl Maria von Weber, Eugene Weigel, Kurt Weill, Jacob Weinberg, Jaromir Weinberger, Felix Weingartner, Hugo Weisgall, John Weldon, Egon Wellesz, Clarence White, Alec Wilder, Friedrich Wildgans, Pierre Wissner, Hugo Wolf, Ermanno Wolf-Ferrari, Stefan Wolpe, Kosçak Yamada, Eugen Zádor, Riccardo Zandonai, Eric Zeisl, Alexander von Zemlinsky, Antonio Zingarelli, Vassily Zolotarev

668

## Librettists

Jules Barbier, Arrigo Boito, Raniero di Calzabigi, Salvatore Cammarano, John Erskine, Charles Favart, John Gay, Antonio Ghislanzoni, William Gilbert, Ludovic Halévy, Zsolt Harsányi, Georges Hartmann, Hugo von Hofmannsthal, Luigi Illica, Johann Friedrich Kind, Camille du Locle, Abbé Metastasio, Pierre Perrin, Lorenzo da Ponte, Phillipe Quinault, Ottavio Rinuccini, Felice Romani, Emanuel Schikeneder, Augustin Eugène Scribe, Modest Tchaikovsky, Apostolo Zeno

## Conductors

Kurt Adler, Kurt Herbert Adler, Peter Herman Adler, Victor Alessandro, Emanuel Balaban, Carl Bamberger, Giuseppe Bamboschek, Thomas Beecham, Artur Bodansky, Karl Böhm, Warwick Braithwaite, Hans von Bülow, Fritz Busch, Cleofonte Campanini, Fausto Cleva, Emil Cooper, Walter Ducloux, Alberto Erede, Richard Falk, Ferenc Fricsay, Wilhelm Furtwängler, Giulio Gatti-Casazza, Philippe Gaubert, Gianandrea Gavazzeni, Boris Goldovsky, Carmago Guarnieri, Vittorio Gui, László Halász, Johannes den Hertog, Alfred Hertz, Margaret Hillis, Eugen Jochum, Georg Jochum, Werner Josten, Herbert von Karajan, Joseph Keilberth, Rudolf Kempe, Erich Kleiber, Otto Klemperer, Hans Knappertsbusch, Ernst Knoch, Erich Korngold, Clemens Krauss, Joseph Krips, Karl Krueger, Rafael Kubelik, Charles Lamoureux, Erich Leinsdorf, Hermann Levi, Franz Liszt, Charles Mackerras, Gustav Mahler, Edwin McArthur, Dmitri Mitropoulos, Pierre Monteux, Jean Morel, Felix Mottl, Karl Muck, Leopoldo Mugnone, František Neumann, Sigismund Noskowsky, Ettore Panizza, Bernhard Paumgartner, Emil Paur, Wilfred Pelletier, Jonel Perlea, Giorgio Polacco,

Felix Prohaska, Albert van Raalte, Karl Rankl, Carl Reinecke, Fritz Reiner, Hans Richter, Carl Rosa, Joseph Rosenstock, Max Rudolf, Victor de Sabata, Harold Malcom Watts Sargent, Franz Schalk, Thomas Scherman, George Schick, Thomas Schippers, Ernst von Schuch, George Sebastian, Anton Seidl, Tullio Serafin, Alexander Smallens, Cesare Sodero, Georg Solti, William Steinberg, Fritz Stiedry, Maurice Strakosch, George Szell, Arturo Toscanini, Auguste Vianesi, Bruno Walter, Felix Weingartner, Albert Wolff, Eugene Ysaye

## Roles for Soprano

Abigaille, Adalgisa, Adele, Adina, Adriana Lecouvreur, Aennchen, Agatha, Aïda, Aithra, Alceste, Alice, Alice Ford, Countess Almaviva, Almira, Alms Collector, Amalia, Amelia, Amelia Boccanegra, Amina, Aminta, Amora, Mrs. Anckarström, Angel More, Angèle, Angelic Voice, Angelica, Suor Angelica, Anita, Anna, Anna Bolena, Donna Anna, Anna Gomez, Anna Reich, Anne, Anne Trulove, Annina, Antigonae, Antonia, Antonida, Arabella, Ariadne, Arianna, Arline, Armida, Arsena, Ascagne, Aspasia, Astaroth, Asteria, Avis, Azema, Barak's wife, Barbarina, Barce, Barena, Baroness, Belinda, Bellangère, La Bergère, Berta, Bertha, Bess, Beth, Bianca, Biancofiore, Lady Billows, Birdie, Blanche, Blonde, Countess Bronislawa, Brünnhilde, Buda, Fraulein Bürstner, Camille, Carolina, Cassandra, Catarina, Caterina, Catherine, La Chauve-Souris, Cherubino, Childrens' Voices, Chloé, Female Chorus, La Chouette, Christine, Chrysothemis, Ciocio San, Cis, Clara, Claretta, Clémence, Clorinda, Clotilde, Clytemnestra, The Golden Cockerel, Columbine, Composer, Concepcion, Concetta, Confidante, Constance Fletcher, Constanze, Countess, Coupava, A Cricket, Crobyle, Cupidon, Dalilah, Danae, Daphne, Daughter of

Cardillac, Desdemona, Despina, Dew Fairy, Dewman, Diana, Diane, Dido, Diemut, Dinorah, Dorabella, Dorotka, Dot, Dressmaker, Duchess of Parma, Duchesse de Krakenthorp, Early, Echo, Eglantine, Electra, Electre, Elektra, Elena, Duchess Elena, Elisabeth, Elisabeth the First, Elisabetta di Valois, Elise, Elisetta, Ellen, Ellen Orford, Elsa of Brabant, Elvira, Donna Elvira, Elf, Emma, Emmie, Empress, Empress of Austria, Errand Girl, Esmeralda, Esquire, Etain, Princess Eudoxia, Euridice, Europa, Euryanthe, Eva, Falcon's Voice, Farmer's Daughter, Fata Morgana, Fatimah, Princess Fedora Romanov, Felice, Fenena, Fiakermilli, Fidelio, Fiora, Fiordiligi, Fiorilla, Fire, Flora, Floriana, Flower Maiden, Frau Fluth, Foreign Woman, Fortune Teller, Francesca da Rimini, Frasquita, Freia, Baroness Freimann, Garcias, Garsenda, Genii, Genoveva, Suor Genoveva, Gerhilde, Gertrude, Gianetta, Gilda, Gingerbread Woman, La Gioconda, Giorgetta, Giovanna, Girl with the Hunch Back, Giulia, Giulietta, Goatherd, Mrs. Gobineau, Gorislava, Gretchen, Gretel, Grimgerde, Mrs. Grose, Gutrune, Lady Harriett Dunham, Heavenly Being, Hedwige, Helena, Hélène, Helmwige, Henrietta, Henrietta M., Hermione, Hester Prynne, Idamante, Ighino, Ilia, Ilka, Inez, Infanta, Iolanthe, Iphigenie, Irene, Iris, Irma, Isabella, Isabelle, Isolde, Isotta, Italian Singer, Jaele, Jano, Jaroslavna, Javotte, Jean, Jemmy, Jenny, Jenny Reefer, Jenufa, Jitka, Mlle. Jouvenot, Julie, Juliet Brook, Juliette, Kathinka, Katya, Klytemnestra, Kostelnika Buryjouka, Kundry, Lady, Lady in Waiting, Lady Macbeth, Laetitia, Lakmé, Laura, Countess Laura, Lauretta, Laurie, Leader of the People, Leïla, Leni, Leonora, Leonora di Gusman, Donna Leonora di Vargas, Lillian Russell, Linda, Lion Tamer, Lisa, Lisette, Little Susanne, Liù, Lorance, Louise, Lucia, Lucieta, Lucile,

Lucrezia Borgia, Lucy Lockit, Ludmilla, Luisa, Lulu, Maddalena, Madeleine, Madeleine de Coigny, Magda, Magda Sorel, Maid Servant, Maiden, Malice, Maliella, Manon, Manon Lescaut, Marcellina, Marchand de Masques, Marenka, Margared, Margarethe, Margherita, Margiana, Marguérite, Marguerite de Valois, Maria, Maria Golovin, Marianne, Marie, Mariette, Marina, Maritana, Marquise de Birkenfeld, The Marschallin, Marta, Mary, Mascha, Mathilde, May, Medea, Mélisande, La Messagera, Messenger of Peace, Micaela, Milada, Milk Woman, Mimi, Minerva, Minerve, Minnie, Mireille, Mona, Mona Lisa, Monica, Morgiana, Mother, Muse of Poetry, Musetta, Myrrha, Naiade, Nanetta, Nanette, Nedda, Nella, Nelly, Newspaper Girl, Niece, Ninetta, Noble Page, Norina, Norma, Norn, Notary's Wife, Nuri, Nurse, Nursing Sister, Countess Olga Sukarev, Princess Olga Yourievna Tokmakov, Olimpia, Olympia, Ophélie, Orphan, Ortlinde, Oscar, Suor Osmina, Overseer, Pamina, Papagena, Parassia, Pastourelle, Pedro, Penelope, Pepa, Perside, Philine, Phryné, Miss Pinkerton, Polly Peachum, Polyxène, Pousette, Prima Donna, Princess, Princess von Werdenberg, Puck, Puppet, Pythie, Queen Mother of Samarkand, Queen of Shemakha, Queen of the Night, Rachel, Regina, Regina Gideens, Rezia, Lady Penelope Rich, Rosa, Rosalinda, Rosario, Rose, Rossetta, Rosette, Rossignol, Rossweisse, Rowan, Rozenn, Rusalka, Princess Saamcheddine, Saffi, St. Settlement, St. Theresa I, Sali, Salome, Salud, Samaritana, Sandman, Santuzza, Sapho, Sappho, Savitri, Schwertleite, Sea Nymph, Selika, Semele, Semiramide, Senta, Serena, Serpina, Servilia, Sesto, Shining One, Sieglinde, Siegrune, Mme. Silberkang, Simona, Singer, Slim Girl, Snyegorochka, Sophie, Sophie Brook, Spirit, Statue d'Athena, Stella, Stephanida Matouta.

Stephano, Street Arab, Sulamith, Susan, Susan B. Anthony, Susanna, Countess Susanna, Suzel, Tatyana, Tebaldo, Telea, Temple Gatekeeper, Teresa, Thaïs, Tina Crome, Tormentilla, Floria Tosca, Toto, Trainbearer, Turandot, Princess Turandot, Undine, Ursula, Valentine, Vanessa, Vendulka, Venus, Violetta Valery, Vitellia, Vivetta, Voice from Heaven, Voice of a Bird, Voice on a Record, Volkhova, Vreli, Waldvogel, Wally, Walter, Waltraute, Madam Wanton, Mrs. Waters, Wellgunde, Wheel of Fortune Woman, Wife, Wife of the Court Attendant, Woglinde, Woman, Woodcutter's Boy, Miss Wordsworth, Xanthe, Xenia, Ygraine, Yniolde, Young Shepherd, Yvette, Zaza, Zdenka, Zelmira, Zerbinetta, Zerlina, Zora

## Roles for Mezzo-soprano

Abbess, Adalgisa, Adelaide, Adelma, Adriano, Agnes, Alcmene, Alice, Altichiara, Andrelux, Angel, Anna Hope, Annie, Annius, Antonia's Mother's Voice, Ariane Ascanio, Aspirant Sisters, Augusta Tabor, Azucena, Baba the Turk, Barbara, Béatrice, Mistress Benton, Beppe, Bersi, Bobilicka, Bostana, Boy, Brangäne, Madam Bubble, Buffoon, Carlotta, Carmela, Carmen, Cassandra's Ghost, Cat, Countess Ceprano, Charlotte, Cheap Jewellery Woman, Child, La Ciesca, Coal Gatherer, Comtesse de Coigny, Columbine, Commère, Cook, Countess, Curra, Czipra, Dalila, Mlle. Dangeville, Mrs. Day, Debora, Desdemona, Didon, Djamileh, Suor Dolcina, Donella, Duenna, Mme. Dufresne, Principessa Eboli, L'Ecureuil, Emilia, Erda, Ericlea, Erika, Fatima, Feklusha, Feodor, Fidalma, Fidès, Filipievna, Flora Bervoix, Flosshilde, Forewoman, ˙ Countess Frances of Essex, Frasquita, Fricka, Frugola, Genii, Gerhilde, Gertrude, Gertrude S., Gräfin Geschwitz, Giovanna, Glasha, Gloster Heming, Governess, Grandmother, Grimgerde, Frau Grubach, Hadassa, Hänsel, Hécube, Helmwige, Herodias, Mrs. Herring, Housewife, Indiana Elliott, Innkeeper, L'Innocente, Isabel Wentworth, Ismene, Jack, Miss Jessel, Jocasta, Judith, Julie, Junon, Karolka, Kate Pinkerton, Khivria, Klytemnestra, Kontchakovna, Lady, Mme. Larina, Laura, Lazarillo, Leader of the People, La Libellule, Lily, Lola, Lubara, Madame de Croissy, Madelon, Magdalena, Maid, Maid of Honor, Maidservant, Mallika, Manuela, Mara, Marcelline, Marchioness of Montefiore, Margarita, Marie Louise, Marina Mnischek, Martha, Martha Schwerlein, Mayor's Wife, Melanto, Mercedes, Mignon, Mistress of the Novices, Mother Goose, Musician, Myrtale, Naina, Nancy, Natalia, Nejata, Nicklausse, Nicoletta, Mrs. Nolan, Norn, Nurse, Octavian, L'Opinion Publique, Orlovsky, Orphan, Ortlinde, Ortrud, Page, Mistress Page, Palmatica, Lady Pamela, Mrs. Peachum, Pepa, Perfilievna, Pippo, Preziosilla, Princess de Bouillon, Queen, Queen Iceheart, Queen of Sheba, Ragpicker, Frau Reich, Rosa Mamai, Rosina, Rubria, Savoyard, Schwertleite, Secretary, Mrs. Sedley, Sélysette, Shining One, Siebel, Siegrune, Silla, Singer, Smeraldina, Sorceress, Spectre de Clytemnestre, Spirit Voice, Spring, Statue d'Athena, Streetsweeper, Suzuki, Suzy, Taven, Telemaco, Thirza, Thisbe, Tichon Ivanitsch Kabanov, Tisbe, Mrs. Trapes, Urbain, Waltraute, Wild Girl, Witch, Woman, Wowkle, Zayda, Zinida

## Roles for Contralto

Agata, Albine, The Alto, Amelfa, Amneris, Anaide, Angelina, Anna, Annina, Arsace, Aunt, Auntie, Baba, Miss Baggott, Bianca, Madam By-Ends, Cerinto, Children's Voices, Chinese Cup, La Cieca, Clairon, Princess Clarissa, Countess, Daphnis, Death, Dmitri, Dryade, La Belle Dulcinée, Countess of

Eberbach, Elf, Empress Persicaria, Federica, Felicia, Florence Pike, Françoise, Frédéric, Gaea, Geneviève, Gertrude, Gherardino, Goatherd, Gräfin von Helfenstein, Grandmother Buryja, Heavenly Being, Housekeeper, Isabella, Aunt Jane, Katharina, Katherine, Laura, Leda, Shepherd Lehl, Linetta, Lucretia, Maddalena, Madeleine, Maffio Orsini, Maidservant, Maive, Mamma Lucia, Marfa Kabanova, Margret, Maria, Martha, Martinka, Mary, Doña Mercedes, Mirabella, The Moon, Mother, Mother of Louise, Nancy, Noble Page, Norn, Nourrice, Olga, The Omniscient Mussel, Orfeo, Orphan, Page, Pantalis, Pâtre, Pauline, Penelope, Pickthank, Pierotto, Primrose Seller, Princess, Puppet, Queen of the Gypsies, Dame Quickly, Ratmir, Romeo, Rosalia, St. Theresa II, Schoolboy, Serena, Sextus, Shepherd Boy, Shining One, Slave, Statue D'Athena, Suzanne, Ulrica, Ursula, Vanja, Venus, Vera Boronel, Vlassievna, Voice from Above, Wardrobe Mistress, Wife, Witwe Browe, Zita, Zulma

### Roles for Tenor

Abate di Chazeuil, Abbé, Abdallo, Abdisa, Achilles, Adolar, Aegisth, Aeneas, Afanasy Viazemsky, Afra, Albert Herring, Cardinal Albrecht von Brandenburg, Alfonso d'Arcos, Alfred, Alfredo Germont, Count Almaviva, Alwa, Don Alvar, Don Alvaro, Amaryllus, Anatol, Andrea Chenier, Andres, Andrew J., Prince Andrew Khovansky, Anfinomo, Animal Tamer, Apollo, Apparition of a Youth, Arbace, Archer, Arithmetic, Arnold, Arrigo, Artaban, Lord Arthur Bucklaw, Lord Arthur Talbot, Assad, Astrologer, Auguste, Avito, Azriel, Baba Mustapha, Babinsky, Bacchus, Ballad Seller, Balthasar Zorn, Bardolph, Baronelli, Don Basilio, Bayan, Beelzebub, Belmonte, Bénédict, Harry Benn, Sir Benno Robertson, Benvenuto Cellini, Benvolio, Beppe, Beppo, Bernardo

Novagerio, Biasco, Bishop of Budoja, Doctor Blind, Bob Boles, Bobil, Bois-Rosé, Boris Grigorievitch, Boyard Guard, Brighella, Buffoon, Burgomaster, Mr. By-Ends, Don Caeser de Bazan, Doctor Cajus, Calaf, Camille Desmoulins, Canio, Wolfgang Capito, Captain, Captain of Hell's Guard, Cardinal, Don Carlos, Cassio, Cavalier, Celestial Messenger, Chappelou, Charles, Chief Sailor, Male Chorus, Christoph, Cicillo, Clem, Cochenille, Lord Cockburn, Cola Rienzi, Companion, Cook, Marquis de Corcy, Corentino, Cossé, Courier, Crab Man, Don Curzio, Dalibor, Dancing Master, Daniel, Danieli, Da-Ud, David, Dead Composers, Desiré, Devil's Familiar Spirit, Dickson, Doctors, Donald Gallup, Drum-Major, Duke, Duke of Mantua, Duke of Parma, Ritter von Ebelasztin, Mr. Eccles, Edgardo, Edmondo, Edward Plummer, Elder, Eléazar, Graf Elemer, Elvino, Emperor, Emperor Altoum, Enée, Enzo Grimaldo, Eric, Ernani, Ernesto, Eroshka, Erster Bürger, Esquire, Robert Devereux Earl of Essex, Don Eugenio de Zuniga, Eumete, Erimacho, Evander, Executioner, Faust, Federico, Fellah, Fenton, Ferdinand, Fernando, Ferrando, Filch, Filipeto, Finn, Fisherman, Flamand, Flaminio, Flavio, Florestan, Florestein, Fool, Forest Ranger, Fra Diavolo, Francesco, Frantz, Frazier, Fritz Kobus, Froh, Gabriel Adorno, Gabriel von Eisenstein, Don Gaspar, Gastone de Letorières, Gennaro, Georges Brown, Gérald, Gherardo, Giove, Giuseppe, Gobin, Gobrias, Gonsalve, Goro, Chevalier des Grieux, Grigorij, Gritzko, Guard, Prince Guidon, Guillot de Morfontaine, Hadji, Hagenbach, Hämon, Hangman, Harlequin, Haroun, Harry, Harvester, Heinrich der Schreiber, Helenus, Henry B., Henry Morosus Blunt, Herald, Herault de Séchelles, Hermann, Herod Antipas, High Priest of Neptune, Hindu Merchant, Hoffman, Horace Adams, Horn Player,

Hugh the Drover, Hunchback, Sir Huon of Bordeaux, Hylas, Idomeneo, Idreno, Incredibile, Innkeeper, Intendant, Interpreter, Iopas, Iro, Isèpo, Ismaele, Italian Singer, Jacquino, Jafia, Jan Janitzky, Japanese Envoy, Jean, Jenik, Jew, Jo the Loiterer, Joe, John Adams, John of Leyden, Dick Johnson, Jonas, Don José, Josef K., Juan, Judge, Julien, Jupiter, Kilian, King of Fools, King, Knight, Baron Kronthal, Boyar Krutschtschov, Kunz Vogelgesang, Laca Klemen, Laertes, Lamp Lighter, Leandro, Leary, Lord Lechery, Lensky, Léopold, Count Lerma, Leukippos, Lieutenant, Lindoro, Lionel, Livoretto, Loge, Lohengrin, Lord, Lorenzo, Count Loris Ipanov, Lover, Luigi, Lukas, Baron Lummer, Macduff, Captain MacHeath, Maintop, Major-Domo, Malatestino dell'Occhio, Malcolm, Man Servant, Man with the Donkey, Count Mancini, Manfredo, Manrico, Marco, Mario Cavaradossi, Mark, Marlardot, Marouf, Marquis de Chateauneuf, Mars, Masaniello, Master of Ceremonies, Boyar Nikita Matouta, Matteo, Matteo Borsa, Maurizio, Max, Megärus, Memucan, Man in Armor, Menelaus, Méphistophélès, Merchant, Mercure, Mercury, Messenger, Michael Andreievitch Touche, Midas, Midir, Milio Dufresne, Mime, Mingo, Missail, Mitrane, Monostatos, Morphée, Augustin Moser, Muezzin, Muff, Music Master, Mylio, Nadir, Nandro, Don Narciso, Narraboth, Nathanael, Nazarene, Neighbor, Nelson, Nemorino, Nereo, Nerone, Nicias, Nick, Nicola, Nika Magadoff, Noctambulist, Norman, Novice, Nureddin, Oberon, Oedipus, Officer, Old-Clothes Man, Orphée, Osaka, Otello, Don Ottavio, Ottokar, Ovlour, Paco, Painter, Giovanni Pierluigi Palestrina, Pang, Paolino, Paolo il Bello, Parpignol, Parsifal, Peasant, Pedrillo, Pedro, Pélleas, Peter, Peter Grimes, Peter Ibbetson, Peter Ivanov, Phaeton, Philistine Messenger, Philosopher, Piedmontese, Pilgrim, Lt. B. F. Pinkerton, Pisandro, Pittichinaccio, Pliable, Pluton, Poet-Monk, Poisson, Pollione, Pollux, Pong, Priest, Priest's son, Prince, Private Soldier, Prunier, Puppet, Pylade, Quint's Ghost, Radames, Rainbaut, La Rainette, Don Ramiro, Raoul de Nangis, Red Whiskers, El Remondado, Riccardo, Don Riccardo, Count Riccardo Accolai, Rinuccio, Robbins, Robert, Robespierre, Roderigo, Rodolfo, Rodriguez, Roméo, Baron Rouvel, Rudolph, Ruedi, Ruggero, Ruiz, Rustighello, Sacco, Sadko, Sailor, Saint Chavez, Sali, Samson, Sandor Barinkay, Satravan, Scarmuccio, Schmidt, Wassily Ivanovitch Schuisky, Hans Schwalb, Scrivener, Sellem, Sentry, Shepherd, Shillem, Showman, Siegfried, Siegmund, Simon, Simpleton, Singer, King Sisera, Sobinjin, Spalanzani, Junker Spärlich, Reasonable Spectator, Spirit of the Forest, Spirit of the Masque, Splendiano, Spoletta, Sportin' Life, Springer, Squeak, Steersman, Stewa Buryja, Streshner, Kapellmeister Stroh, Student, Student from Krakov, Student from Wittemberg, Sultan Miramoulin, Superstition, Surgeon, Sylvester von Schaumberg, Tallan, Tamino, Tannhäuser, Monsieur Taupe, Tavannes, Tchaplitsky, Tchekalinsky, Tebaldo, Temple Gatekeeper, Tenor, Thaddeus, Thaddeus Stevens, La Théière, Theophilus of Imola, Timorous, Tinca, Tiresias, Titurelli, Titus, Ser Toldo Berandengo, Tom Rakewell, Tonio, Torquemada, Trabucco, Tramp, Trim, Monsieur Triquet, Tristan, Truffaldino, Tsar Berendey, Turiddu, Turnkey, Tybalt, Ulisse, Ulrich Grüsser, Ulrich Eisslinger, Mr. Upfold, Usher, Valzacchi, Vanya Kudrjas, Vasco da Gama, Vasek, Prince Vassily Galatsin, Vaucluse, Captain Vere, Vincent, Vitek, Vladimir Igorevitch, Voice, Wagner, Waiter, Wallenstein, Walter von der Vogelweide, Walther von Stolzing, Watchman, Werther, Wilhelm Meister, William, Young Man, Young Servant, Youth

## Roles for Baritone

Abbate Cospicuo, Admetus, Adonisek, Prince Afron, Agamemnon, Alberich, Albert, Alfio, Don Alfonso, Alfonso XI, Alfonso d'Este, Ali, Count Almaviva, Altair, Amantio di Nicolao, Amfortas, Amonasro, Antonio, Apollon, Apprentice, Arthur Jones, Asmodus, Assan, Assur, Athanael, Avosmediano, Baal Hanan, Baldassare, Captain Balstrode, Barak, Barnaba, Belcore, Ben, Bijou, Billy Budd, Bishop, Old Bohemian, Boniface, Boris Godunov, Borov, Bosun, De Bretigny, Budivoj, Bussy, Cacan, Cacique, The Caliph, Captain of the Guard, Captain, Cardillac, Cardinal Carlo Borromeo, Don Carlo di Vargas, Don Carlos, Cascart, Sir Robert Cecil, Don César de Bazan, Charles Gérard, Cheap Jack, Chorèbe, Chorèbe's Ghost, Chris the Citizen, Christopher Columbus, Cirillo, City Crier, Claudio, Colas, Commandant, Commercial Councillor, Conte Carnero, Conte di Luna, Coppelius, Corporal, Count, Crébillon, Creon, Crespel, Crown, Dalua, El Dancairo, Daniel Webster, Dapertutto, David, Dead Composer, Demas, Doctor of Natural History, Graf Dominik, Donald, Donner, Dositeo, Baron Douphol, Duclou, Dumas, The Dutchman, Count of Eberbach, Empress of China, Enrico, Enterich, Eochaidh, Bishop Ercole Severolus, Escamillo, Eugene Onegin, Doctor Falke, Sir John Falstaff, Herr von Faninal, Fanuèl, Fasolt, Doctor Faust, Fernando, The Dark Fiddler, Fieramosca, Figaro, Fléville, Mister Flint, Herr Fluth, Ford, Foreman, Fouquier-Tinville, Frank, Frédéric, Frederick of Telramund, Friend, Front Line Officer, Gallanthus, Mr. Gedge, Gellner, Georg Danton, Gianni Schicchi, Count Gil, Giorgio Germont, Don Giovanni, Giovanni lo Sciancato, Giovanni Morone, Mr. Gobineau, Golaud, Gregory, Guido di Monforte, Guillaume Tell, Gunther, Hamlet, Handsome, Hans Heiling, Happy,

Harlequin, Háry János, Helmsman, Henry Cuffe, Herald, Hercules, Herman Atlan, Hermann, Herrmann, Hero, Hever, High Priest, High Priest of Brahma, High Priest of Dagon, Hoël, Horace Tabor, L'Horloge Comptoise, Iago, Igor Sviato-slavitch, Jahel, Jake, Jake Wallace, Japanese Envoy, Jesser, Jewish Doctor, Jim, Johannes Kepler, John, John Bunyan, John Sorel, John the Butcher, Jokanaan, Don José de Santarem, Judas Iscariot, Judge Examiner, Junius, Jupiter, Justizrat, Kalman Zsupan, Karnac, King, King Solomon, Mr. Kofner, Kouzka, Kreon, Kruschina, Kuligen, Kurnewal, Kyoto, Lawrence, Lawyer, Leader of the People, Leandro, Lescaut, Lockit, Lord, Lorek, Count Luna, Lysiart, Macbeth, Major-Domo, Doctor Malatesta, Man with the Mule, Mandarin, Mandryka, Manfredo, Manuel, Manufacturer, Manz, Marcello, Marchese d'Obigny, Marco, Marouf, Marquis de Boisfleury, Marti, Cavaliere Marullo, Old Marzci, Mate, Mathieu, Mathis, Matteo del Sarto, Maurizio, Medecin Juif, Fra Malitone, Melot, Mercutio, Merry-go-Round Man, Méru, Messenger, Metifio, Michele, Michelin, Michonnet, Miller, Doctor Miracle, Misgir, Mistrust, Count Monterone, Morbio, Moruccio, Lord Mountjoy, Music Master, Musician-monk, Nabi, Nabucco, Emperor Napoleon, Napoleone, Narum-off, Ned Keene, Nelusko, Count de Nevers, Newby, Nick Shadow, Nilakantha, Notary, Novice's Friend, Count Oberthal, Officer, Official Registrar, Old Gypsy, Olivier, Orest, Oreste, Orfeo, Orphée, Osgood, Ostasio, Prince Ottokar, Overseer, Painter-monk, Paloucky, Pantaloon, Paolo Albiani, Papageno, Paquiro, Count Paris, Passerby, Peasant Perichaud, Peter, Peter I, Graf Peter Homonay, Pierrot, Pietro, Ping, Piram, Pirro, Plutus, Poet, Policeman, Polish Commander, Pompeo, Porgy, Rafaele, Rambaldo, Ramiro, Jack Rance,

Mr. Redburn, Baron Regnard, Renato, de Retz, Sir Richard Forth, Rigoletto, Rodrigo, Ruggiero, Ryan, Sacristan, Count de St. Bris, St. Ignatius Loyola, Samson, Sancho, Baron Scarpia, Schaunard, Schmidt, Schneidebart, Dr. Schön, Schwanda the Bagpiper, Scindia, Sculptor, Sebastiano, Sergeant, Sergio, Servant, Boyar Shaklovity, Sharpless, Shepherd, Sherasmin, Shikeneder, Show-man, Sid, Silvano, Silvio, Simon, Simon Boccanegra, Simon Mago, Singer, de Serieux, Soldier, Song Writer, Sonora, Spirit Messenger, Baron Starbemberg, Hofkapellmeister Robert Storch, John Styx, Taddeo, Tanato, Tarquinius, Taylor, Andrey Tchelkalov, Thoré, Tio Lucas, Tom Cat, Tomes, Count Tomsky, Tonio, Torchbearer, Tramp, Ned Travers, Trojan Captain, Trojan Soldier, Ulysses S. Grant, Undertaker, Valentin, Vanzetti, Varsono-viev, Venetian Merchant, Viking Merchant, Virgil T., Vizier, Vladislav, Wagner, Watchful, Willem, Wolfram von Eschenbach, Workman, Worldly Glory, Wotan, Wozzeck, Prince Yama-dori, Prince Yeletsky, Zurga

### Roles for Bass

Abimilech, Abul Hassan Ali Ebn Bekar, Ahmad, Albert, Albert K., Alcade, Alcindoro, Alessio, Alidoro, Emperor Altoum, Alvise Badoero, Ambrogio, Maître Ambroise, Antinoo, Anton Buis von Müglitz, Antonio, Apollyon, Archer, Archibaldo, Arkel, Count Arnheim, Ashby, Astolfo, Baculus, Le Bailli, Balducci, Ballad Singer, Balthazar, Banquo, Barak, Barbacan, Barbe-bleue, Doctor Bartolo, Don Basilio, The Bass, Benes, Benoit, Bermate, Bernardino, Bertram, di Béthune, Betto di Signa, Billy Jackrabbit, Biterolf, Black Bob, Duke Bluebeard, Doctor Bombasto, Bomely, The Bonze, Borella, Bourdon, Brander, Supt. Budd, Buffoon, Bugler, Cadi, Dr. Caius, Canciano, Cappadocian,

Captain, Captain of the Guard, Count Capulet, Cardinal de Brogny, Cardinal of Lorraine, Caspar, Cecco del Vecchio, Celio, Count Ceprano, Cesare Angelotti, Chamberlain, Cardinal Christoph Madruscht, Il Cieco, Claggert, Collatinus, Colline, Commandant, Commendatore, Compère, Conrad Nachtigall, Constable, Cook, Corporal, Court Attendant, Courtois, Cuno, Customs Officer, Daland, Dandini, Daniel Hizler, Dansker, Mr. Day, Dead Composer, Death, Devil, Devilshoof, Don Diego, Dikoy, Dipsacus, Director-Representative, Doctor, King Dodon, Dositheus, Duke of Verona, Dulcamara, Elder, Elder Ott, Enan the Blind, Envy, Evangelist, Fafner, Sir John Falstaff, Farfallo, Farfarello, Farlaf, Farmer, Father-in-Law, Father of Louise, Le Fauteuil, Kaiser Ferdinand II, Ferrando, Figaro, Filippo II, Fiorello, Fool, Fran-cesco, Franz, Friend, Fritz Kothner, King Frost, Gabriel, Lord Gaultiers Walton, Gaveston, Gazello, Sir George Walton, Geronimo, Geronte di Ravoir, Gessler, Ghost of Nino, Giacomo, Ciarno, Giovanni da Prodica, Government Director, Grand Inquisitor, Gravis, Grech, Greek Captain, Prince Gremin, Doctor Grenvil, Count des Grieux, Padre Guardiano, Gubetta, Guccio, Guglielmo, Gurnemanz, Gypsy, Gzak, Hagen, Haly, Hanezò, Hans Foltz, Hans Sachs, Hans Schwarz, Harvey, Lord Hate-Good, Hector's Ghost, Henry the Fowler, Herald, Hermann, Hermann Ortel, Her-mit, High Priest, High Priest of Babylon, Hobson, Holstein, Hortensio, Hunch-backed Bass Fiddler, Hunding, Huntsman, Imperial Commissioner, Innkeeper, Don Inigo Gomez, Prince Ivan Khovansky, Ivan Susanin, Tsar Ivan Vassilievitch, Jacopo Fiesco, Jago, Jailer, Friar Jean, Jester, Jew, Johann, John Brown, José Castro, Juan Lopez, Junkman, Jurist, Kammer-sänger, Kecal, Keeper of the Madhouse, King, King Marke, King of

675

Clubs, King of Egypt, King of Spain, King of the Ocean, The King's Herald, Klingsor, Knight, Kontchak, Lackey, Graf Lamoral, Larkens, Lartigon, Friar Laurence, Admiral Lefort, Leonato, Leporello, Leuthold, Levis, Lindorf, Lodovico, Lord, Lorenz von Pommerfelden, Lotario, Louis the Sixth, Lowitzky, Lunardo, Luther, MacIrton, Magician, Don Magnifico, Major-Domo, Mamalik, Man Servant, Manus, Maometto, Marcel Marchese di Calatrava, Marco, Marquis of Montefiore, Mars, Masetto, Master of Ceremonies, Matous, Matteo, Matthisen, Maurevert, Mayor, Mayor of Hornachuelos, Mefistofele, Melcthal, Melnik, Man in Armor, Méphistophélès, Merchant, Mercury, Micha, Mitjuch, Monk, Montano, Morales, Morena, Sir Morosus Blunt, Mosé, Musketeer, Mustafa, Narbal, Naval Captain, Nazarene, Nerone, Nettuno, Night Watchman, Nightwatchman's Voice, Nikititsch, Notary, Nourabad, Marchese d'Obigny, Obstinate, Baron Ochs, Officer, Old Bard, Old Hebrew, Old Servant, Colonel Ollendorf, One-Arm, One-Eye, Orator, Oroe, Oroveso, Osmin, Ourrias, Painter, Palémon, Pali, Pantalone, Panthée, Paolo Orsini, Pascoe, Don Pasquale, Mr. Peachum, Peasant, Don Pedro, Peneios, Philosopher, Physician, Pietro, Pilot, Pimen, Pinellino, Pistol, Don Pizzaro, Plunkett, Police Commissioner, Policeman, General Polkan, Pontius Pilate, Pope Pius IV, Prefect, Priam, Priam's Ghost, Priest, Prince de Bouillon, The Prior, Publius, Puppet, Don Quichotte, Quinault, Ragman, Raimondo, Sir Walter Raleigh, Ramfis, Maître Ramon, Rangoni, Lt. Ratcliffe, Raymond, Recorder of Norwich, Herr Reich, Reinmar von Zweter, Repela Riedinger, Robert, Roberto, Count Robinson, Rocco, La Roche, Count Rodolpho, Rodrig, Le Roi d'Ys, Toucher, Kaiser Rudolf II, Russlan, Don Ruy Gomez di Silva, Saint Corentin, St.

Just, Cardinal Salviati, Samuele, Sarastro, Uncle Sarvaor, Saturn, Schilgolch, Schlemil, Sciarrone, Sculptor-monk, Secret Police Agent, Selva, Sergeant, Sergeant of Archers, Shellfish Seller, Shepherd, Sheriff, Simon, Simon Magus, Simone, Sixtus Beckmesser, Skoula, Soldier, Somarona, Sourin, Sparafucile, Reasonable Spectator, Maestro Spinellocchio, Steffano Colonna, Steward, Stromminger, Student from Krakov, Sulpice, Sultan of Khaitan, The Sun, Svietosar, Swallow, Lord Syndham, Tackleton, Talpa, Tansur, Tartaglia, Tcherevik, Tcherevik's Friend, Theater Director, Theologian, Thoas, The Thrasher, Tigellino, Timur, Tiresias, Titurel, Prince Youry Ivanovitch Tokmakov, Tomaso, Tommaso, Tonuelo, Tramp, Tree, Tristan de Mikleford, Trojan Captain, Truchsess von Waldburg, Truffaldino, Trulove, Tschernjakovsky, Tutor, Uberto, van Bett, Vanuzzi, Varlaam, Count Vaudemont, Veit Pogner, Vitellozo, Vladimir Jaroslavitch, Voice of Neptune, Voice of the Temple Watchman, Waiter, Graf Waldner, Count Waldner, Walter Furst, Colonel Washington, Watchman, Wigmaker, William Jennings Bryan, Workman, Wurm, Yousko Velehin, Zaccaria, Zacharias, Zaretsky, Zuane, Zuniga

**Roles for Chorus**

Actors, Actresses, Agricultural Laborers, Ambassadors, Anabaptists, Angels, Animals, Apprentices, Archers, Artists, Attendants, Bacchantes, Bandits, Bodyguards, Boyards, Boyars, Boys, Bridal Couples, Burghers, Burghers' Sons, Caliph's Entourage, Captains, Captives, Capuchin Monks Caribiniers, Carthaginians, Catholic Ladies and Gentlemen, Cavalry, Celestial Phalanxes, Certain Persons Cloth'd in Gold, Cherubs, Les Chiffres, Children, Chorus, Christians, Church-goers, Cigarette Girls, Citizens, Clowns, Comedians, Cossacks,

676

Councillors, Country People, Counts, Court Officials, Court Servants, Courtiers, Creditors, Crowd, Cypriotes, Demimondaines, Demons, Disguised Jews, Doctors, Doleful Creatures, Dragoons, Druids, Drummers, Drunkards, Egyptians, Elders, Elders of Thebes, Electors, Erinnyes, Esquires, Ethiopian Slaves, Eunuchs, Eunuchs of the Harem, Choir of Evil, Evil Spirits, Executioners, Fairies, Farmers, Fauns, Fisherfolk, Fishermen, Flower Maidens, Followers, Friends, Frogs, Furies, Gamblers, Gauls, Geishas, Generals, Gentlemen, Ghosts, Invisible Ghosts, Girls, Gluttons, Choir of Good, Greek Chorus, Greek Soldiers, Greeks, Grenadiers, Guards, Guests, Guildsmen, Gypsies, Hebrews, Highbrows, Huguenot Ladies and Gentlemen, Hunters, Huntresses, Huntsmen, Indians, Inquisitors, Janissaries, Jews, Jokers, Journeymen, Judges, Jury, Knights, Knights of the Grail, Laborers, Ladies, Ladies in Waiting, Ladies of Honor, Laundry Girls, Little Devils, Lowbrows, Madmen, Magi, Magnates, Maidens, Maids, Maids in Waiting, Majas, Majos, Marines, Masks, Masquers, Members of the Revolutionary Tribunal, Men, Men at arms, Merchants, Messengers, Midshipmen, Miners, Ministers, Monks, Franciscan monks, Monsters, Mountaineers, Muleteers, Musicians, Mystic Choir, Naiads, Neighbors, Nibelungs, Night Watch, Nobles, Nobles of the Venetian Republic, Novices, Nuns, Nymphs, Officers, Officials, Old Believers, Old Men, Old Men of Thebes, Opera singers, Pages, Patricians, Peasants, Peddlars, Penitents, People, Phaecian Sailors, Philistines, Pietists, Pilgrims, Pirates, Players, Plebians, Police, Polish Ladies, Polovtsian Chiefs, Populace, Powder Monkeys, Prelates, Priestesses of Diana, Priests, Priests of Neptune, Princes, Princesses, Prisoners, Puritans, Ragpickers, Reapers, Recruits, Relatives, Retainers, Roaring Boys, Romans, Romantics, Sailors, Saints, Samurai, Satraps, Satyrs, Savoyards, Schoolboys, Scythians, Senators, Servants, Shades of Trojans, Sharpers, Shepherds, Shopkeepers, Sicilians, Singers, Sirens, Sisters, Slaves, Smugglers, Soldiers, Spirits, The Stars, Strange Children, Street Folk, Strelitzky, Students, Tartars, Temple Virgins, Theater Personnel, Thessalians, Torchbearers, Tourists, Townspeople, Toysellers, Traders, Travellers, Trees, Trojan Captives, Trojan Prisoners, Trojan Soldiers, Turkish Soldiers, Tyroleans, Vassals, Vendors, Villagers, Wailing Women, Waiters, Warriors, The Watch, Wayfarers, Weeping Women, Whores, Witches, Wits, Wizards, Women, Workmen, Wreckers, Young Men, Young Women, Youths

## Speaking Roles

Abdullah, Abraham, Almanzor, Mr. Archdale, Arlecchino, Artillerymen, Babekan, Bacchus, Beggar, General Blood and Thunder, Cabin Boy, Charlemagne, Coroner, Counsel for the Prosecution, Detectives, Doctor, General Dufla, Countess Estrella, Frosch, Haroun el Rashid, Hungarian Sentry, Hussar, Kaiser Franz of Austria, Major Domo, Man, Mary Ann, Countess Melusine, Nadina, Namouna, Narrator, Pancratius, Representative of the Sailors, Roshana, Russian Sentry, Samiel, Scipio, Selim, Student, Titania, Village Elder

## Silent Roles

Alladine, Andromaque, Annunziata, Astynax, Bear, Bishop of Thelesia, Boleslav Lazinski, Boy, Cleopatra, Clorinda, Crowds, Dr. Thorp, Duncan, Fenella, Fleance, Flute Player, Giuseppe, Duke Godfrey, Graf von Helfenstein, Guide, Hairdresser, Helen of Troy, Jesuits, John, Laïs, Marquis, Massarelli, Tancredi, Wig Maker

## Children's Roles

Le Banc, Boy's Voice, Gay Brook, Harry, Hugh Crome, John Crome, Marie's Child, Norma's Children, Ottoman, Sam, Sofa, Trouble, Wicker Chair.

## Arias for Soprano

A Serpina penserate
A una fonte aflito e solo
Abscheulicher! wo eilst du hin?
Ach, ich fühl's, es ist verschwunden
Ach, ich liebte, war so glücklich
Addio del passato
Addio di Mimi
Addio notre petite table
Ah, Belinda, I am prest with torment
Ah, chi mi dice mai quel barbaro dov'è
Ah! dite alla giovine
Ah! fors è lui
Ah, fuggi il traditore
Ah! j'ai baisée ta bouche
Ah, je ris de me voir si belle
Ah, malgré moi
Ah, non credea mirarti
Ah, non giunge uman pensiero
Ah! perche non posso odiarti
Ahi, casa acerbo!
Allmächtige Jungfrau
Ave Maria
Batti, batti, o bel Masetto
Bei Männern, welche Liebe fühlen
Bel raggio lusinghier
Brahma! gran Dio
La Caleseva
Caro nome
Casta Diva
Chaste fille de Latone
Che volo d'Augelli
Chimes in the Valley
D'Amour l'ardente flamme
Deh vieni non tardar
Depuis le jour
Der Freund ist dein'
Der Hölle Rache kocht in meinem Herzen
Der Kleine Sandmann bin ich
Der Männer Sippe sass hier im Saal
Dew Fairy's song

Di Tanti Palpiti
Dich, teure Hall
Divinités du Styx
Doch dich rührt kein Flehen
Donde lieta usci
Dove sono
Du bist der Lenz
Durch Zärtlichkeit und Schmeicheln
E amore un ladroncello
E quest' asilo ameno e grato
Elle a ful la tourterelle
Elsa's dream
Ernani, involami
Et ta langue elle ne remue plus
Euch Lüften, die mein Klagen
Hoyoto Ho
Ich Sah' das Kind
Il est doux, il est bon
Il était un Roi de Thulé
Il padre adorato ritrovo e lo perdo
Imponete!
In quelle trine morbide
In uomini, in soldati
Isolde's Narrative
Je dis que rien ne m'épouvante
Je suis Titania
Je t'implore et je tremble
Je veux vivre dans ce rêve
Klänge der Heimat
Kommt ein schlanker Bursch gegangen
La Biondina in gondoletta
L'Amour est un oiseau rebelle
Lasciatemi morire
Leise, leise, fromme Weise
Les oiseaux dans la charmille
L'Ora o Tirsi
Ma dell' avido stelo divulsa
Mad scene from Lucia
Martern aller Arten
Mein Herr Marquis
Mi chiamano Mimi
Mi tradì quel alma ingrata
Mild und leise
Music Lesson scene
My man's gone now
Non, ce n'est point un sacrifice
Non mi dir, bell' idol mio

678

Non più di fiori vaghe catene
Non so più, cosa son, cosa faccio
O malheureuse Iphigenie
O mio babbino caro
O patria mia
O toi qui prolongeas
O wär ich schon mit dir vereint
O zittre nicht, mein lieber Sohn
Obéisons quand leur voix appelle
Oh, pourquoi ne m'as-tu regardé?
Ombre légère
Ophelie's mad scene
Or sai chi l'onore
Où va la jeune Hindoue?
Ozean, du ungeheuer
Pace, pace, mio Dio
Padre, germani addio
Per pieta, ben mio, perdona
Piangea cantando
Porgi Amor
Près des ramparts de Séville
Printemps qui commence
Quando m'en vo' soletta
Qui la voce sua soave
Qui sola, vergin rosa
Ritorna vincitor
Salut a toi, soleil de flamme
Se il padre perdei
Sempre libera
Siccome un dì caduto
Sleepwalking scene
Smanie implacabili
So elend und so treu
Son vergin vezzosa
Stizzoso, mio stizzoso
Suicidio!
Summertime, and the livin' is easy
Tacea la notte placida
Traurigkeit ward mir zum Loose
Tu n'as pas voulu
Tutte le feste al tempio
Un bel dì vedremo
Una donna a quindici anni
Und ob die wolke
Vedrai, carino, se sei buonino
Vien, diletto

Vissi d'arte
Voi che sapete
Voi lo sapete
Welche Wonne, welche Lust
Welche Kummer herscht in meiner Seele
When I am laid in earth
Zefiretti, lusinghieri

**Arias for Mezzo-soprano**
A lonely Arab maid
Amour, viens aider ma faiblesse
Belle nuit, o nuit d'amour
Brangäne's Warning
Connais-tu le pays?
Erzählung der Waltraute
Faites-lui mes aveux
Ich lade gern mir Gäste ein
In dem Schatten meiner Locken
Io sono docile
Mon coeur s'ouvre à ta voix
Music lesson scene
O Araby, dear Araby
O mio Fernando
Song of the Drake
Song of the Gnat
Una voce poco fa
Voce di donna o d'angelo
Witch's song

**Arias for Contralto**
Ah! mon fils
Che faro senza Euridice
Che puro ciel
Chiamo il mio ben così
Già i sacerdoti adunansi
Il segreto per esser felice
Nacqui all' affanno, al pianto
Nobles seigneurs, salut!
Nurse's song
O don fatale
O prêtres de Baal
Ombra mai fu
Torna, torna, deh torna, Ulisse
Weiche, Wotan, Weiche!

**Arias for Tenor**
A te o cara
Ach, das leid hab' ich getragen

Addio alla madre
Addio Mignon
Ah! fuyez douce image!
Ah! lève-toi, soleil!
Ah, lo veggio, quel' anima bella
Ah! non credere!
Ah sì ben mio coll' essere
Alles fühlt der Liebe Freuden
Als flotter Geist
Am stillen Herd
Amfortas, die Wunde!
Amor ti vieta
Berceuse
Celeste Aida
Che Gelida manina
Ch'ella mi creda libero
Cielo e mar
Come un bel dì di Maggio
De' miei bollenti spiriti
Deh per questo istante solo
Dell' elisir mirabile
Di quella pira
Dich selig Frau
Dies Bildnis ist bezaubernd schön
Dieu, que ma voix tremblante
Dir, Göttin der Liebe soll mein lied
  ertönen
Donna non vidi mai
Durch die Walder, durch die Auen
É lucevan le stelle
Ecco ridente in cielo
En fermant les yeux
Frisch weht der Wind der Heimat zu
Fuor del mar ho un mar in seno
Hat denn Himmel mich verlassen?
Hier soll' ich dich denn sehen, Constanze
Ho ho! Schmiede, mein Hammer!
Horch, die lerche singt im Hain
I revel in hope and joy again
Ich baue ganz auf deine Stärke
Ich hab' kein Geld, bin Vogelfrei
Ich knüpfte manche zarte Bande
Il mio tesoro intanto
Im Mohrenland gefangen wir
In des Lebens Frühlingstagen
In fernem Land
It ain't necessarily so

Je viens célébrer la victoire
La donna è mobile
La fleur que tu m'avais jetée
Lay of sorrow
Lebewohl mein flandrisch Mädchen
Lohengrin's Farewell
Ma se m'è forza perderti
Magische Töne
Me voici dans son boudoir
Meco all' altar di Venere
Mi par d'udir ancora
Mit Gewitter und Sturm
Morgenlich leuchtend in rosigem Schein
Morir! si pura e bella
Nessun dorma
No! Pagliaccio non son!
Nothung! Nothung!
Nur eine Waffe taugt
O Lola
O Paradiso
O Soave Fanciulla
O tu che in seno agli' angeli
O wie ängstlich, o wie feurig
Ora 'e per sempre addio
Parmi veder le lagrime
Pourquoi me reveiller?
Pur ti riveggo mia dolce Aïda
Quanto e bella
Questa o quella
Rachel! Quand du Seigneur
Recondita armonia
Rienzi's prayer
Rom' Erzählung
Rosa del Ciel
Salut, demeure chaste et Pure
Se il mio nome saper
Sigfried's Erzählung
Siegmund heiss ich
Simpleton's lament
Sogno, soave e casto
Song of India
Sonst spielt ich mit Szepter und Kron
There's a boat that's leaving soon for
  New York
Torna la pace al core
Tu se' morta, se' morta mia vita
Un' aura amorosa

Una furtiva lagrima
Unis dès la plus tendre enfance
Vesti la giubba
Vi ricordo o boschi ombrosi
Viva il vino spumeggiante
Wenn der Freude Thränen fliessen
When zephyrs waft me peace
Wie stark ist nicht dein Zauberton
Winterstürme wichen

## Arias for Baritone

A red-headed woman
A tanto amor
A woman is a sometime thing
Adamastor, re dell' onde profonde
Ah! per sempre io ti perdei
Ah, pescator, affonda l'esca
Aprite un po' quegli occhi
Avant de quitter ces lieux
Bannis la crainte et les alarmes
Blick ich umher
Conoscete, signor Figaro, questo foglio
    chi vergò?
Cortigiani, vil razza dannata
Credo in un dio crudel
Deh, vieni alla finestra
Der Vogelfänger bin ich ja
Di provenza il mar
Die Frist ist um
È sogno o realtà?
Eccomi a vostri piedi
Ein Mädchen oder Weibchen
Eri tu, che macchiavi
Femme sensible
Figlia dei re
Figlia, tal nome palpita
Già mi dicon venal
Ho capita, signor, si
I got plenty o' nuttin'
Il cavallo scalpita
It takes a long pull to get there
Ja, das Schreiben und das Lesen
Largo al factotum
Mad scene of Oreste
Metà di voi quà vadano
Nemico della Patria
Non più andrai

O Carlo, ascolta
O, du mein holder Abendstern
O monumento
O vin, dissipe la tristesse
Pari siamo!
Per me ora fatale
Salomé, Salomé, demande!
Schusterlied
Scintille, diamant
Se a caso Madama
Se vuol ballare
Standin' in de need of prayer
Te Deum
Vedrò mentr' io sospiro
Vision fugitive
Votre toast je peux le rendre
Wahn! Wahn! überall Wahn!
Where seek to hide
Wie oft in Meers tiefsten Schlund

## Arias for Bass

A un dottor della mia sorte
Ach, ich hab' sie ja nur auf die Schulter
    geküsst
Ah, del Tebro
Ah! I am suffocating!
Ah, pietà, Signori miei!
Ah! se l'error t'ingombra
Als Büblein klein
Berceuse
Cinta di Fiori
Coronation Scene
De noirs pressentiments
Donne mie la fate a tanti
Dormirò sol nel manto
Ein Kobold
Finch' han dal vino
Fünftausend Thaler
Ha! welch' ein Augenblick!
Ha, wie will ich triumphieren
Hark, the tolling bell
Hat man nicht auch Gold beneben
Herz, versage nicht geschwind
I have attained the highest power
Il lacerato spirito
In diesen heil'gen Hallen
Infelice e tu credevi

King Marke's soliloquy
La calunnia
Le vendetta
Le jour est levé
Madamina
Manca un foglio
Monstre affreux!
'Neath almond trees in blossom
Non siate ritrosi
Notte e giorno faticar
O Isis und Osiris
Patter song
Piff! Paff!
Pogner's Address
Rivolgete a lui lo sguardo
Sempre in contrasti
Si la rigeur et la vengeance
Son imbrogliato io già
Song of the Viking
Splendon più belle in ciel
Udite, udite, o rustici!
Vallons de l'Helvétie
Varlaam's song
Vi ravviso o luoghi ameni
Vous qui du Dieu vivant
Vous qui faites l'endormie
Wer ein Liebchen hat gefunden
Wie duftet doch der Flieder

**Duets for two Sopranos**
Barcarola (*Les Contes d'Hoffmann*)
Che soave zeffiretto
Mira, O Norma

**Duets for Soprano and Mezzo-soprano**
Abends will ich schlafen gehen
Clapping game song
Threatful gather clouds about me

**Duets for Soprano and Contralto**
Che fiero momento
Giorno d'orrore
Su, e con me vieni, o cara

**Duets for Soprano and Tenor**
Ah! che la morta ognora
Das süsse Lied verhallt

D'un pensiero e d'un accento
È il sol dell' anima
Fuggiam gli argori inospiti
Già nella notte densa
Ich setz den Fall
Il nome vostro ditemi
In mia man alfin to sei
Isolde! Tristan! Geliebte!
La Fatal pietra
Libiamo, libiamo ne' lieti calici
Non la sospiri la nostra casetta
O Dieu, Dieu de nos pères!
O holdes Bild
O namenlose Freude
O terra addio
Parigi, o cara noi lasceremo
Qual cor tradisti
Sono andati?
To you my soul I give
Tornami a dir che m'ami
Trinke, liebchen, trinke schnell
Un dì felice eterea
Va crudele, al dio spietato
Vieni fra queste braccia
Vieni la sera
Welch' ein Geschick
Wer uns getraut?

**Duets for Soprano and Baritone**
Bess, you is my woman now
Crudel, perche finora?
Imponete
Là ci darem la mano
Quanto amore
Te souvient-il du lumineux voyage

**Duets for Soprano and Bass**
Death of Don Quixote
Il core vi dono
Io son ricco e tu sei bella
La vergine degli angeli

**Duet for Mezzo-soprano and Baritone**
Dunque io son, tu non m'inganni

**Duets for Contralto and Tenor**
Ai nostri monti
Mal reggendo all' aspro assalto

## Duets for Tenor and Baritone

Del tempio al limitar
Enzo Grimaldo, Principe di Santafiore
Invano, Alvaro!
La Minaccie
Mein freund, in holder jungendzeit
O mimi, tu più
Secondate aurette amiche
Si pel ciel marmoreo giuro
Solenne in quest' ora

## Duets for Tenor and Bass

Giusto cielo, rispondete
Le veau d'or
Nume, custode e vindici
Obbligato, obbligato
Tu che a Dio spiegasti l'ali
Vivat Bacchus

## Duets for Baritone and Bass

O statua gentilissima!
Suoni la tromba!

## Trios

(Arranged according to voices as indicated
   by the initials preceding the item)
STB: Alerte! Alerte!
SSMs: Bald prangt den Morgen zu
   verkünden
SST: Pria di partir
   Protegga il giusto cielo
SSBar: Soave sia il vento
SMsT: Er kommt, er kommt, o
   Wonne meiner Brust
   Ha, seht es winkt
   Mein Aug' bewacht
STBar: O sommo Carlo
STB: Deh non volerli vittime
   Io muojo
   Non imprecare

MsTBar: Zitti, zitti, piano
CBarBar: Sittencommissions Couplets
TTB: Marsch, Marsch, Marsch!
TBarB: E la Fede delle femine
TBB: O diese Sonne

## Quartets, Quintets, Sextet

(Arranged according to voices as indicated
   by the initials preceding the item)
SSST: Andrò ramingo e solo
SSTBar: Addio dolce svegliare
SSTB: Mir ist so wunderbar
SCTBar: Bella Figlia dell' amore
STBarB: Er sterbe
   Piango su voi
SSMsTBar: Der arme kann von Strafe
   sagen
SSTBarBar: Ah sì! che feci
SSTBB: È scherzo ed è follia
SMsTTB: Selig wie die Sonne
SSTBarB: Sento, oh Dio
SCTBarB: Chi mi Frena?
MsTBarBB: Buona sera mio Signore
SMsTBarBB: Fredda ed immobile

## Choruses

Anvil Chorus
Bridal Chorus
By Wisla's blue waters
Cantiamo facciam brindisi
Chi mai dell' Erebo
Duidu
Gloire immortelle de nos aieux
Gloria all' Egitto e ad Iside
Heil diesem Hause
O welche Lust
Pilgrim's Chorus
Placido è il mar, andiamo
Va, pensiero
Wach'auf! es nahet gen den Tag